THE PAPERS OF ULYSSES S. GRANT

THE PAPERS OF

ULYSSES S. GRANT

Volume 12: August 16–November 15, 1864

Edited by John Y. Simon

ASSOCIATE EDITOR

David L. Wilson

EDITORIAL ASSISTANT

Sue E. Dotson

———

SOUTHERN ILLINOIS UNIVERSITY PRESS

CARBONDALE AND EDWARDSVILLE

Library of Congress Cataloging in Publication Data (*Revised*)

Grant, Ulysses Simpson, Pres. U.S., 1822–1885.
    The papers of Ulysses S. Grant.

    Prepared under the auspices of the Ulysses S. Grant Association.
Bibliographical footnotes.
    CONTENTS: v. 1. 1837–1861—v. 2. April–September 1861.
—v. 3. October 1, 1861–January 7, 1862.—v. 4. January 8–March 31,
1862.—v. 5. April 1–August 31, 1862.—v. 6. September 1–December 8, 1862.—v. 7. December 9, 1862–March 31, 1863.—v. 8.
April 1–July 6, 1863.—v. 9. July 7–December 31, 1863.—v. 10.
January 1–May 31, 1864.—v. 11. June 1–August 15, 1864.—v. 12.
August 16–November 15, 1864.
    1. Grant, Ulysses Simpson, Pres. U.S., 1822–1885. 2. United
States—History—Civil War, 1861–1865—Campaigns and battles
—Sources. 3. United States—Politics and government—1869–1877
—Sources. 4. Presidents—United States—Biography. 5. Generals—
United States—Biography. I. Simon, John Y., ed. II. Wilson, David
L. 1943–. III. Ulysses S. Grant Association.
E660.G756 1967   973.8′2′0924   67–10725
ISBN–0–8093–1118–6 (v. 12)

To Bell I. Wiley (1906–1980)

Contents

———

Maps and Illustrations

—

Introduction

FOR THE THREE MONTHS covered in this volume, Lieutenant General Ulysses S. Grant remained with the Army of the Potomac before the besieged city of Petersburg, Va., leaving only briefly for visits to Washington, to confer with Major General Philip H. Sheridan in the Shenandoah Valley, and to visit his family in Burlington, N.J. Although Grant himself was most closely associated with the stalemated Petersburg campaign, this pressure against the declining strength of General Robert E. Lee made possible the victories of Sheridan in the Shenandoah and the continuing advance of Major General William T. Sherman in Georgia, which culminated in the occupation of Atlanta on September 2.

The fall of Atlanta represented the first major achievement of Grant's grand strategy, based upon his assumption that unrelenting pressure applied by all the armies of the United States would inevitably lead to a major breakthrough in at least one theater of war. This victory also influenced the presidential campaign. With dissatisfaction over the course of the war rising in the North, Grant feared a Democratic victory, even though presidential candidate George B. McClellan had disavowed the peace plank in the platform. Evidence that the war was not a failure improved chances for the reelection of President Abraham Lincoln, something Grant believed essential to victory. By late September, in writing to give permission to use his letters for political purposes, Grant noted that for Lincoln "to attempt to answer all the charges the opposition will bring against him will be like setting a maiden to work to prove her chastity—" The reelection of Lincoln by a substantial majority, free of disorder at the polls, Grant regarded as "worth more to us than a victory in the field."

Through these months, Grant's official and private correspondence combined show him very much in control of military affairs, those immediately under his supervision at Petersburg and throughout the nation, and also capable of managing the affairs of his own family with the same steady hand. One day in October, he advised his son Fred to "*pitch in*" when provoked by other boys at school but to avoid those likely to start a fight; on the same day, he wrote to Lee, concluding correspondence concerning Confederate treatment of black troops. "I shall always regret the necessity of retaliating for wrongs done our soldiers but regard it my duty to protect all persons received into the Army of the United States, regardless of color or Nationality." Grant had only one set of principles for both public and private conduct and applied them with the same clearheaded determination. What he wrote to Lee foreshadowed his policy for twelve years as general and president during Reconstruction.

Confederate treatment of captured black troops enabled Grant to maintain federal policy concerning prisoners. An earlier gentlemanly practice of exchanging man for man, based upon accounts kept by both sides, had broken down under the pressure of conflict. Grant believed that letting prisoners return to combat increased the killing and lengthened the war. Although the policy originated in Washington, he accepted responsibility, which brought with it blame for deplorable conditions in prison camps North and South. The policy reflected the logic of war, something Grant understood better than most, and the same logic dictated the devastation of the Shenandoah Valley, a granary repeatedly tapped by the Confederacy, as well as Sherman's harsh treatment of civilians in Georgia. From the start, Grant had never found any romance in war; his only goal was to end it quickly, at the least cost.

Grant was little closer to Richmond on November 15 than he had been three months earlier. Yet as the grand strategist of the war, he understood his progress toward victory better than any other man in the country and took full responsibility for Sherman's plan to cut through Georgia as well as the stalemated army at Petersburg. Nobody could then foresee the exact schedule and method of ending the war, but political and military events had eliminated any reasonable expectation of defeat.

We are indebted to W. Neil Franklin and Karl L. Trever for searching the National Archives; to Mary Giunta, Anne Harris Henry, and Sara Dunlap Jackson for further assistance in the National Archives; to Harriet Simon for proofreading; and to Stephen R. Alvin, Jr., Cynthia L. High, Wayne Lutton, Tamara Melia, Patricia Ann Owens, and Eric A. Topham, graduate students at Southern Illinois University, for research assistance.

Financial support for the period during which this volume was prepared came from Southern Illinois University and the National Historical Publications and Records Commission.

JOHN Y. SIMON

March 31, 1982

Editorial Procedure

1. Editorial Insertions

A.   Words or letters in roman type within brackets represent editorial reconstruction of parts of manuscripts torn, mutilated, or illegible.

B.   [. . .] or [— — —] within brackets represent lost material which cannot be reconstructed. The number of dots represents the approximate number of lost letters; dashes represent lost words.

C.   Words in *italic* type within brackets represent material such as dates which were not part of the original manuscript.

D.   Other material crossed out is indicated by ~~cancelled type~~.

E.   Material raised in manuscript, as "4th," has been brought in line, as "4th."

2. Symbols Used to Describe Manuscripts

AD	Autograph Document
ADS	Autograph Document Signed
ADf	Autograph Draft
ADfS	Autograph Draft Signed
AES	Autograph Endorsement Signed
AL	Autograph Letter
ALS	Autograph Letter Signed
ANS	Autograph Note Signed
D	Document
DS	Document Signed
Df	Draft

DfS   Draft Signed
ES   Endorsement Signed
LS   Letter Signed

3. Military Terms and Abbreviations

Act.   Acting
Adjt.   Adjutant
AG   Adjutant General
AGO   Adjutant General's Office
Art.   Artillery
Asst.   Assistant
Bvt.   Brevet
Brig.   Brigadier
Capt.   Captain
Cav.   Cavalry
Col.   Colonel
Co.   Company
C.S.A.   Confederate States of America
Dept.   Department
Div.   Division
Gen.   General
Hd. Qrs.   Headquarters
Inf.   Infantry
Lt.   Lieutenant
Maj.   Major
Q. M.   Quartermaster
Regt.   Regiment or regimental
Sgt.   Sergeant
USMA   United States Military Academy, West Point, N.Y.
Vols.   Volunteers

4. Short Titles and Abbreviations

ABPC   *American Book-Prices Current* (New York, 1895–)
CG   *Congressional Globe* Numbers following represent the Congress, session, and page.
J. G. Cramer   Jesse Grant Cramer, ed., *Letters of Ulysses S.*

	Grant to his Father and his Youngest Sister, 1857–78 (New York and London, 1912)
DAB	*Dictionary of American Biography.* (New York, 1928–36)
Garland	Hamlin Garland, *Ulysses S. Grant: His Life and Character* (New York, 1898)
HED	*House Executive Documents*
HMD	*House Miscellaneous Documents*
HRC	*House Reports of Committees* Numbers following *HED, HMD,* or *HRC* represent the number of the Congress, the session, and the document.
Ill. AG Report	J. N. Reece, ed., *Report of the Adjutant General of the State of Illinois* (Springfield, 1900)
Johnson, Papers	LeRoy P. Graf and Ralph W. Haskins, eds., *The Papers of Andrew Johnson* (Knoxville, 1967–)
Lewis	Lloyd Lewis, *Captain Sam Grant* (Boston, 1950)
Lincoln, Works	Roy P. Basler, Marion Dolores Pratt, and Lloyd A. Dunlap, eds., *The Collected Works of Abraham Lincoln* (New Brunswick, 1953–55)
Memoirs	*Personal Memoirs of U. S. Grant* (New York, 1885–86)
O.R.	*The War of the Rebellion: A Compilation of the Official Records of the Union and Confederate Armies* (Washington, 1880–1901)
O.R. (Navy)	*Official Records of the Union and Confederate Navies in the War of the Rebellion* (Washington, 1894–1927) Roman numerals following *O.R.* or *O.R.* (Navy) represent the series and the volume.
PUSG	John Y. Simon, ed., *The Papers of Ulysses S. Grant* (Carbondale and Edwardsville, 1967–)
Richardson	Albert D. Richardson, *A Personal History of Ulysses S. Grant* (Hartford, Conn., 1868)
SED	*Senate Executive Documents*
SMD	*Senate Miscellaneous Documents*
SRC	*Senate Reports of Committees* Numbers following *SED, SMD,* or *SRC* represent the number of the Congress, the session, and the document.
USGA Newsletter	*Ulysses S. Grant Association Newsletter*

Young	John Russell Young, *Around the World with General Grant* (New York, 1879)

5. Location Symbols

CLU	University of California at Los Angeles, Los Angeles, Calif.
CoHi	Colorado State Historical Society, Denver, Colo.
CSmH	Henry E. Huntington Library, San Marino, Calif.
CSt	Stanford University, Stanford, Calif.
CtY	Yale University, New Haven, Conn.
CU-B	Bancroft Library, University of California, Berkeley, Calif.
DLC	Library of Congress, Washington, D.C. Numbers following DLC-USG represent the series and volume of military records in the USG papers.
DNA	National Archives, Washington, D.C. Additional numbers identify record groups.
IaHA	Iowa State Department of History and Archives, Des Moines, Iowa.
I-ar	Illinois State Archives, Springfield, Ill.
IC	Chicago Public Library, Chicago, Ill.
ICarbS	Southern Illinois University, Carbondale, Ill.
ICHi	Chicago Historical Society, Chicago, Ill.
ICN	Newberry Library, Chicago, Ill.
ICU	University of Chicago, Chicago, Ill.
IHi	Illinois State Historical Library, Springfield, Ill.
In	Indiana State Library, Indianapolis, Ind.
InFtwL	Lincoln National Life Foundation, Fort Wayne, Ind.
InHi	Indiana Historical Society, Indianapolis, Ind.
InNd	University of Notre Dame, Notre Dame, Ind.
InU	Indiana University, Bloomington, Ind.
KHi	Kansas State Historical Society, Topeka, Kan.
MdAN	United States Naval Academy Museum, Annapolis, Md.
MeB	Bowdoin College, Brunswick, Me.
MH	Harvard University, Cambridge, Mass.

MHi	Massachusetts Historical Society, Boston, Mass.
MiD	Detroit Public Library, Detroit, Mich.
MiU-C	William L. Clements Library, University of Michigan, Ann Arbor, Mich.
MoSHi	Missouri Historical Society, St. Louis, Mo.
NHi	New-York Historical Society, New York, N.Y.
NIC	Cornell University, Ithaca, N.Y.
NjP	Princeton University, Princeton, N.J.
NjR	Rutgers University, New Brunswick, N.J.
NN	New York Public Library, New York, N.Y.
NNP	Pierpont Morgan Library, New York, N.Y.
NRU	University of Rochester, Rochester, N.Y.
OClWHi	Western Reserve Historical Society, Cleveland, Ohio.
OFH	Rutherford B. Hayes Library, Fremont, Ohio.
OHi	Ohio Historical Society, Columbus, Ohio.
OrHi	Oregon Historical Society, Portland, Ore.
PCarlA	U.S. Army Military History Institute, Carlisle Barracks, Pa.
PHi	Historical Society of Pennsylvania, Philadelphia, Pa.
PPRF	Rosenbach Foundation, Philadelphia, Pa.
RPB	Brown University, Providence, R.I.
TxHR	Rice University, Houston, Tex.
USG 3	Maj. Gen. Ulysses S. Grant 3rd, Clinton, N.Y.
USMA	United States Military Academy Library, West Point, N.Y.
ViHi	Virginia Historical Society, Richmond, Va.
ViU	University of Virginia, Charlottesville, Va.
WHi	State Historical Society of Wisconsin, Madison, Wis.
Wy-Ar	Wyoming State Archives and Historical Department, Cheyenne, Wyo.
WyU	University of Wyoming, Laramie, Wyo.

Chronology

———

AUG. 16. USG reported continued fighting north of the James River as Maj. Gen. Winfield S. Hancock probed C.S.A. lines with inconclusive results. The siege of Petersburg, Va., continued.

AUG. 17. USG directed Maj. Gen. George G. Meade to attack the Weldon Railroad the following day.

AUG. 18–19. Maj. Gen. Gouverneur K. Warren suffered heavy losses in the battle of the Weldon Railroad but held his position, cutting a major C.S.A. supply route.

AUG. 20. USG directed Hancock to abandon his probe north of the James River.

AUG. 21. C.S.A. Maj. Gen. Nathan B. Forrest briefly occupied Memphis.

AUG. 21. U.S. forces repulsed a C.S.A. counterattack on the Weldon Railroad.

AUG. 22. USG canceled an attack planned for Maj. Gen. Benjamin F. Butler north of the James River.

AUG. 23. USG suspended offensive operations on the Weldon Railroad.

AUG. 25. Hancock's 2nd Army Corps suffered heavy losses during the battle of Reams' Station, Va.

AUG. 27. USG left for a visit with Julia Dent Grant at Fort Monroe, Va., bringing her to City Point, Va., the following day.

AUG. 30. USG testified before the court of inquiry investigating the battle of the Crater.

AUG. 31. USG escorted Julia Grant to Fort Monroe on her way to Burlington, N.J.

Aug. 31.   Maj. Gen. George B. McClellan nominated for president by the Democratic Party.

Aug. 31–Sept. 1.   USG at Norfolk, Va.

Aug. 31–Sept. 1.   C.S.A. Gen. John B. Hood defeated by Maj. Gen. William T. Sherman in the battle of Jonesboro, Ga. At the conclusion, C.S.A. forces evacuated Atlanta.

Sept. 1–2.   USG conferred with Assistant Secretary of the Navy Gustavus V. Fox regarding a possible expedition against Wilmington, N.C.

Sept. 2.   Atlanta occupied by U.S. forces, and, on Sept. 4, USG directed U.S. batteries at Petersburg to fire a salute in honor of the capture.

Sept. 7.   Sherman ordered civilians to evacuate Atlanta.

Sept. 8.   McClellan accepted the Democratic nomination for president although disavowing the "peace plank" in the Democratic platform.

Sept. 10.   USG expressed his willingness to send an expedition against Wilmington in cooperation with the Navy.

Sept. 10.   USG considered the possibility of a further campaign in Ga., and, on Sept. 12, sent Lt. Col. Horace Porter to confer with Sherman at Atlanta.

Sept. 15.   USG traveled to visit Maj. Gen. Philip H. Sheridan to expedite the campaign in the Shenandoah Valley.

Sept. 16.   USG at Baltimore.

Sept. 16.   C.S.A. cav. raided Coggins' Point, Va., driving off the cattle of the Army of the Potomac.

Sept. 16–17.   USG conferred with Sheridan at Charles Town, W. Va.

Sept. 17.   John C. Frémont withdrew as a presidential candidate.

Sept. 18.   USG visited his family at Burlington, returning via Philadelphia.

Sept. 19.   USG arrived at City Point.

Sept. 19.   Sheridan won the third battle of Winchester or Opequon Creek, Va., and, on Sept. 20, USG ordered a salute fired in honor of the victory.

Sept. 20.   USG conferred with Fox and Rear Admiral David D. Porter about the Wilmington expedition.

Sept. 20.   C.S.A. President Jefferson Davis left Richmond for Ga. to attempt to redeem C.S.A. fortunes there.

SEPT. 22. Sheridan again defeated Lt. Gen. Jubal A. Early at the battle of Fisher's Hill, Va.

SEPT. 24. USG conferred with Meade to plan another offensive at Petersburg.

SEPT. 25. Davis visited Hood's hd. qrs. at Palmetto, Ga.

SEPT. 29–OCT. 2. USG launched a two-pronged offensive at Petersburg, fighting the battles of Pecble's Farm, Va., and Fort Harrison or Chaffin's Farm, Va., extending the siege lines west and north of Petersburg.

SEPT. 29. USG, at Chaffin's Farm, directed the battle north of the James River.

SEPT. 29. USG at Signal Hill and at Deep Bottom, Va.

SEPT. 30. USG at Deep Bottom.

OCT. 1. USG at the junction of Varina and New Market roads north of the James River.

OCT. 2. USG at Deep Bottom.

OCT. 2–3. USG corresponded with C.S.A. Gen. Robert E. Lee, insisting that captured Negro soldiers be exchanged on the same basis as white soldiers.

OCT. 4. USG stated that Sherman was capable of making his way to the Atlantic Coast from Atlanta.

OCT. 5. U.S. forces held off C.S.A. forces during the engagement of Allatoona, Ga.

OCT. 6–9. USG traveled to Washington to expedite recruits going to the front.

OCT. 7. C.S.A. forces repulsed at Chaffin's Farm with heavy losses.

OCT. 11. USG again recommended the replacement of Maj. Gen. William S. Rosecrans in Mo.

OCT. 11. Republicans won elections in Pa., Ohio, and Ind.

OCT. 12. USG directed Butler to make a reconnaissance in force on his front.

OCT. 12. President Abraham Lincoln worried about Sherman's proposed march to the sea, and the next day USG stated that "Shermans proposition is the best that can be adopted. . . ."

OCT. 16–17. Secretary of War Edwin M. Stanton visited the front at Petersburg and conferred with USG.

OCT. 17. USG prepared supplies to meet Sherman's army on the coast.

OCT. 18–20. USG corresponded with Lee about providing mutual relief for prisoners of war.

OCT. 19. Early attacked U.S. forces in the battle of Cedar Creek, Va., with initial gains, only to be defeated decisively after Sheridan rallied his forces in the last major battle in the Shenandoah Valley. On Oct. 20, USG ordered a salute fired in honor of the victory.

OCT. 21. USG and Meade toured the front along the Weldon Railroad.

OCT. 23. C.S.A. Maj. Gen. Sterling Price defeated at the battle of Westport, Mo., the last major battle west of the Mississippi River.

OCT. 24. USG sent troops to New York City to maintain order during the presidential election.

OCT. 24. USG instructed Meade to prepare his forces for an offensive movement on Oct. 27.

OCT. 25. USG approved a proposal to organize the 1st Veteran Army Corps.

OCT. 27. As Butler made a diversion north of the James River, USG came under fire south of the river while observing the engagement at Hatcher's Run, Va. (also known as Burgess' Mill or Boydton Plank Road). C.S.A. forces maintained control of the Southside Railroad.

OCT. 30. USG sent Chief of Staff Brig. Gen. John A. Rawlins to Mo. to ensure that Rosecrans forwarded troops to Maj. Gen. George H. Thomas.

NOV. 1. USG ordered Butler to New York City to take charge of troops sent to maintain order during the election.

NOV. 5. USG prepared for a possible C.S.A. attack on Nov. 8, the day soldiers voted in the presidential election.

NOV. 6. USG opened correspondence with C.S.A. Agent of Exchange Robert Ould about a plan to exchange C.S.A. cotton for goods to provide relief for prisoners held in the North.

NOV. 7. The second and last session of the C.S.A. Congress opened in Richmond, Va.

NOV. 8. Lincoln reelected president.

NOV. 12. USG continued correspondence with Ould regarding sale of cotton to provide money for relief of C.S.A. prisoners.

Nov. 13. USG conferred with Porter and Fox at City Point about the Wilmington expedition.

Nov. 14. USG at Fort Monroe and returned to City Point that evening.

Nov. 14. Rawlins in Washington planned to return to City Point the following day.

Nov. 15. USG instructed Thomas that Hood should "be pressed with such force as you can bring to bear."

Nov. 15. USG prepared to leave City Point for a visit to Burlington.

The Papers of Ulysses S. Grant
August 16–November 15, 1864

To Maj. Gen. Henry W. Halleck

(Cipher)   City Point Va. Aug. 16th *1864.* [*6:30* P.M.]
MAJ. GEN. HALLECK, WASHINGTON,

The fighting North of the river to-day has resulted favorably for us so far as it has gone but there has been no decisive results. The enemy have been driven back somewhat from their position of the morning with a conciderable loss in killed and wounded and about four hundred prisoners, well ones, left in our hands. Two brig. Gens. Chambliss[1] & Gherarde,[2] were killed and their bodies left in our hands. We also have quite a number of wounded prisoners. I have releived the 5th Corps from the trenches and have it ready to march round Petersburg if the enemy can be induced to throw troops enough North of the James to justify it.

Since moving North of the river our losses will probably reach near one thousand in killed & wounded very many however only slightly wounded owing to so much of the fighting being taking place in thick woods. The enemy have lost about as many that have fallen into our hands.

U. S. GRANT
Lt. Gen.

ALS (telegram sent), CSmH; telegram received (on Aug. 18, 1864, 8:00 P.M.), DNA, RG 107, Telegrams Collected (Bound). *O.R.*, I, xlii, part 1, 18; *ibid.*, I, xlii, part 2, 210.

1. John R. Chambliss, Jr., born at Hicksford, Va., in 1833, USMA 1853, resigned the year after graduation to become a Va. planter. A militia officer before the war, he led the 13th Va. Cav. as col. until appointed brig. gen. as of Dec. 19, 1863. At the time of his death on Aug. 16, 1864, he commanded a cav. brigade under Maj. Gen. William H. F. Lee. See telegram to Maj. Gen. Winfield S. Hancock, Aug. 16, 1864.

2. On Aug. 16, Maj. Gen. Winfield S. Hancock telegraphed to USG. "A Brig Gen supposed to be Brig. Gen. Gherarde is dead within our lines Sso reports my chief of staff   Gherarde commands that brigade of Gen Wrights who is on leave" Telegram received, DNA, RG 108, Letters Received. *O.R.*, I, xlii, part 2, 215. Victor J. B. Girardey, born in France in 1837, brought to Augusta,

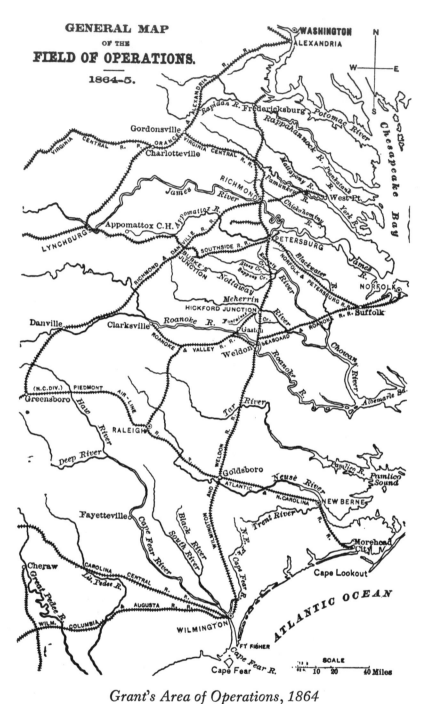

Grant's Area of Operations, 1864

From *Andrew A. Humphreys,* The Virginia Campaign of '64 and '65 (*New York, 1883*)

Ga., at age five, served as a staff officer for Brig. Gen. Ambrose R. Wright, and for Brig. Gen. William Mahone, receiving special notice for service at the Crater and an appointment as brig. gen. shortly before his death on Aug. 16.

To Maj. Gen. Benjamin F. Butler

By Telegraph from City Pt
Dated Aug 16 *1864.*

To Gen Butler,

Our troops are now near Whites tavern. You will perceive from the map this is between the enemy at NewMarket & Richmond. They still however have the road clear to Chapins farm. If one thousand (1000) of your men at Dutch Gap could be sent under arms & threaten an advance it might have the effect to start the enemy on the retreat. In making such demonstration troops would have to start bearing down the river to avoid the batteries near Cox's House.

U. S. Grant
Lt Gen

Telegram received (at 10:20 a.m.), DLC-Benjamin F. Butler; copies, DLC-USG, V, 45, 59, 68; DNA, RG 108, Letters Sent. *O.R.*, I, xlii, part 2, 231. On Aug. 16, 1864, 11:15 a.m., Maj. Gen. Benjamin F. Butler telegraphed to USG. "Your despatch rec'd   I have directed the available force which will amount to about twelve hundred (1200) men at Dutch Gap to make the demonstration you suggest,   We shall move in that direction with considerable vigor   The only doubt I have is whether the enemy's Iron clads may be able to sweep the plain in front of Dutch Gap—I have ordered Col Wooster commanding at Deep bottom also to make an advance up the Kinsland road towards G its Junction with three mile creek as a feint at the time we open at Dutch Gap"   Telegram received, DNA, RG 107, Telegrams Collected (Unbound); *ibid.*, RG 108, Letters Received. *O.R.*, I, xlii, part 2, 231.

At 6:00 p.m., Butler, "Hatcher's Signal Station," signaled to USG. "We are advancing from Dutch Gap." Signal received, DNA, RG 107, Telegrams Collected (Unbound); telegram received, *ibid. O.R.*, I, xlii, part 2, 231. On the same day, USG telegraphed to Butler three times. "What was the result of the effort to advance at Dutch Gap. Quite a number of prisoners have been taken by Birney & Hancock today. But not without loss on our side." Telegram received (at 6:10 p.m.), DLC-Benjamin F. Butler. "It is now getting so late & the troops under Hancock being at a stand still it will be necessary to use caution about advancing." Telegram received (at 6:30 p.m.), *ibid.*; copies, DLC-USG, V, 45, 59, 68; DNA, RG 108, Letters Sent. *O.R.*, I, xlii, part 2, 231. "Has any men been taken from Wilcox div within 3 days.? If not have you any information fixing its presence here within this line." Telegram received, DLC-Benjamin F. Butler; copies, DLC-USG, V, 45, 59, 68; DNA, RG 108, Letters Sent. *O.R.*, I, xlii, part 2, 230. At 10:00 P.M., Butler telegraphed to USG. "Wilcox Div is all here Lane & McGowan are on north side of the James where they have been for some weeks Thomas & Scales are on the right of Picketts Div. in our front here where they also have been for some six weeks or more. I had not heard from them for a day or two, but tonight have had a man from McGowan & have heard direct from Thomas & Scales" Telegram received, DNA, RG 107, Telegrams Collected (Unbound); *ibid.*, RG 108, Letters Received. Printed as sent at 10:00 A.M. in *O.R.*, I, xlii, part 2, 231. On the same day, 11:15 P.M., Butler telegraphed to USG. "As soon as arrangements could possibly be made to get the men rested from their work, at five o'clock—I put on board the Steamer Mount Washington, kindly loaned me by the Navy, nine hundred and fifty of the working party at Dutch Gap, and landed about three quarters of a mile below, at Aikens, by which I ~~was~~ I was enabled to turn the enemy's Battery at H. Cox's, and under cover of the gun boats, which you heard, Major Ludlow advanced, turning the enemy's line, capturing it after a smart skirmish in which we lost one man killed, and we now occupy the work on the brow of the hill which you saw—It is a very strong line for the enemy—Our line of pickets extend from Cox's house at the turn of the river, above Dutch Gap to the North East and about a half a mile toward Three Mile Creek—We have not men enough to occupy all the works— The right has been occupied by rifle pits and one piece of Artillery, the line extending to Three Mile Creek, but there is nothing now between us and Three Mile Creek—Major Ludlow thinks this position a very strong one, if occupied by the Rebels to oppose any advance on our part I have directed it to be held to night—If you propose to go up to Deep Bottom to morrow, you can easily examine it yourself, or one of the Engineers may be sent up to examine it—We have captured a prisoner there and he says he is from one of Beauregards Brigades, (Johnson's old)—I have a report from Col Wooster Com'dg at Deep Bottom, that he advanced a strong skirmish line until his entire line passed Kingsland Road, his right resting on Four Mile Creek, and advancing beyond it as far as W. H. Ammon's beyond the NewMarket Road, and his left beyond Buffin's house—He developed only a strong skirmish line and two or three Companies of Infantry He captured a prisoner of the 3rd North Carolina which Regiment belonged to Johnson's Division & Stuart's Brigade, which was supposed to have been captured with its General—I have also another prisoner who claims to belong to the 10th Va of the same Brigade who says his Brigade is out there, and has been encamped there for some time—At nine o'clock Col Wooster retired to his original position— With reference to this prisoner, I have never from all the prisoners or deserters heard of this Brigade on this line before, and know not where they came from— Col Wooster had no killed and non[e] seriously wounded—It would seem that there is no difficulty in advancing any body of troops in that direction Our movement has certainly been successful as a reconnoisance if nothing more—" LS (telegram sent), DNA, RG 107, Telegrams Collected (Unbound); telegram received, *ibid.*, RG 108, Letters Received. *O.R.*, I, xlii, part 2, 232. At the foot of the telegram received, USG drafted a telegram to Maj. Gen. Winfield S. Hancock. "The position secured by Gen. Butler may turn the whole position now held by the enemy. I will have it examined in the morning and if it does will transfer a portion of your command to it." ADfS, DNA, RG 108, Letters Received; copies, *ibid.*, Letters Sent; DLC-USG, V, 45, 59, 68. *O.R.*, I, xlii, part 2, 222. On the same day, USG telegraphed to Butler. "If you have men to spare to hold the position secured by Maj Ludlow until I can get up there, I will have the ground examined & if it is practicable to get through, will transfer a portion of the force with Gen Hancock." Telegram received (at 11:30 P.M.), DLC-Benjamin F. Butler; copies, DLC-USG, V, 45, 59, 68; DNA, RG 108, Letters Sent. *O.R.*, I, xlii, part 2, 232.

To Maj. Gen. Winfield S. Hancock

City Point, Va. Aug 16. 1864 10 A. M.

MAJ GEN HANCOCK

Your dispatches received. At Whites Tavern You are in rear of the enemy's line, or nearly so and must cause a falling back on the whole front from NewMarket to the left (our right.) The troops not engaged on our right should watch the enemy closely and be prepared to follow up the moment the enemy give way, if they do give way.

The people at Whites Tavern are Union and may be relied on, if You or Birney get an opportunity to question them in person.

U. S. GRANT.
Lt. Genl.

Telegram received, DNA, RG 94, War Records Office, Army of the Potomac; copies, *ibid.*, RG 108, Letters Sent; DLC-USG, V, 45, 59, 68. *O.R.*, I, xlii, part 2, 217. On Aug. 16, 1864, 9:15 A.M., Maj. Gen. Winfield S. Hancock telegraphed to USG. "At eight a. m. our troops on Charles city road were driving the enemy—Our advance being within a mile of Whites tavern—Brig Gen Chambliss was killed & his body fell into our hands—Our loss is not considerable yet. Col Gregg is wounded but not dangerously" Telegram received, DNA, RG 108, Letters Received. Printed as sent at 9:10 A.M. in *O.R.*, I, xlii, part 2, 216.

On Aug. 16, Hancock telegraphed to USG frequently, usually sending a copy to Maj. Gen. George G. Meade. "I send four (4.) more officers & forty ~~(40)~~ nine (49) men" Telegram received, DNA, RG 108, Letters Received. *O.R.*, I, xlii, part 2, 219. At 8:15 A.M. "There is as yet nothing important to note Gens Miles and Gregg are advancing up the charles city road—The enemy were driven from behind Deep creek and are falling back towards White's tavern I do not think I will push the reconnoissance much farther than Whites tavern until I hear from Gen Birney who has swung into the left and is advancing towards the central road—He reports a line of the enemy's works well filled & is moving to the right to see if he can turn the flank He will attack if there is a good opportunity—The enemy's lines along the Heights behind Bailey's creek appear about as yesterday" Telegram received, DNA, RG 107, Telegrams Collected (Unbound); *ibid.*, RG 108, Letters Received. *O.R.*, I, xlii, part 2, 216. Probably shortly after 9:00 A.M. and 9:20 A.M. "One prisoner from Sanders brig reports that the other brigades of Mahones Div were ready to come Gen Gregg found a valuable map on Gen Chambliss body which I will send you when it comes It is said to have the enemy line marked on it" "Gen Birney is still examining the enemys line with a view to attack He finds it protected by a difficult ravine & is crossing the Ravine further to the right—The enemy's line is apparently not continuous from the central to the charles city roads" Telegrams received, DNA, RG 108, Letters Received. *O.R.*, I, xlii, part 2, 216. At 9:30 A.M. "I omitted to state that the prisoners thus far taken on the Charles city road are all cavalry of H. F. Lee's Div" Telegram received, DNA, RG 94, War Records Office, Army of the Potomac; *ibid.*, RG 108, Letters Received. *O.R.*, I, xlii, part 2, 217. Received at 10:15 A.M. "Prisoners just taken report Lane & Wrights brigades in front of Gen Birney—They having arrived there last night" Telegram received, DNA, RG 94, War Records Office, Army of the Potomac; *ibid.*, RG 107, Telegrams Collected (Unbound); *ibid.*, RG 108, Letters Received. *O.R.*, I, xlii, part 2, 219.

At 10:30 A.M., USG telegraphed to Hancock. "I have directed Gen Butler to make a demonstration of an advance with his troops at Dutch Gap. You will perceive this threatens their retreat on Chapins Bluff, whilst Your forces near Whites Tavern threatens their retreat towards Richmond" Copies, DLC-USG, V, 45, 59, 68; (sent at 10:00 A.M.) DNA, RG 94, War Records Office, Army of the Potomac; *ibid.*, RG 108, Letters Sent. *O.R.*, I, xlii, part 2, 217. Hancock sent two telegrams to USG, both received at 12:20 P.M. "Your dispatches have been recd. Gen Birney is advancing in three lines and will make a vigorous attack If the enemy will make a fight where Birney is I will put in my whole force, If they however are entrenched strongly I leave it to Gen Birney's discretion to assault or not—The enemy are strengthening their left apparently at the expense of their right Gen Birney just sends in thirty four prisoners from the following regiments 37 N. C. 38 N. C. 33 N. C. 18th N C. 2d Ga. 10th Ga 64 Ga. 22d Ga 48th Ga—He has carried one line and thinks he has their left He will go forward again—Gen Miles & Gregg report the enemy re inforcing against them from the direction of the central road" Telegram received, DNA, RG 107, Telegrams Collected (Unbound); *ibid.*, RG 108, Letters Received. *O.R.*, I, xlii, part 2, 217–18. "The Pro Mar. at Deep bottom says that an officer from the enemys lines opposite Cammunicated with him to exchange papers this morning He belonged to the 29th Tennessee & says that the 17th of the same state is with them They belong to Longstreets corps but I do not find them on the memorandum ~~from~~ furnished me of Field's Div. He says that the enemy are expecting a flag of truce today at Aikens landing" Telegram received, DNA, RG 94, War Records Office, Army of the Potomac; *ibid.*, RG 108, Letters Received. *O.R.*, I, xlii, part 2, 217. At 12:30 P.M. "Maj Gen Birney reports to me that he has captured the enemy's ravine line in his front—The enemy are doubling on him & I am making an attack now on their right to seize the forts which they hold thinly I think we will seize them—The Infantry command from Charles City has been ordered in on to Gen Birneys right or rather to Connect with it— leaving the cavalry to cover the Charles city road & hold their position if possible" Telegram received, DNA, RG 108, Letters Received. *O.R.*, I, xlii, part 2, 218. At 1:10 P.M. and 1:30 P.M. "This Division of Cavalry is Gen W H. F. Lees

(—'Rooney' Lee)—Gen Lees son not Fitz Lee who is the oldest Division Commander but the one who was in Fort Lafayette—They are both named Fitz Lee but one is known as Fitz Lee & the other as Rooney Lee among the[ir] companions   This com[man]d left Reams Station day bef[ore] yest[er]day at 11 oclock and arrived here yesterday m[orning]   I sent for have a rebel color just recd & some tn prisoners ten officer[s] & one hun 153 men—A staff officer of Gen Birney reports that he has taken three (3) colors but has only got hold of one as yet. . . . Col Dent will return with the prisoners capt[ure]d—except those taken by the Cavalry which have not yet come"   "One Brigade from which Gen Birney took prisoners arrived here last night—An officer of Gen Field's Staff is taken & says there are fifteen thousand (15000) men in my front   A prisoner says that Gen Lee crossed over here from Petersburg last night today   The enemy are attacking Birneys right pretty strongly . . . P. S. Gen Birneys loss is considerable & he has captured some more prisoners"   ALS (telegrams sent— the second incomplete), DNA, RG 107, Telegrams Collected (Unbound); telegrams received, *ibid.*, RG 108, Letters Received. *O.R.*, I, xlii, part 2, 219. At 2:40 P.M. "Gen Birney is pretty heavily engaged on his right & left   I have now three (3) Brigades of my Corps to his right & left   He considers himself pretty hard pressed"   AL (unsigned telegram sent), DNA, RG 107, Telegrams Collected (Unbound). At 3:30 P.M. "Our losses so far as I can ascertain are quite very heavy—for Gen Birney has had Four (4) Brigade Commanders disabled are reported killed or wounded—I have just returned from Gen Birney—He has I think lost a part of the line he took from the enemy—but he has is entrenching the rest & I have ordered him to retake the all of it—I think he is secure—I have formed additional troops on his right & left. A considerable portion of Hills Corps is here. How much I cannot say at this moment   Gen Birney thinks all of it but I could not in any of the these statemts advise credence until I can substantiate them—We have been making a formidable dem demonstration thus far—I have taken numbers of prisoners from Sanders Brigade whose presence I reported this morning Field's Fields & Fields Div still remains here There are more on our right according to the statement of prisoners well disposed to us who were taken this morning—I have made demonstrati[on]s, really attacks, on the en[em]ys right but have always found the enemys entrenchments well manned"   ALS (telegram sent), *ibid.*; telegram received, *ibid.*; *ibid.*, RG 94, War Records Office, Army of the Potomac; *ibid.*, RG 108, Letters Received. *O.R.*, I, xlii, part 2, 220. At 4:15 P.M. and 5:10 P.M. "The force on the Charles City road has been pressed back to this side of Deep Creek by a superior force of Infantry—what Command is not known—Our troops behaved well but were driven back by superior numbers—Gen Gregg is now on the North side of Deep Creek and says he can hold his position. Gen Miles has returned to Gen Birneys right flank, and the Infantry which attacked him on the Charles City road has moved towards Flussers Mill on the enemys left—I have Richmond papers of the 15th   I can telegraph you some items if you have not seen them—though there is nothing important—Dates from Mobile and Atlanta of 13th—Two of our ships reported inside the bar at Mobile—. . . Gen Miles lost say 150 men of 1400 and Gen Gregg quite a number"   "Gen Birney has just sent me the following statement   Prisoners from Hill's Corps state that to prevent their march from Petersburg to this point being observed from the Tower on the Appomattox they were compelled to avoid the turnpike & come by a circuitous route   This was voluntary statement"   ALS (telegrams sent), DNA, RG 107, Telegrams Collected (Unbound); telegrams received, *ibid.*; *ibid.*, RG 108, Letters Received. *O.R.*, I, xlii, part 2, 220–21. The second is not printed. At 5:15 P.M. "Since Gen Miles was with drawn the enemy have pressed Gen Gregg pretty hard & have forced him across Deep Creek where he now holds in the rifle pits—The furthest point gained by our forces was six or seven miles from Richmond, within half a mile of Whites Tavern, where the enemys Inf.y appeared in ~~con~~ force" ALS (telegram sent), DNA, RG 107, Telegrams Collected (Unbound); telegram received, *ibid.*; *ibid.*, RG 94, War Records Office, Army of the Potomac; *ibid.*, RG 108, Letters Received. *O.R.*, I, xlii, part 2, 221. Received at 6:00 P.M. "Gen Miles has returned to the right of Gen Birney. Gen Gregg holding Deep Creek, a strong place on the Charles City Road—An attack upon the Enemy will be made ~~after~~ at 5 oclock on Gen Birneys front—Everything is calm here at present —I have on Gen Birneys line, two brigades of the 2d Corps on the right, & one engaged with him & one on his left   the remainder of the 2d Corps is on the left   The fight has been to the right of Fussers Mill pond. The enemy have lost heavily today according to the reports of their prisoners & other indications—I have the map taken from Gen Chamblins body which is a very perfect map—embracing the complete fortifications of richmond & the surrounding country on both sides of the river—I have not sent it in as I have not had an opportunity since receiving it." ALS (telegram sent), DNA, RG 107, Telegrams Collected (Unbound); telegram received, *ibid.*; *ibid.*, RG 108, Letters Received. *O.R.*, I, xlii, part 2, 221. At an unspecified time. "The following dispatch is just receivd from Genl Birney I have not recd a full report from Col Smith   'Hdqrs 10 A. C. 5 57 P M 16th To GENL HANCOCK—I advanced my skirmishers & after a reconnoissance have concluded not to attack—The enemy have massed in my front & my opinion even after taking the works my force could not do more   Col Smyth 2d Division reports troops and artillery passing 2 hours to my front   I send another flag Captured this morning   4 more are reported   I have not seen them   I would like a statement of previous flags turned over   Signed D B BIRNEY M. G.' " Telegram received, DNA, RG 94, War Records Office, Army of the Potomac; *ibid.*, RG 107, Telegrams Collected (Unbound); *ibid.*, RG 108, Letters Received. *O.R.*, I, xlii, part 2, 221–22.

Also on Aug. 16, USG telegraphed to Hancock. "Telegraph me the latest news from Mobile & Atlanta contained in the Richmond papers of the 15th" Telegram received (at 6:10 P.M.), DNA, RG 94, War Records Office, Miscellaneous War Records; copy, DLC-USG, V, 68. On the same day, Hancock telegraphed to USG. "The following is latest from Atlanta & Mobile—'From Richmond Enquirer, Atlanta Aug 13th—The Enemy yesterday advanced his right about One mile at same time extending his left but hurriedly withdrew early this morning to original position from some Cause unknown—same paper reports atlanta shelled on night of 11th—several Houses struck & no Casualties. '—Mobile Aug 11th   Nothing late from Fort Morgan   The wires are broken—Gen Forrest drove the enemys advance out of Oxford last night—Press dispatch—Heavy firing reported at Fort Morgan Tuesday Wednesday & today. The wire between the City & fort is Cut—Iron Vessels are off Dog river bar this morning   Troops are daily arriving and a good feeling exists'   I do not see any report of Vessels being inside the bar. I was told the paper so reported—" Telegram received, DNA, RG 108, Letters Received; copy, *ibid.*, RG 107, Telegrams Collected (Unbound).

At 7:00 P.M. and 7:50 P.M., Hancock telegraphed to USG. "This evening

Genl Mott by making a strong demonstration on the enemys right brought off the gun left by Genl Birney day before yesterday together with 3 loads of ammunition which have been covered by the enemy since that time   The gun was an 8 inch Siege Howitzer & the ammunition belongs to guns of that calibre" "My Casualties in the entire command including cavalry are at the minimum fifteen hundred (1500)"   Telegrams received, *ibid.*; *ibid.*, RG 94, War Records Office, Army of the Potomac; *ibid.*, RG 108, Letters Received. *O.R.*, I, xlii, part 2, 222.

Also on Aug. 16, USG telegraphed to Hancock. "I have ordered to strawberry plains steamers Ostensibly to bring down the 2d Corps. It is intended as a ruse to make the enemy believe you are withdrawing & to bring them out to attack you   send orders to the strs to return here at 4 a m in the morning"   Telegram received (at 9:20 P.M.), DNA, RG 94, War Records Office, Dept. of the Cumberland; copies, *ibid.*, RG 108, Letters Sent; DLC-USG, V, 45, 59, 68. Printed as received at 9:30 P.M. in *O.R.*, I, xlii, part 2, 222. At 10:00 P.M., Hancock telegraphed to USG. "Your dispatch is received and the necessary steps will be taken to carry out your views"   Telegram received, DNA, RG 107, Telegrams Collected (Unbound); *ibid.*, RG 108, Letters Received. Printed as received Aug. 17 in *O.R.*, I, xlii, part 2, 223.

To Maj. Gen. George G. Meade

(Cipher)   City Point, Aug. 16th/64
Maj. Gen. Meade,

It seems from Gn. Hancocks dispatches that a part of Hills Corps is North of the James. If the enemy reduce again to three Divisions at Petersburg it will be advisable to move Warren on to the Welden road at least and further if it should then appear advisable. The enemy would necessarily have to keep a good part of Beaurigards force to confront the two Corps that would still be left.

U. S. Grant
Lt. Gn.

ALS (telegram sent), CSmH; telegram received, DNA, RG 94, War Records Office, Army of the Potomac. Printed as sent at 6:30 P.M. in *O.R.*, I, xlii, part 2, 211. On Aug. 16, 1864, 7:45 P.M., Maj. Gen. George G. Meade telegraphed to USG. "Until this P. M. there were no indications of movements—I reported this morning that deserters who came in last night said we had in our front 3 Brigades of Mahones Divn. & all of Heths division *both* of *Hills Corps*, besides Beauregards forces—The two remaining brigades of Mahone Wright & Perrin they said had been with drawn & were in the rear—Hancock has taken prisoners from Wright & I have no doubt Perrin is also in his front, but that is all of Hill that has left us, as far as we know—Wilcox's Division of Hill is & has been there for some time.

I send a report from the signal station on the Plank road just received which would seem to indicate a further movement, tho it is very indefinite—If you think it advisable on this information to move Warren I will give him orders to move at early daylight or before, & to attack at the Lead works or where the Welden R. Rd enters the line of works.—I do not think myself he will have much chance of success, unless we get more definite information of the enemys having sent away more troops than we have now." ALS (telegram sent), DNA, RG 94, War Records Office, Army of the Potomac; telegram received, *ibid.*, RG 108, Letters Received. *O.R.*, I, xlii, part 2, 211. The enclosure is *ibid.*, p. 214.

At 10:00 P.M. and 10:15 P.M., USG telegraphed to Meade. "From here it sounds as if there was heavy musketry firing on your front. is it so? Is it not probable that the movement of the Enemys towards his right this evening was in anticipation of a flank movement by you" "Your despatch of 7.45 received. I would not move Warren until we are assured of further movements of the enemy   I think the changes reported by the signal officer on the ~~flan~~ Plank Road either indicates an intention to attack you or is in anticipation of a flank movement to our left." Telegrams received, DNA, RG 94, War Records Office, Army of the Potomac; copies, *ibid.*, RG 108, Letters Sent; DLC-USG, V, 45, 59, 68; Meade Papers, PHi. *O.R.*, I, xlii, part 2, 212. At 10:30 P.M., Meade telegraphed to USG. "There is no musketry firing on my front except the usual picket firing.— The movement of the enemy reported is I think undoubtedly a weakening of his extreme right, probaly with a view of re inforcing to the North of the James— The question with me was whether he had so weakened himself, as to render an attack by Warren likely to be followed by any material advantages, because so long as he holds his present lines we can not do any thing to assist Warrens movements   I am waiting to have your views—Warren has been ordered to be ready to move at 3. a m but the final order has not yet been sent—Just as I had completed the foregoing your despatch of 10.15. arrived—I hardly think the enemy will attack, but his movement is either to prepare for a flank movement on my part as you surmise, or else it is to re-inforce to the North of the James.—" ALS (telegram sent), DNA, RG 94, War Records Office, Army of the Potomac; telegram received, *ibid.*, RG 108, Letters Received. *O.R.*, I, xlii, part 2, 212.

At 11:00 A.M. and noon, Meade had telegraphed to USG. "No reports have been received from Corps Comds. or signal officers indicating any movement or change in the Enemys position in my front, except a part of the 9th corps, where it is reported the enemy have relieved the force in their trenches but not diminished it.—The appearance of Wrights Brigade Mahone's Division in front of Hancock confirms the previous statement of deserters that on Saturday last Two brigades of Mahone's Divn were with drawn & placed in reserve in the rear.—" "The following just received from Prov. Mar. Genl. Dept is forwarded   'We believe that two brigades, Wrights & Perrins of Mahones Division, moved from the enemys extreme right day before yesterday at 2. P. M—that the 3 remaining brigades of Mahone, with Heths Division & Beauregard's two divisions are still in our front.—' One of Kautz men taken prisoner escaped from the enemy last night   He says he was on the P. & R. R. Rd between Petersburgh & Swift run, when the two brigades of Mahones division marched up & took the cars for a station near Drurys bluff.—" ALS (telegrams sent), DNA, RG 94, War Records Office, Army of the Potomac; telegrams received, *ibid.*, RG 108, Letters Received. *O.R.*, I, xlii, part 2, 210–11.

To Maj. Gen. Philip H. Sheridan

(Cipher)   City Point Aug. 16th *1864.* [*1:30* P.M.]
MAJ. GEN. SHERIDAN, WICHESTER VA.

Fitz Lee's Division is not in the Valley. We took quite a number of prisoners from it yesterday North of the James. Kershaw's Division has gone to the valley and possibly two Brigades of Wilcox Division though I do not think it. Some Cavalry has gone but I do not know whose. I would not advise an attack on Early in an intrenched position but would watch him closely with the Cavalry and if he attempts to move ₙNorth follow him. The Hundred days men will have to be discharged at the expiration of their time unless there is a presing necessity for detaining them for a few days on account of immediate active hostilities. The families of most of Mosebys[1] men are know and can be collected. I think they should be taken and kept at Ft. McHenry or some secure place as hostages for good conduct of Mosby and his men. When any of them are caught with nothing to designate what they are hang them without trial.

U. S. GRANT
Lt. Gn.

ALS (telegram sent), CSmH; telegram received (on Aug. 17, 1864, 6:30 A.M.), DNA, RG 107, Telegrams Collected (Bound). *O.R.*, I, xliii, part 1, 811. On Aug. 17, 9:00 P.M., Maj. Gen. Philip H. Sheridan, Berryville, Va., telegraphed to USG. "All of your despatches have been received. Kershaws division is here and Wickhams and Lomax brigades of Fitz Lees cavalry division also another brigade from Reams station   The first cavalry Division captured 300 prisoners yesterday, most of them belonged to Kershaws division. One division of A. P Hills corps is reported here but no prisoners taken   The position that I held in front of Strausburg was a very bad one from which I could be forced at any time precipitately—Winchester is untenable except as a provisioned garrison   I have therefore taken a position near Berryville which will enable me to get in their rear if they should get strong enough to push north   Winchester is now held by the cavalry with one brigade of infantry of the 6th Corps to act with it—The cavalry engagement in front of Front Royal was splendid, it was on open ground —The sabre was freely used by our men—great credit is due to Generals Merrett Custar and Col. Devins. my impression is that troops are still arriving Kershaws and Fitz Lees divisions came through Culpeper   Mosby has annoyed me & captured a few wagons—we hung one & shot six of his men yesterday   I have burned all wheat and hay and brought off all stock, sheep cattle and horses etc South of Winchester. The prisoners captured belong to Kershaws division

SHERIDAN'S OPERATIONS
IN
VALLEY OF VIRGINIA
1864

Maj. Gen. Philip H. Sheridan's Area of Operations,
Summer and Fall, 1864

From Adam Badeau, Military History of Ulysses S. Grant
(New York, 1868–81), II

and Wickhams and Lomax brigades of Fitz Lees cavalry division" Telegram received (on Aug. 18, 1:00 P.M.), DNA, RG 107, Telegrams Collected (Bound); (on Aug. 19) *ibid.*, RG 108, Letters Received; copies, *ibid.*, RG 107, Telegrams Received in Cipher; (2) DLC-Philip H. Sheridan. *O.R.*, I, xliii, part 1, 822.

1. John S. Mosby, born in Va. in 1833, imprisoned for shooting a fellow student at the University of Virginia, practiced law in Va. before the Civil War. Enlisting in the cav., he served on the staff of Brig. Gen. James E. B. Stuart and later organized a co. of partisan rangers in northern Va. Although U.S. officials did not recognize Mosby as an officer of the C.S. Army, C.S.A. officials acknowledged his service as lt. col., 43rd Va. Partisan Rangers Battalion.

To Maj. Gen. Philip H. Sheridan

(Cipher)   City Point Va. Aug. 16th/64 [*3:30* P.M.]
Maj. Gen. Sheridan Winchester Va

If you can possibly spare a Division of Cavalry send them through Loudon County to destroy and carry off the crops, animals ~~and All~~ negroes, and all men under fifty years of age capable of bearing arms. In this way you will get many of Mosby's men. All Male Citizens under fifty can farely be held as prisoners of war and not as citizen prisoners. If not already soldiers they will be made so the moment the rebel army gets hold of them.

U. S. Grant
Lt. Gn.

ALS (telegram sent), CSmH; telegram received (on Aug. 18, 1864, 8:00 P.M.), DNA, RG 107, Telegrams Collected (Bound). *O.R.*, I, xliii, part 1, 811.

To Maj. Gen. William T. Sherman

(Cipher)   City Point Va. Aug. 16th 10 a. m. *1864.*
Maj. Gen. Sherman, Near Atlanta Ga.

Saturday[1] night last I threw the 2d & 10th Corps with a Division of Cavalry to the North of the James for the purpose of employing the enemy and keeping him from sending off any of his forces and to make him recall some from the Shenandoah valley if I could. We have kep ~~the enemy~~ him constantly occupied since and prisoners report with very heavy loss. Two Gen. Officers have been

killed and their bodies left in our hands. I shall keep the enemy so
employed that he will not send troops to Atlanta.

U. S. GRANT
Lt. Gn.

ALS (telegram sent), CSmH; telegram received (misdated as sent on Aug. 17,
1864, 10:00 A.M., received on Aug. 18, 7:00 P.M.), DNA, RG 107, Telegrams
Collected (Bound). *O.R.*, I, xxxviii, part 5, 521.

1. Aug. 13.

To Elihu B. Washburne

City Point Va. Aug. 16th *1864*.

HON. E. B. WASHBURN,
DEAR SIR:

Your letter asking for Autographs to send to Mrs. Adams, the
wife of our Minister to England, was duly received. She had also
sent to Mr. Dana for the same thing and his requisition, he being
with me at the time, was at once filled. I have directed Col. Bowers
to send with this a few of the original dispatches telegraphed from
here. They have all been hastily written and not with the expectation of ever being seen afterwards but will, I suppose, answer as
well as any thing els, or as if they had been written specially for
the purpose of sending.

We are progressing here slowly. The weather has been in-
tolerably warm, so much so that marching troops is nearly death.

I state to all Citizens who visit me that all we want now to insure an early restoration of the Union is a determined unity of sentiment North. The rebels have now in their ranks their last man. The
little boys and old men are guarding prisoners, guarding rail-road
bridges and forming a good part of their garrisons for intrenched
positions. A man lost by them can not be replaced. They have
robbed the cradle and the grave equally to get their present force.
Besides what they lose in frequent skirmishes and battles they are
now loosing from desertions and other causes at least one regiment
per day. With this drain upon them the end is visible if we will but

be true to ourselves. Their only hope now is in a divided North. This might give them reinforcements from Tenn. Ky. Maryland and Mo. whilst it would weaken us. With the draft quietly enforced the enemy would become dispondent and would make but little resistence.

I have no doubt but the enemy are exceedingly anxious to hold out until after the Presidential election. They have many hopes from its effects. They hope a counter revolution. They hope the election of the peace candidate. In fact, like McCawber, the hope *something* to turn up.[1]

Our peace friends, if they expect peace from separation, are much mistaken. It would be but the begining of war with thousands of Northern men joining the South because of our disgrace allowing separatio[n.] To have peace the "on any terms" the South would demand the restoration of their slaves already freed. They would demand indemnity for losses sustained, and they would demand a treaty which would make the North slave hunters for the South. They would demand pay or the restoration of every slave escaping to the North.

Your Truly
U. S. GRANT

ALS, IHi. The final three paragraphs of this letter received wide circulation as Republican campaign material in the presidential election of 1864. See *President Lincoln and General Grant on Peace and War*, broadside, IHi; *Important Letters from Gens. Grant and Sherman*, broadside, ICarbS; *Democratic Statesmen and Generals to the Loyal Sons of the Union* (Union Campaign Documents No. 8: Albany, 1864), p. 93.

1. Wilkins Micawber (a character in Charles Dickens, *David Copperfield*) lives in poverty while waiting for something "to turn up," a phrase indicating unrealistic optimism.

To Abraham Lincoln

(Cipher)   City Point Va. Aug. 17th *1864*. [*9:00* P.M.]
A. LINCOLN PRESIDENT, WASHINGTON

I have thought over your dispatch relative to an arrangement between Gn. Lee and myself for the suppression of insindiaryism

by the respective Armies. Experience has tought us that agreements made with rebels ~~is~~ are binding upon us but are not observed
by them longer than suits their convenience. On the whole I think
the best that can be done is to publish a prohibitory order against
burning private property except where it is a ~~nee~~ Military necessity
~~and~~ or in retaliation for like acts by the enemy. When burning is
done in retaliation it must be done by order of a Dept. or Army
Commander and the order for such burning to set forth the particular act it is in retaliation for. Such an order would be published
and would ~~reach rebel~~ come to the knowledge of the rebel Army.
I think this course would be much better than any agreement with
Gn. Lee. I could publish the order or it could be published by you.
This is respectfully submitted for your consideration and I will
then act as you deem best.

U. S. GRANT
Lt. Gn.

ALS (telegram sent), CSmH; telegram received (on Aug. 18, 1864, 8:00 P.M.),
DNA, RG 94, Letters Received, 2403W 1864; *ibid.*, RG 107, Telegrams Collected (Bound); DLC-Robert T. Lincoln. *O.R.*, I, xlii, part 2, 243. On Aug. 14,
1:50 P.M., President Abraham Lincoln telegraphed to USG. "The Secretary of
War and I concur that you better confer with Gen. Lee and stipulate for a
mutual discontinuance of house-burning—and other destruction of private property. The time ~~for~~ and manner of conference, and particulars of stipulation ~~are~~
we leave, on our part, to your convenience and judgment." ALS (telegram sent),
DNA, RG 107, Telegrams Collected (Bound); telegram received (datelined
1:30 P.M.), *ibid.*, RG 108, Letters Received. *O.R.*, I, xlii, part 2, 167. Lincoln,
Works, VII, 493.

To Maj. Gen. Benjamin F. Butler

City Point Va. Aug. 17th/64

MAJ. GN. BUTLER,

The 5th Corps commence a movement by our left at 4 a. m. in
the morning with the intention of getting on to the Welden road
and to take advantage of any weakness that may be discovered in
the lines of the enemy. If this should lead to a withdrawel from
your front be prepared to throw all your force at Bermuda into the

breach and I will recall every thing from North of the James to reinforce them.

U. S. GRANT

Lt. Gn.

ALS (telegram sent), OClWHi; telegram received (at 10:30 P.M.), DLC-Benjamin F. Butler. *O.R.*, I, xlii, part 2, 255. Also on Aug. 17, 1864, USG telegraphed to Maj. Gen. Benjamin F. Butler. "What is the firing heard up the river this evening?" Copy, DLC-USG, V, 68. At 10:40 P.M., Butler telegraphed to USG. "Telegram recieved The most vigilant watchfulness will be had to ascertain any withdrawal and the promptest movement made to take advantage of it Maj. Ludlow has withdraw without loss from his advanced position near Dutch Gap The firing you hear is from the Gun boats upon the Rams" ALS (telegram sent), DNA, RG 107, Telegrams Collected (Unbound); telegram received, *ibid.*, RG 108, Letters Received. *O.R.*, I, xlii, part 2, 255.

At 10:30 P.M., USG telegraphed to Maj. Gen. Winfield S. Hancock. "Warren moves at 4 a m by our left to Get on to the Weldon road & with instructions to take advantage of any weakness he may discover in the lines of the enemy. This lmay lead to the withdrawal of troops from your front watch closely & take advantage of anything you can." Telegram received (at 10:37 P.M.), DNA, RG 107, Telegrams Collected (Unbound); copies, *ibid.*, RG 108, Letters Sent; DLC-USG, V, 45, 59, 68. *O.R.*, I, xlii, part 2, 250.

At 8:45 P.M., Butler had telegraphed to USG. "We have ~~James~~ now on the North side of the James Field's Division of Longstreets Corps Lane & Conner's Brigades of Wilcox Div of Hill's Corps and Mahones Div of same Corps with Bushrod Johnson's old Brig of Beauregard's command Mahone's Div moved across there from our front at Petersburg on Sunday night making a long detour in order to avoid observation from my signal Tower—" LS (telegram sent), DNA, RG 107, Telegrams Collected (Unbound); telegram received, *ibid.*, RG 108, Letters Received. *O.R.*, I, xlii, part 2, 255.

To Maj. Gen. Winfield S. Hancock

City Point, Va. Aug. 17th/64

MAJ. GEN. HANCOCK,

I have sent Gen. Barnard and Col. Comstock to Dutch Gap to see if the works carried by Gen. Butlers men there last evening, and still held by them, give us any advantage in turning the enemy from that direction.[1] I can not go up until I get their report and likely will not go up at all to-day. Rest your men all you can unless you see some decided advantage to be gained.

U. S. GRANT

Lt. Gen.

ALS (telegram sent), OClWHi; copies, DLC-USG, V, 45, 59, 68; DNA, RG
108, Letters Sent. *O.R.*, I, xlii, part 2, 248.

On Aug. 17, 1864, Maj. Gen. Winfield S. Hancock telegraphed three times
to USG, addressing the second also to Maj. Gen. George G. Meade, as he addressed other telegrams sent to USG that day. "I have now 3 Rebel battle flags
in my possession taken yesterday—" Telegram received, DNA, RG 108, Letters
Received. "a close examination of the Enemys line this morning shows nothing
new, except, that they have been all night strengthening their line on our right
& extending their entrenchments in that direction—" Telegram received, *ibid.*;
(at 9:30 A.M.) *ibid.*, RG 94, War Records Office, Army of the Potomac. *O.R.*,
I, xlii, part 2, 247. "I send you a note just recd. from Gen Birney which I have
not thought proper to act on without referring to you" Telegram received,
DNA, RG 108, Letters Received. *O.R.*, I, xlii, part 2, 248. The enclosure, proposing to recover the dead and wounded, is *ibid.* On the same day, USG telegraphed to Hancock. "Send a flag of truce to the Commanding Officer on the
Enemy's front, where the wounded lay proposing cessation of hostilities there
until the dead and wounded of both parties are collected" Copies, DLC-USG,
V, 45, 59, 68; DNA, RG 108, Letters Sent. *O.R.*, I, xlii, part 2, 248. On the
same day, Hancock telegraphed three times to USG and Meade, first at 3:50
P.M., second at 4:15 P.M. "Between 4 & 6 this P M the dead & wounded be-
twen the lines at Flusser's Mill will be delivered to the Contending parties under
flag of truce" ALS (telegram sent), DNA, RG 107, Telegrams Collected
(Unbound); telegram received, *ibid.*, RG 108, Letters Received. *O.R.*, I, xlii,
part 2, 248. "In sendig in the proposal for flag of truce I addressed it to the
commander immediately in front—It was answered by Gn Field who was in
command of this portion of the line, their right, where the flag went in   Gen
W H F Lee also a few minutes since sent in a message to my extreme right on
th Charles City Road, asking for Gn Chambliss body—I answered that it would
be delivered at Flussers Mills—" ALS (telegram sent), DNA, RG 107, Telegrams Collected (Unbound); telegram received, *ibid.*; (at 9:50 P.M.) *ibid.*, RG
94, War Records Office, Army of the Potomac; *ibid.*, RG 108, Letters Received.
O.R., I, xlii, part 2, 249. "The dead in front of our lines were removed this P M
under flag of truce   the wounded had already been removed by the enemy—
The flag was at two different places a mile apart & as far as the entrenchments
could be observed in either place they were full—Gen Gary of the enemys Cavy
was present during the removal of the dead—several enquiries were overheard as
to Gen Andersons HdQrs & other remarks showing that he is in our front—His
adjt Genl was present—officers of Lanes brigade were also present—It was also
noticed that in speaking of yesterdays fight some of the Confederate officers mentioned the part taken by the 10th Ga Battalion & a staff officer says he is confident the 64th Ga was also mentioned though this regt does not appear on my
roster of Lees Army   there is no doubt but that the enemy have a pretty strong
force here today—The Richmond papers of today which I will send you as soon
as a tug arrives devote some considerable comment on our affair yesterday—One
of them says we attacked on the Charles City road with thirty or forty thousand
men including 2d 9th & 10th Corps—Burnsides niggers leading every attack
They also speak of one attack in heavy force near Phissus Mill." Telegram received (at 10:25 P.M.), DNA, RG 94, War Records Office, Army of the Potomac; *ibid.*, RG 108, Letters Received. *O.R.*, I, xlii, part 2, 249.

1. On Aug. 17, 7:00 A.M., Maj. Gen. Benjamin F. Butler telegraphed to
USG. "We hold our own at Dutch Gap. At what time will you go up and see the

ground? Shall I call for you with the Greyhound?" *Ibid.*, p. 254. On the same day, USG telegraphed to Butler. "I have directed Gen. Barnard & Col. Comstock to go up to Dutch Gap and thought I would not go up myself. They have not yet started but will go as soon as they get breakfast." ALS (telegram sent), OClWHi; telegram received (at 8:35 A.M.), DLC-Benjamin F. Butler. Incomplete in *O.R.*, I, xlii, part 2, 254. At 9:30 A.M., Butler telegraphed to USG. "I am about starting for Bermuda to take a boat for Dutch Gap Will Genl Barnard meet me there & accompany me." Copy, DNA, RG 107, Telegrams Collected (Unbound). On the same day, USG telegraphed to Butler. "Gn. Barnard & Col. Comstock have gone to Dutch Gap. Started before receipt of your despatch." ALS (telegram sent), OClWHi; copy, DLC-USG, V, 68.

At 5:00 P.M., USG telegraphed to Hancock. "Gen. Barnard and Col. Comstock have returned and report that no benefit can arise from an advance from the work carried by Gen. Butler last evening. His troops will be withdrawn to Dutch Gap during the night. Your forces will be left North of the James for some days during which employ the enemy as you deem best." ALS (telegram sent), OClWHi; telegram received (at 9:00 P.M.), DNA, RG 94, War Records Office, Dept. of the Cumberland. Printed as received at 9:20 P.M. in *O.R.*, I, xlii, part 2, 249.

To Maj. Gen. George G. Meade

City Point, Va Aug 17. 1864.

MAJ GEN G. G. MEADE
COMD'G. A. P.
GENERAL

The report of prisoners captured North of the James indicates that all the Cavalry or nearly so, south of Petersburg, has been withdrawn and also three Brigades of Infantry have been sent North of the River. There may have been a further reduction of the Infantry force, but there is no evidence to show it. Under these circumstances no ~~dicisive~~ decisive result could be expected from moving a single corps by our left, but they might get to the Weldon Road and with the Aid of a little Cavalry, cut and destroy a few miles of it. You may therefore start Warren in the morning. I do not want him to fight any unequal battles nor to assault fortifications. His movement should be more a reconnaisance in force with instructions to take advantage of any weakness of the enemy he may discover. The 9th & 18th Corps ~~form~~ form so thin a line on their present front that no assistance can be expected from them further than the number of men they detain by their presence.

Three or four days rations will be sufficient for Gen. Warren to carry with him. If he can not strike the Road near the enemy's line enclosing Petersburg he can strike or feel further South. If he finds the enemy extending along the RailRoad showing front wherever he does, let him remain holding them there and send back for further supplies.

I want if possible to make such demonstrations, as will force Lee to withdraw a portion of his troops from the Valley so that Sheridan can strike a blow against the balance.

Very Respectfully

U. S. GRANT

Lt. Genl.

Copies, DLC-USG, V, 68; (2) Meade Papers, PHi. *O.R.*, I, xlii, part 2, 244. On Aug. 17, 1864, 2:00 P.M., Maj. Gen. George G. Meade wrote to USG. "I have to acknowledge the receipt of your communication of this date per Capt. Dunn A. D. C.—The necessary instructions will be given to Maj. Genl. Warren who will move at 4. a m tomorrow—Genl. Kautz will be directed to place Two regiments of Cavalry (½ his force) under Genl. Warren's orders.—Genl. Warren will be directed to strike the R. Rd. near the enemys works but out of range of them. I anticipate no difficulty in Genl. Warren's making a lodgment on the R. Rd. but I think the enemy will send out all his available Reserves to endeavor to check the work of destruction—It is not believed he can spare a force sufficient to seriously embarrass Genl. Warren tho he may be able to interrupt his work of destroying the Road by keeping him on the alert by his threats—Genl. Warren will be directed to destroy as much of the road as possible, working south & continuing to work till recalled or forced away by the enemy's operations.—" ALS, DNA, RG 108, Letters Received. *O.R.*, I, xlii, part 2, 245.

At 9:00 A.M., Meade had telegraphed to USG. "All quiet on the lines during the night—some little picket firing & mortar practice.—I forward despatch from signal officer, indicating a return of part of the enemys troops that were seen to move yesterday p. m.—" ALS (telegram sent), DNA, RG 94, War Records Office, Army of the Potomac; telegram received, *ibid.*, RG 108, Letters Received. *O.R.*, I, xlii, part 2, 244; (misdated Aug. 27) *ibid.*, p. 541. The enclosure is *ibid.*, p. 244.

On the same day, USG telegraphed to Meade. "~~Maj~~ Mahones Div. and Bushrod Johnson's old Brigade are now North of the James. This leaves the force at Petersburg reduced to what it was when the mine was sprung. Warren may find an opportunity to do more than I had expected." ALS (telegram sent), OClWHi; telegram received (at 10:00 P.M.), *ibid.*, RG 94, War Records Office, Army of the Potomac. *O.R.*, I, xlii, part 2, 245. At 10:30 P.M., Meade telegraphed to USG. "The information contained in your telegram of 10. P. M has been sent to Genl. Warren & he has been directed to strike the Rail Road close to the enemys works, to extend & reconnoitre to the left, and if he finds any weak point to attack.—" ALS (telegram sent), DNA, RG 94, War Records Office, Army of the Potomac; telegram received, *ibid.*, RG 108, Letters Received. *O.R.*, I, xlii, part 2, 245.

To Maj. Gen. Philip H. Sheridan

(Cipher)   City Point, Va. Aug. 17th/64 9 a. m.
Maj. Gen. Sheridan, Winchester Va.

Our movement to the North of James river has execised the enemy a greatdeel, and from statements of prisoners they have lost very heavily. It has too undoubtedly prevented sending reinforcements to the valley. Richmond is now threatened by no mean force on the North and Petersburg by a larger force on the South. It is highly probable that the constant vigilence I shall compell the enemy to keep up will force him to recall a large portion of Early's force. Watch closely and be prepared to move at any moment. If you find Early sending off any of his troops strike suddenly and hard.

U. S. Grant
Lt. Gn

ALS (telegram sent), CSmH; telegram received (on Aug. 18, 1864, 8:00 P.M.), DNA, RG 107, Telegrams Collected (Bound). Printed as received at 7:00 P.M. in *O.R.*, I, xliii, part 1, 822. On Aug. 18, 11:00 P.M., Maj. Gen. Philip H. Sheridan, Charles Town, West Va., telegraphed to USG. "In a previous telegram I informed you that I would give up my position at Cedar Creek and fall back to Berryville. The enemy were massing heavily in Luray valley and Cedar Creek was no place for defensive operations. I now hold with Cavalry the line of the Opequan Creek—A heavy force of the enemys Infantry drove Genl Torbert out of Winchester yesterday evening about dark. He had Wilsons Division of Cavalry and a small Brigade of Infantry—I can not tell the loss, it will be at least 250— No loss of material—All reports I get is to the effect that troops are coming into the valley from Culpepper. There has been no advance toward Martinsburg—I destroyed all the wheat, Hay & Provisions south of Winchester and Berryville and drove off all the cattle. The enemy is very much chagrined at it. If the enemy should go North of the Potomac I will follow him up. There is no occasion for alarm. Genl Grovers Division joined me this morning at Snickers Gap" Telegram received (on Aug. 19, 10:45 A.M.), DNA, RG 107, Telegrams Collected (Bound); *ibid.*, RG 108, Letters Received; DLC-Robert T. Lincoln; copies, DNA, RG 107, Telegrams Received in Cipher; DLC-Philip H. Sheridan. *O.R.*, I, xliii, part 1, 830.

On Aug. 19, 10:30 P.M., Sheridan telegraphed to USG. "All the information received today shows a large concentration of the enemy at Winchester. I receive constant reports of the passage of troops across to this valley from Culpeper—I have taken the defensive until their strength is more fully developed They have made no attempt to pass down the valley to Martinsburg which I hold with a small force of cav. If they cross the Potomac they expose their rear and I will pitch into them   I destroyed every thing that was eatable south of Win-

chester & they will have to haul supplies from well up towards Staunton   Our
losses at Winchester ~~road~~ will be abut two hundred   Guerillas ~~have~~ give me
great annoyance but I am quietly disposing of numbers of them   The enemy
appears to be uncertain as to what course to pursue.   the intentio[n] so far as I
can learn was to send a column direct from Culpeper to the Potomac and Early
to advance at the same time from Martinsburg—this was frustrated by Early
being compelled to fall back and your operations on the north side of the James
I still think that two divisions of infantry have come here and Fitz Lees Cavalry
My force will have to be weakened to supply the place of the hundred days men
serving at Harpers Ferry and in west Virginia   Grover has joined me   I now
can calculate on bringing into action about 22. or 23000 infantry and about
eight cavalry"   Telegram received (on Aug. 20, 7:30 A.M.), DNA, RG 107,
Telegrams Collected (Bound); *ibid.*, RG 108, Letters Received; copies, *ibid.*,
RG 107, Telegrams Received in Cipher; DLC-Philip H. Sheridan. *O.R.*, I, xliii,
part 1, 841.

To Frederick Dent

——

Aug. 17th *1864.*

Mr. Dent,

I have not written to Julia for the last week thinking that she
would be on her way to Philadelphia before the letter would reach.
If not yet gone however I want to say that Col. Porter failed to
procure a house for her at Princeton. I now want her to go to Phila
and either rent a house there and send the children to school, or
board until proper arangements can be made for her elswhere. The
moment I hear she has started from St. Louis I will send Fred.
Dent to assist in making arrangements for settling.

I am in very good health. The Commissioner for the exchange
of prisoners has promised for the last six weeks to return John
Dent by the next flag. My experiance however has been that men
who have committed treason neither regard their word or their oath
afterwards. Their ministers preach the doctrine that an oath given
to a Yankee, even though it is to obtain their freedom when they
are farely captives, has no binding effect. I hope John has been
thoroughly cured of his *sesesh*, sympathies by the long sojorn he
has been forced to submit to with the people he defends.

Yours Truly
U. S. Grant

ALS, DLC-USG.

To Maj. Gen. Henry W. Halleck

———

(Cipher)   City Point, Va. Aug. 18th *1864*. [*8:00* P.M.]
Maj. Gen. Halleck, Washington,

Gen. Warren moved with his Corps this morning to and across the Welden road about one mile south of the Lead works. To that point he met nothing but the enemy's pickets. He advanced from there towards Petersburg meeting the enemy early in his advance. He had conciderable fighting during the day suffering some loss and inflicting loss upon the enemy. I have no report showing the extent of our losses but judge them to be light from the dispatches. Some of the enemy's wounded fell into our hands and a few other prisoners.

                                U. S. Grant
                                Lt. Gn.

ALS (telegram sent), CSmH; telegram received (on Aug. 19, 1864, 6:45 A.M.), DNA, RG 107, Telegrams Collected (Bound). *O.R.*, I, xlii, part 1, 18; *ibid.*, I, xlii, part 2, 261. On Aug. 19, 2:00 P.M., Secretary of War Edwin M. Stanton telegraphed to USG. "The President directs me to express [h]is gratification at your success in pushing across and seizing the Welden road. He thinks that is a a heavy blow to the enemy if you are able to hold it as he hopes you will." ALS (telegram sent), DNA, RG 107, Telegrams Collected (Bound); telegram received, *ibid.*, RG 108, Letters Received. *O.R.*, I, xlii, part 2, 291.

On Nov. 26, 3:00 P.M., Col. James A. Hardie telegraphed to USG. "What date is to be assumed as that of the occupation of the Weldon Railroad?" LS (telegram sent), DNA, RG 107, Telegrams Collected (Bound); telegram received, *ibid.*, RG 108, Letters Received. On Nov. 27, USG telegraphed to Hardie. "The date of our occupation of the Weldon RR is August 18th 1864" Telegram received, *ibid.*, RG 107, Telegrams Collected (Bound); copies, *ibid.*, RG 108, Letters Sent; DLC-USG, V, 45, 70, 107.

To Maj. Gen. Benjamin F. Butler

———

                          City Point, Va, Aug. 18th *1864*.
Maj. Gen. Butler,

I am opposed to exchanges being made until the whole matter is put on a footing giving equal advantages to us with those given to the enemy. In the mean time I direct that no flags of truce be sent to the enemy nor any arrangements or agreements entered into with him without my first being fully advised of what is being done and yielding my ~~sanction~~ consent to it. The Steamer New York will not be permitted to proceed to Aiken's Landing until I receive a report of the full object of her mission and the load she now has on board.[1]

U. S. GRANT Lt. Gn

ALS (telegram sent), OClWHi; telegram received (at 3:35 P.M.), DNA, RG 94, War Records Office, Dept. of Va. and N. C., Army of the James, Unentered Papers. *O.R.*, II, vii, 606. On Aug. 18, 1864, 4:00 P.M., Maj. Gen. Benjamin F. Butler telegraphed to USG. "Telegram received   No exchange has been or will be made by me which will give the enemy any advantage   To Shew that my views and the Lt General are in exact accordance I will send letter written to Gen Hitchcock today—upon this subject with ~~full~~ the endorsements referred to. I have exchanged nobody but wounded men since the first of May except Surgeons —noncombatants and and a few cases of special exchange   A full report will be made to the Lt General of all that was intended to be done in the matter"   ALS (telegram sent), DNA, RG 107, Telegrams Collected (Unbound); telegram received, *ibid.*, RG 108, Letters Received. Printed as sent at 7:00 P.M. in *O.R.*, II, vii, 606. The enclosure is *ibid.* On the same day, Butler wrote to USG. "I have the honor to inclose to you a few of the applications and orders about special exchanges, to which I wish to call your attention; also a copy of a letter written this morning to Major-General Hitchcock, commissioner of exchange at Washington, upon the subject of his indorsement 'that an exchange would be very desirable,' and also a direction from the Secretary of War upon the necessity of making some arrangement about the treating of our prisoners in cases of supposed retaliation. As these papers are original may I ask you the favor that they shall be returned?" *Ibid.*, p. 607. See following telegram.

1. Earlier on Aug. 18, USG telegraphed to Butler. "I see the Steamer New York has arrived. Is she going to Aiken's Landing or elswhere under Flag of Truce?" ALS (telegram sent), OClWHi; copy, DLC-USG, V, 68. *O.R.*, II, vii, 605. On the same day, 3:45 P.M., Butler telegraphed to USG. "Steamer New York is to go to Aiken's Landing under Flag of Truce at which place she is to recieve certain communications and special exchanges among whom is Gen Bartlett and to arrange a meeting between Commissioner Ould and myself for a conference in regard to the treatment of ~~my~~ our prisoners and some cases of retaliation" LS (telegram sent), DNA, RG 107, Telegrams Collected (Unbound); telegram received, *ibid.*, RG 108, Letters Received. *O.R.*, II, vii, 605.

To Maj. Gen. Benjamin F. Butler

City Point Va. Aug. 18th 1864

MAJ. GEN. BUTLER,

I am satisfied that the object of your interview, besides having the proper sanction, meets with my entire approval. I have seen from Southern papers that a system of retaliation is going on in the South which they keep from us and which we should stop in some way. On the subject of exchanges however I differ from Gen. Hitchcock. It is hard on our men held in Southern prisons not to exchange them but it is humanity to those left in the ranks to fight our battles. Every man released, on parole or otherwise, becomes an active soldier against us at once either directly or indirectly. If we commence a system of exchanges which liberates all prisoners taken we will have to fight on until the whole South is exterminated. If we hold those caught they amount to no more than dead men. At this particular time to release all rebel prisoners North would insure Sherman's defeat and would compromise our safety here.

U. S. GRANT
Lt. Gn.

ALS (telegram sent), OClWHi; telegram received, DLC-Benjamin F. Butler. *O.R.*, II, vii, 606–7.

To Maj. Gen. Benjamin F. Butler

City Point, Aug. 18th/64

MAJ. GN. BUTLER,

Wilsons Wharf & Ft Powhattan must be held. No troops however can be had from Washington or Baltimore. They are calling on me for troops to take the place of theirs now soon to be discharged. You will have to send some of your colored troops.

U. S. GRANT Lt. Gn.

ALS (telegram sent), OClWHi; telegram received, DLC-Benjamin F. Butler. *O.R.*, I, xlii, part 2, 286. On Aug. 18, 1864, 5:30 P.M., Maj. Gen. Benjamin F.

Butler had telegraphed to USG. "We are garraisoning Fort Powhattan & Fort Pocohantus (Wilsons Landing) with 100 days men whose time is now quite out—we want two regiments for that purpose—There must be now a large surplus of new regiments of hundred days men and others in and about Washington and Baltimore   Can we not have some of these new one hundred days regiments ordered down—It will not do to lose either of these points—It would shut us off from the river—" LS (telegram sent), DNA, RG 107, Telegrams Collected (Unbound). *O.R.*, I, xlii, part 2, 286.

Earlier on Aug. 18, Butler telegraphed to USG transmitting a signal message of 7:35 A.M. reporting seven railroad cars carrying troops moving toward Richmond. Telegram received, DNA, RG 107, Telegrams Collected (Unbound). The signal message is in *O.R.*, I, xlii, part 2, 287.

At 10:50 A.M., Butler telegraphed to USG. "Did Warren make the move which was contemplated   we have heard nothing on our front. I have heard no report of any result from the rapid firing at Petersburg" LS (telegram sent), DNA, RG 107, Telegrams Collected (Unbound). Printed as received at 11:20 A.M. in *O.R.*, I, xlii, part 2, 286. On the same day, USG telegraphed to Butler. "The firing last night was nothing more I believe than the enemy feeling to ascertain if we had evacuated. Warren moved this morning. At 8.30 the enemy's pickets were falling back before him." ALS (telegram sent), OClWHi; telegram received, DLC-Benjamin F. Butler. On the same day, USG telegraphed to Butler and to Maj. Gen. Winfield S. Hancock. "Our forces reached the Welden road meeting nothing but Cavalry. They captured a few men belonging to the 7th Confederate Cavalry." ALS (telegram sent), OClWHi; telegram received (at 12:15 P.M.), DLC-Benjamin F. Butler; (at 12:10 P.M.) DNA, RG 107, Telegrams Collected (Unbound). *O.R.*, I, xlii, part 2, 286.

At 3:50 P.M., Butler telegraphed to USG. "I am informed from the lookout at Dutch Gap that a Brigade of troops are crossing Cox's Ferry going East" ALS (telegram sent), DNA, RG 107, Telegrams Collected (Unbound). *O.R.*, I, xlii, part 2, 287.

To Maj. Gen. Winfield S. Hancock

City Point Aug. 18th *1864*. [*10:30* A.M.]

MAJ. GN HANCOCK

If you can hold your position with a Div. less than you have send one Div. to-night, starting as soon as you can get it off, to report to Gen. Meade.

U. S. GRANT
Lt. Gn

ALS (telegram sent), OClWHi; telegram received (at 6:47 P.M.), DNA, RG 94, War Records Office, Dept. of the Cumberland. *O.R.*, I, xlii, part 2, 268. On Aug. 18, 1864, 6:40 P.M. and 7:00 P.M., Maj. Gen. Winfield S. Hancock telegraphed to USG, sending a copy of the first to Maj. Gen. George G. Meade.

"The Enemy have been feeling my lines and have made some pretty sharp attacks on my front and right—They still Continue it on my right but at this moment slightly—" Telegram received, DNA, RG 94, War Records Office, Army of the Potomac; *ibid.*, RG 107, Telegrams Collected (Unbound); *ibid.*, RG 108, Letters Received. *O.R.*, I, xlii, part 2, 269. "Your despatch is recd   The enemy are very vigorous—I have just recd a despatch stating that the enemy have possession of the roads in Gen Greggs rear and that they have passed cavalry and infantry towards Malvern Hill threatning my hold on the river which is now essential to me—I can only send a division by shortening my lines so as to render my connection with the River secure—I shall change my lines tonight to meet the new state of things & will send a division if you do not object to my contracting my lines—I will telegraph you a little later—" Telegram received, DNA, RG 107, Telegrams Collected (Unbound); *ibid.*, RG 108, Letters Received. *O.R.*, I, xlii, part 2, 269. At 7:40 P.M., USG telegraphed to Hancock. "I have no objection to your shortning your line to make your position secure." ALS (telegram sent), OClWHi; telegram received (at 7:45 P.M.), DNA, RG 94, War Records Office, Dept. of the Cumberland. *O.R.*, I, xlii, part 2, 269. On the same day, Hancock telegraphed to USG three times, the second at 11:00 P.M., the third at 11:30 P.M. "I will send Gen Motts Division to report to Gen Meade—" "Everything is quiet, at time I am Changing my line a little. The Genl direction being that of the NewMarket road—By withdrawing my right I have taken out a Div. & still have a heavy force on my right with which I shall make a demonstration on the Charles City road tomorrow   The enemy attacked with Considerable force on Gen Birneys right just above Flussers Mill but were repulsed—They attacked Gregg on the roads Coming in from white oak Swamp & drove him though he still holds the intersection of the Charles City & Malvern Hill roads. The enemy holding between the Cross road & Deep bottom Creek—I shall Clear out whatever may be there in the morning—" "The last report I had from the enemy tonight was one that Came from the picket line, just after their repulse to the effect they were moving at Double quick towards my right" Telegrams received, DNA, RG 108, Letters Received. *O.R.*, I, xlii, part 2, 268, 270.

To Maj. Gen. Winfield S. Hancock

City Point Va. Aug. 18th 1864

Maj. Gen. Hancock,

There has been a requisition made for 500 horses for the 2d Cavalry Div. There are now at Washington about 1000 men of this Div. ~~in Washington~~ dismounted. Ask Gregg if he will have 500 men sent with the horses or if he will have the horses sent and leave the men until they can be remounted.

It is reported that the Mail Steamer has been fired into below here. Get a Brigade of Greggs cavalry ready if you can to go down and cut ~~them~~ off the enemy   I will make full enquiries about the matter and inform you.[1] In the mean time have the cavalry ready but do not start them until further orders.

U. S. GRANT, Lt. Gn.

ALS (telegram sent), OClWHi; copies, DLC-USG, V, (misdated Aug. 17, 1864) 45, 59, 68; (misdated Aug. 17) DNA, RG 108, Letters Sent. *O.R.*, I, xlii, part 2, 268. On Aug. 18, Maj. Gen. Winfield S. Hancock telegraphed to USG. "Your Dispatch is rec'd—and Gen Gregg has been sent for to make the arrangements you pr[o]p[os]e—" ALS (telegram sent), DNA, RG 107, Telegrams Collected (Unbound). *O.R.*, I, xlii, part 2, 268. On the same day, Hancock telegraphed to USG. "General Gregg reports that he would prefer having 500 horses sent to City Point, as he has now at this time more than 500 dismounted men." *Ibid.*, p. 269.

On Aug. 17, 2:20 P.M., Maj. Gen. Henry W. Halleck had telegraphed to USG. "Requisitions for five hundred horses to be sent to city-Point for second cavalry division has been recieved. There are about a thousand men here dismounted belonging to that Division. Shall these men be sent with the horses, or be retained here till mounted?" ALS (telegram sent), DNA, RG 107, Telegrams Collected (Bound); telegram received, *ibid.*; *ibid.*, RG 108, Letters Received. On Aug. 18, 2:30 P.M., USG telegraphed to Halleck. "Send horses for the 2d Div. of Cavalry and leave the dismounted men in Washington until they can return mounted." ALS (telegram sent), CSmH; telegram received (on Aug. 19, 7:00 A.M.), DNA, RG 107, Telegrams Collected (Bound).

1. Also on Aug. 18, USG telegraphed to Hancock. "It turns out to be a mistake about there being a rebel battery below here. The firing heard was our gun boats discharging their guns." ALS (telegram sent), OClWHi; telegram received (at 12:10 P.M.), DNA, RG 107, Telegrams Collected (Unbound). *O.R.*, I, xlii, part 2, 269.

To Maj. Gen. George G. Meade

City Point Va. Aug. 18th *1864. 12. M*

MAJ. GEN. MEADE,

If Warren can do no better I would have him close up on Petersburg, with his left West of the Welden road, and intrench and stay there. So long as the enemy is occupied North of the James he can spare no force to drive Warren away. When we withdraw from there Hancock can go to his support and the 10th Corps will relieve the 18th from the trenches giving us an other Corps footloose.

I do not mean this in any way to prevent Warren from taking advantage of any weakness of the enemy according to his judgement.

U. S. GRANT
Lt. Gn

ALS (telegram sent), OClWHi; telegram received, DNA, RG 94, War Records Office, Army of the Potomac. *O.R.*, I, xlii, part 2, 262. On Aug. 18, 1864, 1:15 P.M., Maj. Gen. George G. Meade telegraphed to USG. "Respectfully forwarded —Your telegram of 12 M recd—I will await the developements of the day before sending Warren any instruction based on it—Indeed his orders last night Contemplate his making and retaining a lodgement on the Railroad—" Telegram received, DNA, RG 108, Letters Received. *O.R.*, I, xlii, part 2, 263. The enclosed telegram of 11:00 A.M. from Maj. Gen. Gouverneur K. Warren to Maj. Gen. Andrew A. Humphreys is *ibid.*, p. 273.

At 2:30 A.M., Lt. Col. Cyrus B. Comstock had telegraphed to Meade. "Gen Grant desires me to ask what the heavy firing is" ALS (telegram sent), DNA, RG 108, Telegrams Sent by Comstock; telegram received (at 1:48 A.M.), *ibid.*, RG 94, War Records Office, Army of the Potomac. *O.R.*, I, xlii, part 2, 261. At 2:15 A.M. and 2:30 A.M., Meade telegraphed to Comstock. "The firing is in front of the 9th corps—No report has been made but I have sent for one." ALS (telegram sent), DNA, RG 94, War Records Office, Army of the Potomac; copies, *ibid.*, RG 393, Army of the Potomac, Telegrams Sent; Meade Papers, PHi. *O.R.*, I, xlii, part 2, 261. "The cannonading & mortar practice was along the whole line 18. & 9th Corps No one seems to know how it began or the cause.— It is probably the enemy feeling to see if we are still here.—It is now subsiding.—" ALS (telegram sent), DNA, RG 94, War Records Office, Army of the Potomac; telegram received, *ibid.*, RG 108, Letters Received. *O.R.*, I, xlii, part 2, 261. At 2:30 A.M., Comstock telegraphed to Maj. Gen. Edward O. C. Ord. "Gen Grant desires me to ask what the heavy firing is. & where." ALS (telegram sent), DNA, RG 108, Telegrams Sent by Comstock; telegram received, CU-B. On the same day, Ord telegraphed to Comstock. "There is a heavy cannonade & mortar firing going on on my front—We are replying to the enemy—" ALS (telegram sent), DNA, RG 107, Telegrams Collected (Unbound). At 1:30 P.M., Meade telegraphed to USG. "I have endeavored to ascertain the probable cause of the heavy cannonading last night, but without success—It commenced a little before 2. a m on the right of the 18th corps by the enemy and was quickly taken up by all their batteries to our left, and as quickly responded to by ours—The enemy in the afternoon previous told the pickets of the 9th corps not to be alarmed in the night because they were going to shell the negroes. The probabilities are, that they suspected some movement on our part, which they thought they might interrupt, or they may have suspected we were or had been withdrawing, and they would draw our fire—From all I can learn the casualties on our side are 9th corps 2 killed 10 wounded 18th. corps 5 killed 15 wounded in all 7 killed 25 wounded. I have given orders hereafter our batteries are not to open at night unless there is evidence they are able to accomplish something—" ALS (telegram sent), *ibid.*, RG 94, War Records Office, Army of the Potomac; telegram received, *ibid.*, RG 108, Letters Received. *O.R.*, I, xlii, part 2, 263.

At 10:30 A.M., USG telegraphed to Meade. "Have you heard what progress Gen. Warren is making?" ALS (telegram sent), OClWHi; telegram received,

DNA, RG 94, War Records Office, Army of the Potomac. *O.R.*, I, xlii, part 2, 261. At 10:45 A.M., Meade telegraphed to USG. "Tel. of 10.30 received—The last despatch from Genl. Warren of 8.20 is forwarded—Whenever Genl. Warren reports any thing of importance it will be promptly transmitted.—. . . P. S—I am having the telegraph run out to the Gurley House." ALS (telegram sent), DNA, RG 94, War Records Office, Army of the Potomac; telegram received, *ibid.*, RG 108, Letters Received. *O.R.*, I, xlii, part 2, 262. The enclosure is *ibid.*, p. 272.

On the same day, Meade sent a series of telegrams to USG, beginning at 11:00 A.M. "The following just received from Genl. Warren.—The 7th Va. cavalry is in Rossers brigade, Youngs Division, formerly Hamptons Divn. it being understood Hampton now commands all the cavalry." ALS (telegram sent), DNA, RG 94, War Records Office, Army of the Potomac; copies, *ibid.*, RG 393, Army of the Potomac, Letters Sent; Meade Papers, PHi. *O.R.*, I, xlii, part 2, 262. The enclosure is *ibid.*, p. 272. At 12:30 P.M. "I send the last report just received from Genl. Warren—Since its receipt, quite sharp cannonading is heard in his direction but no report of progress." ALS (telegram sent), DNA, RG 94, War Records Office, Army of the Potomac; telegram received, *ibid.*, RG 108, Letters Received. *O.R.*, I, xlii, part 2, 262. The enclosure is *ibid.*, p. 272. At 3:15 P.M. "I forward the above just recd—No despatch from Warren since the one sent you at 1 15 P. M.—Heavy Musketry firing as well as Cannonading has recently been heard in that direction—" Telegram received, DNA, RG 108, Letters Received. *O.R.*, I, xlii, part 2, 263. The enclosure is *ibid.* At 4:00 P.M. and 4:10 P.M. "The above just recd   Was sent before the attack of which I have reported Musketry & Cannonading—No sounds now. As there appears to be a div. of the Enemys Cavalry on the Railroad I have ordered Kautz to draw in another of his Regts leaving only one (1) between the Black Water swamp and the James." "Just received & forwarded—" Telegrams received, DNA, RG 108, Letters Received. *O.R.*, I, xlii, part 2, 264. The enclosures are *ibid.*, pp. 264, 273. At 5:00 P.M. "Just recd and forwarded. This appears to have been an open fight   The enemy attacking & Warren further reports them moving down on his left flank   He has two (2) divisions besides those reported by him as engaged   I fancy he will not be able to do more than effect a lodgement on the road & that the enemy will vigorously dispute this . . . P. S. There has been no firing since the fight here reported"   ALS (torn telegram sent), DNA, RG 94, War Records Office, Army of the Potomac; telegram received, *ibid.*, RG 108, Letters Received. *O.R.*, I, xlii, part 2, 264. The enclosure is *ibid.*, p. 273.

To Maj. Gen. George G. Meade

City Point Va. Aug. 18th/64 7.40 p m

MAJ. GN. MEADE,

Gen. Hancock will probably send a Div. to-night. I will let you know as soon as he ascertains if it can be spared. The distance between Hancock & Warren is so great that it would take until 12 to-morrow to transfer troops from one to the other and then they would be to much fatigued to do much. Could not reinforcements be sent from the 9th Corps to Warren, if he should want them and let the 2d Corps take their place? If the enemy pile any conciderable force against Warren to-morrow they must do it by taking nearly every thing from their line in front of the 9th & 18th Corps and must be met by an equal reduction of our lines.

U. S. Grant
Lt. Gen.

ALS (telegram sent), OClWHi; telegram received, DNA, RG 94, War Records Office, Army of the Potomac. *O.R.*, I, xlii, part 2, 266.

On Aug. 18, 1864, 6:00 P.M., Maj. Gen. George G. Meade telegraphed to USG. "Warren is directed to maintain his hold & entrench himself—. When may we look for Hancock?" ALS (telegram sent), DNA, RG 94, War Records Office, Army of the Potomac; telegram received, *ibid.*, RG 108, Letters Received. *O.R.*, I, xlii, part 2, 265. Meade wrote his telegram at the foot of a telegram of 4:00 P.M. from Maj. Gen. Gouverneur K. Warren to Maj. Gen. Andrew A. Humphreys, printed *ibid.*, p. 274. On the same day, USG telegraphed to Meade. "I think it will be advisable to hold Hancock where he is until to-mirrow night. I will direct him if he can hold his position to send one Div. to-night." ALS (telegram sent), OClWHi; telegram received (at 6:20 P.M.), DNA, RG 94, War Records Office, Army of the Potomac. *O.R.*, I, xlii, part 2, 265. At 7:15 P.M. and 7:20 P.M., Meade telegraphed to USG. "Warren can hold his own I think, and may perhaps yet push the enemy.—I ought to have mentioned that when he spoke of Ayres Division he referred to the *Maryland* brigade, which he had previously reported as giving way.—" "The following just received from Warren & forwarded." ALS (telegrams sent), DNA, RG 94, War Records Office, Army of the Potomac; telegrams received, *ibid.*, RG 108, Letters Received. *O.R.*, I, xlii, part 2, 265. The enclosure in the second telegram is *ibid.*, pp. 274–75. On the same day, USG telegraphed to Meade. "Gen. Hancock has ordered Gn. Motts Div. to report to you." ALS (telegram sent), DNA, RG 107, Telegrams Collected (Unbound); telegram received (at 8:20 P.M.), *ibid.*, RG 94, War Records Office, Army of the Potomac. Printed as sent at 8:20 P.M. in *O.R.*, I, xlii, part 2, 265. At 9:30 P.M., Meade telegraphed to USG. "I send you the last despatch recieved from Warren—Parke has been ordered to relieve the maximum force he can with Motts division, & push them up at once to Warrens support.—" ALS (telegram sent), DNA, RG 94, War Records Office, Army of the Potomac; telegram received, *ibid.*, RG 108, Letters Received. *O.R.*, I, xlii, part 2, 265. The enclosure is *ibid.*, p. 275.

Probably on Aug. 18, 11:15 P.M., USG telegraphed to Meade. "Tell Warren if the enemy comes out and attacks him in the morning not to hesitate about taking out every man he has to repel it and not to stop when the enemy is repulsed but follow him up as long as he can. to the last. We certainly ought to be satisfied when we can get the enemy to attack us." ALS (telegram sent), CSmH; telegram received, DNA, RG 94, War Records Office, Army of the Potomac. *O.R.*, I, xlii, part 2, 266. Both telegrams sent and received are dated Aug. 19; USG's letterbook copies are dated Aug. 18.

To Maj. Gen. William T. Sherman

———

(Cipher)   City Point Va. Aug. 18th *1864*.
Maj. Gn. Sherman, Near Atlanta Ga.

Richmond papers of the 17th give it as the opinion of Military men that Atlanta can hold out one month yet. In the mean time, like McCawber, the expect something to turn up. If you can hold tight as you are now and prevent raids upon your rear you will destroy most of that Army. I never would advise going backward even if your roads are cut so as to preclude the possibility of receiving supplies from the North but would recommend the accumulation of Ordnance stores and supplies while you can and if it comes to the worst move sSouth as you suggested. I have forced the enemy to move a large force North of the James River and am now moving one Corps by our left around Petersburg. I expect no great results but will probably cut the Welden road again and will also demonstrate to the enemy that he has now the minimum garrison possible to hold his present lines with, and that to hold his roads he must reinforce.

U. S. Grant
Lt. Gen.

ALS (telegram sent), CSmH; copies, DLC-USG, V, 45, 59, 68; DLC-William T. Sherman; DNA, RG 108, Letters Sent; *ibid.*, RG 393, Military Div. of the Miss., Telegrams Received in the Field. *O.R.*, I, xxxviii, part 5, 569. On Aug. 19, 1864, 10:45 A.M., Maj. Gen. William T. Sherman telegraphed to USG. "I have your two despatches of 14th and 16th also that of 18th. I will never take a step backward and have no fears of Hood. I can whip him outside of his trenches and think in time I can compel him to come out   I think at this moment I have a fine cavalry force on the only road which can find him and if necessary will swing my whole army across it also" Telegram received (datelined 11:00 A.M.), DNA, RG 108, Letters Received; copy, *ibid.*, RG 393, Military Div. of the Miss., Telegrams Sent in the Field. *O.R.*, I, xxxviii, part 5, 594.

To Commander Daniel Ammen

City Point, Va., Aug. 18th, 1864.

DEAR AMMEN,—

Your letter of the 2d inst. was duly received. I regret not having made better progress in whipping out the rebellion, but feel conscious of having done the best I know how. This army has fought desperately since leaving Culpeper, and has gained this substantial advantage: the enemy is afraid to fight it on an open field, whilst the Army of the Potomac feels confident of success whenever the terms are anything like equal. Several times we have had decisive victories within our grasp, but let them, through accident or fault, slip through our hands. Our movement from Cold Harbor to the south side of the James was made with such celerity that before the enemy was aware of it, and before he had got a single regiment across the river, our forces had carried the fortifications east of Petersburg. There was nothing—not even a military force—to prevent our walking in and taking possession. The officer charged with the work, for some unaccountable reason, stopped at the works he had captured, and gave the enemy time to get in a garrison and to intrench it. On the 30th of July, again, by a feint north of the James, we drew most of the enemy to that side of the river, and whilst he was there (with my troops quietly withdrawn during the night) a mine, judiciously prepared, was exploded, burying a battery and some three hundred of the enemy, and making a breach in his works into which our men marched without opposition. The enemy was completely surprised, and commenced running in all directions. There was nothing to prevent our men from marching directly to the high ground in front of them, to which they had been directed to go, and there all the enemy's fortifications would have been taken in reverse, and no stand would have been made. It is clear that without a loss of five hundred men we could have had Petersburg, with all its artillery and many of the garrison. But our troops stopped in the crater made by the explosion. The enemy was given time to rally and reoccupy his line. Then we found, true enough, that we had the wolf by the ears. He was hard to hold, and more dangerous to let go. This was so outrageous that I have obtained a court of inquiry to sift the matter. We will peg away, however, and end this matter, if our people at home will but be true to themselves. If they would but reflect, everything looks favorable. The South now have every man in the ranks, including old men and little boys. They have no longer means to replace a man lost; whilst by enforcing the draft we have abundance of men. Give us half the men called for by the draft, and there will hardly be any resistance made. The rebellion is now fed by the bickering and differences North. The hope of a counter-revolution over the draft or the Presidential election keeps them together. Then, too, they hope for a Peace candidate who would let them go. A "peace at any price" is fearful to contemplate. It would be but the beginning of war. The demands of the South would know no limits. They would demand indemnity for expenses incurred in carrying on the war. They would demand the return of all their slaves set free in consequence of the war. They would demand a treaty looking to the rendition of all fugitive slaves escaping into the Northern States, and they would keep on demanding until it would be better to be dead than to submit longer.

My staff officers generally have been sick. I am the only one at headquarters that has escaped entirely. General Rawlins, Col. Badeau and Rowley are now absent, sick, and three others of the staff have been absent, but have returned improved. The health of the troops, however, is generally good.

I will be glad to hear from you at all times.

Yours truly,
U. S. GRANT,
Lt.-G'l.

Daniel Ammen, *The Old Navy and the New* (Philadelphia, 1891), pp. 531–32.

To William H. Seward

City Point, Va, Aug. 19th *1864.*

HON. W. H. SEWARD,
SEC. OF STATE,
WASHINGTON D. C.

DEAR SIR:

I am in receipt of copy of F. W. Morse letter of the 22d of July to you inclosing copy of statement of C. W. G. in relation to desertions from this Army.[1] There are constant desertions, though but few of them go over to the enemy. Unlike the enemy however we do not loose our veterans and men who entered the service through patriotic motives. The men who desert are those who have just arrived and who have never done any fighting and never intended to when they enlisted. They are a class known as "Bounty Jumpers" or "Substitute" men, men who enlist for the money, desert and enlist again. After they have done this until they become fearful of punishment they join their regiments, in the field, and desert to the enemy.

Of this class of recruits we do not get one for every eight bounties paid to do good service. My Provost Marshal Gn. is preparing a statement on this subject which will show the reinforcements received from this class of recruits. Take the other side: the desertions from the enemy to us. Not a day passes but men come into our lines and men too who have been fighting for the South for more than three years. Not unfrequently a commissioned officer comes with them. Only a few days ago I sent a regiment, numbering one thousand men for duty, to Gen. Popes Department composed wholly of deserters from the rebel Army and prisoners who took the oath of allegiance and joined them.

There is no doubt but many prisoners of War have taken the oath of allegiance and enlisted as substitutes to get the bounty and effect their return to the South. These men are paraded abroad as deserters who want to join the south and fight her battles, and it is through our leniency that the South expects to reap great advantages.

We ought not to make a single exchange nor release a prisoner on any pretext whatever until the war closes. We have got to fight until the Military power of the South is exhausted and if we release or exchange prisoners captured it simply becomes a War of extermination.

> I have the honor to be
> Very respectfully
> your obt. svt.
> U. S. GRANT
> Lt. Gn

ALS, Seward Papers, NRU. *O.R.*, II, vii, 614–15.

1. On July 22, 1864, Freeman H. Morse, former U.S. Representative from Maine as a Whig (1843–45) and Republican (1857–61), U.S. Consul, London, wrote to Secretary of State William H. Seward, enclosing a statement of "C. W. G." of London, which quoted James E. Macfarland, secretary of legation to C.S.A. commissioner James M. Mason, as stating that deserters from USG's army wanted to fight against him because he had treated them so badly. On Aug. 10, Asst. Secretary of War Charles A. Dana forwarded copies of this correspondence to USG. ES, DNA, RG 108, Letters Received. Other reports from agent C. W. Geddes are *ibid.*, RG 84, Despatches from U.S. Consuls in London.

To Maj. Gen. Henry W. Halleck

———

(Cipher)   City Point Va. Aug. 19th *1864.* [*7:30* P.M.]
MAJ. GEN. HALLECK, WASHINGTON

Our troops are firmly fixed across the Welden road. There has been little or no fighting to-day either South of Petersburg or North of James River. Gen. Warren reports that the enemy's dead in conciderable numbers were found in his front this morning unburyed.

Gen. Birney telegraphs Gen. Butler as follows,

Hd Qrs. 10th A. C. Aug. 19th 1864

The enemy attacked my line in heavy force last night and were repulsed with great loss. In front of our colored regiment 82 dead bodies of the enemy are counted. The Colored troops behaved handsomly and are in fine spirits. The assault was in Column a Division strong and would have carried works not so well defended. The enemys loss was at least 1000.

Resptly D. B. BIRNEY Maj. Gen.[1]

We have had a greatdeel of rain about Petersburg this week and a very greatful change in the temperature.

U. S. GRANT
Lt. Gen.

ALS (telegram sent), CSmH; telegrams received (2—Aug. 20, 1864, 2:40 P.M.), DNA, RG 107, Telegrams Collected (Bound). *O.R.*, I, xlii, part 2, 292.

1. On Aug. 19, Maj. Gen. Benjamin F. Butler telegraphed to USG transmitting this telegram. "Respectfully forwarded to the Lt Genl Comdg Armies with the request that he will forward to the Hon Secy of War" Telegram received, DNA, RG 108, Letters Received.

To Maj. Gen. Henry W. Halleck

(Cipher)   City Point Va. Aug. 19th *1864*. [8:00 P.M.]
MAJ. GEN. HALLECK, WASHINGTON

Fitz Lee's Cavalry and Kershaws Division of Longstreets Corps have gone from here to the Valley. No other troops have and with the present distribution of troops here the enemy is much more likely to withdraw from the Valley than to send more there. The enemy's loss here this week in killed wounded and captured cannot fall much short of 4,000 if it does not exceed this number. They are now so extended that they are forced to keep every man on the watch and from accounts of prisoners are runing their men to death shifting them from one place to an other. Sheridan has a force about equal to the enemy and if the latter advances will have him at an advantage.

U. S. GRANT
Lt. Gen,

ALS (telegram sent), CSmH; telegram received (on Aug. 20, 1864, 2:50 P.M.), DNA, RG 107, Telegrams Collected (Bound). *O.R.*, I, xlii, part 2, 292; *ibid.*, I, xliii, part 1, 841.

To Maj. Gen. Henry W. Halleck

———

(Cipher)   City Point Va. Aug. 19th/64

MAJ. GN. HALLECK, WASHINGTON

The enemy come out this evening to Warrens right driving in the pickets connecting between him and the left of our old line on the Jerusalem Plank road and forcing back the two right Divisions of Warrens Corps. A heavy fight took place resulting in the re-establishing of our lines and the capture of a good many prisoners. The prisoners were from Heths, Mahones & Hokes Divisions. We also lost conciderable in prisoners.

U. S. GRANT
Lt. Gn.

ALS (telegram sent), CSmH; telegram received (sent at 9:00 P.M., received Aug. 20, 1864, 2:00 P.M.), DNA, RG 107, Telegrams Collected (Bound). Printed as received at 3:00 P.M. in *O.R.*, I, xlii, part 2, 292.

To Maj. Gen. Benjamin F. Butler

———

City Point Va. Aug. 19th/64

MAJ. GEN. BUTLER,

Have you possitive evidence of the presence of Picketts Division any where on our front? I ask because Gen. Halleck telegraphs that evidence which has heretofore proven reliable reports the whole of Longstreets Corps moving from Culpepper into the vally.[1] I know Fields Division is not ~~with~~ here.

U. S. GRANT
Lt. Gen.

ALS (telegram sent), OClWHi; telegram received, DLC-Benjamin F. Butler. *O.R.*, I, xlii, part 2, 322. On Aug. 19, 1864, 8:30 P.M., Maj. Gen. Benjamin F. Butler telegraphed to USG. "I have no positive evidence of Picketts Division lately—That a portion of it withdrew on Monday & Tuesday I have no doubt because some dismounted Cavalry was among a portion of the picket line in our front   But yesterday afternoon troops came back into the Rebel lines who had been there before, because one of the Captains in talking with an officer of the picket line stated to him a circumstance which happened to his Company two

weeks ago—I believe that but a Brigade or two of Picket's Division is before us—
I am surprised at your information that Field's Division is not here—Most of the
Prisoners captured by the 10th Corps were from Brigades of that Division   The
Richmond Sentinel which I sent you yesterday speaks of Benning's Brigade and
another the name of which I do not recollect, both of which are in Fields Div
having made a charge on our lines on Wednesday—You will see by the intercepted signal message of the Rebels ~~Lane's divn is near the Appomattox~~ Lanes
Brigade Wilcox' Division is near the Appomattox"   LS (telegram sent), DNA,
RG 107, Telegrams Collected (Unbound); telegram received, *ibid.*, RG 108,
Letters Received. Printed as received at 9:30 P.M. in *O.R.*, I, xlii, part 2, 323. On
the same day, USG telegraphed to Butler. "My dispatch, as written reads, 'I
know Fields Div. is here.' " ALS (telegram sent), OClWHi; telegram received
(at 9:43 P.M.), DLC-Benjamin F. Butler. USG's letterbook copy of the message
in question (DLC-USG, V, 68) has the word "not" cancelled.

On Aug. 19, Butler had telegraphed to USG transmitting a signal message
received at 9:00 A.M. "A large column of troops are crossing Chaffins farm in
the direction of Cox's Ferry"   Telegram received, DNA, RG 107, Telegrams
Collected (Unbound). On the same day, USG telegraphed to Butler. "Do you
understand the force ~~moving~~ crossing Chapin's farm towards Cox's Ferry to be
moving towards Hancock or towards Petersburg?" ALS (telegram sent),
OClWHi; telegram received, DLC-Benjamin F. Butler. At 10:15 A.M. and 11:00
A.M., Butler telegraphed to USG. "I understand the movement to be toward
Petersburgh   Willl send and ascertain and send word to you"   "~~Signal officer~~
Signal officer upon further examination reports Column of troops heretofore re-
ported as moving toward Cox's Ferry to be principally Cavalry and Waggons
moving in direction of Petersburgh"   ALS (telegrams sent), DNA, RG 107,
Telegrams Collected (Unbound).

At 10:00 A.M., Butler telegraphed to USG transmitting a signal message of
9:45 A.M. from Capt. Lemuel B. Norton to Lt. Col. George A. Kensel, chief of
staff for Butler. "The Signal Officer at Spring Hill reports that at 7.30 A. M.
eight (8) cars loaded with troops passed the Junction towards Petersburg."
Telegram received, *ibid.* On the same day, Butler telegraphed to USG transmitting intercepted C.S.A. signal messages. LS (telegram sent), *ibid.*; telegram
received, *ibid.*, RG 108, Letters Received. *O.R.*, I, xlii, part 2, 322.

On Aug. 19, Lt. Col. Cyrus B. Comstock telegraphed to Butler. "Lt. Gen.
Grant desires that you have the spare ponton bridge now at Deep Bottom thrown
across the river near the lower ponton bridge so as to have two bridges with the
best approaches that can be got for Hancocks use by dark tonight." ALS (telegram sent), DNA, RG 107, Telegrams Collected (Unbound). Misdated Aug.
18 in *O.R.*, I, xlii, part 2, 286. On Aug. 19, 10:00 A.M., Butler telegraphed to
Comstock. "Bridge will be ready at 8 o clock P. M.   there are two approaches on
the North side of River one very steep directly up the hill the other round the base
of the bluffs the last fit for Artillery & Waggons the first entirely ~~practible~~cable
for infantry. I would suggest that Gen. Hancock send a Staff officer to direct the
Waggons and Artillery by the latter road as if the former gets choked it will
entirely block the column by that Route"   ALS (telegram sent), DNA, RG
107, Telegrams Collected (Unbound); telegram received, *ibid.*, RG 108, Letters
Received. *O.R.*, I, xlii, part 2, 322.

On Aug. 19, Butler wrote to USG. "From all I can hear, the Colored troops
belonging to the 9th Army Corps have been very much demoralized by loss of

Officers, and by their repulse of the 30th—I would respectfully suggest that the arrangement which was spoken of, earlier in the season, may be carried out, and they be assigned to me, to take the place of the hundred days men, who are going home—Perhaps, by adding them to the 18th Corps, we can get in condition by and by, to start that Corps out, in an efficient manner, upon the expedition suggested—For long marches in the enemy's country, I much prefer Colored Troops. There are with them, no stragglers—Allow me to suggest, whether the 9th Corps under the circumstances, might not be added to the 5th and 10th, as it has substantially lost its Corps organization, and we might dispose of a troublesome question now pending—" LS, DNA, RG 108, Letters Received. *O.R.*, I, xlii, part 2, 323.

1. On Aug. 19, 10:00 A.M., Maj. Gen. Henry W. Halleck telegraphed to USG. "One of Genl Augur's scouts insists that Longstreet's corps & Fitz Hugh Lee's cavalry have passed through Culpepper on their way to join Early. The information derived from this man has heretofore proved very reliable. If this be true the enemy is too strong for Sheridan." ALS (telegram sent), DNA, RG 107, Telegrams Collected (Bound); telegram received, *ibid.*; *ibid.*, RG 108, Letters Received. *O.R.*, I, xlii, part 2, 291; *ibid.*, I, xliii, part 1, 840.

To Maj. Gen. Winfield S. Hancock

City Point Aug. 19th/64 10.30 a. m.

MAJ. GEN. HANCOCK,

The enemy are moving troops to Petersburg. How many have gone I do not know but probably a Division. If you can find an opportunity to attack any weak point do not hesitate to do so. I think it will be perfectly safe for you to leave any portion of your lines guarded merely with pickets whilst all the balance of the force is being used as an assaulting column.

U. S. GRANT
Lt. Gn

ALS (telegram sent), OClWHi; telegram received (at 10:40 A.M.), DNA, RG 107, Telegrams Collected (Unbound). *O.R.*, I, xlii, part 2, 299. On Aug. 19, 1864, Maj. Gen. Winfield S. Hancock telegraphed to USG. "I have not discovered any thing going out of the enemy's line in my front yet—I am having a careful examination made with a view to assault   If however the lines appear to be well manned I cannot promise success—A movement down the charles city road with 6 or 8000 infantry & the cavalry might be more successful than an assault on the lines here—but if you consider an assault preferable I will make it at the best point I can determine" Telegram received, DNA, RG 108, Letters Received; copy, *ibid.*, RG 107, Telegrams Collected (Unbound). Printed as sent at 12:10 P.M. in *O.R.*, I, xlii, part 2, 300. At 1:10 P.M., USG telegraphed to Hancock. "I did not intend to order ~~that~~ how you should attack or whether you should attack at all. Assault if you think it can be done successfully and in the manner you deem best. All I have to say is that I feel no doubt but you can use all of your force upon any point you deem best except a thin skirmish line." ALS (telegram sent), OClWHi; telegram received, DNA, RG 107, Telegrams Collected (Unbound). Incomplete in *O.R.*, I, xlii, part 2, 300.

At 10:15 A.M., USG had telegraphed to Hancock. "The enemy claim to have captured 600 six hundred prisoners from you on Teusday and numbers at other times making in all near 1000. They also claim to have captured many horses. How far are these statements correct?" ALS (telegram sent), OClWHi; telegram received, DNA, RG 107, Telegrams Collected (Unbound). *O.R.*, I, xlii, part 2, 299. At 11:00 A.M. and 11:40 A.M., Hancock telegraphed to USG. "Gen Gregg reports that he does not know of any horses being Captured in his late fight—He had 300 killed & wounded & a few mired in a Swamp. He has 33 men missing now, of whom he believes to be wounded—" Telegram received, DNA, RG 108, Letters Received. *O.R.*, I, xlii, part 2, 299. "I have sent for the list of missing, & to ascertain the number supposed to have been taken prisoners —I have never heard of any horses being taken, nor have I heard of any prisoners being taken except that I suppose stragglers might have been ~~taken~~ There may have been some loss but it was considered a matter of so small moment that it never was presented to me in the light of ~~men being taken~~ captures by the enemy—When Gen Miles & Gregg were pressed back on the Charles City Road, some men were ~~reported~~ missing, but it was supposed that they had been broken off in the Jungle & had straggled to the rear Gen Miles that evening reported 150 as unaccounted for, the most of whom he supposed he could collect" ALS (telegram sent), DNA, RG 107, Telegrams Collected (Unbound); telegram received, *ibid.*, RG 108, Letters Received. *O.R.*, I, xlii, part 2, 299.

At noon and at 7:00 P.M., Hancock telegraphed to USG, sending a copy of the second to Maj. Gen. George G. Meade, transmitting information from C.S.A. newspapers. Telegrams received, DNA, RG 108, Letters Received; copy (2nd), Meade Papers, PHi. *O.R.*, I, xlii, part 2, 303, 301.

At 12:40 P.M., USG telegraphed to Hancock. "If You can possibly spare a Brigade of Cavalry to go to our left, to support the 5th Corps, send it. There will be no necessity, ~~for~~ in waiting for night to start it." Copies, DLC-USG, V, 45, 59, 68; DNA, RG 108, Letters Sent. Printed as received at 1:00 P.M. in *O.R.*, I, xlii, part 2, 300. At 2:40 P.M., Hancock telegraphed to USG. "I have ordered one (1) brigade of cavalry to report to Genl Meade—The order went out a little before 2. P. M" Telegram received, DNA, RG 107, Telegrams Collected (Unbound); *ibid.*, RG 108, Letters Received. *O.R.*, I, xlii, part 2, 300. On the same day, USG telegraphed to Meade. "I have ordered a Brigade of Cavalry sent to your to be sent to aid Warren. They will start at once. 200 rail-road men will also go to work on the Welden road." ALS (telegram sent), OClWHi; copies, DLC-USG, V, 45, 68, 107; DNA, RG 108, Letters Sent.

To Maj. Gen. Winfield S. Hancock

City Point, Va. Aug. 19th 8 p. m. *1864.*

MAJ. GEN. ~~HALLECK~~, HANCOCK,

I have no information of the withdrawel of any troops from the North side of the river further than I telegraphed you to-day and those proved to be Cavalry and in less numbers probably than a Division. I do not think it advisable to assault unless you feel satisfied that you will gain a decided advantage. I want now principally the enemy so occupied that he cannot send off any of his forces and attacks made only when he leaves a weak place or where he can be surprised. From your discription I hardly think it advisable to let Gen. Miles[1] attack in the morning but you are a better judge of this matter than I am. Exercise your own judgement.

U. S. GRANT
Lt. Gen.

ALS (telegram sent), PPRF; telegram received (at 8:10 P.M.), DNA, RG 107, Telegrams Collected (Unbound). *O.R.*, I, xlii, part 2, 301. On Aug. 19, 1864, 4:25 P.M. and 7:00 P.M., Maj. Gen. Winfield S. Hancock telegraphed to USG. "I have just returned from a Careful examination of my line my Commandars have also made Caraful reconnoisance—but one point is seen where an assault is Considered practicable this being just below the Dam at Flussers mill—The enemys line is about 200 paces from our skirmish line as to whether it Can be held if taken I Cannot say I think I will try at daylight in the morning this place is filled with men as Close as though ~~as~~ on parade—It is about the only place where the pickets do not fire on each other" "Desiring to carry out your wishes here I have had since my last telegraph careful examinations of the enemys line by my Chf of staff & Gen Miles to whom I propose to give the attacking column—They are of the opinion I expressed to you that by putting in a strong force at a certain point on my line we can break through the enemys line probably capturing three or four hundred prisoners and possibly two Guns, but that it is a question as to whether we could hold it at the point to be attacked. It presents no particular feature & is not as high as the surrounding ground It is an important question how many men the enemy have opposite me now—I can only say their pits are well filled I would like to know the latest information you have ~~i~~on this point & I would like your views on the matter of the assault as you know what is occurring elsewhere ~~where~~ as well as here—a rebel paper of 19th speaks of the engagements here and some admitting a thousand casualties claiming that we had a thousand killed They do not claim many prisoners" Telegrams received, DNA, RG 108, Letters Received. *O.R.*, I, xlii, part 2, 300, 301. The second is printed as sent at 7:10 P.M., received at 7:22 P.M. On the same day, Hancock telegraphed to USG. "Your despatch is received—I had almost Completed my preparations for attack & hoped to be Successful but with the proviso that a Div of Infantry had been withdrawn by the enemy. With their force not diminished I should anticipate a fight after Carrying the line without any advantage on my side as my force would be Considerably disorganized by the assault—I suppose I could fight 14.000 men of which three thousand are on picket not including Greggs remaining brigade of Cav.y. after reading Your despatch I have concluded not to assault in the morning but to perfect my arrangements & take advantage of any weakening of the enemy hereafter—The rain tonight softens the Ground so where I wish to place artillery in close proximity to the enemy so making it very difficult to move twelve pounders & I am therefore willing to postpone for the additional The pieces have to be put in position by hand. Gregg has 1600 Cavalry here—" Telegram received, DNA, RG 108, Letters Received. *O.R.*, I, xlii, part 2, 302.

1. Nelson A. Miles, born in Mass. in 1839, a clerk in Boston before the Civil War, was commissioned 1st lt., 22nd Mass., as of Sept. 9, 1861. Involved in every campaign of the Army of the Potomac, conspicuous for gallantry and wounded several times, he was appointed brig. gen. as of May 12, 1864, and commanded the 1st Div., 2nd Army Corps.

To Maj. Gen. Winfield S. Hancock and Maj. Gen. Benjamin F. Butler

---

City Point Va. Aug. 19th/64 9.30 p m

MAJ. GN. HANCOCK, & BUTLER.

Hoke's, Heth's & Mahones Division come out and attacked Warren this evening. A heavy fight ensued with conciderable loss in prisoners captured on each side. As we understand Johnsons Division is also at Petersburg. This leaves Wilcox Pickett & Field, with the possibility of part of Picketts Div. gone to the valley, to guard from Petersburg to the James and to confront you on the North side. There must be a weak point somewhere.

U. S. GRANT
Lt. Gn

ALS (telegram sent), deCoppet Collection, NjP; telegram received (sent at 9:30 P.M., received at 10:20 P.M.), DNA, RG 107, Telegrams Collected (Unbound); DLC-Benjamin F. Butler. Printed as received at 10:40 P.M. in *O.R.*, I, xlii, part 2, 302. On Aug. 19, 1864, 10:40 P.M. and 11:00 P.M., Maj. Gen. Winfield S. Hancock telegraphed to USG. "Your dispatch is received. According to my information which is necessarily imperfect Field & Wilcox are here & wright's brigade of Wilcox's Div. these troops must number nearly as many men as I have now that Mott is absent From what Gen Birney informed me last night I imagined that Pickett had left Gen Butlers front—I shall try & avoid being deceived here by the enemy weaking materially their force & am willing to try whether the weak point is here or not" "That you may know exactly how matters are here I will say that I consider a much larger force necessary here for the offensive than for the defensive & though I should have to contract my lines I can still spare a Div of the 18th Corps and maintain a respectable show here—This is sent you on the supposition that you really feel desirous of calling for some of my force as I have not been able to force the enemy here yet" Telegrams received, DNA, RG 108, Letters Received. The first is printed as received at 11:50 P.M. in *O.R.*, I, xlii, part 2, 302–3.

To Maj. Gen. George G. Meade

City Point Va. Aug. 19th/64

MAJ. GEN. MEADE,

I think Gen. Hancock by detaining a large force North of the James makes our force at Petersburg relatively as strong as it would be ~~with him there.~~ if he was with it. It also seems to be a sensitive point with the enemy. I ~~also~~ am anxious to force the enemy to withdraw from the valley the reinforcements he has sent to Early and think the best way to do it is to threaten as long a line as possible. If therefore there is no necessity for it I shall not withdraw Hancock for the present.

U. S. GRANT
Lt. Gn.

ALS (telegram sent), OClWHi; telegram received (at 8:50 A.M.), DNA, RG 94, War Records Office, Army of the Potomac. Printed as sent at 8:50 P.M. in *O.R.*, I, xlii, part 2, 293. On Aug. 19, 1864, 8:00 A.M., 9:30 A.M., and 11:00 A.M., Maj. Gen. George G. Meade telegraphed to USG. "Ord's reserves consisting of two small brigades were put in Parkes line last night—permitting Wilcox's Division to go to Warren—Motts Division has just arrived and will relieve men of the 9th corps to go to Warren's support—Warren reports at 7. a m, that he has driven the enemys cavalry down to Reams station—that the enemy are in force in his front, having been at work all night entrenching—Reports from Pickets of 9th corps would indicate a movement of the enemy to their right (our left).—" "Your telegram 8-50 recieved—I will confer with Genl. Warren & advise you whether in his judgment & mine, more troops are required on the Welden Road that those sent by Parke—My own impression now is that they are not so long as the enemy is threatened on the North bank of the James." "Parke will be able to send Warren all his white troops amounting to Six thousand—this will be ample for all Warrens purposes unless the enemy reinforce strongly from their troops now north of the James.—I have directed Warren to entrench himself strongly & to connect if possible with the left of the 9th Corps—Also if practicable to push the enemy back to their works around Petersburgh they being now, as I understand it, over a mile or more outside of these works.—" ALS (telegrams sent), DNA, RG 94, War Records Office, Army of the Potomac; telegrams received, *ibid.*, RG 108, Letters Received. *O.R.*, I, xlii, part 2, 293–94. Meade misdated the second and third Aug. 18. On Aug. 19, 12:15 P.M., Meade telegraphed to USG. "I send despatch just received from Warren—I am going to see him—the telegraph now runs to his Hd. Qrs.—" ALS (telegram sent), DNA, RG 94, War Records Office, Army of the Potomac; telegram received, *ibid.*, RG 108, Letters Received. *O.R.*, I, xlii, part 2, 294. The enclosure is *ibid.*, p. 306.

To Maj. Gen. George G. Meade

City Point Va. Aug. 19th 9.30 p. m. *1864.*

Maj. Gn. Meade,

Your dispatch of 8 p. m. just received. I am pleased to see the promptness with which Gen. Warren attacked the enemy when he come out. I hope he will not hesitate in such cases to abandon his lines and take every man to fight a battle and trust to regaining them afterwards or to getting better. The enemy must have left their lines guarded by a single Division.

U. S. Grant
Lt. Gn.

ALS (telegram sent), OClWHi; telegram received (at 11:40 P.M.), DNA, RG 94, War Records Office, Army of the Potomac. *O.R.*, I, xlii, part 2, 294. On Aug. 19, 1864, 8:00 P.M. and 9:45 P.M., Maj. Gen. George G. Meade telegraphed to USG. "I left Warren's at 4. p. m all quiet—at 4.30 the enemy drove in the picket line he had established connecting with our works on the Jerusalem Plank road, and turning his right flank interposed their masses between Warren & Parke—Warren immediately attacked them and after a severe fight drove them back & re-established his lines—I send you his despatch just received.—The roads are in a very bad condition & if it continues to rain there will be trouble in supplying Warren.—" "I send despatch just received from Warren—I think he is not aware that 3 of his regiments that were on picket are now in connection with Parkes pickets on the old line—This I get from Parke who said he could not find out whether these three regiments had any connection with the rest of the 5th corps—If Warren has included them in the missing it will reduce his losses in this respect. I have telegraphed him to enquire—I expect he will be attacked again in the morning as the enemy are very tenacious of their hold on the Weldon Road & will not be likely to give it up without great effort." ALS (telegrams sent), DNA, RG 94, War Records Office, Army of the Potomac; telegrams received, *ibid.*, RG 108, Letters Received. *O.R.*, I, xlii, part 2, 294, 295. The enclosures are *ibid.*, pp. 307–8.

At 10:11 P.M., USG telegraphed to Meade. "Can you not spare Motts Div. from the line to reinforce Warren? The enemy have evidently taken every thing from their line and would think of no attack except to dislodge our troops from the rail-road. I will bring Hancock back to-morrow night and then the 10th Corps will releive the 18th giving us more troops footloose." ALS (telegram sent), OClWHi; telegram received, DNA, RG 94, War Records Office, Army of the Potomac. *O.R.*, I, xlii, part 2, 295. At 11:00 P.M., Meade telegraphed to USG. "It will not be possible to withdraw Mott from the lines for it would leave the whole of the line recently held by the 5th corps to be held by the colored division of the 9th corps less than 4000 strong.—Warren I think has men enough provided the enemy do not re-inforce from the James   Warren with his own corps & the 3 divisions of the 9th ought to have, after his losses nearly 20,000 men, and I can not believe the enemy can have over 12,000—With this preponderance he ought not only to maintain his lodgment on the R. Rd. but should be able to drive the enemy into his fortifications   I have suggested to him to try it tomorrow morning as the best way to stop any further flanking by the enemy— I have however left it to his discretion dependant on the temper of his men of which he is a better judge than I am.—Instead of relieving the 18th corps who are familiar with the line they now occupy—I would suggest the 10th relieving Mott & the colored division of the 9th that is holding the lines up to the Plank road   Then Hancock could go to the Weldon Road & the 9th hold between the Plank & Weldon Road.—" ALS (telegram sent), DNA, RG 94, War Records Office, Army of the Potomac; telegram received, *ibid.*, RG 108, Letters Received. *O.R.*, I, xlii, part 2, 295.

To Maj. Gen. Benjamin F. Butler

City Point Aug. 20th/64

MAJ. GEN. BUTLER.

The 10th Corps, in fact all the troops from North of the James are ordered to return to-night. When this change is made it will probably induce the enemy to strengthen his weak point in your front before we can take advantage of it. If you can get through however I should like it very much.

In regard to sending you the Colored troops of the 9th Corps it is now impossible. The 18th Corps and Colored troops of the 9th are holding all of our line at Petersburg ~~and~~ whilst the White troops of the 9th are operating with the 5th Corps.

U. S. GRANT
Lt. Gen.

ALS (telegram sent), OClWHi; telegram received (at 4:00 P.M.), DLC-Benjamin F. Butler. *O.R.*, I, xlii, part 2, 350. On Aug. 20, 1864, 1:40 P.M., Maj. Gen. Benjamin F. Butler telegraphed to USG. "Two deserters from Pickett's Division have just come in—One a very intelligent man—He informs me that six Regts have been taken from Picketts Division and sent across the James River—That on our left opposite Port Walthall they have reduced the line so that the line of battle is scarcely stronger than the skirmish line, ~~that~~ being one man in every twenty feet—I believe this statement—I think the weak point now is in front of our line, and if we had the 10th Corps here I have no doubt we could go out on the left—At least, I should be inclined to try it—~~A~~ I do not think we have over thirty five hundred men between the two rivers That you may judge for yourself I will send you the deserter with yesterdays paper—Please question him— Allow me also to call your attention to the fact that the last of the 100 day's Regiments go away from me to day—Certainly in the absence of the 10th Corp I have no one whom I can send to Fort Powhattan or Fort Pocahontas—Allow me to suggest that as the Colored troops of the 9th Corps are so much demoralized & broken up for want of officers ~~that~~ if they could be sent to me by putting the weaker ones in Powhattan & Pocahontas they might be recruited up & got into condition" LS (telegram sent), DNA, RG 107, Telegrams Collected (Unbound); telegram received, *ibid.*, RG 108, Letters Received. Printed as received at 2:25 P.M. in *O.R.*, I, xlii, part 2, 349.

To Maj. Gen. Winfield S. Hancock

———

Dated Aug 20 *1864*. 9 50 a. m.

To Maj Genl Hancock

You may withdraw from the north of the River tonight marching by way of Bermuda Hundred & across the Appomattox at the Pontoon Bridge back to your old camp—Leave the 10th corps to cover the crossing of the 2nd corps & cavalry—after you are entirely out of the way the 10th corps will return to their places at once or may take up a shorter line & hold it until tomorrow night as you and Genl Birney may deem most advisable—if any thing through the day should give you an advantage where you are this order will not be observed

U S Grant
Lt Genl

Telegram received, DNA, RG 107, Telegrams Collected (Unbound); copies, *ibid.*, RG 108, Letters Sent; DLC-USG, V, 45, 68, 107. Printed as sent at 9:40 P.M. in *O.R.*, I, xlii, part 2, 334.

On Aug. 20, 1864, Maj. Gen. Winfield S. Hancock telegraphed to USG and Maj. Gen. George G. Meade. "A deserter from 44th Alabama Law's brigade Field's Div. came in this morning he states that the enemy have one brigade in single rank & seven or eight Guns on the high hill on the New Market road to the right & left their troops are deployed in the usual order, does not know of any change in troops   He saw a ~~brigade~~ brigade moving to our right—a little before dark last night but does not know where the came from or who they were —Says the talk among the men is that two Divisions are there and there is no doubt but what Kershaw's Div. has gone to Early but they are looking for it back—Thinks Picketts is still across the James—His regiment has about a hundred (100) muskets, started with nearly nine hundred (900) many of whom have deserted—says alabama is full of deserters   His reg't. was under marching order night before last during the firing at Petersburg   He knows that this morning beside all of Field's Div. Sanders late Perrin's brigade and wrights brigade of Mahone's Div. are there also McGowan's brigade of Wilcox Div. Gen Lee was there the evening the enemy attacked Gen Birney—From his account this attack was a general affair the whole line being under orders to advance if the attack on our right was successful—He says they knew that the 10th Corps and part of the 2d Corps are here"   Telegram received (at 10:45 A.M.), DNA, RG 94, War Records Office, Army of the Potomac; *ibid.*, RG 108, Letters Received. *O.R.*, I, xlii, part 2, 334.

At 12:10 P.M., Hancock telegraphed to USG. "Is there a pontoon bridge at Bermuda Hundred? I am ordered to march to Bermuda Hundred, but it is not stated whether a bridge has been thrown there or whether I am to cross at Point of Rocks." *Ibid.* At 12:40 P.M., USG telegraphed to Hancock. "You will cross at Pt of Rocks. If materil for a bridge at Broadway Landing can be raked together one will be thrown across there. Of this you will soon be advissed." Telegram received (datelined 4:25 P.M.), DNA, RG 107, Telegrams Collected (Unbound); copies, *ibid.*, RG 108, Letters Sent; DLC-USG, V, 45, 68, 107. Printed as sent at 1:50 P.M. in *O.R.*, I, xlii, part 2, 335. At 1:45 P.M., USG telegraphed to Hancock. "A pontoon will be laid at Broadway landing this evening & will be ready for you two hours after dark." Telegram received (marked as sent at 3:10 P.M., received at 3:35 P.M.), DNA, RG 107, Telegrams Collected (Unbound); copies, *ibid.*, RG 108, Letters Sent; DLC-USG, V, 45, 68, 107. Printed as sent at 3:10 P.M., received at 3:35 P.M., in *O.R.*, I, xlii, part 2, 335. At 2:45 P.M., Hancock telegraphed to USG. "I sent you a despatch this morning asking ~~whether~~ whether I was to go back by way of Bermuda Hundred Landing as might implied from the order whether it was intended I should cross at Point of Rocks by the usual route—Thinking, you may not have received the despatch I repeat the substance"   Telegram received, DNA, RG 107, Telegrams Collected (Unbound); *ibid.*, RG 108, Letters Received. *O.R.*, I, xlii, part 2, 335. At 3:00 P.M., Lt. Col. Cyrus B. Comstock telegraphed to Hancock. "Lt. Gen. Grant desires me to say that there will be two bridges for you to cross the Appomattox on, one at Pt. of Rocks the other at Broadway, and that thus with the two bridges at Deep Bottom you will have two roads for your movement. I think but one of the bridges at Deep Bottom is prepared for wagons." ALS (telegram sent), DNA, RG 108, Telegrams Sent by Comstock; telegram received (at 3:37 P.M.), *ibid.*, RG 107, Telegrams Collected (Unbound). *O.R.*, I, xlii, part 2, 335. At 4:00 P.M., USG telegraphed to Hancock. "The words Bermuda Hundred, should not have occurred in my despatch. As Col Comstock telegraphed there will be two bridges across the Appomattox one at Pt of Rocks & one at Broadway & you should take the best route & from Deep Bottom to them." Telegram received (at 4:26 P.M.), DNA, RG 107, Telegrams Collected (Unbound); copy, DLC-USG, V, 68. *O.R.*, I, xlii, part 2, 335. At 4:20 P.M., USG telegraphed to Hancock. "There will be a bridge for you at Broadway on the Appomattox & the old bridge at Pt of Rocks giving you two lines to move on." Telegram received, DNA, RG

107, Telegrams Collected (Unbound); copies, *ibid.*, RG 108, Letters Sent; DLC-USG, V, 45, 68, 107. *O.R.*, I, xlii, part 2, 336.

At 9:30 P.M., Hancock telegraphed to USG and Meade. "My Chief of Staff who is at Gen Butlers HdQrs informs me that the roads are knee deep in water in some places   He says that the troops canot be over before morning— However I have directed them to proceed under the orders to their destination The Night is very dark & of course there will be a great deal of difficulty on that account   One Division complete is over & the other is crossing as is the cavalry. Gen Birney will cross tonight—The 2d Corps & the Cavalry will be over at 11 oclock" ALS (telegram sent), DNA, RG 107, Telegrams Collected (Unbound); telegram received, *ibid.*, RG 94, War Records Office, Army of the Potomac; *ibid.*, RG 108, Letters Received. *O.R.*, I, xlii, part 2, 336.

On the same day, Hancock telegraphed to USG three times. "Reports from Gen Gregg as to losses etc, have not been recd beyond that sent last night   The following are the numbers of missing including stragglers & those supposed to be captured exclusive of the Cavalry operating on this side of this river—This includes the 14th inst. Missing unaccounted for, 9 officers and 540 men— Supposed to be captured 7 officers and 363 men   The report of the Cavalry as to men & horses will be furnished as soon as recd. The losses were given by Gen Gregg last night and are supposed to be correct   They are trifling" ALS (telegram sent), DNA, RG 107, Telegrams Collected (Unbound); telegram received, *ibid.*, RG 108, Letters Received. *O.R.*, I, xlii, part 2, 333. "The following is Genl Greggs report of men & horses missing Corrected from that of last night—I send it that the report may be Complete—men thirty six (36) Horses thirty five (35)   The greater part of those horses were swamped in Deep Creek and abandoned. It is not known whether any of them lived to be extricated by the enemy   While in the swamp many were shot—" Telegram received, DNA, RG 108, Letters Received. *O.R.*, I, xlii, part 2, 333–34. "Richmond sentinal of 20th says about 3 oclock this Evening 19th the arrangements being Completed our forces attacked in front & flank Warrens Yankee Corps which had made a temporary lodgement on the Weldon R. R. 2 miles below here driving them 2 miles Capturing over two thousand prisoners including Gen Hayes & a number of stand of Colors. No news from any other sources—" Telegram received, DNA, RG 108, Letters Received; copy, *ibid.*, RG 107, Telegrams Collected (Bound). *O.R.*, I, xlii, part 2, 336. A telegram from Hancock to USG dated only "20" was probably sent on Aug. 20. "Your despatch is recd." ALS (telegram sent), DNA, RG 107, Telegrams Collected (Unbound).

To Maj. Gen. George G. Meade

By Telegraph from City Point
Dated Aug 20 *1864.*

To Maj Gen Meade

I have ordered Gen Hancock to withdraw from the north side of the River tonight & move back to his old position   when there you can send him to the support of ~~Greg~~ Warren with the other brigade of Greggs cavalry. If the enemy come out to attack we will have advantage of position If they hold their lines only & persist in sending more troops to the valley we can extend still further I am not so particular about holding the Weldon Road permanently as I am to destroy it effectually & to force the Enemy to attack us with advantages on our side. two hundred Rail Road men with Hancock were orderd yesterday were ordered to report to Warren they must be near there now & will destroy more Rail Road in a day than a Division of troops

U S GRANT
Lt Gen

Telegram received (at 1:10 P.M.), DNA, RG 94, War Records Office, Army of the Potomac; copies, *ibid.*, RG 108, Letters Sent; DLC-USG, V, 45, 68, 107; (2) Meade Papers, PHi. Printed as sent at 1:10 P.M. in *O.R.*, I, xlii, part 2, 327. On Aug. 20, 1864, 1:45 P.M., Maj. Gen. George G. Meade telegraphed to USG. "Your telegram of 1.10 received.—The working party referred to passed here at 9.30 a m, and are without doubt now with Warren, but I fear like Gregg's cavalry they will report themselves exhausted & unfit for service from long marching—the roads are very bad & very trying to man & horse. Hancock will not probably be here before 8 or 9 tomorrow morning & will then also be tired & exhausted I propose to detain him on the plank road, and let him hold as far to the left of that road as practicable—thus freeing the 9th corps to operate with Warren on the Welden R. Rd. & covering the left flank—If the idea of extending beyond the Welden R. R. is entertained it is absolutely essential, a strongly forti-fied line should be constructed & held between that R. Road & the Jerusalem plank road—Hancock can make such line to meet the line now held by Warren & part of the 9th corps.—As it is made & strengthened Hancock can extend to the base & free more of the 9th or 5th corps—If such line is not made any force on the R. Rd is liable to have both flanks turned—with this line the enemy will be compelled to maneuvre on our left flank, where we can collect available reserves to meet him.—" ALS (telegram sent), DNA, RG 94, War Records Office, Army of the Potomac; telegram received, *ibid.*, RG 108, Letters Received. *O.R.*, I, xlii, part 2, 328. At 3:40 P.M., USG telegraphed to Meade. "You can use the 2d Corps as you propose. I have no idea of extending further to the left unless as stated in my dispatch the enemy should persist in sending more troops to the valley. I want to hold the Welden road though permanently if easy done and to thoroughly destroy it if it cannot be held." ALS (telegram sent), OClWHi; tele-gram received, DNA, RG 94, War Records Office, Army of the Potomac. *O.R.*, I, xlii, part 2, 328.

At 10:00 A.M., Meade telegraphed to USG. "I send you two despatches from Genl. Warren—one received at 1. a m this day, from which I hoped War-ren would be able to take the offensive this morning. Not hearing from him, a call was made for information to which was sent the despatch of Col Locke A. A. G. now forwarded.—A deserter who came in last night asserts as many have done previously that the enemy are mining on Beauregards front.—" ALS (telegram sent), DNA, RG 94, War Records Office, Army of the Potomac; copies, *ibid.*, RG 393, Army of the Potomac, Letters Sent; (2) Meade Papers, PHi. *O.R.*, I, xlii, part 2, 326. The second enclosure is *ibid.*, p. 338. At 11:30 A.M. and 12:50 P.M., Meade telegraphed to USG. "I forward despatch just received from Genl. Warren from which you will see all hopes of any offensive movement on his part are at an end; and that it is now questionable, whether he can establish a line with his present force from the Welden road to the Plank road.—Instructions have been sent to him to employ Greggs cavalry & the working party from City Point in destroying the R Rd & not to detach any part of his Infantry.—" "I send two despatches recieved this a m—Your attention is called to the statement of the deserter from Finnegan's brigade, which is directly in conflict with the report from Genl. Hancock this a m—both parties averring of their own knowledge that Wright & Perrin of Mahone are at the same time in front of Hancock & Warren.—" ALS (telegrams sent), DNA, RG 94, War Records Office, Army of the Potomac; telegrams received, *ibid.*, RG 108, Letters Received. *O.R.*, I, xlii, part 2, 326. The enclosures are *ibid.*, pp. 338–39, 327.

At 8:15 P.M., USG telegraphed to Meade. "Richmond paper of today claim to have captured two thousand prisoners from Warren's. Is this not far above his estimate? What number did Warren capture & what does he estimate the loss of the enemy at." Telegram received (on Aug. 20, 4:00 A.M.), DNA, RG 94, War Records Office, Army of the Potomac; copies, *ibid.*, RG 108, Letters Sent; DLC-USG, V, 45, 68, 107; (2) Meade Papers, PHi. *O.R.*, I, xlii, part 2, 328. At 8:30 P.M., Meade telegraphed to USG. "Warrens return of casualties for the 18th shows 392 missing   His report this morning which I forwarded to you gave 1500 as all the losses of his corps yesterday but did not discriminate between the killed wounded & missing—I have sent your telegram to him with directions to let me know the missing in his corps & the 9th on the 20th   His losses I know from reports of others were nearly all in prisoners.—No succinct report of the affair has been made and I have sent you all I have received.—" ALS (telegram sent), DNA, RG 94, War Records Office, Army of the Potomac; telegram received, *ibid.*, RG 108, Letters Received. *O.R.*, I, xlii, part 2, 328–29.

To Maj. Gen. Edward O. C. Ord

By Telegraph from City Point
Dated Aug 20 1864.

To MAJ GEN ORD.

Statements of deserters and refugees go to show that the enemy are mining in your front,   Can you not Countermine against them.

U S GRANT
Lieut Genl

Telegram received, Ord Papers, CU-B; copies (sent at 12:40 P.M.), DLC-USG, V, 45, 68, 107; DNA, RG 108, Letters Sent. *O.R.*, I, xlii, part 2, 353. On Aug.

20, 1864, Maj. Gen. Edward O. C. Ord telegraphed to USG. "I have had reports of the mines in my front for some time,   have two (2) counter mines going now   cant hear much yet in them"   Telegram received, DNA, RG 108, Letters Received; copy, *ibid.*, RG 107, Telegrams Collected (Unbound). *O.R.*, I, xlii, part 2, 353.

Also on Aug. 20, USG telegraphed to Ord. "What is meaning of the heaving firing going on"   Telegram received, Ord Papers, CU-B. On the same day, Ord telegraphed to USG. "I suppose it means the same this morning as yesterday and the day before. Previous to the first the rebels in Warrens front called out to our men that they were going to shell Burnsides niggers and they (Warrens' men) must not mind it—They have ~~had us~~ shelled us every morning since—" ALS (telegram sent), DNA, RG 107, Telegrams Collected (Unbound); telegram received, *ibid.*, RG 108, Letters Received.

To Maj. Gen. Philip H. Sheridan

(Cipher)   City Point, Va. Aug. 20th *1864.* [*9:00* P.M.]
MAJ. GEN. SHERIDAN, CHARLESTOWN VA.

As stated in previous dispatches no Division or Brigade has gone from Lee's Army to the valley except Kershaws & Fitz Lee's. We have had prisoners and deserters fixing every single Brigade within the last three days. Warren's Corps is now intrenched across the Welden road. I shall endeavor to stay there and to employ the enemy so actively that he can not detach further. It is possible that a few regiments may have been detached from different Divisions and sent against you but I have no evidence of it.

U. S. GRANT
Lt. Gn.

ALS (telegram sent), CSmH; telegram received (on Aug. 21, 1864, 5:00 P.M.), DNA, RG 107, Telegrams Collected (Bound). *O.R.*, I, xliii, part 1, 856.

On Aug. 20, 10:00 P.M., Maj. Gen. Philip H. Sheridan telegraphed to USG. "I have nothing important to communicate—The enemy have not gone down the valley further than BunkerHill and that far only with cavalry—I left everything on that direction, for them but they have not accepted the invitation as yet   I will probably tomorrow learn something of their strength and intentions   Averill this morning moved from Sheperdstown on a stampeding report and without orders—I dont yet know where he went but by his movement gives unnecessary alarm. I hope to be able to manage this affair—The enemy do not know exactly what to do and appear to be in doubt—Can you be certain of what has come here —Taking all the reports which reach me they are very unsatisfactory" Telegram received (Aug. 21, 3:30 A.M.), DNA, RG 107, Telegrams Collected (Bound); *ibid.*, RG 108, Letters Received; copies, *ibid.*, RG 107, Telegrams Received in Cipher; DLC-Philip H. Sheridan. *O.R.*, I, xliii, part 1, 856-57.

To Edwin M. Stanton

(Cipher)   City Point Va. Aug. 21st 1864
HON. E. M. STANTON, SEC. OF WAR, WASHINGTON.

Please inform Gen. Foster that on no circumstances will he be authorized to make exchange of Prisoners of War. Exchanges simply reinforce the enemy at once whilst we do not get the benefit of those received for two or three months and loose the majority entirely. I telegraph this from just hearing that some five or six hundred more prisoners had been sent to Gn. Foster.

U. S. GRANT
Lt. Gn.

ALS (telegram sent), CSmH; telegram received (sent at 5:00 P.M., received on Aug. 22, 1864, 7:00 A.M.), DNA, RG 107, Telegrams Collected (Bound). *O.R.*, I, xxxv, part 2, 254; *ibid.*, II, vii, 662.

To Maj. Gen. Henry W. Halleck

(Cipher)   City Point Va. Aug. 21st 1864 [*11:00* A.M.]
MAJ. GEN. HALLECK, WASHINGTON,

Taking possession of the Welden road has made the enemy apparently very nervous. They have been constantly attacking to regain possession. I can not report acurately the result but apparently our losses have been light in killed & wounded whilst the enemys loss in that respect must have been heavy from the fact of his being repulsed so often. The second day however we lost heavily in captures from the fact that the enemy enveloped Warren's right before he was aware of it. I withdrew the troops from North of the James last night and now the 2d Corps are in must be nearly in supporting distance of Warren.

U. S. GRANT
Lt. Gn.

ALS (telegram sent), CSmH; telegram received (at 6:00 P.M.), DNA, RG 107, Telegrams Collected (Bound). *O.R.*, I, xlii, part 1, 18; *ibid.*, I, xlii, part 2, 353–54.

To Maj. Gen. Henry W. Halleck

(Cipher)   City Point Va. Aug. 21st/64 [*1:30* P.M.]
MAJ. GN. HALLECK, WASHINGTON.

The enemy come out and attacked Warren between 10 & 11
a. m. but were repulsed with great ease. No loss reported on our
side except ~~Col~~. Gen. Cutler slightly wounded[1] & Col. Duchane
killed.[2] Gen. Warren reports 400 prisoners captured that he knows
of. There may be more. I am expecting a heavy attack this after
noon and preparing for it.

U. S. GRANT
Lt. Gn.

ALS (telegram sent), CSmH; telegram received (on Aug. 22, 1864, 7:00 A.M.),
DNA, RG 107, Telegrams Collected (Bound); *ibid.*, Telegrams Collected (Unbound). *O.R.*, I, xlii, part 1, 19; *ibid.*, I, xlii, part 2, 354.
    On Aug. 21, 10:15 P.M., Lt. Col. Theodore S. Bowers wrote to Capt. George
K. Leet. "I never before saw Grant so intensely anxious *to do something*. He appears determined to try every possible expedient. His plans are good, but the
great difficulty is that *our troops cannot be relied on.* The failure to take advantage of opportunities pain and chafe him beyond anything that I have ever
before known him to manifest." Quoted in Leet to Lt. Col. William R. Rowley,
Aug. 23, Rowley Papers, IHi.

    1. On Sept. 13, 10:30 A.M., USG telegraphed to Maj. Gen. Henry W.
Halleck. "Gen. Cutler has been relieved from duty with the Army of the Potomac
by the consolidation of his Division with other Divisions of his Corps, and he
ordered to report by letter to the Adj. Gn. for orders. I would like to have the
General ordered to visit the different recruiting rendezvous in the Eastern &
Middle states for the purpose of pushing forward recruits, convalescents and all
others whos duties are at the front." ALS (telegram sent), CSmH; telegram received (at 12:30 P.M.), DNA, RG 107, Telegrams Collected (Bound). *O.R.*,
I, xlii, part 2, 804. See *ibid.*, p. 805. At the end of the year, Bvt. Maj. Gen. Ly-
sander Cutler commanded the draft rendezvous at Jackson, Mich. *Ibid.*, I, xlv,
part 2, 469.
    2. Col. Nathan T. Dushane, 1st Md., commanding 2nd Brigade, 2nd Div.,
5th Army Corps, was killed Aug. 21 during a C.S.A. counterattack on U.S. positions on the Weldon Railroad.

To Maj. Gen. Benjamin F. Butler

———

By Telegraph from City Pt.
Dated Aug 21 *1864.*

To GEN BUTLER

Gen Ord has extended so as to hold a greater front to relieve as many as possible of the A. P. to go to Gen Warrens support to hold what he now does two or three more batteries ought to be sent to him. Have you got them to spare. If so send them two will probably be enough.

U. S. GRANT
Lt Genl

Telegram received (at 1:45 P.M.), DLC-Benjamin F. Butler; copies, DLC-USG, V, 45, 68, 107; DNA, RG 108, Letters Sent. *O.R.,* I, xlii, part 2, 375. On Aug. 21, 1864, 1:00 P.M., USG telegraphed to Maj. Gen. Benjamin F. Butler. "The enemy is evidently massing everything he can to drive our troops from the Weldon road. To do this he is undoubtedly leaving his intrenched lines almost to their own care Have a reconnoissance made & if with the 10th corps you can break through do it" Telegram received (at 1:40 P.M.), DLC-Benjamin F. Butler; copies, DLC USG, V, 45, 68, 107; DNA, RG 108, Letters Sent O R , I, xlii, part 2, 376. At 2:00 P.M., Butler telegraphed to USG. "Gen Birny and myself are at this moment consulting upon the movement which you sugest and will try and do it tomorrow morning. If we do any thing I must have all the batteries I have left. I have but seven in all on the line and in reserve on this side of the River. Will send the one at Springhill to Ord Gen Hancock has twelve." LS (telegram sent), DNA, RG 107, Telegrams Collected (Unbound); telegram received, *ibid.,* RG 108, Letters Received. *O.R.,* I, xlii, part 2, 376.

To Maj. Gen. Benjamin F. Butler

———

By Telegraph from City Pt.
Dated Aug 21 *1864.*

To GEN BUTLER

The last despatch from Gen Warren was dated at 11 a m. He then stated that the enemy had attacked from the North & West but were too easily repulsed. He did not get them close enough for his firer to have full effect. He captured however (400) prisoners that he knew of. I hope there is a mistake in the intercppted signal[1]

U. S. GRANT. Lt Genl

Telegram received (at 3:20 P.M.), DLC-Benjamin F. Butler; copies, DLC-USG, V, 45, 68, 107; DNA, RG 108, Letters Sent. *O.R.*, I, xlii, part 2, 376. On Aug. 21, 1864, 3:50 P.M., USG telegraphed to Maj. Gen. Benjamin F. Butler. "The operator at Gen Warrens HdQrs this moment in reply to a question from me says every attack of the enemy has been repulsed & Warrens position is now stronger than ever." Telegram received (at 3:40 P.M.), DLC-Benjamin F. Butler; copies, DLC-USG, V, 45, 68, 107; DNA, RG 108, Letters Sent; *ibid.*, RG 393, 10th Army Corps, Telegrams Received. *O.R.*, I, xlii, part 2, 376.

1. Butler had telegraphed to USG a C.S.A. signal message received at 2:20 P.M. "The enemy was ~~drove~~ driven from Weldon road. We are still pursuing him." Telegram received, DNA, RG 107, Telegrams Collected (Unbound).

To Maj. Gen. George G. Meade

By Telegraph from City Point 12.45 p m
Dated Aug 21st *1864.*

To MAJOR GEN MEADE

If the enemy are moving to turn Warrens left why can he not move out & attack between them and Petersburg & either cut their force in two or get in rear of it? If the roads are impassable for our Artillery it must be so for the enemys & it becomes an infantry fight. I will telegraph Ord either to assault or extend so as to relieve more men—the enemy evidently intend to use nearly their entire force to drive Warren away & we can either penetrate his line or hold ours with a very small force

U S GRANT
Lt Gen

Telegram received, DNA, RG 94, War Records Office, Army of the Potomac; copies, *ibid.*, RG 108, Letters Sent; DLC-USG, V, 45, 68, 107; (2) Meade Papers, PHi. *O.R.*, I, xlii, part 2, 355. On Aug. 21, 1864, noon and 1:00 P.M., Maj. Gen. George G. Meade telegraphed to USG. "Ord reports the enemy leaving his front —it is probably Martins brigade of Hokes Division the only one left of that division in front of Ord last night, as reported by Deserters—The enemy now holds his entrenched line with Johnstons Division & part of Heths that is between the Appomatox & the plank road—I have asked Ord if he can not assault in his front, whether he cannot extend to his left so as to relieve part of Motts Division 2d corps now holding from Burnsides mine to the Plank road   Hancock is now at the strong House west of the Plank road, slashing trees to make an obstacle to the enemys interposing between the Plank road & Warren   If I can get a line

of obstacle to be held by a skirmish line I can throw more troops to Warren's support—Warren reports the enemy moving to his left—I have sent him your despatch having previously advised him the way to stop the enemys flanking was to
assume the offensive & make him look out for his flanks   The difficulty of Warren's position is, the roads are *impassable* and his artillery can not be moved—It
is absolutely essential he should maintain his position, and I have no doubt of his
ability to do so unless the enemy should bring so superior a force as to turn his
left flank in which case we can not get our men to stand—they dont mind any
orders when they find themselves outflanked but move off bodily to the rear in
spite of orders.—" "Tel 12.45. received—Instructions have gone to Warren em-
bodying the spirit of your suggestions that is to assume the offensive. Ord has
reported he can spare 800 men and he has been—requested to extend his left with
that amount & Mott allowed to extend his left proportionately   this will free so
many men for Warren—I shall move Hancock up as soon as he can make any
thing of an obstacle to prevent the enemys getting in between Warrens position
and the Plank road   Telegraphic communication with Warren is interrupted
just now—The main roads running in to Petersburgh are passable—it is the cross
roads which by the passage of artillery & trains have since the rains, become impassable"   ALS (telegrams sent), DNA, RG 94, War Records Office, Army of
the Potomac; telegrams received, *ibid.*, RG 108, Letters Received. *O.R.*, I, xlii,
part 2, 355, 356.

At 9:45 A.M., Meade had telegraphed to USG. "I send you two despatches
from Genl. Warren—one in reply to your telegram about prisoners, the other in
relation to the firing just heard which has apparently ceased. The batteries on the
lines held by the 2d. & 18. corps can be opened, if still deemed necessary—"
ALS (telegram sent), DNA, RG 94, War Records Office, Army of the Potomac;
telegram received, *ibid.*, RG 108, Letters Received. The enclosed telegrams of
5:30 A.M. and 9:00 A.M. from Maj. Gen. Gouverneur K. Warren to Maj. Gen.
Andrew A. Humphreys are in *O.R.*, I, xlii, part 2, 366, 367. On the same day,
USG telegraphed to Meade. "Is the firing now heard on Warrens front? If so the
enemy should be opened upon by the 9th & 18th Corps and their lines threatened"
Telegram received, DNA, RG 94, War Records Office, Army of the Potomac;
copies, *ibid.*, RG 108, Letters Sent; DLC-USG, V, 45, 68, 107; (2) Meade
Papers, PHi. *O.R.*, I, xlii, part 2, 354. At 10:00 A.M., 10:25 A.M., and 10:55
A.M., Meade telegraphed to USG. "I send a despatch from Warren explanatory
of the firing—which has been resumed within the last few minutes—Hancock is
moving up—also Parke with his 4th Division—Warren on the defensive ought to
be able not only to hold his position but to punish the enemy severely, and undoubtedly would, if we could only get our troops to act with the audacity the
enemy show." "I have ordered Ord & Mott to £ open with their batteries & make
all the demonstrations they can against the enemy"   ALS (telegrams sent),
DNA, RG 94, War Records Office, Army of the Potomac; telegrams received,
ibid., RG 108, Letters Received. *O.R.*, I, xlii, part 2, 354. The enclosure in the
first is *ibid.*, p. 368. "I take pleasure in sending accompanying despatch from
Warren—. . . As soon as I see Hancock & Parke & arrange about their movements I shall go out to Warren"   ALS (telegram sent), DNA, RG 393, Army
of the Potomac, Telegrams Sent; copies, *ibid.*, Letters Sent; Meade Papers, PHi.
On the same day, USG telegraphed to Meade. "It is hard to say what ought to be
done without being on the field but it seems to me that when the enemy comes
out of his works and attacks, and is repulsed, he ought to be followed vigerously
to the last minuet with every man. Holding a line is of no importance whilst

troops are operating in front of it." ALS (telegram sent), CSmH; telegram received (at 11:20 A.M.), DNA, RG 94, War Records Office, Army of the Potomac. Printed as sent at 11:20 A.M. in *O.R.*, I, xlii, part 2, 355.

To Maj. Gen. George G. Meade

By Telegraph from City Point 1 10 p m
Dated Aug 21st *1864.*

To MAJ GEN MEADE

Do you not think it likely the enemy are preparing for a heavy attack on Warren this afternoon   if such is the case would it not be better to move Hancock up to his support at once & leave the ~~starting~~ slashing to troops that will be set free by Ord—I have directed Ord either to assault on his front or to extend & relieve Mott favoring the latter—You will know very soon which he thinks best

U S GRANT
Lt Genl

Telegram received, DNA, RG 94, War Records Office, Army of the Potomac; copies, *ibid.*, RG 108, Letters Sent; DLC-USG, V, 45, 68, 107; (2) Meade Papers, PHi. *O.R.*, I, xlii, part 2, 356. On Aug. 21, 1864, 1:30 P.M., Brig. Gen. Seth Williams telegraphed to USG. "The following has just been received from General Warren—General Meade left here half an hour since for General Warrens Head Quarters—It is expected that we shall again have telegraphic communication with General Warrens HeadQuarters in a few moments—" ALS (telegram sent), DNA, RG 94, War Records Office, Army of the Potomac; telegram received, *ibid.*, RG 108, Letters Received. *O.R.*, I, xlii, part 2, 356. The enclosure is *ibid.* At 2:30 P.M. and 5:25 P.M., Maj. Gen. George G. Meade, Jones's House, Plank Road, and Weldon Railroad, telegraphed to USG. "Tel 1.10 received—I had just ordered one division of Hancocks to Warrens left   I have now ordered the other one—the third Motts is holding our entr[en]chments—I have sent you a despatch from Warren announcing another repulse of the enemy. As soon as I get on the field & Hancock is up I will assume the offensive before if practicable—Hancocks people however are very weary and will not [b]e fit for much today & will not much more than get into position—The c[on]dition of the roads is a great draw back   Every thing has to be packed ac[ro]ss the plank road" "Hancocks men are so exhausted with their long march that nothing can be expected of them this afternoon—Having moved Hancock over to the left, I have placed Parke on the right and he is extending to make the line & connection over to the plank road—The enemy appear to have abandoned their intention of turning Warrens left & now show some signs of a movement on his right   My solicitude in desiring to have a line of slashings across to the plank road, is based on the fact that the enemy may move on Warren's left and turn our entrenchments resting on the plank road, which can not be held if turned—a̶n̶ This would compel the abandonment of this position, and might embarrass us to recover our entrenchments—If the enemy do not make this move before night Parke I think will prepare the line so as to prevent it—" ALS (telegrams sent), DNA, RG 94, War Records Office, Army of the Potomac; telegrams received, *ibid.*, RG 108, Letters Received. *O.R.*, I, xlii, part 2, 357.

To Maj. Gen. George G. Meade

(Cipher)   City Point Va. Aug. 21st *1864*. [*8:30* P.M.]
MAJ. GEN. MEADE,

Between the Appomattox and Bakers [*Bake-House*] Creek the enemy are supposed to be very weak. Gen. Butler is preparing two assaulting columns to-night with the view of breaking that c̶o̶l̶u̶m̶ line at daylight in the morning. If successful he will endeavor to clear out the entire line of the enemy South from the Howlett House and establish him self, with all his force, on the line of Swift Creek. With the 10th Corps he ought to be able to hold his ground all day, if he gets through, and could only then be driven away b̶u̶t̶ by drawing largely from Petersburg. I cannot say now what is best to be done with your forces in connection with this but notify you so that you can take advantage of any weakening of the enemy. I shall hear and inform you the result of Butler's efforts and can tell better then the best directions to give.

U. S. GRANT
Lt. Gn.

ALS (telegram sent), CSmH; telegram received, DNA, RG 94, War Records Office, Army of the Potomac. *O.R.*, I, xlii, part 2, 357.

To Maj. Gen. George G. Meade

City Point Va. Aug. 21st/64 10. p. m.
MAJ. GN. MEADE,

Your dispatch of 9.30 p. m. just received. I sent you a dispatch in cipher from which you will se̶e̶n̶ when received that I do not expect offensive operations to-morrow except in case of a success in

Butler's front making it practicable. If ~~you~~ we can retain hold of the rail-road it will be a great advantage. Has much of the rail-road been destroyed? After the men get well rested it will be well to support the Cavalry with a ~~d~~Division of Infantry to destroy as much of the road as we can if an advantage is not gained in the mean time making it unnecessary. If Butler does not succeed in the morning he will relieve the 18th Corps from the lines leaving it loose. With that as a reserve our lines will be strong.

U. S. GRANT
Lt. Gn.

ALS (telegram sent), PPRF; telegram received, DNA, RG 94, War Records Office, Army of the Potomac. *O.R.*, I, xlii, part 2, 358. On Aug. 21, 1864, 9:20 P.M. and 11:00 P.M., Maj. Gen. George G. Meade telegraphed to USG. "I have just returned from the front—I found it impracticable to arrange any offensive movements for tomorrow.—Warren expressed every confidence in his command defending itself against any attack but advised against attacking.—Hancocks men are completely exhausted with their march & nearly a third behind on the road—Parke's people will be working all night on the connecting line Under these circumstances, I gave orders to act on the defensive but in the event of the enemys attacking again to follow up their repulse. I think now we have thinned our line from the Appomatox to the plank road as much as we ought to do—Ord proposes to send more men but I do not think it judicious to weaken him any more, because the enemy finding an accumulation on our left might mass & by a bold assault break through our weakened line—I dont think this probable but it is possible. Warren reports taking some 400 prisoners today.—" "Your despatch in cipher received—I will be prepared tomorrow to act according to developments. Prisoners say that Genl. W. H. F Lee was mortally wounded today I send this for what it is worth. The R Rd. party have been at work today but I have received no report of their progress—Greggs cavalry Division are protecting them—In case it is necessary a supporting force of Infantry will be sent." ALS (telegrams sent), DNA, RG 94, War Records Office, Army of the Potomac; telegrams received (the first at 9:30 P.M.), *ibid.*, RG 108, Letters Received. *O.R.*, I, xlii, part 2, 358.

To Maj. Gen. Edward O. C. Ord

By Telegraph from City Point
Dated Aug 21 *1864*. 1 P. M.

To MAJ GEN E O C ORD.

The enemy evidently intend to use nearly their entire force to drive us from the weldon road. This will enable us either to penetrate their line or to hold ours with a very small force. Either make an attempt to break through on your front or extend so as to relieve Motts Div to go to Warren   I am in inclined to believe the latter to be the best policy but leave it to your judgement

U. S. Grant
Lt Genl

Telegram received, Ord Papers, CU-B; copies, DLC-USG, V, 45, 68, 107; DNA, RG 108, Letters Sent. *O.R.*, I, xlii, part 2, 384. On Aug. 21, 1864, Maj. Gen. Edward O. C. Ord telegraphed to USG. "I have ordered portions of my men to relieve Mott's division by Gen. Meade's order—My parapet front line in places does not cover my men—having been washed down by rain. Hence there is danger of reducing too much my trench guard, having no reserves of either infantry or artillery. I should like two or three batteries from Genl. Butler—Parke having withdrawn three batteries and I have none to replace them. I have no battery to prevent the enemy's crossing near Fort Clifton—" ALS (undated telegram sent), DNA, RG 94, War Records Office, Army of the Potomac; telegram received, *ibid.*, RG 108, Letters Received. *O.R.*, I, xlii, part 2, 384. On the same day, USG telegraphed to Ord. "Gen Butler will send you one battery   Gen Hancock has a surplus of Artillery and will supply you all you want if you will call on him"   Telegram received (at 3:30 P.M.), Ord Papers, CU-B; copies, DLC-USG, V, 45, 68, 107; DNA, RG 108, Letters Sent.

To Maj. Gen. Philip H. Sheridan

(Cipher)   City Point Va. Aug. 21st *1864.*
Maj. Gen. Sheridan, Charlestown Va.

In striping Loudon County of supplies &c. impress from all loyal persons so that they may receive pay for what is taken from them. I am informed by the Asst. Sec. of War that Loudon County has a large population of Quakers who are all favorably disposed to the Union. These people may be exempted from arrest.

U. S. Grant
Lt. Gen

ALS (telegram sent), CSmH; telegram received (sent at 10:30 A.M., received at 6:00 P.M.), DNA, RG 107, Telegrams Collected (Bound). *O.R.*, I, xliii, part 1, 869–70. On Aug. 20, 1864, Asst. Secretary of War Charles A. Dana telegraphed to USG. "There is in Loudoun county a considerable settlement of Quakers favorable to the Union, but never disturbed nor conscripted by the rebels. No doubt they would be very willing to have their produce & animals impressed, but ought they not to be personally excepted from the late order to

Gen. Sheridan?" ALS (telegram sent), DNA, RG 107, Telegrams Collected (Bound); telegram received (datelined 5:00 P.M.), *ibid.*, RG 108, Letters Received. *O.R.*, I, xliii, part 1, 856.

To Maj. Gen. Philip H. Sheridan

Cipher   City Point, Va. Aug. 21st 5 p. m. *1864.*
MAJ. GN. SHERIDAN, CHARLESTOWN VA.

We have had prisoners or deserters from every Division and Brigade of Lee's & Beaurigard's Armies in the last few days except Fitz Lee's Cavalry & Kershaws Division. These we know have gone to the valley. A man employed by the Provost Marshal visits Orange Court House regularly and gets accurate reports from there. Not a regiment has passed there in the last two weeks going either way. To-day several attacks of the enemy on our forces occupying the Welden road have been repulsed with very little loss to us and with conciderable to them in killed wounded and captured. If operations planned for to-morrow are as successful as I hope they will be, I think the troops from the valley, or a portion of them, are more likely to be withdrawn than to be reinforced from here.

U. S. GRANT
Lt. Gn

ALS (telegram sent), CSmH; telegram received (on Aug. 22, 1864, 6:30 A.M.), DNA, RG 107, Telegrams Collected (Bound). *O.R.*, I, xliii, part 1, 870.

On Aug. 22, 10:30 P.M., Maj. Gen. Philip H. Sheridan, Harpers Ferry, telegraphed to USG. "Yesterday the enemy crossed Opequan Creek at different points in the vicinity of Smithfield or Middle Way & advanced on my position at Welch's Spring about two miles west of Charlestown—Skirmishing took place during the day in front of both Gen Crooks command & the Sixth army Corps. The skirmishing was at one time rather sharp in front of the latter command as the line was pressed forward & drove the enemy from a crest in our front which they occupied early in the day. The Cavalry skirmished some with the enemy at Berryville & Summit Point. This however did not amount to much—As my position at best in front of Charlestown was a bad one & much being dependent upon this army I withdrew my command without loss or opposition last night & took up a new line in front of Halltown—This morning the enemy followed my rear guard in & we have been skirmishing with them during the day—My loss yesterday was about two seventy five—None of the enemy have crossed the river—Various reports have come to me in reference to a column of the enemy being at Culpepper

& Warrenton but I place no reliance on the report—We have disposed of quite a number of Mosebys men" Telegram received, DNA, RG 107, Telegrams Collected (Unbound); copies, *ibid.*; *ibid.*, Telegrams Received in Cipher; DLC-Philip H. Sheridan. *O.R.*, I, xliii, part 1, 880.

To Maj. Gen. Henry W. Halleck

———

(Cipher)   City Point Va. Aug. 22d *1864*. [*9:30* P.M.]
Maj. Gn. Halleck, Washington

There is no place from which troops can be withdrawn to send Gen. Burbridge that I know of. I do not think Wheeler[1] can get to Ky. to do much harm nor do I think he can be spared from Hood's Army. John Morgan I ~~do not~~ think has no command. If Wheeler does go however Burbridge must pick up all his force and leave every thing els, except very important points, unguarded and go in pursuit.

                                    U. S. Grant
                                    Lt. Gn.

ALS (telegram sent), CSmH; telegram received (on Aug. 23, 1864, 2:00 P.M.), DNA, RG 107, Telegrams Collected (Bound). *O.R.*, I, xxxix, part 2, 283. See *ibid.*, p. 279.

1. Joseph Wheeler, born in Ga. in 1836, USMA 1859, resigned from the U.S. Army as of April 22, 1861, then commanded the 19th Ala. Appointed chief of cav., Army of Ky., on Oct. 13, 1862, he rose in rank to maj. gen. as of Jan. 22, 1863, and commanded the cav. of the Army of Tenn. In Aug., 1864, Gen. John B. Hood sent Wheeler's cav. to Tenn. to break U.S. supply and communication lines; Wheeler was unsuccessful.

To Maj. Gen. Henry W. Halleck

———

(Cipher)   City point Va. Aug. 22d/64 10 p. m.
Maj. Gn. Halleck, Washington,

Every thing quiet to-day. There were indications all day of the enemy collecting his strength to attempt to drive our forces from the rail-road. The effort may be made to-morrow. I suspended

about 2 a. m. to-day the order for an attack which had been prepared and was to have been made at day light. Yesterdays operations cost the enemy very dearly in killed wounded and captured
whilst our loss was very small.

U. S. GRANT
Lt. Gn

ALS (telegram sent), CSmH; telegram received (on Aug. 23, 1864, 2:00 P.M.),
DNA, RG 107, Telegrams Collected (Bound). *O.R.*, I, xlii, part 1, 19; *ibid.*, I,
xlii, part 2, 390.

To Maj. Gen. Benjamin F. Butler

By Telegraph from City Point
Dated Aug 22 *1864.*

To MAJ GEN BUTLER

Prisoners & deserters taken this morning rept the enemys loss
yesterday very heavy   I think it most likely the troop's seen going
towards Petersburg are likely troops getting back from the north
side of the river[1]   Gen W H F Lee is reptorted mortally wounded
in yesterday's engagement

U S GRANT
Lt Gen

Telegram received, DLC-Benjamin F. Butler; copies, DLC-USG, V, 45, 68, 107;
DNA, RG 108, Letters Sent. *O.R.*, I, xlii, part 2, 410. On Aug. 22, 1864, 10:10
A.M., Maj. Gen. Benjamin F. Butler telegraphed to USG. "Signal Office reports
6 50   Six trains passed during night toward *Richmond*   fifteen Cars loaded
with troops 6 45 A M Toward Richmond   2500 Cavalry toward Petersburgh
20 Cars with troops toward Petersburgh   Is it not relieving the fild troops in the
trenches with fresh troops from the North side of James"   ALS (telegram sent),
DNA, RG 107, Telegrams Collected (Unbound); telegram received, *ibid.*, RG
108, Letters Received. *O.R.*, I, xlii, part 2, 410. On the same day, Capt. Lemuel
B. Norton telegraphed to USG. "The signal officer at Spring Hills reports that
six trains of cars passed the Junction last night towards Richmond & that 6-45
this a. m. a train of fifteen cars loaded with troops passed in same direction"
Telegram received, DNA, RG 108, Letters Received.
    At 12:35 A.M., Butler telegraphed to USG. "Scouts report that [at] 5 o clock
this evening [the] absent troops made [the]ir appearance again in their [o]ld
places in front of our lines. The officer in charge of Picket line reports it as fully
maned. I sent to Gen Birney for his opinion of the Movement and he telegraphs as

follows . . . Shall we move at two oclock as proposed" ALS (telegram sent), *ibid.*, RG 107, Telegrams Collected (Unbound); telegram received, *ibid.*, RG 108, Letters Received. Printed as received at 12:40 A.M. in *O.R.*, I, xlii, part 2, 409. The enclosure is *ibid.*, p. 379. At 1:30 A.M., USG telegraphed to Butler. "Your dispatch of 12.35. a m. rec'd. Under the circumstances I think you had better not move." Telegram received, DLC-Benjamin F. Butler; copies, DLC-USG, V, 45, 68, 107; DNA, RG 108, Letters Sent. *O.R.*, I, xlii, part 2, 409. At 9:20 A.M., Butler telegraphed to USG. "I send the following from Signal Officer —What can it mean? The night trains were very heavy—These troops did not cross chafins ‡Farm this morning" Telegram received, DNA, RG 108, Letters Received. *O.R.*, I, xlii, part 2, 409. The enclosed signal message reported 20 railroad cars carrying troops, 27 wagons, and 100 cav. moving toward Petersburg. *Ibid.* On the same day, USG twice telegraphed to Butler. "The troops reported moving towards Petersburg must be the same that were opposed to the 2d & 10th Corps, north of the James They probably crossed the river during the night so as to escape observation" "I think it will be well to hold the 10th ready to make the effort that was proposed for this morning for a day or two before moving it The enemy may be induced to move most of his troops from your front in the hope of driving us from the Weldon road" Telegrams received, DLC-Benjamin F. Butler; DLC-USG, V, 45, 68, 107; DNA, RG 108, Letters Sent. *O.R.*, I, xlii, part 2, 409, 410. At 11:10 A.M., Butler telegraphed to USG. "I will keep the sharpest possible look out upon the movements of the enemy in my front and will be all ready to move at once day or night At 10 35. 27 waggons 14 ambulan[ces] and 300 cavalry passed toward Petersburgh 13. waggons toward Richmond." ALS (telegram sent), DNA, RG 107, Telegrams Collected (Unbound). Printed as received at 11:25 A.M. in *O.R.*, I, xlii, part 2, 410. On the same day, Butler telegraphed to USG. "When they get all their troops on the south side ~~we sha~~ we may be able to get out and have them all before us" ALS (telegram sent), DNA, RG 107, Telegrams Collected (Unbound); telegram received, *ibid.*, RG 108, Letters Received. *O.R.*, I, xlii, part 2, 411. The enclosed signal message, reporting nine railroad cars carrying troops moving toward Petersburg at noon, is *ibid.*, p. 410.

1. All copies read at this point: "I think it most likely the troops seen going towards Richmond are wounded men going to hospitals. Those moving towards Petersburg are likely troops getting back from the North side of the river."

To Maj. Gen. Benjamin F. Butler

City Point Va. Aug. 22d *1864*.

Maj. Gen. Butler,

I see by yesterdays Chronicle that there is a large number of negro men at Newbern who will not enlist. Newspaper articles are not entirely reliable authority to act upon but as the Chief Qr. Mr. is much in want of about 1000 men to release the same number of enlisted men with I thought I would enquire of you if this was so and if it is to send them here for employment not to be enlisted.

U. S. GRANT

Lt. Gn.

ALS (telegram sent), CSmH; telegram received (incomplete), DLC-Benjamin F. Butler. *O.R.*, I, xlii, part 2, 411. On Aug. 22, 1864, 10:30 P.M., Maj. Gen. Benjamin F. Butler telegraphed to USG. "Telegram recieved in relation to the unployed negros at Newbern. I have reason to believe that there is truth in the report   I will send an energetic Staff officer to investigate report and bring up the Negros." ALS (telegram sent), DNA, RG 107, Telegrams Collected (Unbound); telegram received, *ibid.*, RG 108, Letters Received. *O.R.*, I, xlii, part 2, 411.

To Maj. Gen. George G. Meade

———

By Telegraph from City Point
Dated Aug 22 *1864.*

To M GENL MEADE

2500 Cavy were seen moving toward P.Burg this morning. They will probably try to get to Warrens left today either to drive in the working party on the R.R. or to operate on this rear. Do you not think it advisable to move a Div of Infy a few miles down the Road to be ready for them

U. S. GRANT

Lt Genl

Telegram received, DNA, RG 94, War Records Office, Army of the Potomac; *ibid.*, RG 107, Telegrams Collected (Unbound); copies, *ibid.*, RG 108, Letters Sent; DLC-USG, V, 45, 68, 107; (2) Meade Papers, PHi. *O.R.*, I, xlii, part 2, 391. On Aug. 22, 1864, Maj. Gen. Benjamin F. Butler had telegraphed to USG. "My Signal officers reports that a column of about twenty five (2500) was seen at 9-30 A. m. on turn pike opposite R.R. Junction going towards Petersburg" Telegram received, DNA, RG 108, Letters Received. At 11:20 A.M. and 12:30 P.M., Maj. Gen. George G. Meade telegraphed to USG. "I find the enemy have left Warrens flank (left) and apparently his front between this point and the works in front of Petersburgh—I also find that Warren is occupying the most favorable point in case a permanent lodgment on the R. Rd. is determined on— There is not object therefore in advancing him unless it is intended to attack the enemys works—I have accordingly directed him to remain in his present position pushing his skirmishers forward till they feel the enemys   Parkes corps is on the right completing the line from here to the plank road—Hancock has one division in reserve and the other I have sent to assist in destroying the Rail Road

U.S. Signal Corps officers on Cobb's Hill Lookout Tower near Dutch Gap
provided information about movements between Petersburg and Richmond.
Photograph attributed to Mathew B. Brady. *Courtesy National Archives.*

Field telegraph battery wagon of the Army of the Potomac near Petersburg in Sept., 1864. Photograph attributed to David Knox and Alexander Gardner. *Courtesy National Archives.*

& covering the working party—I understand the R. Rd. men yesterday became alarmed & mostly deserted the work—The enemys cavalry will undoubtedly endeavor to interfere with this work—I should be glad to know if these dispositions meet your views—also whether you propose to reinforce the entrenched line held by Ord & Mott by any of Butlers troops, for I feel a little uneasy about this line" ALS (telegram sent—misdated Aug. 24), *ibid.*, RG 94, War Records Office, Army of the Potomac; telegram received (dated Aug. 22), *ibid.*; *ibid.*, RG 108, Letters Received; copies (2—dated Aug. 21 and Aug. 24), *ibid.*, RG 393, Army of the Potomac, Letters Sent; (3—one dated Aug. 21 and two Aug. 24) Meade Papers, PHi. Dated Aug. 22 in *O.R.*, I, xlii, part 2, 391–92. "My telegram of 11.20 has been delayed by the wire out of order—Since writing it Warrens pickets report the enemy in position entrenched about a mile back from the position occupied yesterday—I have directed any signal despatches for me to be sent to you, as they may indicate movements requiring your action.—" ALS (telegram sent), DNA, RG 94, War Records Office, Army of the Potomac; telegram received, *ibid.*, RG 108, Letters Received. *O.R.*, I, xlii, part 2, 392. The signal messages transmitted according to Meade's instructions are in DNA, RG 108, Letters Received. A number are printed in *O.R.*, I, xlii, part 2, 395–98.

Also on Aug. 22, USG telegraphed to Meade. "The object in relieving the 18th Corps is that from being kept so long in the Appomattox bottom A great many are now sick & the number is increasing very rapidly—Having the 18th Corps free will give the same reserve as having any other Corps free would" Telegram received, DNA, RG 94, War Records Office, Army of the Potomac; copies, *ibid.*, RG 108, Letters Sent; DLC-USG, V, 45, 68, 107; (2) Meade Papers, PHi. *O.R.*, I, xlii, part 2, 393. At 3:30 P.M., Meade telegraphed to USG. "Warrens Skirmishers are in contact with the enemys about a miles from here & the same distance from the enemys outer works on the R.R. They do not report any very heavy force and there is no indication at this moment of any attack notwithstanding the reports of Sig officer would seem to indicate an accumlation of troops about the Lead works which are on the R.R. inside the outer entrenchments   a despatch from Gen Ord asks for reserves of infantry & artillery in case it is ~~anticiptated~~ anticipated he may be attacked   I have directed him to call on Gen Hunt for the artillery as he has batteries in reserve but I have no infantry to send to him—your despatch giving reason for relieeiving the 18th by the 10th Corps was not recd by me till after sending my dispatch of 11-20 which must be my excuse for referring in that dispatch to the subject—The R.R. men have done very little work & that very indifferently—Hancocks Div. will soon be at work in addition" Telegram received, DNA, RG 108, Letters Received; copy, *ibid.*, RG 393, Army of the Potomac, Letters Sent. *O.R.*, I, xlii, part 2, 392.

On Aug. 22, 7:30 A.M., Meade telegraphed to USG. "I send a despatch just received from Warren   He has been instructed to follow the enemy & Hancock to move up after him. I shall go to the front in a short time" Telegram received, DNA, RG 108, Letters Received; copies (misdated Aug. 23), *ibid.*, RG 393, Army of the Potomac, Letters Sent; Meade Papers, PHi. On the same day, Lt. Col. Cyrus B. Comstock telegraphed to Meade. "Lt. Gen. Grant desires me to say that in consequence of the reports of deserters, that the enemies line in front of Butler had been reoccupied by the original force, no attempt will be made from Butlers front." ALS (telegram sent), DNA, RG 108, Telegrams Sent by Comstock; telegram received (at 8:00 A.M.), DNA, RG 94, War Records Office, Army of the Potomac. *O.R.*, I, xlii, part 2, 390. At 8:15 A.M., Meade telegraphed to USG. "Col Comstocks telegram received. If the 10th corps is brought this side of the Appomatox I beg leave to renew my suggestion that it relieve the 2d. corps holding to the left of the 18th—This would leave some reserve for the line of the 10th & 18th corps & would enable the concentration of the 2d. corps for further operations.—" ALS (telegram sent), DNA, RG 94, War Records Office, Army of the Potomac; telegram received, *ibid.*, RG 108, Letters Received. *O.R.*, I, xlii, part 2, 390–91.

Also on Aug. 22, USG twice telegraphed to Meade. "2 trains of cars loaded with Troops moving to P.Burg have been reported this morning by the signal officers at Spring Hill" Telegram received, DNA, RG 94, War Records Office, Army of the Potomac; copies, *ibid.*, RG 108, Letters Sent; DLC-USG, V, 45, 68, 107; (2) Meade Papers, PHi. *O.R.*, I, xlii, part 2, 392. "Cars were runing constantly between pRichmond and Petersburg and this morning several trains have been seen to pass heavily loaded with troops going South. Warren may be attacked this evening." ALS (telegram sent), Havemeyer Collection, NHi; telegram received, DNA, RG 94, War Records Office, Army of the Potomac; *ibid.*, Miscellaneous War Records. *O.R.*, I, xlii, part 2, 393.

To Maj. Gen. George G. Meade

By Telegraph from City Pt
Dated Aug 22 1864.

To Maj Gen Meade

It is my desire to hold the Weldon Road if it can be held & to Thoroughly destroy it as far south as possible   I donot expect to attack the Enemy behind his intrenchments unless he sends off a large part of his force—There is no necessity therefore for Warren ~~to~~ moving from where he is unless he gains a better position by doing so. I intend to send all of the 10Th Corps that can be spared from Bermuda to take the place of the 18th Corps & to place the latter back on high ground where it will support our whole line from the Appomattox to the PlankRoad & will at the same time be loose to go whereever it may be needed—Thinking It possible however that the Enemy might during today or tomorrow Concentrate all his forces to drive Warren away I have directed Gen Butler to hold the 10th Corps where it is to make the attack Contemplated for this morning should the Enemy do so

U S Grant
Lt Genl

Telegram received, DNA, RG 94, War Records Office, Army of the Potomac; copies, *ibid.*, RG 108, Letters Sent; DLC-USG, V, 45, 68, 107; (2) Meade Papers, PHi. *O.R.*, I, xlii, part 2, 391.

On Aug. 22, 1864, 9:30 P.M., Maj. Gen. George G. Meade telegraphed to USG. "I left the Welden R. Rd. at 6 p m   At that time all was quiet. Genl. Miles Comdg. Divn. 2d. corps had progressed within 1½ miles of Reams station destroying the rail road as he moved.—Hearing the enemys cavalry occupied Reams station I directed Genl. Gregg to send all his available cavalry force to assist Genl. Miles in occupying the place—Since my return a despatch from Genl. Gregg announces the occupation of Reams station by his command—Col Spear Comdg. Brigade of Kautz cavalry drove the enemys cavalry on the Vaughn & Bond roads in the direction of Petersburgh till he came to a bridge destroyed by by the enemy after crossing it at which point the pursuit ceased—Prisoners report the death yesterday of Genl. Sanders Comdg. brigade & the wounding severely of Genl. W. H. F. Lee—but I place no reliance on the reports of prisoners in such matters as they are generally only camp rumours.—" ALS (telegram sent), DNA, RG 94, War Records Office, Army of the Potomac; telegram received, *ibid.*, RG 108, Letters Received. *O.R.*, I, xlii, part 2, 393.

To Maj. Gen. Henry W. Halleck

(Cipher)   City Point Va. Aug. 23d *1864*. [6:00 P.M.]
Maj. Gn. Halleck, Washingtn

Our position on the Welden rail-road now seems entirely secure. One Division of Infantry & the Cavalry have been working south destroying the road as they go. They met some opposition to-day from the enemy's Cavalry and were consequently further reinforced. Prisoners taken since the last repulse of the enemy repeat the report of W. H. F. Lee being mortally wounded, Gen. Clingman loosing a leg and Gen. Saunders ~~being~~ killed.[1] These reports however may not be reliable.

U. S. Grant
Lt. Gn,

ALS (telegram sent), CSmH; telegram received (on Aug. 24, 1864), DNA, RG 107, Telegrams Collected (Bound); *ibid.*, Telegrams Collected (Unbound). *O.R.*, I, xlii, part 1, 19; *ibid.*, I, xlii, part 2, 418.

1. Maj. Gen. William H. F. Lee was not mortally wounded; Brig. Gen. Thomas L. Clingman was seriously wounded; Brig. Gen. John C. C. Sanders was killed.

To Maj. Gen. Benjamin F. Butler

By Telegraph from City Pt
Dated Aug 23 *1864.*

To MAJ GENL BUTLER

You ~~can~~ may now send the 10th Corps or as much of it as can be spared from Bermuda 100 to relieve as far as possible the 18th Corps,   when the 18th is relieved let them go into Camp on the high ground in rear of their present position—so long as we hold the Weldon Road it is prudent for us to keep all the force we can south of the Appomattox—

U S GRANT
Lt Genl

Telegram received, DLC-Benjamin F. Butler; copies, DLC-USG, V, 45, 68, 107; DNA, RG 108, Letters Sent. *O.R.*, I, xlii, part 2, 436–37. On Aug. 23, 1864, 1:00 P.M., Maj. Gen. Benjamin F. Butler telegraphed to USG. "Telegram receivd   I will immediately proceed to relieve the 18th corps Division by Division —and encamp ~~the~~ ~~m~~at corp as a reserve so that fewer men can hold the ~~position~~ trenches, than if they were not so encamped." ALS (telegram sent), DNA, RG 107, Telegrams Collected (Unbound); telegram received, *ibid.*, RG 108, Letters Received. Printed as sent at 12:35 P.M., received at 1:00 P.M., in *O.R.*, I, xlii, part 2, 437.

At 8:25 P.M., Butler telegraphed to USG. "My Chief Paymaster is here with a small amount of money. There are now two payments due near all my troops and will be thee a Week from to Day   The money will go but little way as so many of the troops have instalments of bounties and recruiting bounties due them so that it takes so much for each soldier that but few can be paid. For example four month pay is 58 dollars but an instalment of bounty is 50 dollars and some have two instalments due so that in fact we can pay nearly twice as many if we do not pay the bounties. Now as the bounties are gratuities should we not endeavor to pay as many as we can then pay proper so that many may get a little for their wants and not a few get a good deal. If you see no objection I will order the pay master to pay only the pay proper, till he gets more money. Another thing after next wednesday as new muster day nobody can be paid on the old rolls, and must wait nearly a month for the new rolls and returns which is an additional reason for paying as many as possible during this week" ALS (telegram sent), DNA, RG 107, Telegrams Collected (Unbound); telegram received (datelined 9:25 P.M.), *ibid.*, RG 108, Letters Received. On the same day, Lt. Col. Theodore S. Bowers telegraphed to Butler. "Genl Grant directs me to say that he approves of the policy suggested by you & that you are authorized to issue the necessary order" Telegram received (at 10:00 P.M.), DLC-Benjamin F. Butler.

To Maj. Gen. George G. Meade

By Telegraph from Ft Powhattan
Dated August 23rd *1864.* [*1:15* P.M.]

To MAJ GEN MEADE

I think with you it would be imprudent to send Gen Miles with his small force beyond the support of the main army to destroy the R R   If we can hold our present position until the Roads get in good order Ord can be sent with the 18th corps & cavalry to complete the work possible as far as Hicks ford at least so far as to inconvenience the Enemy in hauling around the break & so that it would take considerable time to repair it

U S GRANT
Lt Gen

Telegram received (at 2:15 P.M.), DNA, RG 94, War Records Office, Army of the Potomac; copies, *ibid.*, RG 108, Letters Sent; DLC-USG, V, 45, 68, 107; (2) Meade Papers, PHi. Printed as sent at 2:15 P.M. in *O.R.*, I, xlii, part 2, 420. On Aug. 23, 1864, 10:30 A.M., noon, and 6:00 P.M., Meade telegraphed to USG. "I have nothing new to report this morning—Reports from deserters & observed movements of the enemy led to the belief of the probability of an attack on Motts front last night.—Every preparation that was practicable was made to meet it. I have called on Genl. Warren for his views as to holding his present position with his own & the 9th corps extending to the Plank road—It becomes a question, on which I desire your views how far ~~the~~ Miles Division 2d Corps should go down the R. Rd. destroying it—This division is small less than 4000 effectives & has a brigade of cavalry about 1000 strong.—From reports of deserters there is reason to believe the enemy sent infantry down the Rail Road on Sunday night & we know the has two divisions of cavalry available for operations, besides troops now on the road that can be sent up from the South to meet Miles advance—In my judgement therefore Miles ought not to go beyond support from Warrens position say Rowanty creek some 10 miles which point he will probably reach today—He has ~~& can~~ no artillery with him & it can not be got over to him and he can not carry any trains, or reserve ammunition—He should therefore return or be reinforced—If Warren replies he can take care of himself, and it is deemed the line from the plank road to the Appomatox is secure, Gibbons division can be sent to Miles & another brigade of cavalry, but this is extending very far & leaves no means of repairing any casualty should the enemy, by a successful movement penetrate our line at any point—I should be pleased to have your instructions upon these points.—" "I have a despatch from Warren advising me he has so strengthened his position, he feels secure against any attack without the aid of the 2d. corps. In deciding upon the movements of this corps 2d an important consideration must be held in view—the present condition of all but the main & old

roads—all others, country & cross roads, are impassible for artillery & wagons—
the rain of last evening will I fear keep them so for some days or until we have
fair weather, a warm sun & drying winds.—The question therefore of supplying
any large force at a distance from the main army or carrying supplies enters into
the expediency of movements—With pack mules we can keep up supplies, if the
troops are not too far removed from the trains—the trains can not be taken along.
—This despatch is intended as as continuation of the one sent this a. m—asking
your views." "I have examined the line from the strong house to Warrens right—
It can be held securely by two divisions of the 9th corps leaving two divisions in
reserve   Warren can hold his line securely with three divisions leaving him one
in reserve—Under these circumstances, as Miles has had a skirmish with the
enemys cavalry & from prisoners learned that a division of cavalry was in his
front, I have ordered Gibbon down to Reams station & sent Hancock down to
take charge of the two divisions of infantry & the cavalry & to destroy the Rail
Road as far as practicable—" ALS (telegrams sent), DNA, RG 94, War Records
Office, Army of the Potomac; telegrams received, *ibid.*, RG 108, Letters Received.
O.R., I, xlii, part 2, 418–20.

   Also on Aug. 23, USG telegraphed to Meade. "The Richmond papers of
22nd claim to have captured from Warren on Saturday morning twenty seven
hundred prisoners   Did Warren lose any such number   No report yet recvd
shows it"   Telegram received, DNA, RG 94, War Records Office, Army of the
Potomac; copies, *ibid.*, RG 108, Letters Sent; DLC-USG, V, 45, 68, 107; (2)
Meade Papers, PHi. *O.R.*, I, xlii, part 2, 419. At 10:45 a.m., Meade telegraphed
to USG. "Warrens official returns show as follows—. . . Aug. 18—66 [*killed*].
478 [*wounded*]. 392 [*missing*]. Aug 19. 46 [*killed*]. 218 [*wounded*]. 2,457
[*missing*]. Genl. Warren was in hopes many of the above missing were stragglers
—It should be observed the above report is exclusive of the 9th corps who also
lost prisoners on the 19th. it is therefore probable the Richmond papers are not
far in error.—" ALS (telegram sent), DNA, RG 94, War Records Office, Army
of the Potomac; telegram received, *ibid.*, RG 108, Letters Received. *O.R.*, I, xlii,
part 2, 419.

To Julia Dent Grant

City Point Aug. 23d *1864*.

Dear Julia,

   Fred starts in the morning for Philadelphia to meet you and to
remain with you until arrangements are made for your housekeeping. I should like however very much to see you and the children before you settle dow so if you choose you may come down
here bringing them with you. There is no possible place however
for you to stay. You would have to remain aboard of the boat and
return with it next day. I would go back with you as far as Fortress

Monroe. If you do come you had better let Dr. Brinton's Mother know what kind of a house you want and she would let it be known so I think you would find no difficulty on your return. If possible you want to rent a furnished house. If not you will have to take one and furnish it your self. In that case I will have to get you some more money. I can spare $1000 from this months pay and unless Mr. Jones has bought more Horse rail-road stock I have about $1.400 with him. This would give you $3.400 to start with. At present rates it would take five or six thousand to furnish a house. I have not been so well for the last week as usual though to-day feel better.

Kisses for your self and the children.

ULYS.

ALS, DLC-USG.

To Abraham Lincoln

City Point Va. Aug. 24th *1864*.

A. LINCOLN
PRESIDENT OF THE UNITED STATES,
DEAR SIR:

I have heretofore recommended Lt. Col. Theador[e] S. Bowers my Asst. Adj. Gen. for appointment in the Adj. Gen's Dept. of the regular army. I find howeve he is not eligible for the appointment he not belonging to the regular army. I would therefore most respectfully recommend his appointment as Asst. Quartermaster to fill the vacancy created by the promotion of Gen. Hancock out of the Dept. as a step to make him eligible for the other place. I would then urge the appointment of Capt. T. S. Bowers A. Q. M as Maj. & A. A. Gen. in the Regular army to fill the vacancy now existing.

Col. Bowers has served directly with me from his first enlistment in 1861, first as a private soldier detailed as a clerk in the office, next as Aid de Camp, then as Judge Advocate and since the fall of Vicksburg as Asst. Adj. Gn.

But few men are better qualified for the office and none are possessed of higher moral worth. He has too this great merit; he has never asked directly nor through friends for this advancement nor for any other promotion he has had in this war.

> I have the honor to be, very respectfully your obt. svt.
> U. S. GRANT
> Lt. Gn.

ALS, Mrs. Walter Love, Flint, Mich. On Aug. 27, 1864, President Abraham Lincoln endorsed this letter. "Let Gen. Grant be obliged in the matter within." AES, *ibid*. Theodore S. Bowers received an appointment as maj. and adjt., U.S. Army, as of Jan. 6, 1865.

To Maj. Gen. Henry W. Halleck

(Cipher) City Point, Aug. 24th *1864*.
MAJ. GN. H. W. HALLECK, WASHINGTON

Yesterday evening the enemy engaged our Cavalry which was protecting the party destroying rail-road near Reams station. Gen. Gregg was about one & a half miles West from the station and maintained his position the fight lasting from 4.30 p. m. till 9 p. m. He reports his loss at 75. Earlyier in the afternoon Col Spear[1] Comd.g Brigade of Kautz Cavalry had a sharp engagement with the enemy's Cavalry on the Bond road, near Reams station, and notwithstanding largely superior forces against him maintained his ground inflicting heavy loss on the enemy. He reports over One hundred & eighty of the enemy's dead left upon the field. The road is now thoroughly destroyed to Reams station. The force on the road was largely reinforced last night and will push on the work.

I send to-day a Richmond paper of the 23d directed to the Sec. of War. You will see from that that great dispondency was caused by the last affair on the Welden road. In Richmond they have reports of five Generals being killed in that action but the death of but two of them, Saunders & Lamar,[2] is positively confirmed.

> U. S. GRANT
> Lt. Gen,

ALS (telegram sent), CSmH; telegram received (sent at 10:30 P.M., received Aug. 25, 1864, 6:00 A.M.), DNA, RG 107, Telegrams Collected (Bound). *O.R.*, I, xlii, part 1, 19–20; *ibid.*, I, xlii, part 2, 441–42.

1. Col. Samuel P. Spear, 11th Pa. Cav., a soldier in the prewar U.S. Army, commanded the 2nd Brigade, Kautz's Div. See *ibid.*, I, xlii, part 1, 833–35.
2. Col. Thompson B. Lamar, 5th Fla., killed on Aug. 21.

To Maj. Gen. Benjamin F. Butler

City Point Va August ~~1.20 P. M.~~ 24 1.20 P. M. [*1864*]

MAJ GEN BUTLER

Has a Division of the 10th Corps started yet to replace the 18th. Gen Ord has just asked Meade for any spare troops he may have stating that there are indications of an attack and that a number of deserters having gone over to the enemy last night who may have given information of his weakness, makes him fear the result. If a Division of Birney has not gone, how long will it take, to get one there?

U. S GRANT Lt. Gen.

Copies, DLC-USG, V, 45, 68, 107; DNA, RG 108, Letters Sent. *O.R.*, I, xlii, part 2, 455. On Aug. 24, 1864, 1:45 P.M. and 2:06 P.M., Maj. Gen. Benjamin F. Butler telegraphed to USG. "General Ord telegraphs me that his look outs inform him that large bodies of troops supposed to be five thousand (5000) are concentrating in front of his lines and asking for one division of General Birneys command which I have ordered, he fearing attack either today or to night—Deserters say that Mahones divisions was relieved by Picketts which was cut up in the fight of Sunday—The fact that Mahones division was in the fight appears in to days Examiner which I have sent you That There has been some change in my front between the James and appomattox would appear from the fact that for the first time in many weeks picket firing was started on our left near Port Walthall." LS (telegram sent), DNA, RG 107, Telegrams Collected (Unbound); telegram received, *ibid.*, RG 108, Letters Received. *O.R.*, I, xlii, part 2, 455–56. "Orders was sent this morning for one Div to move & I suppose it is En route. I will hurry it along." Copy, DNA, RG 107, Telegrams Collected (Unbound). *O.R.*, I, xlii, part 2, 456.

Also on Aug. 24, 1:38 P.M., Butler transmitted to USG a telegram from Maj. Gen. David B. Birney to Maj. Robert S. Davis, adjt. for Butler. "Deserter in today say that Picketts Division has been Ordered to relieve Mahone which is badly Cut up from sundays fight" LS (telegram sent), DNA, RG 107, Telegrams Collected (Unbound); telegram received, *ibid.*, RG 108, Letters Received. Printed as received at 1:28 P.M. in *O.R.*, I, xlii, part 2, 458.

On Aug. 25, 5:30 A.M., Butler telegraphed to USG. "The enemy made an attack on my Picket line this Morning at daylight which has been kept up at intervals ever since. They have not forced it back. Prisoners captured Say Mahones Division has reinforced Picket. I suppose is relieving Picket" ALS (telegram sent), DNA, RG 107, Telegrams Collected (Unbound); telegram received, *ibid.*, RG 108, Letters Received. At 8:45 A.M., Butler telegraphed to USG. "The Signal officer at Spring Hill reports that at 8 A. M 'fourteen cars heavily loaded with troops passed the Junction towards Petersburg.' Forwarded for the information of Lt General Grant I think this is Pickets division going to take Mahones place" ALS (telegram sent), *ibid.*, RG 107, Telegrams Collected (Unbound); telegram received, *ibid.*, RG 108, Letters Received. Printed as received at 9:15 A.M. and in variant form in *O.R.*, I, xlii, part 2, 497. On the same day, Butler telegraphed to USG. "The enemy made a charge on our picket line early this morning because of the information of some deserters who went over ~~the~~ last night, saying that our troops were all moving away—Thereupon Gen Pickett is reported saying that he wanted to straighten his line near Ware Bottom Church, and made a charge for that purpose with a very strong skirmish line— For the moment our pickets were pressed back but they recovered, and charged in return and retook all our own picket line and part of theirs—The loss of the enemy is pretty large—Ours I have not yet learned, but it is trifling—We have captured fifteen prisoners—" LS (telegram sent), DNA, RG 107, Telegrams Collected (Unbound); telegram received, *ibid.*, RG 108, Letters Received. *O.R.*, I, xlii, part 2, 498. At 12:30 P.M., Butler telegraphed to USG. "Gen Birney reports that he has reestablished his picket line which was forced back by a charge from the Enemy that in a charge in return he has taken fifty prisoners two commissioned officer We have also five deserters Our loss in killed and wounded is trifling—It was a plucky little affair on the part of Gen Foster. As all seems to be going right now I will availing myself of your kind permission at two oclock start North A telegram will reach me at Willards or at 5th Avenue if you should desire to communicate with me. I have turned over the command to Gen Ord the Senior officer during my absence." ALS (telegram sent), DNA, RG 107, Telegrams Collected (Unbound); telegram received, *ibid.*, RG 108, Letters Received. *O.R.*, I, xlii, part 2, 498. At 8:06 P.M., Col. John W. Shaffer, chief of staff for Butler, telegraphed to Lt. Col. Theodore S. Bowers. "General Birneys report of ~~off~~ the attack on his line this morning Shews our loss at one killed 1~~2~~6 wounded and 14 missing—the Enemys loss ~~must of been more than o~~ in killed and wounded must of been more than double our loss as they attacked us in our rifle Pits—We Captured Sixty one (61) Prisoners" ALS (telegram sent), DNA, RG 107, Telegrams Collected (Unbound); telegram received, *ibid.*, RG 108, Letters Sent. *O.R.*, I, xlii, part 2, 498.

To Maj. Gen. George G. Meade

City Point Aug. 24th *1864.*

MAJ. GN. MEADE,

Richmond papers of yesterday shew great dispondency over the affair on the Welden road and report five Generals killed but only know positively of two of them, Saunders & Lamar, being actually dead. They seem to be unable to learn any thing official of the affair but have to depend entirely upon citizens going from Petersburg to Richmond for information. They say however we have not seen the end of that affair yet.

U. S. GRANT

Lt. Gn.

ALS (telegram sent), CSmH; telegram received (at 10:50 A.M.), DNA, RG 94, War Records Office, Army of the Potomac. *O.R.*, I, xlii, part 2, 442. Maj. Gen. George G. Meade transmitted this telegram to corps and div. commanders.

On Aug. 24, 1864, 8:15 A.M. and 10:20 A.M., Meade telegraphed to USG. "Late last night I received a despatch from Genl. Gregg reporting that he had been engaged with ~~the~~ his whole cavalry force with the enemys cavalry about 1½ miles west of Reams station on the Dinwidie C. H. road—Genl. Gregg maintained his ground the fight lasting from 4.30 P. M till 9. p. m with ~~a~~ reported casualties about 75.—Earlier in the afternoon Col. Spear comd. brigade Kautz Divn. had a sharp engagment with the enemys cavalry on the Bond road also in the vicinity of Reams station—on which occasion notwithstanding the largely superior force of the enemy col Spear held his ground, inflicting heavy loss he reporting over 180 of the enemys dead on the field.—The infantry division of the 2d. corps had reached Reams station, thoroughly destroying the Rail Road up to that point—It will be joined early this morning by the 2d. division, when Genl. Hancock will take charge of the whole comman Infantry & cavalry & push the work of destruction, as far as in his judgement it is practicable & expedient to go.—On the rest of the lines under my Charge all was quiet—Maj Genl Ord reports the desertion to the enemy of a man who was believed to have been collecting information." ALS (telegram sent), DNA, RG 94, War Records Office, Army of the Potomac; telegram received, *ibid.*, RG 108, Letters Received. *O.R.*, I, xlii, part 2, 442. "If you will be at your Hd. Qrs this morning & have no objection I propose visiting City Point." ALS (telegram sent), DNA, RG 393, Army of the Potomac, Cav. Corps, Letters Received; telegram received, *ibid.*, RG 107, Telegrams Collected (Unbound). Lt. Col. Theodore S. Bowers drafted his reply at the foot of the telegram received. "Gen Grant directs me to say that he will be at his Headquarters, and will be pleased to see you"   ADfS, *ibid.*

At 11:30 A.M., Meade telegraphed to USG. "Deserters & prisoners have reported the wounding of the following named Confederate Generals in Warrens affairs—W. H. F. Lee—Clingman, Sanders & Harris—if to these ~~are~~ is added Lamar reported dead in the Richmond papers, it would just make Five.—There is no doubt the enemy suffered severely in his attacks on the 21st. A deserter told me his brigade Kirklands had lost 300 men.—" ALS (telegram sent), *ibid.*, RG 94, War Records Office, Army of the Potomac; telegram received, *ibid.*, RG 108, Letters Received. *O.R.*, I, xlii, part 2, 442–43. At 4:30 P.M., Meade telegraphed to USG. "I forward the above   I think Gen Lee meant last saturday when he tried & could not get us away. I hope he will try again—Ord seems to think now he will not be attacked"   Telegram received, DNA, RG 108, Letters Received. *O.R.*, I, xlii, part 2, 451. The enclosure is *ibid.*

Also on Aug. 24, Meade telegraphed to USG transmitting a telegram from

Maj. Gen. Edward O. C. Ord to Meade reporting C.S.A. movements. Telegram received, DNA, RG 108, Letters Received. *O.R.*, I, xlii, part 2, 443.

To Maj. Gen. Henry W. Halleck

(Cipher) City Point Va. Aug. 25th *1864.* [*11:00* A.M.]
MAJ. GN. HALLECK, WASHINGTON,

It is understood in Richmond that Fitz Lee has been ordered back from the valley with his Cavalry Division. I have no doubt of the truth of the rumor. If the men of the 2d Division now in Washington can be remounted and returned here and horses sent to remount those here without horses we will be strong enough and can render their Cavalry almost useless.

U. S. GRANT
Lt. Gen.

ALS (telegram sent), CSmH; telegram received (at 6:00 P.M.), DNA, RG 107, Telegrams Collected (Bound). *O.R.*, I, xlii, part 2, 466.

To Maj. Gen. Henry W. Halleck

City Pt. Va.
2 30 P m aug 25. [1864]

MAJ GEN HALLECK,
CHF OF STF.

Picketts & Fields Divns are here. You can say this to Gen Sheridan, & That there is no doubt about it.

One Regt from each of the four brigades of Picketts Divn were detached a couple of weeks ago, & for some time I did not know but they might have gone to the valley. These Regts are now back.

U. S. GRANT
Lt. Genl.

Telegram received (at 6:00 P.M.), DNA, RG 107, Telegrams Collected (Bound); copies, *ibid.*, Telegrams Received in Cipher; *ibid.*, RG 108, Letters Sent; DLC-USG, V, 45, 68, 107. *O.R.*, I, xlii, part 2, 466; *ibid.*, I, xliii, part 1, 905.

To Maj. Gen. Henry W. Halleck

(Cipher)   City Point Va. Aug. 25th *1864*. [*8:00* P.M.]
MAJ. GEN. HALLECK, WASHINGTON,

I see by the Richmond ~~papers~~ Examine[r] of to-day that Gen.
Canby is about exchanging the prisoners captured at Fort Gaines.
I hope Gen. Canby will be instructed to make no more exchanges.
It is giving the enemy reinforcements at a time when they are of
immense importance to him.

U. S. GRANT
Lt. Gn.

ALS (telegram sent), CSmH; telegram received (marked as sent at 7:30 P.M.,
received Aug. 26, 1864, 7:00 A.M.), DNA, RG 107, Telegrams Collected
(Bound). *O.R.*, II, viii, 811.

To Maj. Gen. Henry W. Halleck

(Cipher)   City Point Va. Aug. 25th 9 p. m. *1864*.
MAJ. GEN. HALLECK, WASHINGTON

Up to last accounts this after noon from Gen. Hancock, who
is South of Reams Station, he had been attacked several times to-
day but had repulsed every assault. Since the last dispatch very
heavy and continuous Artillery firing has been heard in that direction continueing until dark. When I hear from there will telegraph
you again.

U. S. GRANT
Lt. Gn.

ALS (telegram sent), CSmH; telegram received (Aug. 26, 1864, 7:00 A.M.),
DNA, RG 107, Telegrams Collected (Bound). Entered in USG's letterbooks as
sent at 8:30 P.M. and so printed in *O.R.*, I, xlii, part 2, 466.

To Maj. Gen. George G. Meade

By Telegraph from City Point
Dated Aug 25 1864.

To GEN MEADE

I think it adviseable to get all our forces back on to the line we now hold & strengthen it well. When that is done we can detach fifteen or twenty thousand men & start them early in the morning so as to make a march of 20 miles & destroy the road at that distance   We may be able at the same time to send the Army Gunboats upo the Chowan with a detachments of troops to destroy the triangle between the Nottoway & Roanoke

U S GRANT
Lt Gen

Telegram received, DNA, RG 94, War Records Office, Army of the Potomac; copies, *ibid.*, RG 108, Letters Sent; DLC-USG, V, 45, 68, 107; (2) Meade Papers, PHi. *O.R.*, I, xlii, part 2, 468. On Aug. 25, 1864, 3:00 P.M., Maj. Gen. George G. Meade telegraphed to USG. "I send a despatch just received from Hancock—I have ordered Motts reserves & Wilcoxs division 9. corps down the plank road to the branching off of the Reams Sta road—to watch Hancocks rear & move up to his support if necessary—If the enemy will only attack either Hancock & Warren we are all right, but he may bother us by maneuvering & getting between the two forces." ALS (telegram sent), DNA, RG 94, War Records Office, Army of the Potomac; telegram received, *ibid.*, RG 108, Letters Received. *O.R.*, I, xlii, part 2, 468. The enclosure is *ibid.*, p. 482. On the same day, Maj. Gen. Andrew A. Humphreys telegraphed to Lt. Col. Theodore S. Bowers. "General Meade has just gone to Gen'l. Hancock's HeadQrs. The force of cavalry between the plank road and James river is still small. The cattle should not return to Coggin's point." Copies, DNA, RG 393, Army of the Potomac, Letters Sent; Meade Papers, PHi. *O.R.*, I, xlii, part 2, 467.

To Maj. Gen. George G. Meade

By Telegraph from City Pt
Dated Aug ~~20~~ 25. *1864.*

To MAJ. GEN MEADE

I desire to hold the Weldon railroad as long as possible— Redoubts should be constructed on warrens left and the line generally strength~~enene~~dened   It is not intended to keep any more troops south of the Appomattox than is necessary to hold the line

U. S. GRANT

Lt. Genl

Telegram received, DNA, RG 94, War Records Office, Army of the Potomac; copies, *ibid.*, RG 108, Letters Sent; DLC-USG, V, 45, 68, 107; (2) Meade Papers, PHi. Printed as sent at 6:00 P.M. in *O.R.*, I, xlii, part 2, 469. On Aug. 25, 1864, 7:15 P.M., Maj. Gen. George G. Meade telegraphed to USG. "Your despatch of 6. P. M just received on my return Do you mean to hold to the Welden R. Rd. or to the Jerusalem plank road, as the line we now hold—I presume as you said this morning to build the redoubts on the R. Rd. that you mean the line now held by Warren—but to prevent misunderstanding ask for explicit instructions—when I left Hancock had repulsed several attacks of the Enemy—Wilcox was moving up to his support—After leaving I heard rapid & continuous artillery firing which is now going on—No report from Hancock—He was directed to withdraw after dark as he could not work any more on the R. Rd for the presence of the Enemy" ALS (telegram sent), DNA, RG 94, War Records Office, Army of the Potomac; telegram received, *ibid.*, RG 108, Letters Received. *O.R.*, I, xlii, part 2, 469. On the same day, USG telegraphed to Meade. "I meant by my dispatch that we would hold our present line to and West of the Welden rail-road." ALS (telegram sent), Kohns Collection, NN; telegram received (at 7:35 P.M.), DNA, RG 94, War Records Office, Army of the Potomac. *O.R.*, I, xlii, part 2, 469.

Also on Aug. 25, USG telegraphed to Meade. "I think from last dispatches received from Gn. Hancock he had better be instructed to fall back at once to our main line." ALS (telegram sent), Kohns Collection, NN; copies, DLC USG, V, 45, 68, 107; DNA, RG 108, Letters Sent. *O.R.*, I, xlii, part 2, 468.

To Maj. Gen. George G. Meade

City Point Aug. 25th *1864.*

MAJ. GEN. MEADE,

Please inform Gen. Hancock that I have detailed Private John H. McGuire of the 116th Pa. Vols. 2d Corps Forage Master ~~temporarily~~ for ~~detach~~ special service. He is from Upperville Va. and well acquainted with the ground over which Mosby roams and knew many of his men before the War. Many of them were boys partly educated at the school of which he was principal. I have ordered him to report to Gen. Sheridan.

U. S. GRANT

Lt. Gn.

ALS (telegram sent), CSmH; telegram received, DNA, RG 94, War Records Office, Army of the Potomac.

To Maj. Gen. George G. Meade

By Telegraph from City Point
Dated Aug 25 1864.

To MAJ. GEN MEADE

I feel too unwell today to go to the front. Think I will take a boat this evening and go to Fortress Monroe & return tomorrow night.[1] Would it not be safe for Hancock to pick up all the force he has on the Railroad & make one days march towards Weldon and destroy there a few miles of road & return by a road further East than the one he goes on.

U. S. GRANT
Lt. Gen.

Telegram received, DNA, RG 94, War Records Office, Army of the Potomac; copies, *ibid.*, RG 108, Letters Sent; DLC-USG, V, 45, 68, 107; (2) Meade Papers, PHi. *O.R.*, I, xlii, part 2, 467. On Aug. 25, 1864, 10:00 A.M. and 2:00 P.M., Maj. Gen. George G. Meade telegraphed to USG, the second time from hd. qrs., 5th Army Corps. "Every thing is ~~comparitively~~ apparently quiet this morning—Last evening the signal officers reported large bodies of the Enemy moving along the Welden R. Rd. near the Lead works going southwardly & this morning they report the disappearance during the night of camps from our front—This intelligence has been communicated to Genl. Warren & Hancock & the latter instructed to move with caution & be on the alert, and in case he finds the Enemy interposing between himself & Warren to return & rejoin the army   The last despatch from Hancock is 6. A M in which he reports that in consequence of the above intelligence he has this morning ceased work on the R. Rd. till he can satisfy himself the road is clear of the enemy & his rear unthreatened. The road has been thoroughly destroyed some 3 miles beyond Reams station & within two miles of Rowanty creek—If it is determined to maintain a permanent lodgement on the Welden Road, it will be necessary to erect some redoubts & in other ways strengthen the position & our lines—If the lines from the plank road to the Appomatox can be made secure—I see no difficulty in holding the Welden Road with the 5th. 9th & part of the 2d. corps,—and perhaps extending beyond to the Lynchburgh road.—I do not deem it advisable however to commence the proposed works involving considerable labor, unless it is settled the position is to be maintained.—. . . Is it intended the 18. corps on being relieved are to return to Bermuda Hundred or will any portion be left as a reserve to the 10th corps—" "Hancock reports the enemy passing his left & threatening the plank road in his rear—I dont think he can destroy much more of the R. Rd. than he has, if the enemy interrupt him, because his force is so small that he must keep it in hand to meet attacks & have but small working parties—Movements reported by signal officers in connection with statements of deserters in this morning lead to the conclusion that Lee is about making an effort to get us away from the R. Rd. This will take I think the form of passing our left & threatening our rear on the plank road—I am making preparations to meet this contingency—Should Hancock be pressed or the Enemy interposed between him & Warren, I shall withdraw him to the Plank road—" ALS (telegrams sent), DNA, RG 94, War Records Office, Army of the Potomac; telegrams received, *ibid.*, RG 108, Letters Received. *O.R.*, I, xlii, part 2, 466–67.

1. On Aug. 25, USG telegraphed to Meade and Maj. Gen. Edward O. C. Ord. "I leave here at four P M for Fortress Monroe   Will start back tomorrow evening"   Telegram received, DNA, RG 94, War Records Office, Army of the Potomac; Ord Papers, CU-B. On the same day, USG telegraphed to Meade and Ord. "I shall not go to Fort Monroe as I had thought of doing"   Telegram received (at 5:55 P.M.), DNA, RG 393, Army of the Potomac, Cav. Corps, Letters Received; copies, *ibid.*, RG 108, Letters Sent; DLC-USG, V, 45, 68, 107. At 3:00 P.M. and 5:00 P.M., USG had telegraphed to Secretary of War Edwin M. Stanton. "I start at 4 p. m. for Fortress Monroe. Will start from there to return to-morrow night." "There are indications of the enemy attacking us this evening or in the morning. I shall not therefore go to Fortress Monroe as I telegraphed you this morning." ALS (telegrams sent), CSmH; telegrams received (at 9:00 P.M. and Aug. 26, 7:00 A.M.), DNA, RG 107, Telegrams Collected (Bound). *O.R.*, I, xlii, part 2, 465. The second is printed as received at 7:15 A.M.

To Maj. Gen. George G. Meade

By Telegraph from City Point 11.20 P. M
Dated Aug 25 *1864.*

To MAJ GEN MEADE

The enemy having carried Hancocks rifle pits have probably captured a good many prisoners   in that case & finding too that Hancock is being reenforced they will be likely to return tonight with their prisoners, & attack Warren in the morning. Warren ought to be well on his guard.

U. S GRANT
Lt. Gen

Telegram received, DNA, RG 94, War Records Office, Army of the Potomac; copies, *ibid.*, RG 108, Letters Sent; DLC-USG, V, 45, 68, 107; (2) Meade Papers, PHi. *O.R.*, I, xlii, part 2, 470. On Aug. 25, 1864, 10:00 P.M., Lt. Col. Cyrus B. Comstock telegraphed to Maj. Gen. George G. Meade. "Lt Gen Grant requests me to ask if anything has been heard from Hancock since your despatch of 6 P. M." ALS (telegram sent), DNA, RG 108, Telegrams Sent by Comstock; telegram received, DNA, RG 94, War Records Office, Army of the Potomac. *O.R.*, I, xlii, part 2, 469. At 10:30 P.M., 11:20 P.M., and 11:50 P.M., Meade telegraphed to USG. "A staff officer has just arrived from Hancock leaving him at 7. P. M   At that time the enemy having massed assaulted Hancock with great vehemence in front & on both flanks—carrying I regret to say his entrenched line on his right flank—At the time the staff officer left Hancock had rallied his men, reformed them & was preparing to retake his line which he hoped to do—The road in his rear leading to the plank road was yet open & the staff officer met Wilcoxs column about 2 miles from the scene of action & hurried them up—I have sent orders to Warren & Parke to immediately send Crawford's & Whites Divisions to Hancocks support & to assist him in withdrawing—Hancock was authorised several times during the day to withdraw, if the security of his command required it, or if the enemy interposed between him & Warren—On my return here at 7.30 finding a despatch from him intimating he desired orders to withdraw specific orders were sent, but altho' the operator acknowledged the receipt & said they were delivered, I fear the enemy at that time had possession of the road between the operator & Hancock.—I am in hopes the arrival of Wilcox has enabled Hancock to recover his entrenchments and that he will withdraw, as soon as it is dark—Should the enemy follow tomorrow the reinforcements carried by Crawford may enable Hancock to punish him.—" "Another staff officer has arrived from Genl. Hancock, who left him at 8. P. M   At that time all was quiet—Hancock had been unable to recover that portion of his line which the enemy got possession of—The staff officer reports the fighting very severe & desperate—He can form no idea of our losses tho thinks they must be considerable—I regret to state he reports the loss of 8 pieces of artillery   It appears the enemy got possession of a salient in the line where two batteries were parked—The staff officer says from the number of attacks repulsed the enemys losses must be far greater than ours—Genl. Hancock was making his preparations to with draw when this officer left, and as his rear was all open no difficulty in this operation is anticipated—The wounded will all be brought off but the dead can not be buried.—I have directed the reinforcements ordered to be halted and held in readiness for movement tomorrow in case Hancock is followed or attacked.—" "On learning that Hancock was withdrawing I ordered Parke & Warren to halt the reinforcements on the way to him & communicate with him, as to the necessity of their advancing farther & in case he did not require them, to recall them.—Warren felt perfectly secure, without these reserves   with them he will be prepared for any attack—I think it probable the enemy may follow up Hancock on the plank road, tho if he has been as severely punished as the accounts from Hancock would indicate he will most probably be satisfied with Hancocks withdrawal & the capture of the guns—I have already reported that it was the opinion of the staff officers that the loss in prisoners was small.—" ALS (telegrams sent), DNA, RG 94, War Records Office, Army of the Potomac; telegrams received, *ibid.*, RG 108, Letters Received. *O.R.*, I, xlii, part 2, 469–70, 471.

To Maj. Gen. Edward O. C. Ord

City Point Va. Aug. 25th *1864.*

MAJ. GEN. ORD, 18TH CORPS,

I have just received the dispatch to Gen. Pickett which was intercepted by our Signal Officers.[1] If there is to be any blowing up it will probably be in front of the 18th Corps. The men who are likely to be exposed however ought to be notified so they will not be stampeded. If we can be on ~~the~~ our guard when a mine is sprung the enemy ought to be repulsed with great slaughter. Where do you understand from the dispatch the explosion was to take place?

U. S. Grant
Lt. Gn.

ALS (telegram sent), Ritzman Collection, Aurora College, Aurora, Ill.; telegram received, Ord Papers, CU-B. *O.R.*, I, xlii, part 2, 511.

On Aug. 25, 1864, Maj. Gen. Edward O. C. Ord telegraphed to USG. "I think Maj Gen. Birney & 10th Corps on this side (south) of Appomattox should act in concert with Gen. Meade and therefore in that matter should be under his orders—I endeavored so to act and offered Gen. Meade all my reserves (3000) last evening if needed." ALS (telegram sent), DNA, RG 107, Telegrams Collected (Unbound). Dated Aug. 26 in *O.R.*, I, xlii, part 2, 534. On Aug. 26, USG telegraphed to Maj. Gen. George G. Meade. "You are authorized at all times until further orders to assume command and direct the movement of all troops operating against Petersburg South of the Appomattox." ALS (telegram sent), PPRF; telegram received, DNA, RG 94, War Records Office, Army of the Potomac; (dated Aug. 25 and sent to Ord) Ord Papers, CU-B. *O.R.*, I, xlii, part 2, 520.

1. On Aug. 25, Col. John W. Shaffer telegraphed to USG transmitting an intercepted message of 2:00 P.M. from C.S.A. Maj. Gen. George E. Pickett to Gen. Pierre G. T. Beauregard. "I have felt the enemy's line in my front and discover them in force along my line." Telegram received (at 4:10 P.M.), DNA, RG 108, Letters Received; copy, *ibid.*, RG 107, Telegrams Collected (Unbound). *O.R.*, I, xlii, part 2, 500. On the same day, Shaffer telegraphed to USG transmitting an intercepted message of 2:30 P.M. from Beauregard to Pickett. "Your despatch of date 2 P. m. recd. Be prepared to blow up your mine at any time— A. S. Hokes two divisions are ordered to you—Pontoon bridge across appomattox must be captured as soon as practicable" ALS (telegram sent), DNA, RG 107, Telegrams Collected (Unbound); telegram received (at 4:05 P.M.), *ibid.*, RG 108, Letters Received. Shaffer sent copies of both intercepted messages to Ord; USG telegraphed to Meade transmitting the second. Telegram received, *ibid.*, RG 94, War Records Office, Army of the Potomac; copies (2), Meade Papers, PHi. *O.R.*, I, xlii, part 2, 468.

To Maj. Gen. Philip H. Sheridan

(Cipher)   City Point Aug. 25th/64 11 a m.
Maj. Gn. Sheridan, Harper's Ferry Va.

I have good authority for believing that orders have gone to the valley for the return of Fitz Lee's Cavalry. This is the general

talk among the southern soldiers and a man sent to Richmond by
the Provost Marshal learns the same fact. It is also natural that
this should be so after the reverse the enemy's Cavalry met with
the evening of the 23d. Since that our troops have quietly destroyed
the Welden road working South, the enemy's Cavalry falling back
before ours without offering resistence. If this should be so it will
give you a great advantage in harrassing the enemy and possibly
you might send entirely around to his rear and destroy his trains
supplies &c.

U. S. GRANT

Lt. Gn.

ALS (telegram sent), CSmH; copies, DLC-USG, V, 45, 68, 107; DNA, RG 108,
Letters Sent. *O.R.*, I, xliii, part 1, 905. On Aug. 25, 1864, 11:00 P.M., Maj.
Gen. Philip H. Sheridan, Halltown, telegraphed to USG. "There is not much
doubt of the presence here of two divisions of Longstreets corps—Gen Anderson
commanding—The enemy succeeded this evening in getting Shepardstown   I
do not know whether they will attempt to cross or not. I ordered two divisions of
cavalry to make a reconnoissance this morning on the enemys flank—They met
Breckenridges corps at Blue Spring or Leetown marching towards Shepardstown
Our cavalry skirmished with this corps sharply during the afternoon with but
little loss. The cavalry ~~of~~ were forced to give up Shepardstown, all but one
brigade coming back to Halltown,   This brigade, it is supposed, crossed at the
Shepardstown Ford   I cannot say whether or not the enemy will attempt to cross
in the morning,   They must be very strong to do so; my information is that
Early marched with that intention, but reports are very unreliable—The enemy
are in very strong force   I will not give up this place and hope to be able to
strike the enemy divided   I hardly think that they will attempt to go to Washington"   Telegram received (on Aug. 26), DNA, RG 108, Letters Received;
copies, *ibid.*, RG 107, Telegrams Received in Cipher; DLC-Philip H. Sheridan.
O.R., I, xliii, part 1, 905–6.

To Julia Dent Grant

———

City Point Va. Aug. 25th *1864.*

DEAR JULIA,

If you can locate yourself comfortably and get the children in
good schools Philadelphia will be as good a place as any for our
permanent home. I have a horror of living in Washington and
never intend to do it. Philadelphia is within five and a half hours
of Washington and in time of peace it would not be necessary for

me to be there more than one each week and not always that. If you can rent a comfortable place for the present after a while we may be able to buy one of our own.

I hope you will leave word what you want and come on to Ft. Monroe for a few days. I sent a letter this morning directed to Fred in relation to a house in Philadelphia which can be got. I regret that I can not be at home to arrange your commencement for you. But my position is one that must be filled by myself whilst the War lasts. I think then I will be entitled to a good long rest.

Kisses for your self and the children.

ULYS.

ALS, DLC-USG.

To Edwin M. Stanton

City Point Va. Aug. 26th *1864*.
HON. E. M. STANTON SEC. OF WAR, WASHINGTON,

There are some 700 men in the 1st N. Y. Mounted Rifle Regt. who are willing to reenlist for three years. All but some forty or fifty of them come within the limit and can be reenlisted without further authority. This number however will not be within the limit, the last of them, until about the 15th of Sept. Can I have the authority to reenlist them also for three years and the number of days they have yet to serve to bring them within the limit. Please answer as soon as you can.

U. S. GRANT
Lt. Gn.

ALS (telegram sent), CSmH; telegram received (at 5:30 P.M.), DNA, RG 107, Telegrams Collected (Bound). On Aug. 27, 1864, Secretary of War Edwin M. Stanton telegraphed to USG. "You are fully authorised to exercise your own discretion as to the enlistment of the 1st New York Mounted Rifles, and any other troops under your command. Please report your action to the Department so as to keep up the record." ALS (telegram sent), *ibid.*; telegram received, *ibid.*, Telegrams Collected (Unbound); *ibid.*, RG 108, Letters Received.

On Aug. 26, USG twice telegraphed to Maj. Gen. Edward O. C. Ord. "Reinlist and furlough all of the first N. Y. Mounted Rifle Regt who have less then one (1) year to serve. let them go home at once. There are some forty (40) or fifty (50) men in the regiment who have a few days over one year to serve who express a willingness to reinlist if they can be allowed the bounty & furlough. I will telegraph at once for the authority to let them go also" Telegram received, *ibid.*, RG 393, Dept. of Va. and N. C., Telegrams Received; DLC-Benjamin F. Butler; copies, DLC-USG, V, 45, 68, 107; DNA, RG 108, Letters Sent. "In furloughing the first N. Y. Mtd Rifles make their furloughs commence from the 7th of Sept. Send them armed with orders to report to Gen Dix for duty until their furloughs commence. One half of the officers can go with the portion of the regt furloughed, & the balance will have an equal leave when those going now returns." Telegram received (at 3:00 P.M.), *ibid.*, RG 393, Dept. of Va. and N. C., Telegrams Received; copies, *ibid.*, RG 108, Letters Sent; DLC-USG, V, 45, 68, 107. On Aug. 27, USG telegraphed to Ord. "You may re-inlist all of the 1st N. Y. Mnt'd Rifles reg't who have less than one year to serve from the twenteenh (20) of Sept. for three (3) years from the date when they came within the limit & furlough them with the balance of the veterans of their reg't." Telegram received, Ord Papers, CU-B; copies, DLC-USG, V, 45, 68, 107; DNA, RG 108, Letters Sent.

To Maj. Gen. Henry W. Halleck

(Cipher)   City Point, Va. Aug. 26th 10 a. m. *1864.*
Maj. Gen. Halleck, Washington,

I have no report of casualties yet from operations of yesterday near Reams Station. Orders were given during the day for Gn. Hancock to return. But being pressed by the enemy he could not do so until night. Frequent assaults were repulsed but just before night the enemy carried one point of the line and captured eight pieces of Artillery. The Staff officer who gives the only report I have yet thinks the enemy were very severely punished and that our loss in prisoners will be small. During the night Gen. Hancock returned to his place in line without opposition Yesterday morning the enemy drove in Gen. Butlers Pickett line. ~~They~~ The Picket guard soon rallied however, ~~and~~ drove the enemy back and re-established their line. The result was One killed, sixteen wounded & fourteen missing on our side. Two commissioned Officers & fifty-nine enlisted men were captured from the enemy. What their casualties were in killed and wounded we do not know.

U. S. Grant
Lt. Gn.

ALS (telegram sent), CSmH; telegram received (at 6:30 P.M.), DNA, RG 107, Telegrams Collected (Bound). *O.R.*, I, xlii, part 1, 20; *ibid.*, I, xlii, part 2, 517.

To Maj. Gen. George G. Meade

———

By Telegraph from City Point
Dated Aug 26 *1864.*

To MAJ. GEN MEADE

I think the chances are that Warren will be attacked in rear this afternoon by the same force that attacked Hancock yesterday. There will probably be a demonstration on his front by all the force occupying the lines in his front   if Warren can prepare for both a front & rear attack The enemy will be most severly handled   The cavalry out to watch the enemy well & give full notice of the direction from which he comes & when they are forced back into our lincs thcy should fight on foot with our infantry   If Warrcn can be further reenforced by putting Hancocks men on the line & relieving some now there it ought to be done.

U S GRANT
Lt Gen

P. S. I give this as my view from the intercepted despatch of Beauregard[1]

U S GRANT

Telegrams received (2—at 12:30 P.M.), DNA, RG 94, War Records Office, Army of the Potomac; copies, *ibid.*, RG 108, Letters Sent; DLC-USG, V, 45, 68, 107; (2) Meade Papers, PHi. *O.R.*, I, xlii, part 2, 518–19. On Aug. 26, 1864, 2:00 P.M., Maj. Gen. George G. Meade telegraphed to USG. "I have just recd your despatch in reference to an attack upon Warren   all you suggest has been done   Warren is prepared and Greggs cavalry is well out watching all approaches   I have sent you the information by the safe guard showing how terribly the enemy was punished yesterday & that they retired last night to Petersburg leaving their dead & wounded on the field—This may be owing to their intention to attack at some other point but I dont think it will be on Warren— Previous to your dispatch I had directed Hancock to relieve Ferrero's Div of Colored troops not to increase warren's defensive force but to use these troops in the construction of Warrens redoubts as they work so much better than the white troops & save the latter for fighting"   Telegram received, DNA, RG 108, Letters Received; copies, *ibid.*, RG 94, War Records Office, Army of the Potomac; *ibid.*, RG 393, Army of the Potomac, Letters Sent; (2) Meade Papers, PHi. *O.R.*, I, xlii, part 2, 519.

Also on Aug. 26, USG telegraphed to Meade. "Is anything heard from Gn Hancock this morning?" ALS (telegram sent), Kohns Collection, NN; copies, DLC-USG, V, 45, 68, 107; DNA, RG 108, Letters Sent. At 10:00 A.M., Meade telegraphed to USG. "Hancocks troops were withdrawn without molestation or being followed—He is now near the Williams House—He reports his command at present unserviceable.—A report from Genl. Gregg Comd. Cavalry on Warrens left & Hancocks rear reports the enemy pressing his pickets a little this morning with a view he thinks of picking up stragglers—Warren's & Parke's troops have returned to their former position & every preparation has been made to meet any further offensive movements of the enemy.—All else quiet.—" ALS (telegram sent), *ibid.*, RG 94, War Records Office, Army of the Potomac; telegram received, *ibid.*, RG 108, Letters Received. *O.R.*, I, xlii, part 2, 517. At 10:15 A.M., Meade telegraphed to USG. "I forward a despatch just received from Maj. Genl. Hancock.—" ALS (telegram sent), DNA, RG 393, Army of the Potomac, Cav. Corps, Letters Received; telegram received, *ibid.*, RG 108, Letters Received. The enclosure is in *O.R.*, I, xlii, part 2, 525–26. At noon, USG telegraphed to Maj. Gen. Henry W. Halleck transmitting a copy of this enclosure. Telegrams received (2), DNA, RG 107, Telegrams Collected (Bound); copy, *ibid.*, Telegrams Received in Cipher.

At 12:30 P.M. and 1:00 P.M., Meade telegraphed to USG. "A safe guard that was left on the battle field remained there till after day light this a. m. At that time the enemy had all disappeared leaving their dead on the field unburied—This shows how severely they were punished, and doubtless hearing of the arrival of reinforcements they feared the results today if they remained" "Since sending my last dispatch I have conversed with the safe guard referred to—He did not leave the field till after sun rise—At that time nearly all the enemy had left moving towards Petersburg—He says they abandoned not only their dead but their wounded also—He conversed with an officer who said their losses were greater than ever before during the war The safe guard says he was over a part of the field & it was covered with the enemys dead & wounded—He has seen a great many battle fields but never saw such a sight. very few of our dead nearly all of the enemy All our wounded are brought off but our dead unburied—I have instructed Gregg to make an effert to send a party to the field & bury our dead I should judge from all accounts the enemy will most likely be quiet for some time" Telegrams received, *ibid.*, RG 108, Letters Received; copies, *ibid.*, RG 94, War Records Office, Army of the Potomac; *ibid.*, RG 393, Army of the Potomac, Letters Sent; (2) Meade Papers, PHi. *O.R.*, I, xlii, part 2, 517–18. At 1:00 P.M., USG telegraphed to Halleck transmitting copies of both telegrams. Telegrams received (2), DNA, RG 107, Telegrams Collected (Bound); copies (entered as sent separately at 1:00 P.M. and 2:00 P.M.), *ibid.*, Telegrams Received in Cipher.

At 9:15 P.M., Meade telegraphed to USG. "The usual quiet has prevailed along the lines today—This p. m Signal officers reported the movement of considerable bodies of the enemy artillery & infantry passing the Lead Works into Petersburgh, some turning apparently to the left or the enemys right—This was undoubtedly the force that attacked Hancock yesterday returning to their entrenchments. The following disposition of troops will be made tomorrow—The 2d. Corps one division in the trenches from the left of the 10th Corps to the Strong house—with one division in reserve on the Jerusalem plank road & one division in reserve in rear of of the point of junction of the 2d. & 10th corps.—Three divisions of the 9th corps on the line between the Strong house & the right of 5th corps The 4th Division colored in reserve at the Gurley House to be employed in constructing the field works to be built to strengthen the line.—Three divisions of the 5th corps on the line covering the Weldon R Rd & extending down that road to the Perkins house—A fourth division in reserve.—By this arrangement each corps has a reserve which can in case of emergency be concentrated at any point threatened. Maj. Genl. Birney comdg. 10th corps has reported part of this corps being in the trenches occupied by the 18th altho' the balance yet to relieve part of the 18." ALS (telegram sent), *ibid.*, RG 94, War Records Office, Army of the Potomac; telegram received, *ibid.*, RG 108, Letters Received. *O.R.*, I, xlii, part 2, 519.

1. On Aug. 26, Col. John W. Shaffer, chief of staff for Maj. Gen. Benjamin F. Butler, telegraphed to Lt. Col. Theodore S. Bowers. "The following Rebel signal message was intercepted by our signal officer at Miles house lookout at 11 a. m. Aug. 26th 'To Gen Pickett—Hokes mine failed to explode from some namless cause in the Gallery—It will be tried again soon—Have your reinforcements arrived (signed) G. T. Beauregard'" Telegram received, DNA, RG 107, Telegrams Collected (Unbound); *ibid.*, RG 108, Letters Received. *O.R.*, I, xlii, part 2, 518. On the same day, Shaffer telegraphed to Bowers transmitting an intercepted message from Maj. Gen. George E. Pickett to Gen. Pierre G. T. Beauregard. "So much the better. only one (1) division has arrived yet from richmond" Telegram received, DNA, RG 108, Letters Received. On the same day, USG telegraphed to Meade and to Ord enclosing the first intercepted message. "The signal dispatch intercepted is evidently a hoax as was the one intercepted yesterday to blind us from some really intended attack Today I suspect it will be against Warren" Telegrams received (2—one at 1:50 p.m.), *ibid.*, RG 94, War Records Office, Army of the Potomac; Ord Papers, CU-B; copies, DLC-USG, V, 45, 68, 107; DNA, RG 108, Letters Sent; (2) Meade Papers, PHi. *O.R.*, I, xlii, part 2, 518.

To Maj. Gen. Edward O. C. Ord

City Point Aug. 26th/64

Maj. Gn. Ord,

The term of service of two regiments of one hundred days men now serving at Wilsens Wharf has expired and they must be discharged. I think one good Colored regiment will be sufficient to take their place. Please have them relieved and and sent off as soon as possible.

U. S. Grant
Lt. Gn

ALS (telegram sent), OClWHi; telegram received, Ord Papers, CU-B. On Aug. 26, 1864, USG telegraphed to Maj. Gen. George G. Meade. "The term of service of the 148th regiment Ohio hundred day men on duty at this post expired yesterday and they must be discharged If the 36th Colored Volunteers can be spared from the ninth (9) Corps please send them here If this regiment is on any duty from which it Cannot be taken then send any other colored regiment" Telegram received, DNA, RG 94, War Records Office, Army of the Potomac; copies (2), Meade Papers, PHi. At 9:30 p.m., Meade telegraphed to USG. "The

36th regiment of Colored Troops is in the 18th. Army Corps. Under these circumstances shall I send one of the colored regiments of the 9th Corps to City-Point" Copy (telegram sent), DNA, RG 94, War Records Office, Army of the Potomac; copies, *ibid.*, RG 393, Army of the Potomac, Letters Sent; Meade Papers, PHi. On the same day, USG telegraphed to Meade. "I will direct Gen Ord to releive the regiment on duty here." ALS (telegram sent), Kohns Collection, NN; telegram received (at 10:30 P.M.), DNA, RG 94, War Records Office, Army of the Potomac. Also on Aug. 26, USG telegraphed to Maj. Gen. Edward O. C. Ord. "In addition to the Colored reg't ordered to relieve the troops at Wilsons Wharf send the 36th Colored to relieve the reg't now on duty at this place" Telegram received, Ord Papers, CU-B; copies, DLC-USG, V, 45, 68, 107; DNA, RG 108, Letters Sent. On the same day, Ord telegraphed to USG. "telegrams relating to relieving 100 day troops ~~and at~~ at Wilsons—and a Regiment at city point are recieved—will be obeyed—some delay will ensue as the 36th Colored has gone to deep bottom—and will from the limited command there have to be relieved by another Regiment . . . Carrs division has not yet relieved Fosters it will do so in part to morrow" ALS (telegram sent), *ibid.*, RG 107, Telegrams Collected (Unbound); telegram received, *ibid.* On Aug. 27, Ord telegraphed to Lt. Col. Theodore S. Bowers. "The only colored regiments I brought away with me went to Deep Bottom—The 36th is one of them and has only three of its officers for duty with companies The 10th & 37th I had to leave near Petersburg. Shall I order them to Wilson's & City Point respectively? They can get there sooner than any other colored regiments." ALS (telegram sent), *ibid.*; telegram received, *ibid.* On the same day, Bowers telegraphed to Ord. "You can send the 10th & 37th as you propose—they will answer as well as any" Telegram received, CU-B.

On Aug. 26, Ord had telegraphed to USG. "Genl. Birney is bringing ~~over~~ to this side over 12000 Infantry to relieve 7.600 of my corps—of these 7600—1600—will go to deep bottom—and 2800 to spring hill south of appomattox—leaving me with 3200—to relieve over 10000—after relieving my front with Similar numbers to what I have in the trenches—Genl Birney will have a reserve of ~~over~~ about five thousand—Can he not station those at or near his rear and let me take Carrs division ~~now~~ 2800 to relieve Turners 4500—as it is I have no force to relieve Turners Division—There will be but little rest for Amc's Div. if it has to do all the duty in the Peninsula—" ALS (telegram sent), DNA, RG 107, Telegrams Collected (Unbound); telegram received, *ibid.*, RG 108, Letters Received. *O.R.*, I, xlii, part 2, 534–35. On the same day, USG telegraphed to Ord. "You can take any or all of the 18th corps to relieve the 10th if that may be necessary." ALS (telegram sent), Kohns Collection, NN; telegram received, Ord Papers, CU-B. *O.R.*, I, xlii, part 2, 535.

To Maj. Gen. Philip H. Sheridan

(Cipher)   City Point Va. Aug. 26th *1864*. [*2:30* P.M.]
MAJ. GEN. SHERIDAN, HALLTOWN VA.

I telegraphed you that I had good reason for believing that Fitz Lee had been ordered back here? I now think it likely that all

troops will be ordered back from the Valley except what they beleive to be the minimum number to detain you. My ~~R~~reason for
supposing this is based upon the fact that yealding up the Welden
road seems to be a blow to the enemy he can not stand. I think I
do not overstate the loss of the enemy in the last two weeks at
10,000 killed & wounded. We have lost heavily but ours has been
mostly in captures when the enemy gained temporay advantages.

Watch closely and if you find this theory correct push will all
vigor   Give the enemy no rest and if it is possible to follow to the
Va Central road follow that far. Do all the damage to rail-roads &
crops you can. Carry off stock of all discretions and negroes so as
to prevent further planting. If the War is to last another year we
want the Shenandoah valley to remain a barren waste.

U. S. Grant
Lt. Gn.

ALS (telegram sent), CSmH; telegram received (marked as sent at 3:00 P.M.,
received Aug. 27, 1864), DNA, RG 107, Telegrams Collected (Bound). Printed
as received at 12:10 A.M., Aug. 27, in O.R., I, xliii, part 1, 916–17; (incomplete)
ibid., I, xliii, part 2, 202. On Aug. 27, 2:30 P.M., Maj. Gen. Philip H. Sheridan,
Halltown, telegraphed to USG. "The enemy fell back from my front last night
taking position at Smithfield and Leetown. Their demonstrations to cross the
river up towards Williamsport so far are feints   It is more than probable that
your theory about drawing them back will prove itself correct   I will watch
closely. I captured 101 prisoners yesterday   Since Kershaw came into the valley
I have captured nearly five hundred (500) of his men." Telegram received (on
Aug. 28), DNA, RG 108, Letters Received; copies, ibid., RG 107, Telegrams
Received in Cipher; DLC-Philip H. Sheridan. O.R., I, xliii, part 1, 932. On Aug.
28, 2:00 P.M., USG telegraphed to Sheridan. "If you are so situated as to feel
the enemy strongly without compromising the safety of your position I think it
advisable to do so. I do not know positively that any troops have returned yet
from the valley but think you will find the enemy in your immediate front weaker
than your are. We are quiet here the enemy apparently having abandoned the
idea of driving us from the Welden road, at least with his present force." ALS
(telegram sent), CSmH; telegram received, DNA, RG 107, Telegrams Collected
(Bound). O.R., I, xliii, part 1, 939.

To Maj. Gen. George G. Meade and
Maj. Gen. Edward O. C. Ord

By Telegraph from City Point
Dated Aug 27 *1864.*

To Gen Meade

Telegraph me at Ft. Monroe all occurrences whilst I am down
there[1]   especially telegraph any news you may get from Atlanta
through Richmond papers[2]

U S Grant
Lt Gen

Telegram received, DNA, RG 393, Army of the Potomac, Cav. Corps, Letters
Received; Ord Papers, CU-B; copies, DLC-USG, V, 45, 68, 107; DNA, RG 108,
Letters Sent; (2) Meade Papers, PHi. On Aug. 27, 1864, USG telegraphed to
Maj. Gen. George G. Meade. "I leave here in a few minutes for your Hd Qrs &
Gen Warrens" Telegram received (at 9:20 A.M.), DNA, RG 94, War Records
Office, Army of the Potomac; copies (2), Meade Papers, PHi. *O.R.*, I, xlii, part
2, 542.

On Aug. 28, 11:00 A.M., Meade telegraphed to USG. "I have nothing particular to report this morning—There was a little more brisk firing than usual
about 3. a m apparently on the lines of Mott & Birney—as no report has been
received of it—it is presumed to have been without consequence—A flag of
truce sent in to Ream's station yesterday by Genl. Gregg proposing to send a
working party to bury our dead, was declined by Genl. Wade Hampton on the
ground that his people were then engaged in burying our dead estimated at Two
hundred in number & that our wounded had all been removed—A congratulatory
order of Genl. Lee in yesterdays Petersburgh paper claims nine guns seven colors
& Two thousand prisoners as the result of the battle at Reams." ALS (telegram
sent), DNA, RG 94, War Records Office, Army of the Potomac; telegram received, *ibid.*, RG 107, Telegrams Collected (Unbound). *O.R.*, I, xlii, part 2, 556.
On the same day, USG telegraphed to Meade. "It is reported that Gen Ord has
withdrawn the guard detail for the Commissary Depot at Cedar Level station
Will you please send a guard detail to report to Capt Smith C. S." Telegram received, DNA, RG 393, Army of the Potomac, Cav. Corps, Telegrams Received;
copies (2), Meade Papers, PHi.

1. On Aug. 27, USG telegraphed to Meade and to Maj. Gen. Edward O. C.
Ord. "I leave this evening for Fortress Monroe. Will be back to-morrow night."
ALS (telegram sent), Kohns Collection, NN; telegram received, DNA, RG 94,
War Records Office, Army of the Potomac. Printed as sent at 5:50 P.M. in *O.R.*,
I, xlii, part 2, 542.

2. Also on Aug. 27, USG telegraphed to Ord. "Please telegraph me any news
the Richmond paper you have has from Atlanta." ALS (telegram sent), Kohns
Collection, NN; telegram received (at 5:55 P.M.), DNA, RG 94, War Records

Office, Miscellaneous War Records. On the same day, Col. John W. Shaffer, chief of staff for Maj. Gen. Benjamin F. Butler, telegraphed to USG. "The following is from the Richmond Examiner of the 27th. . . . Atlanta Aug 25th   For some cause the yankee's batteries are silent this morning. Last night a shell struck the presbyterian Church on marietta st, and exploded in the basement where a number of citizens had sought shelter. a fragment of shell cut off the arm of a Citizen lying in bed in the basement. no other casualties reported. The Enemy has again destroyed the Georgia R R below Decatur. Lt Colonel G R. Henry Jr has been temporarily appointed Provost Marshal Genl of the army   Col G W Gordon of Eleventh Tennessee Regt has been appointed Brigadeir Genl & assigned to the Command of Vaughans brigade' "   Telegram received, *ibid.*, RG 108, Letters Received. On the same day, Shaffer telegraphed to Ord. "I have just recd a signal dispatch that Eighteen Cars heavily loaded with troops have just passed the Junction Enroute to Richmond and send a copy to Gen Grant"   Telegram received (at 4:50 P.M.), *ibid.*, RG 107, Telegrams Collected (Unbound).

To Abraham Lincoln

(Cipher)   City Point Va. Aug. 29th *1864.* [*10:30* A.M.]
A. Lincoln, President, Washington

It was the Richmond papers of the 26th which contained the news of Fort Morgan being in our possession. Seeing a dispatch which said the news could not be found in the papers of the 27th, as had been reported to me, I asked ~~g~~Gen. Ord who reported to me ~~having~~ ᵣ the information which I telegraphed to Washington if he had read the Article alluded to. He replied that he read the Article himself but it was in the paper of the 26th instead of 27th as I reported. There is no question ~~of the~~ about the fall of Fort Morgan being reported in the Richmond papers nor do I suppose there to be any doubt of the facts reported.

U. S. Grant
Lt. Gn.

ALS (telegram sent), Lamon Papers, CSmH; telegram received (11:50 A.M.), DNA, RG 107, Telegrams Collected (Bound). On Aug. 27, 1864, USG had telegraphed to Maj. Gen. Henry W. Halleck. "Richmond Papers of this morning state that Fort Morgan is in our possession. It is not stated whether the Fort was surrendered or whether it was blown up." Telegram received, *ibid.*, RG 94, War Records Office, Miscellaneous War Records; (on Aug. 26, 7:00 A.M.) *ibid.*, RG 107, Telegrams Collected (Bound); (2) *ibid.*, Telegrams Collected (Unbound). On Aug. 27, Maj. Gen. Edward O. C. Ord had telegraphed to USG.

"Richmond examiner of today Says 'Ft Morgan is in possession of the Enemy whether blown up or Surrendered is not known" ALS (telegram sent), *ibid.*; telegram received, *ibid.* On Aug. 28, President Abraham Lincoln telegraphed to USG. "There appears to be doubt whether the report of Fort Morgan being in our possession is in the Richmond papers. Did you see the Richmond paper containing the statement?" LS (telegram sent, drafted by Secretary of War Edwin M. Stanton), *ibid.*, Telegrams Collected (Bound); telegram received (at 9:15 A.M.), *ibid.*, Telegrams Collected (Unbound); *ibid.*, RG 108, Letters Received. Lincoln, *Works*, VII, 521. On the same day, Lt. Col. Horace Porter telegraphed to Ord. "Did you yourself See the fall of Fort Morgan announced in a Richmond paper and of what date?" ALS (telegram sent), DNA, RG 107, Telegrams Collected (Unbound); telegram received, *ibid.* On the same day, Ord telegraphed to Porter. "I saw it myself in the paper of the 26th inst" Telegram received, *ibid.* On Aug. 29, USG telegraphed to Lincoln. "Since my dispatch of this morning I have received the Richmond sentinel of the 27th. It contains the following dispatches. *From Mobile.* The report of the surrender of Fort Morgan was most unexpected, and we await some explanation of so unfortunate an occurrence. The press of Mobile is hopeful and confident of their ability to hold the City." ALS (telegram sent), Lamon Papers, CSmH; telegram received (at 12:03 P.M.), DNA, RG 94, War Records Office, Miscellaneous War Records; (at noon) *ibid.*, RG 107, Telegrams Collected (Bound); DLC-Robert T. Lincoln. At 3:15 P.M., Maj. Gen. George G. Meade telegraphed to USG conveying the same information. ALS (telegram sent), DNA, RG 94, War Records Office, Army of the Potomac; telegram received, *ibid.*, RG 108, Letters Received.

On Aug. 30, Ord telegraphed to USG. "Have you the papers (Richmond) containing the details of the surrender of Fort Morgan If not shall I send it to you—" ALS (telegram sent), *ibid.*, RG 107, Telegrams Collected (Unbound); telegram received (at 8:20 P.M.), *ibid.* On the same day, Lt. Col. Theodore S. Bowers telegraphed to Ord. "Gen Grant directs me to say that he has not received a Richmond paper giving the details of the surrender of Fort Morgan & would thank you for one—he also directs that you send him the statement of the paper by telegraph before sending by orderly—" Telegram received (at 9:05 P.M.), Ord Papers, CU-B; DNA, RG 107, Telegrams Collected (Unbound). At 9:30 P.M., Ord telegraphed the newspaper account to Bowers. ALS (telegram sent), *ibid.*; telegram received, *ibid.* On the same day, USG telegraphed to Halleck transmitting the newspaper account. Telegrams received (2—on Aug. 31, 5:20 P.M.), *ibid.*, Telegrams Collected (Bound); *ibid.*, Telegrams Collected (Unbound). Printed as received on Aug. 30, 5:20 P.M., in *O.R.*, I, xxxix, part 2, 321.

To Abraham Lincoln

(Cipher)   City Point Va. Aug. 29th *1864.* 3.10 p. m.
A. LINCOLN PRESIDENT WASHINGTON,

Your dispatch of 1.40 p. m. in relation to permitting Col. Worthington to come here is received. I should be very sorry to see the Col. He has nearly worried the life out of me at times when I could not prevent an interview.

U. S. GRANT

Lt. Gn.

ALS (telegram sent), Lamon Papers, CSmH; telegram received (at 6:30 P.M.), DNA, RG 107, Telegrams Collected (Bound); DLC-Robert T. Lincoln. On Aug. 29, 1864, 1:40 P.M., President Abraham Lincoln telegraphed to USG. "Col. T. Worthington, of Ohio is here wishing to visit, you. I will send him if you say so; otherwise not." ALS (telegram sent), DNA, RG 107, Telegrams Collected (Bound); telegram received, *ibid.*, Telegrams Collected (Unbound); *ibid.*, RG 108, Letters Received. Lincoln, *Works*, VII, 523. Thomas Worthington of Ohio, USMA 1827, dismissed as col., 46th Ohio, in 1862, wrote several pamphlets after the Civil War severely criticizing U.S. leadership at the battle of Shiloh.

To Edwin M. Stanton

City Point, Va. Aug 29. 1864

HON. E. M. STANTON
SECRETARY OF WAR
WASHINGTON D. C.
SIR

I have the honor to acknowledge the receipt of your communication of date 26th inst. in relation to the services of George A Lamb, scout etc. I have no knowledge of Lamb, and no recollection of his having reported to me or furnished me information at Vicksburg or elsewhere. I have employed but few scouts during the War, because I found the statements of such persons unreliable and for the same reason paid but little attention to the reports brought to me by scouts claiming to have been sent out, by officers in our service. Whilst I cannot say positively that Lamb did not report to me at Vicksburg, I have no recollection of his having done so, and am confident, that he furnished me no information of Value,

Very Respectf. Your obt sert

U. S GRANT. Lt. Gen—

Copies, DLC-USG, V, 45, 68, 107; DNA, RG 108, Letters Sent. On Aug. 26, 1864, Asst. Secretary of War Charles A. Dana wrote to USG. "An account has

been presented to this Department by George A. Lamb, for his services as a
Scout or spy, on a trip into Texas during the year 1863, made by order of Capt
Pierre, Chief of Scouts of the then 'Army of The Frontier.' He alleges, that on
his return from Texas, he reported to you at Vicksburg 'giving a full exposition
of the enemy's position and movements.' The Secretary of War instructs me to
request, that you will cause this Department to be informed whether this statement of Lamb is correct, and also to be furnished with any information under
your control, which will enable the settlement of his accounts." LS, *ibid.*, Letters
Received.

To Maj. Gen. Henry W. Halleck

City Point, Va. Aug. 29th *1864.*

MAJ. GEN. H. W. HALLECK,
CHIEF OF STAFF OF THE ARMY,
GENERAL,

Your letter of the 27th is just received. I think with you it
would be hazardous and productive of no special good to send
Granger past Mobile towards Atlanta. Granger would not be the
right man to trust with an Army cut loose from its base of supplies. Again, the movement Sherman is now making, result as it
may, can not be influanced by any thing that can be done at Mobile
in obedience to orders sent from here now.

On the subject of exchanges I have no special objection to
Commanders making of exchanges after battles of the men they
have respectively captured. But I do not understand these to be the
class of exchanges that have been made either by Canby or Foster.
They have given men that will go immediately into the ranks to
fight against us whilst we get nothing of the sort in return. Such
exchanges are very much against us.

I think now that Sheridan is superior to Early besides the latter
being where it must take a good part of his force to collect supplies
for the balance. He can at least feel the enemy and ascertain. If he
can only get the Early to retreating then all of Crooks force can be
sent to Western Va. With the balance the enemy can be followed
as far as may prove prudent, I hope to the Va. Central rail-road.

If this can be done the 6th Corps might be brought here and the 19th left for other service. My greatest alarm now is that Wheeler may go into Ky. He is easily whipped if boldly attacked by half his numbers but I fear that Burbridge will not be able to raise even such a force. The only chance I know for him is to call upon the Governer of Ky. for all the aid he can give. There is no doubt but Burbridge will fight with whatever force he has.

I can not believe that Gn. Heintzel[man's] fears are well founded. The class of people who would threaten what he apprehends make a great noise but it is hard to believe that states so largely represented in the Union Army have not friends to the soldiers enough left at home to prevent violence.

The only way any soldier can ever be taken from Gen. Rosecrans is by sending a staff officer directly to him to execute the order in person. I do not know that he has any troops to spare but it would be all the same if he had double the number he has.

> Very respectfully
> your obt. svt.
> U. S. GRANT
> Lt. Gn.

ALS, deCoppet Collection, NjP. *O.R.*, I, xxxix, part 2, 313. On Aug. 27, 1864, Maj. Gen. Henry W. Halleck wrote to USG. "In a letter just received from Genl Sherman, he advises that Granger should not attack Mobile, but move directly up the Alabama river to Selma or Montgomery. He says the capture of Mobile will only weaken our active forces by the garrison required to hold it, whereas garrisoned by the enemy & threatened by our gun-boats, Hood's forces are weakened to the amount of that garrison. I think Sherman has entirely overestimated Granger's forces, and under-estimated the difficulty of passing Mobile and ascending the Alabama some hundred and fifty or two hundred miles. Possibly something of the kind might have been effected if A. J. Smith's column had moved on Selma or Montgomery; but I now learn from Sherman that he was ordered to strike the Tennessee at Eastport or Decatur. It will not do to attempt too many things at once with our rapidly diminishing armies. If Canby weakens the line of the Miss. too much, in order to reënforce Granger, Kirby Smith may cross and reënforce Hood. I fear that as it is he will send small parties across to meet at some place of rendezvous and then march to Atlanta. Genl Canby and Admiral Farragut both understand that the main object of their operations is to assist Sherman, and I think it will be better to let them work out the problem as circumstances may require rather than to embarrass them with orders based on a supposed state of things which may be essentially different when the orders are received. I have directed Genl Canby to permit no more exchanges of prisoners of war. That part of the Cartel which authorizes commanders to exchange on the field troops just captured, man for man, has been considered heretofore as still in effect. I do not see any objection to it, as it can give no advantage to either party & saves our men from barbarous treatment by the rebels. To exchange their healthy men for ours who are on the brink of the grave from their hellish treatment, of course gives them all the advantage. Nevertheless it seems very cruel to leave our men to be slowly but deliberately tortured to death. But I suppose there is no remedy at present. Horses and men for the 2d cavalry Division are being sent down as rapidly as possible. The hundred days men in West Va. are nearly all discharged & that country is nearly defenceless. The people of that country are in a panic about rebel raids and beg for troops. I have none to send them, and must leave it to Sheridan to keep the enemy occupied. Genl Heintzelman reports unfavorably of the condition of affairs in his Dept. He is firmly of opinion that the plots of the copperheads to release the rebel prisoners were frustrated only by sending additional guards, & that such attempts will be made at the earliest favorable opportunity. At the request of the Governor of Colorado, I telegraphed to Genl Rosecrans to send the regiment of Colorado Cavalry now at Kansas City to operate against the hostile Indians on the plains and to protect the overland mail route, but he replied, as usual, that he could not spare any troops. The authorities of Colorado & the Post Office & Interior Depts. are very urgent for more troops in that direction, but it is impossible to give them." LS, DNA, RG 108, Letters Received. *O.R.*, I, xxxix, part 2, 306–7; (incomplete) *ibid.*, II, vii, 685.

To Maj. Gen. George G. Meade

By Telegraph from City Point
Dated Aug 29 *1864.*

To Maj Gen Meade

I will direct work to be commenced on the Rail Road extension at once.[1] I do not want to give up the Welden Road if it can be avoided until we get Richmond. That may be months yet   To facilitate operations wagons returning from near the Norfolk RR & from the Welden Road should throw in a light load of Rails & bring them to present depot   No Rails should be brought from the Norfolk Road East of where the proposed Road will intesect it unless the Engineers deem it expedient to haul in wagons all the Rails that will be required   when the Road is fimished to that point a train of cars could be run down the Road & used to bring up the Rails   again if the wagons were to be used exclusively in placing Rails where they are wanted 4 parties could work at a time 1 from the Norfolk Road 1 north the other south & 1 from the city Point

Road   The manner of doing the work will be submitted to the
Engineers

U S GRANT

Telegram received (at 1:00 P.M.), DNA, RG 94, War Records Office, Army of
the Potomac; copies, *ibid.*, RG 108, Letters Sent; DLC-USG, V, 45, 68, 107;
(2) Meade Papers, PHi. *O.R.*, I, xlii, part 2, 564. On Aug. 29, 1864, 11:45
A.M., Maj. Gen. George G. Meade telegraphed to USG. "I have nothing of importance to report this morning.—The 13 in mortar has been placed in battery on
the right of the 10th corps front & from time to time throws shells at the R. Rd.
Depot in Petersburgh. The difficulty of supplying the troops on the Welden R.
Rd & the advantage of greater facility in moving troops from left to right of our
extended line, has caused my attention to be called to the expediency of extending
the City Point R. Rd—to the Weldern Rd. in rear of our lines.—A survey by
the Engineers proves the scheme quite feasible & there is ample material in the
shape of rails & ties on the Norfolk road—The labor therefore would consist in
the transportation of this material—the grading & laying of the track—The Engineers estimate it would require a month to complete the work but I am of the
opinion, by placing a large force on it, it could be done in a shorter time   The
question of its expediency is greatly dependant on the proposed future operations,
and is therefore submitted to you for your judgement   If it is contemplated the
army will remain in its present position for any considerable time, over the period
three weeks required to construct the road I think it would pay, as unless this is
done we shall have to build at least two cordury roads between the plank road &
Welden R. Rd—. . . Report from signal officer just in indicates a movement of
the enemys infantry from their right to left—Troops are seen passing in that
direction this morning—" ALS (telegram sent), DNA, RG 94, War Records
Office, Army of the Potomac; telegram received, *ibid.*, RG 108, Letters Received.
O.R., I, xlii, part 2, 564.

Also on Aug. 29, USG telegraphed to Meade. "If Capt. Mechler can possibly be spared ~~order~~ direct him to report here for orders. I want an Engineer
officer to report to Gn. Sheridan for duty." ALS (telegram sent), Kohns Collection, NN; telegram received (at 1:00 P.M.), DNA, RG 94, War Records Office, Army of the Potomac. *O.R.*, I, xlii, part 2, 564. At 3:00 P.M., Meade telegraphed to USG. "I can not possibly spare Maj. Michler—Two officers Capts.
Mendell & Turnbull have recently been taken away.—Maj. Duane's health is
precarious & I am daily expecting his being obliged to leave on this account—
Michler is the only officer of experience I have to act as Chief Engineer—In our
present position the Engineers are very much occupied   Besides field-works—
there are the surveys for roads—the obtaining a knowledge of the topography of
the country—~~min~~ counter mining—and a variety of miscellaneous duties, which
are constantly arising, and would prevent the reduction of the Engineering force
of this army—If it is deemed imperative to take an officer from this army—I
would prefer the detachment of Capt. Harwood but I hope some one may be found
other than those now here." ALS (telegram sent), DNA, RG 94, War Records
Office, Army of the Potomac; telegram received, *ibid.*, RG 108, Letters Received.
O.R., I, xlii, part 2, 565. At 4:30 P.M., USG telegraphed to Col. Edward D.
Townsend. "Please order Capt Turnbull of the Eng. Corps to report to Gn.
Sheridan for duty. Capt. T. was ordered from here to Baltimore for temporary
duty and I suppose is still there." ALS (telegram sent), CSmH; telegram received

(at 6:30 P.M.), DNA, RG 94, Letters Received, 908A 1864; *ibid.*, RG 107, Telegrams Collected (Bound). On Aug. 31, Townsend telegraphed to USG. "Orders were sent Capt. Turnbull, Engineers, to report to Genl Sheridan according to your telegram. Captain Turnb[ull] reports unfit for field service and sends surgeons certificate." ALS (telegram sent), *ibid.*, Telegrams Collected (Unbound); telegram received, *ibid.*, Telegrams Collected (Bound); *ibid.*, RG 108, Letters Received. On Sept. 1, USG telegraphed to Townsend. "Capt F. A. Farquhar who was recently sent from here to report to the chief Engineer appears to be the only available officer to send to Genl Sheridan. If he is through with his work at Wash or can possibly be spared from it please order him to report to Sheridan" Telegram received, *ibid.*, RG 94, Letters Received, 911A 1864; *ibid.*, RG 107, Telegrams Collected (Bound); *ibid.*, Telegrams Collected (Unbound); copies, *ibid.*, RG 108, Letters Sent; DLC-USG, V, 45, 68, 107. On Sept. 2, 2:40 P.M., Maj. Gen. Henry W. Halleck telegraphed to USG. "Capt Farquhar has been appointed asst to Prof. Mahan at West-Point & cannot be spared. Lieut Allen, a recent graduate, can be sent to Genl Sheridan, but he ought to have an engineer of more experience. There is none available unless taken from the Army of the Potomac or from Genl Sherman." ALS (telegram sent), DNA, RG 107, Telegrams Collected (Bound); telegram received, *ibid.*; *ibid.*, Telegrams Collected (Unbound); *ibid.*, RG 108, Letters Received. On Sept. 4, 8:30 P.M., USG telegraphed to Halleck. "I cannot send Sheridan an Engineer Officer from here very well   We will have to assign to him the young Officer of whom you spoke—" Telegram received (at 10:30 P.M.), *ibid.*, RG 107, Telegrams Collected (Bound); copies, *ibid.*, Telegrams Received in Cipher; *ibid.*, RG 108, Letters Sent; DLC-USG, V, 45, 68, 107. 1st Lt. Vanderbilt Allen was so assigned; see *O.R.*, I, xliii, part 2, 102.

On Aug. 29, USG telegraphed to Meade. "I presume our cavalry is so desposed that the Enemy cannot, come around Warrens flank & attack in rear without our having timely notice   if they should make such an attack Warren should move with every man he has & trust to getting back his position after a battle" Telegram received (at 1:20 P.M.), DNA, RG 94, War Records Office, Army of the Potomac; copies, *ibid.*, RG 108, Letters Sent; DLC-USG, V, 45, 68, 107; (2) Meade Papers, PHi. Printed as sent at 1:20 P.M. in *O.R.*, I, xlii, part 2, 565. At 1:20 P.M., Meade telegraphed to USG. "Your despatch of 1.20 received —Kautz division of cavalry watches our rear from the Jerusalem plank road to the James—Greggs Division pickets from the Jerusalem plank road west around our rear & to Warrens left—Any movement of the enemy such as you indicate would therefore be known—There is no indication of any such movement—Perhaps my despatch of this a m may have been accidentally either erroneously written or mis-apprehended   I desire to say the enemys infantry had been seen passing from the vicinity of Lead works towards Petersburgh apparently moving to their left—I have 4 divisions of Infantry in reserve ready to meet any movement in our rear or on the left.—" ALS (telegram sent), DNA, RG 94, War Records Office, Army of the Potomac; telegram received, *ibid.*, RG 108, Letters Received. *O.R.*, I, xlii, part 2, 565.

At 4:15 P.M., Lt. Col. Theodore S. Bowers telegraphed to Meade and to Maj. Gen. Edward O. C. Ord transmitting a telegram of 1:30 P.M. from Capt. George K. Leet to Bowers. "Scouts who left Mine Run Thursday night are just in & report following. Welkhams [*Wickham's*] & Youngs cavalry brigades passed up the valley early part of last week. Corses & Andersons brigades started for

Richmond early part of last week. Andersons brigade recalled & is still in valley. Thought to be no infantry now in the valley but part of Ewells old corps & two or three brigades of Longstreets corps. Gen Ed Johnson of Ewells corps gone to Atlanta. ~~Anderson~~ understood that Beauregard has gone to Atlanta with troops from valley. Gen Lomax is in Richmond but not known whether his brigade is there. Prominent secessionists of Orange county say Richmond cannot be held a month with Weldon road in our possession. Rumor of important movement of Infy in valley when scouts left but no particulars could be had. Other scouts will be in Wednesday." Telegram received (marked as sent at 6:15 P.M.), DNA, RG 94, War Records Office, Army of the Potomac; (received at 7:05 P.M.) *ibid.*, RG 107, Telegrams Collected (Unbound); Ord Papers, CU-B; copies (2), Meade Papers, PHi. *O.R.*, I, xlii, part 2, 567; *ibid.*, I, xliii, part 1, 952. At 11:00 P.M., Maj. Gen. Philip H. Sheridan telegraphed to Leet. "The report of the scouts, from Mine Run is inaccurate. Prisoners were yesterday captured from Wickham and Lomax. Lomax is in command of the Valley Cavalry, and Fitz Lee in command of all Cavalry in the Valley. Breckenridge's Corps I saw myself this evening. Ewell's Corps I have not been able to locate for two days. Kershaw's Division was here Sunday Morning. I do not Know what Corse and Anderson belong to unless to some of the Divisions of Longstreet's Corps; they do not belong to Kershaw. Early was here today." Telegram received, DNA, RG 107, Telegrams Collected (Bound); copies, *ibid.*, Telegrams Received in Cipher; DLC-Philip H. Sheridan. *O.R.*, I, xliii, part 1, 953.

On Sept. 4, 7:30 P.M., USG telegraphed to Leet, Washington. "Send me the name of the scout who was at Gordonsville and brought back the report that Early was coming to Richmond. I want to know so as to judge how far it is reliable." ALS (telegram sent), CSmH; telegram received (at 10:30 P.M.), DNA, RG 107, Telegrams Collected (Bound). On Sept. 5, 2:30 P.M., Leet telegraphed to USG. "The information contained in dispatch of 29th ult. was obtained by the scouts from an Agent named Cammack—an old man who lives near Orange CourtHouse. Scouts in this morning, who derive their information from same source, report following. 'No troops have passed to or from the Valley since Fitz Hugh Lee's Cavalry went up. Force of Infantry now there is Ewells old Corps, Breckenridges Division and Andersons Brigade of Fields Division. Have been steadily falling back of late, but no signs of their leaving the Valley.' This information is to the 3d inst. and Mr. Babcock, who has charge of scouts, thinks it reliable" ALS (telegram sent), *ibid. O.R.*, I, xliii, part 2, 28.

1. On Aug. 29, Bowers wrote to Brig. Gen. Rufus Ingalls. "You will please extend the City Point. RailRoad, with the least practicable delay to the Weldon RailRoad, the extension to pass in the rear of our present lines and at points giving the greatest accommodations to our troops. Telegrams marked 'A.' and 'B.' on the subject are respectfully enclosed for your information" Copies, DLC-USG, V, 45, 68, 107; DNA, RG 108, Letters Sent. *O.R.*, I, xlii, part 2, 565–66. Bowers enclosed the correspondence between USG and Meade. A letter of Aug. 29, 3:00 P.M., entered in Meade's letterbook (PHi) as addressed to USG was written to Ingalls as the content indicates. *O.R.*, I, xlii, part 2, 566.

To Maj. Gen. Edward O. C. Ord

————

By Telegraph from City Pt
Dated Aug 29 *1864.*

To MAJ GENL ORD

If you can raise from four to six hundred cavalry send them under a good office from Deep Bottom to sweep down the River to Wilsons Wharf   from that point they can be ferried over the River and return by this side—there will be no necessity for them to take forage with them.   the object of sending them is to catch up all the Enemies Scouts & parties that are now said to be near the River with Torpedoes ready to plant   I want them to destroy & use all forage & wheat Stacks but to keep out of houses—

U. S. GRANT
Lt Genl

Telegram received, Ord Papers, CU-B; DNA, RG 94, War Records Office, Dept. of the Cumberland; copies, *ibid.*, RG 108, Letters Sent; DLC-USG, V, 45, 68, 107. *O.R.*, I, xlii, part 2, 585. On Aug. 29, 1864, Maj. Gen. Edward O. C. Ord, "Hatchers," twice telegraphed to USG, first at 2:50 P.M. "I cannot raise more than two hundred men & do think it advisable to send that small across the river as the enemys pickets are reported to have been strengthened at Deep Bottom" "I cannot raise more than three hundred cavalry this evening by raking together all in this neighborhood   The best officer I have is Capt Ellis [*Allis*] who does not know much about the country but I will put him across the river if you say so"   ALS (telegrams sent), DNA, RG 107, Telegrams Collected (Unbound); telegrams received, *ibid.*; *ibid.*, RG 108, Letters Received. *O.R.*, I, xlii, part 2, 585–86. At 3:30 P.M., Lt. Col. Theodore S. Bowers telegraphed to Ord. "Gen Grant directs me to say that he thinks theree hundred cavalry will be sufficient for the purpose if it can get out from Deep Bottom and that he think the Infantry can enable it to get out"   Telegram received, Ord Papers, CU-B; (at 4:00 P.M.) DNA, RG 107, Telegrams Collected (Unbound). *O.R.*, I, xlii, part 2, 586. At 3:35 P.M., Ord telegraphed to USG. "I have ten (10) officers & two Hundred fifty one (251) Cavy about half the men scattered on orderly & other duties— Gen Birney reports over six hundred (600) Cavalry—I have telegraphed him for Two hundred (200)—Probably he is away or Considers himself not under my orders as no answer has been recd to my telegram—Is it worth while your ordering him to send me Two Hundred (200) Cavy.—They would arrive here some time tomorrow a. m.—I shall wait your orders whether to send my Two Hundred Cavy on the Scout from Deep Bottom—" ALS (telegram sent), DNA, RG 107, Telegrams Collected (Unbound); telegram received, *ibid.*; *ibid.*, RG 108, Letters Received. *O.R.*, I, xlii, part 2, 586. At 3:45 [P.M.], Bowers telegraphed to Ord. "a force two hundred is not sufficient—Postpone the ~~expeditton~~ expedition until a larger force is available." Telegram received, Ord Papers, CU-B;

DNA, RG 107, Telegrams Collected (Unbound). *O.R.*, I, xlii, part 2, 586. At 4:05 P.M., Ord telegraphed to USG. "Gen Birney now reports that he has no Cavy mounted except small company that relieved my escort on the river as pickets and the usual provost Guard and Orderlies—He left the cavy that was at Deep bottom there and all the rest is dismounted in trenches" ALS (telegram sent), DNA, RG 107, Telegrams Collected (Unbound); telegram received, *ibid.*; *ibid.*, RG 108, Letters Received. *O.R.*, I, xlii, part 2, 586.

At 8:45 P.M., Ord telegraphed to Bowers. "Gen Birney wishes to put two hundred (200) pdr parrotts on the R R where the thirteen (13) inch Mortar is. Shall I direct him to do so?" ALS (telegram sent), DNA, RG 107, Telegrams Collected (Unbound); telegrams received (2), *ibid.*; *ibid.*, RG 94, War Records Office, Army of the Potomac. *O.R.*, I, xlii, part 2, 587. Bowers endorsed the telegram received. "Respectfully referred to Maj. Gen Meade, who will give Gen Birney such orders as he may deem proper" AES, DNA, RG 107, Telegrams Collected (Unbound). *O.R.*, I, xlii, part 2, 587. At 10:15 P.M., Bowers telegraphed to Ord. "Your despatch in relation to the Parrotts has been referred to Gen Meade with directions to give Gen Birney such orders on the subject as he may after examing the ground deem proper—" Telegram received, Ord Papers, CU-B; DNA, RG 94, War Records Office, Miscellaneous War Records.

To Maj. Gen. Philip H. Sheridan

(Cipher)   City Point, Vn. Aug. 29th *1864.* [*1:30* P.M.]
MAJ. GEN. SHERIDAN, HALLTOWN VA.

If it is ascertained certainly that Breckenridge has been detached to go into Western Virginia attack the remaining force vigerously with every man you have and if successful in routing him follow your success with the 6th & 19th Corps and send Crooks to meet Breckenridge. This is sent on the strength of a dispatch just received reporting that Breckenridge with 8000 men has gone to Western Va. I know nothing of the truth of the report.

U. S. GRANT
Lt. Gn.

ALS (telegram sent), DLC-USG, I, C; telegram received (at 3:00 P.M.), DNA, RG 107, Telegrams Collected (Bound). *O.R.*, I, xliii, part 1, 952. On Aug. 29, 1864, 11:00 P.M., Maj. Gen. Philip H. Sheridan telegraphed to USG. "There is not one word of truth in the report of Breckinridge being in West Va   It is a copperhead report   I saw his corps at the crossing of Opequan Creek this evening. It came down to dislodge Meritts Division of Cavalry   Early and Breckenridge were there in person   They attacked the Cavalry at the ford & forced it back a short distance   I then put in Ricketts Division of Infantry and the enemy fell back to Bunker Hill where their whole force has been concentrated for the last two days. Fitz Lee is here in command of all the Cavalry of the Valley   I had prisoners from Lomax and Wickhams yesterday. I believe no troops have yet left the Valley, but [I] believe they will and that it will be their last campaign in the [S]henandoah—They came to invade and have failed. They must leave [or] cross the Potomac   They acknowledge a loss of sixteen hundred men since the last advance from Strasburg and today their loss was severe   Our loss slight—" Telegram received (on Aug. 30, 3:20 A.M.), DNA, RG 107, Telegrams Collected (Bound); *ibid.*, RG 108, Letters Received; copies, *ibid.*, RG 107, Telegrams Received in Cipher; DLC-Philip H. Sheridan. *O.R.*, I, xliii, part 1, 952. The third sentence of this telegram, as received by USG, reads "morning" instead of "evening." On Aug. 30, 2:20 P.M., Lt. Col. Theodore S. Bowers telegraphed to Maj. Gen. George G. Meade and to Maj. Gen. Edward O. C. Ord transmitting a copy of Sheridan's telegram. Telegram received, DNA, RG 107, Telegrams Collected (Unbound); *ibid.*, RG 108, Letters Received; (misdated Aug. 29) Ord Papers, CU-B; copies (2), Meade Papers, PHi.

To Capt. Melancton Smith

                                                       City Point. Va. Aug 29. 64

CAP'T. M. SMITH U. S. V.
COMMD'G JAMES RIVER FLOTILLA
CAP'T.

There is good reason for believing, that one or more torpedos were planted in the river between this & Wilcox Landing last night. Before sending out any vessels particularily with valuable cargoes, I wish at least to have a search made to see if the suspision entertained is veryfied,   I would be pleased Capt. if you would instruct the Officers in your Command convenient to this locality to search the river from immediately below here to Wilcox landing

                                        Very Respectfully Your obdt servt.
                                        U. S. GRANT. Lt. Gen.

Copies, DLC-USG, V, 45, 68, 107; DNA, RG 108, Letters Sent. *O.R.*, I, xlii, part 2, 567; *O.R.* (Navy), I, x, 406. On Sept. 1, 1864, Capt. Melancton Smith, U.S.S. *Onondaga*, wrote to USG. "I have respectfully to inform you that, since the morning of the 29th Ult; the boats of the U. S. Steamer 'Sassacus' have been employed dragging the river with grapnels below City Point to Harrison's Landing for the Torpedos supposed to have been placed in that vicinity, but have not succeeded in finding any. It is thought that their locality is not correctly defined, or that the parties reporting them have been misinformed. I have ordered a Steamer to patrol the river nightly from City Point to Harrison's Landing to prevent the enemy from indulging in any such diabolical tricks hereafter." LS,

DNA, RG 108, Letters Received. *O.R.*, I, xlii, part 2, 627; *O.R.* (Navy), I, x, 412–13. On Sept. 21, Smith wrote to USG. "I have ordered one of the Gun-boats off the Chickahominy to patrol the river with boats to Jamestown Isd: and another Gun boat to patrol from the mouth of the Chickahominy to Wilcox's Wharf, and have instructed the Commander of the 'Hunchback' to examine the Swash Channel off Jamestown Island every day." LS, DNA, RG 108, Letters Received. *O.R.*, I, xlii, part 2, 952.

Testimony

[*Aug. 30, 1864*]

Lieut. Gen. U. S. GRANT, U. S. Army, being sworn and examined by the JUDGE-ADVOCATE, says:

Question. Will you please to state what in your judgment caused the failure of the attack on the enemy's lines on the 30th of July?

Answer. It seemed to me that it was perfectly practicable for the men, if they had been properly led, to have gone straight through the breach which was caused by the explosion of the mine, and to have gone to the top of Cemetery Hill. It looked to me, from what I could see and hear, that it was perfectly practicable to have taken the men through; but whether it was because the men themselves would not go, or whether it was because they were not led, I was not far enough to the front to be qualified to say.

Question. What orders which you issued were not executed, if any?

Answer. I could send you copies of all the dispatches that I wrote. The orders for the assault were issued by General Meade in obedience to general instructions from me. I saw the detailed order of General Meade before the mine was exploded, and I thought that the execution of that order was practicable. That order I presume you have before you. My order was to General Meade, and then General Meade made his order from what I directed him to do, and sent me a copy of it, and I thought it was all that could be required. I recollect that, failing on the north bank of the river to surprise the enemy as we expected or hoped to do, but instead of that drew a large part of his force to the north side,

I telegraphed to General Meade that we would now take advantage of the absence of that force of the enemy to explode the mine and make an assault on Petersburg.

By the COURT:

Question. From your information how many of the enemy were in Petersburg at the time of this assault?

Answer. My information was that three divisions were left in Petersburg, with one brigade absent from those divisions—Johnson's. From the best evidence none of the enemy's troops crossed the James River until 2 o'clock of the 30th of July, on their way back. Then they had fully sixteen miles to travel to get back, with, however, the advantage of a railroad near them to carry many of the men. The distance I guess at when I say sixteen miles.

O.R., I, xl, part 1, 82. USG testified before the court of inquiry on the battle of the Crater. See telegram to Maj. Gen. Henry W. Halleck, Aug. 1, 1864. On Aug. 29, 1864, Col. Edmund Schriver, judge advocate, telegraphed to USG. "I am directed to acquaint you that the Court of Inquiry instituted by special orders No 258 W. D. for the investigation of the facts & circumstances which attended the unsuccessful assault on the enemys line on the 30th July is now in session and that your testimony is desired   That you may be inconvenienced as little as possible in giving it the court direct me to say that your evidence will be received any day between ten & three oclock on which you may see fit to attend for the purpose"   Telegram received, DNA, RG 108, Letters Received. On the same day, Lt. Col. Cyrus B. Comstock telegraphed to Schriver. "I will attend the Court of Inquiry with Gen. Grant." ALS (telegram sent), *ibid.*, Telegrams Sent by Comstock.

On Aug. 30, Schriver telegraphed to Comstock. "Please ascertain from Genl. Grant the name of the Colonel & his regiment, who was once a Sergeant that knows something important respecting the affair of 30th July, and communicate it to me." ALS (telegram sent), *ibid.*, RG 107, Telegrams Collected (Unbound). On the same day, Comstock telegraphed to Schriver. "Gen. Grant cannot at this moment recall the name of the officer in question. He is Captain comd'g a Penna. Regt. perhaps recently promoted to a majority, was formerly a Sergeant in the 4th Infy & is believed to be in the 9th Corps." ALS (telegram sent), *ibid.* On Sept. 2, 10:00 A.M., USG telegraphed to Maj. Gen. John G. Parke. "Please send me a list of officers now commanding Penna Regiments in the 9th Corps   The one I want to get at is a Capt now Commanding Regiment the number of which I do not know." Telegram received, *ibid.*, RG 94, War Records Office, Army of the Potomac; copy, DLC-USG, V, 68. At 11:20 A.M., Parke telegraphed to USG. "The Pennsylvania regiments in the 9th Army Corps are now commanded as follows: 48th Major O. C. Bosbyshell. 45th Captain Thomas Gregg   100th. Captain J. H Pent[e]cost   50th. Lieut. Colonel E. Overton   51st. Captain Jos. K. ~~Bolton~~ Bolton, Jr" ALS (telegram sent), DNA, RG 94, War Records Office, Army of the Potomac; copy, *ibid.*, RG 393, Army of the Potomac, Letters Sent. USG probably wanted Capt. Theodore

Gregg, 45th Pa., who testified before the court of inquiry on Sept. 3. *O.R.*, I, xl, part 1, 117–18.

On Sept. 9, Maj. Gen. Winfield S. Hancock telegraphed to USG. "the court of Inquiry has completed its labors, and adjourned sine die. I dont understand the despatch from Maxwell,   I am afraid that the cegars have been used up? What is it? t"   Telegram received, DNA, RG 108, Letters Received.

To Maj. Gen. Edward O. C. Ord

By Telegraph from City Pt
Dated Aug 30th *1864.*

To MAJ GEN ORD—

To protect the navigation on the James River I have determined to establish a garrison about the Burkley House on the north bank   Genl Barnard selected the location today & has sent for your engineer officer to direct him as to the works to throw up— You will please furnish the garrison two companies of infantry a section of artilley & one (1) squadron of the 1st N. Y. mntd rifles will be sufficient   I think the artill'y & infantry can be taken from the garrisons of Ft Powhattan & wilsons wharf   Gen'l Martin[1] having but a small commadnd at Wilsons wharf should be assigned to the command of all troops on the river east of City Point & west of Ft Monroe with Hd. Qrs at wilsons wharf—

U. S GRANT
Lt. Gen

Telegram received, Ord Papers, CU-B; (at 10:00 P.M.) DNA, RG 94, War Records Office, Miscellaneous War Records; copies, *ibid.*, RG 108, Letters Sent; DLC-USG, V, 45, 68, 107. *O.R.*, I, xlii, part 2, 597–98. On Aug. 30, 1864, 11:50 P.M., Maj. Gen. Edward O. C. Ord telegraphed to USG. "I will make the details for garrison at Berkely house—the New York Mounted Rifles has all enlisted except about enough to take care of horses of Regiment going on furlough— I have had to replace the two squadrons of it at Deep bottom by a detail from my pro-guard   can detail 50 men more from   The cavalry guard to garrison the Berkely work might be taken from Genl. Birneys, or Kautz cavalry" ALS (telegram sent), DNA, RG 107, Telegrams Collected (Unbound); telegram received, *ibid.*; *ibid.*, RG 108, Letters Received. *O.R.*, I, xlii, part 2, 598. On the same day, Lt. Col. Cyrus B. Comstock telegraphed to 1st Lt. Peter S. Michie. "Gen. Ord will be directed to send a small garrison to the Berkley Place, Harrisons Landing. Gen. Grant It   A work will be erected under your charge & if you will call on Gen. Barnard at these H. Q. tomorrow morning he will give you its general character." ALS (telegram sent), DNA, RG 108, Telegrams Sent by Comstock. *O.R.*, I, xlii, part 2, 598.

On Sept. 1, 1:35 A.M., Comstock telegraphed to Ord. "As the two companies which you sent to the Berkeley Place are insufficient to do any work, the general commanding desires that you send in addition a small colored regiment, which can be relieved after the defenses are completed." *Ibid.*, p. 647.

1. Gilman Marston, born in N. H. in 1811, a graduate of Dartmouth and Harvard Law School, Republican U.S. Representative from N. H. (1859–63), appointed col., 10th N. H., as of June 10, 1861, and brig. gen. as of Nov. 29, 1862. For the orders USG requested, see *ibid.*, pp. 606–7.

To Maj. Gen. George G. Meade

By Telegh from City Pt Aug 31—186[4]

MAJ. GEN MEADE—

As soon as it Can be done I would like to have a column of Cavalry perhaps supported by infantry would be well thrown out west from Warrens position to cut off wagon trains carrying supplies into Petersburg   It should be a rapid sudden dash to gather up all the teams & straggling escorts they could

U. S. GRANT

Lt Gen

Telegram received, DNA, RG 94, War Records Office, Army of the Potomac; copies, *ibid.*, RG 108, Letters Sent; DLC-USG, V, 45, 68, 107; (2) Meade Papers, PHi. *O.R.*, I, xlii, part 2, 601. On Sept. 1, 1864, 10:30 A.M., Maj. Gen. George G. Meade telegraphed to USG. "I have nothing of consequence to report this morning—un-usual quiet prevailing yesterday & last night. The enemy are apparently erecting a battery on the north side of the Appomatox to enfilade the position occupied by the 13 inch mortar. This will be met by a removal of the mortar to a more secure position   Orders will be issued this morning to Brig. Genl. Gregg instructing him to concentrate all the available cavalry of his own & Kautz command after leaving the necessary pickets so as not to attract the enemys attention, and with this command supported by Ayre's Division 5. corps who for this purpose will be ordered to report to him, to proceed at early daylight tomorrow from the left of Warrens line, to the several roads leading into Petersburgh from the west & south west & endeavor to capture or destroy some of the enemys trains, supposed to be passing between stony creek & Petersburgh —It is believed however that *besides* strong escorts to these trains, the enemy is prepared, for an operation of this kind, by the disposition of his cavalry between stoney creek & Petersburgh & by holding in readiness, an infantry reserve to meet the contingency.—" ALS (telegram sent), DNA, RG 94, War Records Office, Army of the Potomac; telegram received, *ibid.*, RG 108, Letters Received. *O.R.*, I, xlii, part 2, 624–25.

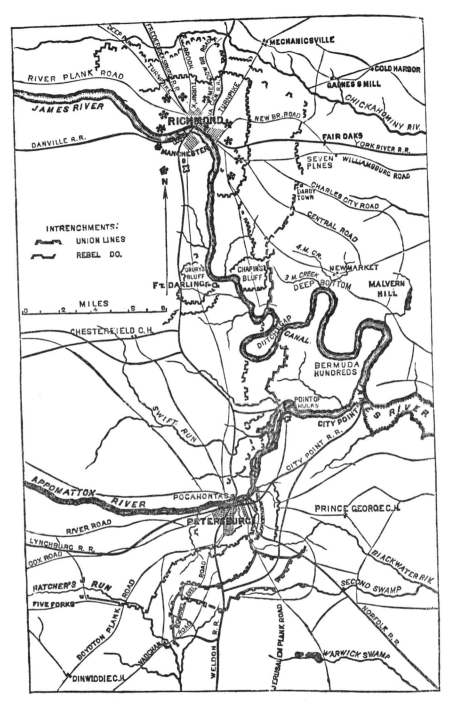

Area of Operations around Richmond and Petersburg

From Horace Greeley, The American Conflict: A History of the
Great Rebellion (*Hartford, Conn., 1866*), II, 594

On Aug. 31, USG telegraphed to Meade. "The depot C. S. at Cedar Level stn. reports that he is still without a guard for stores there—Please order the necessary guard" Telegram received, DNA, RG 94, War Records Office, Army of the Potomac; copies, DLC-USG, V, 68; (2) Meade Papers, PHi. At 9:45 A.M., Meade telegraphed to USG. "General Birney was directed on Sunday to furnish from his command a guard for the depot at Cedar Level station and I supposed the guard was furnished on that day. I will now direct General Hancock to send at once the ~~necessay~~ necessary guard from the Second corps." Copy (telegram sent), DNA, RG 393, Army of the Potomac, Cav. Corps, Letters Received; telegram received, *ibid.*, RG 108, Letters Received.

At 11:00 A.M., Meade telegraphed to USG. "There is nothing of importance to report this morning—The field works on the left are being constructed as rapidly as possible.—" ALS (telegram sent), *ibid.*, RG 94, War Records Office, Army of the Potomac; telegram received, *ibid.*, RG 108, Letters Received. *O.R.*, I, xlii, part 2, 600.

Also on Aug. 31, USG telegraphed to Meade. "I go this morning to Ft Monroe Expect to start back this evening" Telegram received, DNA, RG 94, War Records Office, Army of the Potomac; copies (2), Meade Papers, PHi. *O.R.*, I, xlii, part 2, 601. USG telegraphed the same message to Maj. Gen. Edward O. C. Ord. Telegram received, Ord Papers, CU-B.

To Maj. Gen. Henry W. Halleck

(Cipher)   City Point Va. ~~Aug~~ Sept 1st *1864*. [*3:30* P.M.]
MAJ. GN. HALLECK, WASHINGTON

If A. J. Smith has reached Decatur he had better be ordered by rail to Nashville to get on the track of Wheeler and drive him south. If he has not arrived Chattanooga and all points on the roads not threatened can be stripped to the lowest standard and sent North after ~~him~~. Wheeler.

U. S. GRANT
Lt. Gn.

ALS (telegram sent), CSmH; telegram received (at 3:30 P.M.), DNA, RG 107, Telegrams Collected (Bound). *O.R.*, I, xxxix, part 2, 335.

To Maj. Gen. George G. Meade

City Point Va. ~~Aug.~~ Sept. 1st/64 11.05 a. m.

MAJ. GEN. MEADE,

Your dispatch of 11 a. m. ~~just~~ received. From all information for the last twenty-four hours Early's force is now on its way to Richmond. If this proves true we may expect stiring times within a few days of his arrival and I should not like you to be absent. A dispatch is just in however from Gn. Sheridan and as soon as it is disciphered I may be able to tell better what may be expected and will inform you. If you do go I would prefer your starting immediately so as to be back as early as possible.

U. S. GRANT

Lt. Gn

ALS (telegram sent), CSmH; telegram received, DNA, RG 94, War Records Office, Army of the Potomac. *O.R.*, I, xlii, part 2, 625. On Sept. 1, 1864, 11:00 A.M., Maj. Gen. George G. Meade telegraphed to Lt. Col. Theodore S. Bowers. "I have to ask of the Lt. Genl. Comdg. the favor of a seven days leave to visit my family in Philada, to attend to private affairs the leave to commence on Sunday the 3d. inst.—This application is based on the belief, so far as my knowledge extends, that the operations of this army during that time will admit of my services being dispensed with.—" ALS (telegram sent), DNA, RG 94, War Records Office, Army of the Potomac; copies, *ibid.*, RG 393, Army of the Potomac, Letters Sent; Meade Papers, PHi. *O.R.*, I, xlii, part 2, 625. On the same day, USG telegraphed to Meade. "Sheridan is satisfied that no conciderable force, if any, has been detached from his front, I am willing therefore that you should go for a week, but if it is convenient for you would prefer that you start this evening. Ingalls starts for Washingtn this evening on a special boat and if you will go he will start at any hour that suits your convenience." ALS (telegram sent), deCoppet Collection, NjP; telegram received (at 1:00 P.M.), DNA, RG 94, War Records Office, Army of the Potomac. *O.R.*, I, xlii, part 2, 625. At 1:00 P.M., Meade telegraphed to USG. "Your telegram just received I will be ready to leave this evening with Ingalls, and will endeavor to return before the end of the week Whom shall I leave in command during my absence—Maj. Genl. Parke is the ranking officer—" ALS (telegram sent), DNA, RG 94, War Records Office, Army of the Potomac; telegram received, *ibid.*, RG 108, Letters Received. *O.R.*, I, xlii, part 2, 626. On the same day, USG telegraphed to Meade. "Genl Parke being the senior officer will be left in command" Telegram received (at 2:30 P.M.), DNA, RG 94, War Records Office, Army of the Potomac; copies, *ibid.*, RG 108, Letters Sent; DLC-USG, V, 45, 68, 107; (2) Meade Papers, PHi. *O.R.*, I, xlii, part 2, 626.

To Maj. Gen. Philip H. Sheridan

(Cipher)   City Point Va. Sept. 1st *1864.*
Maj. Gen. Sheridan, Charlestown Va.

Some refugees ~~are just~~ who left Richmond last night are just in. One an intelligent young man of Northern birth says that on last Sunday he met an acquaintance of his who has long been a Sutler in the Army; that he knew of his having gone some time ago to Earlys in the Valley with a supply of tobacco. He says that when they met on Sunday the Sutler told him that of of Early's troops were on their way back. He does not know what point they had reached on their return but the fact of the whole force returning was spoken of as if there was no doubt about it.

U. S. Grant
Lt. Gn.

ALS (telegram sent), CSmH; telegram received (at 3:40 p.m.), DNA, RG 107, Telegrams Collected (Bound). *O.R.*, I, xliii, part 2, 3. On Sept. 2, 1864, 10:00 a.m., Maj. Gen. Philip H. Sheridan telegraphed to USG. "I am satisfied that no troops have yet gone from this valley. On the 29th Averill drew out Rhodes corps. on the 28th Merritt drew out Breckenridges corps. Yesterday the cavalry drove Fitz Lees cavalry picket in over the Jordan-Spring road, Berryville Pike, Millwood Pike, crossed the Front Royal Pike and got around nearly as far as Strausburg Pike   That no troops have left here is,—up to this time—almost unquestionable. There is a report among the people that Early has been ordered back to Richmond with troops, but no troops have yet gone   Kershaw was encamped yesterday on the road from Summit Point to Winchester, near where it crosses the Opequan. Averill is over the Williamsport line near Martinsburg; with his advance south of that place   Troops here are in front of Charlestown covering Smithfield Pike, Summit Point road and Berryville Pike" Telegram received, DNA, RG 107, Telegrams Collected (Bound); *ibid.*, RG 108, Letters Received; copies, *ibid.*, RG 107, Telegrams Received in Cipher; DLC-Philip H. Sheridan. *O.R.*, I, xliii, part 2, 12.

On Sept. 1, Capt. George K. Leet, Washington, telegraphed to Lt. Col. Theodore S. Bowers. "Scouts just up report as follows, to 30th ult. No signs of any movements from the Valley. One passenger train running daily between Staunton & Richmond—Up in morning and down at night—Three freight trains weekly through to Staunton. No troops seen on Railroad but returning convalescents. Trains on Fredk Railroad only run to Hanover Junction. Building Bridge over North Anna—will be done 15th inst. when trains will be run to Hamilton Crossing. Gen. Lee reported severely wounded at Weldon R. R. fight." ALS (telegram sent), DNA, RG 107, Telegrams Collected (Bound). *O.R.*, I, xliii, part 2, 4.

To Maj. Gen. Philip H. Sheridan

(Cipher)   City Point Va. Sept. 1st 9. p. m./64

MAJ. GEN. SHERIDAN, CHARLESTOWN VA.

The frequent reports of Averell's falling back without much fighting or even skirmishing and afterwards being able to retake his old position without opposition presents a very bad appearance at this distance. You can judge better of his merrits than I can but it looks to me as if it was time to try some other officer in his place. If you think as I do in this matter releive him at once and name his successer.

U. S. GRANT
Lt. Gn.

ALS (telegram sent), CSmH; telegrams received (2—at 9:00 P.M.), DNA, RG 107, Telegrams Collected (Bound). *O.R.*, I, xliii, part 2, 3.

On Sept. 13, 1864, Brig. Gen. William W. Averell wrote to Lt. Col. Cyrus B. Comstock. "Since I have been in this department I have unfortunately incurred the displeasure of a few small politicians and they have left no stone unturned to injure me publicly & privately. The most atrocious slanders have been circulated regarding my official conduct and private character—I have endured the contumely that these few active enemies have heaped upon me with indifference until the present time, conscious of the rectitude of my conduct and always relying upon the confidence of my superiors and the respect of my comrades. But recently I have become aware that the mind of Genl Grant has been poisoned by these slanderous reports and his judgement prejudiced against me. I think it is my duty now to request an investigation   Knowing that the regular correspondence of the General must very much embarrass him I enclose a letter which I have written to him asking that you will be good enough to lay it before him at some opportune moment when he he can give it that attention which I would like it to recieve. My dear Comstock I rely upon your friendship and discretion in this matter. Read the letter and endeavor to present it to the General under favorable circumstances so that he will be inclined to send some one to investigate this matter   It touches my honor very closely: to tamely submit to the humiliation of having my character & competency passed upon with the evidence of such men to direct the judgement is unendurable is impossible   If there is any one hope in my breast that is supreme over all others it is that this rebellion may be put down by whipping the south honestly and fairly by destroying their military force & power entirely. It is the only proper way. It is this belief which has been always the main spring of my action—Is it not then dreadful that after all my hardships & sufferings I should be believed every thing that is bad by the Genl Comdg our armies without a chance for defence. We shall see better times here before this reaches you   Please let me hear from you soon   Believe me sincerely yr friend & classmate" ALS (press), DNA, RG 393, Dept. of West Va., 2nd Cav. Div., Telegrams Sent. *O.R.*, I, xliii, part 2, 79.

To Julia Dent Grant

———

Sept. 1st *1864.*

DEAR JULIA,

After you left yesterday we started back up the river but the captain stating that there was some danger of getting aground runing at night I told him he might run over to Norfolk where I spent the evening until 12 at night with Gen. Shepley[1] & family. Starting out about daylight we had a severe storm. If it extended up the bay, you must have been seasick. We arrived here about 9 this morning. Was Jess glad to get back to his Ma? Tell him I believe he likes his Ma better than he does me & Jeff Davis (the pony) put together. I hope you will very soon get to house keeping and find yourself pleasantly situated.

Gen. Meade left here this evening for Philadelphia and will call on you. Love and kisses for you and the children.

                         Good night
                         ULYS.

ALS, DLC-USG.

1. Son of a U.S. Senator, George F. Shepley, born in Me. in 1819, graduated from Dartmouth, studied law at Harvard, then became a Democratic lawyer-politician in Me. Appointed col., 12th Me., as of Nov. 16, 1861, and brig. gen. as of July 18, 1862, his Civil War career was closely tied to that of Maj. Gen. Benjamin F. Butler, who arranged for Shepley's appointment as commandant of New Orleans, then military governor of La. In Aug., 1864, Shepley commanded the District of Eastern Va. with hd. qrs. at Norfolk.

To Maj. Gen. Henry W. Halleck

———

(Cipher)   City Point, Va. ~~Aug~~ Sept. 2d *1864.*

MAJ. GN. HALLECK, WASHINGTON.

I understand some of the states have been authorized to raise regiments complete towards filling their quotas? I would like to have such regiments to the number of twelve sent to Memphis as soon after the 5th inst. as practicable. If this number of troops can be raised for Memphis it will enable Gn. Canby to operate against

Mobile with a force that can either capture the city and open up communication with Sherman from the South or force the enemy to keep a large force for its defence.

U. S. Grant

Lt. Gn.

ALS (telegram sent), CSmH; telegram received (sent at 10:10 A.M., received at 12:20 P.M.), DNA, RG 107, Telegrams Collected (Bound).

To Commanders

———

City Point Va. Sept. 2d *1864.*

To Commander A. P. & all Corps Commanders,
A dispatch just received from Superintendent of Telegraph in Dept. of Cumberland of this date announces the occupation of Atlanta by our troops.[1] This must be by the 20th Corps which was left by Sherman on the Chattahoocha whilst with the balance of his army he march to the south of the City.

U. S. Grant

Lt. Gn.

ALS (telegram sent), CSmH; telegram received (at 8:45 P.M.), DNA, RG 94, War Records Office, Miscellaneous War Records; (2) *ibid.*, Army of the Potomac; *ibid.*, RG 393, 10th Army Corps, Telegrams Received; Ord Papers, CU-B.

1. On Sept. 2, 1864, Capt. John C. Van Duzer, U.S. Military Telegraph, Marietta, Ga., telegraphed to Maj. Thomas T. Eckert, sending a copy to USG. "Our advance entered at Atlanta two hours since—I will have line in there before we stop" Telegram received, DNA, RG 108, Letters Received. On the same day, USG telegraphed to Maj. Gen. Edward O. C. Ord and to Maj. Gen. John G. Parke transmitting this telegram. Telegram received, Ord Papers, CU-B; (2) DNA, RG 94, War Records Office, Army of the Potomac. Also on Sept. 2, Maj. Gen. Henry W. Slocum, Atlanta, telegraphed to Secretary of War Edwin M. Stanton, sending a copy to USG. "General Sherman has taken Atlanta; The twentieth (20) corps occupies the city: The main army is on the Macon road near EastPoint. A battle was fought near that point, in which Gen. Sherman was successful Particulars not known" Telegram received, *ibid.*, RG 107, Telegrams Collected (Unbound); (on Sept. 3) *ibid.*, RG 108, Letters Received. Printed as received on Sept. 2, 10:05 P.M., in *O.R.*, I, xxxviii, part 5, 763. On Sept. 3, 8:00 P.M., Lt. Col. Theodore S. Bowers telegraphed to Ord and all corps commanders transmitting this telegram. Telegram received, Ord Papers, CU-B; DNA, RG 107, Telegrams Collected (Unbound); copy, *ibid.*, RG 393, 9th Army Corps, Letters Received. On Sept. 2, 9:30 P.M., USG telegraphed to Slocum.

"Whilst you are cut off from communication with Gen. Sherman telegraph your situation daily to Gn. Halleck" ALS (telegram sent), CSmH; telegram received (on Sept. 3, 4:00 P.M.), DNA, RG 107, Telegrams Collected (Bound). *O.R.*, I, xxxviii, part 5, 763.

On Sept. 4, Ord telegraphed to USG transmitting a report of the battles near Atlanta from the *Richmond Examiner* of the previous day. ALS (telegram sent), DNA, RG 107, Telegrams Collected (Unbound); telegrams received (2), *ibid.*; *ibid.*, RG 108, Letters Received. See telegram to Maj. Gen. William T. Sherman, Sept. 4, 1864. On Sept. 5, 5:15 P.M., Maj. Benjamin C. Ludlow, Dutch Gap, signaled to USG. "Hood abandoned Atlanta on night of Sept. 1st. Rebel army fallen back to Lovejoys Station seven miles from Jonesboro. Rebel paper. I will send you the paper." ALS (signal sent), DNA, RG 107, Telegrams Collected (Unbound); telegram received, *ibid.*

To Maj. Gen. John G. Parke

By Telegraph from City Point
Dated Sept 2 *1864.*

To Maj Gen. J. G. Parke Comdg A. P

Gen. Gregg need not make any further effort to reach the Enemys wagon train in the direction he did this morning. Keep Warren & Gregg ready however to move out and attack the Enemy if he should feel his way up near our left

U S Grant
Lt. Gen

Telegram received (at 9:15 A.M.), DNA, RG 94, War Records Office, Army of the Potomac; copies, *ibid.*, RG 108, Letters Sent; DLC-USG, V, 45, 68, 107. *O.R.*, I, xlii, part 2, 655. On Sept. 2, 1864, 8:20 A.M., Maj. Gen. John G. Parke telegraphed to USG. "The following telegrams show the result of the operations of the Cavalry Column this Morning. Shall Gen Gregg make another dash in heavier Column at some point two or three miles lower down? The brigade that made the dash out was 2.600 or 2.800 strong." Telegram received (marked as sent at 6:30 A.M.), DNA, RG 94, War Records Office, Army of the Potomac; copies, *ibid.*, RG 393, Army of the Potomac, Letters Sent; Meade Papers, PHi. Printed as received at 8:40 A.M. in *O.R.*, I, xlii, part 2, 654. The enclosures are *ibid.*, pp. 669–70.

Also on Sept. 2, USG telegraphed to Parke. "What was the result of the Cavalry movement this morning as to losses on each side?" ALS (telegram sent), Kohns Collection, NN; telegram received, DNA, RG 94, War Records Office, Army of the Potomac. *O.R.*, I, xlii, part 2, 655. At 3:15 P.M. and 7:15 P.M., Parke telegraphed to USG. "Genl. Gregg has not yet reported the losses—He has been telegraphed for them. It is reported by him & by Genl. Warren that no movements of the enemy have been observed—as the following despatches show."

ALS (telegram sent), DNA, RG 94, War Records Office, Army of the Potomac; telegram received, *ibid.*, RG 108, Letters Received. *O.R.*, I, xlii, part 2, 655. The enclosures are *ibid.*, pp. 665, 670. "The parties sent out by Gen Gregg found no evidences of any movement of the enemy going on—The signal officer on the Weldon Rail road Saw no movements during the day other than those reported   It is probable the Brigade of Infantry seen going out the squirrill level road reinforced the infantry & cavalry posted at the intersection of the Boydtown plank road & the road the cavalry moved on—Greggs Cavalry got within three or four hundred yards of the plank road   It was not intended to strike it so near Petersburg—A branch road from the one they were on enters the plank road a mile further from the town   No other enters it this side of R̶a̶w̶ Rowanty swith [*Creek*]" Telegram received, DNA, RG 108, Letters Received; copies, *ibid.*, RG 393, Army of the Potomac, Letters Sent; Meade Papers, PHi. Printed as received at 7:25 P.M. in *O.R.*, I, xlii, part 2, 655.

To Edwin M. Stanton

(Cipher)   City Point Va. Sept. 3d *1864*. 9 p. m.
HON. E. M. STANTON, SEC. OF WAR, WASHINGTON

I have Richmond paper of to-day. It contains rumor of a battle at Atlanta but says that the War Dept. having no official n̶o̶t̶i̶c̶e̶ o̶f̶ [information] it declines to form an opinion from [the] rumors. I have no doubt, however, but Sherman has gained a great success there. Before the dispatch of last night was received announcing the occupation of Atlanta by our troops, i̶t̶ [the fact] was known b̶y̶ [to] our picketts. The rebels hallo̶w̶[o]ed over to our men that Sherman had whipped Hood—the[at the] latter [had] l̶o̶o̶s̶i̶n̶g̶ [lost] 40.000 men—and that our troops a̶r̶e̶ [were] in Atlanta. All quiet here.

U. S. GRANT
Lt. Gn.

ALS (telegram sent), CSmH; telegrams received (2), DNA, RG 107, Telegrams Collected (Bound). Bracketed words not in USG's hand. On Sept. 3, 1864, 8:00 P.M., Secretary of War Edwin M. Stanton had telegraphed to USG. "The telegraph line between Nashville and Chattanooga being broken we have had nothing South of Nashville today and i̶t̶ the next intelligence from Atlanta may come through the Richmond papers. If you get any-thing from that source please f̶o̶r̶w̶a̶r̶d̶ transmit to this Department" ALS (telegram sent), *ibid.*; telegram received, *ibid.*, Telegrams Collected (Unbound); *ibid.*, RG 108, Letters Received. *O.R.*, I, xlii, part 2, 674.

To Julia Dent Grant

City Point Va. Sept. 3d *1864.*

DEAR JULIA,

I have but little to say except that I am well and hope that you have succeeded in getting a nice pleasant house.—I shall expect a letter from you to-morrow evening. I received this evening the money you left with Capt. Leet for me.—Tell Jess I shall not forget his failing to stop with me. Fred or Buck would have staid I know. I wrote to Bass Sappington last night telling him to commence suit against White at once.

Love and kisses for you and the children.

ULYS.

ALS, DLC-USG.

To Maj. Gen. Henry W. Halleck

(Cipher)   City Point Va. Sept. 4th *1864.* [*8:00* P.M.]
MAJ. GN. HALLECK, WASHINGTN,

Gen. Payne must be removed from Paducah. He is not fit to have a command where there is a solitary family within his reach favorable to the Government. His administration will result in large and just claims against the Government for destruction of private property taken from our friends. He will do to put in an intensely disloyal district to ~~schurge~~ scourge the people but even then it is doubtful whether it comes within the bounds of civilized warfare to use him.

U. S. GRANT
Lt. Gn.

ALS (telegram sent), CSmH; telegram received (at 10:30 P.M.), DNA, RG 107, Telegrams Collected (Bound). *O.R.,* I, xxxix, part 2, 342. After his removal from command of the District of Western Ky. as of Sept. 11, 1864, Brig. Gen. Eleazer A. Paine received no other command and resigned as of April 5, 1865.

On Aug. 16, 1864, Brig. Gen. Henry Prince, Columbus, Ky., wrote to USG. "From the time of taking command here by your orders, I have conducted, without ostentation, the necessary business of this district, and have occupied myself assiduously, being a stranger to it, in the endeavor to become acquainted with it—a slow work—sufficiently to form a judgment in the first person of its condition as respects the rebellion and the course which ought to be pursued. The utmost activity of the troops consistent with the nature of them, the immense changes which have taken place in them, and the good of the district and the cause, has been kept up. The utmost care and fidelity and purity in applying the restrictions of trade prescribed by authority over me, have been observed. But the absence of noise and pretense on my part appears to have led to the impression that nothing was being achieved, and a new commander of the district, imbued with that idea, and with the theory that the sickest patient requires the most violent dosing, has, unannounced, superseded me. To being superseded I make no objection, but a policy calculated, in my belief, to spread ruin and devastation, and having no good in it, is being pursued at the moment that an improvement in the feeling of the citizens toward the Government was making itself apparent to me. They were getting tired of the rebel reign of terror, propagated by guerrillas, and were meditating on the comfort of being relieved from them and of having a government. The new policy propagates a new reign of terror by means of soldiers and hired assassins and unsettles every nook of society. The facts which I shall state to illustrate the mode of proceeding are only some which are well and thoroughly known to me. This new commander took from my custody at Columbus, Ky., a man named Kesterson, whom I had captured and whom I was holding in prison for trial, conducted him to Paducah, Ky., and publicly killed him there, in semblance of an execution, without authority of law or any proper justification. One Gregory, a citizen heading a gang employed by the new commander and acting under his orders, took a man named Bryant from his bed, near Dublin, in the district, conducted him to Mayfield, and there publicly killed him in semblance of an execution, without authority of law or any proper justification. The first of these acts was committed on the 27th day of July, 1864; the second on the 2d day of this present month. He has sent under guard from this neighborhood quiet and peaceable citizens, who had taken the oath of allegiance, and actually banished them to Canada. The main object of my writing this letter is to show that I have not been, to any extent whatever, a participator in these acts, which are patent to the public here, and to ask to be relieved—which has occurred from other authority while I am writing. I beg leave, in vindication of myself, to add my protest against them in the name of God and of all my countrymen who respect the rights of mankind." *Ibid.*, pp. 260–61.

To Maj. Gen. John G. Parke

City Point Va. Sept. 4th/64

MAJ. GN. PARKE, COMD.G A. P.

A scout sent from Washingtn to Gordonsville and who left the latter place on the 1st inst. reports that Early's forces commenced passing there on the 28th on their way to Richmond and were still passing when he left.[1] They avowed the purpose of driving us from the Weldon road. Breckinridge was left in the Valley with orders to hold it. A close watch must be kept upon the enemy and every preparation made to receive an attack. My own impression is that if the enemy attacks, and I expect it, he will hold his present lines from the James River to the Welden road with a force not exceeding three Divisions. With the balance they will likely march entirely around our left and attack in rear near the Jerusalem Plank road. Should they do so all our troops to the left of the point of attack should be instructed to move at once against the enemy leaving only garrisons for the enclosed works. All troops to the right should also be taken to face the enemy leaving not to exceed 2000 men to the mile to hold the intrenchments. With proper vigilence the Cavalry will be able to give timely notice of the point of attack if made.

U. S. GRANT
Lt. Gn.

ALS (telegram sent), CSmH; telegram received (at 6:00 P.M.), DNA, RG 94, War Records Office, Army of the Potomac; *ibid.*, RG 393, 10th Army Corps, Telegrams Received. *O.R.*, I, xlii, part 2, 682. On Sept. 4, 1864, USG telegraphed to Maj. Gen. John G. Parke. "A line should be selected at once in rear of our present line & facing from it which can be taken at any time if the enemy should come in from the rear—Some preparation should also be taken to make it defensable   If Major Duane is not able for such duty no one could select such a line better than Genl Humphreys" Telegram received, DNA, RG 94, War Records Office, Army of the Potomac; copies, *ibid.*, RG 108, Letters Sent; DLC-USG, V, 45, 68, 107. *O.R.*, I, xlii, part 2, 682. On the same day, Parke telegraphed to USG. "Your two despatches recd. Immediate arrangements will be made to meet the contingency promptly   The lookout at Friends House reported today a column of troops 2500 strong moving on the Road from Richmond to Petersburg" Telegram received, DNA, RG 108, Letters Received; copies, *ibid.*, RG 393, Army of the Potomac, Letters Sent; Meade Papers, PHi. *O.R.*, I, xlii, part 2, 683. Also on Sept. 4, Lt. Col. Cyrus B. Comstock telegraphed to Col. John W. Shaffer, chief of staff for Maj. Gen. Benjamin F. Butler. "Lieut Genl Grant desires me to ask if any Rebels Troops have been seen from the Point of Rocks Observetory Moving from Richmond towards Petersburg today   If so in what force and at what times" Telegram received, DNA, RG 94, War Records Office, Army of the Potomac. *O.R.*, I, xlii, part 2, 692. At 7:30 P.M., Maj. Robert S. Davis telegraphed to Comstock. "There have been no troops seen moving from the signal tower." *Ibid.*

1. A telegram of Sept. 3, 10:20 P.M., from Maj. Gen. Christopher C. Augur to Maj. Gen. Henry W. Halleck is *ibid.*, I, xliii, part 2, 18. On Sept. 4,

noon, Halleck telegraphed to USG. "A scout from Gordonsville says that Early was at that place on the 27th on his way from Richmond to withdraw a part of his forces from the valley to assist in recapturing the Weldon road." ALS (telegram sent), DNA, RG 107, Telegrams Collected (Bound); telegram received, *ibid.*; *ibid.*, RG 108, Letters Received. *O.R.*, I, xliii, part 2, 21.

To Maj. Gen. Philip H. Sheridan

(Cipher)   City Point Va. Sept. 4th *1864*. [*10:00* A.M.]
MAJ. GN. SHERIDAN, CHARLESTOWN VA,

In clearing out the Arms bearing community from Louden County and the subsistence for Armies exercise your own judgement as to who should be exempt from arrest and as to who should receive pay for their stock grain &c. It is our interest that that County should not be capable of subsisting a hostile Army and at the same time we want to inflict as little hardship upon Union men as possible.

                                             U. S. GRANT
                                             Lt. Gn.

ALS (telegram sent), CSmH; telegram received (at noon), DNA, RG 107, Telegrams Collected (Bound). *O.R.*, I, xliii, part 2, 22.

To Maj. Gen. William T. Sherman

(Cipher)   City Point Va. Sept. 4th *1864*. 9 p. m.
MAJ. GEN. SHERMAN, ATLANTA GA.

I have just received your dispatch announcing the capture of Atlanta.[1] In honor of your great victory I have ordered a salute to be fired with shotted guns from every battery bearing upon the enemy. The salute will be fired within an hour amidst great rejoicing.

                                             U. S. GRANT
                                             Lt. Gen.

ALS (telegram sent), CSmH; (facsimile) Grant Cottage, Mount McGregor, N. Y.; telegram received, DNA, RG 107, Telegrams Collected (Bound). *O.R.*,

I, xxxviii, part 1, 87. On Sept. 6, 1864, 3:00 P.M., Maj. Gen. William T. Sherman, Jonesboro, Ga., telegraphed to USG. "I have your despatch and shall announce it to the troops in general orders. We are gradually falling back to Atlanta feeding high on the corn fields of the Confederacy. I will be in Atlanta in a day or two and will communicate fully with you. I have always felt that you personally take more pleasure in my success than in your own and I appreciate the feeling to its fullest extent" Telegram received (on Sept. 8, 11:00 P.M.), DNA, RG 107, Telegrams Collected (Bound); (on Sept. 9) *ibid.*, RG 108, Letters Received; copies, *ibid.*, RG 107, Telegrams Received in Cipher; *ibid.*, RG 393, Military Div. of the Miss., Telegrams Sent in the Field. Printed as received on Sept. 8 in *O.R.*, I, xxxviii, part 5, 808.

On Sept. 4, 9:00 P.M., USG telegraphed to Maj. Gen. John G. Parke. "Direct every battery bearing upon the enemy, and within reach of his lines, to fire a salute in honor of Sherman's victory in capturing Atlanta. Let it be done tonight as soon as word can be got to the different commanders." ALS (telegram sent), IC; copies, DLC-USG, V, 45, 68, 107; (3) DNA, RG 94, War Records Office, Army of the Potomac; *ibid.*, RG 108, Letters Sent; *ibid.*, RG 393, 10th Army Corps, Telegrams Received.

1. On Sept. 3, 6:00 A.M., Sherman telegraphed to Maj. Gen. Henry W. Halleck reporting the capture of Atlanta. This telegram was transmitted to USG on Sept. 4, 2:40 P.M., then transmitted to Maj. Gen. George G. Meade and all corps commanders. Telegram received, *ibid.*, RG 107, Telegrams Collected (Unbound); *ibid.*, RG 108, Letters Received. *O.R.*, I, xxxviii, part 5, 777.

To Maj. Gen. Christopher C. Augur

(Cipher)   City Point Va. Sept. 5th/64 9 p. m.
MAJ. GEN. AUGUR, WASHINGTN D. C.

For some time back bounty and substitute men have been deserting to the enemy immediately on their arrival here to take advantage of Cooper's Gen. Order No 65[1] promising to send such persons through their lines at the nearest point to their homes. Richmond papers of to-day announce that they now have several hundred such deserters who are to be sent off. I think the route that will be taken by many of them will be to cross the Bay into Accomac or els the Potomac above Point Lookout. I wish you would have a close lookout kept for them and send all you get back here for trial.

U. S. GRANT
Lt. Gn.

ALS (telegram sent), CSmH; telegram received (on Sept. 6, 1864, 1:20 P.M.), DNA, RG 107, Telegrams Collected (Bound). *O.R.*, I, xliii, part 2, 29. On Sept. 6 or 7, 10:30 A.M., Maj. Gen. Christopher C. Augur telegraphed to USG. "I have received your telegram, and will attend to the line this side of PontLookout. Accomack is beyond my control." ALS (telegram sent—dated Sept. 7), DNA, RG 107, Telegrams Collected (Bound); telegram received (dated Sept. 6), *ibid.*, RG 108, Letters Received.

1. General Orders No. 65, Aug. 15, issued by Gen. Samuel Cooper, C.S.A. adjt. and inspector gen., are in *O.R.*, IV, iii, 591.

To Maj. Gen. John G. Parke

By Telegraph from City Point
Dated Sept 5 1864.

To MAJ GEN. PARKE

Cal spear reports that the Enemy made his appearance at different points between Sycamore Chur & Cox Mills   I think it advisable to send a brigade of cavalry in that direction to feel the Enemy & drive what force he has in that quarter entirely off   this should be done at once

U S GRANT
Lt Gen.

Telegram received (at 10:30 A.M.), DNA, RG 94, War Records Office, Army of the Potomac; copies, *ibid.*, RG 108, Letters Sent; DLC-USG, V, 45, 68, 107. *O.R.*, I, xlii, part 2, 697. On Sept. 6, 1864, 8:40 P.M., Maj. Gen. John G. Parke telegraphed to USG. "Colonel Lewis 3d. N. Y. Cavalry reports that he found to day, but one small party of the enemy, five in number, in the region about Sycamore Church & Cox's Mills." Copies, DNA, RG 393, Army of the Potomac, Letters Sent; Meade Papers, PHi. *O.R.*, I, xlii, part 2, 717.

On Sept. 5, Parke telegraphed to USG. "Respectfully forwarded for what it is worth"   Telegram received, DNA, RG 108, Letters Received. *O.R.*, I, xlii, part 2, 703. The enclosed telegram of 10:00 P.M. from Maj. Gen. Winfield S. Hancock to Maj. Gen. Andrew A. Humphreys reporting information from a deserter about C.S.A. movements is *ibid.*, pp. 702–3.

On Sept. 6, Parke telegraphed to USG. "Respectfully forwarded for the information of Lieut Gen Grant. The same information has been received from Several other deserters & appears to be Confirmed by the fact reported by Maj Gen Birney that several Brigades of the Enemy were relieved by others from the trenches in his front last night"   Telegram received, DNA, RG 108, Letters Received. *O.R.*, I, xlii, part 2, 717. The enclosure, reporting the reinforcement of Petersburg, is *ibid.* On the same day, Parke twice telegraphed to USG transmitting similar information from Maj. Gen. David B. Birney. Telegrams received, DNA, RG 108, Letters Received. *O.R.*, I, xlii, part 2, 729–30.

To Jesse Root Grant

City Point, Va. Sept. 5th *1864*.

DEAR FATHER,

Your last letter is just received. Before you receive this it is probable Beverly Simpson will be in service if he comes in atall. If he does enlist however after you receive this tell him to ask to be assigned to a regiment now with the Army of the Potomac. If he is already in service have him write to me and I will assign him to some duty either with me or where it will be equally pleasant for him.

Your theory about delays either with Sherman or myself was not correct. Our movements were co-operative but after starting each have done all that we felt ourselves able to do. The country has been deceived about the size of our Armies and also as to the number of the enemy. We have been contending against nearly equal forces to our own and they always on the defensive and strongly intrenched.—Richmond will fall as Atlanta has done and the rebellion will be suppressed in spite of rebel resistence and Northern countinance and support.

Julia & children are in Philadelphia. If I can get a house there I will make P̶that my home. Julia is very desirous that Jennie should make her home with us if she will and if she will not do that at least spend the Fall and Winter with us.

ULYSSES,

ALS, PPRF.

To Julia Dent Grant

City Pt. Va. Sept. 5th *1864*.

DEAR JULIA,

Dr. Harned,[1] who wrote me the letter in relation to Mr. Chews house in Germantown has written to Mrs. Harned to call upon you and to aid in securing such a house as you want. I hope you will be able to suit yourself in Philadelphia.—You received my telegraphic dispatch did you not? telling you to get boarding in Phila. until such time as you could secure a house, ~~Ggo~~ go to New York or New Jersey as you like.

I am in good health feeling greatly better than for the week or two before you came here. Kisses for yourself and children.

Ulys.

ALS, DLC-USG.

1. Possibly Dr. Joseph E. Harned of Philadelphia, who wrote to USG on March 4 and April 8, 1869, applying (unsuccessfully) for the office of director of the U.S. Mint at Philadelphia and mentioning his service as surgeon in the U.S. Army during the Civil War and as surgeon for the Christian Commission for the last two years of the war. ALS, DNA, RG 56, Asst. Treasurers and Mint Officials, Letters Received.

To Maj. Gen. Henry W. Halleck

(Cipher)   City Point, Sept. 6th/64 [*10:30* P.M.]
Maj. Gn. Halleck, Washington,

Telegraph Gen. Sherman what Gen. Washburn says about threatened movements towards Mo.[1] I think he will stop A. J. Smith and if necessary send him against Price Marmaduke &co.[2]

I only intended that portion of the sick and detailed men of the 19th Corps belonging to ~~that~~ the portion of the command now under Gn. Emery should be ordered North.[3]

U. S. Grant
Lt. Gn.

ALS (telegram sent), CSmH; telegram received (on Sept. 7, 1864, 8:00 A.M.), DNA, RG 107, Telegrams Collected (Bound). *O.R.*, I, xli, part 3, 75.

Also on Sept. 6, USG telegraphed to Maj. Gen. Henry W. Halleck. "Richmond Examiner of this morning states that John Morgan was surprised and killed and his staff captured at Greenville Tenn. on yesterday. It further states that Hoods army was in line of battle at Lovejoy's Station, Confronting Sherman—" Telegram received (at 7:45 P.M.), DNA, RG 107, Telegrams Collected (Bound); copies, *ibid.*, RG 108, Letters Sent; DLC-USG, V, 45, 69, 107. At 7:15 P.M., Maj. Gen. John Gibbon telegraphed to USG reporting this news. Telegrams received (2), DNA, RG 107, Telegrams Collected (Unbound); *ibid.*, RG 108, Letters Received. Also at 7:15 P.M., Maj. Benjamin C. Ludlow, Dutch Gap, signaled or telegraphed the same information. Signal received, *ibid.*, RG 107, Telegrams Collected (Unbound); telegram received, *ibid.*

1. On Sept. 3, Maj. Gen. Cadwallader C. Washburn, Memphis, telegraphed to Halleck. "I am satisfied that a large raid is on foot for Mo. to be lead by Price Marmaduke & Sibley [*Shelby*]—They will have 10 or 12000 men, all mounted— My scouts inform me that six days ago Sibley had returned to Batesville after a successful raid on the rail road between Duvalls Bluff & Little Rock and that rations were being issued then for 10 days for 12000 men Sibley had 4000 men and Price & Marmaduke were said to have crossed the Ark. river & daily expected at Batesville My advices from Steele very vague and unsatisfactory. I had reports that Pine Bluff and Saint Charles were captured & Duvalls Bluff threatened and sent Maj Gen Mower with his division, 4000 strong to the relief of our force. I have just heard from Commodore Phelps U. S. N. at mouth of White river that Saint Charles has been evacuated but Pine Bluff is not captured. I have sent 2000 cavalry to Ark river to cooperate with Gen Steele. ~~Gen~~ A J Smith will lie at Cairo some four or five days en route for Sherman" Telegram received (on Sept. 6), *ibid.*, RG 108, Letters Received. Dated Sept. 4 in *O.R.*, I, xli, part 3, 57.

2. On Sept. 7, 9:00 P.M., USG telegraphed to Halleck. "Stop A. J. Smith at Cairo until Gen. Sherman can be telegraphed to know if he still wants him. If he does not he can be thrown into Mo. to head off Price." ALS (telegram sent), CSmH; telegram received (at 9:30 P.M.), DNA, RG 107, Telegrams Collected (Bound). *O.R.*, I, xli, part 3, 88. On Sept. 8, 10:30 A.M., Halleck telegraphed to USG. "Telegram was sent yesterday morning to stop Smith at Cairo till sherman could be heard from. Telegram sent to him at same time." ALS (telegram sent), DNA, RG 107, Telegrams Collected (Bound); telegram received, *ibid.*; *ibid.*, RG 108, Letters Received. *O.R.*, I, xli, part 3, 99.

3. On Sept. 1, Bvt. Maj. Gen. William H. Emory wrote to Lt. Col. Theodore S. Bowers. "I desire to call the attention of the Lieutenant General Commanding the Armies of the United States to the enormous list of Absent Sick on my Report for August 31st. 1864. viz—: 4187; and on the other hand to the very small number who are present sick viz: 435, and on this to base a suggestion to the General Commanding that the absent sick, most of whom are in the Department of the Gulf shall be immediately sent North.—Our troops have steadily improved in health since they have come North, and I have no doubt, that if those whom we left behind sick were sent to the Northern Hospitals, we should have in one Month an accession to our force of from 2 to 4000 men. If allowed to remain in the Hospitals of the Department of the Gulf I doubt if one tenth of that number will ever rejoin their regiments" LS, DNA, RG 108, Letters Received. *O.R.*, I, xliii, part 2, 7. On Sept. 5, 5:00 P.M., USG telegraphed to Halleck. "Please order all the sick and detailed men from the 19th Corps now in the Dept. of the Gulf ~~ordered~~ to Northern Hospitals or back to the regiments to which they belong." ALS (telegram sent), CSmH; telegram received (on Sept. 6, 1:30 P.M.), DNA, RG 107, Telegrams Collected (Bound). On Sept. 6, 4:00 P.M., Halleck telegraphed to USG. "Your telegram of yesterday is ambiguous. Do you mean to order to northern Hospitals the sick of the whole 19th corps or only of the part of that corps now at the north under Genl Sheridan?" ALS (telegram sent), *ibid.*; telegram received, *ibid.*; *ibid.*, RG 108, Letters Received.

To Maj. Gen. Philip H. Sheridan

(Ciphcr)   City Point Va. Sept. 6th/64 [*9:30* P.M.]
MAJ. GN. SHERIDAN, CHARLESTOWN VA,
From reports of deserters coming in at different times and on difer-
ent parts of our line we learn that Kershaws Division arrived in
Petersburg last night. I think there is no doubt but some troops
have arrived from the valley.

U. S. GRANT
Lt. Gn—

ALS (telegram sent), CSmH; telegram received (on Sept. 7, 1864, 6:00 A.M.),
DNA, RG 107, Telegrams Collected (Bound). *O.R.*, I, xlii, part 2, 717; (printed
as received Sept. 7, 8:00 A.M.) *ibid.*, I, xliii, part 2, 36. On Sept. 8, 10:00 A.M.,
Maj. Gen. Philip H. Sheridan telegraphed to USG. "Your dispatch of the 6th
instant received.—Kershaw has not left the valley nor has any portion of his
command. Yesterday I sent off twenty six prisoners representing his four brigades.—No troops have left here.—I have had prisoners daily, representing each
Division of Early's army, and from other sources I am able to say positively that
no troops have left.—Early's infantry force and my own number about the same.
I have not deemed it best to attack him, but have watched closely, to press him
hard so soon as he commences to detach troops for Richmond.—or This was the
tenor of your telegram to me, after I took the defensive. The right of my infantry
line is at '*Left Point*' [*Summit Point*] my left near Berryville—Early is on West
side of Opequan Creek, his left above Stevensons depot,—his right, Kershaw's
division covering the Berryville pike." Telegram received (at 4:00 P.M.), DNA,
RG 107, Telegrams Collected (Bound); *ibid.*, RG 108, Letters Received; copies,
ibid., RG 107, Telegrams Received in Cipher; DLC-Philip H. Sheridan. *O.R.*, I,
xliii, part 2, 49.

To Maj. Gen. John Gibbon

City Point Va. Sept. 7th *1864*

MAJ. GN. GIBBON, 18TH CORPS HD QRS.
Have you or any of the officers of your Corps a Richmond
paper of this date? If so please telegraph me the news from Atlanta. Picketts last night reported there had been a fight and that
Sherman was worsted.

U. S. GRANT
Lt. Gn.

ALS (telegram sent), OClWHi; telegram received, Ord Papers, CU-B. On Sept.
7, 1864, 4:30 P.M. and 7:15 P.M., Maj. Gen. John Gibbon telegraphed to USG.
"No papers have come in yet. As soon as they do I will send them   A deserter
that came in to day reports that Atlanta has been retaken." ALS (telegram sent),
DNA, RG 107, Telegrams Collected (Unbound); telegram received, *ibid*. "The
Rebels refuse to exchange papers on my Line—Maj. Ludlow sent you Hoods report—I suppose he suceeded in getting a paper"   Telegrams received (2), *ibid*.
On the same day, Maj. Benjamin C. Ludlow, Dutch Gap, signaled to USG transmitting a telegram of Sept. 5 from Gen. John B. Hood, Lovejoy's Station, Ga.,
to Gen. Braxton Bragg. "The enemy withdrew from my front in the direction of
Jonesboro last night." ALS (signal sent), *ibid*.; signal received, *ibid*., RG 393,
24th Army Corps, Letters and Telegrams Received.

On the same day, USG twice telegraphed to Maj. Gen. Henry W. Halleck,
the second time at 7:00 P.M. "Todays Richmond paper contains a despatch from
Hood of the 5th from twenty nine miles south of Atlanta stating that Sherman
withdrew from his front during the night"   Telegram received (at 9:30 P.M.),
ibid., RG 107, Telegrams Collected (Bound); copies, *ibid*., Telegrams Received
in Cipher; *ibid*., RG 108, Letters Sent; DLC-USG, V, 45, 69, 107. "Has any
news been received from Gen Sherman since his dispatch announcing the capture
of Atlanta. Rebel pickets & deserters say, that Hood has recaptured the place"
Copies, *ibid*. At 9:15 P.M., Secretary of War Edwin M. Stanton telegraphed to
USG. "We have had nothing from Atlanta Since ~~Shermans~~ ~~and~~ ~~Howards~~
~~despatches~~ ~~of the~~ 4th. Sunday the 4th at 5 p m. The operator at Louisville reports that the lines ~~from~~ ~~there~~ South of Nashville are down but that the line
works to Atlanta by way Cumberland Gap and Knoxville. He has been asked what
news he has from Atlanta last night or today ~~Th~~ and directed to put the enquiry
through to Atlanta. The Herald of this morning has a despatch of the 5th dated
at Nashville speaking of reports of killed & wounded received from Atlanta that
day"   ALS (telegram sent), DNA, RG 107, Telegrams Collected (Bound);
telegram received (marked as sent at 9:30 P.M.), *ibid*., Telegrams Collected
(Unbound); *ibid*., RG 108, Letters Received.

On Sept. 7, 6:00 P.M., Maj. Gen. Benjamin F. Butler telegraphed to USG.
"I have the honor to report ~~my~~ return to my command and will do myself the
honor to report in person tomorrow"   ALS (telegram sent), *ibid*., RG 107,
Telegrams Collected (Unbound). *O.R.*, I, xlii, part 2, 742. On Sept. 9, USG
telegraphed to Butler. "If you have a Richmond paper of the 8th please telegraph
me the news from atlanta. If it does not rain I will be at your HdQrs about one
(1) P. M." Telegram received (at 10:15 A.M.), MH. At 10:40 A.M., Butler telegraphed to USG. "I got the dispatch of the 8th about an hour since   It contains
the following from Atlanta with the editorial comment. . . . I shall be most happy
to have you dine with me at two P. M." ALS (telegram sent), DNA, RG 94, War
Records Office, Army of the Potomac. At 11:00 A.M., USG telegraphed to Stanton. "The Richmond Dispatch of the 8th contains the following. Hd Qrs. Army of
Tenn. Sept. 6th/64   GEN. B. BRAGG. Sherman has continued his retreat beyond
Jonesboro. (signed) J. B. HOOD, Gen." ALS (telegram sent), CSmH; telegram
received (at 9:30 P.M.), DNA, RG 107, Telegrams Collected (Bound). On the
same day, Lt. Col. Theodore S. Bowers telegraphed to Butler and to all corps
commanders. "Sherman telegraphs from Atlanta under date of the 8th that his
Army is grouping about Atlanta that his Troops are well & in fine spirits and that
after a few days rest they will be impatient to again sally forth in search of the
Enemy. he says his Army has been feeding high on the Cornfields of the Con-

federacy & that he has a months stores on hand & feels no anxiety on account of supplies. wheeler is supposed to be trying to cross the Tennessee River at Lambs ferry closely pursued. Ressegca [*Rousseau*] Granger & Steadman have sufficent force to drive wheeler out of the Country or whip him if they can get a fight out of him—the R. R. to Atlanta will be repaired in a few days" Telegram received, *ibid.*, RG 94, War Records Office, Dept. of Va. and N. C., Army of the James, Unentered Papers; *ibid.*, RG 393, 10th Army Corps, Telegrams Received; copy, *ibid.*, 9th Army Corps, 3rd Brigade, Telegrams Received.

On Sept. 3, Maj. Gen. Edward O. C. Ord had telegraphed to USG. "Genl Butler telegraphs that he will be at Old Point to morrow morning Can you send Genl Gibbon or Humphreys to take my corps and let me go to morrow for 10 or fifteen days—" ALS (telegram sent), *ibid.*, RG 107, Telegrams Collected (Unbound); telegram received, *ibid.* At 9:20 P.M., Bowers telegraphed to Ord transmitting Special Orders No. 88. "Leave of absence for ten days is hereby granted Maj Gen E. O. C. Ord Comd'g 18th Army Corps. Maj General John Gibbon U. S. V. is hereby temporarily assigned to the command of the 18th corps." Telegram received, *ibid.* Revised, entered in letterbooks, and printed as Special Orders No. 87, Sept. 4. *O.R.*, I, xlii, part 2, 691.

On Sept. 4, Ord telegraphed to Brig. Gen. John A. Rawlins. "There is a 100 day regiment at Harrisons Landing whose time expired the 22d and who were ~~return~~ retained until the 7th they say Ought they to be relieved and when—" ALS (telegram sent), DNA, RG 107, Telegrams Collected (Unbound); telegram received, *ibid.* On the same day, USG telegraphed to Ord. "The regiment at Harrisons Landing must be relieved as soon as its time is out." ALS (telegram sent), Kohns Collection, NN; copies, DLC-USG, V, 45, 68, 107; DNA, RG 108, Letters Sent. On the same day, Ord telegraphed to USG. "Shall I send the Regiment of Paines Cold. troops—~~22d~~ which I left with Genl Birny to relieve the Regt. of 100 day men at Powhatan they are not at Harrisons Landing—" Telegram received, *ibid.*, RG 107, Telegrams Collected (Unbound).

Also on Sept. 4, 2:00 P.M., Gibbon telegraphed to Rawlins. "I have arrived here & assumed command of the 18th corps." Telegram received, *ibid.*; *ibid.*, RG 108, Letters Received. *O.R.*, I, xlii, part 2, 694. On Sept. 15, Ord, Bellaire, Ohio, wrote to USG. "I am much better, and expect to start back on the 19th. I hope the supply of recruits will continue to flow in until all the corps are filled up to their maximum—the drain by casualties is so regular that the reinforcements should not be spasmodic; I think it is a mistake post poning, or only partially enforcing the draft—" ALS, DNA, RG 108, Letters Received.

To Maj. Gen. John G. Parke

By Telegraph from 2nd AC
Dated Sept 7 *1864.*

To GEN PARKE

There seems to be a break between the new line taken by Gen Birney & the line occupied by the 2nd Corps,

The break is at the Norfolk road. I wish you would send your Chief of Staff or Chief Eng'r to correct & establish the line that must be held

U S Grant
Lt Gen

Telegram received, DNA, RG 94, War Records Office, Army of the Potomac; copies, *ibid.*, RG 108, Letters Sent; DLC-USG, V, 45, 69, 107. *O.R.*, I, xlii, part 2, 734.

On Sept. 8, 1864, 2:00 P.M., Maj. Gen. John G. Parke telegraphed to USG. "The following dispatch from Maj Gen Hancock and explanatory note from Capt McEntee are thought worth sending" Telegram received, DNA, RG 108, Letters Received; copy, *ibid.*, RG 393, Army of the Potomac, Letters Sent. *O.R.*, I, xlii, part 2, 746. The enclosures discussed the discovery of the Richmond City Home Guards in the C.S.A. lines. *Ibid.*

To Julia Dent Grant

City Point Va. Sept. 7th *1864.*

Dear Julia,

I received a letter from you this evening containing two pieces of news that I regreted to hear: first that you had not succeeded in getting a house, and second, that you had not received a letter from me. I wrote to you the day I returned to City Point and have written regularly every other day since. I had no expectation that you would find difficulty in finding a house. Hope yet that you will succeed. I am sorry that it is not so that I can be absent for a few days to see you comfortably fixed. But you know that of all persons I am the last one who can leave. When this campaign ends I shall have Commanders in the field and will spend most of my time, or at least some of it, at home and visit the different Armies.

Since you left here I have had a fine appetite for the first time since we have been at City Point and feel very strong to what I did. Have you not had a great many calls since you have been in Philadilphia? I should suppose you would have.

Kisses for you and the children.

Ulys.

ALS, DLC-USG.

To Maj. Gen. Philip H. Sheridan

(Cipher) City Point Va. Sept. 8th/64 [*1:00* P.M.]
MAJ. GEN. SHERIDAN, CHARLESTOWN VA.

If you want to attack Early you might reinforce largely from Washington. Whilst you are close in front of the enemy there is no necessity for a large force there. This is not intended to urge an attack because I believe you will allow no chance to escape which promises success.

U. S. GRANT
Lt. Gn.

ALS (telegram sent), CSmH; (facsimile) Grant Cottage, Mount McGregor, N. Y.; telegram received (at 4:30 P.M.), DNA, RG 107, Telegrams Collected (Bound). *O.R.*, I, xliii, part 2, 49.

To Maj. Gen. Henry W. Halleck

(Cipher) City Point Va. Sept. 9th 12 m. *1864*
MAJ. GN. HALLECK, WASHINGTON,

I do not know enough of Price's position and strength to say positively what course Smith should pursue. As a rule it is generally advisable to keep troops together to insure full effect, but if Price is ~~alrea~~ now moving North it would be advisable that Smith should head and hold him until the troops in rear can get up. It probably will be best to give A. J. Smith the problem of ketching Price and let him work it out in his own way.

U. S. GRANT
Lt. Gen.

ALS (telegram sent), CSmH; telegram received (at 9:30 P.M.), DNA, RG 107, Telegrams Collected (Bound). *O.R.*, I, xli, part 3, 113. On Sept. 9, 1864, 10:30 A.M., Maj. Gen. Henry W. Halleck telegraphed to USG. "Sherman consents to Smith's going west & he has halted at Cairo. I have directed him to prepare his command for immediate operations, & to telegraph what line he proposes to operate on. The question seems to be between his landing at Cape Girardeau & returning to join Mower on the white River. Please signify your wishes on this point." ALS (telegram sent), DNA, RG 107, Telegrams Collected (Bound); telegram received, *ibid.*; *ibid.*, RG 108, Letters Received. *O.R.*, I, xli, part 3, 113.

To Maj. Gen. Henry W. Halleck

City Point, Va. Sept 9, '64

MAJ GEN HALLECK
CHIEF OF STAFF OF THE ARMY
WASHINGTON D. C.
GENERAL

Under the construction given to it the War Department Circular No. 61 is giving rise to much dissatisfiaction. According to it, officers and non commissioned officers of the three years organizations who have at times varying from that of original organization to the present, accepted promotions won by merit, often if not always in the belief, that thereby their term of service was not increased, are now held for three years, from their last promotion and remuster. I submit, that such a decision, at this late day is of doubtful expediency, with reference to those officers who previously to the publication of the Circular referred to had accepted promotion as even if good officers they will still feel, that they have been injustly treated and unfairly held.

Since the promulgation of this Circular many valuable officers are refusing promotion, which while purporting to be a reward yet imposes at once without opportunity for forlough another term of three years service.

For the good of the service I therefore respectfully recommend, that the Circular be so changed, that at all remusters arrising from promotions, whether before or after its date, officers shall have the option of being remustered for the unexpired portion of their term of service, or for three years, as they shall choose

I am General
Very Respectfully
Your obt servt
U S GRANT
Lieut. Gen.

Copies, DLC-USG, V, 45, 69, 107; DNA, RG 108, Letters Sent. *O.R.*, I, xlii, part 2, 757. On Sept. 2, 1864, President Abraham Lincoln endorsed a printed copy of War Dept. Circular No. 61. "I am told by Major J. C. Richart, to-day that the two first paragraphs of the within order works badly in the Army. Will Lieut. General Grant please give me his opinion on the question?" AES, Abraham Lincoln Book Shop, Chicago, Ill. Incomplete and misdated Sept. 7 in Lincoln, *Works*, VII, 539. Circular No. 61 is in *O.R.*, III, iv, 566–67. On Sept. 9, USG telegraphed to Lincoln. "I think War Dept Circular number 61 should be so modified as to give officers the option of accepting commissions for the balance of their original term or for three years as they should elect" Telegram received (on Sept. 10, 10:10 A.M.), DNA, RG 107, Telegrams Collected (Bound); copies, *ibid.*, Telegrams Received in Cipher; *ibid.*, RG 108, Letters Sent; DLC-USG, V, 45, 69, 107. USG's recommendation was implemented (with qualifications) in War Dept. Circular No. 75, Sept. 22. *O.R.*, III, iv, 740–41.

To Maj. Gen. Philip H. Sheridan

(Cipher)   City Point Va. Sept. 9th *1864*
MAJ. GEN. SHERIDAN, CHARLESTOWN VA.

It is now satisfactorily ascertained that no force has returned here from the valley except a Brigade of Field's & one of Pickett's. It is doubtful whither the Brigade from Pickett's Division ever reached the valley as it was absent from here but a few days. I would not have you make an attack with the advantages against you but would prefer just the course you seem to be pursuing: that is pressing closely upon the enemy and when he moves follow him up being ready at all times to pounce upon him if he detaches any conciderable force. We are strengthening our position here so that a small force can hold the present line and leave the greater part of the Army to act on a given point when I choose. I feel able now for offensive movements but as reinforcements may be expected daily I prefer to wait a short time to make every blow struck more effective. Are you being reinforced to any conciderable extent?

U. S. GRANT
Lt. Gn.

ALS (telegram sent), CSmH; telegram received (sent at 11:30 A.M., received at 10:00 P.M.), DNA, RG 107, Telegrams Collected (Bound). *O.R.*, I, xliii, part 2, 57. On Sept. 11, 1864, 9:00 P.M., Maj. Gen. Philip H. Sheridan, "Near Berryville," telegraphed to USG. "Your despatch recd. I have nothing important to report. Early still holds his position on west bank of Opequan Creek near Jordan Spring. It is exceedingly difficult to attack him in this position. The Opiquan Creek is a very formidable barrier; There are various crossings but all difficult. The banks are formidable—I have thought it best to remain on the defensive until he detaches unless the chances are in my favor   The troops here are in fine spirits; some of them however have not seen very hard fighting and some of them are not entirely reliable. There is no interest suffering here except the Balt. & O. RailRoad & I will not divide my forces to protect it. We have exterminated three officers and 27 men of Mosbys gang in the last 12 days   The enemy have lost in the various little combats which we have had with them according to their own accounts over *3000* men. Our own losses will not exceed 900. I have had some increase from Crooks convalescents but as yet but few recruits. Yesterday & to-day about ninety came in all—The newspaper accounts about loss of ambulances &c are erronious. Only one ambulance was lost and thirteen horses   same day the bushwackers replaced the horses from captures from Mosbys men. We have had heavy rains for last few days, Potomac is not now fordable"   Telegram received (on Sept. 12, noon), DNA, RG 107, Telegrams Collected (Bound); *ibid.*, RG 108, Letters Received; copies, *ibid.*, RG 107, Telegrams Received in Cipher; DLC-Philip H. Sheridan. *O.R.*, I, xliii, part 2, 69.

On Sept. 13, 7:00 P.M., Sheridan telegraphed to USG. "This morning I sent Genl Gettys Division of 6th Corps with two brigades of cavalry to the crossing of the Summit Point and Winchester road over the Opequan Creek to develope the force of the enemy at the crossing in that vicinity   Rhodes Ramseurs Gordons & Whartons Divisions were found on the west bank. At the same time Genls Wilson and Mackintoshs brigade of Cavalry dashed up the Winchester pike drove the rebel Cavalry at a run, ca[me in] contact with Kershaws d[ivision] charged it and captured the 8th S. C Regiment sixteen officers and 145 men and its battle flag and Col Hennegan Commanding Brigade, with a loss of only two men killed and two wounded. Great credit is due to Genl Wilson Mackintosh 3rd N. J and 2nd Ohio. The charge was a gallant one. A portion of the 2nd Mass reserve Brigade made a charge on the right of line and captured one officer and eleven men of Gordons Division of Infantry. Our loss in the reconnoissance is very light" Telegram received (on Sept. 14, 11:00 A.M.), DNA, RG 107, Telegrams Collected (Bound); copies, *ibid.*, Telegrams Received in Cipher; DLC-Philip H. Sheridan. *O.R.*, I, xliii, part 1, 24; *ibid.*, I, xliii, part 2, 77.

On Sept. 15, 9:30 P.M., Sheridan telegraphed to USG. "I have nothing new to report for yesterday or today—There is as yet no indications of Earlys detaching, and I have reports that a small number of pontoon boats have passed through Winchester to Stevensons Depot, and that W. H. F. Lee's old brigade of Cavalry left Staunton over the flood—These reports were brought by one of our soldiers who escaped from Winchester and I question their reliability—The enemy are greatly chagrined at the capture of Hennegan and the Eighth South Carolina regiment   We got the entire organization   We are now getting some recruits but in small numbers—Our increases have been from returned convalescents   It seems impossible to get at the enemys Cavalry, as it is in poor condition, and is kept close in on their Infantry." Telegram received (on Sept. 16, 4:15 A.M.), DNA, RG 107, Telegrams Collected (Bound); copies, *ibid.*, Telegrams Received in Cipher; DLC-Philip H. Sheridan. *O.R.*, I, xliii, part 2, 89. At 9:30 P.M., Sheridan also telegraphed to Capt. George K. Leet. "Have you any information from your scouts from Culpepper or other points south? Please answer." Telegram received (on Sept. 16, 4:30 A.M.), DNA, RG 107, Telegrams Collected (Bound); (2) *ibid.*, Telegrams Collected (Unbound); copy, DLC-Philip H. Sheridan. *O.R.*, I, xliii, part 2, 89.

To Gustavus V. Fox

City Point Va. Sept 10th. 1864

HON. G. V. FOX
ASST. SEC. OF THE NAVY
DEAR SIR

Your letter of the 9th inst inclosing Copy of instructions to Admiral Farragut was recieved by last nights Mail.[1] I have no suggestions to make different from what those instructions contain. As soon as the land forces can be spared, and the Navy is ready to co.operate, I will send an expedition of sufficient force quietly down the coast not even allowing the command, with the exception of the commanding officer, to know where they are going. The details for landing a force can ~~best~~ be best arranged by Adml. F.—and the commander of the land forces. So soon as all is arranged I will acquaint you with what is done on my part.

Yours Truly
U. S. GRANT
Lt. Gen.

Copies, DLC-USG, V, 45, 69, 107; DNA, RG 108, Letters Sent. *O.R.*, I, xlii, part 2, 769; *O.R.* (Navy), I, x, 450.

On Sept. 1, 1864, 2:00 P.M., Maj. Gen. Henry W. Halleck telegraphed to USG. "Asst Secty Fox, Navy Dept, and Genl Gillmore, go down to see you about a project on Wilmington. It originates in the Navy not the War Dept. I think we have more irons now than we can keep from burning." ALS (telegram sent), DNA, RG 107, Telegrams Collected (Bound); telegram received, *ibid.*; *ibid.*, RG 108, Letters Received. *O.R.*, I, xlii, part 2, 624. At 9:00 P.M., Secretary of War Edwin M. Stanton telegraphed to USG. "The Navy Department appears very anxious that the Army should take Wilmington. At the instance of Captain Fox General Gilmore has been directed to accompany Mr Fox to see you on the subject. Whether any ~~thing~~ operation there be possible and if possible whether expedient to be undertaken now is left wholly to your judgment by the President and ~~with~~ entire satisfaction will be felt with your determination. Fox and Gilmore started for City Point today. I have ordered Bowers appointment ~~in the~~ as Assistant Adjutant General according to your request." ALS (telegram sent), DNA, RG 107, Telegrams Collected (Bound); telegram received (on Sept. 2), *ibid.*, RG 108, Letters Received. *O.R.*, I, xlii, part 2, 624. On the same day, Stanton wrote to USG. "By direction of the President Major General Gilmore has been directed to report to you in company with Assistant Secretary Fox for the purpose of giving you information in relation to Wilmington. When that purpose is accomplished you will direct him to report to the Adjutant General if you have no occasion for his services." ALS, DNA, RG 108, Letters Received.

On Sept. 3, noon, Asst. Secretary of the Navy Gustavus V. Fox telegraphed to USG. "Just returned   does the fall of Atlanta make any change in your views —especially as to the time October first." ALS (telegram sent), CSmH; telegram received, DNA, RG 108, Letters Received. Dated Sept. 2 in *O.R.*, I, xlii, part 2, 654; (dated Sept. 3) *O.R.* (Navy), I, x, 418. On Sept. 3, 6:30 P.M., USG telegraphed to Fox. "It is impossible at this time to say what effect Shermans victory may have on the time of undertaking the enterprise you speak of." ALS (telegram sent), CSmH; telegram received (on Sept. 3), DNA, RG 45, Miscellaneous Letters Received. Printed as received at 11:00 P.M. in *O.R.*, I, xlii, part 2, 674; *O.R.* (Navy), I, x, 418. On Sept. 6, Maj. Gen. Quincy A. Gillmore wrote to Halleck submitting a lengthy plan for closing Wilmington, N. C., to blockade runners, which Halleck endorsed to USG on Sept. 10. *O.R.*, I, xlii, part 2, 731–34.

On Sept. 14, Fox wrote to USG. "Enclosed are certain interrogatories propounded to A. R. Admiral Lee and his answers. The water seems to be scant for the iron-clads to enter, but the wooden ones can enter if the fire of the forts can be kept under. The Hatteras fort was reduced in August 1861 with the Minnesota frigate two miles distant; therefore, I think the Admiral is mistaken in saying that that class of vessels can render no assistance. The particular and last information we require is this: Will the army force and its Commander go to Port Royal? It is necessary to know this, as Farragut goes there to await orders. It seems to me it would be advisable to let them settle the details at that point together, as no other point is so fit in all respects as a rendesvous. In my letter of the 12th instant, I should have said that it was high water on the *15th of September* instead of the 30th." Copy, DNA, RG 45, Confidential Letters Sent. *O.R.* (Navy), I, x, 461. The enclosures are *ibid.*, pp. 419, 441–44.

On Sept. 17, Fox wrote to USG. "I forward herewith a memorandum of information furnished by a refugee from Wilmington, which may be of service to you. The chart to which it refers will be obtained and sent forward as soon as possible. The position A referred to is at the lower end of the sound, north of Federal Point." Copy, DNA, RG 45, Confidential Letters Sent.

On Sept. 19, 10:00 A.M., Fox telegraphed to USG. "Admiral Porter and my self will call up on you at noon tomorrow." ALS (telegram sent), *ibid.*, RG 107, Telegrams Collected (Unbound).

On Sept. 20, 7:00 P.M., USG telegraphed to Fox. "The letter of which you spoke reached here this evening—" Telegram received (at 8:40 P.M.), *ibid.*, RG 45, Miscellaneous Letters Received; copies, *ibid.*, RG 107, Telegrams Received in Cipher; *ibid.*, RG 108, Letters Sent; DLC-USG, V, 45, 69, 107.

On Sept. 24, Fox wrote to USG. "My note of the 17th inst., enclosing the memorandum addressed to Gov. Andrew, signed 'Ritchie,' calls for a chart, which belongs to said memorandum, and is herewith enclosed." Copy, DNA, RG 45, Confidential Letters Sent.

1. No such letter has been found, but on Sept. 7, Secretary of the Navy Gideon Welles wrote to USG. "Herewith are the orders addressed to Rear Admiral Farragut, which conform to the arrangements agreed upon during the visit of the Assistant Secretary to yourself on the 2d inst. Every exertion will be made by this Department to render the expedition successful; and any suggestions which you can offer relative to naval coöperation will be received and acted

upon." Copy, *ibid.*; DLC-Gideon Welles. Instructions of Sept. 5 from Welles to Rear Admiral David G. Farragut for an attack upon the defenses of Cape Fear River are in *O.R.* (Navy), I, x, 430–31.

To Maj. Gen. Henry W. Halleck

(Cipher)   City Point, Va, Sept. 10th/64

MAJ. GEN. HALLECK, WASHINGTON,

The following information is just received from a deserter who left Richmond on Monday[1] but come into our lines to-day. Please communicate it to the Navy Dept.

He says that Capt. Wood[2] of the Tallahassee had been on to Richmond. That on last Monday 200 sailors from the Receiving Ship lying near Drulry's Bluff were sent to Wilmington under the command of Lieut. Murdough[3] to man a new vessel of war that was soon to run out to see.

He adds a piece of Army news that all boys over 16 years of age and old men under 55 had been ordered into Richmond.

U. S. GRANT
Lt. Gn.

ALS (telegram sent), CSmH; telegram received (sent at 6:30 P.M., received at 10:30 P.M.), DNA, RG 107, Telegrams Collected (Bound). *O.R.*, I, xlii, part 2, 769.

1. Sept. 5, 1864.
2. The son of U.S. Army Surgeon Robert C. Wood and grandson of Zachary Taylor, John T. Wood, born in 1830, entered the U.S. Navy as midshipman in 1847, was dismissed as lt. in April, 1861, and entered the C.S. Navy at the same rank. Famous for midnight raids on enemy ships which led to his promotion to commander, Wood took the C.S.S. *Tallahassee* from Wilmington, N. C., in Aug., 1864, for a raid to Nova Scotia and back during which he captured thirty-three ships. *O.R.* (Navy), I, iii, 701–4. See Royce Gordon Shingleton, *John Taylor Wood: Sea Ghost of the Confederacy* (Athens, Ga., 1979), pp. 122–44.
3. William H. Murdaugh, who entered the U.S. Navy as midshipman in 1841, was dismissed with the rank of lt. in April, 1861, and reached the rank of 1st lt. in the C.S. Navy as of Jan. 6, 1864. Like Wood, Murdaugh gained a reputation for skill in planning daring naval operations.

To Maj. Gen. William T. Sherman

City Point Sept 10. 1864 10. a. m.

For GENL SHERMAN

As soon as your men are properly rested and preparations can be made it is desirable that another campaign should be commenced   We want to keep the enemy continually pressed to the end of the war   If we give him no peace whilst the war lasts the end cannot be distant   Now that we have all of Mobile bay that is valuable I do not know but it will be the best move to trace for Canbys troops to act upon Savannah whilst you move on Augusta I should like to hear from you however in this matter

U. S. GRANT
Lt. Genl.

Telegrams received (2—at 11:30 A.M.), DNA, RG 107, Telegrams Collected (Bound); copies (2), *ibid.*, Telegrams Received in Cipher; *ibid.*, RG 108, Letters Sent; *ibid.*, RG 393, Military Div. of the Miss., Telegrams Received in the Field; DLC-USG, V, 45, 69, 107. *O.R.*, I, xxxix, part 2, 355. On Sept. 10, 1864, 9:00 P.M., Maj. Gen. William T. Sherman telegraphed to USG. "I have your despatch of today. My command needs some rest and pay: Our roads are also broken back near Nashville and Wheeler is not yet desposed of; still, I am perfectly alive to the importance of pushing our advantages to the utmost. I do not think we can afford to operate further out on the Railroad, it takes so many men to guard, and even then is nightly broken by the enemys cavalry that swarms about us. Macon is distant 103 miles and Augusta 175 miles. If I could be sure of finding provisions and ammunition at Augusta or Columbus Georgia I can march to Milledgeville and compel Hood to give up Augusta or Macon and Could then turn on the other: The country will afford forage and many supplies but not enough in any one place to admit of a delay; in scattering for forage we lose a great many men picked up by the enemys cavalry   If you can manage to take the Savannah river as high as Augusta or the Chattahoochee as far up as Columbus I can sweep the whole state of Georgia: Otherwise I would risk our whole army by going too far from Atlanta"   Telegram received (on Sept. [11], 11:50 A.M.), DNA, RG 107, Telegrams Collected (Bound); *ibid.*, RG 108, Letters Received; copies, *ibid.*, RG 107, Telegrams Received in Cipher; (sent at 8:00 P.M.) *ibid.*, RG 393, Military Div. of the Miss., Telegrams Sent in the Field. Printed as sent at 8:00 P.M. in *O.R.*, I, xxxix, part 2, 355–56.

Also on Sept. 10, 6:30 P.M., USG telegraphed to Sherman. "Petersburg paper of the 9th contains a dispatch from Mobile of the 7th announcing arrival of Gens. Forrest & Taylor. It is to be hoped that the enemy have found it necessary to call in Forrest's forces." ALS (telegram sent), Stevens Collection, Washington University, St. Louis, Mo.; copies, DNA, RG 107, Telegrams Received in Cipher; *ibid.*, RG 108, Letters Sent; *ibid.*, RG 393, Military Div. of the Miss., Telegrams Received in the Field; DLC-USG, V, 45, 69, 107. *O.R.*, I, xxxix, part 2, 355. On Sept. 12, 1:00 P.M., Sherman telegraphed to USG. "I have Macon papers of the tenth and eleventh. Dick Taylor is in command of the department including Mobile. Forrest and his men have reached Mobile. All well here. The exodus of the people is progressing and matters coming into shape. I will have all official reports of the campaign in and off for Washington by the 15th I dont understand whether you propose to act against Savannah direct from Fort Pulaski or by way of Florida or from the direction of Mobile. If you can take Savannah by a sudden coup de main it would be valuable The enemy is evidently concentrating all his Miss. forces at Mobile & Hood is about Lovejoys Station watching me apprehensive of big raids" Telegram received (at 4:30 P.M.), DNA, RG 107, Telegrams Collected (Bound); *ibid.*, RG 108, Letters Received; copies, *ibid.*, RG 107, Telegrams Received in Cipher; *ibid.*, RG 393, Military Div. of the Miss., Telegrams Sent in the Field. *O.R.*, I, xxxix, part 2, 364.

To Edwin M. Stanton

From City Point Sept 11 *1864.*

HON E M STANTON

Capt N B McLaugher[1] fourth (4) U S Cavalry formerly Col first (1) Mass Vols but mustered out of the Volunteer Service by reason of Expiration of the term of Service of his Regiment has been appointed Colonel of the fifty seventh (57.) Mass By the Governor of his State   This Regiment numbering but six sixty nine (669) men aggregate he cannot be mustered in without Special authority   This Regiment is said to be in a wretched condition for want of a commander—Having no field Officers—I would respectfully recommend that authority be given to muster Capt Mc-Laughter in as its Colonel

U S GRANT
Lieut General

Telegram received (at 11:00 A.M.), DNA, RG 107, Telegrams Collected (Bound); *ibid.*, Telegrams Collected (Unbound); copies, *ibid.*, RG 94, Vol. Service Div., 2017 (VS) 1864; *ibid.*, RG 108, Letters Sent; DLC-USG, V, 45, 69, 107. On Sept. 12, 1864, 9:30 A.M., Maj. Thomas M. Vincent, AGO, telegraphed to USG. "Authority has been granted for the muster of Colonel N. B. McLaughlin as requested." ALS (telegram sent), DNA, RG 107, Telegrams Collected (Unbound); telegram received, *ibid.*

1. Napoleon B. McLaughlen, born in Vt. in 1823, served as private, corporal, and sgt. in the 2nd Dragoons (1850–59), then was commissioned 2nd lt.,

1st Cav., as of March 27, 1861, and capt., 4th Cav., as of July 17, 1862. He served as col., 1st Mass., Oct. 1, 1862, to May, 1864, winning two bvt. promotions, and as col., 57th Mass., as of Sept. 17, 1864.

To Edwin M. Stanton

City Point—12 M
Sept 11, 1864—

Hon E. M. Stanton
Sec War

I hope it is not the intention to postpone the draft to allow time to fill up with recruiting   the men we have been getting in that way are nearly all deserters and out of five reported north as having enlisted we do not get more than one effective soldier

U. S. Grant
Lt. Genl.

Telegram received (at 1:00 P.M.), DNA, RG 107, Telegrams Collected (Bound); copies, *ibid.*, Telegrams Received in Cipher; (2—dated Sept. 10 and 11, 1864) *ibid.*, RG 108, Letters Sent; DLC-USG, V, 45, 69, 107. Dated Sept. 10 in *O.R.*, III, iv, 706. On Sept. 11, 7:55 P.M., Secretary of War Edwin M. Stanton telegraphed to USG. "It is not designed by this Department to delay the [d]raft a single day after the credits are made up, and quota ascertained. and The Provost Marshal General has been directed to lose no time in that work. It is represented that the first recruits were a hard lot, but that recently the volunteers are equal to any that have taken the field during the war. The local authorities have been slack in paying their bounties and this has occasioned some delay. I would like to be glad if you would send me a telegram for publication showing urging the advantage necessity of immediately filling up the army by draft. The most difficulty is likely to be in Ohio, Indiana, and Illinois, from the desire of candidates to retain their men until after the election. We have not got a single regiment from Indiana. Morton came here specially to have the draft postponed, but was peremptorily refused. But the personal interest to retain men until after the election requires every effort to procure men troops in that state even by draft. Illinois is much the same way. Not a regiment or even company there has been sent organized. A special call from you would aid the Department in overcoming the local inertia and pe personal interests that favor delay." ALS (telegram sent), DNA, RG 107, Telegrams Collected (Bound); telegram received, *ibid.*, Telegrams Collected (Unbound); *ibid.*, RG 108, Letters Received. *O.R.*, I, xlii, part 2, 783–84; *ibid.*, III, iv, 709–10.

On Sept. 10, 12:30 P.M., Maj. Gen. Henry W. Halleck telegraphed to USG. "Had not the new Infantry regiments now coming in better be sent to city Point? The facilities for desertion here and with Genl Sheridan are so great that we shall soon lose large numbers. Moreover, we have difficulty in getting officers enough to drill the new artillery regiments. Infantry regiments will not improve here without experienced officers to look after them." ALS (telegram sent), DNA, RG 107, Telegrams Collected (Bound); telegram received, *ibid.*; *ibid.*, RG 108, Letters Received. *O.R.*, I, xlii, part 2, 768. At 6:30 P.M., USG telegraphed to Halleck. "I would like very much to have all the new regiments sent here. They can be made good use of and will improve more rapidly here than they possibly could about the cities." ALS (telegram sent), CSmH; telegram received (at 10:20 P.M.), DNA, RG 107, Telegrams Collected (Bound). *O.R.*, I, xlii, part 2, 768.

On Sept. 8, 2:50 P.M. (sent at 3:57 P.M.), Stanton had telegraphed to USG. "The recruiting returns show an average of about five thousand '5000' ~~per d~~ mustered in per day for the last week." ALS (telegram sent), DNA, RG 107, Telegrams Collected (Bound); telegram received (dated Sept. 9), *ibid.*, Telegrams Collected (Unbound); *ibid.*, RG 108, Letters Received. Dated Sept. 9 in *O.R.*, I, xlii, part 2, 756; (dated Sept. 8) *ibid.*, III, iv, 699.

On Sept. 10, 11:00 P.M., Stanton telegraphed to USG. "The new loan advertised for has proved quite a success. Over Seventy Millions more than twice the Sum asked for have been offered at a premium of four per cent and upwards." ALS (telegram sent), DNA, RG 107, Telegrams Collected (Bound); telegram received, *ibid.*, Telegrams Collected (Unbound); *ibid.*, RG 108, Letters Received. *O.R.*, III, iv, 707.

On Sept. 14, Lt. Col. William L. Duff wrote to Brig. Gen. Marsena R. Patrick. "Please give the necessary directions to your Assistants, to hereafter send all new troops arriving at this point to Bermuda Hundred with instructions to report to Maj. Gen. Butler for orders." Copies, DLC-USG, V, 45, 69, 107; DNA, RG 108, Letters Sent. *O.R.*, I, xlii, part 2, 817.

To Maj. Gen. Henry W. Halleck

(Cipher) City Point Va. Sept. 11th/64 [*10:30* A.M.]
MAJ. GN. HALLECK, WASHINGTON.

If a good competant Inspecting officer can be sent to the Dept. of the Ark. at this time I think it would have a good effect. I understand there are many irregularities between Helena & Little Rock that want correction. Special attention should be called to the manner of guarding and protecting stores on the route between the Miss. & Little Rock.

U. S. GRANT
Lt. Gn.

ALS (telegram sent), CSmH; telegram received (at 1:00 P.M.), DNA, RG 107, Telegrams Collected (Bound). *O.R.*, I, xli, part 3, 148.

On Sept. 21, 1864, 5:30 P.M., USG telegraphed to Maj. Gen. Henry W. Halleck. "Has an Inspector been sent to the Dept. of Ark. to examin[e] into affairs there? If not I will send an officer from here." ALS (telegram sent), CSmH; telegram received (at 7:00 P.M.), DNA, RG 107, Telegrams Collected (Bound). *O.R.*, I, xli, part 3, 281. On Sept. 22, 1:45 P.M., Halleck telegraphed to USG. "Inspectors have been sent to Arkansas and partial reports recieved. If you can spare another competent officer I would advise his being sent also. There seems to have been great rascalities committed under Genl Blunt on the Arkansas & in the Indian country." ALS (telegram sent), DNA, RG 107, Telegrams Collected (Bound); telegram received (marked as sent at 12:35 P.M.), *ibid.*; *ibid.*, Telegrams Collected (Unbound); *ibid.*, RG 108, Letters Received. Printed as sent at 1:45 P.M. in *O.R.*, I, xli, part 3, 296. On the same day, USG telegraphed to Maj. Gen. George G. Meade. "Have you any objection to sparing Col Schriver to go west on a tour of inspection? I want to send an officer to Arkansas & will send him if he can be dispensed with here—It will take probably a month make the tour & unless you are perfectly willing for Col S, I will select some one else." Telegram received (at 10:15 P.M.), DNA, RG 94, War Records Office, Army of the Potomac; copies, *ibid.*, RG 108, Letters Sent; DLC-USG, V, 45, 69, 107; (2) Meade Papers, PHi. At 10:20 P.M., Meade telegraphed to USG. "Col Schriver is at present quite busy, endeavoring to get back into the ranks, men on extra duty—At the same time if it is of importance, he can be spared for the duty you propose" ALS (telegram sent), DNA, RG 94, War Records Office, Army of the Potomac; telegram received, *ibid.*, RG 108, Letters Received. On the same day, USG telegraphed to Meade. "I regard the duty which Col Schriver is now performing of so much importance that unless you have others who can do it as well I will send another officer on Inspection duty" Telegram received (at 11:00 P.M.), *ibid.*, RG 94, War Records Office, Army of the Potomac; copies, *ibid.*, RG 108, Letters Sent; DLC-USG, V, 45, 69, 107; (2) Meade Papers, PHi. At 11:30 P.M., Meade telegraphed to USG. "The duty now being performed by Col Schriver would in his absence be performed by the Senior Corps Inspector—I dont know who this is, but I am quite sure, it will be more efficiently & actively discharged by Col S. than any one else.—" ALS (telegram sent), DNA, RG 94, War Records Office, Army of the Potomac; copies, *ibid.*, RG 393, Army of the Potomac, Letters Sent; Meade Papers, PHi. On the same day, USG telegraphed to Meade. "I will detail some officer for Inspection duty" Telegram received (at 11:40 P.M.), DNA, RG 94, War Records Office, Army of the Potomac; copies, *ibid.*, RG 108, Letters Sent; DLC-USG, V, 45, 69, 107.

On Sept. 24, 8:30 P.M., Halleck telegraphed to USG. "If you have detailed an officer to inspect in Arkansas, and he has not gone, please send him here to take with him certain documents recieved since Col. Sacket left for same purpose." ALS (telegram sent), DNA, RG 107, Telegrams Collected (Bound); telegram received, *ibid.*; (2) *ibid.*, Telegrams Collected (Unbound); *ibid.*, RG 108, Letters Received. *O.R.*, I, xli, part 3, 337. On Sept. 25, USG telegraphed to Halleck. "Can you not detail Gen Seymour to inspect in Arkansas. If not, I will detail Lt Col Babcock and se[nd] him." Telegram received, DNA, RG 94, War Records Office, Miscellaneous War Records; (at 2:45 P.M.) *ibid.*, RG 107, Telegrams Collected (Bound); copies, *ibid.*, RG 108, Letters Sent; DLC-USG, V, 45, 69, 107. *O.R.*, I, xli, part 3, 354. On Sept. 26, 11:15 A.M., Halleck telegraphed to USG. "Genl Seymour is a man of too many prejudices for the delicate task of inspecting West of the Miss. He would make up his opinion without proper examination. Franklin & Baldy Smith are better suited. Col Marcy has made a partial report. Col Sackett is now inspecting. Genl Canby has also been directed to send an Inspector. If you think another should be sent, & cannot spare Col Babcock, I would recommend Smith." ALS (telegram sent), DNA, RG 107, Telegrams Collected (Bound); telegram received, *ibid.*; *ibid.*, RG 108, Letters Received. *O.R.*, I, xli, part 3, 373.

On Oct. 3, Halleck wrote to USG. "In a private letter to me Genl Canby urges the importance of an officer of rank, ability & tact, being sent by you or the Secty of War to examine into all matters of his military Division. In order, he says, to have this inspection or examination produce the proper effect, and the reports made have the proper weight, the officer sent should be entirely in dependant of him and act only up on instructions from higher authority. I presume, from information from other sources, that he alludes mainly to alleged peculations in cotton and illicit trade with the enemy, said to have been countenanced or connived at by officers of high rank. As such an investigation would probably include officers of the Treasury Dept, and perhaps also of the Navy Dept, it is suggested that the appointment of the commissioner should be made and the instructions given by the President himself. Before taking any further action in the matter, it is necessary to determine upon some one to recommend for the duty. The only competent Genl officer that I now think of off duty is W. F. (Baldy) Smith; but I do not know his fitness for so delicate & important a task. The Secty of war has directed me to ask your opinion; or perhaps you can suggest a more suitable person." ALS, DNA, RG 108, Letters Received.

On Sept. 23, Lt. Col. Orville E. Babcock had written to Brig. Gen. Richard Delafield, chief engineer. "Lt. Gen'l Commd'g directs me to inform you that Maj. Gen. W. F. Smith and Lt. Col. N. Bowen are available if you still need Engineer Officers to sent to the Lakes. Col Bowen left yesterday to join Gen Smith." Copies, DLC-USG, V, 45, 69, 107; DNA, RG 108, Letters Sent.

To Maj. Gen. Henry W. Halleck

(Cipher)   City Point Va. Sept. 11th 1864 [*3:00* P.M.]
MAJ. GEN. HALLECK, WASHINGTON

Please order Brig. Gn. Meagher to report to Gn. Sherman for duty reporting by telegraph from Nashville. Orders will reach Gen. Meagher at 129th 5 5th Av. New York.

U. S. GRANT
Lt. Gn.

ALS (telegram sent), CSmH; telegram received (on Sept. 12, 1864, 11:00 A.M.), DNA, RG 94, Letters Received, 951A 1864; *ibid.*, RG 107, Telegrams Collected (Bound). Thomas F. Meagher, born in Waterford, Ireland, in 1823, banished to Tasmania in 1849 as punishment for his work for Irish independence, escaped to the U.S. in 1852 and became well-known as an Irish leader. Organizer and commander of the Irish Brigade, he was appointed brig. gen. as of Feb. 3, 1862. He resigned as of May 14, 1863, in protest against the refusal of the War Dept. to relieve his battered brigade, but the resignation was canceled as of Dec. 23, and Meagher began to push for a command. W. F. Lyons, *Brigadier-General Thomas Francis Meagher* (London, [1869]), pp. 95–97; Robert G. Athearn, *Thomas Francis Meagher: An Irish Revolutionary in America* (Boulder, Colo., 1949), pp. 125–33. See *O.R.*, I, xxxix, part 2, 371; *ibid.*, I, xxxix, part 3, 640–41, 742.

To Julia Dent Grant

City Point, Va. Sept. 11th *1864.*

DEAR JULIA,

I was delighted to receive a letter from you this evening saying that you had a house and to find you writing in so much better [—]. Before I wrote my last letter and before receiving your [gossipping] letters I had written that you wanted Jennie to come and stay with you. I have also written to your father inviting him to make his home with us. I am not particular which house you take. So that you are comfortable and contented I will be satisfied. If you want Hellen[1] to take the house you were going in you take the other. If it is necessary for you to furnish one or two rooms it will make no difference. If you get good furnature it will always come handy for us.—I have written to your father to send Little Rebel in to Mr. Ford to leave him there until I give further directions. I would not have him lost for a great deel. If you get a place to keep him I will have him sent on to you. In the Winter the children could drive him in a sleigh. I will also send you Egypt if you want him. I wrote to your father to let Lewis Dent have Hypodrome if he would accept him; if not to send him to the city and let him be sold for what he would fetch.

It is singular you get no more letters from me. I have written regularly every other day.—Love and Kisses for you and the children.

ULYS.

ALS, DLC-USG.

1. Wife of Lt. Col. Frederick T. Dent.

To Maj. Gen. Henry W. Halleck

(Cipher)   City Point Va. Sept. 12th *1864.*
Maj. Gen. Halleck, Washington,

Gen. Rosecrans telegram of the 11th to the Sec. of War in relation to placing A. J. Smith at Cape Girardeau under his Rosecrans orders is just received.[1] I think it probable Cape Girardeau is the place where Smith should be to watch the movements of Price and to prepare himself for land travel. But in moving into the interior he should go as light as possible purchasing supplies from the loyal and taking from the disloyal. Going to that point he necessarily will be under Gen. Rosecrans orders. You may so instruct him. If Smith is acting now under information which I have not got he need not change his course. If matters have not changed however since his last dispatch direct him to go to Cape Girardeau and report to Gn. Rosecrans. Direct Gen. Rosecrans at the same time that this force is put at his disposal to expell Prices forces from Mo. & Ark. and to cooperate with other troops sent from Memphis for the same purpose.

U. S. Grant
Lt. Gn

ALS (telegram sent), CSmH; telegram received (at 6:10 p.m.), DNA, RG 107, Telegrams Collected (Bound). *O.R.,* I, xli, part 3, 164. On Sept. 13, 1864, 11:30 a.m., Maj. Gen. Henry W. Halleck telegraphed to USG. "In accordance with your previous instructions to me, I directed Genl A. J. Smith to take charge of the expedition against Price, & co., and to select his own line of operations, after consulting with Genl Rosecrans & others. I so informed Genl Rosecrans & directed him to assist Smith all he could. Smith, answered that he would wait for further news of Price before deciding, but thought it probable that he would move by St Louis and Rolla. Is it now your wish that these orders be countermanded, & that Smith report for orders to Genl Rosecrans? Before acting on your telegram of yesterday I wish you to understand precisely what orders have already been given." ALS (telegram sent), DNA, RG 107, Telegrams Collected (Bound); telegram received, *ibid.; ibid.,* Telegrams Collected (Unbound); *ibid.,* RG 108, Letters Received. *O.R.,* I, xli, part 3, 170. At 3:00 p.m., USG telegraphed to Halleck. "My instructions of yesterday to General Smith were in answer to a despatch of Genl Rosecrans to the Secretary of war which was referred to me—With the instructions I had already given Genl Smith I would prefer that they should remain unaltered" Telegram received (at 5:15 p.m.), DNA, RG 107, Telegrams Collected (Bound); copies, *ibid.,* Telegrams Received in Cipher; *ibid.*, RG 108, Letters Sent; DLC-USG, V, 45, 69, 107. *O.R.*, I, xli, part 3, 170.

1. Printed *ibid.*, pp. 154–55. On Sept. 12, 11:20 A.M., Secretary of War Edwin M. Stanton telegraphed to USG. "The following telegram has been received from General Rosecrans. You will please answer it and give to General Rosecrans such instructions as you think the military exigency requires" ALS (telegram sent), DNA, RG 107, Telegrams Collected (Bound); telegram received (marked as sent at 10:45 A.M.), *ibid.*, RG 108, Letters Received. *O.R.*, I, xli, part 3, 164.

To Maj. Gen. Henry W. Halleck

Cipher   City Point Va. Sept. 12th/64 [*3:30* P.M.]
MAJ. GEN. HALLECK, WASHINGTON,

The branch rail-road runing out to the Welden road is now finished and all supplies for the Army are now moved in that way.[1] Every thing is now perfectly quiet except the usual picket firing.[2] The enemy seen to be mining in front of the 10th Corps but it causes no uneasiness.[3] On Friday morning Gen. Hancock moved a portion of his picket line forward and in doing so captured 85 of the enemy's pickets.[4]

U. S. GRANT
Lt. Gn.

ALS (telegram sent), CSmH; telegram received (at 6:45 P.M.), DNA, RG 107, Telegrams Collected (Bound). *O.R.*, I, xlii, part 2, 795.

1. On Sept. 12, 1864, noon, Maj. Gen. George G. Meade telegraphed to USG. "Maj. Genls. Warren, Parke & Hancock, report all quiet on their lines during the past 24 hours. Gen'l. Birney reports the enemy working steadily on a flying sap either a covered way for their pickets or probably to gain the crest of a hill which our pickets occupy with a view of driving them away—Genl. B has begun this morning a counter mine at the Hare house, where the enemy are supposed to be mining   Genl. Birney also reports the enemy throwing up a work on their second line just in rear of the old crater, and that a new battery has been established at the foot of Cemetery Hill from which they opened at 8. a m this morning.—This last is for the purpose of firing at the trains on the Rail Road, which owing to Mr. Wentz supdt. of construction, having failed to communicate with the Chief Engineer at these Hd. Qrs, has been improperly located & is exposed for some distance to the view of the enemy, who has established batteries from which he fires at all passing trains—No damage has yet been done but much annoyance to passers by & the camps in the vicinity." ALS (telegram sent), DNA, RG 94, War Records Office, Army of the Potomac; telegram received, *ibid.*, RG 108, Letters Received. *O.R.*, I, xlii, part 2, 795–96. On the same day,

USG telegraphed to Meade. "I will direct Maj. Wentz to commence relaying the rail-road so as to take it round out of sight of the enemy." ALS (telegram sent), Kohns Collection, NN; telegram received, DNA, RG 94, War Records Office, Army of the Potomac. *O.R.*, I, xlii, part 2, 796.

2. On Sept. 12, 11:40 P.M., Maj. Gen. Benjamin F. Butler telegraphed to USG. "I have rec'd the following despatch from Deep Bottom—'Rebels say on their line that they attacked us at Reams Station last night and were badly whipped—' Have you any information of it? Please answer" Telegram received, DNA, RG 107, Telegrams Collected (Unbound). *O.R.*, I, xlii, part 2, 801. On the same day, Lt. Col. Cyrus B. Comstock telegraphed to Butler. "The Lt Genl Comd'g desires me to say that we have no troops at Reams Station. Reports from Corps Commanders this morning are that all is quiet." Telegram received, DNA, RG 94, War Records Office, Dept. of Va. and N. C., Army of the James, Unentered Papers. *O.R.*, I, xlii, part 2, 802.

3. On Sept. 11, 12:30 [P.M.], Meade telegraphed to USG. "I have nothing of importance to report this morning.—Genl. Birney telegraphs that a deserter reports the enemy mining on his left, our right—and that troops are being moved in rear of the Crater—Genl. Hancock reports, that thro a misconception of his orders by the Comd. officer of the Pickets, the enemy, was enabled last night to recapture a small portion of the line taken from him the night previous—Genls. Parke & Warren report all quiet on their lines." ALS (telegram sent), DNA, RG 94, War Records Office, Army of the Potomac; telegram received, *ibid.*, RG 108, Letters Received. *O.R.*, I, xlii, part 2, 784. On the same day, USG telegraphed to Meade. "Has Gen. Birney taken any steps to countermine against the enemy and or to construct works in rear of where their mine is likely to terminate?" ALS (telegram sent), Kohns Collection, NN; telegram received (at 10.00 P.M.), DNA, RG 94, War Records Office, Army of the Potomac. *O.R.*, I, xlii, part 2, 784. At 10:30 P.M., Meade telegraphed to USG. "I send you a despatch from Birney received on referring yours of 10. P. M to him.—We occupy now a second line the whole length of our line, so that no mine exploded can be of much consequence—There have been so many reports of mining by the enemy since our mine of July 30th that I have ceased to pay much attention to them unless they are accompanied by some very specific details—I will see that all the usual precautions are taken at the point on Birneys front last indicated—" ALS (telegram sent), DNA, RG 94, War Records Office, Army of the Potomac; telegram received, *ibid.*, RG 108, Letters Received. *O.R.*, I, xlii, part 2, 785. The enclosure is *ibid.*, pp. 791–92.

4. On Sept. 11, Lt. Col. Horace Porter telegraphed to Meade. "The Gen. Comdg. wishes to know whether you have received a report of the number of prisoners taken by Gen. Hancock yesterday morning" ALS (telegram sent), DNA, RG 107, Telegrams Collected (Unbound); copies (2—one entered as sent by USG), Meade Papers, PHi. Printed as received at 1:00 P.M. in *O.R.*, I, xlii, part 2, 784. At 1:05 P.M., Meade telegraphed to Porter. "The Prov. Mar. Genl. reports receiving 85 prisoners of war from 2d. corps—These were taken on the night of the 9th & morning of the 10th when Genl. Hancock advanced his picket line—I find in my despatch of this a m to the Lt. Genl. Comd. I inadvertently committed an error—It was on the morning of the 10th & not last night, that the enemy retook a portion of the captured line the operation being effected soon after Hancok's advance, indeed being almost a part of it.—" ALS (telegram sent), DNA, RG 94, War Records Office, Army of the Potomac; telegram received, *ibid.*, RG 108, Letters Received. *O.R.*, I, xlii, part 2, 784.

To Maj. Gen. William T. Sherman

City Point Va. Sept. 12th *1864*.

MAJ. GEN. W. T. SHERMAN,
COMD.G MIL. DIV. OF THE MISS.,
GENERAL.

I send Lt. Col. Porter of my Staff with this. Col. P. will explain to you the exact condition of affairs here better than I can do in the limits of a letter.—Although I feel myself strong enough now for offensive operations I am holding on quietly to get advantage of recruits and convalescents who are coming forward very rapidly. My lines are necessarily very long, extending from Deep Bottom, North of the James, across the peninsular formed by the Appomattox and the James, and South of the Appomattox to the Welden road. This line is very strongly fortified and can be held with comparitively few men. But from its great length necessarily takes many in the aggregate. I propos[e] when I do move to extend my left so as to controll what is known as the South side, or Lynchburg & Petersburg, road; then if possible to keep the Danville road cut. At the same time this move is made I want to send a force of from six to ten thousand men against Wilmington. The way I propose to do this is to land the men North of Fort Fisher and hold that point. At the same time a large Naval Fleet will be assembled there and the Iron Clads will run the batteries as they did at Mobile. This will give us the same controll of the harbor of Wilmington that we now have of the harbor of Mobile. What you are to do with the forces at your command I do not exactly see. The difficulties of supplying your army, except when they are constantly moving, beyond where you are I plainly see. If it had not been for Price's movements Canby could have sent 12.000 more men to ~~Ala~~ Mobile. From your command on the Miss. an equal number could have been taken. With these forces my idea would have been to divide them sending one half to Mobile, the other half to Savanna. You could then move, as proposed in your telegram, so as to threaten Macon & Augusta equally. Which ever one abandoned by the enemy you could take and open up a new base of supplies.—My object now in sending a Staff officer to you is not so much to suggest operations for you as to get your views and have plans matured by the time everything can be got ready. It will probably be the 5th of October before any of the plans here indicated will be executed.

If you have any promotions to recommend send the names forward and I will approve them.

In conclution it is hardly necessary for me to say that I feel you have accomplished the most gigantic undertak[ing] given to any General in this War and with a skill and ability that will be acknowledged in history as unsurpassed if not unequalled. It gives me as much pleasure to record this in your favor as it would in favor of any living man myself included.

Truly yours
U. S. GRANT
Lt. Gn.

ALS, DLC-William T. Sherman. *O.R.*, I, xxxix, part 2, 364–65. On Sept. 12, 1864, 2:30 P.M., USG telegraphed to Maj. Gen. William T. Sherman. "A Staff officer leaves here to-morrow with a communication for you." ALS (telegram sent), CSmH; telegram received (at 5:40 P.M.), DNA, RG 107, Telegrams Collected (Bound).

On Sept. 19, 2:00 P.M., and Sept. 20, 1:00 P.M., Sherman telegraphed to USG. "Your messenger has not yet arrived—Things remain 'statu quo.' Most of the inhabitants are gone and I am exchanging about 2000 prisoners with Hood as a special exchange with the understanding that I get an equal number of my own men back whom I can put right away to duty—He raised the question of humanity but I am not to be moved by such tricks of the enemy—I have taken high ground with Hood on purpose—A deserter just in says Stewarts corps is moving back to Macon with a view of going to Va I have ordered one of my female scouts from New Orleans to Augusta and will send some out from here and give you prompt notice of any of Hoods army going East—I can quickly force him out of Lovejoy but think him better there where I can watch him than further off—I await the arrival of your messenger with impatience. All well but large numbers of our men and officers are being discharged—time out—and we must have recruits" "Col Porter has just come and I have read your letter with much interest I will send East tonight my official reports and will write fully by Col Porter In the mean time all is well and I can watch your movements with interest—I hear that Sheridan is now fighting" Telegrams received (the first on Sept. 19 at 7:30 P.M., the second on Sept. 20, 8:00 P.M.), *ibid.*; *ibid.*, Telegrams Collected (Unbound); *ibid.*, RG 108, Letters Received; copies, *ibid.*, RG 107, Telegrams Received in Cipher; (2) *ibid.*, RG 393, Military Div. of the Miss., Telegrams Sent in the Field. *O.R.*, I, xxxix, part 2, 404, 411. On Sept. 20, Sherman wrote to USG. "I have the honor to acknowledge at the hands of Lt

Col Porter of your staff, your letter of September 12, and accept with thanks the honorable and kindly mention of the services of this Army in the Great Cause in which we are all engaged. I send by Colonel Porter all official Reports which are completed and will in a few days submit a list of names which I deem worthy of promotion. I think we owe it to the President to save him the invidious task of election among a vast number of worthy aspirants, and have ordered my Army commanders to prepare their lists with great care, and to express their preferences based upon claims of actual capacity and service rendered. These I will consolidate and submit in such a form that if mistakes are committed they will at least be sanctioned by the best contemporaneous evidence of merit, for I know that vacancies do not exist equal in number to that of the officers that really deserve promotion. As to the Future, I am pleased to know your Army is being steadily reinforced by a good class of men, and I hope it will go on till you have a force numerically double that of your Antagonist, so that with one part you can watch him and with the other you can push out boldly from your Left Flank, occupy the south shore Rail road, compel him to attack you in position, or accept Battle on your own terms. We ought to ask our Country for the largest possible Armies that can be raised, as so important a thing as the 'Self Existence of a Great Nation' should not be left to the fickle chances of War. Now that Mobile is shut out to the commerce of Our Enemy it calls for no further effort on our part unless the capture of the City can be followed up by the occupation of the whole Alabama River, and the Rail road across to Columbus Georgia, when that place would at once become a magnificent auxiliary to my further progress into Georgia, but until General Canby is much reinforced, and until he can more thoroughly subdue the scattered Armies west of the Mississipi I suppose that much cannot be attempted as against the Alabama River, and Columbus Georgia. The utter destruction of Wilmington North Carolina is of importance only in connection with the necessity of cutting off all Foreign Trade to our Enemy, and if Farrigut can get across the Bar and the move can be made quick, I suppose it will succeed. From my knowledge of the mouth of Cape Fear I anticipate more difficulty in getting the heavy ships across the Bar, than in reaching the Town of Wilmington but of course the soundings of the channel are well known at Washington as well as the draft of his iron clads, so that it must be demonstrated as feasible or else it would not be attempted. If successful I suppose Fort Caswell will be occupied and the Fleet at once sent to the Savannah River. Then the reduction of the City is the only question. It once in our possession, and the River open to us I would not hesitate to cross the State of Georgia with 60000 men, hauling some stores and depending on the Country for the balance. Where a million of People live *my* Army wont starve, but as you know in a Country like Georgia, with few Roads, and innumerable streams, an inferior force could so delay an army and harrass it, that it would not be a formidable object, but if the Enemy knew that we had our boats on the Savannah I could rapidly move to Milledgeville where there is abundance of Corn & Meat, and would so threaten Macon & Augusta that he would give up Macon for Augusta: then I would move to interpose between Augusta and Savannah, and force him to give me Augusta with the only powder mills & factories remaining in the South, or let us have the Savannah River. Either horn of the dilemma would be worth a Battle. I would prefer his holding Augusta as the probabilities are, for then with the Savannah River in Our possession the taking of Augusta would be a mere matter of Time. This Campaign could be made in Winter. But the more I study the Game the more am I convinced that it would be wrong for me to penetrate much further into Georgia without an objective beyond. It would not be productive of much good. I can start east & make a circuit south and back, doing vast damage to the State but resulting in no permant good, but by mere threatening to do so, I hold a rod over the Georgians, who are not over loyal to the South. I will therefore give my opinion that your Army and Canby's should be reinforced to the maximum, that after you get Wilmington, you strike for Savannah & the River,—that Canby be instructed to hold the Mississipi River, and send a force to get Columbus Georgia either by the way of the Alabama or the Apilachicola, and that I keep Hood employed & put my Army in fine order for a march on Augusta, Columbia and Charleston, to be ready as soon as Wilmington is sealed as to Commerce, and the City of Savannah is in our possession. I think it will be found that the movemts of Price & Shelby west of the Mississipi are mere diversions. They cannot hope to enter Missouri save as raiders, and the Truth is Rosecrans should be ashamed to take my troops for such a purpose   If you will secure Wilmington and the City of Savannah from your Center, and let Canby have the Mississippi River and west of it, I will send a force to the Alabama & Apilachicola provided you give me 100000 of the Drafted men to fill up my old Regimts, and if you will fix a day to be in Savannah I will ensure our possession of Macon, and a point on the River below Augusta. The Possession of the Savannah River is more than fatal to the possibility of a Southern Independence. They may stand the Fall of Richmond, but not of All Georgia. I will have a long talk with Col Porter and tell him every thing that may occur to me of interest to you. In the mean time know that I admire your dogged perseverance & pluck more than ever. If you can whip Lee, and I can march to the Atlantic I think Uncle Abe will give us a 20 days leave of absence to see the young folks." ALS, DNA, RG 108, Letters Received. *O.R.*, I, xxxix, part 2, 411–13. On Sept. 21, noon, Sherman telegraphed to USG. "Lieut. Col. Porter will start back in the morning— Will bring you full answer to your letter and also all my official reports of the past. I prefer that Gen. Canby and a [p]art of Farraguts fleet should continue to threaten Mobile City but not attempt its Capture—that a small force with Gunboats ascend the Appalachacola to the Arsenal and up to Columbus if possible— that you take the City of Savannah by a Coup-de Main at the same time or soon after your active movements about Petersburg and the mouth of Cape Fear River—Savannah in our possession and boats at liberty to work up the Savannah I am willing to [s]tart for aAugusta in the manner I propose in my letter of last night which Col. Porter will bring—I beg you to give my personal congratulations to Genl. Sheridan and my earnest hope that he will push Early back on Lynchburg. We cant do much up the Tennessee and Virginia Valley. It is too long—Genl. Burbridge will attempt the capture and destruction of the Salt works about Abingdon from Kentucky and Knoxville—Gen. Schofield has gone to Knoxville to make the necessary arrangements—All well"   Telegram received, DNA, RG 107, Telegrams Collected (Bound); *ibid.*, Telegrams Collected (Unbound); *ibid.*, RG 108, Letters Received; copies, *ibid.*, RG 107, Telegrams Received in Cipher; *ibid.*, RG 393, Military Div. of the Miss., Telegrams Sent in the Field. *O.R.*, I, xxxix, part 2, 432.

To Maj. Samuel S. Seward

City Point Va. Sept. 12th/64

MAJ. SEWARD, 18TH CORPS HD QRS,

Have you got a copy of the portion of Pollard's[1] 3d Volume of the history of the rebellion published in the South. It is entitled If my memory serves me right "The rival Administration. I would like very much to get it if you have it.

U. S. GRANT
Lt. Gn.

ALS (telegram sent), California File, CSmH; copy, DLC-USG, V, 69. On Sept. 12, 1864, Maj. Samuel S. Seward, nephew of Secretary of State William H. Seward and staff officer of Maj. Gen. Edward O. C. Ord, telegraphed to USG. "Gen Gibbon forwarded a copy of 'The Rival Administrations' of Col. Duff yesterday when he comes in he will undoubtedly send it to you." ALS (telegram sent), DNA, RG 107, Telegrams Collected (Unbound).

1. See telegram to Maj. Gen. Benjamin F. Butler, Dec. 2, 1864.

To Edwin M. Stanton

(Cipher)   City Point Va. Sept. 13th *1864*. [*10:30* A.M.]

HON. E. M. STANTON, SEC. OF WAR WASHINGTON,

My dispatch to you on the subject of enforcing the draft was ~~written~~ suggested by reading Sec. Seward's Auburn speach where he intimates that Volunteers were coming in so rapidly that ~~it wou~~ there would be no necessity for a draft,[1] and your dispatch stating that Volunteers were coming in at the rate of 5000 per day. We ought to have the whole number of men called for by the President in the shortest possible time.[2] A draft is soon over and ceases to hurt after it is made. The agony of suspense is worse upon the public than the measure itself.

Prompt action in filling our Armies will have more effect upon the enemy than a victory over them   They profess to believe, and make their men believe, there is such a party North in favor of recognizing southern independence that the draft can not be enforced. ~~Undeceive them and you gain a great triumph~~ Let them be undeceived. Deserters come into our lines daily who tell us that the men are nearly universally tired of the War and that desertions would be much more frequent but they believe peace will be negotiated after the fall elections. The enforcement of the draft and prompt filling ~~of~~ up of our Armies will save the shedding of bloods to an immence degree.

U. S. Grant
Lt. Gn.

ALS (telegram sent), CSmH; telegram received (at 12:30 p.m.), DNA, RG 107, Telegrams Collected (Bound). *O.R.*, I, xlii, part 2, 804; *ibid.*, III, iv, 712–13. On Sept. 13, 1864, 2:10 p.m., Secretary of War Edwin M. Stanton telegraphed to USG. "Mr. Sewards declaration that there would be no draft was unauthorised and most unhappy, for it has already ~~diminished~~ reduced recruiting down to about fifteen hundred per day, and will produce disappointment [a]nd discontent. The draft has been ordered to commence in [e]very state on Monday until the whole number is obtained. No suspension or [d]elay will be permitted." ALS (telegram sent), DNA, RG 107, Telegrams Collected (Bound); telegram received, *ibid.*, Telegrams Collected (Unbound); *ibid.*, RG 108, Letters Received. *O.R.*, III, iv, 713.

1. At a meeting in Auburn, N. Y., on Sept. 3 to celebrate the fall of Atlanta, Secretary of State William H. Seward stated that: "We shall have no draft because the army is being reinforced at the rate of five to ten thousand men per day by volunteers." *New York Times*, Sept. 7, 1864.

2. This sentence and the whole of the second paragraph appeared in contemporary newspapers. *New York Herald*, Sept. 15, 1864.

To Edwin M. Stanton

———

(Cipher)   City Point Va. Sept. 13th *1864*.
Hon. E. M. Stanton, Sec. of War Washington,

I would respectfully recommend that a supervising Inspector of the Treasury Dept. within the lines of the Army, be appointed by the President. The amount of support received by our enemies through either the ignorance or corruption of Treasury Agents and Post Commanders is fearful and should be stopped in some way. Col. A. H. Markland, spl. Agt. of the P. O. Dept. as an officer of the Government thoroughly acquainted with all that has been done in the West from the begining of the War I think would be a good appointment.

U. S. GRANT
Lt. Gen—

ALS (telegram sent), CSmH; telegram received (at 5:30 P.M.), DNA, RG 107, Telegrams Collected (Bound); *ibid.*, Letters Received, Irregular Series. *O.R.*, III, iv, 712. On Sept. 13, 1864, 9:00 P.M., Secretary of War Edwin M. Stanton telegraphed to USG. "Your reccommendation as to Treasury Inspectior will be laid before the Secretary and urged upon him. I agree with you as the necessity of the measure." ALS (telegram sent), DNA, RG 107, Telegrams Collected (Bound); telegram received, *ibid.*, Telegrams Collected (Unbound); *ibid.*, RG 108, Letters Received. On Sept. 15, Secretary of the Treasury William P. Fessenden wrote to Stanton rejecting the suggestion on the grounds that the U.S. Army had adequate control of trade in and around City Point. LS, *ibid.*, RG 107, Letters Received, Irregular Series.

To Bvt. Maj. Gen. Montgomery C. Meigs

City Point, Va. Sept. 13th *1864.*

MAJ. GEN. M. C. MEIGS,
Q. M. GEN. U. S. A.
GENERAL,

Capt. Janes, A. Q. M has been on duty at my Hd Qrs. from the date of his appointment to the present time. Holding the appointment of Asst. Qr. Mr. in the regular Army he is desirous of seeing more varied service in his Dept. than he can do where he ~~is~~ now is. He has requested me to give him a letter to you to secure this change in his services solely with the view of becoming more conversant with the duties of a profession, and Department, which he has taken up for life. Maj. Van Vliet,[1] I understand, has signified that he has a place under him which he would like to assign Capt. Janes to.

I am Gn. Very respectfully
your obt. svt.
U. S. GRANT
Lt. Gn.

ALS, DNA, RG 92, Letters Received from Hd. Qrs.

1. Stewart Van Vliet of N. Y., USMA 1840, began to serve as q. m. capt. during the Mexican War. Appointed brig. gen. as of Sept. 23, 1861, he served as chief q. m., Army of the Potomac, during the Peninsular campaign but, on July 17, 1862, relinquished his commission in the vols., reverting to maj., and began service at New York City, where he remained through the war.

To Maj. Gen. George G. Meade

By Telegraph from City Point
Dated Sept 13 *1864.*

To GEN MEADE

Major Wentz[1] says that before laying the R. R. he tried to see the Chief Engineer but was told that he was sick—

He then stated to the officer of whom he enquired the object of his call. He was replied to—that the work of locating the road had been given to another engineer. This latter he made two efforts to see, but failing he commenced his work supposing the Engineer would come along if it was not laid too suit He now proposes to sink the road five feet where it is, in view of the Rebel Batteries throwing all the earth towards the enemy. This will give an embankment of eleven feet & a cut of five—

I have directed him to go on with the work

U S GRANT
Lt Gen

Telegram received, DNA, RG 94, War Records Office, Army of the Potomac; copies, *ibid.*, RG 108, Letters Sent; DLC-USG, V, 45, 69, 107; (2) Meade Papers, PHi. *O.R.*, I, xlii, part 2, 805. On Sept. 13, 1864, noon, Maj. Gen. George G. Meade telegraphed to USG. "I have nothing of consequence to report this morning.—Your despatch in reference to Maj. Wentz has been referred to Maj. Michler Actg. Chief Engineer, who replies that no one about these Hd. Qrs can be found who ever knew of any visit of Maj. Wentz—that Maj. Duane tho unwell was never so sick that he could not see any one on business, and atho it is not intended to impugn Maj. Wentzs statement, yet there is no doubt that had proper effort been made by him to see either Maj Duane or myself, or had a written or telegraphic communication been made to us, the very serious mistake which has been made in the location of the road could have been avoided as the only condition I had to make was that the road should be laid out of sight of & beyond the range, of the enemys batteries.—The plan proposed & directed to executed by you of sinking the road can be tried, but I fear the noise of the locomotive & cars & the knowledge the enemy now have of the location of the road will prevent its undisturbed use, tho' I do not know any interruption is to be anticipated." ALS (telegram sent), DNA, RG 94, War Records Office, Army of the Potomac; telegram received, *ibid.*, RG 108, Letters Received. *O.R.*, I, xlii, part 2, 805.

1. Erasmus L. Wentz was then serving in the U.S. Military Railroad service as chief engineer and general superintendent, Military Railroads of Va. See *ibid.*, III, iv, 954–56.

To Frederick Dent Grant and Ulysses S. Grant, Jr.

City Point Va. Sept. 13th *1864.*

DEAR FRED. & BUCK,

I was very glad to get your letters the other day and still better pleased to see so few mistakes. There was some mistakes though. Write often to me and when you do write always keep a dictionary by you. When you feel any doubt about how a word should be spelled look at your dictionary and be sure to get it right. Missy did not write? Why did she not? She writes very pretty letters and by writing often now she will write a better letter at twelve years of age than most grown up yong ladies.

I have sent to get Jess' pony brought into town from your grand pa's. If he is left there long I am afraid he will be stolen.

I hope to be up to see you all before many weeks and before many months to be with you most of the time. Is Jess sorry he run off and left his pa the way he did? I thought he was going to be a brave boy and stay with me and ride Jeff Davis. Ask Jess if Jeff aint a bully horse.

Kiss your Ma, little Nelly & Jess for your

PA

ALS, DLC-USG.

To Maj. Gen. Henry W. Halleck

(Cipher)   City Point Va. Sept. 14th/64
MAJ. GEN. HALLECK, WASHINGTON

I will leave here to-morrow morning for the Shenandoah Valley to see Sheridan. Will not pass through Washington either going or coming unless it is ~~de~~ the wish of the President or Sec. of War I should do so. Every thing is very quiet here and all indications are that it will remain so until I take the offensive

U. S. GRANT
Lt. Gen.

ALS (telegram sent), CSmH; telegram received (at 4:00 P.M.), DNA, RG 107, Telegrams Collected (Bound); *ibid.*, Telegrams Collected (Unbound). *O.R.*, I, xlii, part 2, 815; *ibid.*, I, xliii, part 2, 83. On Sept. 14, 1864, 10:20 P.M., Secretary of War Edwin M. Stanton telegraphed to USG. "If any thing [s]hould requires your presen~~t~~ce here notice will be given. At present there is no reason to change your plans." ALS (telegram sent), DNA, RG 107, Telegrams Collected (Bound); telegram received (marked as sent at 10:00 P.M.), *ibid.*, RG 108, Letters Received. Printed as sent at 10:00 P.M. in *O.R.*, I, xlii, part 2, 815; *ibid.*, I, xliii, part 2, 83.

On Sept. 12, President Abraham Lincoln wrote to USG. "Sheridan and Early are facing each other at a dead lock. Could we not pick up a regiment here and there, to the number ~~say~~ of say ten thousand men, and quetly, but suddenly concentrate them at Sheridan's camp and enable him to make a strike? This is but a suggestion—" ALS, Phillips Exeter Academy, Exeter, N. H. Lincoln, *Works*, VII, 548. On Sept. 13, USG wrote to Lincoln. "It has been my intention for a week back to start to-morrow, or the day following, ~~and~~ to see Sheridan and arrange what was necessary to enable him to start Early out of the Valley. It seems to me it can be successfully done." ALS, Phillips Exeter Academy, Exeter, N. H.

On Sept. 14, 1:00 P.M., Maj. Gen. Henry W. Halleck telegraphed to USG. "It is represented to me by reliable business men that the long and continued interruption of the Ohio & chesapeake canal & B & O. railroad is very seriously affecting the supply of provisions & fuel for public and private use in Baltimore, Washington Georgetown & Alexandria. Unless the canal can be opened very soon a sufficient supply of winter's coal cannot be procured before the close of navigation. The gas companies are already thinking to stop their works for want of coal. The canal & railroad have been several times repaired & as often destroyed. They, therefore, urge the great importance of driving Early far enough south to secure these lines of communication from rebel raids, and that if Sheridan is not strong enough to do this, he should be reinforced. I respectfully communicate the substance of these representations for your consideration." ALS (telegram sent), DNA, RG 107, Telegrams Collected (Bound); telegram received, *ibid.*; *ibid.*, RG 108, Letters Received. *O.R.*, I, xliii, part 2, 83–84.

To Maj. Gen. George G. Meade

(Cipher)   ~~Maj. Gen.~~ sept. 14th/64 [*3:00* P.M.]
MAJ. GEN. MEADE.

I shall leave here to-morrow morning for Sheridan's Hd Qrs. Will be gone five days. Gen. Butler also leaves to-day to be absent

a few days.[1] You will therefore assume command of all the forces
operating in this field if ~~any movement should make it necessary.~~
you find it necessary.

U. S. GRANT
Lt. Gn.

ALS (telegram sent), CSmH; telegram received, DNA, RG 94, War Records
Office, Army of the Potomac. *O.R.*, I, xlii, part 2, 816. On Sept. 14, 1864, 10:30
A.M., Maj. Gen. George G. Meade telegraphed to USG. "Reports from corps
comds. indicate nothing extraordinary to report this morning—Maj. Genl. Birney
states that the recent advance of Hancocks picket line, has drawn on his line in-
cessant picket firing increasing his casualties & that he has taken measures to
stop it   There is at present sharp canonading going on in Birneys front which I
presume to be the measure he indicated he would take—A special report of the
cause has been called for—" ALS (telegram sent), DNA, RG 94, War Records
Office, Army of the Potomac; telegram received, *ibid.*, RG 108, Letters Received.
Printed as received at 10:45 A.M. (probably because of the telegrapher's notation on the telegram sent) in *O.R.*, I, xlii, part 2, 815. On the same day, USG
telegraphed to Meade. "What is the heavy firing now heard about"   Telegram
received, DNA, RG 94, War Records Office, Army of the Potomac; (2) Meade
Papers, PHi. *O.R.*, I, xlii, part 2, 815. At 11:10 A.M., Meade telegraphed to USG.
"In reply to your telegram just received, I send you a despatch from Birney recieved simultaneously which confirms the view I took in my last despatch—Maj.
Genl. Birney has been directed to make a special report so soon as his present
experiment is over as to the result & hereafter not to open his batteries under
similar circumstances without first referring to these Hd. Qrs, as I am some what
doubtful of the efficacy of his plan of stopping picket firing & the expenditure of
ammunition is becoming a question of some importance"   ALS (telegram sent),
DNA, RG 94, War Records Office, Army of the Potomac; telegram received,
ibid., RG 108, Letters Received. Printed as received at 11:15 A.M. (actually the
time sent) in *O.R.*, I, xlii, part 2, 815. The enclosure is *ibid.*, p. 829.

1. On Sept. 14, Maj. Gen. Benjamin F. Butler telegraphed to USG. "If you
will permit or see no objection I will go to Fortress Monroe for a day or two as
I am quite unwell and besides desire to arrange transportation for our sick soldiers
from Georgia." ALS (telegram sent), DNA, RG 107, Telegrams Collected (Unbound).

To Maj. Gen. George G. Meade

———

By Telegraph from City Point
Dated Sept 14 *1864.*

To GEN MEADE
Gen Butler reports that the enemy in his front show but little more
within their intrenchments than our picket line—May it not be the

enemy are massing everything on their right for an attack—I think it would be well to push recconnoisances both west & south from our extreme left to ascertain if any movements are in contemplation

If you have occasion to telegraph me after I start in the morning, dispatches directed to Harpers Ferry will reach me—I shall have a Cipher Operator along

U S GRANT
Lt. Gen

Telegram received, DNA, RG 94, War Records Office, Army of the Potomac; copies, *ibid.*, RG 108, Letters Sent; DLC-USG, V, 45, 69, 107; (2) Meade Papers, PHi. *O.R.*, I, xlii, part 2, 816. On Sept. 14, 1864, 8:45 P.M., Maj. Gen. George G. Meade telegraphed to USG. "Your despatch in relation to the thinning of the enemys line in front of Genl. Butler has been received. The Signal officers have reported something of the same kind on my front in the vicinity of the Plank road—also the movements of small bodies of the enemy near the Lead works.—I will direct Warren to send a reconnaissance out in the morning in a westerly direction, sending with him two regiments of cavalry—Our cavalry is out so far to the South that any advance meets the enemy at once, and they have their cavalry so strongly posted, that a mere reconnaissance can not force them back—besides our cavalry is so far in this direction that we ought to have ample warning if our pickets are vigilant.—I do not think the enemy will be likely to attack our immediate left or the rear of it, but may perhaps endeavor to threaten still farther round in the direction of Prince Geo's C. H—so as to try and draw us away from our entrenched lines—This would be running great risk on their part unless they have a very large force—I will be vigilant and keep a sharp look out—" ALS (telegram sent), DNA, RG 94, War Records Office, Army of the Potomac; telegram received, *ibid.*, RG 108, Letters Received. Printed as received at 9:00 P.M. (probably because of the telegrapher's notation on the telegram sent) in *O.R.*, I, xlii, part 2, 816. On the same day, USG telegraphed to Meade. "Telegraph me at Ft Monroe the result of Warrens reconnoisance tomorrow if known by 3 P M. If not known until a later hour telegraph to Baltimore" Telegram received, DNA, RG 94, War Records Office, Army of the Potomac; copies, *ibid.*, RG 108, Letters Sent; DLC-USG, V, 45, 69, 107; (2) Meade Papers, PHi. *O.R.*, I, xlii, part 2, 816.

On Sept. 15, 7:45 A.M. and 8:40 A.M., Meade telegraphed to USG transmitting telegrams from Maj. Gen. Gouverneur K. Warren reporting skirmishes. Telegrams received, DNA, RG 108, Letters Received. *O.R.*, I, xlii, part 2, 839. At 10:00 A.M., Meade telegraphed to USG at City Point "or if Genl. G has left—in cipher to Fortress Munroe.—I send a despatch received from Warren—Genl. Warren has been ordered to with draw his command, as soon as all the information is obtained that is practicable.—I judge from the reports, that Greggs recent movement about the 1st inst shewed the enemy the necessity of holding Poplar Grove Church with some force, to be notified of any advance on our part, and that Warren has met there this force—The fact that he found the roads obstructed and of his not being immediately driven back, are evidences to me that the enemy are not in great force at that point & did not contemplate immediate offensive movements—If he has any such intention he will doubtless mask his movements, by holding all such points of approach as Poplar Grove Church, Ream's &c in such force, as to compel a battle for us to find out what he is about.—" ALS (telegram sent), DNA, RG 94, War Records Office, Army of the Potomac; telegram received, *ibid.*, RG 108, Letters Received. *O.R.*, I, xlii, part 2, 831. The enclosure is *ibid.*, p. 840. At 11:40 A.M., Capt. George K. Leet telegraphed to Meade. "Lt. Gen. Grant directs me to say that the reconnoisance of this morning is satisfactory and the troops can now be withdrawn" ALS (telegram sent), DNA, RG 107, Telegrams Collected (Unbound); telegram received, *ibid.*, RG 94, War Records Office, Army of the Potomac. *O.R.*, I, xlii, part 2, 831.

To Julia Dent Grant

City Point Va. Sept. 14th *1864.*

DEAR JULIA,

Your letter speaking of the new embarassment which has arisen in not being able to send the boys to College without having them board away from home has just reached me. As school does not commence until the begining of next month it will not be necessary for me to write to the principle about it as I shall try to slip up there for a day and see him in person. As to Jess refusing to go to school I think you will have to show him that you are *boss*. How does he expect ever to write letters to his Pa, or get to be Aide de Camp if he does not go to school and learn to write. He will go I know. He was only joking when he said he would not. I hope you will be pleasantly situated. Burlington is said to be a very nice place and nice people. You will soon be more at home there than in Gravois where there is no body except your own family for whom you have much reason to care.—I hope Jennie will come on and at least spend the Winter with you. I have written to your father asking him to make his home with us. Love and kisses for you and the children. Good night.

ULYS.

ALS, DLC-USG.

To Edwin M. Stanton

Baltimore Md Sept. 16th *1864.*

HON. E. M. STANTON,
SEC. OF WAR,
SIR;

The bearer of this, Mr. Lugo, is the person who was tried by Rebel Authorityies as a Spy, condemned to death but afterwards his sentence commuted to banishment but was rescued whilst runing the blockade at Wilmington. He has a proposition for destroying Southern rail-road bridges which may be practicable but which, if adopted, will have to be adopted at Washington. Mr. L. will explain the entire matter to you.

Very respectfully
your obt. svt.
U. S. GRANT
Lt. Gn.

ALS, DNA, RG 107, Letters Received from Bureaus.

On Sept. 12, 1864, noon, Secretary of War Edwin M. Stanton had telegraphed to USG. "The Santiago one of your blockading squadron captured a few days ago the Blockade runner A D Vance from Wilmington. On board of the Vance was found an Italian named Antonzini who was brought in to Hampton roads yesterday on the Santiago. He was found double ironed, had been condemned to death by the rebel government for treason, and was being deported to Bermuda his punishment having been commuted. This morning Mr Fox brought me a letter from Antonzini offering to give information about for the destruction of bridges on the Danville road. I have requested Mr Fox to have him sent direct to you from Fortress Monroe" ALS (telegram sent), *ibid.*, Telegrams Collected (Bound); telegram received, *ibid.*, RG 108, Letters Received. *O.R.*, I, xlii, part 2, 794. The author of an article on Orazio Lugo de Antonzini concludes that his "operations in Richmond, Charleston, and Wilmington in the winter of 1864 establish him as one of the significant Federal secret agents of the Civil War." Meriwether Stuart, "Dr. Lugo: An Austro-Venetian Adventurer in Union Espionage," *Virginia Magazine of History and Biography*, 90, 3 (July, 1982), 358.

To Maj. Gen. George G. Meade

(Cipher)   Harpers Ferry Va. Sept. 16th [*1864*] 9 p m
MAJ. GEN. MEADE, NEAR PETERSBURG VA.

If the enemy makes so rich a hawl as to get our cattle herd he will be likely to strike far to the south or even to the southeast to get around with ~~them~~ it. Our Cavalry should either recover what is lost or els in the absence of so much of the enemy's Cavalry strike the Welden road far to the south of where it has been destroyed.

U. S. GRANT
Lt. Gn.

ALS (telegram sent), CSmH; telegram received (on Sept. 18, 1864, 9:00 A.M.), DNA, RG 94, War Records Office, Army of the Potomac; (on Sept. 16, 10:00 P.M.) *ibid.*, RG 107, Telegrams Collected (Bound); *ibid.*, Telegrams Collected (Unbound). *O.R.*, I, xlii, part 2, 853. On Sept. 16, 10:00 A.M. and 10:30 P.M., Maj. Gen. George G. Meade telegraphed to USG. "Warren's reconnaissance was withdrawn yesterday about 12. m—Signal officers reported the movement of the enemys troops towards our left at various times yesterday from 9. a m till sunset—There were believed to be counter movements to meet an expected advance on our part—This view was confirmed by Warrens pickets on the vaughan road reporting the return of the enemy to Petersburgh & by a deserter this morning, who states his command left the trenches & moved to their right yesterday afternoon & returned during the night.—This morning at day light our cavalry pickets & reserves were strongly attacked between the ~~Jerusalem plank road~~ Blackwater & the James—at the same time a dash was made on the cattle herd at Coggins Point & it is feared this herd & its guard have fallen into the enemys hands—A prisoner taken reports the movement as being executed by Hamptons with 3 brigades of cavalry, who left Stony creek last night, and after crossing the Blackwater, took the shortest & most direct road to Coggins Point.—Immediately on receiving intelligence of this movement Genl. Davies Comd. cavalry was directed to pursue with all his available force and a brigade of Infantry with a battery of artillery was at the same time sent down the Prince Geo. C. H road to reinforce Kautz—Warren reports demonstrations on his front this morning—his pickets being driven in, but at last report—he had resestablished ~~their~~ his line—It is believed this movement was a diversion in favor of the cavalry raid.—This raid was one which I have feared for some time, as with the limited force of cavalry under my command & the great extent of country to be watched, I have always considered Coggins point, an unsuitable position for the cattle herd it being liable to capture at any time by a coup-de-main of the enemy in force—Every effort will be made to recover the herd or a portion of it.—" ALS (telegram sent), DNA, RG 94, War Records Office, Army of the Potomac; telegram received (at 5:00 P.M.), DNA, RG 107, Telegrams Collected (Bound); *ibid.*, Telegrams Collected (Unbound); *ibid.*, RG 108, Letters Received. *O.R.*, I, xlii, part 2, 852. "Nothing definite has been received from the cavalry—except that Kautz reports the enemy retired as soon as they succeeded in driving off the cattle from Coggins Point.—Kautz is in pursuit on the Prince Geo's C. H. road & Davies on the Jerusalem plank road—with all the cavalry that could be collected at the moment—A supporting force of Infantry was sent on both roads   Heavy & distant firing was heard about 9. P. M presumed to be Davies coming up with the enemy, but Hamptons force is so superior to ours & he had so much time to get off—that I fear nothing will come of the pursuit except to harrass the enemy.—Twenty four hundred head of cattle were captured—The affair was evidently the result of a deliberate plan & advantage was taken of Warren's movement, on the presumption our cavalry, was all on the left. A Deserter who came in this morning says he saw troops passing thro' Petersburgh yesterday said to be part of Early's force—that Early had sent back Six thousand men—I send this for what it is worth but Genl. Butlers signal officers reported yesterday troops moving into Petersburgh on the road from Richmond.—With the exception of the cavalry raid & the demonstration on Warren's pickets this morning—the rest of the lines were quiet.—" ALS (telegram sent), DNA, RG 94, War Records Office, Army of the Potomac; telegram received (marked as sent at 8:30 P.M., received Sept. 17), *ibid.*, RG 107, Telegrams Collected (Bound); *ibid.*, Telegrams Collected (Unbound). *O.R.*, I, xlii, part 2, 853. At 8:05 P.M., Brig. Gen. Seth Williams telegraphed to Lt. Col. Ely S. Parker. "In answer to your dispatch of this evening I am instructed to say that it is believed the ~~en~~ raid of the enemy has terminated with the seizure of the cattle herd and that that there is supposed to be now no ~~difficulty in the way~~ obstacle to prevent the rebuilding of the telegraph line to Fort Powhatan—At any rate it is thought the construction party had better endeavor to reopen the communication." ALS (telegram sent), DNA, RG 94, War Records Office, Army of the Potomac; copy, *ibid.*, RG 393, Army of the Potomac, Letters Sent. Printed as received at 8:10 P.M. in *O.R.*, I, xlii, part 2, 852-53.

On Sept. 17, 2:00 P.M., Meade telegraphed to USG, adding a postscript at 3:00 P.M. "I send you the reports of Genls. Davies & Kautz in command of the cavalry sent in pursuit of the enemy, by which you will find the enemy was prepared for any attempt on our part to recapture the cattle—The distance to be marched, over ~~20~~ 15 miles in Davies case & 30 in Kautz would have prevented any infantry force from reaching the scenes of action in time—this consideration together with the undeveloped movements of the enemy towards his right & my left—prevented me from detaching any considerable force of infantry to aid in the attempt to recover the cattle. These movements have been previously reported being the moving of a considerable body of infantry & artillery on the Boydtown plank road on the 15th inst, the return of which is as yet unknown— In addition deserters particularly one from the North side of the James, state it was reported by their officers Lee was making a great flank movement and today Col Sharpe sends information (despatch transmitted) that the Govt. employees in Richmond, had been ordered to Petersburgh   Yesterday I informed you Signal officers North of the appomatox reported the movement into Petersburgh of troops on the Richmond road and a deserter stated he had about the same time seen troops marching through Petersburgh said to be part of Early's forces, who it was stated had sent back Six thousand troops. There may be nothing in all this, but so many reports from different sources—would lead to the conclusion that some movement is on foot   Whether it be offensive, or whether it is that seeing in our journals the reports of large accessions daily recieved by this Army Lee is merely preparing for an anticipated extension of our lines I am unable to say, but the existence of these reports & the movements known have combined to produce caution on my part during your absence—I deem it proper to call your attention to the small force of cavalry under my command—For ordinary purposes & were the enemy without cavalry, it would be ample, but in the presence of the enemys superior forces, this arm of the service is unable to accomplish any thing—In yesterdays operations the lowest estimate of the enemys forces made by prisoners & deserters is 6000, and called suddenly as our troops were without time to draw in pickets & detachments, I question whether the combined commands that went in pursuit amounted to 3000—With this superiority, a knowledge of the country, & preparations made to meet pursuit, it is hardly fair to expect much more than what was accomplished, tho' I hoped the difficulty of driving the cattle & the chances of war might prove more favorable to us.—There is nothing else to report up to this hour . . . P. S. Genl. Birney has just telegraphed, that a deserter in this morning reports Hokes division withdrawn from his front, and that it has gone to Genl. Lee at Reams station—This may mean Genl. W. H. F. Lee Comdg. Cavalry & to cover the withdrawal of the cavalry, or it may be part of an offensive movement.—" ALS (telegram sent), DNA, RG 94, War Records Office, Army of the Potomac; telegram received, *ibid.*, RG 107, Telegrams Collected (Bound); *ibid.*, Telegrams Collected (Unbound); (on Sept. 18) *ibid.*, RG 108, Letters Received. *O.R.*, I, xlii, part 1, 33–34; *ibid.*, I, xlii, part 2, 879–80. The enclosures are *ibid.*, pp. 869, 880, 890, 891, 896–97. At 9:45 [P.M.], Secretary of War Edwin M. Stanton telegraphed to USG, Eutaw House. "A long cipher despatch is coming through from General Meade to you. Shall it be forwarded to you at Baltimore or wait your arrival here" ALS (telegram sent), DNA, RG 107, Telegrams Collected (Bound). At 5:00 P.M., Maj. Gen. Benjamin F. Butler telegraphed to USG. "All is quiet along the entire line. Yesterday afternoon three Brigades of Hamptens Cavalry turned our left—and struck cattle cor[r]al about seven miles below city point Captured about (2000) two thousand head of cattle and one Telegraph construction party A cavalry force was sent out to cut them off also Hancock moved to intercept them with a division of infantry. The result is not yet known. Rumer is that the cattle are recaptured They broke the telegraph line so that we send to Powhatan will advise farther through through ~~city~~ General Wallace to send ~~it~~ to you at Burlington I have just returned but believe I have given you all of interest Line will be up this evening & working" ALS (telegram sent), *ibid.*, Telegrams Collected (Unbound); telegram received (at 12:00 P.M.), *ibid.*, Telegrams Collected (Bound); (on Sept. 18) *ibid.*, RG 108, Letters Received. Printed as sent at 3:45 P.M. and incomplete in *O.R.*, I, xlii, part 2, 892.

On Sept. 18, noon, Butler telegraphed to USG. "All perfectly quiet. The cattle were not recaptured Deserters are coming in all reporting exertions making to fill up the Army. No change in disposition of troops in our front No cannonading of consequence During the morng or last evenig Line repaired and Working to Fortress Monroe" ALS (telegram sent), DLC-USG, I, B; telegram received (at 2:30 P.M.), DNA, RG 107, Telegrams Collected (Bound); *ibid.*, RG 108, Letters Received. *O.R.*, I, xlii, part 2, 905.

On Sept. 19, Meade wrote at length to Lt. Col. Theodore S. Bowers discussing the loss of the cattle. Copy, DNA, RG 393, Army of the Potomac, Letters Sent. *O.R.*, I, xlii, part 1, 34–35.

On Sept. 22, Lt. Col. Michael R. Morgan, chief commissary, wrote to USG. "I have the honor to transmit herewith the report of the officer in charge of the cattle herd at the time of its capture, also the report of the officer who has the general charge of Cattle and Forage of the Subsistence Department of the Armies operating against Richmond, together with a true copy of an official despatch from Headquarters Army of the Potomac to the Assistant Adjutant General at your Headquarters, that it was safe to graze the herd near Coggin's Point. Having some time before been shown a despatch sent to you by General Meade that the cattle was not safe because, if I remember rightly, the Cavalry had been sent over to Deep Bottom, I had them brought in and foraged and kept them in, until I received the despatch of which the enclosed is a copy. I do not attribute any blame in this matter to any officer in the Subsistence Department. I do not know that any one is particularly to blame, but I would prefer to have the matter investigated and I expect an application from Captain Richardson, C S V, for a court of Inquiry." LS, DNA, RG 94, Letters Received, 1629M 1864. *O.R.*, I, xlii, part 1, 25–26. The enclosures are *ibid.*, pp. 26–30.

To Maj. Gen. Henry W. Halleck

Harpers Ferry
Sept 17th 1864

Maj Gen H W Halleck
Chief of Staff—

I leave for Baltimore in a few minutes—Hold all new regiments coming into service in Washington until further orders   It is possible though not probable that Sheridan may want to throw a force suddenly into Hagerstown

U. S. Grant
Lieut Genl

Telegram received (at noon), DNA, RG 107, Telegrams Collected (Bound); copies, *ibid.*, Telegrams Received in Cipher; (dated Sept. 16, 1864) *ibid.*, RG 108, Letters Sent; DLC-USG, V, 45, 69, 107. Dated Sept. 17 in *O.R.*, I, xliii, part 2, 96. On Sept. 17, 1:30 P.M., Maj. Gen. Henry W. Halleck telegraphed to USG. "Despatch from Harper's Ferry recieved. Orders were given some days ago to send all Infantry regiments & recruits in the northern states from Boston, N. Y. Phil & Baltimore to City Point by water, on account of the numerous desertions. Do you mean that these orders be suspended & the new regiments brought here, or simply to retain what are now here & on their way here?" ALS (telegram sent), DNA, RG 107, Telegrams Collected (Bound); telegram received, *ibid. O.R.*, I, xliii, part 2, 96. At 5:00 P.M., USG, Baltimore, telegraphed to Halleck. "I shall not leave Baltimore for Washington until to-morrow evening. In the mean time I shall go to Burlingting N. J. to make arrangements for sending my Children to school." ALS (telegram sent), CSmH; telegram received (at 6:00 P.M.), DNA, RG 107, Telegrams Collected (Bound). *O.R.*, I, xliii, part 2, 96. USG arrived in Burlington, N. J., about midnight that day, received many visits from citizens the next day, and left at 10:00 (apparently in the evening). On his walk to the station, a young woman said to him: "General, you have already done so much for us, that we expect a great deal more." USG replied: "I expect from Gen. Sherman more than from any other man in the country." Correspondence from Burlington, Sept. 18, in *New York Tribune*, Sept. 19, 1864.

To Maj. Gen. Henry W. Halleck

City Point Va
8 30 p m Sept 19th 1864

MAJ GEN HALLECK
CHF. OF STAFF

A large part of the convalescents sent from Alexandria here, belong to the 6th & 19th Corps and have to be immediately returned—Please direct the commanding officer there to caution his Provost Marshal against making this mistake

U S GRANT
Lt Genl

Telegram received (at 9:00 P.M.), DNA, RG 107, Telegrams Collected (Bound); copies, *ibid.*, Telegrams Received in Cipher; *ibid.*, RG 108, Letters Sent; DLC-USG, V, 45, 69, 107. *O.R.*, I, xlii, part 2, 909; *ibid.*, I, xliii, part 2, 110.

On Sept. 18, 1864, noon, USG, Philadelphia, telegraphed to Maj. Gen. Lewis Wallace. "Please detain the Fortress Monroe boat until this 5 p. m. I am now just leaving Philadelphia." *Ibid.*, p. 108. On the same day, USG, Baltimore, telegraphed to Maj. Gen. Henry W. Halleck. "I leave immediately for Fort Monroe & city Point" Telegram received (at 6:15 P.M.), DNA, RG 107, Telegrams Collected (Bound). *O.R.*, I, xliii, part 2, 102.

On Sept. 19, Lt. Col. Cyrus B. Comstock telegraphed to Maj. Gen. Andrew A. Humphreys. "Is it known this morning that the enemy are moving on our left" Telegram received, DNA, RG 94, War Records Office, Army of the Potomac. *O.R.*, I, xlii, part 2, 909. At 9:50 A.M. and 1:15 P.M., Humphreys telegraphed to Comstock. "Gen Kautz reported last night some reported movements of enemys Cavalry towards sycamore Church & coxe's mills   He was directed to move out there at daylight this morning & look after the enemy   No report has been received from him. All measures taken were simply precautionary   It was thought probable that there was nothing in the reported movement. The Comdg Genl requests me to say that he thinks some more extended works than those at City Point should be thrown up the space enclosed by them being too contracted   Gen Benham will be directed to take the matter in hand" "Gen Kautz reports that Capt Spear on duty at Sycamorce church in his morning report states that the enemy are in his front in force but all was quiet—Col Steadman in command of the Brigade sent Gen Kautz at Day light this morning has been directed to look after the enemy there & a report is expected from him this afternoon" Telegrams received, DNA, RG 108, Letters Received; copies, *ibid.*, RG 393, Army of the Potomac, Letters Sent. The first is printed as received at 10:00 A.M., the second at 1:25 P.M., in *O.R.*, I, xlii, part 2, 910, 911.

At 1:00 P.M., Maj. Gen. George G. Meade began a telegram to USG. "Every thing has been quiet since my last despatch till about 7. P. M last evening, when Genl. Kautz reported the appearance of the enemys cavalry in the vicinity of Sycamore church. Genl. Davies was immediately ordered to reinforce Kautz by a brigade of his Division & to push out & ~~feel~~ ascertain what the enemy was doing—A despatch just received from Kautz dated 12. M confirms the previous report of the enemys cavalry being in force near Sycamore church & states he is about sending Col Stedman's brigade of Davies Division to reconnoiter—no reason given why this reconnaissance was not made this morning as ordered.—I am at a loss to account for the appearance of the enemys cavalry at this point unless a dash is intended on our rear—To provide against this, besides the cavalry, I have placed a brigade of Infantry on the Norfolk stage road & one at Prince Geo C. H, and as I am unable to extend any farther have requested Maj. Genl. Butler to place a brigade at the Old C. H as part of the defences of City Point where I have sent a battery of artillery & placed the troops under the command of Brig. Genl. Benham the senior officer present. The signal officers have reported some movements of the enemy indicating a partial return of the troops from their right to left—Hokes division however, withdrawn from their extreme left, has not yet returned, according to the report of deserters in this morning . . . 3. P. M . . . The foregoing was prepared to send in cipher, when information was received you were on your way up the river.—Since writing it—Majr Genl. Butler has telegraphed he will send two brigades to Old C. H. and deserters report that Hoke has returned to the left & is lying in reserve in rear of Bushrod Johnston.—I have directed the Engineers to examine the vicinity of Old C. H. for the location of a work which shall be part of a line either to Prince Geo. C. H. or to Pt. of Rocks, in case it should be desirable to hold either of these lines.—" ALS (telegram sent), DNA, RG 94, War Records Office, Army of the Potomac; telegram received, *ibid.*, RG 108, Letters Received. Printed as received at 3:15 P.M. in *O.R.*, I, xlii, part 2, 910. On the same day, USG, City Point, telegraphed to Meade. "Have just returned" Telegram received, DNA, RG 94, War Records Office, Army of the Potomac. *O.R.*, I, xlii, part 2, 911. At 5:00 P.M. and 5:20 P.M., Meade telegraphed to USG. "I am glad to hear of your return I sent a despatch at 3. P. M since which time nothing has been heard from Genl. Kautz reconnaissance tho his last despatch seemed to intimate a doubt as to the presence of the enemy in force near Sycamore Church, tho' it was twice reported by Col Spear.—In view of the large amount of property about City Point & extending for some distance outside—I deemed it prudent to ask Genl Butler to send a spare brigade if he had one to Old C. H—He telegraphed in reply he would send two As nothing seems to have been developed today—I think one brigade will be ample, as you have returned however, I will leave this question to you.—" "I send a despatch just received from Kautz—It appears Capt Spears report last evening—repeated this morning, is not confirmed by Col Steadmans reconnaissance & that there has been no enemy in that vicinity since the Cattle Raid. I would however suggest if it meets your views one of Butlers brigades being retained for a while at Old C. H. for I notice by the Richmond paper of today, that very highly colored accounts are given of the stores & c at City Point & a sudden dash such as was made the other morning, if made during the night, might occasion trouble.—" ALS (telegrams sent), DNA, RG 94, War Records Office, Army of the Potomac; telegrams received, *ibid.*, RG 108, Letters Received. Printed as received at 5:20 P.M. and 5:30 P.M. in *O.R.*, I, xlii, part 2, 911. The enclosure in the second telegram is *ibid.*, p. 932.

Also on Sept. 19, USG telegraphed to Maj. Gen. Benjamin F. Butler. "Please send me a report of an approximate report of the number of men for duty now between the James & Appomattox." ALS (telegram sent), Kohns Collection, NN; copies, DLC-USG, V, 45, 69, 107; DNA, RG 108, Letters Sent. *O.R.*, I, xlii, part 2, 925. At 6:15 P.M., Butler twice telegraphed to USG. "We have 4500 infantry old troops   4000. New Pennsylvania Troops—2500 Negro Troops—at Deep Bottom & one thousand 1000 at Dutch Gap—2 brigades of a thousand each have gone across River to City Point now on the March"   "The following message has just been received, from spring Hill 'A train of 14 freight & two passenger cars loaded with troops towards Richmond' Trains were running loaded all night last night towards Petersburg from Richmond. A deserters says that he left the Cav'y. force Saturday night upon their way back with the cattle. there were 5 brigades cav. & 2 batteries   they were returning to Hold their lines which were left to a brigade of Infy while they were away   This deserter is intelligent having brought his horse & equipment with him"   ALS and LS (telegrams sent), DNA, RG 107, Telegrams Collected (Unbound); telegrams received, *ibid.*, RG 108, Letters Received. The first is printed as sent at 6:20 P.M. in *O.R.*, I, xlii, part 2, 925. On Sept. 20, USG telegraphed to Butler. "The Points held by the two Brigades you have sent below here I presume are important in view of the late sucessful Raid of the Enemy. I would like however that you should hold it with Troops from the 10th Corps so as to keep all the force possible in Bermuda Hundred"   Telegram received, DNA, RG 94, War Records Office, Army of the Potomac; copies, *ibid.*, RG 108, Letters Sent; DLC-USG, V, 45, 69, 107. *O.R.*, I, xlii, part 2, 948.

To Edwin M. Stanton

(Cipher)   City Point Va. Sept. 20th *1864.* [*11:00* A.M.]
A. L̶i̶n̶c̶o̶l̶n̶ Hon. E. M. Stanton, Sec. of War, Washington.

Please advise the President not to attempt to doctor up a state government i̶n̶ for Georgia by the appointment of citizens in any capacity whatever. Leave Sherman to treat on all questions in his own way the President reserving his power to approve or disapprove of w̶h̶a̶t̶ ̶e̶v̶e̶r̶ ̶i̶s̶ ̶d̶o̶n̶e̶ his action. Through Treasury Agents on the Mississippi and a very bad civil policy in Louisianna I have no doubt the war has been very conciderably protracted and the states bordering on that river thrown further from sympathy with the Government than they were before the river was opened to commerse. This is given as my private views.

U. S. Grant
Lt. Gn.

ALS (telegram sent), CSmH; telegram received (at 3:30 P.M.), DNA, RG 107, Telegrams Collected (Bound); *ibid.*, Telegrams Collected (Unbound). *O.R.*, III, iv, 734. On Sept. 20, 1864, 5:15 P.M., Secretary of War Edwin M. Stanton telegraphed to USG. "The advice you reccommend for the President shall surely be given and enforced as far as I can do. Hurrah for Sheridan!" ALS (telegram sent), DNA, RG 107, Telegrams Collected (Bound); telegram received, *ibid.*, RG 108, Letters Received. At 2:00 P.M., USG telegraphed to Stanton. "Let me urge now the appointment of Gen. Sheridan a Brig. Gen. in the regular army. Please also direct the promulgation of the order appointing him permanently to the Command of the Middle Division." ALS (telegram sent), CSmH; telegram received (at 5:40 P.M.), DNA, RG 107, Telegrams Collected (Bound). *O.R.*, I, xliii, part 2, 118. At 8:00 P.M., Stanton telegraphed to USG. "General Sheridan has been appointed Brigadier in the regular army and assigned to the permanent command of the Middle Military Division the order will be promulgated immediately." ALS (telegram sent), DNA, RG 107, Telegrams Collected (Bound); telegram received, *ibid.*, Telegrams Collected (Unbound); *ibid.*, RG 108, Letters Received.

To Maj. Gen. George G. Meade

City Point Va. Sept 20th/64

Maj. Gen. Meade,

Gen. Lee claims in an official dispatch that in driving back our picketts on the left they captured 90 men from us.[1] In the cavalry fight he claims to have captured 300 prisoners, a large number of horses and some arms besides 2500 cattle. The ~~way our men~~ ease with which our men of late fall into the hands of the enemy would indicate that they are rather willing prisoners.

U. S. Grant
Lt. Gn

ALS (telegram sent), CSmH; telegram received, DNA, RG 94, War Records Office, Army of the Potomac. *O.R.*, I, xlii, part 2, 935. On Sept. 20, 1864, sent at 9:10 A.M., Maj. Gen. George G. Meade telegraphed to USG. "I have sent to Warren & Davies for official reports of their losses on the 16 & 17. inst—Warren's loss in the reconnaissance of the 16th was slight—but on the 17th simultaneously with the cavalry raid a dash was made along the whole length of Warren's picket line & I should not be surprised if they picked up a number of prisoners.

Kautz lost nearly the whole of the 1st D. C. cavalry besides many of his pickets—his estimate however was not as large as Lee reports 300.—" ALS (telegram sent), DNA, RG 94, War Records Office, Army of the Potomac; telegram received, *ibid.*, RG 108, Letters Received. *O.R.*, I, xlii, part 2, 935.

1. *Ibid.*, I, xlii, part 1, 852.

To Maj. Gen. George G. Meade

(Cipher)   City Point, Va. Sept. 20th/64 [*11:00* A.M.]
MAJ. GN. MEADE,

Gen. Gregg told me on the way up to Baltimore that his Division of Cavalry now numbered 6000 for duty. This gives us a Cavalry force of over 9000 men all told. I want such disposition made of the Cavalry at once as will give from three to four thousand ready for a service which I will make know to you either by letter or by calling on you.

U. S. GRANT
Lt. Gen

ALS (telegram sent), CSmH; telegram received, DNA, RG 94, War Records Office, Army of the Potomac. *O.R.*, I, xlii, part 2, 935. On Sept. 20, 1864, 12:30 P.M., Maj. Gen. George G. Meade telegraphed to USG. "Genl. Greggs last official report for the 10th inst gives the aggregate present for duty officers & men 38.98—Thirty eight hundred & ninety eight—Kautz does not make any returns, but I understood from him that his Four regiments averaged about Four hundred for duty—as one the 1st—D. C. has been nearly destroyed in the recent raid I should estimate Kautz at not more that 1500 effectives   This allowing for increase of recruits since last return would give at the outside about 5,500 for all the cavalry available for duty. I will instruct Genls. Davies & Kautz to hold their commands in readiness for your orders, in the absence of these orders I do not know of any different disposition—except to concentrate Davies Division about 4000 & leave the picketing from the infantry left to Kautz. . . . I have called for returns from Davies & Kautz to date"   ALS (telegram sent), DNA, RG 94, War Records Office, Army of the Potomac; telegram received, *ibid.*, RG 108, Letters Received. *O.R.*, I, xlii, part 2, 936.

At 11:00 A.M. and 11:10 A.M., Meade telegraphed to USG. "I have nothing of particular importance to report this morning beyond what has already been communicated in special despatches. The enemy yesterday opened from a heavy gun, said to be a 7 inch Brooks, placed in their second line on cemetery ridge back of the Mine.—Measures are being taken to reply to this piece and silence it.—There seems to be reliable evidence that Hoke's division has returned to the left of the enemys line, but instead of resuming its former position in the trenches, it is massed in rear behind cemetery ridge.—" ALS (telegram sent), DNA, RG

94, War Records Office, Army of the Potomac; telegram received, *ibid.*, RG 108, Letters Received. Printed as received at 11:15 A.M. in *O.R.*, I, xlii, part 2, 935–36. "I propose to visit you at City Point today, if you are going to be at your quarters & you have no objection." ALS (telegram sent), DNA, RG 94, War Records Office, Army of the Potomac; copy, *ibid.*, RG 393, Army of the Potomac, Letters Sent. *O.R.*, I, xlii, part 2, 936. On the same day, USG telegraphed to Meade. "I shall be at home all day & will be glad to see you here   Adm'l Porter & the asst Secy of the Navy will be here"   Telegram received, DNA, RG 94, War Records Office, Army of the Potomac; copies (2), Meade Papers, PHi. *O.R.*, I, xlii, part 2, 936. See letter to Gustavus V. Fox, Sept. 10, 1864.

To Maj. Gen. Philip H. Sheridan

City Point Va. Sept 20th [*1864 2:00* P.M.]

MAJ. GEN SHERIDAN

~~HARPERS FERRY~~ WINCHESTER—

I have just received the news of your great victory and ordered each of the Armies here to fire a salute of one hundred (100) guns in honor of it at seven 7 A. M. tomorrow morning—If practicable push your success and make all you can of it

U. S. GRANT
Lieut. Genl.

Telegram received (at 5:40 P.M.), DNA, RG 107, Telegrams Collected (Bound); *ibid.*, Telegrams Collected (Unbound); copies, *ibid.*, Telegrams Received in Cipher; *ibid.*, RG 108, Letters Sent; DLC-USG, V, 45, 69, 107. *O.R.*, I, xliii, part 2, 118. On Sept. 21, 1864, Maj. Gen. Philip H. Sheridan issued a circular to his troops quoting the first sentence of USG's telegram. Copies, DLC-Philip H. Sheridan; OFH.

On Sept. 20, USG telegraphed to Maj. Gen. George G. Meade, Maj. Gen. Benjamin F. Butler, and to all corps commanders transmitting a telegram of the same date from Secretary of War Edwin M. Stanton to USG. "The following despatch has just been received giving further particulars of Sheridans great victory—A salute of One hundred guns has just been given—" Telegram received, DNA, RG 94, War Records Office, Army of the Potomac; *ibid.*, RG 108, Letters Received; *ibid.*, RG 393, 10th Army Corps, Telegrams Received; DLC-S. Phillips Lee; copies, DNA, RG 393, 10th Army Corps, Miscellaneous Telegrams Received; *ibid.*, 9th Army Corps, 3rd Brigade, Telegrams Received; (2) Meade Papers, PHi. Enclosed was a telegram from Brig. Gen. John D. Stevenson, Harpers Ferry, 11:40 A.M., to Stanton. "Just received following official from Gen Sheridan dated one A. M. this Morning   'Gen, We fought Early from daylight until between six & seven P. M. We drove him from Opaquan Creek through winchester and beyond the Town. We captured from twenty five hundred to three thousand prisoners five (5) pieces of artillery nine (9) battle flags. All the rebel wounded & dead. Their wounded in winchester amounts to some three thousand (3.000) we lost in killed Genl David Russell Comdg Div sixth A. C. Wounded Genls Chapman McIntosh & Upton. The Rebels lost in killed the following Genl officers: Genl Rhodes Genl Wharton Genl Gordon and Genl Ramseur We just sent them a whirling through winchester, and we are after them tomorrow. This army behaved splendidly. I am sending forward all Medical supplies subsistence stores and all ~~amb~~ambulances" Copies, DNA, RG 108, Letters Received; *ibid.*, RG 393, 10th Army Corps, Miscellaneous Telegrams Received; *ibid.*, 9th Army Corps, 3rd Brigade, Telegrams Received; DLC-S. Phillips Lee; (2) Meade Papers, PHi. *O.R.*, I, xliii, part 2, 124. On the same day, USG telegraphed to Butler and Meade. "Fire a salute of One hundred guns in honor of Sheridan's great victory in the Shenandoah Valley. The salute may be fired at ~~day light~~ 7 O'clock to-morrow morning from shotted guns at such points as you may select." ALS (telegram sent), Munson-Williams-Proctor Institute, Utica, N. Y.; telegram received, DNA, RG 94, War Records Office, Army of the Potomac. *O.R.*, I, xlii, part 2, 948. Also on Sept. 20, 10:00 P.M., USG telegraphed to Maj. Gen. Henry W. Halleck. "Has the news of Gn. Sheridans battle been sent to Gn. Sherman? If not please telegraph him." ALS (telegram sent), CSmH; telegram received (at 10:45 P.M.), DNA, RG 107, Telegrams Collected (Bound).

On Sept. 19, telegrams of noon and 2:35 P.M. from Stevenson to Stanton reporting Sheridan's battle were sent to USG. Telegrams received, *ibid.*, Telegrams Collected (Unbound); (1) *ibid.*, RG 108, Letters Received. *O.R.*, I, xliii, part 2, 114, 115. At 7:30 P.M., Sheridan telegraphed to USG. "I have the honor to report that I attacked the forces of Genl Early over the Berryville pike at the crossing of Opequan Creek, and after a most stubborn and sanguinary engagement, which lasted from early in the morning, until five (5) O Clock in the evening completely defeated him and driving him through Winchester, capturing about twenty five hundred (2500) prisoners—five (5) of Artillery, nine (9) Army Flags and most of their wounded—The rebel Genlerals Rhodes and Genl Gordon were killed, and three other general Officers wounded Most of the enemys wounded and all their killed fell into our hands. Our losses are severe, among them Genl D A Russell Com'dg Division in Sixth (6th) Corps, who was killed by a cannon ball. Generals Upton, McIntosh and Chapman were wounded I cannot yet tell our losses The conduct of the Officers and men was most superb—They charged and carried every position taken up by the rebels from Opequan Creek to Winchester—The rebels were strong in numbers and very obstinate in their fighting—I desire to mention to the Lieut Genl Commanding the Army the gallant conduct of Generals Wright, Crook, Emory, Torbert and the Officers and men under their command—to them the country is indebted for this handsome victory—A more detailed report will be forwarded" Telegrams received (2—on Sept. 20, 7:30 A.M.), DNA, RG 107, Telegrams Collected (Bound); *ibid.*, Telegrams Collected (Unbound); DLC-Robert T. Lincoln; copies, *ibid.*, RG 84, Instructions from Dept. of State, Spain; *ibid.*, RG 107, Telegrams Received in Cipher; DLC-Philip H. Sheridan. *O.R.*, I, xliii, part 1, 24–25; *ibid.*, I, xliii, part 2, 110.

On Sept. 20, 9:00 P.M. and 9:30 P.M., Sheridan, Strasburg, telegraphed to USG. "I have the honor to report my command at Strasburg—My troops were so much fatigued by their work yesterday that I was only able to follow the enemy a short distance south of Winchester last night—My Infantry marched from Winchester to Strasburg today—I could not get ready to attack the enemy before night—Early was badly whipped yesterday—Have not yet received full reports—The enemy left in Winchester over three thousand (3000) wounded— We captured five pieces of Artillery a number of caissons four thousand stand of small arms—The estimate of Earlys loss yesterday is over seven (7) thousand (7000) He lost the following General officers—Rhodes and Goodwin killed— Gordon wounded mortally—Terry, Haines [*Hays*], Fitz Lee and Bradly Johnson wounded Genl Ramsuer reported by citizens as wounded This is doubtful— My casualties will be about four thousand (4000) No accurate returns received—Col Duvall Comdg. division in Crooks army was wounded—Genl Chapman was slightly wounded.—He is now on duty—" Telegram received (on Sept. 21), DNA, RG 107, Telegrams Collected (Bound); *ibid.*, Telegrams Collected (Unbound); copies, *ibid.*, Telegrams Received in Cipher; DLC-Philip H. Sheridan. *O.R.*, I, xliii, part 1, 25; *ibid.*, I, xliii, part 2, 118–19. "In consequence of a report received from Averill that Early had marched two Divisions of his command down to Martinsburg I changed the programme that I spoke about when I saw you at Charlestown and moved directly up the Berryville pike—The information that Early had marched two Divisions to Martinsburg was incorrect and I found his whole force (excepting Kershaws Division which was at Front Royal) in my front—I then attempted by swinging around my left flank to cut him off from Winchester This move would have been entirely successful if it had not been for unfortunate giving way of a part of Ricketts Division sixth Corps and a portion of the 19th Corps which came back in confusion—This mishap was soon remedied by the good conduct of Uptons Brigade of the first Division sixth Corps—The enemy then attempted to turn my right flank but Genl Crooks, who was up to that time held in reserve, went in and turned their left— Our whole line then advanced beautifully routing the enemy at every point— From the best sources of information that I have, Earlys strength is much greater than your estimate—The people of Winchester say that Early had yesterday on the field 28,000 Infantry—One of my staff who was captured yesterday and released by Early near this place this morning and saw all their force, estimates it to be at least that number—I can scarcely think however that it is as high as these figures—The engagement was a very handsome one, the lines at different points being in the open field" Telegram received (on Sept. 21, 2:00 P.M.), DNA, RG 107, Telegrams Collected (Bound); copies, *ibid.*, Telegrams Received in Cipher; DLC-Philip H. Sheridan. *O.R.*, I, xliii, part 1, 25–26; *ibid.*, I, xliii, part 2, 119.

To Julia Dent Grant

Sept. 20th *1864*.

DEAR JULIA,

I got back here last evening all well. Found two letters from you on my return. The scene at the house on Sunday[1] morning was what I had to go through the whole way. It is but little pleasure now for me to travel. I was very sorry I did not bring the children with me all the way to Baltimore. The rail-road company were kind enough to send me down in a extra train with the same fine car they gave me from Phila when you was along. It had to go immediately back and the children could have made the trip as well as not. I come up from Ft. Monroe on the Steamer New York. The son of the owner of the boat was aboard and told me that the citizens of Phila intended to raise their subscription for a house for you to $60,000

Love and kisses for you and the children.

ULYS.

ALS, DLC-USG.

    1. Sept. 18, 1864.

To Edwin M. Stanton

(Cipher)   City Point, Va. Sept. 21st/64 [*10:30* P.M.]
HON. E. M. STANTON, SEC. OF WAR.

I informed Gen. Sheridan that I would direct the new regiments coming into the field to be stopped at Washington so that he could order them as he desired the Dept. of Washington being within his command. I think it would hardly be advisable to send troops down the Baltimore road unless he should order it. Now that Sheridan is at Strasburg he may want troops sent East of the Blue Ridge if he wants them al all. Before sending any ~~troops~~ new regiments here it will probably be well to hear from Sheridan.

U. S. GRANT
Lt. Gn.

ALS (telegram sent), CSmH; telegram received (at 11:00 P.M.), DNA, RG 107, Telegrams Collected (Bound); *ibid.*, Telegrams Collected (Unbound). *O.R.*, I, xliii, part 2, 130. On Sept. 21, 1864, 4:00 P.M., Secretary of War Edwin M. Stanton telegraphed to USG. "There are several thousand men here not needed for Washington, chiefly new troops. I requested General Halleck to ask you whether they ~~should~~ ought not to be thrown forward to Sheridan. I have had

Transportation ready for that purpose. I see by General Hallecks telegram that he gives an opinion about the quality of the troops without asking the question I directed. If you think they will be of service to Sheridan please say so and they can be forwarded speedily." ALS (telegram sent), DNA, RG 107, Telegrams Collected (Bound); telegram received, *ibid.*, Telegrams Collected (Unbound); *ibid.*, RG 108, Letters Received. *O.R.*, I, xliii, part 2, 129–30. See following telegram.

To Maj. Gen. Henry W. Halleck

(Cipher)   City Point Sept. 21st/64 [*4:00* P.M.]
MAJ. GEN. HALLECK, WASHINGTON

It was not in contemplation to send any troops from Washington to join Sheridan in the pursuit of Early. I thought it possible though not probable that Early might turn North or send his Cavalry North when Sheridan commenced his movement and in that case wanted troops in Washington so that a force might be thrown suddenly into Hagerstown to head them off. I think it will be safe now to send all new organizations here. They will become fitted for service here faster than elswhere and will have less chance of deserting. I hope Sheridan will wipe out all the stain the Valley of the Shenandoah has been to us heretofore before he gets through.

U. S. GRANT
Lt. Gen.

ALS (telegram sent), CSmH; telegram received (at 7:00 P.M.), DNA, RG 107, Telegrams Collected (Bound). *O.R.*, I, xliii, part 2, 130. On Sept. 21, 1864, 2:00 P.M., Maj. Gen. Henry W. Halleck telegraphed to USG. "A veteran regiment was sent from here yesterday to Johnson's Island, as additional guard for prisoners of war, against [r]ebel raids from Canada. There are several new [r]egiments here detained by [y]our direction to await movements of Genl Sheridan. I think they would not be of much use to him in the pursuit of the enemy. [S]hall I retain them here for the present, or send them to City Point." ALS (telegram sent), DNA, RG 107, Telegrams Collected (Bound); telegram received, *ibid.*; *ibid.*, Telegrams Collected (Unbound); *ibid.*, RG 108, Letters Received. *O.R.*, I, xxxix, part 2, 436.

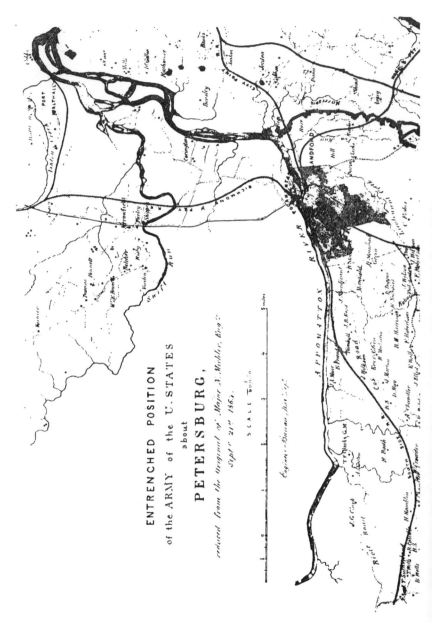

U.S. Lines at Petersburg as of Sept. 21, 1864
RG 77, G458, National Archives

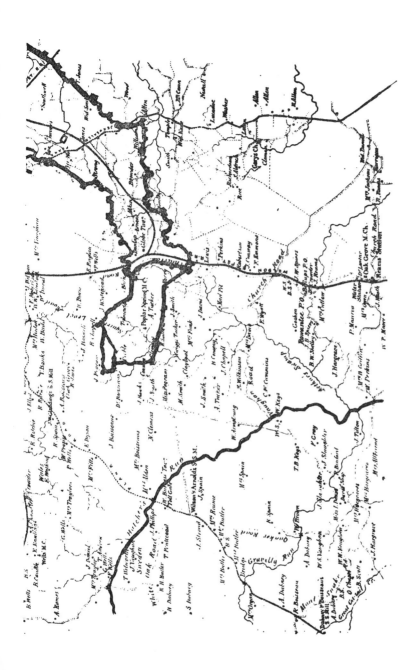

To Maj. Gen. Benjamin F. Butler

————

City Point Va. Sept. 21st/64

MAJ. GN. BUTLER,

Further news from Sheridan is better than the first we heard.[1] In pursuing the enemy up the Valley Lee may be induced to detach from here. Put every one on the lookout for any movements of the enemy. Should any forced be detached we must either manage to bring them back or gain an advantage here.

U. S. GRANT
Lt. Gn

ALS (telegram sent), PPRF; telegram received (at 1:00 P.M.), DNA, RG 94, War Records Office, Dept. of Va. and N. C., Army of the James, Unentered Papers. *O.R.*, I, xlii, part 2, 960. On Sept. 21, 1864, 1:20 P.M., Maj. Gen. Benjamin F. Butler telegraphed to USG. "Telegram recieved   Orders will be given for the utmost vigilance to watch any movement of the enemy and prompt advantage of it taken." LS (telegram sent), DNA, RG 107, Telegrams Collected (Unbound); telegram received, *ibid.*, RG 108, Letters Received.

At 1:40 P.M., Butler telegraphed to USG. "I have an old regiment, dismounted, the 1st Md. Cavalry. Our ea Cavalry force is very much diminished here. Is it possible to mount them. May I request the you to order the horses from the Cavalry Bureau to mount them. By an order of the War Dept. 8 companies of the our Cavalry, armed with Henry Rifles, have been orderd to the other army, and these are to replace them—" LS (telegram sent), *ibid.*, RG 107, Telegrams Collected (Unbound). *O.R.*, I, xlii, part 2, 960. On the same day, USG telegraphed to Butler. "Your request for horses to mount the 1st Md. Cavalry, will receive immediate attention." Copies, DLC-USG, V, 45, 69, 107; DNA, RG 108, Letters Sent. *O.R.*, I, xlii, part 2, 960.

Also on Sept. 21, Butler telegraphed to USG, transmitting a signal message received at 1:13 P.M. "The following Message has just been rec'd from springhill: 'A train of six Cars loaded with troops towards Petersburg' " Telegram received, DNA, RG 107, Telegrams Collected (Unbound); *ibid.*, RG 108, Letters Received. *O.R.*, I, xlii, part 2, 960.

1. At 10:00 A.M., Secretary of War Edwin M. Stanton telegraphed to USG transmitting a telegram of 8:00 A.M. from Brig. Gen. John D. Stevenson, Harpers Ferry, to Stanton. "Reliable news from front—Our army was Crossing Cedar Creek yesterday at 3 P. M. No fighting—The following list of rebel Generals killed & wounded is Correct—Gens. Rhodes Ramesur Gordon Terry, Goodwin, Brad Johnson & Fitz Lee—From all I can learn the prisoners will approximate Five thousand (5000). The indications are that the rebels will not make a stand Short of Staunton. They are evidently too much demoralized to make another fight—" Telegram received, DNA, RG 107, Telegrams Collected (Unbound); *ibid.*, RG 108, Letters Received. *O.R.*, I, xliii, part 2, 137–38. On the same day, USG telegraphed to Maj. Gen. George G. Meade, Butler, and all corps

commanders transmitting this telegram. Telegram received, DNA, RG 94, War Records Office, Army of the Potomac; *ibid.*, Dept. of Va. and N. C., Army of the James, Unentered Papers; *ibid.*, RG 393, 10th Army Corps, Telegrams Received; Ord Papers, CU-B; copies, DNA, RG 393, 10th Army Corps, Miscellaneous Telegrams Received; *ibid.*, 9th Army Corps, 3rd Brigade, Telegrams Received; (2) Meade Papers, PHi.

To Elihu B. Washburne

City Point Va
Sept 21st 1864

HON. E. B. WASHBURNE—

I have no objection to the President using any thing I have ever written to him as he sees fit—I think however for him to attempt to answer all the charges the opposition will bring against him will be like setting a maiden to work to prove her chastity—

U. S. GRANT
Lieut. Genl

Telegram received (at 10:30 A.M.), DLC-Robert T. Lincoln; DNA, RG 107, Telegrams Collected (Bound); copy (marked as sent at 10:00 A.M.), *ibid.*, Telegrams Received in Cipher. *O.R.*, I, xlii, part 2, 951. On Sept. 20, 1864, 8:30 P.M., U.S. Representative Elihu B. Washburne telegraphed to USG. "you recollect the answer you wrote to the letter of the Pres. I took to you at culpeper the copper heads charge that the Pres has interfered with your arrangements, but that correspondence completely contradicts the charge and the publication would justify both your and the President   have you any objection to its publication   please answer by telegraph" Telegram received, DNA, RG 107, Telegrams Collected (Unbound). *O.R.*, I, xlii, part 2, 934. See letter to Abraham Lincoln, May 1, 1864.

To Edwin M. Stanton

(Cipher)   City Point Va. Sept. 22d/64 [*6:30* P.M.]
HON. E. M. STANTON SEC. OF WAR.

The record of Col. Stokes where he has served in this war has been exceedingly good. He was appointed to his last position on my recommendation and according to my judgment he performed the duties assigned to him admirably and entirel[y] in the interests of Government. You probably will recollect that serious charges were made against Col. Stokes for acts said to have been committed some years ago whilst connected with the Ill. C. R. R. Mr Osborn, pres. of the road and Gen. Burnside who was also connected with the road, substantiated the charges. My endorsment on these papers ~~was as follows~~ will be found with the A. G of the Army.[1] I would be very glad to see Col Stokes clear up the charges against him.

U. S. GRANT

Lt. Gn.

ALS (telegram sent), CSmH; telegram received (sent at 6:00 P.M., received Sept. 23, 1864, 10:40 A.M.), DNA, RG 107, Telegrams Collected (Bound). On Sept. 22, 2:40 P.M., Secretary of War Edwin M. Stanton telegraphed to USG. "Col Stokes is here with letters from General Canby Strongly in his favor and askend a reconsidration of his case at least so far as to afford him opportunity of being heard upon the charges against him. The letters of General Canby will be forwarded to you. You will please signify what course you think should be pursued in respect to him." ALS (telegram sent), *ibid.*; telegram received, *ibid.*, Telegrams Collected (Unbound); *ibid.*, RG 108, Letters Received. On the same day, Col. Edward D. Townsend wrote to USG. "The Secretary of War instructs me to forward to you for remark two letters from Major General Canby, in relation to the dismissal of Lieutenant Colonel James H. Stokes." LS, *ibid.* The enclosures are *ibid.* On Sept. 28, Townsend wrote to USG. "The Secretary of War directs me to send the enclosed affidavit of Colonel J. H. Stokes, to be considered in connection with the two letters from General Canby, forwarded a few days since." LS, *ibid.* The enclosure, twenty-three pages addressed by Stokes to Townsend on Sept. 23, is *ibid.* See telegram to Edwin M. Stanton, Jan. 31, 1865.

1. On Aug. 1, Asst. Secretary of War Charles A. Dana had referred to USG papers charging Lt. Col. James H. Stokes with improperly taking $6300 from the office of the Illinois Central Railroad at the time of his discharge as auditor in Aug., 1860, charges supported by William H. Osborn, president, and Maj. Gen. Ambrose E. Burnside, formerly treasurer of the Illinois Central. On Aug. 10, USG endorsed these papers. "Respectfully returned to the Secretary of War. At the time I recommended (then Captain) James H. Stokes for the appointment of Lieutenant Colonel and Inspecting Quarter Master I knew nothing of him only as I had met him and heard of him in the service. As an officer he stood high for capacity and efficiency. The confidential communications of Gen. Burnside and of Mr. Osborn, brought to my attention within, show Stokes to be an unfit person for the position he holds, or for any position in the military service of the Government. I therefore recommend that he be mustered out." ES, *ibid.*, RG 94, Letters Received, S1593 1864. Stokes was mustered out of service on Aug. 22. See letter to Edwin M. Stanton, July 20, 1865.

To Maj. Gen. Henry W. Halleck

(Cipher)   City Point Sept. 22d/64 [*11:30* A.M.]
Maj. Gen. Halleck, Washington

Of 1438 men sent from here yesterday 1019 had to be sent back to Alexandria. More than half the men coming from there have to be sent immediately back as t not belonging to any regiments here. The officers in charge of Camp Distribution are grosely negligent of their duties and ought to be punished with stopage of pay for it.

U. S. Grant
Lt. Gn.

ALS (telegram sent), CSmH; telegram received, DNA, RG 107, Telegrams Collected (Bound). Printed as sent at 11:30 P.M. in *O.R.*, I, xlii, part 2, 963. See following telegram. On Sept. 25, 1864, 3:10 P.M., Maj. Gen. Henry W. Halleck telegraphed to USG. "It is ascertained that the men returned from city Point, were not sent from Alexandria, but from New York direct. The error resulted from the neglect of the officers of Genl Sheridan's command to make returns to the Adjt Genls office." ALS (telegram sent), DNA, RG 107, Telegrams Collected (Bound); telegram received, *ibid.*; (marked as sent at 12:20 P.M.) *ibid.*, Telegrams Collected (Unbound); *ibid.*, RG 108, Letters Received. Printed as sent at 3:10 P.M. in *O.R.*, I, xlii, part 2, 1008.

On Sept. 22, 1:40 P.M., Halleck telegraphed to USG. "Genl Woodbury was placed in command of the District of West Florida, including the fortifications at Key West & Tortugas, with special reference to his qualifications as an engineer officer to defend those works against a naval attack. Some one of similar [qu]alifications should fill the vacancy created by his death. Brig Genl Newton is recommended by Genls Sherman & [T]homas. Genl Delafield also approves. The garrisons being small, the command is an important one. [Th]e Secty of War wishes your opinion." ALS (telegram sent), DNA, RG 107, Telegrams Collected (Bound); telegram received, *ibid.*; *ibid.*, Telegrams Collected (Unbound); *ibid.*, RG 108, Letters Received. At 6:30 P.M., USG telegraphed to Halleck. "Gen. Newton, Gen. Vogdes or Gen. Benham either can be taken to fill Gen. Woodberry's place in Florida. Gen. Newton will probably be the best officer to send." ALS (telegram sent), CSmH; telegram received (marked as sent at 6:00 P.M., received Sept. 23, 10:40 A.M.), DNA, RG 107, Telegrams Collected (Bound).

To Maj. Gen. Henry W. Halleck

(Cipher)   City Point, Va, Sept. 22d/64 [*9:30* P.M.]
MAJ. GEN. HALLECK, WASHINGTON.

Will it not be practicable to open in a short time the rail-road from Washington to Strasburg? If this can be done it seems to me advisable that the latter place should be held. Before giving any directions on the subject I will await your views.

U. S. GRANT
Lt. Gen.

ALS (telegram sent), CSmH; telegram received (on Sept. 23, 1864, 10:40 A.M.), DNA, RG 107, Telegrams Collected (Bound). *O.R.*, I, xliii, part 2, 141. On Sept. 23, 2:00 P.M. and 4:30 P.M., Maj. Gen. Henry W. Halleck telegraphed to USG. "It is believed that a large portion of the ties on the Manassas Gap R. R. are too much decayed to be used. [T]he R. R. Bureau think the road can be put in running order in about [a] week through the gap. The bridges across the branches of the Shenandoah [w]ill take somewhat longer. I have ordered a R. R. officer with a cavalry [de]tachment to examine the road, and [as] soon as he reports will [tel]egraph more fully. The country is wooded and [f]ull of guerrillas, and it will probably require a pretty large force to guard the road. About five thousand troops have been sent from here to [Ge]neral Sheridan via Harper's Ferry last night & to-day. Col. McKelvey reports that [th]e men erroneously sent to city Point were not sent from Alexandria, but from New York [&] the east direct. On their arrival at Alexandria the matter will be fully investigated." ALS (telegram sent), DNA, RG 107, Telegrams Collected (Bound); telegram received, *ibid.*; *ibid.*, Telegrams Collected (Unbound); *ibid.*, RG 108, Letters Received. *O.R.*, I, xliii, part 2, 151. "I now learn that Manassas gap R. R. can be put in running order to Piedmont, sixteen miles from Front Royal, in three days. From there to Front Royal all the iron of the track has been carried away & it will require about a week to replace it. From Front Royal to Strasburg [a]ll the bridges which are very long have been destroyed & the rails removed. But it is thought that Front Royal will serve all the purposes for the defence of the valley that Strasburg would, a ponton bridge being established across the river at that place. Before any decision is arrived at in regard to the location of a Depot a competent engineer officer should be sent to examine the relative merits of Front Royal & Strasburg. Winchester is not susceptible of defence without a very large garrison to occupy the surrounding heights. I would also remark that the Orange R R. to Culpepper & the Rapidann can be repaired in three days. I will have every thing in readiness to begin the work on either road the moment I recieve your orders. We can picket it from Alexandria to Thoroughfare Gap, but Genl Sheridan must defend it beyond. To put it in operation within the time specified it will require working parties all along the road at the same time." ALS (telegram sent), DNA, RG 107, Telegrams Collected (Bound); telegram received, *ibid.*; *ibid.*, RG 108, Letters Received. *O.R.*, I, xliii, part 2, 151–52.

To Maj. Gen. Benjamin F. Butler

By Telegraph from City Pt
Dated Sept 22 *1864.*

To MAJ GEN BUTLER

Please let the troops you have near this place remain where they are for the present ~~if~~ & if it does not make too much change in your present front send the remainder of the brigades now here. I am having a line of fortifications laid out & commenced for contingencies which may arise & which I will explain when I see you.

U. S. GRANT.
Lt Genl

Telegram received (at 4:40 P.M.), DNA, RG 94, War Records Office, Army of the Potomac; copies, *ibid.*, RG 108, Letters Sent; DLC-USG, V, 45, 69, 107. Printed as sent at 4:40 P.M. in *O.R.*, I, xlii, part 2, 974.

On Sept. 22, 1864, Lt. Col. George A. Kensel, act. chief of staff for Maj. Gen. Benjamin F. Butler, telegraphed to USG. "The following message has just been recd from Spring Hill 'The Enemy have a large force at work Strengthening their breastworks on different places on their lines.'" Telegram received, DNA, RG 108, Letters Received. See *O.R.*, I, xlii, part 2, 974.

To Maj. Gen. George G. Meade

Sept. 22d/64

MAJ. GN. MEADE,

You may put the 2 Cav.y Div. on duty again. Col. Sharp[1] has news from Richmond saying that nothing was known there of Early's disaster but it was understood that his force might be looked for back in a few days. Also that if we did not attack soon Lee would. I think our policy for the present will be to hold ourselves ready to receive an attack. If not engaged to-morrow I will go out to see you and inform you fully of what my general plans now are.

U. S. GRANT
Lt. Gn.

ALS (telegram sent), CSmH; telegram received (at 1:00 P.M.), DNA, RG 94, War Records Office, Army of the Potomac. *O.R.*, I, xlii, part 2, 963–64. On Sept. 22, 1864, noon, Maj. Gen. George G. Meade telegraphed to USG. "I have nothing particular to report as having occurred during the past 24 hours. The Trimonthly Return for the 20th shows an aggregate present for duty in the 2d Cavalry Divn. officers & men 4203—Kautz return for same date shows an aggregate of 1493 making in all 5,696—A little over my estimate of that date.—This return of the 20th also shows an aggregate off & men in this army of 47,712 being a gain over the return of the 10th of 4320.—If you do not propose any immediate use of the 2d Cav. Divn. now in reserve—I would suggest its being again put on picket duty, as Kautz's command is inadequate from numbers & morale to the task of properly watching the Country from the Blackwater to the James.—" ALS (telegram sent), DNA, RG 94, War Records Office, Army of the Potomac; telegram received, *ibid.*, RG 108, Letters Received. *O.R.*, I, xlii, part 2, 963.

At 7:05 P.M., Meade telegraphed to Lt. Col. Theodore S. Bowers. "I learn that the 198th regiment Pennsylvania Volunteers Colonel H. G. Sickel has arrived at City Point. Colonel Sickel formerly served in the Army of the Potomac and if consistent with the views of the Lieutenant General commanding I should be glad to have the regiment assigned to my command. Should it be directed to report to me I propose to place it in the 5th Army Corps" Copy (telegram sent), DNA, RG 94, War Records Office, Army of the Potomac; telegram received, *ibid.*, RG 108, Letters Received. *O.R.*, I, xlii, part 2, 964. On the same day, Capt. George K. Leet telegraphed to Meade. "~~The 198th~~ Gen. Grant directs me to say that the 198th Penna. Vols. will be assigned to your command" ALS (telegram sent), DNA, RG 107, Telegrams Collected (Unbound); telegram received, *ibid.*, RG 94, War Records Office, Army of the Potomac. *O.R.*, I, xlii, part 2, 964. At 10:30 P.M., Meade endorsed the telegram received. "Let this regiment when it reports be assigned to the 5th corps." AES, DNA, RG 94, War Records Office, Army of the Potomac. *O.R.*, I, xlii, part 2, 964.

At 10:30 P.M., Meade telegraphed to USG. "I send you for what it is worth a despatch just received from Genl. Hancock—" ALS (telegram sent), DNA, RG 94, War Records Office, Army of the Potomac; telegram received, *ibid.*, RG 108, Letters Received. The enclosure is in *O.R.*, I, xlii, part 2, 967.

1. George H. Sharpe, born in 1828 in Kingston, N. Y., graduated from Rutgers (1847), studied law at Yale (1847–49), served as an attaché at the U.S. legation in Vienna (1851–52), and practiced law at Kingston. In 1861, he served briefly as capt., 20th N. Y. State Militia, and was appointed col., 120th N. Y., as of Aug. 22, 1862. Assigned as deputy provost marshal gen., Army of the Potomac, by Maj. Gen. Joseph Hooker, Sharpe retained that position through the war. See *ibid.*, I, xxv, part 2, 167.

To Maj. Gen. Philip H. Sheridan

(Cipher)   City Point Va. Sept. 22d *1864.* [*10:00* P.M.]
MAJ. GEN. SHERIDAN, STRASBURG VA.

I congratulate you and the Army serving under you for the great victory just achieved. It has been most opportune in point of time and effect. It will open again to the Government and to ~~community~~ the public the very important ~~thorough~~ line of road from Baltimore to the Ohio and also the Chesapeake Canal ~~and~~ ~~b~~Better still, it wipes out much of the stain upon our arms by previous disasters in that locality. May your good work continue is now the prayr of all loyal men.

U. S. GRANT
Lt. Gn.

ALS (telegram sent), CSmH; telegram received (on Sept. 23, 1864, 10:40 A.M.), DNA, RG 107, Telegrams Collected (Bound). *O.R.*, I, xliii, part 1, 61–62; *ibid.*, I, xliii, part 2, 142. On Sept. 22, 12:50 A.M., Brig. Gen. John D. Stevenson, Harpers Ferry, telegraphed to Secretary of War Edwin M. Stanton, sending a copy to USG. "Capt Ellis inspector General toberts staff just arrived from Genl. Sheridans with captured Battle Flags and goes by train to Washington—Sheridan holds Strasburg   Enemy holds Fishers Hill—A heavy recconissance was being made as he left at three (3) P. M yesterday   Result not known" Telegram received, DNA, RG 107, Telegrams Collected (Unbound). *O.R.*, I, xliii, part 2, 148.

On Sept. 21, 8:30 P.M., Maj. Gen. Philip H. Sheridan telegraphed to USG. "I have the honor to report that Genl. Wilson's Cavalry Division charged the enemy at Front Royal this morning and drove them from Front Royal up the Luray Valley for a distance of Six miles. I directed two brigades of the 1st. Cavalry Div. with Genl. Wilson's Div. to follow the enemy up that valley and to push them vigorously. The enemy's Infy. occupy a very strong fortified position in my front across the Strasburg Valley. Heavy fighting occurred during the day between the 6th Corps and the Enemy, and late in the evening a sharp fight took place between a brigade of the 2d Div. 6th Corps and two or three regts. of 3rd Div. 6th Corps, in which the Enemy was driven from a strong crest and the crest held." Telegram received (on Sept. 22, 2:00 P.M.), DNA, RG 107, Telegrams Collected (Bound); copies, *ibid.*, Telegrams Received in Cipher; (2) DLC-Philip H. Sheridan. *O.R.*, I, xliii, part 1, 26; *ibid.*, I, xliii, part 2, 130–31.

On Sept. 22, 3:00 P.M., Stanton telegraphed to USG. "You will see by Sheridan's despatch to General Augur that he wants some troops. About five thousand will, go forward to him this evening." ALS (telegram sent), DNA, RG 107, Telegrams Collected (Bound); telegram received, *ibid.*, RG 108, Letters Received. *O.R.*, I, xliii, part 2, 141. See *ibid.*, p. 131.

At 5:40 P.M., Maj. Gen. Edward O. C. Ord telegraphed to USG. "Richmond

Papers of today acknowledge Early's reverse in a report from Gen Early. He states that on the morning of the 19th the Enemy advanced on winchester near which place he made his attack which was resisted from Early in the day until near night when he was compelled to retire. after night he fell back to Newtown and this morning to Fisher's Hill. our (Rebel) loss reported to be severe Maj Gen Rhodes and Brig Gen Goodwin killed. train and supplies brought off safely. the above report is dated Hd Qurs army Northern Va sept 20th. signed R E LEE. I send you the paper." ALS (telegram sent), DNA, RG 107, Telegrams Collected (Unbound); telegram received, *ibid.*; *ibid.*, RG 108, Letters Received.

At 11:30 P.M., Sheridan telegraphed to USG. "I have the honor to report that I achieved a most signal victory over the army of Genl. Early at Fisher's Hill today. I found the rebel army posted with its right resting on the north fork of the Shenandoah & extending across the Strasburg valley westward to North mountain occupying a position which appeared almost impregnable. After a great deal of maneuvering during the day Gen Crooks command was transferred to the extreme right of the line on North Mountain & he furiously attacked the left of the Enemy's line carrying everything before him. While Crook was driving the enemy in the greatest confusion and sweeping down behind the breastworks the 6th & 19th Army Corps' attacked the rebel works in front & the whole rebel army appeared to be broken up. They fled in the utmost confusion. 16 pieces of artillery were captured also a great many caissons, artillery horses Etc, Etc. I am tonight pushing on down the valley—I cannot say how many prisoners I have captured nor do I know either my own or the enemy's casualties. Only darkness has saved the whole of Early's Army from total destruction. My attack could not be made until 4 oclock in the evening which left but little daylight to operate in—The 1st & 3rd Cavy Divns. went down the Luray valley today and if they push on vigorously to the main valley the result of this day's engagement will be still more signal. The victory was complete A more detailed report will be made as soon as I can obtain the necessary data." Telegrams received (2), *ibid.*, RG 107, Telegrams Collected (Bound); copies (2), DLC-Philip H. Sheridan. Printed as received on Sept. 23 in *O.R.*, I, xliii, part 1, 26–27; *ibid.*, I, xliii, part 2, 142. On Sept. 23, USG telegraphed to Maj. Gen. George G. Meade, Maj. Gen. Benjamin F. Butler, and all corps commanders, transmitting a copy of Sheridan's telegram. Telegrams received (2), DNA, RG 94, War Records Office, Army of the Potomac; *ibid.*, RG 393, 10th Army Corps, Telegrams Received; DLC-S. Phillips Lee; copies, DNA, RG 393, 9th Army Corps, 3rd Brigade, Telegrams Received; (2) Meade Papers, PHi. On the same day, USG telegraphed to Butler and Meade. "Order a salute of One hundred guns, shotted, at day light to-morrow morning in honor of Sheridan's second great victory." ALS (telegram sent), Mrs. Gordon Singles, Arlington, Va.; copies, DLC-USG, V, 45, 69, 107; DNA, RG 108, Letters Sent; (2) Meade Papers, PHi. *O.R.*, I, xlii, part 2, 978. At 10:00 P.M., Meade telegraphed to USG. "I congratulate you & the country most heartily on the glorious news from Sheridan.—I have ordered a salute of 100 shotted guns from Hancocks batteries, the centre of my line, at Sunrise tomorrow." ALS (telegram sent), DNA, RG 94, War Records Office, Army of the Potomac; telegram received, *ibid.*, RG 108, Letters Received. *O.R.*, I, xlii, part 2, 978. At 9:20 P.M., Butler telegraphed to USG. "Glorious news. It will be so foggy at daylight that we cannot see what to fire at. May I say 8 A. M. tomorrow instead of Day break—" Telegram received, DNA, RG 107, Telegrams Collected (Unbound); *ibid.*, RG 108, Letters Received. *O.R.*, I, xlii, part 2, 985. On the same day, USG telegraphed to Butler and Meade. "You can make the salute tomorrow morning at your own hour" Telegram received, DNA, RG 94, War Records Office, Miscellaneous War Records; *ibid.*, Army of the Potomac; copies (2), Meade Papers, PHi. *O.R.*, I, xlii, part 2, 985.

At 8:00 P.M., USG telegraphed to Sheridan. "I have just received the news of your second great victory and ordered a hundred guns in honor of it. Keep on and your work will cause the fall of Richmond," Telegram received (at 9:30 P.M.), DNA, RG 107, Telegrams Collected (Bound); copies, *ibid.*, Telegrams Received in Cipher; *ibid.*, RG 108, Letters Sent; DLC-USG, V, 45, 69, 107. *O.R.*, I, xliii, part 2, 152. At 8:00 A.M., Sheridan had telegraphed to USG. "I cannot as yet give any definite account of the results of the battle of yesterday—Our loss will be light. Genl. Crook struck the left flank of the enemy doubled it up advancing down along their lines—Ricketts division of sixth 6 army corps swung in and joined Crook—Gettys and Wheatons divisions taking up the same movement following by the whole line and attacking beautifully carrying the works of the enemy The rebels threw down their arms and fled in the greatest confusion abandoning most of their artillery—It was dark before the battle ended—I pursued on after the enemy during the night to this point with the sixth and nineteenth Corps and have stopped here to rest the men and issue rations—If Gen. Torbert has pushed down the Luray valley according to my directions he will achieve great results—I do not think that there ever was an army so badly routed—The Valley soldiers are hiding away and going to their homes—I cannot at present give you any estimate of prisoners—I pushed on regardless of everything The number of pieces of artillery reported captured is sixteen (16)" Telegrams received (2—on Sept. 24, 9:00 A.M.), DNA, RG 107, Telegrams Collected (Bound); copies (2), DLC-Philip H. Sheridan. *O.R.*, I, xliii, part 1, 27; *ibid.*, I, xliii, part 2, 152. At 10:00 P.M., Sheridan telegraphed to USG. "I have the honor to request the promotion of Brevet Maj Gen Crook to the full rank of Maj. Gen. His good conduct and the good conduct of his command turned the tide of battle in our favor both at Winchester and Fishers Hill. I also respectfully ask the promotion of Colonel J. H. Duvall commanding a Division of General Crooks command. Col Duvall was wounded in the battle at Winchester These promotions are meritorious" Telegrams received (2—on Sept. 24, 8:00 P.M.), DNA, RG 107, Telegrams Collected (Bound); (2) *ibid.*, Telegrams Collected (Unbound); *ibid.*, RG 108, Letters Received; copies, *ibid.*, RG 107, Telegrams Received in Cipher; (3) DLC-Philip H. Sheridan. *O.R.*, I, xliii, part 2, 153. On Sept. 25, 11:30 A.M., USG endorsed this telegram. "Forwarded to the Sec. of War with the request that these promotions be made." AES (telegram sent), DNA, RG 108, Letters Received; telegram received, DNA, RG 107, Telegrams Collected (Bound); (2—marked as sent at 11:00 A.M.), *ibid.*, Telegrams Collected (Unbound). *O.R.*, I, xliii, part 2, 153.

On Sept. 23, 10:00 P.M., Secretary of War Edwin M. Stanton telegraphed to Julia Dent Grant, Burlington, N. J. "Sheridan fought another great battle yesterday and won a splendid victory" ALS (telegram sent), DNA, RG 107, Telegrams Collected (Bound). *O.R.*, I, xliii, part 2, 151.

To Maj. Gen. William T. Sherman

City Point Va. Sept. 22d *1864.* [*10:00* P.M.]
MAJ. GEN. W. T. SHERMAN, ATLANTA GA.

Do you not require a good Cavalry leader? It has seemed to me that you have during your campaign suffered for want of an officer in command of Cavalry whose judgement and dash both could be relied on. I could send you Gen. Ayres[1] who I believe would make a capital commander and know him to be one of our best officers in other capacities.

U. S. GRANT
Lt. Gen.

ALS (telegram sent), CSmH; telegram received (on Sept. 23, 1864, 10:40 A.M.), DNA, RG 107, Telegrams Collected (Bound); *ibid.*, RG 393, Military Div. of the Miss., Telegrams Received. Printed as received at 10:30 A.M. in *O.R.*, I, xxxix, part 2, 438. On Sept. 23, 10:00 P.M., Maj. Gen. William T. Sherman telegraphed to USG. "I do want very much a good Cavalry officer to command and have been manoeuvreing three months to get Genl. Mower here but Genl Canby has sent him up White River—My present Cavalry need Infantry guards and picket and it is hard to get them within ten miles of the front If you think Ayres would do I would like him but if it be Romain B Ayres he is or was as bad a growler as Granger—I would prefer Gregg or Wilson   Still any body with proper rank would be better than Garrard—Killpatrick is well enough for small scouts but I do want a man of sense and courage to manage my Cavalry and will take any one you have tried—" Telegram received (on Sept. 24, 10:45 A.M.), DNA, RG 107, Telegrams Collected (Bound); (2) *ibid.*, Telegrams Collected (Unbound); (on Sept. 25) *ibid.*, RG 108, Letters Received; copies, *ibid.*, RG 107, Telegrams Received in Cipher; *ibid.*, RG 393, Military Div. of the Miss., Telegrams Sent in the Field. *O.R.*, I, xxxix, part 2, 442. On Sept. 25, 2:00 P.M., USG telegraphed to Maj. Gen. Philip H. Sheridan. "Send either Torbert or Wilson to report to Sherman to command his Cavalry. Report by telegraph which you send. ~~because it will be~~ Sherman is absolutely without a man that can command Cavalry." ALS (telegram sent), CSmH; telegram received (at 6:30 P.M.), DNA, RG 107, Telegrams Collected (Bound). Printed as received at 6:55 P.M. in *O.R.*, I, xliii, part 2, 170. See telegram to Maj. Gen. Philip H. Sheridan, Oct. 3, 1864.

On Oct. 4, 11:30 A.M., USG telegraphed to Secretary of War Edwin M. Stanton. "Gen. Wilson has been selected to go West to command Sherman's Cavalry. As he is junior to the officers now serving with it I would respectfully request that he be Breveted a Maj. Gen. and assigned to duty with that rank." ALS (telegram sent), CSmH; telegram received (at 1:00 P.M.), DNA, RG 107, Telegrams Collected (Bound). *O.R.*, I, xxxix, part 3, 63. See *ibid.*, p. 104. Also at 11:30 A.M., USG telegraphed to Sherman. "Gen. Wilson has been ordered to report to you and that he may have rank to command your Cavalry I have asked that he be ~~app~~ Breveted a Maj. Gn. and assigned with that rank. I believe that Wilson will add fifty per cent to the effectiveness of your Cav.y." ALS (telegram sent), CSmH; telegram received (at 1:30 P.M.), DNA, RG 107, Telegrams Collected (Bound); (on Oct. 10) *ibid.*, RG 94, Generals' Papers and Books, James H. Wilson. *O.R.*, I, xxxix, part 3, 64.

Also on Oct. 4, Brig. Gen. James H. Wilson, Washington, telegraphed to Brig. Gen. John A. Rawlins and wrote to USG. "Am on my way to command Sherman's cavalry & as the Generals with it are all my seniors I want ample & complete authority. I think it should be reorganized as a corps with efficient brigade & division commanders as in the east. As soon as I get there I'll make nominations & with Shermans approval hope to get the officers I need. Please answer before I leave here" Telegram received, DNA, RG 107, Telegrams Collected (Unbound); *ibid.*, RG 108, Letters Received. *O.R.*, I, xxxix, part 3, 87. "I arrived here late last night on my way to take command of Genl. Sherman's cavalry. As a matter of course I am not well enough informed as to its condition to say exactly what will be necessary to render it entirely efficient but I am confident a number of new officers to command the brigades & divisions—and a thorough organization similar to that of the cavalry in the East, will be needed. Every cavalry General in that army being my senior—I shall necessarily receive but little assistance through them. My services here have made me acquainted With a class of young officers, capable to doing any thing—and they with such as can be made available west, will enable me to put the Western cavalry forces on a footing of invincibility. I am confident a corps organization will be extremely beneficial—in fact, nearly indispensable as a preliminary to efficiency. I have already experienced some difficulties in a small way, from having been placed in a command that made other men envious. While this is disagreeable, if possible I hope to avoid the recurrence of it, by having full and complete authority, to do whatever may conduce most to the public interests—and which Genl. S. will approve. It's a big job and will require vigorous means and measures. I depend upon you and General Sherman for the necessary support. Before leaving Harrisonburg I had a long talk with Sheridan. he thought he could not supply his army from Martinsburg, with his means, and move thro' any of the upper gaps against Early's present position—and therefore, that if the campaign should be regarded necessary against Charlottesville or Gordonsville, it will be necessary to transfer himself to the Rail roads this side the mountains. He however thinks that his troops could be better used still by joining you on the James. The measures he is taking in the Valley will effectively render it useless to the enemy—and impossible as a theatre of further operations against us this year. The rail road from here to Manassas Gap—is one of very steep grades, badly broken beyond Front Royal—and said to be almost useless as a supply line from *the steep grades.* The army when I left—noon 1st of Sept—was amply supplied—cattle and sheep were abundant—some grain and long forage—The mills, barns, and grain stacks were being burned in large numbers as far down as Mt. Jackson and all the way from Stanton. No enemy in the valley, except small bands not yet able to get away. Rumors among the people in the Upper valley that Petersburg was to be given up. Remember me to the staff, and particularly Genl. Rawlins." ALS, DNA, RG 108, Letters Received.

On Oct. 15, Wilson, Nashville, telegraphed to USG. "I want Col R S S McKenzie Comdg a Conn Regt in uptons Brigade to command a Brigade of Cavy now here organizing—This meets with Gen Thomas' approval   Please send him at once   Gen upton would also like a command here as soon as he recovers from his wound   I can give him a Div of Cavy   He cannot obtain Div of Infy for a year yet" Telegram received, *ibid.*, RG 107, Telegrams Collected (Bound); *ibid.*, Telegrams Collected (Unbound); *ibid.*, RG 108, Letters Received. On Oct. 24, Wilson, Gaylesville, Ga., telegraphed to Rawlins. "Genl Sherman has given me ample power in the reorganization of the Cavalry & authorizes me to ask if my requests for Gen Upton and Col McKensie have been granted we are very £ short of Commissioned officers & I hope the Lieut General will give me those asked for as well as some others that have been tested." Telegrams received (2—one on Oct. 27, 12:15 A.M.), *ibid.*, RG 107, Telegrams Collected (Unbound); *ibid.*, RG 108, Letters Received. Misdated Oct. 27 in *O.R.*, I, lii, part 1, 649. On Oct. 26, Wilson wrote to Rawlins. "I wish I could write you as fully as I wish—but there is some danger of letters falling into other hands than those intended. This is for you and General Grant—that you may be correctly informed of the condition of the Cavalry question out West. I have been assigned to the command of all the Cavalry forces of the Military Division of the Mississippi, and an order subject to the Presidents approval has been issued by Genl. Sherman constituting them 'The cavalry corps &c.' with instructions to mount arm and bring into the field the largest possible force that can be made available, leaving such police force as may be needed in Middle Tennessee. The last return shows a nominal cavalry force of nearly 60.000 men, but in reality there are not over fiveteen thousand mounted including all that are behind. There are *three* divisions here in the field formerly belonging to the Army of the cumberland—and commanded by Kilpatrick, McCook & Garrarde mounting about 1500 men each, *forty five hundred in all.* They have about twice as many dismounted guarding rail roads *and in block houses.* Colonel Garrard commands a division formerly attached to the Army of the Ohio—five regiments are at the remount camp at Louisville preparing for the field, leaving only parts of two regiments in the field near Atlanta. There are besides, Grierson's & Hatch's divisions in West Tennessee—and a part of Winslow's. The majority of the last went with Mower to Missouri and have not returned In addition to this there are five new Indiana regiments averaging 750 men, now at Nashville & below never mounted—They are splendid materials, in for three years and should be brought out at once; and still further in addition, *two* divisions of Tennessee cavalry not counted in the returns. They are to be left in Tennessee. From this you will see—There are *six divisions* actually organized, materials enough to make another or fill up the old ones, besides Winslow's division absent in Missouri & the Two Tennessee Divisions. These divisions average about ten regiments each—and ought to yield under thorough organization five hundred men for duty—or an aggregate of thirty thousand—under even tolerable organization *twenty thousand* for the field. But what are the facts now? We can't raise *six* thousand, and because horses, arms & equipments have not been furnished. General Sherman estimates that Forrest (now commanding all the cavalry of Beauregards Mil.y Divsion) has *twenty* six thousand (26000) men mounted and menacing his communications—the bulk of it *concentrated* under himself and Wheeler some where between here and Decatur. Armstrong, Gholson Fergusson, Jackson & Roddy are on Beauregard's right flank, South of the Coosa—menacing the rail road between Alatoona and the Chattahoochee. From this hasty sketch you may readily perceive how vastly superior the enemy is to us in the numbers of his mounted troops—actually in the field and concentrated for service; and how necessary it will be to have activity on the part of the Cavalry Bureau—*and an inexorable policy* of *concentration* on the part of Genl. Sherman. If we can organize and get *out of* Tennessee our *six divisions*, and assume the offensive against Beauregard's communications & cavalry—ravaging the rich regions of Alabama, Georgia & the Carolinas, we shall soon destroy their cavalry and establish the invincibility of our own. General Grant's telegram to Genl. Sherman on the 15th looks exactly to the adoption of this policy—and I hope he will repeat it in orders to Genl. Sherman. The latter says he don't expect any thing from the Cavalry—and that all I can do with it will be entirely to my credit—but if Genl. Thomas is left in Tennessee, the Infantry forces must necessarily be more or less divided between him & Genl. Sherman—If the cavalry force is divided *equally* between them we shall effect nothing. Cavalry is useless for defence. It's only power is in a vigorous offensive. Therefore I urge its *concentration* south of the Tennessee and hurling it into the bowels of the South, in masses that the enemy can't drive back as it did Sooy Smith & Sturgis. We shall certainly be able to do this if the enemy doesn't cross the Tennessee—or assume such an offensive as to throw *us* on the defensive—Neither of which are very probable. My main efforts are now directed to mounting McCook, Garrard, & Kilpatrick—and I am doing all in my power to urge that forward. Hatch on The Tennessee has been ordered to move his mounted force via Nashville—to this place and to send his dismounted men to Nashville for remount—Grierson is ordered to collect his division and what remains of Winslow's, thoroughly organize it—keep it well in hand and well fed till the word is given him to move via Columbus, Selma, &c. to join us in the field; General Johnson has been directed to collect the loose regiments and temporarily organize them into a division under General Upton, if we can get him. So that the New Organization will be: . . . And 'Independent Brigade in the district of Vicksburg—under some good officer to be sent there hereafter. If we get into the field fairly and Beauregard on the defensive so that the troops North of the Tennessee can also shove south, I anticipate but little difficulty in carrying out this policy—But should we be thrown on the defensive you will allow the difficulties will be greatly increased. From the above sketch you will also see the absolute necessity of my having the assistance of some more good officers—At present I have but one brigade commander who is a general officer. Garrard, Elliott, & Knipe are to be assigned to infantry for which they are better fitted— We have abolished department chiefs of Cavalry—so that I have the whole matter of organization under my special and exclusive control—General R. W. Johnson is at Nashville charged with the duty of mounting remounting and preparing for the field all the cavalry on this line and superintending it elsewhere. The Inspectors of the Cavalry Bureau at Memphis, Louisville & Nashville are the officers whose duty it is to provide remounts and anticipate demands for the same. I have already asked Genl. Grant twice by Telegraph for Genl. Upton and Col. McKenzie (to be promoted by Brevet)—Custer, Pennington & Reno. Custer I don't expect much to get but Pennington, now colonel of the 3d New Jersey & Reno, now captain of Regular cavalry have been recommended and ought to be promoted—The Cavalry of the Army of the Potomac has already acchieved an acknowledged superiority over that of the enemy and officers detached from it will not disable it, but will carry a prestige with them highly advantageous to us out west. I don't think either that it will discourage our own officers for we shall have a large field for promotion. Please lay these suggestions before the General —and ask him to do what he can for me. All I wish is to get my tools in an efficient condition. I shall then answer for the consequences. I have read this letter to Genl. Sherman and he concurs in what I have said. I would like therefore to have the officers sent to me whom I have designated—and horses, arms & equipments sufficient to put my troops in the field—And the policy of concentration

adopted so firmly that I may be able to ~~Out number~~ exceed Forrest in numbers
and organization. General Sherman sends his very kindest regards to you and the
General. Dr. Kittoe is very well, and wishes to be most kindly remembered by
all. He would be very much pleased with an order to report to the Genl. as Medical Inspector—or to go North on a tour of duty. The Old gentleman will not
complain, or ask for any thing—but he evidently looks with some trepidation
upon the prospect of a campaign this Winter, and I think is getting rather too
old for such work.—Remember me most kindly to Colonels Bowers, Babcock,
Badeau, Porter & Comstock." ALS, USG 3. On Oct. 27, Rawlins telegraphed to
Wilson. "MacKenzie and Upton are both seriously wounded. You will have to
Officer your Cavalry from Officers of Gen. Sherman's Command." Copies, DLC-
USG, V, 45, 70, 107; DNA, RG 108, Letters Sent.

1. Romeyn B. Ayres, born in 1825 in N. Y., USMA 1847, served in the
Mexican War and reached the rank of 1st lt., 3rd Art., before the Civil War. As
capt., 8th Art., as of May 14, 1861, and brig. gen. as of Nov. 29, 1862, Ayres
participated in all major campaigns of the Army of the Potomac through the
close of the war.

To Maj. Gen. George G. Meade

By Telegraph from City Point
Dated Sept 23d *1864.*

To MAJ GEN MEADE

If Gen Hancock is going to take his leave of absence he had better
start in the morning—Gen Gibbon has been relieved from duty
with the 18th Corps & will be back to the 2d on day after tomorrow

U S GRANT
Lt Gen

Telegram received, DNA, RG 94, War Records Office, Army of the Potomac;
copies, *ibid.*, RG 108, Letters Sent; DLC-USG, V, 45, 69, 107; (2) Meade
Papers, PHi. *O.R.*, I, xlii, part 2, 977. On Sept. 22, 1864, USG had telegraphed
to Maj. Gen. George G. Meade. "You may exercise your pleasure about Giving
Gen Hancock a leave of absence   it is impassible to say however that there will
be no Genl Engagement while he proposes to be absent"   Telegram received,
DNA, RG 94, War Records Office, Army of the Potomac; copies, *ibid.*, RG 108,
Letters Sent; DLC-USG, V, 45, 69, 107; (2) Meade Papers, PHi. On Sept. 23,
4:30 P.M., Meade telegraphed to USG. "Genl. Hancock in his application for
leave—stated he did not desire it, if any movements were impending—I referred
the question to you not for authority to grant the leave, but for information as to
whether in your judgement & with your knowledge—I would be justified in
allowing a Corps Commander to be absent for Twenty days—I considered your
despatch of yesterday, as a reply, but awaited Genl. Gibbon's return before com-

municating it to Genl. Hancock—I will however do so at once.—" ALS (telegram sent), DNA, RG 94, War Records Office, Army of the Potomac; copies, *ibid.*, RG 393, Army of the Potomac, Letters Sent; Meade Papers, PHi.

At 11:00 A.M. and 11:30 A.M., Meade had telegraphed to USG. "The quiet of the 'lines' has not been disturbed during the past 24 hours—The 2d Cavalry Division have been placed on duty & in connection with Kautz division are watching & picketing the country from the Jerusalem plank road to the James—the infantry picketing the rear from the Jerusalem plank road to the Welden Rail Road." "The signal officer on Weldon R Rd reports that at 10.20 a m today 6 Regts of Infantry followed by 3 Ambulances moved to our left on the Squirrel level road.—I have a copy of the Richmond Inquirer of the 22d with an official despatch from Lee—reporting the falling back of Early from Winchester to Fisher's hill & acknowledging the death of Genls. Rodes & Godwin & the wounding of Fitz Lee—The losses reported to be severe—Three pieces of artillery were lost, but the trains & supplies brought off safely.—" ALS (telegrams sent), DNA, RG 94, War Records Office, Army of the Potomac; telegrams received, *ibid.*, RG 108, Letters Received. Printed as received at 11:10 A.M. and 11:40 A.M. in *O.R.*, I, xlii, part 2, 978.

To Sylvanus Cadwallader

City Point Va. Sept. 23d/64

S. CADWALLADER,

SIR:

For two years past I have seen more of you personally probably than of all other correspondents put together. I have read your accounts of operations in the field and that of most, if not all, engaged in reporting from the Army. Now that you are about to leave the field to return in another capacity it affords me pleasure to bear testimony that in all your correspondence you have as much, if not more than any other in the profession, stuck to the lagitimate duties assigned to you, i. e. reported facts without giving political bearing, you have avoided building up one Gen. one Brigade or larger command, at the expense of others. Had your course been pursued by all of the profession from the start much of the mortification felt by many would have been avoided and all would have been received as friends and not, as often happens, as something to be dreaded and avoided.

Wishing you success and advancement in the profession of

arms, and a speedy return to your civil pursuits by the Suppression of the rebellion and restoration of the Union, I remain,

Yours Truly

U. S. GRANT

Lt. Gn.

ALS, DLC-Sylvanus Cadwallader. On Sept. 19, 1864, the office of the provost marshal, Milwaukee, prepared a notice informing correspondent Sylvanus Cadwallader of the *New York Herald* that he had been drafted, to report Oct. 3. DS, *ibid.* By Sept. 30, however, Cadwallader had furnished a substitute. DS, *ibid.* In the interim, USG had been joined by several of his staff officers in writing letters praising Cadwallader. *Ibid.*

To Julia Dent Grant

Sept. 23d *1864.*

DEAR JULIA,

I forgot or neglected to write last night and as I only got up a few minuets before time for the Mail to start will have to write very hurriedly. All are well. Col. Hillyer writes me that Rawlins will be back in a few days much improved. Bowers has gone West to bury his mother.

Love and kisses for you and the children. I do hope you will soon be fixed so that you will not have to move again.

ULYS.

ALS, DLC-USG.

To Maj. Gen. Benjamin F. Butler

By Telegraph from City Point
Dated Sept 24 *1864.*

To MAJ GENL. BUTLER

During your absence & when an attack was anticipated at the suggestion of Genl Ord I. directed Genl Meade to hold himself responsible for all the line south of the appottomax & that all Troops occupying such Lines would obey his Orders—It was under this Circumstances that Genl Meade directed Genl Birney, to send all Prisoners & deserters to his Provost Marshal. The 2nd Corps relieving the 10th tonight will make it unnecessary either to repeat or withdraw the Order—

All Prisoners & Deserters taken by either army however should be sent to the Provost Marshal Genl at City Point as soon as questioned   I. suppose they have been so disposed of heretofore

U S GRANT
Lt Genl

Telegram received, DNA, RG 94, War Records Office, Army of the Potomac; copies, *ibid.*, RG 108, Letters Sent; DLC-USG, V, 45, 69, 107. *O.R.*, I, xlii, part 2, 1003. On Sept. 24, 1864, Maj. Gen. Benjamin F. Butler had telegraphed to USG. "There is as is as I understand a colored reg't's at City Point intended for Maj Gen Birney Will you please have them ordered to him" Telegram received, DNA, RG 107, Telegrams Collected (Unbound). On the same day, USG telegraphed to Butler. "GThe 2d Corps will relieve the 10th from the trenches to-night. Instruct Gn. Birney to Place his mass his corps in rear of its present position when relieved out of sight of the enemy." ALS (telegram sent), *ibid.*; telegram received (at 12:45 P.M.), *ibid.*, RG 94, War Records Office, Army of the Potomac. *O.R.*, I, xlii, part 2, 1002. At 1:05 P.M., Butler telegraphed to USG. "The telegram in relation to the 2nd Corps received & preparatory proper orders orders forwarded—" LS (telegram sent), DNA, RG 107, Telegrams Collected (Unbound). *O.R.*, I, xlii, part 2, 1002.

To Maj. Gen. George G. Meade

By Telegraph from City Point
Dated Sept 24 *1864.*

To MAJ GEN MEADE

The order giving you command of all the forces south of the Appomattox was given by telegraph whilst Gen Butler was absent & may know not have been known of by him

Your order to Gen Birney was right but as troops of A. P. take up the whole of the line occupied by the 10th A C. tonight it will only be necessary for me to inform Gen Butler why you gave Birney the orders you did

U S GRANT
Lt Gen

Telegram received, DNA, RG 94, War Records Office, Army of the Potomac; copies, *ibid.*, RG 108, Letters Sent; DLC-USG, V, 45, 69, 107; (2) Meade Papers, PHi. *O.R.*, I, xlii, part 2, 988. On Sept. 24, 1864, 3:00 P.M., Maj. Gen. George G. Meade telegraphed to USG. "I beg leave to refer to you a despatch just received from Genl. Birney. When you directed me to take command of all the troops & line now occupied by Genl. Birney—I requested him to send to these Hd. Qrs any deserters that might come in, that I might be apprised of the position & forces of the enemy in the immediate front I was directed to defend. It would appear Maj. Genl. Butler has, with a knowledge of this fact, countermanded, without any reference to me this order—I beg you will decide whether I had the authority to act as I have done & if so you will notify Maj. Genl. Butler of your decision & request him to rescind his order" ALS (telegram sent—at 3:30 P.M.), DNA, RG 94, War Records Office, Army of the Potomac; telegram received, *ibid.*, RG 108, Letters Received. *O.R.*, I, xlii, part 2, 987–88.

To Maj. Gen. George G. Meade

By Telegraph from City Point
Dated 24 *Sept* 1864.

To MAJ GEN MEADE

The Infantry commander at the front from here out ~~abo~~ about old ch reports to Gen Benham that for the last nights The cavalry pickets have come back near to the Infantry saying that the Enemy in front were too strong for them   Have you heard of any force of the Enemy in that direction   if there is such a force it ought to be driven away

U S GRANT
Lt Gen

Telegram received (at 7:30 P.M.), DNA, RG 94, War Records Office, Army of the Potomac; copies, *ibid.*, RG 108, Letters Sent; DLC-USG, V, 45, 69, 107; (2) Meade Papers, PHi. Variant text in *O.R.*, I, xlii, part 2, 988. On Sept. 24, 1864, 7:30 P.M., Maj. Gen. George G. Meade telegraphed to USG. "I have not heard of any enemy in the direction reported by the cavalry pickets to Genl. Benhams infantry, and I dont believe there is any force there or has been—but since the cattle raid Kautz cavalry have been some what demoralized & I have no doubt they come in on some such pretext. I have sent your despatch to Kautz—" ALS (telegram sent—at 8:00 P.M.), DNA, RG 94, War Records Office, Army of the Potomac; telegram received, *ibid.*, RG 108, Letters Received. *O.R.*, I, xlii, part 2, 988.

To Edwin M. Stanton

(Cipher)   City Point Va. Sept. 25th *1864*. [*10:00* P.M.]
HON. E. M. STANTON, SEC. OF WAR, WASHINGTON

There is no objection whatever to Hooker for either Heintzelman's or Rosecran's place. If both places are to be made vacant, and I would advise it, I would suggest Hooker for the Dept. of the Mo. and Gen. ~~G. M. Dodge if he has sufficiently recovered from his wound~~, Q A Gillmore[1] for the other. If but one vacancy is to be made give that to Hooker.

U. S. GRANT
Lt. Gen.

ALS (telegram sent), CSmH; telegram received (at 11:00 P.M.), DNA, RG 107, Telegrams Collected (Bound); *ibid.*, Telegrams Collected (Unbound). On Sept. 25, 1864, 8:00 P.M., Secretary of War Edwin M. Stanton telegraphed to USG. "It is important to remove Heintzleman from any command, and perhaps Rosecranz. Have you any objection to ~~giving~~ Hooker being assigned to the place of one of them. There is no vacant Major Generalship ~~Edwin M Stanton See of War~~ for Crooks but I am disposed to muster out Heintzleman and make a vacancy. Crook, shall have the first [t]hat occurs. Duval ~~will~~ shall be ~~appointed~~ promoted immediately." ALS (telegram sent), *ibid.*, Telegrams Collected (Bound); telegram received, *ibid.*, RG 108, Letters Received. On Sept. 28, 4:30 P.M., USG telegraphed to Stanton. "If assignments have not already been made in place of Rosecrans & Hentzleman I would change my former recommendation substituting Gen. Burnside for Gn. Gilmore for the Dept. Commanded by H. If but one removal is to be made give Hooker the place." ALS (telegram sent), CSmH; telegram received (at 7:00 P.M.), DNA, RG 107, Telegrams Collected (Bound).

1. Name not in USG's hand.

To Maj. Gen. George G. Meade

(Cipher)   City Point Sept. 25th/64
MAJ. GEN. MEADE,

Thusday[1] will be the day upon which efforts will be made in the direction indicated in our conversation of yesterday. I want a Brigade of Cavalry well commanded to report to Gen. Butler. I think it will be well to start the Brigade you select on a scout tomorrow morning to push out East keeping about the route followed by Hampton when on his cattle raid, further out if they can, and come in to the James river and up to City Point crossing over to Bermuda Hundred after night. They should ride slowly and preserve their horses except when they may come upon the enemy. It is not necessary that the Cavalry Commander should know the object of his reporting to Gen. Butler or even that he is to report to him until his arrival at City Point.

U. S. GRANT
Lt. Gn

ALS (telegram sent), CSmH; telegram received (at 1:00 P.M.), DNA, RG 94, War Records Office, Army of the Potomac. *O.R.*, I, xlii, part 2, 1009. On Sept. 25, 1864, 11:30 A.M., Maj. Gen. George G. Meade telegraphed to USG. "In accordance with your verbal order given yesterday the 10th a c was last night relieved by the two divisions of the 2d corps hitherto posted in the rear or held in reserve. As this change has given to the 2d—Corps with an effective strength of less than 15,000 men a line of over Five miles to hold—I have deemed it proper to order the following changes of position—The 2d corps to hold the line from the appomatox to Fort Crawford on the Jerusalem plank road.—The 9th corps to hold with two divisions from Fort Crawford to include Fort Howard—Such portion of these two divisions as may not be required on this line to be held in reserve in the rear—The 3d division of the 9th corps to be held near the Avery House as a reserve to the 2d corps.—The 5th corps to hold from Fort Howard round to the Gurley House—The present pickets of the 5th corps to the rear to be maintained, they now extending to a line South from the Gurley House.—From this point the cavalry to watch & picket the rear over to the James. Garrisons & artillery to be assigned to the enclosed works on the *front* line—The rest of the troops to be held ready for withdrawal & movement elsewhere." ALS (telegram sent), DNA, RG 94, War Records Office, Army of the Potomac; telegram received, *ibid.*, RG 108, Letters Received. *O.R.*, I, xlii, part 2, 1008. At 12:30 P.M., Meade telegraphed to USG. "The following report just received is forwarded for your information.—" ALS (telegram sent), DNA, RG 94, War Records Office, Army of the Potomac; telegram received, *ibid.*, RG 108, Letters Received. *O.R.*, I, xlii, part 2, 1009. The enclosure, reporting C.S.A. movements on the Weldon Railroad, is *ibid*.

At 5:30 P.M., Meade telegraphed to USG. "I will send Kautz with his division about equal to one of Greggs brigades—His command is a good one and as he belongs to Butlers army it would seem proper to send him.—What time do you desire him to be at City Point—and is it necessary he should go to that place, as this is somewhat out of his way—He might be directed to return to Prince Geo. C. H, and from thence sent over to Genl. Butler.—" ALS (telegram sent), DNA, RG 94, War Records Office, Army of the Potomac; telegram received, *ibid.*, RG 108, Letters Received. *O.R.*, I, xlii, part 2, 1010. On the same day, USG telegraphed to Meade. "Sending Kautz to Butler it will not be necessary that he should make a scout around—He can be relieved by Gregg & allowed to fall back within our lines where he is & report to Genl Butler for orders. If he is relieved on tuesday it will be early enough" Telegram received, DNA, RG 94, War Records Office, Army of the Potomac; copies, *ibid.*, RG 108, Letters Sent; DLC-USG, V, 45, 69, 107; (2) Meade Papers, PHi. *O.R.*, I, xlii, part 2, 1010. Some copies in USG's letterbooks do not reflect the changes in wording incorporated in the telegram as sent.

At 7:00 P.M., USG telegraphed to Meade. "I have learned from a source independent of the Provost Marshal's information that the enemy are preparing to evacuate Petersburg. In all probability it will be impossible to to discover any such move in time to benefit by it but I advise you that you may keep a lookout." ALS (telegram sent—misdated Sept. 23), CSmH; telegram received, DNA, RG 94, War Records Office, Army of the Potomac. *O.R.*, I, xlii, part 2, 1010. At 8:30 P.M., Meade telegraphed to USG. "I will keep a sharp look out thro' Pickets & signal officers for any movements indicating what you state in your despatch." ALS (telegram sent), DNA, RG 94, War Records Office, Army of the Potomac; copy, *ibid.*, RG 393, Army of the Potomac, Letters Sent. *O.R.*, I, xlii, part 2, 1010.

On Sept. 26, noon, Meade telegraphed to USG. "The changes in the disposition of the troops as reported in my despatch yesterday, were made last night.— Particular vigilance has been enjoined on the Pickets & signal officers to detect any movements of the enemy—The accompanying reports received this morning are sent for your information." ALS (telegram sent), DNA, RG 94, War Records Office, Army of the Potomac; telegram received, *ibid.*, RG 108, Letters Received. *O.R.*, I, xlii, part 2, 1028. The enclosed reports from signal officers are *ibid.*, pp. 1028–29. At 3:45 P.M., Meade telegraphed to USG transmitting further reports from signal officers. Copy (telegram sent), DNA, RG 94, War Records Office, Army of the Potomac; telegram received, *ibid.*, RG 108, Letters Received. *O.R.*, I, xlii, part 2, 1029.

On Sept. 24, 10:40 A.M., U.S. Representative Elihu B. Washburne telegraphed to USG. "Gov. Seward and myself start for City Point at one o'clock today on naval steamer." ALS (telegram sent—misdated 1863), DNA, RG 107, Telegrams Collected (Unbound); telegrams received (2), *ibid.* On Sept. 25, Lt. Col. Cyrus B. Comstock telegraphed to Maj. Gen. Benjamin F. Butler. "Genl. Grant was just starting for yours Hd. Qrs when a Telegram informed him that visitors from washington were on the way so that he Cannot leave—If Con[v]enient he would like to have you Come over to see him at once" Telegram received, *ibid.*, RG 94, War Records Office, Dept. of Va. and N. C., Army of the James, Unentered Papers. On the same day, Butler telegraphed to Comstock. "I will be over as soon as I can get a tug—" ALS (telegram sent), *ibid.*, Army of the Potomac. At 1:15 P.M., Lt. Col. Ely S. Parker telegraphed to Meade. "Please send an ambulance to the R. R. station for Gov. Seward, Mr Washburn & Gen Grant, who leave here for your Hdqrs in a few minutes—" ALS (telegram sent), *ibid.*, Miscellaneous War Records; telegram received, *ibid.*, Army of the Potomac. *O.R.*, I, xlii, part 2, 1009. On Sept. 26, Comstock telegraphed to Asst. Secretary of State Frederick W. Seward. "Will you send a Carriage to meet the Baltimore at the Wharf at twelve (12) to-morrow for Governor seward & party." Telegram received, DNA, RG 107, Telegrams Collected (Bound); *ibid.*, Telegrams Collected (Unbound).

1. Sept. 29.

To Maj. Gen. George G. Meade

———

By Telegraph from City Point
Dated Sept. 25 1864.

To MAJ GEN MEADE

Has Gregg returned yet   I will have to send a cavalry commander
to sherman and think of sending Gregg   at present & to this time
there has not been an officer with the cavalry in the west who it was
safe to trust without Infantry to guard from danger   the Rebels
are equally ~~bad~~ bad off   with Either Gregg Torbert or Wilson in
command of shermans cavalry they could travel over that western
country with impunity

U. S. GRANT Lt Gen

Telegram received, DNA, RG 94, War Records Office, Army of the Potomac;
copies, *ibid.*, RG 108, Letters Sent; DLC-USG, V, 45, 69, 107; DLC-David M.
Gregg; (2) Meade Papers, PHi. *O.R.*, I, xlii, part 2, 1008. On Sept. 25, 1864,
noon, Maj. Gen. George G. Meade telegraphed to USG. "Genl. Gregg has returned.—In reference to your proposition to send him West, I have to call your
attention to the fact that there is no other General officer of cavalry with this
army but Genl—Davies one of the youngest & most recently promoted—whereas
with Genl Sheridans army are Torbert—Averill—Merritt—Custer—Devins Chapman & McIntosh.—" ALS (telegram sent), DNA, RG 94, War Records Office,
Army of the Potomac; copies, *ibid.*, RG 393, Army of the Potomac, Letters Sent;
(misdated Sept. 12) Meade Papers, PHi. *O.R.*, I, xlii, part 2, 1008–9.

To Julia Dent Grant

———

Sept. 25th *1864.*

DEAR JULIA,

I have rec'd two letters from you written since I left Burlington one enclosing the ribons sent by Missy. Kiss her for me. My
visit was a very pleasant one and General Sheridan by his briliant
victories has added much to it. In a few days more I [s]hall make
another stir here and shall hope before many weeks to so wind up
matters that I will be able to spend at least a portion of my time at
home. Have you heard any thing more about your house in Phila-

delphia? I want to see you settled. It is probable that going into a new house you will want many things notwithstanding you get it furnished. Write to me as soon as you move about what you will require and I will raise the funds for it. Now that you are going into a house of your own I want you to get every thing of the very best and for the most comfort. Have you thought any more about letting one of the boys go to Paris to receive an education? Since I have learned more about Dr. Evans[1] I am more in favor of having one of them go. If Buck would be contented I would prefer sending him because Fred. will go to West Point as soon as he is old enough. I can assure you one of our boys going under Dr. E's auspices would go under the most favorable auspices. Love and kisses for you and the children. If you want Jess to come down here and stay a week or two with me I will let Bill[2] go up after him after you get settled. Will Buck take it hard leaving his little female acquaintances? Kisses again for you and the children.

ULYS.

ALS, DLC-USG.

1. Probably Thomas W. Evans, born in Philadelphia in 1823, who began to practice dentistry in Paris in 1847 and eventually became closely acquainted with Napoleon III. According to Evans, he visited the U.S. in Aug.–Sept., 1864, in order to advise the emperor concerning recognition of the C.S.A., and Evans visited USG's hd. qrs. Sept. 5–9, spending much time with USG. Edward A. Crane, ed., Memoirs of Dr. Thomas W. Evans: The Second French Empire (New York, 1906), pp. 133–37. See New York Herald, Sept. 10, 1864.

2. For William Barnes, Negro servant of USG, see Jesse R. Grant, In the Days of My Father General Grant (New York and London, 1925), pp. 210–11; letter to Maj. Isaac S. Stewart, Dec. 1, 1864. On May 4, 1874, Barnes, Washington, D. C., wrote to USG. "I do most respectfully ask that you would have me appointed in the State or some other Department of the government, before you leave the City, as I will always cherish what ever place you give me, and feel thankful to you. I am now working by the day in the machine shop. please pardon me for asking you to approve my application to the Secretary of State." ALS, DNA, RG 59, Letters of Application and Recommendation. On May 7, 1875, Barnes wrote to Secretary of State Hamilton Fish. "I most respectfully make application for a position as laborer in the State Department. I was born in St, Louis Mo, age 32 years, I am qualified to give satisfaction in any such position you assign me to. Hoping you may favor my application," ALS, ibid.

To Maj. Gen. Philip H. Sheridan

(Cipher)   City Point Va. Sept. 26th/64 [*6:30* P.M.]
MAJ. GN. SHERIDAN, WOODSTOCK VA.

Lee has sent no troops from here since your first victory except
two regiments & one City Battalion to Lynchburg. This I think is
reliable. Your victories have created the greatest consternation. If
you can possibly subsist your Army to the front for a few days more
do it and make a great effort to destroy the roads about Charlotte-
ville and the canal where ever your Cavalry can reach it.

U. S. GRANT
Lt. Gn.

ALS (telegram sent), CSmH; telegram received (at 9:50 P.M.), DNA, RG 107,
Telegrams Collected (Bound). Printed as received at 9:20 P.M. in *O.R.*, I, xliii,
part 2, 177.

On Sept. 24, 1864, 6:00 P.M. and 11:30 P.M., Maj. Gen. Philip H. Sheridan, "Two miles from Edenburg Va," and six miles south of New Market, telegraphed to USG. "The result of the battle of Fishers Hill gives us twenty pieces
of Artillery, Eleven hundred (1100) prisoners of War. A large amount of
Artillery ammunition, caissons, limbers &c &c. Early expected to stay at Fishers
Hill and had placed all his Artillery ammunition behind the breastworks. A large
amount of entrenching tools, small arms and debris was also taken—No accurate
list received. I have been disappointed in the cavalry operations, which were to
have formed a part of this battle—My advance was near Mount Jackson last
night,   The whole army is now moving forward   The country and small towns
through this Valley have a great many of the Enemy's wounded—" Telegram
received (on Sept. 25, 1:40 P.M.), DNA, RG 107, Telegrams Collected (Bound);
ibid., Telegrams Collected (Unbound); copies (2), DLC-Philip H. Sheridan.
O.R., I, xliii, part 1, 27–28; *ibid.*, I, xliii, part 2, 162. "I have the honor to report
that I drove the enemy from Mount Jackson to six miles beyond New Market
without being able to bring on an engagement   The enemy move[d] rapidly. I
had no cavalry present to hold them—Genl. Torbert attacked Wickhams men at
Luray and captured hundred prisoners—I have found rebel hospitals in all the
towns from Winchester to this place all containing a number of wounded. I am
now eighty miles from Martinsburg and find it Exceedingly difficult to supply
this army. The engagements of Winchester [&] Fishers Hill broke up my original
plan of pushing up the valley with a certain amount of supplies and then returning. There is not sufficient in the valley to live off the country. I should have
mentioned some days ago that Kershaws Division left for Richmond about the
16th or 17th of September. When I last heard from it it was at Sperryville. It is
reported to me that it has returned to the valley   No other troops have left Early
either of Cavalry or Infy. Breckenridge has gone in person to command the Dept.
of the South west." Telegram received (on Sept. 26, 8:00 A.M.), DNA, RG
107, Telegrams Collected (Bound); copies, *ibid.*, Telegrams Received in Cipher;

(2) DLC-Philip H. Sheridan. _O.R._, I, xliii, part 1, 28; _ibid._, I, xliii, part 2, 163. See _ibid._, p. 153.

On Sept. 25, USG telegraphed to Maj. Gen. George G. Meade and Maj. Gen. Benjamin F. Butler. "Gen. Stevenson at Harper's Ferry reports having received already from Sheridan's battles 8000 prisoners." ALS (telegram sent), Kohns Collection, NN; telegram received, DNA, RG 94, War Records Office, Army of the Potomac; _ibid._, Dept. of Va. and N. C., Army of the James, Unentered Papers. No telegram to USG conveying this information has been found; Brig. Gen. John D. Stevenson had telegraphed to Secretary of War Edwin M. Stanton that the number of prisoners was around 3,000. _O.R._, I, xliii, part 2, 159, 168. In USG's letterbooks, the number of prisoners appears as 9,000. On Sept. 25, 11:30 P.M., Sheridan, Harrisonburg, telegraphed to USG. "I pressed the enemy hard yesterday at the same time pushed forward Col Powells cavalry through Timberville struck the valley pike in his rear—This latter movement stampeded him so badly that late last night he gave up the valley pike and struck off toward Keezletown and Port Republic leaving the entire valley south free. All my infantry arrived at Harrisonburg at 4 p m today Col Powells cavalry reached Mount Crawford—Tto-night. Torberts cavalry overtook me this evening. Its operations up the Luray valley on which I calculated so much were an entire failure. They were held at Milford by two small brigades of Fitz Lees Cavalry and then fell back towards Front Royal until after they had learned of our success at Fishers Hill—They then proceeded up the valley again encountering the enemys cavalry at Luray capturing some 75 or 80 men and horses then joined me via New Market—Powells cavalry whipped a portion of the enemys cavalry near Harrisonburg yesterday captured and burned nine wagons—I find at this place 450 wounded—I am now 94 miles from Martinsburg and 104 miles from Harpers Ferry—I will send a column of cavalry to Staunton tomorrow morning and will probably follow the enemy in the direction of Port Republic with the Infantry. Every hour brings me additional information of the demoralization of Earlys army—Reports late this evening say that he is moving towards Charlottsville. Other reports are that he is going to ~~reenforce~~ Waynesboro—The part that I expected the cavalry to accomplish at Fishers Hill was a complete failure—I have relieved Averill from his command—Instead of following the enemy when he was broken at Fishers Hill so that there was not a cavalry organization left, he went into camp and let me pursue the enemy for a distance of fifteen miles with Infantry during the night—Early burned quite a number of wagons on his way up the valley, he also abandoned two caissons on the Keezletown road not far from this place" Telegram received (on Sept. 27, 8:00 A.M.), DNA, RG 107, Telegrams Collected (Bound); copies, _ibid._, Telegrams Received in Cipher; (2) DLC-Philip H. Sheridan. _O.R._, I, xliii, part 1, 28–29; _ibid._, I, xliii, part 2, 170–71.

On Sept. 26, 7:00 P.M., Sheridan telegraphed to USG. "I see it going the rounds of the papers that the 19th Corps was late in coming in to the battle at Winchester I was entirely unconsious of this until I saw it in the papers—The statement was made by R L Shelby—I wish to say that it is incorrect and that this correspondent was arrested by my order on a previous occasion for writing untruthful accounts" Telegram received (on Oct. 1, 9:30 A.M.), DNA, RG 107, Telegrams Collected (Bound); copies, _ibid._, Telegrams Received in Cipher; (2) DLC-Philip H. Sheridan. _O.R._, I, xliii, part 1, 29; _ibid._, I, xliii, part 2, 176–77. See _ibid._, pp. 146–47. On the same day, 10:20 P.M., Stevenson telegraphed to

Stanton, sending a copy to USG. "Gen Chapman just arrived from Front reports Gen Sheridan left NewMarket yesterday morning sunday. That advance of army was five miles ahead pushing for Harrisonburg with utmost dispatch, had been Joined by Torberts Cavalry through Luray Gap   Torbert encountered the main body of Rebel Cavalry between Front Royal & Luray C H, The Enemy retiring up Luray Valley losing some 72 prisoners Torbert going through Gap and joined Sheridan at NewMarket pushing immediately forward to take the Advance of the Army. To-night Sheridan is undoubtedly at Harrisonburg—The Enemy were still in the utmost disorder having only nine pieces of artillery as they passed through New Market—In their trains they have seventeen hundred wounded from the Winchester fight—Our men in best of spirits—They say sheridan is the bearer of peace propositions to Jeff Davis—Genl Chapman rode on horseback ninety miles. His wound not very serious. I send to army in morning a wagon train and five hundred (500) wagons with supplies"   Telegram received, DNA, RG 107, Telegrams Collected (Unbound). *O.R.*, I, xliii, part 2, 183.

On Sept. 29, 7:30 P.M., Sheridan telegraphed to USG. "In my last dispatch I informed you that I pressed Early so closely through New Market at the same time sending cavalry around his flank, that he gave up the valley and took to the mountains passing through Browns Gap—I kept up the pursuit to Port Republic destroying 75 wagons and four caissons. I sent Genl. Torbert, who overtook me at Harrisonburg, to Staunton with Wilsons Division of Cavalry and one Brigade of Merritts—Torbert entered Staunton on the 26th and destroyed a large quantity of rebel government property, harness, saddles, small arms, hard bread, flour, repair shops, etc. etc. He then proceeded to Waynesborous destroying the Iron Bridge over the south branch of the Shenandoah, seven miles of track, the Depot buildings, Govt Tannery, and a large amount of leather, flour and stores etc. etc. at that place—He found the Tunnel ~~destroyed~~ defended by Infantry and retired via Staunton destroying according to your original instructions to me—This morning I sent arounds Merritts and Custers Divisions via Piedmont to burn Grain etc, pursuant to your instructions. My impression is that most of the troops which Early had left passed through the mountains to Charlottsville   Kershaws Division came to his assistance and I think passed along the west base of the Mountain to Waynesboro. The advance of my Infantry is at Mt Crawford eight miles south of Harrisonburg   I will go on and clear out the valley—I am getting from 25 to forty prisoners daily who come in from the mountains on Each side and deliver themselves up—From the most reliable accounts Earlys army was completely broken up, and is dispirited—It will be exceedingly difficult for me to carry the Infantry column over the mountain and strike at the Central road. I cannot accumulate sufficient rations to do so, and think it best to take some position near Front Royal, and operate with the Cavalry and Infantry—I will however stay here for a few days. Kershaw had not reached Richmond but was somewhere in the vicinity of Gordonsville when he received orders to rejoin Early. The destruction of the grain and forage from here to Staunton will be a terrible blow to them—All the grain forage etc in the vicinity of Staunton was retained for the use of Earlys army. All in the lower part of the valley was shipped to Richmond for the use of Lees army—The country from here to Staunton was abundantly supplied with forage & grain etc etc"   Telegram received (on Oct. 1, 10:00 A.M.), DNA, RG 107, Telegrams Collected (Bound); copies, *ibid.*, Telegrams Received in Cipher; (2) DLC-Philip H. Sheridan. *O.R.*, I, xliii, part 1, 29–30; *ibid.*, I, xliii, part 2, 209–10.

On Oct. 2, Capt. George K. Leet, Washington, telegraphed to USG. "Scouts who returned from Stafford and Spottsylvania Co's. this morning report following. A week ago yesterday one division of infantry—generally supposed to be Kershaws—was sent by rail from Richmond to Gordonsville and last tuesday it was marched from Gordonsville to join Early. Some Cavalry—probably a brigade —has gone from Richmond to Early's support recently. Officer in charge of Scouts says the above came to him ~~through two different~~ from two sources." ALS (telegram sent), DNA, RG 107, Telegrams Collected (Bound).

To Maj. Gen. William T. Sherman

Cipher   City Point Va. Sept. 26th/64 [*10:00* A.M.]
MAJ. GN. SHERMAN, ATLANTA GA.

It will be better to drive Forrest from Middle Tennessee as a first step and do any thing els that you may feel your force sufficient for. When a movement is made on any part of the Sea Coast I will advise you. If Hood goes to the Alabama line will it not be impossible for him to subsist his Army?

U. S. GRANT
Lt. Gn.

ALS (telegram sent), Bixby Collection, MoSHi; telegram received (at 2:00 P.M.), DNA, RG 107, Telegrams Collected (Bound). *O.R.*, I, xxxix, part 2, 478. On Sept. 26, 1864, 10:00 P.M., Maj. Gen. William T. Sherman telegraphed to USG. "I have your dispatch of to day   I have already sent one Division [( ]Newtons) to Chattanooga and another [( ]Corses) to Rome. Our Armies are much reduced, and if I send back much more I will not be able to threaten Georgia much There are men enough to the rear to whip Forrest, but they are necessarily scattered to defend the road. Cant you expedite the sending to Nashville of the recruits that are in Indiana and Ohio? They could occupy the Forts   Hood is now on the West Point road twenty four miles south of this and draws his supplies by that road. Jeff Davis is there to day and superhuman efforts will be made to break my roads. Forrest is now Lieut General and commands all the enemys cavalry" Telegram received (on Sept. 27, 3:15 A.M.), DNA, RG 107, Telegrams Collected (Bound); *ibid.*, RG 108, Letters Received; copies, *ibid.*, RG 107, Telegrams Received in Cipher; *ibid.*, RG 393, Military Div. of the Miss., Telegrams Sent in the Field; DLC-William T. Sherman. *O.R.*, I, xxxix, part 2, 479.

To Maj. Gen. William T. Sherman

(Cipher)   City Point Va. Sept. 26th *1864.* [*6:30* P.M.]
MAJ. GEN. SHERMAN, ATLANTA GA.

Jeff Davis was in Richmond on last Thursday.[1] This I think is beyond doubt. I have evidence that Sheridan's victory has created the greatest consternation and alarm for the safety ~~for~~ of the City. I ~~shall~~ will give them an other shake before the end of the week.

U. S. GRANT
Lt. Gn.

ALS (telegram sent), CSmH; telegram received (at 9:20 P.M.), DNA, RG 107, Telegrams Collected (Bound). *O.R.,* I, xxxix, part 2, 479. On Sept. 27, 1864, 10:00 A.M., Maj. Gen. William T. Sherman telegraphed to USG. "Jeff Davis was certainly at Macon on the 23rd for he made a very significant speech which is given at length and which I ordered to be telegraphed as far as Louisville— Forrest has burned the Bridge over Elk river near Athens but I think Rousseau can keep him off the Chattanooga road,   still all recruits should be sent to Nashville with dispatch—" Telegram received (at 7:00 P.M.), DNA, RG 107, Telegrams Collected (Bound); *ibid.,* RG 108, Letters Received; copies, *ibid.,* RG 107, Telegrams Received in Cipher; *ibid.,* RG 393, Military Div. of the Miss., Telegrams Sent in the Field. *O.R.,* I, xxxix, part 2, 488. At 10:30 P.M., USG telegraphed to Sherman. "I have directed all recruits and new troops from the Western states to be sent to Nashville to receive there further orders from you. I was mistaken about Davis being in Richmond on Thursday last. He was then on his way to Macon." ALS (telegram sent), CSmH; telegram received (at 3:00 P.M.), DNA, RG 107, Telegrams Collected (Bound); *ibid.,* Telegrams Collected (Unbound); *ibid.,* RG 393, Military Div. of the Miss., Telegrams Received. Printed as received at 2:00 P.M. in *O.R.,* I, xxxix, part 2, 489.

1. Sept. 22.

To Edwin M. Stanton

City Point Va. Sept. 27th, *1864.*

HON. E. M. STANTON
SEC'Y OF WAR
WASHINGTON D. C.
SIR

The exercise of the right of suffrage, by the Officers and soldiers of Armies in the field, is a novel thing; it has I believe, generally been considered dangerous to constitutional liberty and subversive of Military discipline. But our circumstances are novel and exceptional. A very large proportion of the legal voters of the United States, are now either under arms in the field, or in hospitals, or otherwise engaged in the Military service of the United States. Most of these men, are not regular soldiers in the strict sense of that term, still less are they mercenaries, who give their services to the Government simply for its pay, having little understanding of political questions, and feeling little or no interest in them. On the contrary, they are American Citizens, having still their homes and social and political ties, binding them to the States and Districts, from which they come, and to which they expect to return. They have left their homes temporarily, to sustain the cause of their country, in the hour of its trial. In performing this sacred duty, they should not be deprived of a most precious privelege. They have as much right to demand that their votes shall be counted, in the choice of their rulers, as those citizens, who remain at home; Nay more, for they have sacrificed more for their country.

I state these reasons in full for the unusual thing of allowing Armies in the field to vote, that I may urge on the other hand, that *nothing more*, than the fullest exercise of this right, should be allowed; for any thing not but absolutely necessary to this exercise cannot but be dangerous to the discipline of the Armies, and dangerous to the liberties of the country. The Officers and Soldiers, have every means of understanding the questions before the country. The newspapers are freely circulated, and so, I believe, are the documents prepared by both parties, to set forth the merits and claims of their candidates.

Beyond this nothing whatever should be allowed. No political meetings, no harangues from soldiers or citizens and no canvassing of camps or regiments for votes.

I see not why a single individual, not belonging to the Armies, should be admitted into their lines, to deliver tickets. In my opinion, the tickets should be furnished by the Chief Provost Marshal of each Army, and by them, to the Provost Marshal (or some other appointed Officer) of each brigade or regiment, who shall, on the day of the election, deliver tickets irrespective of party, to whoever may call for them. If however it shall be deemed expedient to admit Citizens to deliver tickets, then it should be most possitively prohibited, that such Citizens should electioneer, harangue, or canvass the regiments in any way. Their business should be, and only be, to distribute, on a certain fixed day, tickets to whoever may call for them.

In the case of those states whose soldiers vote by proxy, proper state authority could be given to Officers belonging to regiments so voting, to secure and forward votes.

As it is intended that all soldiers entitled to vote shall exercise that privelege according to their own convictions of right, unmolested and unrestrincted, there will be no objection to each party sending to Armies, easy of access, a number of respectable gentlemen, to see that these views are fully carried out. To the Army at Atlanta and those Armies on the sea coast from Newbern to New Orleans, not to exceed three Citizens, of each party, should be admitted.

> I am Sir
> Very respectfully
> Your obd't. serv't.
> U. S. GRANT
> Lieut. General.

LS, DNA, RG 94, Letters Received, 1362A 1864. *O.R.*, I, xlii, part 2, 1045–46. Noted on the docket: "Enclosed is application of Geo. H. Ketcham, & J. Mabbitt, to go to Atlanta, to collect votes of N. Y. soldiers." DNA, RG 94, Letters Received, 1362A 1864.

On Sept. 24, 1864, Secretary of War Edwin M. Stanton wrote to USG. "I send you enclosed a letter from Belmont which you will please read and favor me with your views as to the proper regulation of the matter." ALS, *ibid.*, RG 108, Letters Received. On Sept. 21, August Belmont, chairman, and Frederick D. Prince, secretary, National Democratic Executive Committee, wrote to Stanton. "Several of the States in the Union, have provided by law for the exercise, by their qualified votes in the Military Service, of their rights of Suffrage, when on actual duty, wherever they happen to be on the day of Election. The Executive Committee of the National Democratic Committee, respectfully ask that you will authorize the admission, within the military lines—under Such regulations as your Department may adopt—of Such persons as may be designated by our Chairman to deliver tickets. The Committee make this request believing that it was intended—and that it is but just—that our Soldiers Should have the oppertunity to exercise the Same freedom of choice they would have at home. Their faithful Services in the cause of their country entitle them to this privilege. The near approach of Some of the Elections, will, we hope, induce you to give this matter your prompt attention." Copy, *ibid*.

On Sept. 30, 9:00 P.M., Stanton telegraphed to USG. "Your letter in respect to ticket agents reached me this morning. The number of one to each army will be too ~~small~~ few to do the work, but it should of course be restricted to the ~~smallest~~ ~~possible~~ narrowest limit compatible with fair distribution. The regulation prohibiting canvassing &c is all right and will be made an express condition. ~~To~~ ~~avoid~~ ~~trouble~~ ~~with~~ The [c]redentials ~~we~~ to authorize a pass from the Department might be from either the State Executive or State Committe. ~~With~~ ~~these~~ ~~suggest~~ I propose [t]o direct the Adjutant General to issue passes in accordance with these suggestions. Hooker has been assigned to relieve Heintzleman." ALS (telegram sent), *ibid*., RG 107, Telegrams Collected (Bound); *ibid*., Telegrams Collected (Unbound); *ibid*., RG 108, Letters Received. *O.R*., III, iv, 750. On Oct. 1 or 2, USG telegraphed to Stanton. "My letter on the subject of appointing Agts to superintend elections in the Army only gave general views. What ever order you make on the subject will be cheerfully carried out. ~~I~~ ~~have~~ ~~no~~ ~~objection~~ ~~to~~ ~~passes~~ ~~being~~ ~~given~~ ~~to~~ ~~Lord~~ ~~Mahon~~ ~~Hon.~~ ~~Mr.~~ ~~Stanhope~~ ~~&~~ ~~Capt.~~ ~~Hayter~~ ~~to~~ ~~visit~~ ~~this~~ ~~Army.~~" ALS (telegram sent), CSmH; telegram received (marked as sent Oct. 2, 10.30 A.M., received at noon), DNA, RG 107, Telegrams Collected (Bound). Dated Oct. 1 in *O.R*., III, iv, 752. On Sept. 30, 1:20 P.M., Asst. Secretary of War Charles A. Dana had telegraphed to USG. "Permission to visit your lines is asked for Lord Mahon the Hon. Mr. Stanhope & Capt. Hayter of the British army. Have you any objections?" ALS (telegram sent), DNA, RG 107, Telegrams Collected (Bound); telegram received, *ibid*., RG 108, Letters Received. On the same day, USG telegraphed to Dana. "There is no objection." Telegram received (at 5:00 P.M.), *ibid*., RG 107, Telegrams Collected (Bound); *ibid*., Telegrams Collected (Unbound). On Oct. 2, Stanton wrote to USG. "I enclose to you a copy of an order relating to elections which I hope will be found to meet your views. If any modifications or changes occur to you as essential please notify me by telegraph" ALS, *ibid*., RG 108, Letters Received. The enclosure is in *O.R*., III, iv, 751–52.

To Maj. Gen. Henry W. Halleck

(Cipher)   City Point Va. Sept. 27th *1864*. [*11:00* A.M.]
MAJ. GN. HALLECK, WASHINGTON.

From Richmond papers of yesterday I gather that firing was heard from Stanton on Sunday[1] morning. People were leaving Stanton in great alarm. No troops have passed through Richmond to reinforce Early. All that have left ~~that~~ so far as can be learned is two regiments and a city battalion have gone to Lynchburg. I shall make a break here on the 29th.

U. S. GRANT
Lt. Gn.

ALS (telegram sent), CSmH; telegram received (at 3:00 P.M.), DNA, RG 107, Telegrams Collected (Bound); *ibid.*, Telegrams Collected (Unbound). *O.R.*, I, xliii, part 2, 186.

1. Sept. 25, 1864.

To Maj. Gen. Henry W. Halleck

(Cipher)   City Point, Va. Sept. 27th *1864*. [*11:00* A.M.]
MAJ. GN. H. W. HALLECK, WASHINGTON.

I wish you would have every effort made to send troops to Nashville to receive further orders from there from Gn. Sherman. Order all recruits and new regiments from Iowa Wisconsin, Illinois, Indiana and Ohio, now ready, to be sent at once. Also recruits for general distribution from Michigan if there are any. If there are any new regiments in Western Pa. send them also.

                              U. S. GRANT
                              Lt. Gn.

ALS (telegram sent), CSmH; telegram received (marked as sent at noon, received at 2:00 P.M.), DNA, RG 107, Telegrams Collected (Bound); *ibid.*, Telegrams Collected (Unbound).
   On Sept. 26, 1864, Maj. Gen. George G. Meade telegraphed to USG. "Parke has a letter from Wilcox from Detroit of the 21st inst.—saying the 6 Michigan regts are ready to leave & it is understood are going or have been ordered to the A. P—but the Gov. wants to keep them longer in order to fill them to the maximum—Cant you have them pushed on [and] let their recruits be sent after them— I thought you would like to know wh[at] Wilcox writes—" ALS (telegram sent), *ibid.*; telegram received, *ibid.*, RG 108, Letters Received. On the same day, USG telegraphed to Maj. Gen. Henry W. Halleck. "Please direct the six Michigan regiments to come forward without delay to the Army of the Potomac and let the recruits for the same be sent after them as fast as collected." Telegram received (at 7:30 P.M.), *ibid.*, RG 107, Telegrams Collected (Bound); copies, *ibid.*, RG 108, Letters Sent; *ibid.*, Letters Received; DLC-USG, V, 45, 69, 107. On Sept. 27, USG telegraphed to Meade. "I have directed Gen Halleck to order forward to the A of P The ~~6th~~ six (6) Michigan Regiments mentioned by you yesterday & the recruits to be sent after them as fast as collected" Telegram received (at 12:20 P.M.), DNA, RG 94, War Records Office, Army of the Potomac; copies, *ibid.*, RG 108, Letters Sent; DLC-USG, V, 45, 69, 107; (2) Meade Papers, PHi. *O.R.*, I, xlii, part 2, 1046. At 1:00 P.M., Halleck telegraphed to USG. "The six Michigan regiments will not make three. A consolidation was ordered a week ago, but is not yet completed, the fragments being scattered over the state. Sherman telegraphs urging that all new troops from the west be sent to protect his communications. These regiments, however, will, by your orders, be sent to city

Point No reply has been recieved from you in regard to repair of Rail Roads."
ALS (telegram sent), DNA, RG 107, Telegrams Collected (Bound); telegram
received, *ibid.*; *ibid.*, RG 108, Letters Received. *O.R.*, I, xliii, part 2, 186. At
6:00 P.M., USG telegraphed to Halleck. "You may send the three Michigan regiments to Sherman if they can be got off soon." ALS (telegram sent), CSmH; telegram received (at 10:00 P.M.), DNA, RG 94, Vol. Service Div., A1198 (VS)
1864; *ibid.*, RG 107, Telegrams Collected (Bound). On Sept. 28, USG telegraphed to Meade. "The 6 Michigan Regts is so insufficient in numbers that
they will hardly make three (3) full regiments—I have therefore ordered their
consolidation & in consequence of the urgenceny of more troops with Sherman, I
have directed that they be sent to him" Telegram received (at 11:10 A.M.),
ibid., RG 94, War Records Office, Army of the Potomac; copies, *ibid.*, RG 108,
Letters Sent; DLC-USG, V, 45, 69, 107; (2) Meade Papers, PHi.

To Maj. Gen. Henry W. Halleck

(Cipher) City Point Va. Sept. 27th *1864*. [6:00 P.M.]
MAJ. GEN. HALLECK, WASHINGTON,

I think the road towards Sheridan should be put in order as far
as protection can be furnished for it. Washington being protected
as much by troops sent out on the road south as if the same troops
were in the city can be stripped conciderably lower than would be
justifyable to send the troops elswhere. After reaching Manassas
Junction I would like Sheridan to decide which road should be
opened. If he moves as I expected him, to Charlottesville, the road
to Culpepper would be the one to repair.

U. S. GRANT
Lt. Gn.

ALS (telegram sent), CSmH; telegram received, DNA, RG 94, War Records
Office, Dept. of the Cumberland; (at 10:00 P.M.) *ibid.*, RG 107, Telegrams Collected (Bound). *O.R.*, I, xliii, part 2, 187. On Sept. 27, 1864, 11:30 A.M. and
6:30 P.M., USG had telegraphed to Maj. Gen. Henry W. Halleck. "I have said
no more on the subject of opening rail-road communications with Gen. Sheridan
because whilst he is moving it is hard to say where he will want it. If Gen.
Augur can protect the road to the Rappahannock however I think it will be advisable to open the road that far." ALS (telegram sent), CSmH; telegram received, DNA, RG 94, War Records Office, Dept. of the Cumberland; (at 3:00
P.M.) *ibid.*, RG 107, Telegrams Collected (Bound). Printed as received at 2:00
P.M. in *O.R.*, I, xliii, part 2, 186. "Now that Sheridan has pushed so far up the
valley Gen. Augur should send if it is possible a force of Cavalry and Infantry out
by Culpepper with scouts as far to the front as they can go to watch if any troops
move North on the East side of Blue Ridge to get in upon Sheridan's rear." ALS

(telegram sent), CSmH; telegram received, DNA, RG 94, War Records Office, Dept. of the Cumberland; (marked as sent at 6:00 P.M., received at 10:00 P.M.) *ibid.*, RG 107, Telegrams Collected (Bound). *O.R.*, I, xliii, part 2, 187.

At 2:00 P.M., Bvt. Maj. Gen. Montgomery C. Meigs had telegraphed to USG. "We wait military protection to open the Manassas Gap Railroad. Reports of time needed ~~being~~ say three days to Piedmont, seven days to Front Royal, fourteen days to Strasburg. The cost of wagan trains from Harper's Ferry or Martinsburg to Strasburg will be very heavy, and it is very difficult to supply hay and grain for the animals. They consume in the rear what the Manassas Gap Railroad would enable us to deliver near to the front. If the military movements needed to ~~run~~ cover the road can be made, it will be very advantageous to open this road at once. Can you order dispositions to make this safe and practicable?" LS (telegram sent), DNA, RG 107, Telegrams Collected (Unbound); telegram received, *ibid.*; *ibid.*, RG 108, Letters Received. *O.R.*, I, xliii, part 2, 187. At 6:00 P.M., USG telegraphed to Meigs. "I have given no orders until to-day about repairing rail-roads because I did not know whether Gn. Sheridan would have the road to Culpepper or the one to Strasburg opened. Gen. Augur, and other Departments in the Middle Division will have to furnish the troops to guard the road when open." ALS (telegram sent), CSmH; telegram received (at 10:00 P.M.), DNA, RG 92, Consolidated Correspondence, Grant; *ibid.*, RG 107, Telegrams Collected (Bound). *O.R.*, I, xliii, part 2, 187.

To Maj. Gen. Benjamin F. Butler

City Point, Va. Sept. 27th/64

MAJ. GN. BUTLER,

The Surgeon Gn. informs me that the only two ocean Steamers at the disposal of the Medical Dept. suitable for transporting sick and wounded have been applied for by your and wants to know if they are essential. Please inform me by note with Col. Dent who is now on the way to your Hd Qrs. what they are wanted for so that I can reply.

U. S. GRANT
Lt. Gn.

ALS (telegram sent), OClWHi; copies, DLC-USG, V, 45, 69, 107; DNA, RG 108, Letters Sent. See *O.R.*, I, xlii, part 2, 1024. On Sept. 26, 1864, Brig. Gen. Joseph K. Barnes, surgeon gen., telegraphed to USG. "Major General Butler applies for the Atlantic and Baltic—the *only two sea going* Hospital Transports at the control of this Department—Will Lt. Genl. Grant decide if they can be spared, and order accordingly—" LS (telegram sent), DNA, RG 107, Telegrams Collected (Unbound); telegram received, *ibid.*; *ibid.*, RG 108, Letters Received. On Sept. 28, 4:30 P.M., USG telegraphed to Barnes. "I have called on Gn.

Butler to know why he wanted the two Ocean Hospital Steamers of which you telegraphed but have received no reply. Until you hear from me on the subject you need not send them." ALS (telegram sent), CSmH; telegram received (at 7:00 p.m.), DNA, RG 107, Telegrams Collected (Bound); *ibid.*, Telegrams Collected (Unbound). *O.R.*, I, xlii, part 2, 1064.

On Oct. 28, Barnes telegraphed to USG. "The Quartermaster at Fortress-Monroe has seized the Hospl. Transports, 'Atlantic' and 'Baltic' by order of Genl Butler—Surgeon Dalton telegraphs for all available transports for sick and wounded at City-Point and these vessels are urgently required for the purpose— Please countermand General Butlers order—" LS (telegram sent), DNA, RG 107, Telegrams Collected (Unbound); telegram received, *ibid.*, RG 108, Letters Received.

To Maj. Gen. Benjamin F. Butler

City Point, Va. Sept. 27th *1864.*

Maj. Gen. B. F. Butler,
Comd.g Army of the James River,
General,

Prepare your Army according to the verbal instructions already given for moving on the morning of the 29th inst. Your lines between the James & Appomattox rivers can be held with new regiments and such Artillery as you deem necessary. All garrisons from your command, below the mouth of the Appomattox, will be left as they are now. The movement should be commenced at night and so as to get a conciderable force North of the James River ready to assault the enemy's lines in front of Deep Bottom and from about Aikins hHouse, or such other point above Deep Bottom and where the two assaulting columns will be in easy supporting distance of each other as soon as the enemy's line is broken, at the dawn of day. If one good Division from each of your two Corps are over in time for this with the balance of these Corps following; with a pontoon bridge for each, it will answer. The object of this movement is to surprise and capture Richmond if possible. This can not be done if time is given the enemy to move forces to the North side of the river. Success will depend on prompt movement at the start. Should the outter line be broken the troops will push for Richmond with all promptness following roads as near the river as possible. It is impossible to point out the line of march for an Army in the presence of an enemy because the enemy may interpose such an obstacle on our route as to make it impracticable.—It is known that the enemy has intrenched positions on the bank of the river, between Deep Bottom & Richmond, such as Chapin's Farm, which are garrisoned. If these can be captured in passing they should be held by suitable garrisons. If not Captured troops should be left to hold them in their position and should intrench to make themselves strong. It will be necessary therefore to have your Engineer troops, with their tools well up with the advance. Should you succeed in getting to Richmond the interposition of the whole Army (rebel) between you and your supplies need cause no alarm. With the Army under Gen. Meade supplies could be cut off from the enemy in the event of so unexpected a move and communications opened with you either by the South side or from the White House before the supplies you would find in the city would be exhausted. In case you reach Richmond the details for Garrisoning and holding the place are left to you, or the senior officer with the troops that get in. One thing I would say however; all the bridges connecting the city with the south side should be destroyed at once are held beyond a peradventure. As the success of this enterprise depends entirely on celerity the troops will go light. They will take only a single blanket rolled and carried over the shoulder, three days rations in Haversacks and sixty rounds of Ammunition in box and on the person. No wagons will be taken. They will be supplied however with six days rations, ~~and~~ half forage for the same time, and forty rounds of extra ammunition per man, to follow if they should be required. No wagons will cross the James River until ordered by you. The whole of the force under Gn. Meade will be under Arms at 4 a. m. on the 29th ready to attack Petersburg or move on to the south side road as circumstances may determine. As against any force now North of the James you can go to Richmond even without a surprise. If the enemy resists you by sufficient force to prevent your advance it is confidantly expected that Gen. Meade can gain a decisive advantage on his end of the line. The prize sought is either Richmond or Petersburg or a position which will secure the fall of the latter. Please furnish me a copy of your detailed instructions.

> I am General, very respectfully
> your obt. svt.
> U. S. GRANT
> Lt. Gn.

ALS, DLC-Benjamin F. Butler. *O.R.*, I, xlii, part 2, 1058–59.

On Sept. 27, 1864, 11:30 A.M., USG telegraphed to Maj. Gen. Benjamin F. Butler. "Make all your changes of troops at once ready for the execution of orders verbally communicated ~~at once~~ so as to have troops as fresh as possible." ALS (telegram sent), CSmH; telegram received, DNA, RG 94, War Records Office, Army of the Potomac; *ibid.*, RG 107, Telegrams Collected (Unbound). *O.R.*, I, xlii, part 2, 1058. On the same day, Butler telegraphed to USG. "Telegram received. The dispositions are being made—" LS (telegram sent), DNA, RG 94, War Records Office, Army of the Potomac. Printed as sent at noon in *O.R.*, I, xlii, part 2, 1058.

On Sept. 26, 2:00 P.M., Lt. Col. George A. Kensel, act. chief of staff for Butler, telegraphed to USG. "Gen Butler has just gone to Wilsons Wharf—" Telegram received, DNA, RG 107, Telegrams Collected (Unbound).

Also on Sept. 26, Lt. Col. Cyrus B. Comstock telegraphed to Maj. Gen. George G. Meade. "The Lt Gen Comdg wishes you would so arrange it that the battalion of 1st N. Y Vol Engineers lately serving with 10th Corps may be spared from Petersburg & directed to report to Genl Butler" Telegram received (at 9:55 P.M.), *ibid.*, RG 94, War Records Office, Army of the Potomac; copies (2), Meade Papers, PHi. *O.R.*, I, xlii, part 2, 1029. At 10:15 P.M., Meade telegraphed to Comstock. "The battallion of 1st N. Y. Vols Engrs, came with the 10th corps & I presumed went with it when relieved.—I find however upon enquiry that two cos remained with Capt Gillespie by whose authority detained I dont know—I have allowed them to be at once sent to Genl. Butler—" ALS (telegram sent), DNA, RG 94, War Records Office, Army of the Potomac; copy, *ibid.*, RG 393, Army of the Potomac, Letters Sent. *O.R.*, I, xlii, part 2, 1030.

On Sept. 27, 9:20 A.M., Butler telegraphed to USG transmitting information from a signal officer that ten railroad cars carrying troops had gone to Petersburg. Telegram received, DNA, RG 107, Telegrams Collected (Unbound). *O.R.*, I, xlii, part 2, 1060.

To Maj. Gen. George G. Meade

City Point, Va. Sept. 27th *1864.*

MAJ. GEN. G. G. MEADE,
COMD.G A. P.
GENERAL,

On the morning of the 29th inst. a movement will take place intended to surprise and capture the works of the enemy North of the James River and between Malvern Hill and Richmond. The troops engaged in this will be taken exclusively from the 10th and 18th Army Corps.—Although these troops will be instructed to push directly for Richmond, if successful in breaking through the outer line of Rebel Works, it is hardly expected that so much can be accomplished. But as against the force now kept North of the James River by the enemy, Gen. Butler can force his way to Richmond and will do it unless they largely re-enforce from Petersburg. As a co-operative movement with this you will please have the Army of the Potomac under Arms at 4 O'Clock a. m. on the 29th ready to move in any direction. They should have three or four days rations in Haversack and Sixty rounds of Ammunition on the person, including that in Cartridge boxes.—It was my intention to give specific instructions for a concentration of all the force you could spare, on your left, and for a demonstration as if to extend our lines in that direction. But on reflection I will leave the details to you stating me[ar]ly that I want every effort used to convince the enemy that the "South side Road" and 'Petersburg' are the objects of our efforts. ~~and~~ Should the enemy draw off such a force from the defences of Petersburg as to justify you in moving either for the South side road or Petersburg I want you to do it without waiting for instructions and in your own way. One thing however I would say: if the road is reached it, or a position commanding it, should be held at all hazards. If it becomes necessary to maintain the position against an attack draw off from our present defences what force you deem necessary, always keeping the garrisons detailed for the inclosed works on the line intact however.

All trains should be harnassed, hitched and ready to move at a moments notice. The accumulation of supplies at depots along the rail-road should also be stopped, and as far as practicable that now on hand in depot should be got in wagons.

At the begining of this move I shall be on the North side of the river. Up to 8 a. m. however dispatches may be directed to me at City Point, after that hour, until otherwise directed, at Deep Bottom.

> I am Gn. very respectful[l]y
> your obt. svt.
> U. S. GRANT
> Lt. Gn.

ALS, deCoppet Collection, NjP. *O.R.*, I, xlii, part 2, 1046–47. On Sept. 27, 1864, 9:00 P.M., USG telegraphed to Maj. Gen. George G. Meade. "If troops can be moved to-morrow so as to give the appearance of Massing on our left it would serve to deceive the enemy. I think also it will be advisable to send scouts some distance to the Southeast to discover if the enemy are moving Cavalry around towards the James River." ALS (telegram sent), CSmH; telegram received (marked as sent at 9:30 P.M., received at 10:00 P.M.), DNA, RG 94, War Records Office, Army of the Potomac. *O.R.*, I, xlii, part 2, 1047. At 10:30 P.M., Meade telegraphed to USG. "Do you refer to movements within or without our lines.—I can send two divisions of the 9th corps tomorrow beyond our left & beyond where Warren was the other day—If attacked they can be supported by two of Warrens divisions—This is what I proposed to do under your instructions, the next day, but it will no doubt have much more effect tomorrow than the next day, tho it will also be more likely to bring on an engagement.—" ALS (telegram sent), DNA, RG 94, War Records Office, Army of the Potomac; telegram received, *ibid.*, RG 108, Letters Received. *O.R.*, I, xlii, part 2, 1047. On the same day, USG telegraphed to Meade. "What I ment was to move troops within our lines, not openly but so the enemy would likely get glimpses of them and think there was a concentration on our left. The 10th Corps moving to Bermuda Hundred to-night will be missed from its position in the morning and if the enemy can be deceived into thinking they have gone around to the left it will aid us" ALS (undated telegram sent), CSmH; telegram received (at 11:15 P.M.), DNA, RG 94, War Records Office, Army of the Potomac. *O.R.*, I, xlii, part 2, 1048.

At 9:55 A.M., Maj. Gen. Edward O. C. Ord had telegraphed to USG. "A Lieut Deserter from the rebels is in this morning—states that the belief among them is that should Lynchburg which is strongly fortified be captured—it would give you the Danville road and want of food would compel the evacuation of their Lees present position—that they have not force enough to reinforce Lynchburg and their fears are that Richmond will be approached from that quarter—this Lieut is an intelligent officer from Va and I am sure speaks candidly—" ALS (telegram sent), DNA, RG 107, Telegrams Collected (Unbound); telegram received, *ibid.*; *ibid.*, RG 108, Letters Received. *O.R.*, I, xlii, part 2, 1062–63.

To Edwin M. Stanton

From City Point Sept 28 *1864.*

HON E. M. STANTON
SECY OF WAR,

The Richmond Whig [o]f this morning contains the following Charlottesville   Sept 28th 64   The fight near Port Republic on Monday was an engagement between our Cavalry & that of the enemy—They came over the River and were driven back three (3) miles by our Cavalry to and across the River—The enemies Cavalry entered Stanton about eight (8) P M on Monday—A force appeared at Waynesboro about nine (9) oclock this morning and then went back about one (1) mile from town—No damage has been done up to four (4) P M—The smoke seen indicates that they are burning the Rail Road track between Christiana Creek & Stanton—There has been no serious fighting up to four (4) oclock this evening—This despatch should probably have been dated 27th but I give it as given in the Richmond papers

U. S. GRANT
Lieut Genl

Telegram received (at 11:00 P.M.), DNA, RG 107, Telegrams Collected (Bound); copies, *ibid.*, RG 108, Letters Sent; DLC-USG, V, 45, 69, 107. *O.R.,* I, xliii, part 2, 196.

On Sept. 28, 1864, USG telegraphed to Maj. Gen. Benjamin F. Butler. "Have you seen a Richmond Paper of to-day? If so what news does it contain from the Valley?" ALS (telegram sent), OClWHi; telegram received, DNA, RG 94, War Records Office, Miscellaneous War Records. At 7:00 P.M., Butler drafted his reply at the foot of the telegram received. "The Richmond papers are gone to you   They say that a passenger that came down by cars says he had heard that Early repulsed Sheridan but the War department had no news   Stock jobbing news" ADfS, *ibid.*; telegram received, *ibid.*, RG 108, Letters Received.

To Maj. Gen. Henry W. Halleck

(Cipher)   City Point, Va. Sept. 28th/64 [9:00 A.M.]
MAJ. GN. HALLECK, WASHINGTON,

Every thing indicates that the enemy are going to make a last and spasmodic effort to regain what they have lost and especially against Sherman. Troops should be got to ~~Sh~~ Sherman as rapidly as his lines of communications will carry them. If there are no troops in the Western states then send him from further East.

U. S. Grant
Lt. Gn.

ALS (telegram sent), CSmH; telegram received (at 4:00 P.M.), DNA, RG 107, Telegrams Collected (Bound); *ibid.*, Telegrams Collected (Unbound). *O.R.*, I, xli, part 3, 433.

To Maj. Gen. Henry W. Halleck

City Point Va. Sept. 28th *1864*.

Maj. Gen. H. W. Halleck,
Chief of Staff of the Army,
General,

The enclosed letter from General Howard has been written under a misapprehension of all the facts. How far Gen. Canby has been authorized to exercise control over the "Dept. of the Tenn." I do not know, but in placing a commander at Vicksburg it was by my direction. Gen. Slocum being ordered to the Army operating against Atlanta I deemed it important that he should be replaced at Vicksburg by an officer of rank and experience. Gen. Sherman had no such officer to spare. Gen. A. J. Smith was not ordered to Mo. by Gen. Canby but by my direction under the belief that Price had passed the line held by Steele and was making his way to Mo.

General Canby should, when he gives any order affecting the troops in the 'Dept. of the Tenn.' inform Gen. Howard of the orders he had given and the necessity for thm and when troops are taken out of the Dept. to which they belong they should be returned as soon as the exigency for which they are taken ceases to exist.

Very respectfully
your obt. svt.
U. S. Grant
Lt. Gen.

ALS, deCoppet Collection, NjP. *O.R.*, I, xli, part 3, 433–34. USG enclosed a letter of Sept. 16, 1864, from Maj. Gen. Oliver O. Howard, East Point, Ga., to

Brig. Gen. John A. Rawlins. "Considerable confusion and embarrassment have arisen in this Army and Department, from the conflict of Orders resulting from Genl Canby assuming the entire command of Troops belonging here. I am informed that a portion of Genl Blairs Corps, is ordered to the Dept of the Gulf, and attached permanantly to the 19th Corps; that fragments of several regiments represented here by detachments, have been also transferred to the Dept of Arkansas, and ordered to report to Genl Steele; that Genl Mower's Division has recently been sent up White River; that Genl A. J. Smiths Division has ordered somewhere into Missouri; that Genl Canby has given his own commander to the District of Vicksburg. From every little stampeding report Genl Washburn, Commdg Disct of West Tennessee is ordered or requested to send troops across the river to different points. In all these cases the Department commander is not consulted or even informed. I have no personal end to subserve but it is unfair to this gallant Army to dissipate it and absorb it little by little in positions where it can do little good. I know too, that Gen'l Grant and Genl Sherman, coincide with me in the policy of concentrating force rather than scattering it. If my command is too large, I beg that organizations may be removed rather than fragments of Regiments Brigades, and Divisions, as is now the case. It is desired to make this column for the field from 25.000 to 30.000 strong, but not having any control of the troops on the Mississippi I cannot effect this. If permitted, with the approval of Maj Genl Sherman, I can reorganize the Department so as to get a Field force of 30.000, and at the same time have the Posts now occupied by the troops on the Mississippi garrisoned with sufficient strength. I can also have a moveable force properly organized, to spare in case of emergency. I do not object to assisting Maj Genl Canby, nor that the necessary Military control of the Mississippi River be in his hands, but would like to preserve this Army from complete absorption, and be able while held responsible to make proper returns." Copy, DNA, RG 108, Letters Received. *O.R.*, I, xxxix, part 2, 392–93. On the same day, Maj. Gen. William T. Sherman endorsed this letter. "I agree with Genl Howard that the operation of recent orders, giving to Genl Canby the troops left on the Mississippi is having a disorganizing effect on the Army of the Tennessee." Copy, DNA, RG 108, Letters Received.

On Sept. 30, Maj. Gen. Henry W. Halleck wrote to USG. "Yours of the 28th enclosing Gen'l. Howard's of the 16th inst. is just received. Gen'l. Howards statements are all wrong from beginning to end. The correspondence between Gen'l's Sherman and Canby and the War Department put this matter in a very different and satisfactory light. At Gen'l. Sherman's request Gen'l. Canby was authorized to direct the movements of all troops on the east bank of the Missisippi to operate on either side. They were to continue to report to Howard as being in his Department, but neither he nor Sherman were to give them orders, except in case of emergency. Copies of all orders given by Gen'l. Canby to such troops were to be, and have been sent to Gen'l. Sherman. Parts of regiments on the river were collected to be sent to Atlanta; but were stopt at Memphis to assist Steele in Arkansas. Gen'l. Dana was placed in command at Vicksburg by the direct order of the Secretary of War to root out some of the rascalities at that place, and I believe he is doing it pretty effectually. It is very possible that the reported operation of the rebels in Arkansas may turn out only a 'little stampede,' but it would have been unwise for Gen'l Canby, under the circumstances, to neglect any means of Meeting that 'stampede.' In a letter to me Gen'l. Sherman says that as soon as the fragments of regiments and brigades belonging to the Department of the Tennessee can be sent to Gen'l. Howard it may be well to detach the others and make a new Department on the Missisippi River, leaving Howard simply in command of his Army in the field; but for the present he prefers that no change be made. Should he and Canby's troops connect on the Alabama or Appalachicola river, it will be necessary to make a reorganization of Departments and Commands. Sherman has been kept fully advised of what Canby is doing, or proposes to do." LS, *ibid.* *O.R.*, I, xli, part 3, 496–97.

To Maj. Gen. William T. Sherman

[*Sept. 28, 1864, 8:30* A.M.]

MAJ. GN. SHERMAN, ATLANTA GA.

It is evident from the tone of the Richmond press, and all other sources, that the enemy intend making a desperate effort to drive you from where you are. I have directed all new troops from the West, and from the [*East*] too if none are ready in the West, to be sent to you. If Burbridge is not too far on the way towards Abbingdon I think he had better be recalled and his surplus troops sent into Tennessee.

U. S. GRANT

Lt. Gn

ALS (telegram sent), CSmH; telegram received (at 4:00 P.M.), DNA, RG 107, Telegrams Collected (Bound). *O.R.*, I, xxxix, part 2, 502. On Sept. 28, 1864, 9:30 P.M., Maj. Gen. William T. Sherman telegraphed to USG. "Your despatch is just received. I send back to Stevenson and Decherd Gen Thomas to look to Tennessee, and have ordered a Brigade of the Army of the Tennessee up to Eastport, and the cavalry across to that place from Memphis to operate against the flank of any force going into Tennessee by way of the fords near Florence. I want Appalachacola Arsenal taken, also Savannah, and if the enemy does succeed in breaking up my roads I can fight my way across to one or the other place: but I think it better to hold on to Atlanta and strengthen to my rear, and therefore am glad you have ordered troops to Nashville Forrest has got into Middle Tenn. and will I feel certain get on my main road tonight or tomorrow: but I will guard well from this, back to Chattanooga, and trust to troops coming up from Kentucky to hold Nashville & forward to Chattanooga" Telegram received (on Sept. 29, 1:10 A.M.), DNA, RG 107, Telegrams Collected (Bound); (incomplete) *ibid.*, Telegrams Collected (Unbound); *ibid.*, RG 108, Letters Received; copies, *ibid.*, RG 107, Telegrams Received in Cipher; *ibid.*, RG 393, Military Div. of the Miss., Telegrams Sent in the Field. *O.R.*, I, xxxix, part 2, 502.

To Julia Dent Grant

Sept. 28th/64

DEAR JULIA,

This letter is from the young lady in Lexington Ky. you have heard Wilson say so much about and in answer to some of his nonsece which he made a pretext to write to her.

The photograph is also hers. Save it for I know Wilson will want it some day. The other Photograph is of Dr. Rodgers[1] who officiated 42 years ago last 27th of Apl.

All well. I will write no more. In the morning we fight another great battle and I do not feel like writing any thing more than answers to the many dispatches I will receive. troops will be moving all night preparitory for the great struggle which will commence at the dawn of day. You will hear however through the telegraph all about it before this reaches you. Love and kisses for you and the children.

ULYS.

ALS, DLC-USG.

1. See P. F. Greene, "John George Rogers, M. D.: A Biography of the Man Who Delivered President Grant," *The Ohio State Medical Journal*, 59, 1 (Jan., 1963), 36, 38; *ibid.*, 59, 2 (Feb., 1963), 142, 144.

To Abraham Lincoln

Deep Bottom Va.
Sept. 29th/64 1.40 p. m.

A. LINCOLN, PRESIDENT

Your dispatch just received. I am taking steps to prevent Lee sending reinforcements to Early by attacking him here. Our advance is now within six miles of Richmond and have captured some very strong enclosed forts some fifteen or more pieces of Artillery and several hundred prisoners. Although I have been at the front

I can give no estimate of our losses. About 600 wounded men however have been brought in.

U. S. Grant
Lt. Gn.

ALS (telegram sent), OClWHi; telegram received (marked as sent at 2:00 p.m.,
received at 3:30 p.m.), DNA, RG 107, Telegrams Collected (Bound); DLC-
Robert T. Lincoln. *O.R.*, I, xlii, part 2, 1090–91; *ibid.*, I, xliii, part 2, 208. On
Sept. 29, 1864, 9:40 a.m., President Abraham Lincoln telegraphed to USG.
"I hope it will lay no constraint on you, nor do harm any way, for me to say I
am a little afraid lest Lee sends re-enforcements to Early, and thus enables him
to turn upon Sheridan." ALS (telegram sent), DNA, RG 107, Telegrams Collected (Bound); telegram received, *ibid.*, Telegrams Collected (Unbound);
(marked as sent at 10:00 a.m.) *ibid.*, RG 108, Letters Received. *O.R.*, I, xlii,
part 2, 1090; *ibid.*, I, xliii, part 2, 208. Lincoln, *Works*, VIII, 29.

To Maj. Gen. Henry W. Halleck

Chapin's Farm
Sept. 29 *1864*, 10.45 o'clock, A. *M.*

Maj. Gen. Halleck, Washington

Gen. Ord's corps advanced this morning and carried the very
strong fortification and long line of intrenchments below Chapins
farm with some fifteen pieces of Artillery and from two to three
hundred prisoners.[1] Gen. Ord was wounded in the leg though not
dangerously.[2] Gen. Birney advanced at the same time from Deep
Bottom and carried the New Market road and intrenchments and
scattered the enemy in every direction though he captured but few.
He is now pushing on towards Richmond. I left Gn. Birney where
the Mill road intersects the New Market & Richmond road.[3] This
whole country is filled with field fortifications this far.

U. S. Grant
Lt. Gen.

ALS (telegram sent), DNA, RG 94, War Records Office, Army of the Potomac;
telegram received (at 1:15 p.m.), *ibid.*, RG 107, Telegrams Collected (Bound);
ibid., Telegrams Collected (Unbound); OClWHi; DLC-Robert T. Lincoln. *O.R.*,
I, xlii, part 1, 20–21; (received at 12:55 p.m.) *ibid.*, I, xlii, part 2, 1091. Several telegrams received and copies indicate that the same message was sent to

Maj. Gen. Winfield S. Hancock, Maj. Gen. George G. Meade, and Maj. Gen. John G. Parke.

1. On Sept. 29, 1864, Maj. Gen. Edward O. C. Ord telegraphed to USG. "The men have used up their ammunition rapidly and more ought to be sent forward." Telegram received, DNA, RG 108, Letters Received. On the same day, Lt. Col. Ely S. Parker wrote to Lt. Col. John B. Howard, q. m. "The Lt. Genls. orders were positive that the men were to have sixty rounds of ammunition upon their persons and forty rounds per man to be put in wagons together with six days rations. Three days cooked rations were to be carried by each man. The Lt. Gen. presumes that these instructions were carried out, and it only needs that the wagons be ordered forward—" ALS (telegram sent), *ibid.*, RG 107, Telegrams Collected (Unbound); copies, *ibid.*, RG 108, Letters Sent; DLC-USG, V, 45, 69, 107.

2. Also on Sept. 29, Ord (or someone writing for him) twice telegraphed to USG. "Gen Ord has just returned with a flesh wound in the right leg   He says that in order to hold what we have gained on account of the heavy work they have had to do if possible they should be reinforced   I have the remnant of Stannards Div. in the large work at Chafins farm with directions Heckman to push in toward, Richmond with his Division. he appeared unable to get beyond the work about one half mile north of the south end of the Chafin farm works. The rebels did reinforce Chafins farm before we took it and most of them fell back to the other work or across the river. Stannard has directions to destroy the Pontoon bridge if he can reach it with artillery. The rebel Gun boats are below him throwing shells at him. Gen Burnham is dead. Stannards Division the 1st Captured the works   his losses are very heavy   I left them at 10 oclock" Telegram received, DNA, RG 108, Letters Received; copy, *ibid.*, RG 107, Telegrams Collected (Unbound). *O.R.*, I, xlii, part 2, 1115. "The Docter says I will be about thirty days off duty. Can I go home & take one Aide with me? Gen Butler has not returned from the front or I would ask him. Please let me know your answer and I will call for the proper papers, as I pass in the Mail boat tomorrow morning" LS (telegram sent), DNA, RG 107, Telegrams Collected (Unbound); telegram received, *ibid.*, RG 108, Letters Received. On Sept. 30, Capt. George K. Leet issued Special Orders No. 100 granting the leave as requested. LS, *ibid.*, RG 94, War Records Office, Army of the Potomac. *O.R.*, I, xlii, part 2, 1148.

3. On Sept. 29, 10:35 A.M., USG wrote to Maj. Gen. David B. Birney. "Gen. Ord, has carried the very strong works and some 15 pc's Artillery and his Corps is now ready to advance in conjunction with you. Gen. Ord was wounded & has returned to his Headquarters, leaving Gen. Hickman in Command of the Corps. Push forward on the road I left you on." Copies, DLC-USG, V, 45, 69, 107; DNA, RG 108, Letters Sent. *O.R.*, I, xlii, part 2, 1114.

To Maj. Gen. Henry W. Halleck

Deep Bottom Va.

Sept. 29th *186[4]*, 4 *o'clock*, P. M.

[*Maj. Gen. Halleck, Washington*]

Kautz Cavalry was in sight of Richmond at last account on the Darby road. A Division of Infantry has been sent to his support   I did not expect to carry Richmond but was in hope of causing the enemy so to weaken the Garrison of Petersburg as to be able to carry that place. The great object however is to prevent the enemy sending reenforcements to Early.

U. S. GRANT
Lt. Gn

ALS (telegram sent), CSmH; telegram received (at 6:00 P.M.), DNA, RG 107, Telegrams Collected (Bound); *ibid.*, Telegrams Collected (Unbound). *O.R.*, I, xlii, part 1, 20; *ibid.*, I, xlii, part 2, 1091. An undated telegram from Lt. Col. Orville E. Babcock to Capt. Melancton Smith was probably sent about the same time. "The force which crossed this morning have captured the enemys works at Deep bottom & the lower end of chapins farm. At last account our force were still advancing & some were in sight of Richmond   we captured 16 Guns some heavy. Rebel rams are shelling our troops"   Telegram received, DNA, RG 107, Telegrams Collected (Unbound).

To Maj. Gen. Henry W. Halleck

(Cipher)   City Point Va. Sept. 29th *1864*. [*8:00* P.M.]

MAJ. GEN. HALLECK, WASHINGTON,

I have just received copies of letters & telegrams from Gen. Allen on the subject of supplying Forts Smith & Gibson. I think it advisable to order Gen. Steele to keep open the route from Little Rock to these Forts and supply them that way or els abandon them altogether. The first thing for Steele to do is to dismiss his Chief QuarterMaster and put a live man in his place. The idea that animals should starve in Arkansas when the enemy can come and

supply man and beast is simply rediculous. Please give the necessary orders both to Gn. Steele & Q. M. Gen. Meigs.

U. S. GRANT

Lt. Gn.

ALS (telegram sent), CSmH; telegram received (at 8:30 P.M.), DNA, RG 107,
Telegrams Collected (Bound). *O.R.*, I, xli, part 3, 468–69. On Sept. 30, 1864,
1:00 P.M., Maj. Gen. Henry W. Halleck telegraphed to USG. "Stevenson &
Kelley were both reenforced yesterday. It has not been possible for sometime to
communicate with Genl Steele or the inspectors sent to report upon affairs in his
Dept. Genl Canby was authorised if his inspector found complaints against Steele
well founded to place J. J. Reynolds in command. This will avoid the delay of
referring back here for the President's order. An inspector is now in Arkansas
with authority to remove & arrest Steele's chf Qr Mr. & Com. if he deems it best
to do so. This cavalry inspector's report is not so bad as was anticipated, and
many of the other complaints may prove unfounded. I think all proper measures
have been taken to remove, without too hasty action, such evils as shall be found
to really exist. Steele has encountered numerous enemies in Jew traders & cotton speculators, & should not be too summarily condemned." ALS (telegram
sent), DNA, RG 107, Telegrams Collected (Bound); telegram received, *ibid.*;
ibid., RG 108, Letters Received. *O.R.*, I, xli, part 3, 496; (incomplete) *ibid.*, I,
xliii, part 2, 218.

On Sept. 12, USG had telegraphed to Bvt. Maj. Gen. Montgomery C. Meigs.
"I have been told by an officer traveling over the route between the Miss. river
and Little Rock, Ark. that the arrangements for supplying the Army are
wretchedly deficient and show the grossest neglect of the interests of Government on the part of many of the officers, both post commanders & Quartermasters.
Can you send and Inspector to look into this matter? Either Col. Biggs or Bingham would be good officers to send." ALS (telegram sent), CSmH; telegram received (marked as sent on Sept. 11, received on Sept. 12, 2:10 P.M.), DNA, RG
92, Consolidated Correspondence, Grant; *ibid.*, RG 107, Telegrams Collected
(Bound). Dated Sept. 12 in *O.R.*, I, xli, part 3, 157. Also on Sept. 12, 8:30 P.M.,
Meigs telegraphed to USG. "Col Bingham & the other Inspectors have all been
ordered to report here for instructions   As soon as Col Bingham arrives he will
be sent on the inspection of the route to Little Rock unless some other suitable
officer reports & is despatched there earlier.. As Col Rutherford Chief of one of
the divisions of this office has been sent away by the Secretary upon a special tour
of inspection to detach Col Biggs now would too much cripple us here—Col Carr
was nominated for ~~promoti~~ promotion as Chief Qur Master dept of Arkansas upon
reports of Inspectors ~~found~~ which are contradicted by reports since received. I
fear that there will be difficulty in supplying troops at Fort Smith & above that
point. They ask for wagon transportation from Fort Leavenworth for twelve
hundred tons per month. The cost & difficulty of supplying this quantity by
wagons over such route this winter will be enormous. At such expense should
the present positions of troops on the upper Arkansas be maintained. They report
it impracticable to supply Fort Smith & Gibson by the River   It seems to me
nearly impracticable to supply them by wagon from Fort Leavenworth—" ALS
(telegram sent), DNA, RG 107, Telegrams Collected (Unbound); *ibid.*, RG
108, Letters Received. On Sept. 27, Meigs wrote to USG. "I enclose copies of

dispatches relative to the supply of the troops at Forts Smith and Gibson. I doubt the possibility of supplying any large force at these posts by wagon transportation from Fort Leavenworth during the winter. Capt. Edwards, who built our steamers on the Tennessee at Bridgeport, has been to Little Rock to make arrangements for providing steamers suitable for this route. His report is in the hands of Col. Parsons, and the measures he proposes will be carried out. The estimates from Fort Smith, received by the way of Kansas, through Gen. Curtis' Chief Quartermaster, call for transportation of 1250 tons of supplies per month, and assert that the only practicable route is from Fort Leavenworth. On this route, we have just lost by capture 2002 wagons ~~and~~ five ambulances, 1253 mules, and 40 artillery horses, beside some sutlers' trains. Gen. Allen, as you will see by the enclosed, doubts the possibility of replacing these captured trains. The loss is a very heavy one; and if the Rebels have retained and not destroyed the trains, they have made an acquisition most valuable to them. In view of the great cost of supplying these troops, and of the doubt of its practicability, I lay the case before you, after consulting the Secretary. Should the attempt be made to keep up the garrisons of these outlying posts during the winter? Is there any sufficient advantage in their occupation to justify incurring so great an expense, especially when officers of experience doubt the possibility of accomplishing the result desired. Gen. Thayer reports eight or ten thousand Rebels concentrating to attack him—six thousand of them mounted. If they have this force of mounted men, the trains will find the Rebels as great an obstacle as the winter roads. I send this by the hands of Colonel Bingham, who has just seen Gen. Allen, and who may be able to give you some information. The matter is pressing. I sent, some days since, Col. Crittenden, recently appointed Inspector of this Department, to make an inspection of the routes of supply in Arkansas, with authority to give any orders needed to cure abuses and to arrest and suspend for trial any Quartermaster guilty of such practice. I could not wait the arrival of Col. Bingham, or I should have sent him on this duty according to your suggestion." LS, DNA, RG 108, Letters Received. Meigs enclosed copies of two letters from Brig. Gen. Robert Allen, Louisville, and a telegram from Capt. Henry C. Hodges, Fort Leavenworth, reporting the capture of the 202 wagons. Copies, *ibid.*

On Sept. 28, Meigs telegraphed to USG transmitting a telegram from Col. James L. Donaldson, chief q. m., Dept. of the Cumberland, concerning food supplies. Telegram received, *ibid. O.R.,* I, xxxix, part 2, 490.

To Maj. Gen. Henry W. Halleck

(Cipher)   City Point Va. Sept. 29th/64 [*9:00* P.M.]
MAJ. GEN. HALLECK, WASHINGTON,

If Gen Rosecrans does not send forward the regiments belonging to Sherman as ordered arrest him by my orders unless the President will authorize his being releived from command altogether.[1] Operations to-day prevented getting Richmond papers and consequently from hearing from Sheridan. Up to 4 p. m. on Teusday[2] he was all right. At that time he was engaged burning railroad track between Churche's [*Christian's*] Creek and Staunton. I am satisfied no troops have gone from here against him and they can not in the next two days. By that time he will be through and on his way to a position which he can defend and supply himself. Stevenson can I think spare troops enough for Kelly.[3] If he can not send Stevenson a new regiment or two to defend Harpers Ferry and let his older troops go to Kelly.

U. S. Grant

Lt. Gn.

ALS (telegram sent), CSmH; telegram received (at 10:00 P.M.), DNA, RG 107, Telegrams Collected (Bound). Incomplete in *O.R.*, I, xli, part 3, 469; *ibid.*, I, xliii, part 2, 209. On Sept. 29, 1864, 3:30 P.M., Maj. Gen. Henry W. Halleck telegraphed to USG. "No effort has been omitted to push troops forward to Nashville, subject to Genl Sherman's orders. Every new regiment and recruit in the western states were assigned to his army. I have just learned that Genl Rosecrans has ordered to St Louis a Veteran Ill. regiment belonging to Genl Sherman, and also a Wisconsin regiment en route to Nashville. He had no authority for this, but on the contrary I refused to permit him to stop troops belonging to Genl Sherman. I have telegraphed him to forward them on immediately, but I presume he will, as usual, disobey orders. Four regiments of hundred days men ordered north for muster out I have permitted him to retain. Genl Canby telegraphs that the forces now under Steele & Rosecrans are greatly superior to those of the enemy. He says that he has approved Steele's plan of operations, but does not state what that plan is. Genl Kelley is threatened at Grafton & Clarkesburg by a considerable raid under Echols. I have ordered Genl Stevenson at Harper's Ferry to send him reinforcements. We have but a single small regiment of cavalry here for scouting. Another small one has been out on the line towards Strasburg. It will be sent towards Culpepper immediately on arrival. Every thing is ready to open the road as soon as I get definitive information of Sheridan." ALS (telegram sent), DNA, RG 107, Telegrams Collected (Bound); telegram received, *ibid.*; *ibid.*, Telegrams Collected (Unbound); *ibid.*, RG 108, Letters Received. Incomplete in *O.R.*, I, xli, part 3, 468; *ibid.*, I, xliii, part 2, 209.

1. On Sept. 28, Maj. Gen. William S. Rosecrans telegraphed to Halleck, sending a copy to USG, regarding the C.S.A. threat in Mo. Telegram received, DNA, RG 108, Letters Received. *O.R.*, I, xli, part 3, 440.

2. Sept. 27. See telegram to Edwin M. Stanton, Sept. 28, 1864.

3. On Sept. 28, Bvt. Maj. Gen. Benjamin F. Kelley, Cumberland, Md., telegraphed to Halleck, sending a copy to USG, regarding a C.S.A. movement toward Beverly, West Va. Telegram received, DNA, RG 108, Letters Received. *O.R.*, I, xliii, part 2, 204–5; (misdated Sept. 25) *ibid.*, p. 176.

To Maj. Gen. Benjamin F. Butler

Signal Hill, Sept. 29th/64 12 m

MAJ. GN. BUTLER,

After riding forward to what was Gn. Birney's front at the time, the intersection of New Market & Mill road, I turned to the left and visited the works captured by the 18th Corps. From there I returned to Signal Hill expecting to meet you. Being desirous of keeping in communication with Gn. Meade I shall now return to Deep Bottom where any communication will reach me. If our troops do not reach Richmond this afternoon my opinion is that it will be unsafe to spend the night North of the enemy's lower bridge. I think it advisable to select a line now to which the troops can be brought back to-night if they do not reach Richmond. I have not yet heard of any movements of troops South of the James. My desire to be informed on this subject prevents me riding forward to where you are. Please communicate to me all progress made.

Yours &c.

U. S. GRANT

Lt. Gn.

ALS, DLC-Benjamin F. Butler. *O.R.*, I, xlii, part 2, 1109–10. On Sept. 29, 1864, 8:30 A.M., "Grovers House," and 12:50 P.M., "At Junction of New Market & Varina," Maj. Gen. Benjamin F. Butler telegraphed and wrote to USG. "Birney has advanced from Deep Bottom and taken the Main line of works at the Signal tower New Market Heights which commands the road and is advancing. This lets out Kautz who starts is starting   By means of Cavalry we have communicated across to Ords colum who Col Rand of the 4 Mass Cavalry reports to have carried the enemys Main line of works in his front and is advancing rapidly Paines division took their line handsomely with Considerable loss—" ALS (telegram sent), DNA, RG 94, War Records Office, Army of the Potomac; telegram received (at 9:30 A.M.), DNA, RG 107, Telegrams Collected (Unbound); *ibid.*, RG 108, Letters Received. *O.R.*, I, xlii, part 2, 1109. "Birney is this moment making his attack—will inform you at once   16 cars from Petersburgh with troops for Richmond   Have sent word to Gen Meade   The enemys works do not cross the Varina Road but Run nearly parallell with it to within three miles of Richmond   We shall try the works   if they are carried it is the last obstacle" ALS (undated), DNA, RG 108, Letters Received. *O.R.*, I, xlii, part 2, 1110.

On Sept. 28, 1:00 P.M. and 4:00 P.M., USG had telegraphed to Butler. "I see a pontoon train going being towed up the river. Will it not attract attention and put the enemy on his guard?" ALS (telegram sent), CSmH; copies, DLC-USG, V, 45, 69, 107; DNA, RG 108, Letters Sent. *O.R.*, I, xlii, part 2, 1079. "Nothing has been said about troops now at Dutch Gap. I expect all of them except a small Garrison for the fort to join your forces." ALS (telegram sent), CSmH; telegram received, DNA, RG 107, Telegrams Collected (Unbound). *O.R.*, I, xlii, part 2, 1079. At 5:00 P.M., Butler telegraphed to USG. "The whole force save one hundred & fifty men were withdrawn last night   The enemy have been shelling the empty place all day"   Telegram received, DNA, RG 108, Letters Received. *O.R.*, I, xlii, part 2, 1079. On the same day, USG telegraphed to Butler. "Make any change you please in Garrisons below the Appomattox   I only intended to be understood that all points now Garrisoned would continue to be Garrisoned." ALS (telegram sent), OClWHi; telegram received, DNA, RG 94, War Records Office, Army of the Potomac. *O.R.*, I, xlii, part 2, 1079.

To Maj. Gen. Benjamin F. Butler

Deep Bottom, Sep't. 29th. *1864* 3.50 P. M.

MAJ. GEN. BUTLER

I send you a dispatch, just received from Gen Meade.[1] It would seem probable the enemy have sent, but one Division from Petersburg. It would be well under such circumstances, to hold all the ground we can to night and feel out to the right, in the morning. This is not intended to prevent as rapid a push forward to night, as can be made.

U. S. GRANT.
Lt. Gen.

Copies, DLC-USG, V, 45, 69, 107; DNA, RG 108, Letters Sent. *O.R.*, I, xlii, part 2, 1110. On Sept. 29, 1864, 1:35 P.M. and 4:45 P.M., USG wrote to Maj. Gen. Benjamin F. Butler. "If Gen. Birney has not been successful in carrying the works in his front I think it will be advisable to move out to the Central road. From the inclosed dispatches you will see that all must be done to-day that can be done towards Richmond." "I will now return to City Point at which place dispatches will reach me telegraphed from here. Please say to Gn. Barnard, that I will send a boat here for him. If the enemy do not reinforce by more than a Division we will give them another trial in the morning, flanking instead of assaulting works." ALS, DLC-Benjamin F. Butler. *O.R.*, I, xlii, part 2, 1110, 1111.

1. See telegram to Maj. Gen. George G. Meade, Sept. 29, 1864, 1:30 P.M.

To Maj. Gen. Benjamin F. Butler

City Point Va. Sept. 29th *1864*. 11 p. m.

MAJ. GEN. BUTLER, DEEP BOTTOM

Gen. Meade will attack at day light in the morning. If the enemy have datached largely he may be able to carry Petersburg. If so I can send two corps using rail-road & steamers for the Infantry. On account of this attack I want to remain here through the day. I will go to Deep Bottom however to meet you leaving here at 5 a. m.

U. S. GRANT

Lt. Gn.

ALS (telegram sent), PPRF; telegram received, DLC Benjamin F. Butler. *O.R.*, I, xlii, part 2, 1111. On Sept. 29, 1864, 9:10 P.M. and 10:00 P.M., Maj. Gen. Benjamin F. Butler telegraphed to USG. "I am holding the line pointed out by Col Comstock and Gen Barnard to wit from near grave yard at Cox ferry, up to the white house thence to the Fort taken by Ords corps thence along the lines of the enemy taken by us a cross New Market road thence with the ~~Route~~ right refused extending to the Darby town or Central road thence by a cavalry picket a cross that Road, with a small Brigade in reserve at the Junction of the Kingsland and Varina Road—Kautz has advanced up the Central Road to the inner line of Redoubts nearest Richmond thence he has flanked to the right and has cut connections and we have not heard further from him   Col Babcock has reported the other events to you   If Gen Meade does not attack why can we not have another corps. The danger is that the Enemy may cross the river below us and get in our rear as we have no Cavalry to Picket the line to dutch Gap—" ALS (telegram sent), DNA, RG 94, War Records Office, Army of the Potomac; telegram received, *ibid.*, RG 108, Letters Received. *O.R.*, I, xlii, part 2, 1111. "Can you meet me as early as Sunrise tomorrow Morning at Deep Bottom   I desire to Consult you   I would not say this early ~~did~~ were it not that any move should be made early" ALS (telegram sent), DNA, RG 107, Telegrams Collected (Unbound); telegram received, *ibid.*, RG 108, Letters Received. *O.R.*, I, xlii, part 2, 1111.

To Maj. Gen. George G. Meade

Deep Bottom Sept. 29th/64 1.30 p. m.

MAJ. GEN. MEADE

Reinforcements are begining to come from Petersburg. I doubt whether it will be advisable for you to make any advance this evening but this I leave to your judgement. The works carried this morning are very formidable equal to Warren's enclosed works. One that I was in had two 8 or 9 in. Columbiads and a number of small rifle guns besides one One hundred pound Parrott.[1] Since writing the above of have rec'd reports of large forces moving from Petersburg towards Richmond. If this continues it may be well for you to attack this evening.

U. S. GRANT

Lt. Gen

ALS (telegram sent), Abraham Lincoln Book Shop, Chicago, Ill.; telegram received, DNA, RG 94, War Records Office, Army of the Potomac. *O.R.*, I, xlii, part 2, 1092. On Sept. 29, 1864, 3:30 P.M., Maj. Gen. George G. Meade telegraphed to USG. "Gregg has been out in a westerly & Southwesterly direction & on each road has found the enemy in force—A reconnaissance in Fereros front between the Jerusalem Plank road & Strong house found the enemys works occupied in Force—Signal officers report no movement or change in the enemy in our front—Under these circumstances I take it the troops seen going to Richmond are Hokes Division which was in reserve on the enemys left—I shall not therefore make a movement to the left today as it would hardly amount to any thing it being now so late—I have however sent a brigade of Infantry to reconnoitre at Poplar Spring Church, where the enemy are reported entrenched   I have also sent out parties to hunt for roads, and shall be prepared to advance at daylight tomorrow—We are all delighted to hear of the brilliant success of the movements today.—" ALS (telegram sent), DNA, RG 94, War Records Office, Army of the Potomac; telegram received, *ibid.*; (incomplete) *ibid.*, RG 108, Letters Received. *O.R.*, I, xlii, part 2, 1093.

On Sept. 28, 11:30 A.M., Meade had telegraphed to USG. "A Division of the 9th corps was this morning after day light & at places within view of the enemy, moved from near the Avery House to the Gurley House.—No other movements or events of importance to report.—I send a despatch just received from Warren—Pebles farm is just north of Poplar Spring church the works being constructed are to hold the Squirrel level road & the one next to it.—I am coming in to see you as soon as I can get a train.—" ALS (telegram sent), DNA, RG 94, War Records Office, Army of the Potomac; telegram received, *ibid.*, RG 108, Letters Received. *O.R.*, I, xlii, part 2, 1064. On the same day, USG telegraphed to Meade. "Heavy firing both of Artillery & Musketry is heard here distinctly. Does it mean anything like an attack?" ALS (telegram sent), OClWHi; telegram received (at 9:10 P.M.), *ibid.*, RG 94, War Records Office, Army of the Potomac. *O.R.*, I, xlii, part 2, 1065. At 9:15 P.M., Meade telegraphed to USG. "The firing is apparently on the Plank road—The musketry has ceased & the artillery slackened—No report has been received—I imagine it is a stampede   I have called on Hancock for particulars, which I will transmit as soon as received." ALS (telegram sent), DNA, RG 94, War Records Office, Army of the Potomac; telegram received, *ibid.*, RG 108, Letters Received. *O.R.*, I, xlii, part 2, 1065. Meade also transmitted to USG two telegrams from Maj. Gen. John G. Parke concerning the firing. *Ibid.*, pp. 1077–78.

On Sept. 29, 7:00 A.M., Meade telegraphed to USG. "I forward a despatch from Genl. Hancock—all I have this morning.—" ALS (telegram sent), DNA, RG 94, War Records Office, Army of the Potomac; telegram received, *ibid.*, RG 108, Letters Received. The enclosure is in *O.R.*, I, xlii, part 2, 1100. At 9:30 A.M. (sent at 10:35 A.M.), Meade telegraphed to USG. "Warren reports 4. Rgts. Infy. rebel moving down Squirrel level road   Gregg has sent commands towards Reams Stn and is moving on the Wyatt road feeling for the enemys left. —Signal officers report the enemy having struck their camps in the vicinity of the Lead works but no movement perceptible.—" ALS (telegram sent), DNA, RG 94, War Records Office, Army of the Potomac; copies, *ibid.*, RG 393, Army of the Potomac, Letters Sent; (2) Meade Papers, PHi. *O.R.*, I, xlii, part 2, 1091. At 9:30 A.M., Lt. Col. Orville E. Babcock telegraphed to Meade. "We are now on enemies first line   Genl Order has Carried Chapins farm   Our lines still advancing" ALS (telegram sent), DNA, RG 94, War Records Office, Army of the Potomac; telegram received, *ibid.* Printed as received at 10:35 A.M. in *O.R.*, I, xlii, part 2, 1092. At 9:30 A.M. and 10:30 A.M., Babcock telegraphed to Lt. Col. Ely S. Parker. "Just arrived here. Enemys first line taken without firing a gun. No particulars." Telegram received, DNA, RG 107, Telegrams Collected (Unbound). *O.R.*, I, xlii, part 2, 1109. "Ord carried works on Chapin Farm— Captured 15 pieces of Artillery. Ord slightly wounded. Genl Burnham killed. Our line advancing" ALS (telegram sent), DNA, RG 107, Telegrams Collected (Unbound). At noon, Brig. Gen. Seth Williams, adjt. for Meade, telegraphed to USG. "The following despatch has just been received from Major Fisher chief Signal officer. MGeneral Meade has gone to General Warren's HeadQuarters." ALS (telegram sent), *ibid.*, RG 94, War Records Office, Army of the Potomac; copy, *ibid.*, RG 393, Army of the Potomac, Letters Sent. *O.R.*, I, xlii, part 2, 1092. The enclosure is *ibid.* On the same day, Williams sent at least three additional telegrams to USG reporting information from signal officers. Telegrams received, DNA, RG 108, Letters Received. *O.R.*, I, xlii, part 2, 1093–94.

1. At 8:15 P.M., Babcock telegraphed to Col. Henry L. Abbot, 1st Conn. Art. "Genl Ord captured some heavy guns to-day, and two columbiads and one one hundred pounder are still in the works, but orders have been given to destroy them if we have to fall back. The Genl says if you have facilites for moving such guns he wishes you to send and take them away. They are about three miles (good road) from Aiken's Landing. You can take your party there at once and commence. Please reply." ALS (telegram sent), DNA, RG 107, Telegrams Collected (Unbound). Printed as received at 9:00 P.M. in *O.R.*, I, xlii, part 2, 1113. At 9:10 P.M., Abbot replied to Babcock. "I had already started two sling carts for the guns. Will bring them to Aiken's Landing as soon as possible and embark them there at leisure, being covered by the gun-boats." *Ibid.*

To Maj. Gen. George G. Meade

By Telegraph from City Point Va 11.30 P M
Dated Sept 29 *1864.*

To MAJ GEN MEADE

You need not move out at day light in the morning, but be prepared to start at say 8 oclock if you find the enemy still further reduced, or if ordered. I will start up to Deep Bottom at five 5 a. m. & may be able to judge of force sent to the north side by the Enemy. when you do move out, I think it will be advisable to manoever to get a good position, from which to attack and then if the enemy is routed, follow him into Petersburg or where circumstances seems to direct. I do not think it advisable to try to extend our line to the Southside road, unless a very considerable part of the enemy is drawn across the James & then only when we are able to withdraw Butler's force rapidly & send it to you.

U S GRANT.
Lt Genl.

Telegram received (incomplete), DNA, RG 94, War Records Office, Army of the Potomac; copies, DLC-USG, V, 45, 69, 107; DNA, RG 108, Letters Sent; (2) Meade Papers, PHi. *O.R.,* I, xlii, part 2, 1094. On Sept. 29, 1864, 10:30 P.M. (sent at 11:15 P.M.), Maj. Gen. George G. Meade telegraphed to USG. "Gregg after his reconnaissance returned to Col. Wyatt's, where about 4. P. M he was attacked by Hampton with whom he had quite a sharp affair till dark— having one piece of artillery disabled—casualties not great—A Brigade of Infantry was sent to his support but was not engaged—The Infantry brigade sent to Poplar Spring church found the enemy in position & in force—their artillery commanding the road leading westward from the church.—Hancock reports the enemy moving on the road from Petersburgh to Port Walthal threatening our right on the Appomatox.—My Signal officer reports that not over 7000 Infantry have been observed moving towards Richmond & that nearly 5000 have moved to our left.—I do not see indications sufficient to justify my making an attempt on the Southside R. Rd—I find I can only raise 16000 men in the 4 divisions of the 5th & 9th corps whereas when I took the Welden Rd. I had 6 divisions of these two corps & afterwards two divisions of the 2d corps. I can throw a force out to Poplar Spring church & engage the enemy if you deem it advisable—but this will only be extending our lines without a commensurate object unless the engaging the enemy is so deemed.—" ALS (telegram sent), DNA, RG 94, War Records Office, Army of the Potomac; telegram received, *ibid.,* RG 108, Letters Received. *O.R.,* I, xlii, part 2, 1094.

To Julia Dent Grant

City Point, Va. Sept. 29th *1864.*

DEAR JULIA,

I have been out all day on the battle field and well up towards Richmond. Our troops surprised and captured a very long line of strong fortifications and took some fifteen or twenty cannon. The distance was too great to Richmond or it would have been taken. Before morning I presume the enemy will have his fortifications around Richmond well maned and we will have to stay out for the present. Our advance troops were within three miles the last I heard from them.—I have just received your letter written on the blank part of Jennie's. You [are] right to tell the principal of the school you propose to send the children too that you understand the citizens of Phila are about presenting you with a house and if they [do] you will go there and take the children with you. If I was going to be at home all the time the boys might go to boarding school. But for me and them both to be away will leave you to lonesome. I feel that the time is now near when I shall be able to spend a good part of each week at home. I hope I shall not be disappointed. Good night dear Julia. I shall be very busy to-night and to-morrow to. There will be heavy fighting commencing at daylight in the morning if the enemy do not commence it to-night. I shall attack then south of Petersburg and East of Richmond at that time.

ULYS.

ALS, DLC-USG.

To Edwin M. Stanton

(Cipher)   City Point Va. Sept. 30th *1864.* [*3:30* P.M.]
HON. E. M. STANTON SEC. OF WAR.

Gen. Warren attacked and carried enemy's line to-day on their extreme right capturing a number of prisoners. He immediately prepared to follow up his success. Petersburg paper of to-day has rumor which it says is not confirmed that one brigade of Sheridans Cavalry was ambushed & destroyed at Swift Run Creek. Early was to have attacked Sheridan at Mount Sidney on the 28th.

U. S. Grant
Lt. Gen.

ALS (telegram sent), CSmH; telegram received (at 5:00 P.M.), DNA, RG 107, Telegrams Collected (Bound). *O.R.*, I, xlii, part 1, 21; *ibid.*, I, xlii, part 2, 1117.

To Maj. Gen. Henry W. Halleck

(Cipher)   City Point, Va, Sept. 30th 10.30 a. m. *1864.*
MAJ. GEN. HALLECK, WASHINGTON

I have heard no firing yet this morning. Before daylight I went up to Deep Bottom and found all quiet there. Gen. Meade moved out from his left this morning and must soon encounter the enemy. Rosser's Brigade of Cavalry have gone to join Early. This Brigade numbers about 1400 horses. Yesterday an Infantry force left Petersburg in the Lynchburg cars. It may be however they are going by way of Burkesville to Richmond. Nothing heard from Sheridan through southern sources since Teusday[1] evening.

U. S. Grant
Lt. Gn.

ALS (telegram sent), Schoff Collection, MiU-C; telegram received (at 11:40 A.M.), DNA, RG 107, Telegrams Collected (Bound). *O.R.*, I, xlii, part 2, 1117.
    On Sept. 30, 1864, 5:00 P.M., USG twice telegraphed to Maj. Gen. Henry W. Halleck. "Gen. Butler reported at 3 P. M. that the enemy had just made an assault in three columns on his line near Chaffin's Farm and had been repulsed. No report from Meade since he carried the enemy's line near Poplar Grove Church." "A refugee from Richmond just come in to Butlers lines says the greatest consternation is felt in the City and citizens generally are anxious that the City should be evacuated by the Military. He No further news from Sheridan is reported. I think lack of supplies is forcing him back. Trains move west" ALS (telegrams sent), CSmH; telegrams received (at 8:00 P.M.), DNA, RG 107, Telegrams Collected (Bound). Printed as received at 9:30 P.M. in *O.R.*, I, xlii, part 2, 1117. The first is also printed *ibid.*, I, xlii, part 1, 21. On the same day, Maj. Gen. Benjamin F. Butler had telegraphed to USG. "A refugee from Richmond who has been identified by one of my Agents states that great excite-

ment exists in Richmond and that the people talk among themselves of endeavoring to have the authorities evacuate the city if possible—To the best of his knowledge and information no troops arrived in the city from Petersburg or otherwise up to 10 P. M—yesterday." LS (telegram sent), DNA, RG 107, Telegrams Collected (Unbound); telegram received, *ibid.*, RG 108, Letters Received. *O.R.*, I, xlii, part 2, 1142.

1. Sept. 27.

To Maj. Gen. Benjamin F. Butler

City Point Va. Sept. ~~2~~30th *1864.*

MAJ. GEN. BUTLER,

Indications are that not more than one Division of troops have been moved from Petersburg. Reconnoisances might be made towards the Charles City road and preparations made to move out that way in a day or two if thought advisable ~~leaving~~ breaking for the time all connection ~~back~~ with the river. I do not say this will be advisable but get such information as you can about roads &c. Meade has moved out South with two Divisions and sent two more further East to try and flank the enemy. As soon as anything is reported I will inform you.

U. S. GRANT
Lt. Gn.

ALS (telegram sent), CSmH; telegram received, DLC-Benjamin F. Butler. *O.R.*, I, xlii, part 2, 1142.

On Sept. 30, 1864, Maj. Gen. Benjamin F. Butler telegraphed to USG. "A Despatch was sent here for you which by accident was not delivered." Telegram received, DNA, RG 107, Telegrams Collected (Unbound). On the same day, USG telegraphed to Butler. "Has any thing been heard of Kautz this morning? I begin to feel some uneasiness about him." ALS (telegram sent), CSmH; telegram received, DLC-Benjamin F. Butler. *O.R.*, I, xlii, part 2, 1142. At 3:00 P.M., Butler telegraphed to USG. "Kautz has returned and is picketting on our right from the Darbytown Road to ~~the~~ New Market, and is holding the former road in force—He was not able to get through—The enemy here massed on Gen Birney's left which is about the center of our line, nearly opposite the large fort which we took, and made a determined assault in three lines with a very heavy fire of Artillery, but were repulsed—Just now" ALS (telegram sent), DNA, RG 94, War Records Office, Army of the Potomac; telegram received, *ibid.*, RG 108, Letters Received. *O.R.*, I, xlii, part 2, 1142–43.

At 3:50 P.M., Butler telegraphed to USG. "The enemy have assaulted my lines three (3) times at the fort taken yesterday but have been ~~e~~Each time handsomely repulsed—Gen. Stannard is Seriously wounded—If you will Send me a good Brig Gen to Command his Division you will Confer a great favor—" Telegram received, DNA, RG 108, Letters Received; copy, *ibid.*, RG 94, War Records Office, Army of the Potomac. *O.R.*, I, xlii, part 2, 1143. On the same day, USG telegraphed to Butler. "I will send Brig. Gn. Humphreys of the 9th Corps to take command of Stannards Div. until some General officer returns. A column of troops numbering from two to three thousand men were reported moving ~~from~~ on the Richmond Pike towards Petersburg this afternoon." ALS (telegram sent), CSmH; telegram received, DNA, RG 94, War Records Office, Army of the Potomac; *ibid.*, RG 107, Telegrams Collected (Unbound). *O.R.*, I, xlii, part 2, 1143. See *ibid.*, p. 1137. On the same day, Lt. Col. Orville E. Babcock telegraphed to Maj. Gen. John G. Parke. "The Lt Genl desires that you send Col Humphrys down here to night—The Genl wishes to assign him to ~~a~~ the command of a division in 18th Corps in place of Stannard wounded to-day. He will give him back to you again. I think he will be a fine man for the division will he not." ALS (telegram sent), DNA, RG 107, Telegrams Collected (Unbound). *O.R.*, I, xlii, part 2, 1137. On Oct. 2, 8:45 P.M., Parke wrote to USG. "I was exceedingly sorry that Col. Humphrey had left before I rec'd. Col. Babcock's Tel.—& most sorry to lose him—I hope he may yet be Brevetted or Promoted & returned to us. Col. Sigfried has left today—a valuable officer, and I should be glad to have him Brevetted & returned to us. His name is on my list—His record is good, & the service is the loser by his going out—" ALS, DNA, RG 107, Telegrams Collected (Unbound).

On Sept. 30, USG sent two additional telegrams to Butler. "Gen. Warren carried the enemy's works beyond Sycamore Church handsomely capturing a number of prisoners. He is now preparing for a further advance on the enemy. Be well on your guard to act defensively. If the enemy are forced from Petersburg they may push to oppose you." ALS (telegram sent), CSmH; telegram received, DLC-Benjamin F. Butler. *O.R.*, I, xlii, part 2, 1143. "The Navy having no torpedoes here I have ordered your Ordnance officer, Lt. Cress [*Kress*], to Fortress Monroe to fix up what you want. He will be able to get them ready and return to Aikin's Landing by 4 p. m. to-morrow." ALS (telegram sent), CSmH; telegram received, DLC-Benjamin F. Butler; (at 5:30 P.M.) DNA, RG 107, Telegrams Collected (Unbound).

To Maj. Gen. Benjamin F. Butler

City Point Va. Sept. 30th/64

MAJ. GEN. BUTLER, DEEP BOTTOM.

Gen. Meade's forces met with some success to-day capturing a few prisoners, two redouts and some rifle pitts. But later this evening in moving two Divisions of the 9th Corps to flank the enemy they were attacked furiously by two Divisions of Hills Corps and forced back somewhat leaving some of their wounded and some other prisoners in the hands of the enemy. A division of the 5th Corps moved up to their assistance and checked any further advance and it is thought with heavy slaughter of the enemy. This would look as if no heavy force had been sent North of the James. I think it will be advisable for you to reconnoitre up the Darbytown road and if there appears to be any chance for an advance make it.

U. S. GRANT
Lt. Gen.

ALS (telegram sent), DLC-Asher Collection; telegram received (marked as sent at 11:00 P.M.), DNA, RG 94, War Records Office, Dept. of Va. and N. C., Army of the James, Unentered Papers. *O.R.*, I, xlii, part 2, 1144. On Sept. 30, 1864, 7:50 P.M., Maj. Gen. Benjamin F. Butler had telegraphed to USG. "The telegraph now is within half a mile of my Head Quarters and nearer Wietzals—We are making the best preparation we can for defence—We have repulsed the enemy in all his attacks with little loss on our side and heavy on theirs—We are much weaker than you suppose—I would be very glad of any reinforcements—The remainder of Fields Division, three (3) brigades have crossed and are in our front with Hokes Division—Heth was ordered to start but I can hear nothing of him—The city local reserves are in our front, down to the clerks in the Naval Department known as the Naval Battalion and the clerks in the Express companies and the policemen—We have got now before us everything there is—A few more men and we can push through the Darbytown line unless Lee quits Petersburg If he does, it is a question of legs which will get here first—I feel no doubt of being able to hold until you come if Lee and all come—These assaults appear to be directed to the recapture of the big fort—It is evident that that capture troubles the enemy much Indeed the prisoners say they are told it shall be taken if it costs every man they have got and all we have got—Be it so—So far as I am concerned it shall not be taken except upon ~~such~~ those terms I congratulate you upon Warrens success I hope he has been successful in the attack we have just heard—I have no accurate map so that I cannot appreciate the value of his success" LS (telegram sent), DNA, RG 94, War Records Office, Army of the Potomac; telegram received, *ibid.*; *ibid.*, RG 108, Letters Received. *O.R.*, I, xlii, part 2, 1143–44. At 10:00 P.M., USG telegraphed to Maj. Gen. George G. Meade transmitting this telegram. Telegram received, DNA, RG 94, War Records Office, Army of the Potomac; copies (2), Meade Papers, PHi. See following telegram.

At 11:30 P.M., Butler telegraphed to USG. "From an officer who is to take the oath of allegience I recieve the following information upon which I rely—That before me there is Heth Wilcox Field and Hokes Division Picket still at Bermuda Early having Kershaws Rhodes (Earlys old) and Breckenbriges forces. Before Petersburg is Andersons old Division Mahone comd'g—and Bushrod Johnson—Lee is comd'g in person on the North side of the James. We shall be attacked in the morning and we shall make the best fight we can but it is respectfully suggested that the immediate movement of a Division or two by rail to City Point and thence by boat to Aikens Landing is necessary They have as many men as we have with the advantage of being the attacking party— We shall be ready for them at daylight—Hokes Division has suffered so heavily that I dont think it will go in again This information which I believe is reliable is submitted to the Lieut Genl—We have as the result of to days fighting 209 prisoners 18 officers two battle flags" LS (telegram sent), DNA, RG 107, Telegrams Collected (Unbound); telegram received (on Oct. 1, 2:15 A.M.), *ibid.*, RG 108, Letters Received. *O.R.*, I, xlii, part 2, 1144–45.

To Maj. Gen. Benjamin F. Butler

City Point Va. Sept. 30th/64

MAJ. GEN. BUTLER, DEEP BOTTOM,

Your dispatch received since mine was sent to you. Without abandoning the position now occupied by Meade I cannot reinforce you. You might however put a new regiment in at Deep Bottom and move that force to the front If the enemy continues to hold his present force at Petersburg I will to-morrow or Sunday night withdraw a Corps rapidly, using rail-road & steamers to get them to you without fatigue and make another push. Is there not a conciderable number of the 18th Corps back in their old camps who ought to be up with their regiments?

U. S. GRANT
Lt. Gen.

ALS (telegram sent), CSmH; telegram received (marked as sent at 11:10 A.M.), DNA, RG 94, War Records Office, Army of the Potomac. *O.R.*, I, xlii, part 2, 1145. On Sept. 30, 1864, 11:15 P.M., USG telegraphed to Maj. Gen. Benjamin F. Butler. "Whilst in your present position Wilsons Wharf & Powhattan can be reduced to small garrisons and Harrisons Landing can be abandoned altogether if this will give you reinforcements to do any good." ALS (telegram sent), CSmH; telegram received, DNA, RG 94, War Records Office, Army of the Potomac. *O.R.*, I, xlii, part 2, 1144. On Oct. 1, 12:30 A.M., Butler telegraphed to USG. "Since writing my despatch of 11.30 P. M—I have received yours of 11. P. M—saying that two Divisions of Hill's Corps are before Petersburg—I don't think that can be—I have drawn all the available old men with the exception of two hundred men from Forts Powhattan and Pocahontas—Gen Ord was notified at his Head Quarters to forward all the men in his camp to day—I see no reason to alter my despatch of 8.30. P. M—I will put the Officer upon his life as to the truth of his information before sending this despatch—P. S. I have examined this man upon his life and he says he is willing to put it upon the question of all the Divisions I have named, except Wilcox Division of Hill's Corps, to wit; Heth, Field, and Hoake—He believes strongly from what he has heard, that Wilcox is here, but he says he does not *know* it—We have numbers of prisoners from Field and Hoake's Divisions and all report Heth here—" LS (telegram sent—misdated Sept. 30), DNA, RG 107, Telegrams Collected (Unbound); telegram received (at 2:15 A.M.), *ibid.*, RG 108, Letters Received. Misdated Sept. 30 in *O.R.*, I, xlii, part 2, 1145. On Oct. 1, USG telegraphed to Maj. Gen. George G. Meade transmitting this telegram and Butler's telegram of 11:30 P.M. Telegram received (at 4:30 A.M.), DNA, RG 94, War Records Office, Army of the Potomac; copies (2), Meade Papers, PHi.

To Maj. Gen. George G. Meade

City Point Va. Sept. 30th/64 [*8:10* A.M.]

MAJ. GEN. MEADE,

Gen. Butlers forces will remain where they are for the present ready to advance if found practicable. You may move out now and see if an advantage can be gained. It seems to me the enemy must be weak enough at ~~one~~ one or the other places to let ~~him~~ us in.

U. S. GRANT
Lt. Gen.

ALS (telegram sent), CSmH; telegram received (at 8:25 A.M.), DNA, RG 94, War Records Office, Army of the Potomac. Printed as sent at 8:15 A.M. in *O.R.*, I, xlii, part 2, 1118. On Sept. 30, 1864, 8:30 A.M. (sent at 8:50 A.M.), Maj. Gen. George G. Meade telegraphed to USG. "In accordance with your despatch of 8.15 I have sent orders to Warren to move out to the Poplar Spring Church & to Parke to endeavor to get around & come up on Warrens left & if practicable out flank the enemy.—A contraband who left Petersburgh this morning says that troops were sent on the Lynchburgh road yesterday and that Heths division went to Chapins farm—No other news or indications of movement, except an ambulance train seen to move this morning to our left—" ALS (telegram sent), DNA, RG 94, War Records Office, Army of the Potomac; telegram received, *ibid.*, RG 108, Letters Received. *O.R.*, I, xlii, part 2, 1118.

Also on Sept. 30, Brig. Gen. Seth Williams frequently telegraphed to USG transmitting information received from signal officers, prisoners, and deserters. Telegrams received, DNA, RG 108, Letters Received. *O.R.*, I, xlii, part 2, 1118–19, 1120–21, 1124.

At 4:40 A.M., Lt. Col. Orville E. Babcock telegraphed to USG, Deep Bottom. "Do you wish me to go to Genl Meade's this morning. I did not learn your wishes last night." ALS (telegram sent), DNA, RG 107, Telegrams Collected (Unbound).

At 12:45 P.M., Babcock, Globe Tavern, telegraphed to Lt. Col. Ely S. Parker. "General Warren is now at Poplar Grove Church; has drawn the enemy's fire, developing their force. He is trying to advance still. General Parke is trying to go around Warren's left. General Gregg is still farther to the left on the Vaughan road but has a very heavy force in his front. Signal officers report a massing of troops, infantry and artillery, on our left." *O.R.*, I, xlii, part 2, 1133.

At 2:10 P.M., Babcock telegraphed to USG. "Gen Warren has carried Enemys line, taken some prisoners, number not known. We have a Petersburg paper of 30th—No news from Georgia—Forrest said to have taken Sulphur springs with 800 prisoners—Enemy claim to have ambuscaded a Brigade of Sheridans Cavalry at Swift Run Creek & destroyed them. No official Confirmation, but little said of yesterdays fight. I will bring in the paper. Expect to leave here at 5 P. M.— Early was to attack Sheridan On 28th at Mount Sidney" Telegram received, DNA, RG 108, Letters Received. *O.R.*, I, xlii, part 2, 1133–34.

At 2:25 P.M., Meade telegraphed to USG. "Genl. Griffin, Warren reports has carried the enemys work on the Peebles farm, in handsome style taking a number of prisoners—Warren is getting his command in position looking to his connection on the Welden R Rd & Parke is forming on his left.—Gregg reports the enemys cavalry have left his immediate front & as far as he can ascertain are across the Rowanty creek—I have directed him to watch the Jerusalem Plank road & notified Hancock to have his reserves ready to meet any cavalry demonstrations on the Norfolk or Prince Geo C. H. Roads where I now have only small cavalry & infantry Pickets.—Benham must look out for the old C. H. road" ALS (telegram sent), DNA, RG 94, War Records Office, Army of the Potomac; telegram received, *ibid.*, RG 108, Letters Received. *O.R.*, I, xlii, part 2, 1119. On the same day, Parker wrote to Brig. Gen. Henry W. Benham, Engineer Brigade, transmitting a copy of Meade's telegram. "I enclose dispatch from Gen. Meade for your information. You will at Once place strong pickets of Infantry on the old C. H. road, and watch it closely. Should you require any Cavalry to assist in the picket duty, the 5th U. S. Cavalry at these Headquarters, will be placed at your disposal. Please return the dispatch by the Orderly." Copies, DLC-USG, V, 45, 69, 107; DNA, RG 108, Letters Sent. *O.R.*, I, xlii, part 2, 1126. On Oct. 1, Parker wrote to Benham. "Please have the kindness to send to these headquarters, without delay, a statement by regiments (exclusive of the Engineer Brigade) of the troops under your command guarding the defenses of City Point. It is essential that the number of each regiment, or skeleton of a regiment, with their supposed strength, be communicated to these headquarters." *Ibid.*, I, xlii, part 3, 10. The statement sent is *ibid.* On Sept. 30, 3:00 P.M. and 3:15 P.M., USG telegraphed to Meade. "If the enemy can be broken and started follow him up closely. I cant help believing that the enemy are prepared to leave Petersburg if forced a little." "If the enemy's Cavalry has left Greggs front he ought to push ahead and if he finds no obsticle turn ~~the~~ his Infantry." ALS (telegrams sent), CSmH; telegrams received (the first at 3:25 P.M.), DNA, RG 94, War Records Office, Army of the Potomac. *O.R.*, I, xlii, part 2, 1119. At 4:15 P.M., Meade, Peebles' Farm, telegraphed to USG. "In accordance with your instructions I have directed Genl Gregg to send a brigade of cavalry on the left of the Infantry & endeavor to turn the enemys left—The other brigade to support it if necessary & to keep a look out on our immediate rear, where from all indications the enemys cavalry with drew—Genl Parke is advancing towards the Boydtown road in a N. W. direction—I should have mentioned in my last despatch, that Genl Ayres had taken a small work in advance & on the right of the one taken by Griffin, and also that Genl. Griffin had secured one piece of artillery—Warrens casualties will be about one hundred killed & wounded among the former Col Welsh of Michigan—The number of prisoners not known but not so large as at first supposed." ALS (telegram sent), DNA, RG 94, War Records Office, Army of the Potomac; telegram received, *ibid.*, RG 108, Letters Received. *O.R.*, I, xlii, part 2, 1120.

To Maj. Gen. George G. Meade

By Telegraph from City Point Va
Dated Sept 30 *1864.* [*9:40* P.M.]

To MAJ GEN MEADE

You need not advance tomorrow unless in your judgement an advantage can be gained, but hold on to what you have & be ready for an advance. we must be greatly superior to the enemy in numbers on one flank or the other & by working around at each end we will find where the enemy's weak point is. Genl Butler was assaulted three times this afternoon, but repulsed all of them. I will direct him to feel up the darbytown road tomorrow.

U S GRANT
Lt Genl

Telegram received (at 10:35 P.M.), DNA, RG 94, War Records Office, Army of the Potomac; copies, *ibid.*, RG 108, Letters Sent; DLC-USG, V, 45, 69, 107; (2) Meade Papers, PHi. *O.R.*, I, xlii, part 2, 1121. On Sept. 30, 1864, 9:00 P.M., Maj. Gen. George G. Meade had telegraphed to USG. "About 4. P. M—Genl. Parke was advancing to the Boydtown plank road, when he was vigorously attacked by the enemy, said by prisoners to have two divisions of Hills Corps— Potters Division 9th corps was forced back, requiring Hartranft on his left to retire a short distance   Warren sent Griffin to Parke's support and the enemy were checked—Parke has lost in prisoners & ~~left~~ wounded left in the advanced position held—The fighting for some time till after dark was very severe, and after the 9th Corps rallied & Griffin attacked it is believed the enemy suffered heavily   I have directed Genl. Warren to entrench himself in his position & extend if practicable to the Welden Rd—and Genl Parke to entrench on Warren's left—I do not think it judicious to make another advance tomorrow unless re-inforced or some evidence can be obtained of the weakening of the enemy—" ALS (telegram sent), DNA, RG 94, War Records Office, Army of the Potomac; telegram received, *ibid.*, RG 108, Letters Received. *O.R.*, I, xlii, part 2, 1121.

On the same day, USG twice telegraphed to Meade. "Whilst the enemy are concentrating all their strength at two point to resist attacks do you not deem it safe to take one Div. of the 2d Corps out of the line to aid you? I would not do this however until just before an advance was going to be made." "Two new regiments and a part of an other have gone to you. Can they not be put in the line so as to spare some old troops to reinforce the left?" ALS (telegrams sent), CSmH; telegrams received (at 10:30 P.M.), DNA, RG 94, War Records Office, Army of the Potomac. *O.R.*, I, xlii, part 2, 1120, 1122. At 11:30 P.M., Meade telegraphed to USG. "The new regiments were ordered on arrival to be placed in the trenches on the Welden R. R—One arrived this P. M which together with the extension of the Colored Division 9th. Corps—enabled a brigade of the 5th Corps to be relieved.—I have ordered Hancock to hold his line with two divisions and to hold the 3d. in reserve ready for contingencies. I have directed Warren &

Parke to advance their pickets well supported at daylight & endeavor to ascertain the positions & strength of the enemy. I presumed Fields & Hoke's divisions that were in reserve, would be sent to the northern side of the James—this would leave 4 divisions on this side   Two were engaged this p. m—the other two holding the lines." ALS (telegram sent at midnight), DNA, RG 94, War Records Office, Army of the Potomac; telegram received, *ibid.*, RG 108, Letters Received. *O.R.*, I, xlii, part 2, 1122. On Oct. 1, 3:00 A.M., USG telegraphed to Maj. Gen. Benjamin F. Butler transmitting a copy of Meade's telegram of 11:30 P.M. "The following despatch from Gen Meade is forwarded for your information. Under existing curcumstances you must discharge the Idea of rececving reinforcements, and if attacked make the best defence you can with the troops you have"   Telegram received, DNA, RG 393, 10th Army Corps, Miscellaneous Telegrams Received; copies, *ibid.*, RG 108, Letters Sent; DLC-USG, V, 45, 69, 107. *O.R.*, I, xlii, part 3, 30.

To Julia Dent Grant

————

City Point, Va. Sept. 30th *1864*.

DEAR JULIA,

I have just rec'd your letter in regard to starting the children to school in Wilmington. My last letter I think entirely answers it but I write again to make sure. I would not send the children to school in Burlington. I [presume] there is a doubt when you will go [to] Phila and you want the children with you whilst I am away. If I was at home all the time it would make no diffirence, but housekeeping you will be lonesome with them and me both absent. We have been having great battles here such as at the begining of the War would have thrilled the whole country. Our advantages have been large and no doubt the enemy feel badly over it. One fort taken yesterday they regarded as impregnable, but our troops got over the river and surprised and drove them back so rapidly that the fort was taken almost before they were aware of it. In it they had some of their finest guns, 8 in. Columbiads and Rifled guns, one of them a One hundred pounder.

I try to look at everything calmly, believe I do, therefore believe all we want to produce a speedy peace is a unity of sentiment in the North. My dispatches from Sherman shows he is doing a very greatdeel there. Gov. Brown, of Ga. (Vice President Stevens of the so called Confederacy backing him,) wants to call a session of the Legislature to take Ga. out really from the Confederacy.[1] If this is done it will be the end of rebellion, or so nearly so that the rebelling will be by one portion of the South against the other.—Love & kisses for you and the children.

ULYS.

P. S. I have a pair of very handsome pistols and the great sanitary Fair coat both of which I shall send to you by Express in a day or two. As soon as you get to housekeeping, in your own house, you had better call in all the swords, guns &c. now scattered over the country.

ALS, DLC-USG.

1. On Sept. 15, 1864, Maj. Gen. William T. Sherman telegraphed to Maj. Gen. Henry W. Halleck that Governor Joseph E. Brown of Ga. and C.S.A. Vice President Alexander H. Stephens wished to visit him. Although Sherman had spoken to some Unionists about the possible withdrawal of Ga. from the C.S.A., nothing came of his efforts. See *O.R.*, I, xxxix, part 2, 381, 395–96, 488, 501; *Memoirs of Gen. W. T. Sherman* (4th ed., New York, 1891), II, 137–40; Joseph H. Parks, *Joseph E. Brown of Georgia* (Baton Rouge, 1977), 295–300.

To Maj. Gen. Henry W. Halleck

———

(Cipher)   City Point Va. Oct. 1st/64 10. a. m.
MAJ. GN. HALLECK, WASHINGTON,

The enemy assaulted Gen. Butlers line North of James River three times yesterday afternoon and were repulsed each time Gn. Butler reports with heavy loss. Late in the evening Potter[1] Division 9th Corps whilst moving to get to the left of Warren near Poplar Grove Church was vigirously assaulted by a superior force and driven back until reinforced by Griffin's[2] Div. when the enemy were checked Gen. Meade thinks with heavy loss. Potter lost from his Division a conciderable number killed wounded & captured. The enemy are now threatning our left in conciderable force. Our line extends full two miles West of the Weldon rail-road with the

left turned back. ~~to the road~~ The troops intrenched themselves
during the night.

U. S. Grant

Lt. Gn

ALS (telegram sent), CSmH; telegram received (at 6:00 p.m.), DNA, RG
107, Telegrams Collected (Bound). *O.R.*, I, xlii, part 1, 21; *ibid.*, I, xlii, part 3,
3–4.

1. The son of Episcopal Bishop Alonzo Potter, Robert B. Potter was born
in 1829 in Schenectady, N. Y., attended Union College, and practiced law in
New York City. Enlisting as a private in the N. Y. Rifles, he was appointed maj.,
51st N. Y., as of Oct. 14, 1861, and won distinction in the N. C. expedition and
at Antietam. Appointed brig. gen. as of March 3, 1863, he commanded the 2nd
Div., 9th Army Corps, at Vicksburg and in the campaigns of 1864.

2. Charles Griffin, born in 1825 in Granville, Ohio, USMA 1847, held the
rank of 1st lt., 2nd Art., when the Civil War began, and commanded a battery
with the army in Va. until his appointment as brig. gen. as of June 9, 1862.
Briefly removed from command for denouncing Maj. Gen. John Pope during the
battle of Second Bull Run, Griffin was known for intemperate language as well
as valor. He held brigade and div. command, 5th Army Corps, Army of the
Potomac, and commanded the 1st Div. in the 1864 campaigns.

To Maj. Gen. Benjamin F. Butler

———

City Point Va. Oct. 1st/64 [*11:00 p.m.*]

Maj. Gn. Butler, Deep Bottom.

I think it will be advisable to select a line which can be held
with one of your corps as now composed giving you an outlet at
Deep Bottom or Aikins'. The other corps could be kept on the
North side as well as elswhere but held ready for any imergency.
The line now held it seems to me would always expose you to a
flank or rear attack and would cause the enemy to prepare so that
no surprise on that side could again be made. The strong works
about Chapins farm should be held or leveled however. Sheridan
for want of supplies, if there should be no other reason, will be
forced to fall back. The enemy may take advantage of such occation to bring the remnant of Early's force ~~back~~ here, relying upon
his ability to get it back to the Valley before Sheridan could fit up

and return. In such case he could fall upon either flank, as now exposed, and inflict great damage.

U. S. Grant
Lt. Gn.

ALS (telegram sent), OClWHi; telegram received, DLC-Benjamin F. Butler. *O.R.*, I, xlii, part 3, 31–32. On Oct. 1, 1864, 11:55 P.M., Maj. Gen. Benjamin F. Butler, "Junction of Varina & NewMarket Roads," telegraphed to USG. "Will prepare to take up such line as you propose tomorrow. As Gen Barnard and Col. Comstock have been over the ground as well as yourself please advise me what line to take as to its extent and advanced posts. Of course it must be a much shorter one than the present" ALS (telegram sent), DNA, RG 393, Dept. of Va. and N. C., Telegrams Sent (Press); telegram received, *ibid.*, RG 108, Letters Received. *O.R.*, I, xlii, part 3, 32.

At 6:00 A.M., Butler had telegraphed to USG. "All Quiet so far. I have sent for 2d N. H. & Genl Marston from Fort Pocahontas—Shall we see you today I have ordered the Greyhound to report to you" ALS (telegram sent), DNA, RG 107, Telegrams Collected (Unbound). *O.R.*, I, xlii, part 3, 30. On the same day, USG telegraphed to Butler. "I will try to get out to your Hd Qrs. some time before 12 O'clock. Before starting I want to hear the result of Gen. Meades movements." ALS (telegram sent), CSmH; copies, DLC-USG, V, 45, 69, 107; DNA, RG 108, Letters Sent. *O.R.*, I, xlii, part 3, 30. At 6:55 A.M., Butler telegraphed to USG transmitting a telegram of Maj. Gen. David B. Birney. "The rebels have evacuated the small battery in front of my left and have gone apparently to the next redoubt toward my right—My picket line is being advanced" LS (telegram sent), DNA, RG 107, Telegrams Collected (Unbound); telegram received, *ibid.*, RG 108, Letters Received. *O.R.*, I, xlii, part 3, 30. At 10:45 A.M., USG telegraphed to Butler. "From deserters and prisoners captured it is ascertained that Johnson's Mahones Heth's & Wilcox Divisions are about Petersburg. I start for your Hd Qrs. as soon as I can write some dispatches." ALS (telegram sent), CSmH; copies, DLC-USG, V, 45, 69, 107; DNA, RG 108, Letters Sent. *O.R.*, I, xlii, part 3, 31.

At 7:15 P.M. and 8:30 P.M., USG telegraphed to Butler. "Prisoners were yesterday taken from Anderson's Brigade, Fields Div. The presence of Wilcox, Heth's, Mahone's & Johnson's Division was also shown about Petersburg. This shows that the enemy have divided Divisions and possibly Brigades to give the appearance of force at all points." ALS (telegram sent), CSmH; telegram received, DLC-Benjamin F. Butler. *O.R.*, I, xlii, part 3, 31. "Please inform me the result of the reconnoisance up the Central road this afternoon." ALS (telegram sent), CSmH; copies (entered erroneously as addressed to Maj. Gen. George G. Meade), DLC-USG, V, 45, 69, 107; DNA, RG 108, Letters Sent. At 8:55 P.M., Butler telegraphed to USG. "I have received no official report of the reconnoissance. Lt Michie who was with it has returned. Genl Terry penetrated as far as the entrenchentsments on the Darbytown Road without opposition. Genl Kautz Crossed the Charles City Road without opposition as far as the line of forf fortifications which he found held in consederable force but not large force of infantry. Genl Kautz Crossed the Charles City Road and exchanged shots with the enemy at a point in the fortifications where they Cross that road. Genl Birney advanced his pickets along the NewMarket road & drove their skirmishers into their works capturing some prisoners who were all of Local defence Battalions. I have seen one or two of them. All is quiet" Telegram received, *ibid.*, Letters Received; copy, *ibid.*, RG 107, Telegrams Collected (Unbound). *O.R.*, I, xlii, part 3, 31.

To Maj. Gen. George G. Meade

City Point Va. Oct. 1st 1864

MAJ. GN. MEADE,

The movements reported in Gen. Crawford's[1] front would indicate that the enemy had felt there this morning to see if they could strip that part of their line. Finding they could they have reinforced their right from ~~that part of the line~~ there this evening. I think Crawford should be directed to push out in the morning directly down the rail-road, leaving but a pickett line in his rear, and either make the enemy hold that part of his line strongly or go through. Hancock ought to do the same thing on his front.

U. S. GRANT
Lt. Gn.

ALS (telegram sent), deCoppet Collection, NjP; telegram received, DNA, RG 393, Army of the Potomac, Cav. Corps, Letters Received. *O.R.*, I, xlii, part 3, 6. On Oct. 1, 7:30 P.M., Maj. Gen. George G. Meade endorsed this telegram. "Respectfully referred to Brig. Genl Crawford—Genls. Parke & Warren are ordered to attack early tomorrow morning   Genl Crawford will watch the enemy in his front & take advantage of any opportunity that may present itself, in conformity with previous instructions—either to attack or maneuvre so as to compel the enemy to keep a force in his front—" AES, DNA, RG 393, Army of the Potomac, Cav. Corps, Letters Received. *O.R.*, I, xlii, part 3, 6.

At 2:30 P.M. and 7:00 P.M., Meade telegraphed to USG. "Ayres this morning at 8. a m repulsed the attack made by the enemy—Since then Crawfords pickets on the Welden R Rd—have been felt and the signal officer has seen the enemy filing in to their works across & to the right of this road—Prisoners & deserters report positively Wilcox Heth & part of Mahone as present also bodies of dismounted Cavalry Dearings brigade & perhaps other portions of Hampton's command—Gregg who was ordered up to Warren's left on withdrawing was attacked—he repulsed the attack, and is now ordered to fight their cavalry as long as they show fight & then to join us or send such parts as he can spare   One of the prisoners told me had seen a column of 9th corps men going into Petersburgh said to be 700 in number & I fear from what I hear it is true   They were taken when Potter was driven back.—Mott's division is now arriving by rail & going forward—I shall see Warren & Parke & then determine what I will do, being most desirous to attack unless I should not deem it judicious to do so—It is raining hard & roads east of Welden R. Rd—getting bad.—" "Genl. Motts division did not reach the scene of operations till near 6. P. M that is the last brigade—The first got there a little before 4—There was considerable delay in getting the cars for them.—This made it so late that in connection with the character of the weather, no movement was made.—The enemy made no demonstration after Ayres repulsing them till 5. P M when Gregg was attacked—with what result I have not heard yet.—Prisoners were yesterday taken from Andersons brigade of *Fields* division, over 60 of them, proving the presence of that brigade, in addition to Wilcox, Heth, & possibly part of Mahone leaving the balance of Mahone & Johnston to hold the entrenchments—There has been some firing about the Strong House, feeling I presume to see if we hold our lines—I have given orders to Parke & Warren to advance at daylight tomorrow, and endeavor to affect a lodgment, on the Boydtown plank road.—" ALS (telegrams sent), DNA, RG 393, Army of the Potomac, Cav. Corps, Letters Received; telegrams received, *ibid.*, RG 108, Letters Received. *O.R.*, I, xlii, part 3, 5, 6–7.

At 8:00 P.M., Meade telegraphed to USG. "You have mis apprehended the information as to Crawford's ~~part~~ front. The enemy first felt his pickets, & then were seen to man the rifle Pits & works in his front, which they had before abandoned probably to take part in the attack on his Ayres. Crawfords instructions are to watch their movements & to advance, if he sees any weakening of their lines to attack otherwise to threaten. As his forces only consists of a picket line & two new unreliable regiments, I directed him to take one of Ferrero's brigades of Colered troops holding the lines to his right. Th~~is~~ese instructions he has for tomorrow & [are] I think in conformity with the views expressed in your telegram just recd." Telegram received, DNA, RG 108, Letters Received. *O.R.*, I, xlii, part 3, 7. On the same day, USG telegraphed to Meade. "I did misunderstand the movements of the enemy in Crawfords front. I thought they first threatened our left. Have you heard the result of the attack on Greggs Cavalry yet?" Copies, DLC-USG, V, 45, 69, 107; DNA, RG 108, Letters Sent. *O.R.*, I, xlii, part 3, 7.

At 10:15 P.M., Meade telegraphed to USG. "I send you a despatch just received from Genl Gregg—The Davis House where he now is—is about 3 miles south & West from here on the Vaughan road—" ALS (telegram sent), DNA, RG 107, Telegrams Collected (Unbound); telegram received, *ibid.*, RG 108, Letters Received. *O.R.*, I, xlii, part 3, 7. The enclosure is *ibid.*, p. 29.

1. Samuel W. Crawford, born in 1829 in Pa., graduated from the University of Pennsylvania in 1846, began to practice medicine in 1850, and entered the U.S. Army in 1851 as asst. surgeon. After commanding a battery at Fort Sumter, he was appointed maj., 13th Inf., and brig. gen. as of April 25, 1862. Thereafter he held brigade and div. command in the Army of the Potomac; on Oct. 1, 1864, he commanded the 3rd Div., 5th Army Corps.

To Maj. Gen. George G. Meade

City Point Va. SOct. 1st/64

MAJ. GEN. MEADE,

I start in a few minuets for Gen. Butler's Hd Qrs. Dispatches directed to Deep Bottom will reach me. There is one regt. of new

troops here assigned to you that might be ordered out and put in
the line. You will be able to judge best as to the propriety of further
offensive operations

U. S. GRANT

Lt. Gn.

ALS (telegram sent), CSmH; telegram received (at 10:30 A.M.), DNA, RG
393, Army of the Potomac, Cav. Corps, Letters Received. *O.R.*, I, xlii, part 3,
4. On Oct. 1, 1864, 8:00 A.M. and 9:20 A.M., Maj. Gen. George G. Meade telegraphed to USG. "I forward despatches from Genl—Parke—Hancock & Signal
officer From them you will see the enemy haved not left Parkees front at last
report, and that they are being re-inforced this morning—From the deserters
statement I feel confirmed in the view expressed last evening that I have two
divisions in the lines against me & two meeting my attack on the left—Parts of
these in the lines were or will be sent to the point threatened.—I am awaiting a
report from Warren & Parke & Gregs as to the reconnaissances ordered this
morning—Parke & Warren were ordered to advance if they deemed it practicable
and the substance of Genl. Butlers despatch sent to them—If I advance I will
send up Hancocks Division & put in all the troops I can get hold of.—" "I send
you a despatch from Prov. Mar—indicating 4 divisions in my front.—I also forward a report from Warren just received indicating the enemy not only in force
in his front, but menacing him—This may be policy I have ordered Motts Division to the left—As soon as he reaches there I will assume the offensive—This
leaves the line from the Appomatox to the Welden R. Rd. to be held by two
divisions of Hancock & the colored troops—less than 15,000.—" ALS (telegrams
sent), DNA, RG 393, Army of the Potomac, Cav. Corps, Letters Received; telegrams received, *ibid.*, RG 94, War Records Office, Army of the Potomac. *O.R.*,
I, xlii, part 3, 4. The enclosures with the first telegram are *ibid.*, pp. 9, 11, 25;
for the second, *ibid.*, pp. 8, 18.

To Maj. Gen. George G. Meade

———

Junction Varina & New Market
October 1st 1864

MAJ. GEN. MEADE.

Prisoners have been captured here from Heth's Div. Gen Butler is of the opinion, that it has gone back however. You may now
correct and strengthen your line and advance no further, unless a
very favorable chance presents itself. A reconnoisance of two Brigades of Inf'y and Kautz's Cavalry, is now out on the Central Road
probably at this time within five miles of Richmond.

U. S. GRANT. Lt. Gen.

Telegram, copies, DLC-USG, V, 45, 69, 107; DNA, RG 108, Letters Sent. *O.R.*,
I, xlii, part 3, 5. On Oct. 1, 1864, 11:30 A.M., Maj. Gen. George G. Meade telegraphed to USG. "I send two despatches just received for your information   I
have no doubt Wilcox & Heth ᵃare in front of Warren & Parke & that part if not
all of Mahone will be there today   As soon as Mott gets up we will try them
again" ALS (telegram sent), DNA, RG 393, Army of the Potomac, Cav. Corps,
Letters Received; telegram received (dated only Oct.), *ibid.*, RG 94, War Records Office, Army of the Potomac; (2) *ibid.*, RG 107, Telegrams Collected (Unbound). *O.R.*, I, xlii, part 3, 5. The enclosures are *ibid.*, pp. 9, 22.

On Oct. 1, Brig. Gen. Seth Williams twice telegraphed to USG, the second
time at 3:30 P.M., transmitting information received from blacks and a signal
officer. Telegrams received (the first at 11:45 A.M.), DNA, RG 108, Letters
Received. *O.R.*, I, xlii, part 3, 6, 9. An incomplete and undated telegram received of the first is in DNA, RG 107, Telegrams Collected (Unbound).

To Maj. Gen. Lewis Wallace

City Point, Va. Oct. 1st *1864.*

DEAR GENERAL,

Your letter asking to come down here when any active operations were to take place was received tu late to send you back word
in time for you to get down here for the operations which have just
taken place. Then too I did not exactly know how far these operations would go. I should have made no move at this but for the position Sheridan was in. He was getting Early where Lee might
have reinforced him rapidly if left alone. My efforts have been to
prevent this mainly and in this have been successful. Our move
North of the James was a complete surprise and resulted in the
capture of about 500 prisoners, fifteen pieces of Artillery and almost the annihilation of one Division of the enemy. We also captured miles of strong intrenchments and several works which we
continue to hold. South of Petersburg we extended our line some
two miles towards the Southside road capturing one piece of Artillery and strong intrenchments, inflicting a heavy loss on the
enemy besides but suffered probably an equal loss there.—I shall
be glad to see you at any time and had I supposed present operations were going to be as extensive as they have turned out would
have sent for you. Engagements preparing for late moves at the

time of receipt of your letter, and absence in the field most of the time since, must be my excuse for not writing to you immediately on receipt.

Yours Truly
U. S. GRANT

ALS, Wallace Papers, InHi.

To Gen. Robert E. Lee

———

October 2d *1864*.

GEN. R. E. LEE,
COMD.G ARMY N. VA.
GENERAL,

Your letter of yesterday proposing to exchange prisoners of War belonging to the Armies operating in Va. is received. I could not of a right accept your proposition further than to exchange those prisoners captured within the last three days and who have not yet been delivered to the Com.y Gen. of Prisoners. Among those lost by the Armies operating against Richmond were a number of Colored troops. Before further negociations are had upon the subject I would ask if you propose delivering these men the same as White soldiers.

Very respectfully
your obt. svt.
U. S. GRANT
Lt. Gen.

ALS, DNA, RG 109, Adjt. and Inspector Gen., Letters Received. *O.R.*, II, vii, 909. On Oct. 1, 1864, Gen. Robert E. Lee wrote to USG. "With a view of alleviating the sufferings of our soldiers, I have the honour to propose an exchange of the prisoners of war belonging to the armies operating in Virginia man for man, or upon the basis established by the Cartel." LS, DNA, RG 109, Adjt. and Inspector Gen., Letters Received. *O.R.*, II, vii, 906–7. See letter to Gen. Robert E. Lee, Oct. 3, 1864.

To Maj. Gen. Henry W. Halleck

(Cipher)   City Point Va. Oct. 2d/64 8.30 p. m.
MAJ. GN. HALLECK, WASHINGTON.

~~T~~Gen. Butler on the right of the James and Gen. Meade Southwest of Petersburg occupy the same positions as yesterday. There
has been but very little fighting to-day. A few prisoners however
have been captured. Last ~~evening two brigades~~ evening Gen. Butler sent two Brigades of Infantry with a little cavalry within a few
hundred yards of the inner line of works East of Richmond meeting with no oposition.

U. S. GRANT
Lt. Gen.

ALS (telegram sent), CSmH; telegram received (at 9:00 P.M.), DNA, RG
107, Telegrams Collected (Bound). *O.R.*, I, xlii, part 1, 22; *ibid.*, I, xlii, part 3,
35–36.

To Maj. Gen. Benjamin F. Butler

By Telegraph from City Point
Dated Oct 2d *1864*. 12.30 a m

To MAJ GENL BUTLER

I will send Barnard & Comstock up in the morning, but do not
let this make any difference in you plans for the morrow.

Genl Meade will feel in the morning to ascertain what is in his
front at different points in his line & if there is chance for an attack
on his left he will make it

His Main object in feeling at different points in his front will
be to ascertain whether the enemy has stripped any portion of his
line—

U S GRANT
Lt Genl

Telegram received, DLC-Benjamin F. Butler; copies, DLC-USG, V, 45, 69, 107;
DNA, RG 108, Letters Sent. *O.R.*, I, xlii, part 3, 48. See telegram to Maj. Gen.
Benjamin F. Butler, Oct. 1, 1864. On Oct. 2, 1864, USG telegraphed to Butler.

"If you desire an engineer officer to report either to your self or one of your Corps Comdrs for the present occation I can send either Comstock or Babcock Please answer" Telegram received, DLC-Benjamin F. Butler. On the same day, Lt. Col. Cyrus B. Comstock telegraphed to Butler. "Can your Engineer officer meet Genl Barnard and myself at Deep bottom at ten thirty a m." Telegram received, DNA, RG 107, Telegrams Collected (Unbound). Butler drafted his reply at the foot of the telegram received. "I will send down Capt Mhie [*Michie*] I should be very glad to meet Gen Grant there myself and will ride down if he will come up or I will ride down to meet you. I am sending a long Cipher dispatch to the Genl which I think it important to Consult him upon." ADf, *ibid.*

At 9:45 A.M., Butler telegraphed to USG. "Upon consultation with Generals Birney and Wietzel we are of opinion from what we learn from the reconnoisance of yesterday that we can go in with one corps and certainly with both by the Darbytown road and Charles City road. There are no troops there except the militia composed of the employees of the several Departments of the Government and as we made two reconnoisances in that neighborhood which are supposed by them to be cavalry reconnoisances only thier attention will be drawn from that place especially if as you believe Lee looks upon this as the fient and the real attack to be made on the south side. My judgement is that this plan is more hopeful than any other especially in view of the several attempts that have been made by the Army of the Potomac to turn the right and the want of successful accomplishment   To do this we ought to have a corps sent to take our place behind our skirmish line on the line we now hold while we advance—A corps can then hold that line they marching in with the light of our fires and we marching out. I am very strongly of opinion that this plan would succeed from the investigations I have made and I trust the Lieut General has confidence enough in my means of obtaining information that I am not decieved as to the facts. As the corps would not be expected to advance one step after they get their place and as it is only about ten (10) miles directly from Petersburg to the left of our line here they might make the march in the early night so as to let us out by two (2) o clock in the morning which would be sufficiently early. I have examined carefully the proposition of the Lieut Genl as to taking up a line to hold here with a single corps and I find it very difficult in view of the possible return of Early, to find a tenable line that would have any advantage over our line at Deep Bottom and Dutch Gap—" LS, *ibid.*, RG 393, Dept. of Va. and N. C., Telegrams Sent (Press). *O.R.*, I, xlii, part 3, 48.

To Maj. Gen. George G. Meade

City Point Va. Oct. 2d/64

MAJ. GEN. MEADE,

You may shorten your line to the extent you deem necessary to be able to hold it. All you do hold West of the Welden road be prepared to give up when ever the forces holding it are necessary to defend any other part of the line. I have just returned from Deep Bottom. When I left the enemy were reported advancing down the New Market road.

U. S. GRANT
Lt. Gn.

ALS (telegram sent), OClWHi; telegram received, DNA, RG 393, Army of the Potomac, Cav. Corps, Letters Received. *O.R.*, I, xlii, part 3, 36.

On Oct. 2, 1864, 8:00 A.M., Maj. Gen. George G. Meade telegraphed to USG. "I forward despatch just received from Maj. Genl. Parke being all the information I have to report.—Parke's & Warren's losses in killed wounded & missing were yesterday estimated at 2500—As Mott only brings 4500, the actual reenforcement is about 2000.—" ALS (telegram sent—at 8:10 A.M.), DNA, RG 393, Army of the Potomac, Cav. Corps, Letters Received; telegram received, *ibid.*, RG 108, Letters Received. *O.R.*, I, xlii, part 3, 36. The enclosure is *ibid.*, p. 44. At 8:45 A.M., Meade telegraphed to USG. "Three deserters have just been brought from Johnstons division on the enemy's left—They report a thin line of one rank in the rifle pits & one says that a brigade of Johnstons has been taken out leaving only three brigades in the line—He does not know where this brigade went to but heard Richmond—Two prisoners have been sent in by Genl. Gibbon on the plank road They state they belong to Mahones Division—that their division is in the trenches extending from Johnstons right to the Welden R Rd They say ~~they~~ their regiment was taken out the trenches last night At just before day this morning they drove in our pickets—that our pickets colored troops on left of plank road, fell back without resistan[ce.] These men followed on & in trying to get back through the woods got in rear of Gibbons pickets & were captured—They ~~a~~state their Division fills the rifle pits quite well & that they have two ranks I have had no official report from Ferrero.—" ALS (telegram sent), DNA, RG 107, Telegrams Collected (Unbound); telegram received, *ibid.*, RG 108, Letters Received.

At 11:00 A.M., Meade, Globe Tavern, telegraphed to USG. "Parke & Warren report the enemy having withdrawn from some of the positions occupied yesterday—Signal officers report their main line of works as far as seen heavily manned—The inference is the enemy refuse battle outside their works to which they have retired awaiting attack—Without your orders I shall not attack their entrenchments but on being satisfied they are not outside of them I will take up the best position I can connecting with the Welden R Rd—& extending as far to the left as practicable having in view the protection of my left flank and then entrench—I should be glad to know your views & orders—" ALS (telegram sent), *ibid.*, RG 393, Army of the Potomac, Cav. Corps, Letters Received; telegram received, *ibid.*, RG 108, Letters Received. *O.R.*, I, xlii, part 3, 36. At 11:10 A.M., USG telegraphed to Meade. "Carry out what you propose in despatch of 11 a. m. that is intrench & hold what you can but make no attack against defended fortifications—" Telegram received (at 12:30 P.M.), DNA, RG 107, Telegrams Collected (Unbound); *ibid.*, RG 393, Army of the Potomac, Cav. Corps, Letters Received; copies, *ibid.*, RG 108, Letters Sent; DLC-USG, V, 45, 69, 107; (2) Meade Papers, PHi. *O.R.*, I, xlii, part 3, 36.

At 8:00 P.M., Meade telegraphed to USG. "The following despatches from the chief signal officer are sent for your information" Telegram received, DNA, RG 108, Letters Received. The enclosures are in *O.R.*, I, xlii, part 3, 37–38.

To Julia Dent Grant

October 2d *1864.*

DEAR JULIA,

You had better send the children to "Day School" where you can take them away at any time whilst you stay in ~~Wilm~~Burlington. I will send you some money as soon as I can draw it. By all means send to Galena for the girl you had there if you want her.[1] Twenty-five or thirty dollars that it will cost to get her East is nothing to the comfort of having a good cook. I want of all things good cooking when I get back home. It makes the greatest difference in my feeling well. These I believe are answers to all your questions.—Our battles can scarcely be regarded as closed for the present though there has been but little fighting to-day.—I write so often that I have but little to say. Love & kisses for you and the children. If there is a chance for sending Jess down here you might let him come. By the time he would get tired, say in a week or two I think I might find time to run home even if it was but for a day.— I get letters from you now almost dayly. You get all of mine do you not?

ULYS.

ALS, DLC-USG.

1. On Dec. 20, 1864, Julia Dent Grant wrote to U.S. Representative Elihu B. Washburne. "I am going to ask a favor of you, an infliction you must by this time have become accustome to. I want you whilst in Galina make enquery for one *Maggie Cavinaugh*. She lived with me whilst I was in Galina. I want to get her to come here & live with me, here. I will fully satisfy her as to wages & will pay her expenses here of course. I am getting to be such an old scolder (since I have such an indiferent cook) that I really fear for the The Genl's peace of mind when he comes home (After Richmond is taken) & beg for his sake you will put some one on Maggie's track & have her looked up & carefully shiped to your friend & admirer . . . Let me wish you a happy Christmass with your family— Fred is going to City Point" ALS, DLC-Elihu B. Washburne.

To Gen. Robert E. Lee

October 3d *1864*.

GEN. R. E. LEE,
COMD.G ARMY N. VA.
GENERAL,

Your letter of this date is received. In answer I have to state that the Government is bound to secure to all persons received into her Armies the rights due to soldiers. This being denied by you in the persons of such men as have escaped from Southern Masters induces me to decline making the exchanges you ask. The whole matter however will be refered to the proper authority for their decession and whatever it may be will be adhered to.

Very respectfully
your obt. svt.
U. S. GRANT
Lt. Gen.

ALS, DNA, RG 109, Adjt. and Inspector Gen., Letters Received. *O.R.*, II, vii, 914. On Oct. 3, 1864, Gen. Robert E. Lee wrote to USG. "In my proposition of ~~yesterday~~ of the 1st Inst: to exchange the prisoners of War belonging to the armies operating in Viga I intended to include all captured soldiers of the U. S. of whatever nation Colour under my Control—Deserters from our Service, & negroes belonging to our Citizens ~~are were~~ are not Considered Subjects of exchange & ~~are~~ were not included in my proposition. If there are any Such among those stated by you to have been Captured around Richmond, & they ~~will~~ can not be ~~exchanged~~ returned" ALS, MoSHi; LS, DNA, RG 109, Adjt. and Inspector Gen., Letters Received. *O.R.*, II, vii, 914.

To Edwin M. Stanton

Cipher   City Point Va. Oct. 3d/64 [7:00 P.M.]
HON. E. M. STANTON SEC. OF WAR, WASHINGTON
I will follow Sheridans suggestion of bringing the 6th & 19th Corps here, and yours as to bringing them by rail from Front Royal. Please let the work be pushed on the rail-road.

U. S. GRANT
Lt. Gn.

ALS (telegram sent), CSmH; telegram received (at 8:00 P.M.), DNA, RG 107, Telegrams Collected (Bound). *O.R.*, I, xliii, part 2, 266. On Oct. 3, 1864, 11:30 A.M., Secretary of War Edwin M. Stanton telegraphed to USG. "My intelligence from telegraphic operators is that the Front Royal Road is very little broken and might be put in running order before Sheridan could get his ~~fifth~~ sixth and nineteenth corps there say in three days. With a rapid accumulation of rolling stock of the government and Baltimore road they could be moved at once to Alexandria and with an adequate supply of water transportation reach you by Saturday morning if you conclude to adopt Sheridans suggestion of sending them to you." ALS (telegram sent), DNA, RG 107, Telegrams Collected (Bound); telegram received, *ibid.*, RG 108, Letters Received. *O.R.*, I, xliii, part 2, 265.

On Oct. 2, 11:00 A.M., both Stanton and Maj. Gen. Henry W. Halleck telegraphed to USG. "The rail road and telegraph corps have reached Manassas. If they are to go to Front Royal it will be a loss of time and laber to proceed to the Rappahannock as they are ordered by General Halleck. I understand you as leaving the route to be selected by Sheridan and understand him as choosing the road to Front Royal   But General Halleck does not so understand the matter. Would it not be well for you to direct specifically the route from Manassas immediately?" ALS (telegram sent—misdated Oct. 3), DNA, RG 107, Telegrams Collected (Bound); telegram received, *ibid.*, RG 108, Letters Received. *O.R.*, I, xliii, part 2, 257. "I have recieved no reply from Genl Sheridan in regard to his future line of supplies, but infer from his despatch of sept 29th to you that he will not go to Charlottesville. Our construction party has passed Manassas Junction towards the Rappahannock. In view of Sheridan's last despatch would it not be better to put the working party on the road towards Front Royal?" ALS (telegram sent), DNA, RG 107, Telegrams Collected (Bound); telegram received, *ibid.*; *ibid.*, RG 108, Letters Received. *O.R.*, I, xliii, part 2, 257–58. At 4:30 P.M., USG telegraphed to Halleck. "Please direct the construction party at work on rail-road to open the road to Front Royal." ALS (telegram sent), CSmH; telegram received (at 6:00 P.M.), DNA, RG 107, Telegrams Collected (Bound). *O.R.*, I, xliii, part 2, 258.

On Oct. 3, Brig. Gen. John D. Stevenson, Harpers Ferry, telegraphed to Stanton, sending a copy to USG, reporting C.S.A. cav. movements. Telegram received, DNA, RG 107, Telegrams Collected (Unbound); *ibid.*, RG 108, Letters Received. *O.R.*, I, xliii, part 2, 270.

To Maj. Gen. Benjamin F. Butler

City Point Va. Oct. ~~2~~ 3d *1864.*

MAJ. GEN. BUTLER, DEEP BOTTOM

Your dispatch received. Send me a list of all the promotions, by Brevet & otherwise you would like made from your command, stating the particular services for which Brevets are asked, and I will take pleasure in recommending them. Gn. Sherman is preparing such a list from his Army & Gn. Meade has already sent one from

his. In the matter of breaking the enemy's line as suggested by you
I think it practicable but think that will keep. To bring any troops
from the left a good long line now held must be ~~brough~~ abandoned.

U. S. Grant

Lt. Gn.

ALS (telegram sent), OClWHi; telegram received, DLC-Benjamin F. Butler.
O.R., I, xlii, part 3, 66. On Oct. 3, 1864, 11:30 A.M. and 1:05 P.M., Maj. Gen.
Benjamin F. Butler telegraphed to USG. "All quiet during night. An attempt was
made on Kautz ~~Pickets~~ and Birneys Pickets on the Darby town & New Market
Roads last evening which were easily repulsed and By Birney with the capture of
17 Prisoners   Lt Mikie is at work on the new line ~~on~~ with one thousand Colored
troops   Will you telegraph to the Secretary of War for a brevet Majority for
Mcky in his corps   I wish him as my chief engineer   If gallant unwearied and
most meritorious services are ever deserving they are in his case   Also an order
that he be put on duty in his Brevet rank   I have set Ludlows extra men at
Dutch Gap at work on the Redoubt ~~near~~ on Signal Hill near him. ~~I wish we cou~~
Four Regiments of Pickets Division are ~~over here from~~ the Bermuda lines—between Appomattox & James Leaving about twenty five hundred men there. I
believe I could Break through on the left with three thousand Negros   Can we
not have the other Corps here." ALS (telegram sent), DNA, RG 107, Telegrams
Collected (Unbound); telegram received, *ibid.*, RG 108, Letters Received. *O.R.*,
I, xlii, part 3, 65. "Dispatch recieved   Will send forward a list of deserving officers. We will hold where we are. Will keep you advised daily and oftener if
anything happens of interest." ALS (telegram sent), DNA, RG 393, Dept. of
Va and N. C., Telegrams Sent (Press); telegram received, *ibid.*, RG 108, Letters Received. *O.R.*, I, xlii, part 3, 66.

On Oct. 6, Butler wrote at length to USG concerning the staff of Bvt. Maj.
Gen. Godfrey Weitzel and making recommendations for promotions. *Ibid.*, pp.
97–98. See *ibid.*, p. 351. Also on Oct. 6, Weitzel telegraphed to Lt. Col. Cyrus B.
Comstock. "General Butler has put me on duty according to my brevet rank. Does
this entitle me to the pay and staff of a major-general without the orders being
approved at Washington?" *Ibid.*, p. 100. On the same day, Comstock telegraphed
to Weitzel. "The President must assign to duty according to brevet rank, but his
confirmation will make the assignmt good from its date. I think you would be
justified in selecting your staff, at once but of course this is subject to ~~your own~~
approval of your own assignmt about which there is no question." ALS (telegram
sent), DNA, RG 107, Telegrams Collected (Unbound).

To Maj. Gen. Benjamin F. Butler

City Point Va. Oct. 3d *1864.*

Maj. Gen. Butler, Deep Bottom,

If all remains quiet I shall go to Washington to-morrow. I send
you copy of dispatch to Gn. Meade which explains what I want

done. As much of present foothold North of the James as can be held I want held. Please telegraph me the situation of affairs daily. I wrote a letter to Gn. Lee, in reply to one from him, which has not yet been answered. Should this, or any other communication come from inside the rebel lines directed to me in my absence direct ~~that they~~ it to be received and sent to you. You will be at liberty to open any such communication, and, if immediate action is required, to act. I would prefer however my absence should not be known across the lines.

U. S. GRANT
Lt. Gn.

ALS (telegram sent), OClWHi; telegram received, DLC-Benjamin F. Butler. *O.R.*, I, xlii, part 3, 66. USG enclosed a copy of his telegram of noon to Maj. Gen. George G. Meade. Telegram received, DLC-Benjamin F. Butler.

To Maj. Gen. Benjamin F. Butler

City Point Va. Oct. 3d/64

MAJ. GN. BUTLER, DEEP BOTTOM

A dispatch is just received from Sheridan up to the 1st inst. The enemy have entirely left his front and come to Charlottesville & Gordonsville. He cannot reach them so that we may now confidantly expect the return here of at least Kershaw's Div. and Rasser's Cavalry. It will require very close watching to prevent being surprised by this reinforcement. I will have 40.000 reinforcements here in ten days.

U. S. GRANT
Lt. Gn.

ALS (telegram sent), OClWHi; telegram received, DLC-Benjamin F. Butler. *O.R.*, I, xlii, part 3, 66. On the reverse of this telegram appears a fragment written by USG, then cancelled. "~~this force you may do it. I have ordered back the 6th Corps and all as much as possible, of the Cavalry.~~" ADfS, OClWHi. On Oct. 3, 1864, 7:30 P.M., Maj. Gen. Benjamin F. Butler telegraphed to USG. "Dispatch relating to Sheridan recieved. Will watch with the utmost Vigilance Can we not have the 19th Corps? All quiet tonight" ALS (telegram sent), DNA, RG 107, Telegrams Collected (Unbound). *O.R.*, I, xlii, part 3, 67. At 10:10 P.M., USG telegraphed to Butler. "The 19th will come here—" Telegram received, DLC-Benjamin F. Butler. *O.R.*, I, xlii, part 3, 67.

To Maj. Gen. George G. Meade

(Cipher)   Copy to Gn. Butler, Deep Bottom

City Point Va. Oct. 3d/64 [*noon*]

MAJ. GEN. MEADE,

I shall go to Washington to-morrow and see if I cannot devise means of getting promptly into the field the large number of recruits that I understand are now in depots all over the North. Will be gone three or four days. In my absence would like to have present lines held if possible but if necessity requires it, all, or as much as is necessary, West of the Weldon road may be abandoned. One corps, or as many troops as possible, from the Army of the James, will be held footloose to operate on the defensive at any place threatened. Gen. Butler, the Senior officer present, will command during my absence.

U. S. GRANT, Lt. Gn.

ALS (telegram sent), CSmH; telegram received, DNA, RG 393, Army of the Potomac, Cav. Corps, Letters Received. *O.R.*, I, xlii, part 3, 51. On Oct. 3, 1864, 3:30 P.M. (sent at 4:00 P.M.), Maj. Gen. George G. Meade telegraphed to USG. "I regret to learn you are compelled to go to Washington. Am I to understand the forces North of the James are withdrawn or going to be—The holding a corps foot loose causes me to ask the question. Can not Hancock be relieved up to the Jerusalem plank road—which would give me his two divisions as a reserve on the left & would make me quite secure" ALS (telegram sent), DNA, RG 393, Army of the Potomac, Cav. Corps, Letters Received; telegram received, *ibid.*, RG 108, Letters Received. *O.R.*, I, xlii, part 3, 51.

At noon (sent at 2:00 P.M.) and 10:00 P.M. (sent at 10:30 P.M.), Meade telegraphed to USG. "Yesterday after my report Genl. Motts Division advanced on the left, and developed the enemys position, which was found to be a strong line of rifle pits & batteries running in a South westerly direction evidently to cover the Boydtown plank road & South Side R. Rd.—Finding I did not have the force to hold the position in case I secured it on the Boyd town plank road, Mott was withdrawn & placed on the left & rear of the 9th corps;—and the line occupied extending our former line from Fort Wadsworth on the Welden R. Rd. to the Pegram House—a distance of about two & a half miles. The enemy offered no opposition to these movements, except keeping our skirmish line actively engaged advancing & retiring, and opening with artillery on such parts of our lines as were exposed. The casualties were small tho' several officers were wounded on the skirmish line.—Genl. Ayres on Warrens right advanced and took a small redoubt at the W. A. Davis house without great resistance—this work being part of the line previously taken from the enemy & in advance of the line subsequently held by them—It being not well placed for our purposes, it was subsequently abandoned by Ayres when the final rectification of our line was made.—We now hold securely to the Pegram House with our left refused & the cavalry to the rear on the Vaughan & Ducking roads.—The left is a little over a mile from the Boyd town plank road & believed to be not over two miles from the South Side R. Rd.—Genls. Parke & Warren are busily occupied entrenching in this position, and rendering it such that should the enemy turn the left they will have an available force to meet the movement. I send you two despatches from Signal officers showing the enemy are re-inforcing & moving to their right— whether with a view to attempt to dislodge us or simply to resist an advance can not at present be told.—" "Nothing of importance has occurred to day—excepting the driving in of Parke's pickets in front of the Pegram House, our extreme left, about 3. P. M—the line was however immediately re-established.—My lines on the left are now so secure against any attack that I propose tomorrow to return Motts Division to the 2d corps line   Redoubts are being constructed on the new line not only in front but on the flank & in rear—I do not think the enemy will attempt to disturb us now." ALS (telegrams sent), DNA, RG 393, Army of the Potomac, Cav. Corps, Letters Received; telegrams received (the second on Oct. 4), *ibid.*, RG 108, Letters Received. *O.R.*, I, xlii, part 3, 50–51.

To Maj. Gen. Philip H. Sheridan

From City Point 7 p. m Oct 3d. *1864.*

MAJ GEN P H SHERIDAN
HARRISONBURG VA

You may take up such position in the valley as you think can, and ought to be held, and send all the force not required for this, immediately here. Leave nothing for the subsistence of an army on any ground you abandon to the enemy. I will direct the R R to be pushed toward Front Royal so that you, may send your troops back that way. Keep all of Crook's forces and the new troops that have been sent to you

U. S. GRANT
Lt Genl

Telegram received (at 8:00 P.M.), DNA, RG 107, Telegrams Collected (Bound); copies, *ibid.*, Telegrams Received in Cipher; *ibid.*, RG 108, Letters Sent; DLC-USG, V, 45, 69, 107. *O.R.*, I, xliii, part 2, 266. Secretary of War Edwin M. Stanton endorsed this telegram. "General Halleck will please give orders for water transportation of Sixth and Nineteenth Corps from Alexandria to City Point, and make such other needful arrangements as the within dispatch requires for the transportation of the troops." *Ibid.* On Oct. 1, 1864, 10:00 A.M. and 9:30 P.M., Maj. Gen. Philip H. Sheridan telegraphed to USG. "I have ordered Gen Wilson to report to Sherman,   He is the best man for the position   I have defended the valley from Stanton down to Mt Crawford and will continue. The destruction of mills grain forage foundries etc etc etc is very great. The cavalry report to me that they have collected 3000 head of cattle and sheep between Staunton and Mt Crawford   The difficulty of transporting this army through the mountain passes on to the railroad at Charlottesville is such that I regard it as impracticable with my present means of transportation   The rebels have given up the valley excepting Waynesboro which has been occupied by them since my cavalry was there—I think that the best policy will be to let the burning of the crops of the valley be the end of this campaign & let some of this army go somewhere else" "A despatch just recd from Gen. Halleck in which you expect me to reach Staunton & ~~Waynesboro~~ or Charlottesville   I have been to Stanton & Waynesboro with the cavalry destroyed the iron bridge on South River at Waynesboro throwing it into the river, also the bridge over christian creek and the railroad from Staunton to Waynesboro—My judgement is that it would be best to terminate this campaign by the destruction of the crops etc etc in this valley and the transfer of the troops to the army operating against Richmond. If the Orange & Alexandria railroad is opened it will take an army corps to protect it. If the FrontRoyal road is opened it will take as many troops to protect it as there is no enemy in the valley to operate against   Early is without doubt fortifying at Charlottesville holding RockFish Gap—It is no easy matter to pass these mountain gaps & attack Charlottesville, hauling supplies through difficult passes fourteen miles in length & with a line of communication from 135 to 145 miles in length without the organization of supply trains, ordnance trains & all the appointments of an army making a prominent advance—At present we are organized for a raid up the valley with no trains except the corps trains—all the regimental wagons had to be used as supply wagons to subsist us as far as this place & cant do it at that   I am ready & willing to cross the Blue Ridge but know from present indications that the enemy will strongly fortify at Charlottesville & Gordonsville and that these places cannot be taken without the expenditure of a largely supirior force to keep open the line of communication   With my present means I cannot accumulate supplies enough to carry me through to the O. & A. R. R." Telegrams received (on Oct. 3, 3:45 P.M. and 9:00 A.M.), DNA, RG 107, Telegrams Collected (Bound); *ibid.*, RG 108, Letters Received; copies, *ibid.*, RG 107, Telegrams Received in Cipher; (2) DLC-Philip H. Sheridan. *O.R.*, I, xliii, part 2, 249.

On Oct. 7, 9:00 P.M., Sheridan, Woodstock, telegraphed to USG. "I have the honor to report my command at this point tonight. I commen[ced] moving back from Pt Republi[c] Mount Crawford Bridgwater & Harrisonburg yesterday morning   The grain & forage in advance of these points had previously been destroyed. In moving back to this point the whole country from the Blue Ridge to the North Mountain has been made untenable for a rebel army. I have destroyed over two thousand barns filled with wheat hay & farming implements over seventy mills filled with flour & wheat, have driven in front of the army over four herd of stock and have killed & issued to the troops not less than 3,000 sheep. This destruction embraces the Luray valley and Little Fort valley as well as the main valley. A large number of horses have been obtained, a proper estimate of which I cannot now make. Lt. Jno. R. Meigs, my Engr. officer was murdered beyond Harrisonburg near Dayton. For this atrocious act all the houses within an area of five miles were burned. Since I came into the valley from Harpers Ferry up to Harrisonburg every train, every small party & every straggler has been bushwhacked by people, many of whom have protection papers from commanders who have been hitherto in that valley. From the vicinity of

Harrisonburg over 400 wagon loads of refugees have been sent back to Martinsburg. most of these people were Dunkers & had been conscripted   The people here are getting sick of the war,   Heretofore they have had no reason to complain because they have been living in great abundance. I have not been followed by the enemy up to this point; with the exception of a small force of rebel cavalry that showed themselves some distance behind my rear guard today,   A party of one hundred of the 8th Ohio Cavalry which I had stationed at the bridge over the North Shenandoah near Mt Jackson was attacked by McNeil with 17 men while they were asleep & the whole party dispersed or captured. I think that they will all turn up. I learn that 56 of them had reached Winchester   McNeil was mortally wounded & fell into our hands—This was fortunate as he was the most daring and dangerous of all the bushwhackers in this section of the country. I would have preferred sending troops to you by B & O R R. It would have been the Quickest & most concealed way of sending them. The keeping open of the road to Front Royal will require large guards to protect it against a very small number of partisan troops; it also obliges me to have a ponton ~~bridge~~ train, if it is to be kept open, to bridge the Shenandoah to keep up up communication with Winchester; however in a day or two I can tell better. I sent a party of Cavalry through Thornton Gap & directed the balance of the Division of Cavy which I have in the Luray valley to take post at Millwood, occupying Chester Gap & Front Royal. Thornton Gap I have given up as of no value. With this disposition of forces I will move Infantry round the Mountains via Strasburg as soon as possible. Tomorrow I will continue the destruction of wheat, forage Etc., down to Fisher's Hill. When this is completed the valley from Winchester up to Staunton 92 miles, will have but little in it for man or beast. In previous dispatches I have used *lower* valley when I should have said *upper* valley; or in other words, in my last dispatch, I intended to say that the grain & forage from Staunton up to Lexington, had been sent to Richmond, and that the grain & forage from Staunton to Strasburg had been left for the wintering of Early's army. Yesterday Col. Powell captured a guerrilla camp on the mountains with ten wagons & teams."
Telegram received (on Oct. 8), DNA, RG 107, Telegrams Collected (Bound); copies, *ibid.*; *ibid.*, Telegrams Received in Cipher; (2) DLC-Philip H. Sheridan. *O.R.*, I, xliii, part 1, 30–31; *ibid.*, I, xliii, part 2, 307–8.

To Miss E. Glanky

City Point, Va. Oct. 3d 1864.

Miss E. Glanky,
My ~~d~~Dear Miss,

Your very kind letter of the 26th of September, with the beautiful saddle cloth worked by your mother, has been received. I feel very greatful for such marks of esteem from strangers and only regret that your kindness should be so taxed.

The devotion to the cause of our country, exibited in your letter, if it was general in the land, ~~we~~ would ~~have~~ stop desertions from the Army and the rebellion would soon be suppressed. You have given one brother to the cause and regret that you have not another to tender his services? Let all the ladies of the land express the same sentiments and able bodied young men will be ashamed to stay at home whilst the war continues.

I regret that I have not a photograph to send to you, as you request, but I will save your letter, so as to keep your address, and as soon as I can procure one will send it to you

Very truly yours,
U. S. GRANT
Lt. Gn. U. S. A.

ALS, PPRF.

To Maj. Gen. Henry W. Halleck

(Cipher)   City Point Va. Oct. 4th *1864*. [*2:00* P.M.]
MAJ. GEN. HALLECK, WASHINGTON

In moving Sheridan's forces here move one Division of Cavalry as fast as possible. Send all the Cavalry horses that can possibly be raised in the mean time. There is danger of the enemy returning a portion of their Cavalry here and annoying us greatly with raids on our rear and along the river. Is it not possible to get all the new troops now in depot to the front at once? I hear of thousands of men all over the North.

U. S. GRANT
Lt. Gen.

ALS (telegram sent), CSmH; telegram received (at 3:30 P.M.), DNA, RG 107, Telegrams Collected (Bound). *O.R.*, I, xliii, part 2, 273. See telegram to Maj. Gen. Henry W. Halleck, Oct. 5, 1864.

On Oct. 4, 1864, Maj. Gen. Henry W. Halleck wrote to USG. "I percieve from your despatch which passed through last evening to Genl Sheridan, that you propose to withdraw a large portion of his troops from the valley. This will make it necessary to adopt a line of defence against rebel raids. If troops can be spared for that purpose, some point South of the Potomac should be fortified strong enough to resist any *coup de main*, and garrisoned with a force which can operate against a rebel advance either down the Shenandoah or the Loudon valley. Winchester & Strasbourg are both reported as indefensible except by very extensive lines and large garrisons. I do not know that Front Royal has been examined by Engineer officers in regard to its defensive character. I am of opinion, however, that the proper position for such occupation can be found at Manassas Gap or in its vicinity, so that the garrison may operate on either side of the Blue ridge, as occasion may require. The place so selected and fortified should have several months supplies and be capable of making a strong and long resistance to an attacking force. It can be communicated with by the Manassas R. R. which must be protected by entrenched garrisons at Thoroughfare Gap & Manassas Junction, and by cavalry pickets on Broad Run & a cross to Chester Gap & Strasburg or Woodstock. In order to keep up communication on this line to Manassas Gap and the Shenandoah valley, it will be necessary to send South all Secesh inhabitants between that line and the Potomac, and also to completely clean out Moseby's gang of robbers who have so long infested that district of country. And I respectfully suggest that Sheridan's cavalry should be required to accomplish this object before it is sent elsewhere. The two small regiments under Genl Augur have been so often cut up by Moseby's band that they are cowed, & useless for that purpose. If these dispositions are approved & carried out, it will not be necessary to keep so large a force at Harpers Ferry and guarding the canal & B & O Railroad. As soon as we can open the road to Piedmont I will send Cols Alexander & Thom to of the Engrs to examine the localities above mentioned with reference to fortifications, and to confer with Genl Sheridan. I will also send Genl S. a copy of this letter. I have no doubt that Genl Crook might be able to select some points in the great North Mountain or Aleghany Ridge by which a small force could prevent rebel cavalry raids into West Va., and thus avoid the necessity of keeping up so many posts there." ALS, DNA, RG 108, Letters Received. *O.R.*, I, xliii, part 2, 272–73.

To Maj. Gen. Henry W. Halleck

Confidential   City Point Va. Oct. 4th *1864.*
Maj. Gen. H. W. Halleck,
Chief of Staff of the Army,
Washington D. C.
General,

Your letter of the 2d instant in relation to the movements of the Western Armies, and the preparations ordered by the Staff officers of Gen. Canby is received. When this campaign was commenced nothing els was in contemplation but that Sherman, after capturing Atlanta, should connect with Canby at Mobile. Drawing the 19th Corps from Canby however, and the movements of Kirby Smith demanding the presence of all of Canby's surplus forces in an other direction, has made it impossible to carry out the plan as early as was contemplated. Any conciderable force to co operate with Sherman, on the sea coast, must now be sent from here. The question is whether under such circumstances Augusta & Savannah would not be a better line than Selma, Montgomery & Mobile. I think Savannah might be taken by surprise with one Corps from here and such troops as Foster could spare from the Dept. of the South. This is my view but before giving positive orders I want to make a visit to Washington and consult a little on the subject. All Canby can do with his present force is to make demonstrations on Mobile, or up the Appalachacola towards Columbus. He can not possibly have the force to require the transportation your letter would indicate he has called for, or to consume the supplies.

Either line indicated would cut off the supplies from the rich districts of Ga. Ala. & Miss. equally well. Which ever way Sherman moves he will undoubtedly encounter Hoods Army and in crossing to the Sea Coast will sever the connection between Lee's Army and this District of Country.

I wrote to Sherman on this subject sending my letter by a Staff officer. He is ready to attempt (and feels confidant of his ability to succeed) to make his way to either the Savannah river or any of the navigable streams emptying into the Atlantic or Gulf, if he is only certain of finding a base open for him when he arrives. The supplies Canby was ordering I presume were intended for the use of Sherman's Army. I do not deem it necessary to accumulate them in any great quantity until the base to which he is to make his way is secured.

> Very respectfully
> your obt. svt.
> U. S. GRANT
> Lt. Gn.

ALS, Schoff Collection, MiU-C. *O.R.*, I, xxxix, part 3, 63–64.

On Oct. 1, 1864, 1:00 P.M., Maj. Gen. William T. Sherman telegraphed to USG. "Hood is evidently on the west side of Chattahoochee below Sweet-water. If he tries to get on my road this side of the Etowah I shall attack him but if he goes over to the Selma & Taledega road why would it not do for me to leave Tenn to the force which Thomas has and the reserves soon to come to Nashville and for me to destroy Atlanta and then march across Georgia to Savannah or Charleston breaking roads and doing irreparable damage? We cannot remain on the defensive" Telegram received (at 7:00 P.M.), DNA, RG 107, Telegrams Collected (Bound); *ibid.*, RG 108, Letters Received; copies, *ibid.*, RG 107, Telegrams Received in Cipher; *ibid.*, RG 393, Military Div. of the Miss., Telegrams Sent in the Field. *O.R.*, I, xxxix, part 3, 3.

On Oct. 2, Maj. Gen. Henry W. Halleck wrote to USG. "Some time since General Sherman asked my opinion in regard to his operations after the capture of Atlanta. While free to give advice to the best of my ability, I felt it my duty to refer him to you for instructions, not being advised of your views on that subject. I presume from his despatches that you have ~~already~~ corresponded upon the subject, and perhaps his plan of future operations has already been decided upon. At one time he seemed most decidedly of opinion that he ought to operate by Montgomery and Selma and connect himself with Canby and Farragut on the Alabama river, thus severing the northern part of Georgia and Alabama and all of Mississippi from the rebel confederacy. This view was taken in his letters to General Canby, copies of which were sent to the Adjutant General's office, and in this opinion I fully concurred and so wrote both to him and Canby, directing them, however, to make no important movements till they received your instructions. I judge from a despatch just recieved from General Sherman that he is now proposing to move eastwardly towards Augusta or Millen, expecting to connect with the coast by the Savannah river. Whether this is simply a suggestion, or change of opinion, on his part, or the result of his consultation with you, or of your orders to him, I have no means of knowing. All I wish to say or know upon the subject is, that, if any definite plans have been adopted, it is desireable that the Sect'y of War or myself should be informed of that plan as early as possible. Large requisitions ~~from Genl Canby~~ have been recieved within the last day or two from Genl. Canby's staff officers for water transportation, and Quartermaster, commissary and medical stores to be sent to Mobile and Pensacola, for an army of thirty or forty thousand men. Indeed, in the single article of forage, the amount asked for is more than can possibly be furnished in the northern and eastern states and more than all the available sea-going vessels in northern ports could float! On receiving these requisitions I directed Genl Meigs to take active measures to fill them, so far as possible, but to make no shipments till further orders. Now if General Sherman is going to move east to connect with the coast by the Savannah river, these stores should not be shipped to Mobile or Pensacola, but to Hilton Head and transportation be sent to New Orleans to move all available troops to that point. Moreover, operations at Mobile should in that case be limited to a mere demonstration and continued only so long as they may serve to deceive the enemy. It is exceedingly important that some definite conclusion should be arrived at as early as possible, for the expenses of the water transportation, and especially of the demurrage of large fleets, are ~~perfectly~~ enormous. Perhaps it may be desirable that I should give my reasons in brief for concurring with General Sherman in his first proposed plan of operations. In the first place that line of connection with the coast is the shortest and most direct. 2d. By cutting off a smaller slice of rebel territory it is not so directly exposed and leaves a smaller force to attack in rear. 3d. It does not leave Tennessee and Kentucky so open to rebel raids   4th. The Alabama river is more navigable for our gunboats than the Savannah. 5th. This line is more defensible for General Canby's troops than the other. 6th. Montgomery, Selma and Mobile are in a military point of view more important than Augusta, Millen and Savannah. 7th. Mobile can be more easily captured than Savannah. And 8th. this line will bring within our control a more valuable and important section of country than that by the Savannah. There is a section of country from fifty to one hundred and fifty miles wide extending from Selma west to Maridian and thence north on both sides of the Tombigbee to Columbus, Aberdeen and Okalona, more rich in agricultural products than any equal extent of country in the confederacy. Slave labor has been but very little disturbed in this section, and the large crops of this year are being collected at Demopolis, Selma, Montgomery, and other points, for the use of the rebel army. By moving upon that line they will be converted to our use or be destroyed; by moving on Augusta they will be left for the use of Hood's forces. I do not write this for the purpose of influancing your adoption of a particular plan of campaign, or of changing your decision if you have not already made one. It is proper, however, to remark that I have taken every possible means to obtain correct information on the subject, and present these conclusions only after thorough examination, and the most mature consideration" LS, DNA, RG 108, Letters Received. *O.R.*, I, xxxix, part 3, 25–26.

To Maj. Gen. Benjamin F. Butler

Dated Oct 4 *1864.*

City Point

To MAJ GEN BUTLER—

I will be up to see you in the morning. The difficulty of holding more than we now have, I think should keep us from further offensive operations, until we get more men. We will have at least thirty thousand (30.000) additional veteran troops in the next ten days besides all the new troops that may come.

U S GRANT.

Lt Genl.

Telegram received, DLC-Benjamin F. Butler. *O.R.*, I, xlii, part 3, 78.

On Oct. 4, 1864, USG telegraphed to Maj. Gen. Benjamin F. Butler and to Maj. Gen. George G. Meade. "I have changed my mind about going to Washington today will put it off for several days" Telegram received, DNA, RG 107, Telegrams Collected (Unbound); (at 10:30 A.M.) *ibid.*, RG 393, Army of the Potomac, Cav. Corps, Letters Received; copies (2), Meade Papers, PHi. *O.R.*, I, xlii, part 3, 69. On the same day, Butler telegraphed to USG. "Telegram recieved All quiet in my lines Have moved my head Qrs to near Varina. Have a good wharf at Varina to land horses Should be pleased to have you ride up & Visit us. Can show you a new Rebel line which shews we were not a moment too soon Ought we not to make that move before Early gets up" ALS (telegram sent), DNA, RG 107, Telegrams Collected (Unbound); telegram received, *ibid.*, RG 108, Letters Received. *O.R.*, I, xlii, part 3, 77.

Also on Oct. 4, USG telegraphed to Butler. "I see the Correspondent H. J. W. of the New York Times states that two thousand (2000) negroes of Burnhams brigade charged into a ditch in front of one of the rebel works & not one of them returned—" Telegram received, DNA, RG 107, Telegrams Collected (Unbound). *O.R.*, I, xlii, part 3, 78. At 10:40 P.M., Lt. Col. George A. Kensel telegraphed to Lt. Col. Theodore S. Bowers that the newspaper contained a typographical error: the loss was 200. ALS (telegram sent), DNA, RG 107, Telegrams Collected (Unbound).

To Maj. Gen. George G. Meade

By Telegraph from City Point
Dated Oct. 4 *1864.*

To MAJ GEN MEADE

I find that Gen Benham has got little or no work done yet on the line of fortification He was directed to build. I have directed Less elaborate works than he contemplated to be speedily thrown up[1] until they are done this place is in danger of a cavalry raid particularly if the Enemy's Cavy returns here before we get ours back.

I would like to have daily scouting parties sent to the south east to see that no movement is being made.

U S GRANT
Lt Gen

Telegram received (at 11:00 P.M.), DNA, RG 393, Army of the Potomac, Cav. Corps, Letters Received; copies (2), Meade Papers, PHi. *O.R.*, I, xlii, part 3, 69. On Oct. 5, 1864, 11:00 A.M., Maj. Gen. George G. Meade telegraphed to USG. "Your despatch of 11. P. M yesterday in reference to Genl. Benham's operations states precisely the instructions previously given that officer—viz to construct first redoubts covering the main approaches—then to slash between & finally connect the redoubts with infantry parapets—All of these works were to have the minimum profile.—I have to day ordered an assistant to report to him.—Every thing is quiet along the lines & the works progressing favorably." ALS (telegram sent), DNA, RG 94, War Records Office, Army of the Potomac; telegram received, *ibid.*, RG 108, Letters Received. *O.R.*, I, xlii, part 3, 80.

On Oct. 4, 11:00 A.M. (sent at 11:20 A.M.), Meade telegraphed to USG. "Every part of my line is reported quiet & no indications of movements beyond the accompanying despatch from Signal officers." ALS (telegram sent), DNA, RG 393, Army of the Potomac, Cav. Corps, Letters Received; telegram received, *ibid.*, RG 108, Letters Received. *O.R.*, I, xlii, part 3, 69. The enclosure is *ibid.*

On the same day, USG telegraphed to Meade. "Can you give me the military record of Col. E. G. Marshall, 14th Heavy N. Y Artillery, who commanded a Brigade in the 9th Corps and was captured on the 30th of July." ALS (telegram sent), OClWHi; telegram received (at 7:55 P.M.), DNA, RG 94, War Records Office, Army of the Potomac. On Oct. 5, 9:10 A.M., Brig. Gen. Seth Williams telegraphed to USG transmitting the information. ALS (telegram sent), *ibid.*; copy, *ibid.*, RG 393, Army of the Potomac, Letters Sent.

On Oct. 5, 11:30 A.M., Meade telegraphed to USG. "I have directed Gregg to send a regiment to of Cavalry to be posted on the telegraph road in advance of Old. C. H. to patrol to the front & watch for movements on the part of the Enemy —I have one now doing the same duty at Prince Geo. C. H.—a detachment on the Norfolk road & a regiment on the plank road—so that we ought to recieve timely notice. So soon as the works on the left are completed & the working parties returned to the ranks I will relieve Gregg & station him between the Jerusalem plank road & the James, this will be I think in a day or two.—" ALS (telegram sent), *ibid.*, Cav. Corps, Letters Received; telegram received, *ibid.*, RG 108, Letters Received. *O.R.*, I, xlii, part 3, 80.

1. On Oct. 4, Lt. Col. Cyrus B. Comstock wrote to Brig. Gen. Henry W. Benham. "The Lt. Gen. Commd'g. desires me to say, that the defensive line around City Point, should be so finished as to be capable of defense within four days from to morrow, that the redoubts or lunettes should at first only have, that part of the parapet next the revetment for a thickness of three or four feet completed; that the connecting line between these stronger works, should be merely a breast work without exterior ditch and that if possible this work should be completed or made defensible in a shorter time, than that above mentioned." Copies, DLC-USG, V, 45, 69, 107; DNA, RG 108, Letters Sent. See also *O.R.*, I, xlii, part 3, 72.

To Julia Dent Grant

Oct. 4th *1864.*

DEAR JULIA,

You mus be getting tired receiving so many letters from me with so little in them. I have really nothing to write however except that I am well and believe that I shall be able to pay you an other visit before the month is out. Have you heard from home yet? If they will not write about anything els I want at least to hear that Little Rebel has not been stolen. Gen. Rawlins has returned very much improved in appearance. Bowers has not returned and I fear is sick.

Love and kisses for you and the children. Do not neglect to

have Fred study French. It will be great assistance to him if he goes to West Point. The other children must continue their German.

ULYS.

ALS, DLC-USG.

To J. Russell Jones

———

City Point, Va. Oct. 4th *1864.*

DEAR JONES,

Your letter of Sept. 30th is just received. In answer to your querry I would state that I have never felt any desire to give up my residence in Ill. and if I was free to locate myself permanently it would be in Chicago. My duties however are likely to keep me in the East, at least for some time, and I had to locate my family some place. I selected Philadelphia because there they will have the benefit of good schools for the children and at the same time I will be able to visit them occationally.

Our efforts the other day secured us a position two & a half miles further around towards the Lynchburg rail-road and also two lines of the enemy's fortifications around Richmond. Another equal surprise on the North side of James river will carry us into Richmond. I believe the enemy look upon the city as doomed.

Yours Truly
U. S. GRANT

ALS, ICHi.

To Maj. Gen. Henry W. Halleck

———

(Cipher) City Point Va. Oct. 4th [5]/64 [*10:30* P.M.]
GEN HALLECK WASH[1]

Longstreet has been reported as having gone to the valley but he took no troops. Kershaw's Division of his Corps started back to

Richmond before Sheridan's first fight but was turned back from about Gordonsville. Rassers Brigade of Cavalry has gone but no other troops of any kind. Whe have had prisoners and deserters I believe from every brigade of Lee's Army within the last few days and know the location of every ~~brigade~~ Division—at this time.

U. S. GRANT, Lt. Gn.

ALS (telegram sent), CSmH; telegram received (marked as sent Oct. 5, 1864, received Oct. 6, 7:30 A.M.), DNA, RG 107, Telegrams Collected (Bound). Dated Oct. 5 in *O.R.*, I, xliii, part 2, 288. On Oct. 5, 2:30 P.M., Maj. Gen. Henry W. Halleck telegraphed to USG. "Scouts in this morning from Culpepper state Longstreet had joined Early with five thousand men, besides Picketts Division and Rosser's Brigade of Cavalry. All new troops have been sent forward as rapidly as we could get them out of the hands of the State authorities. There has been no neglect on this point." ALS (telegram sent), DNA, RG 107, Telegrams Collected (Bound); telegram received, *ibid.*; *ibid.*, RG 108, Letters Received. *O.R.*, I, xliii, part 2, 288. On Oct. 4, 12:30 P.M., Maj. Gen. Christopher C. Augur telegraphed to USG transmitting a telegram from Col. Henry M. Lazelle, 16th N. J. Cav., reporting the same C.S.A. reinforcements. Telegram received, DNA, RG 108, Letters Received. *O.R.*, I, xliii, part 2, 275.

On Oct. 5, 10:30 P.M., USG telegraphed to Halleck. "I will start to Washington in the morning and will meet Adm.l Porter there or bring him down with me on Saturday." ALS (telegram sent—dated Oct. 4), CSmH; telegram received (marked as sent Oct. 5, received Oct. 6, 8:00 A.M.), DNA, RG 107, Telegrams Collected (Bound). Dated Oct. 5 in *O.R.*, I, xlii, part 3, 79. On Oct. 5, 9:00 A.M., USG telegraphed to Asst. Secretary of the Navy Gustavus V. Fox. "Will you send twenty (20) good sound launches with oars to Brig. Gen. C. K. Graham Comdg army gunboats at Pt. of Rocks. You will understand their purpose." ALS (telegram sent), CSmH; telegram received, DNA, RG 45, Miscellaneous Letters Received; (at 3:30 P.M.) *ibid.*, RG 107, Telegrams Collected (Bound). Misdated Oct. 4 in *O.R.* (Navy), I, x, 525. On Oct. 5, 6:00 P.M., Fox telegraphed to USG. "Launches ordered by telegraph from here Philadelphia & New York   Vessels beginning to arrive at Hampton Roads   Admiral Porter returns from the West tomorrow & will go direct to you   The information and maps I sent you some time since were furnished by a northern man who left the South very lately and he has resided at W. thirty years   He knows the sentiments of people on the coast & has other information and as Govr Andrews vouches for him I will send him down in the boat that carries Adml Porter"   Telegram received, DNA, RG 108, Letters Received; copy, *ibid.*, RG 45, Confidential Letters Sent. *O.R.* (Navy), I, x, 525; (misdated Sept. 5) *ibid.*, p. 431; (misdated Sept. 5) *O.R.*, I, xlii, part 2, 697. On Oct. 6, Fox telegraphed to USG. "Rear Admiral Porter arrived to day and leaves to-morrow afternoon for City Point." Copy, DNA, RG 45, Miscellaneous Letters Sent.

On Oct. 6, Maj. Gen. Benjamin F. Butler telegraphed to USG transmitting a report from a signal officer of trains going to Petersburg in the morning. Telegram sent, *ibid.*, RG 107, Telegrams Collected (Unbound); *ibid.*, RG 108, Letters Received. *O.R.*, I, xlii, part 3, 97. On the same day, Lt. Col. Ely S. Parker telegraphed to Butler and to Maj. Gen. George G. Meade. "Gen Grant has just started for Washington" Telegram received, DNA, RG 107, Telegrams Collected (Unbound); (at 10:20 A.M.) *ibid.*, RG 393, Army of the Potomac, Cav. Corps, Letters Received. *O.R.*, I, xlii, part 3, 91.

1. Not in USG's hand.

To Edwin M. Stanton

———

City Point Va
4 30 P. m. Oct. 10 1864.

HON. EDWIN M. STANTON,
SECRETARY OF WAR,

Our Entire loss in the enemy's attack on our lines on Friday the 7th inst. does not Exceed three hundred (300) in killed, wounded and missing. The enemy's loss is Estimated by Gen. Butler at one thousand (1.000). The Richmond Whig of the 8th speaking of this battle has the following "The gallant Genl. Gregg Comd'g a Texas brigade fell in the advance, Among other casualties we have to report Gen Bratton of S. C. badly wounded, Col. Haskill 7th S. C. Infy. Severely wounded in face, & Maj. Haskin of S. C. Artly also wounded.

Rumor states that Gen. Geary had been killed"[1]

Since Friday there has been no fighting whatever.

U. S. GRANT Lt Genl

Telegrams received (2—at 6:20 P.M.), DNA, RG 107, Telegrams Collected (Bound); copies, *ibid.*, Telegrams Received in Cipher; *ibid.*, RG 108, Letters Sent; DLC-USG, V, 45, 69, 107. *O.R.*, I, xlii, part 1, 22; *ibid.*, I, xlii, part 3, 151–52. On Oct. 10, 1864, 10:30 A.M., Secretary of War Edwin M. Stanton telegraphed to USG. "Bogus Despatches are for electioneering purposes being published in New York and Philadelphia representing a great disaster and loss of thirty thousand men in your army Friday. Please favor me with a report that I can publish of the ~~re~~ true condition of things immediately" ALS (telegram sent), DNA, RG 107, Telegrams Collected (Bound); telegram received (marked as sent at 11:00 A.M.), *ibid.*, RG 108, Letters Received.

On Oct. 7, 9:00 A.M., Butler had telegraphed to USG, Washington. "at 6 45 this morning The enemy have attacked and driven Kautz Back—And are now advancg on our right toward the rear in strong force. They have just ~~driven~~ opened fire upon Fort Harrison" ALS (telegram sent), *ibid.*, RG 107, Telegrams Collected (Unbound); telegram received, *ibid.*; (at 5:00 P.M.) *ibid.*, Telegrams Collected (Bound); *ibid.*, RG 108, Letters Received; *ibid.*, RG 393, Army of the Potomac, Cav. Corps, Letters Received. *O.R.*, I, xlii, part 3, 107. At

10:00 A.M., Butler telegraphed to Brig. Gen. John A. Rawlins. "I have ordered my despatch to General Grant to be duplicated to you   Nothing has changed since that despatch   I have thrown my right back Put Spring hill near New Market in fighting order and am waiting   Deserters report no new troops in my front but a large portion with drawn from Chaffins for this demonstration on the right   The force moving I make out to be Laws Bennings & Greggs brigades infantry a Battallion of Artillery and Lomax brigade of Cavalry. The shelling of Ft Harrison still goes on with viger. If I can learn with a little more certainty about this movement on my right I shall take the Offensive with two divisions of Birney. . . . I will direct the operator to take off at City point any dispatch I may send to Genl Grant" ALS (telegram sent), DNA, RG 107, Telegrams Collected (Unbound); telegram received, *ibid.*, RG 108, Letters Received. *O.R.*, I, xlii, part 3, 107.

At 10:00 A.M., Rawlins telegraphed to Butler and to Maj. Gen. George G. Meade. "Please furnish these Head Qrs with any information you desire to have forwarded to Gen Grant & it will be sent forward with all possible haste if you have not already sent to him." Telegram received, DNA, RG 94, War Records Office, Army of the Potomac; copy, *ibid.*, RG 107, Telegrams Collected (Unbound). At 10:30 A.M. (sent at 10:40 A.M.), Meade telegraphed to Rawlins. "I have nothing of importance to communicate to the Lt. Genl—Comdg. Deserters & refugees in this morning together with reports of signal officers would indicate no change in the enemys position in my front, & no movement on their part up to 8. P. M last evening—One deserter from Scales brigade Wilcoxs Division stated his brigade had returned day before yesterday from Chafin's farm.—I do not see where Lee can get re-inforcements to attack Genl Butler—" ALS (telegram sent), *ibid.*, RG 393, Army of the Potomac, Cav. Corps, Letters Received; telegram received, *ibid.*, RG 108, Letters Received. *O.R.*, I, xlii, part 3, 102; (misdated Oct. 4) *ibid.*, p. 68.

At 11:00 A.M., Lt. Col. Cyrus B. Comstock telegraphed to Bvt. Maj. Gen. Godfrey Weitzel. "How do things stand?" ALS (telegram sent), DNA, RG 108, Telegrams Sent by Comstock. At 11:30 A.M., Weitzel telegraphed to Comstock. "On my front the enemy is only shelling my key point, Fort Harrison. I see no movements of enemy's troops as yet. I have drawn out a little reserve of six regiments from my line to send to Birney if necessary. From the other points all I hear is that Kautz has been driven in, and that the enemy was on right and rear of Birney. I have heard nothing from there during the last half hour and at this moment all is quiet there." ALS (telegram sent), *ibid.*, RG 107, Telegrams Collected (Unbound); telegram received, *ibid.*, RG 108, Letters Received. *O.R.*, I, xlii, part 3, 114.

At noon, Butler telegraphed to USG. "Kautz Cavalry were driven in with some loss   [Bir]ney easily repulse[d] the En[em]y on his right and I am now waitng for a little further information when I propose to assume the offensive with two divisions of Birney   I think this is only an attempt to hold the darby town road far down as possible" ALS (telegram sent), DNA, RG 107, Telegrams Collected (Unbound); telegram received (at 5:00 P.M.), *ibid.*, Telegrams Collected (Bound); *ibid.*, RG 108, Letters Received. *O.R.*, I, xlii, part 3, 108. At 12:20 P.M., Butler telegraphed to Rawlins, sending a copy to USG, transmitting a telegram of 11:15 A.M. from Maj. Gen. David B. Birney. "I have repulsed the attack of the enemy on our right flank with great slaughter. The troops seem [to] be Field's & Pickett's Divisions. I send you a batch of prisoners. I am extending my right flank. The enemy seem to be entrenching on Darby road" Telegram received, DNA, RG 107, Telegrams Collected (Bound); (2) *ibid.*, Telegrams Collected (Unbound); (2) *ibid.*, RG 108, Letters Received; copy, *ibid.*, RG 107, Telegrams Received in Cipher. *O.R.*, I, xlii, part 3, 110. At 6:00 P.M. and 10:00 P.M., Butler telegraphed to USG. "At 6 45 this mornig the Enemy ~~moved~~ having moved fields and Hokes dvisions from the left at Chaffins farm round to our right at Darby town Road attacked with ~~spirt~~ spirit Kautz Cavalry in these entrenchments and drove him back with small loss—of men but with the loss of his artillery. The enemy suffered very considerable loss in this attack The Enemy then swept down the entrenchments toward Birney who having thrown back his ~~left~~ right waited their assaul and repulsed it with very heavy loss on the part of the enemy. ~~At three~~ The enemy in the mean time advanced toward NewMarket but were met by a force at the Signal Tower. At three P. M. I took the offensive sending Brney with two divisions up the Darby Town Road. The Enemy has retreated as he advanced and he now has reached and occupies the entrenchments which the enemy took from Kautz and were fortifying for themselves   Our loss has been small not one eighth of the enemies. We have about a hundred prisoners   Will telegraph again tonight if any thing of interest occurs"   "Birney has regained Kautz old position, and holds the enemy in the inner line of intrenchments around Richmond extending from the Darby town Road to connect with Weitzel on the left near Fort Harrison   There has bee[n] no movement at Petersburgh to day. We have much the best of this days work A thousand at the least of the Enemy killed & wounded a hundred prisoners and a bloody repulse. Gen Gregg commanding Fields division is reported by a lady who saw the body as killed   No news by Richmond papers save that they boast that Hood is at Marietta strongly entrenched"   ALS (telegrams sent), DNA, RG 107, Telegrams Collected (Unbound); telegrams received (at 9:00 P.M. and 11:20 P.M.), *ibid.*, Telegrams Collected (Bound); *ibid.*, Telegrams Collected (Unbound); (second) *ibid.*, RG 108, Letters Received. *O.R.*, I, xlii, part 3, 108.

At 10:30 P.M., USG, Washington, telegraphed to Meade. "Make such demonstration on your left in the morning as to detain the enemy's forces there and prevent any concentration North of the James." ALS (telegram sent), USMA; telegram received, DNA, RG 94, War Records Office, Army of the Potomac; *ibid.*, RG 107, Telegrams Collected (Unbound). *O.R.*, I, xlii, part 3, 102.

On Oct. 8, 10:30 A.M. and 5:00 P.M., Meade telegraphed to Rawlins, sending copies to Butler. "I have nothing very particular to communicate this A. m. Deserters from the enemy report no change in positions of troops or indications of movements   The enemy is apparently engaged in fortifying against a further advance. By direction of the Lt Gen Comdg received last night I am this morning advancing my pickets & making threatening demonstrations along my front with a view of preventing any detachments by the enemy"   "The reconnoitering parties sent forward This morning along the front from the Jerusalem plank Road to the extreme left drove the enemys pickets into their works which we found well manned—From prisoners taken today & from Several deserters who Came in This A. M. I am of the opinion there are in front of me, Heths Wilcoxs Mahones & B. Whartons Div extending from the appomattox to the South Side R. R. in the order enumerated—Heth on their right & Wharton on the left—The lines advanced today will be withdrawn after dark—" Telegrams received, DNA, RG 108, Letters Received. Printed as sent at 10:50 A.M. and 6:40 P.M. in *O.R.*, I, xlii, part 3, 119.

Also on Oct. 8, 1:35 P.M., Butler telegraphed to USG. "Our success yesterday was a decided one, although the Rebel papers claim a victory—They admit

Gen Gregg killed and Gen Bratton wounded—Gen Gregg was in command of Field Division—The Richmond Examiner of this morning ~~repo~~ contains an official despatch from Gordonsville last night states that a Yankee Cavalry force yesterday burnt the railroad bridge over the Rapidan and made their escape—No movement on the Petersburg side—No more troops have been sent over from Lee—The movement of yesterday was made under his eye—All quiet to day—" LS (telegram sent), DNA, RG 107, Telegrams Collected (Unbound); telegram received, *ibid.*, Telegrams Collected (Bound). *O.R.*, I, xlii, part 3, 142.

On Oct. 9, USG telegraphed to Butler and to Meade. "I am at City Pt" Telegram received, DLC-Benjamin F. Butler. *O.R.*, I, xlii, part 3, 143. At 7:10 P.M., Butler telegraphed to USG. "I am glad to hear of your safe return   All Quiet along my lines   I got 75 deserters yesterday   Shall have about same number by the mornig have twenty odd now   I am sorry to say Birny is so sick with Dysentery that I must let him go home Or lose him—Shall I have the pleasure of seeig you in the moring—" ALS (telegram sent), DNA, RG 107, Telegrams Collected (Unbound). *O.R.*, I, xlii, part 3, 150. On the same day, USG telegraphed to Butler. "I will be up to see you in the morning"   Telegram received, DLC-Benjamin F. Butler.

1. In the engagement of Oct. 7 on the Charles City Road, Brig. Gen. John Gregg was killed, Brig. Gen. John Bratton was wounded, Col. Alexander C. Haskell, 7th S. C. Cav., and his brother, Maj. John C. Haskell, commanding an art. battalion, were wounded, and Brig. Gen. Martin W. Gary emerged unhurt.

To Maj. Gen. Henry W. Halleck

Butlers Hd Qrs
Varina 1. p. m
Oct 10 1864

Maj Gen Halleck
Chf of Staff

I find our losses the other day were much less than first reported—

400 will cover our entire loss in killed wounded and captured The enemys loss very many more.

About 150 were captured and a great many dead fell into our hands—The loss of the enemy could not be less than ten or 1200

U S Grant
Lt Genl

Telegram received (at 3:45 P.M.), DNA, RG 107, Telegrams Collected (Bound); (2) *ibid.*, Telegrams Collected (Unbound); copies, *ibid.*, Telegrams Received in

Cipher; *ibid.*, RG 108, Letters Sent; DLC-USG, V, 45, 69, 107. *O.R.*, I, xlii, part 1, 22; *ibid.*, I, xlii, part 3, 152.

On Oct. 10, 1864, noon (sent at 12:10 P.M.), Maj. Gen. George G. Meade telegraphed to USG. "Nothing of importance occurred on the lines yesterday & last night—There was occasional picket firing, and during the night a few discharges of artillery in the vicinity of the Jerusalem Plank road.—No indications of movements by the enemy reported either by deserters or signal officers." ALS (telegram sent), DNA, RG 393, Army of the Potomac, Cav. Corps, Letters Received; telegram received, *ibid.*, RG 108, Letters Received. *O.R.*, I, xlii, part 3, 152.

Also on Oct. 10, 6:30 P.M., Maj. Gen. Benjamin F. Butler telegraphed to USG transmitting a signal message. "The Enemy are sending up signal lights direction North of west" Telegrams received (2), DNA, RG 107, Telegrams Collected (Unbound). A telegram from USG to Butler, dated only Oct., may have been sent in reply. "Your dispatch reporting the enemy throwing up Signal lights just recd. I cannot conceive the object. The enemy will bear watching." Telegram received (at 7:20 P.M.), DLC-Benjamin F. Butler.

On Oct. 11, USG telegraphed to Butler. "Did Gen. Weitzel attempt what he proposed for last night?" ALS (telegram sent), OClWHi; telegram received, DLC-Benjamin F. Butler. On the same day, Butler telegraphed to USG. "No— because they moved a force of Texas Troops there and it would have involved more Cost than it was worth" LS (telegram sent), DNA, RG 94, War Records Office, Army of the Potomac; telegram received, *ibid.*, RG 108, Letters Received.

To Julia Dent Grant

City Point, Va.
Oct. 10th/64

DEAR JULIA,

I wanted to draw my pay whilst in Washington and send you some money. But really I had no time not even to write to you. I will send my pay account to Capt Leet to-morrow or next day and direct him to send you a draft for Eight or nine hundred of the money.

I have received two letters from Fred, but none from you for about a week. I am glad to hear that Jess goes to school and learns so fast. I expect he will be writing to me next year. Mr. Rodgers of New York, Mr. Felt of Galena[1] and three or four other gentlemen are here on a visit. I am terribly bothered just at this time about matters in the West. I hope all will end well. Love and kisses for you and the children

ULYS.

ALS, DLC-USG.

1. Charles K. Rogers of New York City and Lucius S. Felt of Galena. For the former, see letter to Elihu B. Washburne, Dec. 12, 1863.

To Edwin M. Stanton

―――――

(Cipher)   City Point Va. Oct. 11th/64 [*12:30* P.M.]
HON. E. M. STANTON, SEC. OF WAR, WASHINGT[ON]

On reflection I do not know but safety[1] demands the removal of Rosecrans and the appointment of a subordinate General in his place. In conversation I said that I doubted the propriety of making any change during present complications. But present movements of Hoods Army, specially if he should go on to the Miss. river, may make it necessary to have a commander in Mo. who will co-operate. The best General now in Mo. to take that command would be Reynolds, if he is there, if not then Mower would come next. Probably more activity could be insured by sending Sheridan to Mo. place Meade where Sheridan is and put Hancock in command of the Army of the Potomac. I send this more to get your views before anything positive is done than to ask the change at once. It ought to be made however as soon as what is thought best can be agreed upon.

U. S. GRANT
Lt. Gn.

ALS (telegram sent), CSmH; telegram received (at 3:30 P.M.), DNA, RG 107, Telegrams Collected (Bound). *O.R.*, I, xli, part 3, 773. On Oct. 11, 1864, 7:00 P.M., Secretary of War Edwin M. Stanton telegraphed to USG. "Whatever your judgment dictates as best in view of the western operations now developing will have my cordial acquiescence. Sheriden is no doubt the best man, but his presence here will spare to you thousands of troops that would be required by any other commander. Have you considered whether any thing would be accomplished by sending Hooker to the field as Division commander including ~~Kansas an~~ Missouri and if you choose Kansas, ~~and Arkans~~ and Arkansas or either of them. I have no wish on ~~that~~ this point but only suggest it for consideration if you have not already thought of ~~th~~ it. ~~Ans~~" ALS (telegram sent), DNA, RG 107, Telegrams Collected (Bound); telegram received, *ibid.*, RG 108, Letters Received.

1. In USG's letterbooks, the word "safety" was replaced with "that a proper regard for the present and future interests of the service[.]" Copies, DLC-USG, V, 45, 69, 107; DNA, RG 108, Letters Sent. The revision appears in the *O.R.*; nonetheless, USG wrote and Stanton received the original wording.

To Maj. Gen. Henry W. Halleck

(Cipher)   City Point Va. Oct. 11th *1864.* [*9:30* P.M.]
MAJ. GEN. HALLECK, WASHINGTON,

After sending the 6th Corps and one Division of Cavalry here I think Sheridan should keep up as advanced a position as possible towards the Va. Central road and be prepared with supplies to advance onto that road at Gordonsville & Charlottesville at any time the enemy weakens himself sufficiently to admit of it. The cutting of that road and the Canal would be of vast importance to us.

U. S. GRANT
Lt. Gen.

ALS (telegram sent), CSmH; telegram received (on Oct. 12, 1864, 9:00 A.M.), DNA, RG 107, Telegrams Collected (Bound). Printed as received at 9:30 A.M. in *O.R.*, I, xliii, part 2, 339. On Oct. 13, noon, Maj. Gen. Henry W. Halleck telegraphed to USG. "The substance of your despatch of the 11th was immediately sent to Genl Sheridan. Numerous guerrilla parties in his rear frequently interrupt communication with him. The condition of the Manassas Gap R. R. is much worse than represented by the Engineers. Now that elections are over in Ohio & Indianna we will be able to send several additional regiments to Nashville for Sherman. Matters in Missouri seem to be in a muddle. Nothing yet heard of Steele & J J. Reynolds. I have directed Schofield to send to Thomas every thing that can be spared from Kentucky." ALS (telegram sent), DNA, RG 107, Telegrams Collected (Bound); telegram received, *ibid.*; *ibid.*, RG 108, Letters Received. *O.R.*, I, xliii, part 2, 354. See *ibid.*, p. 345.

To Maj. Gen. Benjamin F. Butler

City Point, Va Oct 11. 1864

MAJ GEN B. F. BUTLER
COMMD'G. ARMY OF THE JAMES
GENERAL

I enclose you the letter of the President to me, together with all other papers relating to the exchange of Naval Prisoners of War, now in the James River, and turn the whole matter over to you to conduct. In our conversation yesterday I explained the point in Sec. Welle's Correspondence which the President was afraid might involve us in trouble, if sustained by him. In conducting this exchange ignore all, that has heretofore been done in the matter, but make the exchange, man for man, yielding no point ~~before~~ heretofore insisted ~~on~~ upon.

Very Respectfully
Your obt servt.
U. S. GRANT.
Lt Gen.

Copies, DLC-USG, V, 45, 69, 107; DNA, RG 108, Letters Sent; USG 3. *O.R.*, II, vii, 965.

On Sept. 9, 1864, Secretary of the Navy Gideon Welles wrote to USG. "Enclosed herewith is an official Communication, which the Department desires may be forwarded through the lines as early as practicable, addressed to the Hon S. R. Mallory, Richmond Va." Copy, DNA, RG 45, Miscellaneous Letters Sent. *O.R.*, II, vii, 790. The enclosure, discussing the exchange of naval prisoners, is *ibid.*

On Sept. 30, Capt. Melancton Smith, Norfolk, telegraphed to USG. "Will not the Present disposition of our forces interfere with the exchange of naval prisoners at aikens Landing. Inquiry by sec'y. Welles." ALS (telegram sent), DNA, RG 45, Area 7. On the same day, USG telegraphed to Smith. "For next few days it will be wholly unpracticable to make any exchanges of Prisoners" Telegram received, *ibid.*, RG 107, Telegrams Collected (Unbound).

On Oct. 4, 8:10 P.M., Secretary of War Edwin M. Stanton telegraphed to USG. "By direction of the President a correspondence between the Secretary of the Navy and Mr Mallory in relation to the exchange of Naval prisoners has been referred to you with authority in your discretion to arrest or consummate the exchange under the supervision of General Butler and in accordance with the principles maintained by him in his correspondence with Mr Ould—. The correspondence with a letter of instructions to you from the President will be forwarded by special messenger" ALS (telegram sent), *ibid.*, Telegrams Collected (Bound); telegram received (dated Oct. 5), *ibid.*, Telegrams Collected (Unbound); *ibid.*, RG 108, Letters Received. Dated Oct. 5 in *O.R.*, II, vii, 924. Perhaps about the same date, Stanton drafted an undated telegram to USG. "I transmit herewith a telegram received from Major General Butler and refer that portion of it which relates to the exchange of prisoners to your consideration. The President directs me to say that you are authorized to take such measures as you deem proper in regard to exchanging prisoners and—that the whole matter is committed to your judgment and discretion. The policy of the Government so far as it has been clearly defined in the instructions heretofore given to General Butler and in its approval of the views heretofore expressed by you. The cases of exchange mentioned by General Butler stand on their special and exceptional grounds and were made by Commanding generals without instruction or authority from this Department. In respect to naval prisoners this Department has no control over the action of the Navy Department and has not been consulted." ADf, DLC-Edwin M. Stanton. See *O.R.*, II, vii, 924–25. On Oct. 5, President Abraham Lincoln wrote to USG. "I enclose you copy of a correspondence in regard to a contemplated exchange of Naval prisoners through your lines and not very distant from your Head Quarters. It only came to the knowledge of the War Department and of myself yesterday, and it gives us some uneasiness. I therefore send it to you with the statement that as the numbers to be exchanged under it are small, and so much has already been done to effect the exchange, I hope you may find it consistent to let it go forward under the general supervision of Gen Butler, and particularly in reference to the points he holds vital in exchanges. Still you are at liberty to arrest the whole operation, if in your judgment the public good requires it." Copy, DNA, RG 108, Letters Received. *O.R.*, II, vii, 924. Lincoln, *Works*, VIII, 36. The enclosures are printed in *O.R.*, II, vii, 661–62, 790, 867–69. On Oct. 8, 1:00 P.M., Brig. Gen. John A. Rawlins telegraphed to Welles. "The Naval prisoners on board the 'Circassian' directed to be turned over to Genl Grant in your dispatch to Capt Smith have been received but the instruction mentioned to be sent by the President by mail to Genl Grant have not yet reached here. Are they different from those directed to Admiral Dahlgren and the communications in explanation of them [se]nt to Capt Smith and by him delivered with the prisoners. If so will you please have them forwarded at once as exchanges for Army prisoners are now going on" Telegram received, DNA, RG 107, Telegrams Collected (Bound); *ibid.*, Telegrams Collected (Unbound). On Oct. 10, Welles wrote to USG. "With regard to the proposed exchange of Naval prisoners, the Department desires to call your attention to the case of the Officers and crew of the rebel Steamer 'Alabama,' whom we regard as prisoners of war and hold that we are entitled to equivalents for them. The principal facts are stated in the accompanying copy of a letter addressed on the 27th of August last by the Assistant Secretary of the Navy, to Major General Butler.—It is supposed Captain Melancton Smith has turned over to you the several letters of this Department respecting the proposed exchange. In addition to those therein mentioned as on parole, seventeen others of our seamen captured in the 'Queen City' have reported themselves at Mound City—having been paroled." Copy, *ibid.*, RG 45, Miscellaneous Letters Sent. *O.R.*, II, vii, 960. The enclosure is *ibid.*, p. 961. On the same day, Commander Edward T. Nichols, U.S.S. *Mendota*, wrote to USG. "Understanding from Captain Smith that the matter of exchange of Naval prisoners had been transferred to you, I have the honor to enclose for your information, the accompanying letter. Captain Smith is at present absent and I know not when he will return. May I ask of you the favor to return the letter of Mr Ould." ALS, DNA, RG 45, Subject File RE. On Oct. 11, Asst. Secretary of the Navy Gustavus V. Fox telegraphed to Rawlins. "Will you notify the Department when the Exchange of Naval prisoners is Complete and the terms names &c So that action can be taken by the Navy Department" Telegram received, *ibid.*, RG 108, Letters Received. At 5:20 P.M., Rawlins telegraphed to Maj. Gen. Benjamin F. Butler transmitting this telegram. Copies, DLC-USG, V, 45, 69, 107; DNA, RG 108, Letters Sent.

On Oct. 14, USG telegraphed to Butler. "Has any agreement been entered into for the exchange of the Naval prisoners now in the river. I would like to get them off our hands if possible." Telegram received (at 4:30 P.M.), *ibid.*, RG 107, Telegrams Collected (Unbound). *O.R.*, II, vii, 983. At 4:45 P.M., Butler telegraphed to USG. "No agreement has yet been made. Major Mulford is now out meeting Mr Ould" LS (telegram sent), DNA, RG 107, Telegrams Collected (Unbound). *O.R.*, II, vii, 983. On Oct. 15, USG telegraphed to Butler. "I think it probably be advisable whilst Maj. Mulford is here to get the Naval prisoners on hand put through the lines. Points of difference may serve a good purpose hereafter." ALS (telegram sent), OClWHi; telegram received (at 4:30 P.M.), DLC-Benjamin F. Butler. *O.R.*, II, vii, 989. On the same day, Butler telegraphed to USG. "The proposition for Exchange of naval prisoners is accepted by the Rebels—I have just returned from a ride" LS (telegram sent), DNA, RG 107, Telegrams Collected (Unbound). *O.R.*, II, vii, 989.

On Oct. 17, Lt. Col. John E. Mulford, asst. agent for exchange, twice telegraphed to USG. "I have recd. the following from Maj. Gen. Butler 'To LT COL JNO E MULFORD You will exchange the naval prisoners upon the terms stated in my letter to Mr Ould I do not Care except to get them off our Hands (sgd) BENJ F BUTLER MAJ GEN' Will you please order the naval prisoners up to Varina to report to me on board Su New York by 7 oclock tomorrow Morning" ALS (telegram sent), DNA, RG 107, Telegrams Collected (Unbound); telegram received (at 7:00 P.M.), *ibid.*, RG 108, Letters Received. "The Lady from Richmond is on board my boat I can send her to City Point by mail boat tomorrow morning Shall I do so" ALS (telegram sent), *ibid.*, RG 107, Telegrams Collected (Unbound).

To Maj. Gen. William T. Sherman

By Telegraph from City Point [*Oct.*] 11. *1864* [*11:00* A.M.]
To MAJ GEN'L SHERMAN

Your dispatch received.[1] Does it not look as if Hood was going to the invasion of Middle Tennessee, using the Mobile & Ohio and Memphis & Charleston Roads to supply his base on the Tennessee about Florence or Decatur? If he does this, he ought to be met and prevented getting north of the Tennessee. If you were to cut loose I do not believe you would meet Hood's Army but would be bushwhacked by all the old men, little boys and such railroad guards as are still left at home.—Hood would probably strike for Nashville, thinking by going north he could inflict greater damage upon us than we could upon the enemy by going south. If there is any way of getting at Hood's army, I would prefer that, but I must trust to your own judgment.—I find I shall not be able to send a force from here to act with yours on Savannah; your movements therefore will be independent of mine, at least until the fall of Richmond takes place.—

I am afraid General Thomas, with such lines of road as he has to patrol, could not prevent Hood's going North.—With Wilson turned loose with all your Cavalry you will find the rebels put much more on the defensive than heretofore.—

L<small>T</small> G<small>EN</small> G<small>RANT</small>.—

Telegram received, DNA, RG 94, War Records Office, Dept. of the Cumberland; (at 3:00 P.M.) *ibid.*, RG 107, Telegrams Collected (Bound); copies, *ibid.*, Telegrams Received in Cipher; *ibid.*, RG 108, Letters Sent; DLC-USG, V, 45, 70, 107. *O.R.*, I, xxxiv, part 1, 35; *ibid.*, I, xxxvi, part 1, 39; *ibid.*, I, xxxviii, part 1, 28; *ibid.*, I, xxxix, part 3, 202.

On Oct. 11, 1864, 11:00 A.M., Maj. Gen. William T. Sherman, Kingston, Ga., telegraphed to USG. "Hood moved his army from Palmetto Station across by Dallas and Cedartown and is now on the Coosa south of Rome. He threw one Corps on my road at Ackworth and I was forced to follow. I hold Atlanta with the 20th Corps, and have strong detachments along my line: These reduce my active force to a comparatively small army. We cannot remain here on the defensive. With 25.000 men and the bold Cavalry he has he can constantly break my road: I would infinitely prefer to make a wreck of the road and of the country from Chattanooga to Atlanta, including the latter City. Send back my wounded and worthless and with my effective Army move through Georgia smashing things to the sea. Hood may turn into Tennessee and Kentucky but I believe he will be forced to follow me. Instead of being on the defensive I would be on the offensive; instead of guessing at what he means to do he would have to guess at my plans. The difference in war is full twenty five per cent. I can make Savannah, Charleston or the mouth of Chattahoochie. Answer quick as I know we will not have the telegraph long." Telegram received (at 6:00 P.M.), DNA, RG 107, Telegrams Collected (Bound); *ibid.*, Telegrams Collected (Unbound); *ibid.*, RG 108, Letters Received; copies, *ibid.*, RG 107, Telegrams Received in Cipher; (marked as sent at 10:00 A.M.) *ibid.*, RG 393, Military Div. of the Miss., Telegrams Sent in the Field. *O.R.*, I, xxxiv, part 1, 35–36; *ibid.*, I, xxxvi, part 1, 39; *ibid.*, I, xxxviii, part 1, 28; (printed as sent at 10:00 A.M.) *ibid.*, I, xxxix, part 3, 202. At 11:30 P.M., USG telegraphed to Sherman. "Your dispatch of to-day received. If you are satisfied the trip to the sea coast can be made holding the line of the Tennessee river firmly you may make it destroying all the rail-road South of Dalton or Chattanooga as you think best." ALS (telegram sent—misdated Oct. 12), PPRF; telegram received (on Oct. 12, 7:55 A.M.), DNA, RG 107, Telegrams Collected (Bound). *O.R.*, I, xxxiv, part 1, 36; *ibid.*, I, xxxvi, part 1,

39; *ibid.*, I, xxxviii, part 1, 28; *ibid.*, I, xxxix, part 3, 202. Entered erroneously in USG's letterbooks as sent on Oct. 12.

1. On Oct. 9, 7:30 P.M., Sherman, Allatoona, telegraphed to USG. "It will be a physical impossibility to protect this road now that Hood, Forrest, Wheeler and the whole batch of Devils are turned loose without home or habitation. I think Hoods movements indicate a direction to the end of the Selma and Talladega road to Blue Mountain about sixty miles South west of Rome from which he will threaten Kingston, Bridgeport and Decatur Ala. I propose we break up the road from Chattanooga and strike out with wagons for Milledgeville Millen and Savannah—Until we can repopulate Georgia it is useless to occupy it, but the utter destruction of its roads, houses and people will cripple their military resources ьBy attempting to hold the roads we will lose a thousand men monthly and will gain no result—I can make the march and make Georgia howl We have over 8000 cattle and 3,000,000 pounds of bread but no corn, but we can forage in the interior of the state" Telegram received (on Oct. 10, 11:00 A.M.), DNA, RG 107, Telegrams Collected (Bound); *ibid.*, RG 108, Letters Received; copies, *ibid.*, RG 107, Telegrams Received in Cipher; *ibid.*, RG 393, Military Div. of the Miss., Telegrams Sent in the Field. *O.R.*, I, xxxix, part 3, 162. At 6:00 P.M., Capt. Lewis M. Dayton, Allatoona, had telegraphed to USG. "I am directed by General Sherman to inform you that he is here and all is well" Copy (signed L. M. Rony), DNA, RG 107, Telegrams Received in Cipher.

On Oct. 10, noon, Sherman, Cartersville, telegraphed to USG. "Dispatch about Wilson just rec'd. Hood is now crossing Coosa twelve miles below Rome bound west. If he passes—over to the Mobile and Ohio road had I not better execute the plan of my letter sent by Col. Porter, and leave Thomas with the troops now in Tennessee to defend the State? He will have an ample force when the reinforcements ordered reach Nashville." Telegram received (at 5:20 P.M.), *ibid.*, Telegrams Collected (Bound); *ibid.*, Telegrams Collected (Unbound); *ibid.*, RG 108, Letters Received; copies, *ibid.*, RG 107, Telegrams Received in Cipher; *ibid.*, RG 393, Military Div. of the Miss., Telegrams Sent in the Field. *O.R.*, I, xxxiv, part 1, 35; *ibid.*, I, xxxvi, part 1, 38; *ibid.*, I, xxxviii, part 1, 27; *ibid.*, I, xxxix, part 3, 174.

To Edwin M. Stanton

(Cipher)   City Point Va. Oct. 12th *1864*. [*noon*]
HON. E. M. STANTON, SEC. OF WAR, WASHINGTON.

I agree with you that Sheridan cannot well be replaced in his present position. I have also concidered well the matter of sending Hooker to Mo. and on mature reflection do not believe he will do. We want there a man who will push the enemy with viger without waiting to get up supplies from a given base. There are no better men to command Division in such a pursuit of an enemy than Smith and Mower who are already there. To give a proper head is now the question. After thinking over all the Generals who can possibly be spared I have made up my mind that Crook is the man to send. ~~and supply His place with Logan~~. I would recommend Gen. Logan for Crooks place. He is an active fighting General and under Sheridan will make a first class Commander for that Department.

U. S. Grant
Lt. Gn.

ALS (telegram sent), CSmH; telegram received (at 3:30 P.M.), DNA, RG 107, Telegrams Collected (Bound). *O.R.*, I, xli, part 3, 801.

To Maj. Gen. Henry W. Halleck

(Cipher)   City Point, Va. Oct. 12th/64 [*noon*]
Maj. Gn. Halleck, Washington,

Please send my dispatch of yesterday in relation to what Sheridan should do to him. Thomas should be prepared ~~also~~ to concentrate a force on Hood wherever he ~~prevents~~ presents himself in the Tenn. river and should take the supplies of the country without compunction. I think if Crook goes to Mo. he will drive price out of the country in time to send A. J. Smith & Mower to Tenn. before Hood can get far even if Sherman's movements do not turn him as I think they will. Canby's forces will also be relieved for operations wherever they may be needed.

U. S. Grant
Lt. Gn

ALS (telegram sent), CSmH; telegram received (at 4:30 P.M.), DNA, RG 107, Telegrams Collected (Bound). *O.R.*, I, xxxix, part 3, 222; (incomplete) *ibid.*, I, xliii, part 2, 345.

To Maj. Gen. Henry W. Halleck

(Cipher)   City Point Va. Oct. 12th/64 [2:30 P.M.]
MAJ. GEN. HALLECK, WASHINGTON.

Seventy-five deserters from the enemy come into Gen. Butler's lines North of the James on Sunday; thirty-five more yesterday, & thirty-three to-day. This is in addition to what come in on other parts of the line of which I have no reports as to actual numbers. There were other deserters each of these days however.

U. S. GRANT
Lt. Gn

ALS (telegram sent), CSmH; telegram received (marked as sent Oct. 11, 1864, 2:30 P.M., received 4:00 P.M.), DNA, RG 107, Telegrams Collected (Bound). *O.R.*, I, xlii, part 3, 176. On Oct. 11, 11:41 P.M., Maj. Gen. Benjamin F. Butler telegraphed to USG. "We have thirty three deserters from the enemy this morning—ten and a sergeant from a Georgia Battallion lately from Mattaox Station on Richmond & Danville Road—now in our front water B two from the iron clad Va—eighteen from local defense troops and three negros—" ALS (telegram sent), DNA, RG 107, Telegrams Collected (Unbound). *O.R.*, I, xlii, part 3, 161.

On Oct. 12, 12:25 P.M., Maj. Gen. Henry W. Halleck telegraphed to USG. "The disposable recruits at Fort Columbus have been assigned to the Seventh Infty with a view to that regiment being Sent to the army of the Potomac. That one of old regts of Infty most in need of recruits should this meet with your approbation. please designate the regt you wish returned. Please inform me also whether you wish it to await the arrival of the Seventh." Telegram received, DNA, RG 107, Telegrams Collected (Bound); (2) *ibid.*, Telegrams Collected (Unbound); (2) *ibid.*, RG 108, Letters Received; copy, *ibid.*, RG 94, Letters Sent. *O.R.*, I, xlii, part 3, 175. At noon, USG telegraphed to Halleck. "I will send a regiment of regulars immediately to take the place of the 7th. Please order the latter here without waiting the arrival of one to relieve it." ALS (telegram sent), OClWHi; telegram received (at 2:15 P.M.), DNA, RG 107, Telegrams Collected (Bound). Printed as received at 2:05 P.M. in *O.R.*, I, xlii, part 3, 175. On the same day, USG telegraphed to Maj. Gen. George G. Meade. "Send to New York the regiment of regulars most in need of recruits. The 7th regulars well filled up will take the place of the one you send." ALS (telegram sent), OClWHi; telegram received, DNA, RG 94, War Records Office, Army of the Potomac. At 5:10 P.M., Meade telegraphed to USG. "In compliance with the instructions contained in your telegram of this date I have ordered the 17th. U. S. Infantry to proceed to the city of New York and report to the Superintendent of the recruiting service that regiment being reported to me as the most in need of recruits of any of the regular regiments" Copy (telegram sent), *ibid.*; telegram received, *ibid.*, RG 108, Letters Received. At 9:00 P.M., USG telegraphed to Halleck. "The 17th U. S. Infantry has been designated to relieve the 7th in New

York. This regiment will leave here to-morrow." ALS (telegram sent), CSmH; telegram received (on Oct. 13, 1:40 P.M.), DNA, RG 107, Telegrams Collected (Bound); *ibid.*, Telegrams Collected (Unbound). *O.R.*, I, xlii, part 3, 176.

To Maj. Gen. Benjamin F. Butler

City Point Va. Oct. 12th/64

MAJ. GEN. BUTLER,

I think it advisable to send out a strong ~~Infantry~~ reconnoisance of Infy and Cavalry to drive the enemy from the work they are doing on the Central road. Such a reconnoisance should not go far enough to endanger their being cut off however. Weitzel should at the same time hold as much force as he can ready to move to the support of the reconnoitering party if attacked by a superior force.

U. S. GRANT
Lt. Gen.

ALS (telegram sent), OClWHi; telegram received, DNA, RG 107, Telegrams Collected (Unbound). *O.R.*, I, xlii, part 3, 183. On Oct. 12, 1864, Maj. Gen. Benjamin F. Butler had telegraphed to USG transmitting a telegram of 9:30 A.M. from Brig. Gen. August V. Kautz. "The reports from the picket on the Darby Road are that the Enemys is very busy fortif~~y~~esying on that Road very near to our Pickets—The officer on Picket thinks they are building a fort at a point less than half a mile from the old Line of intrenchments   The fact that no deserters or Refugees have come in yesterday or today on my line indicate that there is some truth in the report of the people living on the Charles City Road that the Enemy have a Close picket line between that Road & the Long Bridge road—a few of the E'my showed thmsevls in front of fussels mill last night but left without any other demonstration—The new Road through the swamp will be finished today"   Telegram sent, DNA, RG 107, Telegrams Collected (Unbound); telegram received, *ibid.*, RG 108, Letters Received. *O.R.*, I, xlii, part 3, 182.

At 1:25 P.M., 2:30 P.M., 4:00 P.M., and 5:00 P.M., Butler telegraphed to USG. "In compliance with your instructions in regard to the reconnoisance orders have been issued which went out at half past twelve (12½) to day copies of which I will forward. We are delayed moving at once by the fact of a flag of truce being out. We shall be all ready to move if the flag of truce returns in season." LS (telegram sent), DNA, RG 107, Telegrams Collected (Unbound); telegram received (marked as sent at 12:50 P.M.), *ibid.*, RG 108, Letters Received. Printed as received at 2:00 P.M. in *O.R.*, I, xlii, part 3, 183. "I have the honor to enclose for your information copies of Orders Sent to Major Generals Terry and Weitzel preliminary to the movement you have directed   We are waiting return of flag of truce to move"   ALS (telegram sent), DNA, RG 393, Dept. of Va. and N. C., Telegrams Sent (Press). *O.R.*, I, xlii, part 3, 183. "I am all ready to move but the enemy still detain my flag on the Picket line in front of Battery Harrison   I Suppose that having moved my troops into position is all I can do till flag returns   I am in doubt whether to move to night it is so late" ALS (telegram sent), DNA, RG 107, Telegrams Collected (Unbound); telegram received, *ibid.*, RG 108, Letters Received. Printed as received at 4:35 P.M. in *O.R.*, I, xlii, part 3, 183. "My flag is still out   I have sent for it. It is raing and I submit to you whether any movement best be made till morning—Am all ready—" ALS (telegram sent), DNA, RG 107, Telegrams Collected (Unbound); telegram received, *ibid.*, RG 108, Letters Received. *O.R.*, I, xlii, part 3, 183.

    At 5:00 P.M., USG telegraphed to Butler. "Your despatches recd. Postpone the movement. It is now too late." Telegram received, DLC-Benjamin F. Butler; copies, DLC-USG, V, 45, 69, 107; DNA, RG 108, Letters Sent. *O.R.*, I, xlii, part 3, 184. At 7:30 P.M. (sent at 8:00 P.M.), Butler telegraphed to USG. "If you see no objection I will order that movement at day break tomorrow so as to strike the Enemies Pickets at sunrise giving the men their Coffee before they Start." ALS (telegram sent), DNA, RG 94, War Records Office, Dept. of Va. and N. C., Army of the James, Unentered Papers; telegram received, *ibid.*, RG 108, Letters Received. Printed as received at 8:00 P.M. in *O.R.*, I, xlii, part 3, 184. At 8:10 P.M., USG telegraphed to Butler. "I fully approve of your making the movemnt ordered for this afternoon early in the morning" Telegram received, DLC-Benjamin F. Butler; copies, DLC-USG, V, 45, 69, 107; DNA, RG 108, Letters Sent. *O.R.*, I, xlii, part 3, 184.

To Maj. Gen. Benjamin F. Butler

City Point Va. Oct. 12th/64

Maj. Gen. Butler,

    Your correspondence with Judge Ould on the subject of exchanges & also the affidavits upon which you rely for proof of the unwarrantable conduct of the enemy in employing prisoners of War ~~in~~ at work on fortifications, under fire, and your letter informing Mr. Ould of the steps taken to retaliate ~~is~~ are received, and the whole approved. I will forward the whole to the Sec. of War with my approval indorsed.

U. S. Grant
Lt. Gn.

ALS (telegram sent), OClWHi; telegram received, DLC-Benjamin F. Butler. *O.R.*, II, vii, 967. On Oct. 12, 1864, 1:30 P.M., Maj. Gen. Benjamin F. Butler had telegraphed to USG. "I send by Orderly copies of correspondence between ~~Mr Ould~~ myself and Mr Ould. I also enclose the affadavits upon which my action is based. The notification to Mr ould of my action will actually get to him be-

fore it is consumated   I think you will agree with me that the evidence is con-
clusive. You will find a copy of the advertisement of which I speak in one of my
letters in the Richmond Examiner which I sent you yesterday—If you approve my
action may I ask you to forward the papers with your approval to the War Dept"
LS (telegram sent), DNA, RG 107, Telegrams Collected (Unbound); telegram received, *ibid.*, RG 108, Letters Received. *O.R.*, II, vii, 966. The enclosures are
ibid., pp. 967–69. On the same day, USG endorsed these documents. "Respectfully forwarded to the Sec. of War for his information. I have approved of the re-
taliatory measures proposed by Gn. Butler and accordingly sent to Dutch Gap
this evening all the prisoners of War now with this Army." AES, DNA, RG 107,
Letters Received from Bureaus. *O.R.*, II, vii, 969. On the same day, USG telegraphed to Butler. "The prisoners you ask for will be sent up to you immediately.
Be certain that the enemy are working our prisoners in the trenches and go ahead.
I would not so employ them however without knowing that the enemy was doing
the same thing." ALS (telegram sent), OClWHi; telegram received, DNA, RG
107, Telegrams Collected (Unbound). *O.R.*, II, vii, 967.

Also on Oct. 12, Butler sent to USG copies of correspondence regarding
naval prisoners and Negro prisoners forced to work. *Ibid.*, pp. 969–70. On the
same day, USG endorsed these documents. "Respectfully forwarded to the Sec.
of War. I have notified Gn. Butler of my approval of the steps taken to effect the
exchanges heretofore agreed upon by the Sec. of the Navy." AES, DNA, RG
107, Letters Received from Bureaus. *O.R.*, II, vii, 970. See letter to Gen. Robert
E. Lee, Oct. 20, 1864; Richard J. Sommers, "The Dutch Gap Affair: Military
Atrocities and Rights of Negro Soldiers," *Civil War History*, XXI, 1 (March,
1975), 51–64.

To Maj. Gen. George G. Meade

City Point Va. Oct. 12th/64

MAJ. GEN. MEADE,

I understand that it has been discovered that the enemy have
undermined Fort Sedgewick: Do you not think it advisable to intrench in rear of it and let the enemy explode their mine and attack?

U. S. GRANT
Lt. Gen.

ALS (telegram sent), OClWHi; telegrams received (2—at 10:00 P.M.), DNA,
RG 393, Army of the Potomac, Cav. Corps, Letters Received. Printed as sent at
10:00 P.M. in *O.R.*, I, xlii, part 3, 176. On Oct. 12, 1864, noon and 11:00 P.M.,
Maj. Gen. George G. Meade telegraphed to USG. "The enemy opened his batteries about 8. P. M last evening on Hancocks front & was replied to by our's—
The firing lasted for an hour   no casualties reported on our side. A Deserter
came in to Hancocks lines last night & reported the completion of a mine on his
front   measures have been taken to prepare for the reported mine & to detect it.—
Another deserter reported the relieving of Wise brigade Johnstons division by

Harris brigade Mahone's division hitherto in reserve. Greggs reconnaissance yesterday proceeded as far as the crossing of Rowanty Creek within 3 miles of Stoney Creek depot—At Rowanty Creek the enemys infantry was found in such force as not to permit the further advance of the reconnoiting party—Fourteen prisoners, including one commd. off were taken by this reconnaissance. From them & citizens no information of any large body of the enemy at Stoney Creek could be obtained. From refugees & contrabands from Sussex it is learned the enemy have at Stoney Creek a regiment of Infy. & a battery of artillery with some cavalry—These people state that it was reported forces from No. Carolina were concentrating at Welden—numbers & organisation unknown.—" "I have received no information of the enemys having certainly undermined Fort Sedgewicke—The only information in reference to the enemys mining operations was contained in a telegram from Maj. Genl. Hancock the substance of which was transmitted in my report this a m to the effect that a deserter said the enemy had completed a mine on his front—Genl. Hancock said the deserter had been detained that he might identify the spot—An Engineer officer was sent to take the necessary steps to meet the contingency—Since then I have heard nothing from Genl. Hancock—Some time ago it was reported the enemy were mining under Fort Sedgewicke—at that time a line was made in the rear & every preparation made to let the enemy blow it up—These still exist—At the time it was considered not likely from the conformation of the ground that a mine could be placed there owing to the distance to be galleried—Since then our pickets have been considerably advanced & we command all the ground in front for 200 yards, and I should think could readily detect the existence of a mine in that locality.— I will however refer your despatch to Maj Genl. Hancock with directions to make the preparations indicated.—" ALS (telegrams sent), DNA, RG 393, Army of the Potomac, Cav. Corps, Letters Received; telegrams received, *ibid.*, RG 108, Letters Received. *O.R.*, I, xlii, part 3, 176, 177.

On Oct. 11, 11:30 A.M., Meade had telegraphed to USG. "Nothing unusial has occurred on my lines during the past 24 hours beyond picket firing and occasional interchange of Artillery Shots on the Jeresalem Plank Road. ~~Dester~~ Deserters yesterday Stated it was reported in their Camp that Maj Gen Whiting with ten thousand (10 000) men from North Carolina was at Stoney Creek. I have directed General Gregg to Send a reconnoitering party in that direction to endeavor to ascertain Something positive about this" Telegram received, DNA, RG 108, Letters Received; copies (2), *ibid.*, RG 393, Army of the Potomac, Letters Sent; (2) Meade Papers, PHi. *O.R.*, I, xlii, part 3, 158.

On Oct. 13, noon, Meade telegraphed to USG. "Since the receipt of your telegram of 10. P. M yesterday Maj. Genl. Hancock reports, the deserter as locating Battery 21 to the east of Fort Sedgewicke as the objective point of the enemys mine—He states however that only about 100 yards of gallery had been excavated when he left beginning inside the enemys works—This leaves over 400 yards of gallery to be excavated passing across a deep ravine commanded by our pickets—The probabilities are that the works referred by the deserter, are some of the counter-mining precautions taken by the enemy of which we have had numerous reports all along their lines ever since the explosion of the Burnside mine—Genl. Hancock has however taken & will take all proper precautions, but he does not deem the contingency sufficiently probable to justify the withdrawal of the garrison of Fort Sedgewicke or Battery 21—He will however prepare a second line in rear of these works & construct listening galleries & trenches in their front so as to be ready whenever it may be deemed essential to occupy the rear line.—A deserter who came in to the 9th corps this a m, reports a conversation between Genls. Heth & Archer as to a proposed attack on the colored troops on our left & rear—in which Genl. Heth said the cavalry could do all that was proposed—We are fully prepared on this part of the line for any attack and should like to have it made   Nothing else of importance to report except that the desertions to the enemy of newly arrived substitutes & recruits is very much on the increase.—One was shot in the 2d. corps a few days ago. between the lines in the act of deserting." ALS (telegram sent), DNA, RG 393, Army of the Potomac, Cav. Corps, Letters Received; telegram received, *ibid.*, RG 108, Letters Received. *O.R.*, I, xlii, part 3, 197–98.

On the same day, USG telegraphed to Meade. "Is the 199th Pa Infy Vols in your Comd & if so where is it stationed"   Telegram received, DNA, RG 94, War Records Office, Army of the Potomac. At noon, Meade telegraphed to USG. "The 199th Pa. vols is not with this army—The 198th & 210th Pa. vols were recently assigned and are now with the 5th corps—I also understand Genl. Benham has the 200th & 205th Pa. with him"   ALS (telegram sent), *ibid.*; copy, *ibid.*, RG 393, Army of the Potomac, Letters Sent.

To Maj. Gen. William T. Sherman

(Cipher)   City Point Va. Oct. 12th 1864. [*1:00* P.M.]
MAJ. GEN. SHERMAN, KINGSTON GA.

On reflection I think better of your proposition. It will be much better to go South than to be forced to come North. You will no doubt clean the country where you go of rail-road tracks and supplies. I would also move every wagon, horse, mule and hoof of stock as well as the negroes. As far as arms can be supplied either from surplus on hand or by capture I would put them in the hands of negro men. Give them such organization as you can. They will be of some use.

U. S. GRANT
Lt. Gen.

Telegram received (at 4:00 P.M.), DNA, RG 107, Telegrams Collected (Bound); copies, *ibid.*, Telegrams Received in Cipher; *ibid.*, RG 108, Letters Sent; DLC-USG, V, 45, 70, 107; (typescript) E. B. Long, Laramie, Wyo. *O.R.*, I, xxxix, part 3, 222.

To Julia Dent Grant

City Point, Va. Oct. 12th *1864.*

DEAR JULIA,

I have just rec'd your letter written the 5th inst. at the same time your letter of the 9th. Of course I am satisfied with the disposition you have made of the children. I want them to go to school all the time. Fred. must study French and Buck & Nelly German. I am glad to hear Jess is such a good boy. I know he will learn very fast. I received a letter from Mr. Ford saying that he had sent out and got Little Rebel and now has him at his stables in town. If you say so I will send and have him expressed to you. The other horse I heard nothing about. I send by the same Mail with this Pay Accounts for Capt. Leet to get cashed with instructions to send you a draft for $800 00[1]   I received a letter from Mr. Jones saying the citizens of Chicago were about purchasing a fine residence for us there. We cant live at both places so that I do not know that it will be desirable to have a house there.—Clothing has been sent to John Dent so that I do not think he can be suffering on that account. I am perfectly willing however to send more to him. The Commissioner for the exchange of prisoners has promised several times that John should be released. His word has not been kept however. The pretext upon which he has been retained is that he is a lessee of a plantation from Govt. This has been frequently denied but I believe some one in the South has given such evidence against him as to determine them to retain him. I have been terribly embarrassed for several days with the movements and demonstrations of the enemy in the West. Here I feel easy. Love and kisses for you and the children.

ULYS.

ALS, DLC-USG.

1. On Oct. 12, 1864, USG wrote to Capt. George K. Leet. "Enclosed please find my Pay account for Sept. I wish you would draw the money getting a check for $800.00 payable to Mrs. U. S. Grant and mail it to her. The balance take in cash and the first opportunity you have send it to me. Mrs. Grant's address is Burlington, N. J. *P. S.*—My Servants are same as previously described." Stan. V. Henkels, Catalogue No. 1194, June 8, 1917, p. 22.

To John Robertson

City Point, Va. Oct 12, *1864*

COL. JNO ROBERTSON
ADJUTANT GENERAL OF THE STATE OF MICHIGAN
DETROIT, MICH.
COLONEL

Your communicatio[n] of date 3d inst, in relation to the order relieving Col. H. R Mizner from the Command of the 14th Reg't Mich. Inf'y. Vols. and requesting that the order be revoked and that Col Meizner be restored to the Reg't, is received. In reply I have to respectfully inform you, that the origina[l] papers in the case were forwarded to the Adjutant Genera[l] of the Army, Washington, where the order was issued, and where it is supposed they are now on file. The following history of the case, is made up from the records of my Office.

"Aug 15, Mizner, Henry H.
Col. 14th Michigan Inf'y.

TO THE ADJT. GENERAL DATED CAMP 14 REGIMENT MICH. INF'Y. JULY 20, 1864

His Regiment having once been mounted, but dismounted by Gen. Grants order of March 1864, he requests, that it be again mounted, giving as a reason 'intense dissatisfactio[n] of the men, who' ask to be remounted, or released from their enlistment."

On this letter of Col Mizner, of which the above is an abstract or, brief, Maj. Gen George H. Thomas Commanding Department and Army of the Cumberland and in whose Command the 14th Michigan is serving, made the following endorsement

"Headquarters Dept. of the Cumberland
Near Atlanta, Ga. Aug 4. 1864

Respectfully forwarded disapproved. For the past twelve ~~years~~ months Col Mizner has acted, as though he had his own personal agrandizement at heart, rather than the good of the service. The order for the dismounting of the mounted Infantry Reg't by (then) Maj. Gen. Grant, was imperative and I had no particular desire, that the 14th Michigan should be exempt from the operations of the order any more than any other Infantry Regiment. The telegram to Col Mizner, that it was not intended to dismount his Regiment, was sent him before Gen. Grant issued his order dismounting them. It was true at the time, but contained no pledge for the future. Since the dismounting of his Regiment Col. Mizner has expressed great dissatisfaction, and been very importunate on the subject of getting his Regiment mounted. The Regiment is now rendering good service in its legitimate capacity as an Infantry Regiment, and in order, that its efficiency and the good of the service may be promoted, I would respectfully recommend, that Col. Mizner be relieved from the Command of the 14th Michigan Infantry and ordered to duty with his Regiment in the regular Army.

(Signed) GEORGE H THOMAS

Maj. Gen. Commanding"

The papers were sent by Gen. Thomas to the Adjutant General of the Army by whom they were refered to me, and by me returned with the following endorsement.

"Headquarters Armies of the U. S.

City Point Va Aug 17. *1864*

Respectfully returned. I approve the recommendation of Maj. Gen George H Thomas, that Col. Henry R. Meizner be relieved from duty in the Volunteer service, and ordered to report to his proper Regiment for duty.

(sgd) U S GRANT

Lt Gen."

It may be proper to state for your better information, that owing to the scarcity of Cavalry i[n] the Department, Gen, Rosecrans, mounted a number of Infantry Regiments. It afterwards became impossible to procure enough horses to keep the mounted force mounted. Thousands of the Cavalry proper, were in dismounted Camps, and early last spring, I ordered, that all Infantry Regiments be dismounted and their horses turned into the Quarter-Masters Dept. for the purpose of mounting the Cavalry, which could not be used as Infantry. This course was an absolute necessity and no Regiments were excepted. Believing that Gen Thomas fully understood the case, and was acting for the good of the service, I approved his recommendation, and nothing has since transpired to change the views, I then entertained.

Very Respectfully, Your obt servt.

U. S. GRANT. Lt. Gen.

Copies, DLC-USG, V, 45, 69, 107; DNA, RG 108, Letters Sent. On Oct. 3, 1864, Mich. AG John Robertson wrote to USG. "I am directed by His Excellency the Governor of this State, to respectfully call your attention to the case of Captain Henry R. Mizner 18th U. S. Infantry late Colonel of the Fourteenth Regiment Michigan Infantry now in the Army of the Cumberland, whose leave of absence has been revoked, and ordered to join his Regiment in the regular Army, in accordance with an Order of which the enclosed is a copy—Since the publication of the Order the Governor has made enquiries at the War Department for information as to the cause of the removal of Colonel Mizner from the command of his Regiment and was referred to you, hence the reason for writing to you on this subject. The Governor is very anxious that he should be re-instated if possible as Colonel of the 14th, as that Regiment is very much in need of his services, and will suffer in its efficiency by his being removed from it. Not knowing the reasons for his removal he can only ɵin his behalf, refer to his record as being a good one, so far as it has come within his knowledge—The Regiment was in a very bad condition when he took command of it, and in a very shorttime was made a good and efficient one, and has done good service under his command previous to and through the whole of General Sherman's Campaign up to the capture of Atlanta, where he led it in a successful charge on a part of the enemy's works, capturing many prisoners, several guns, and a stand of colors—The Governor hopes and most respectfully asks, that unless there is some objection that cannot be removed consistently with the good of the service, that you will direct his reinstatement to the command of his Regiment as he considers it necessary for its welfare and efficiency and consequently for the good of the service—" LS, *ibid.*, Letters Received.

To Edwin M. Stanton

———

(Cipher)   City Point Va. Oct. 13th *1864.* [*3:30* P.M.]
HON. E. M. STANTON, SEC. OF WAR, WASHINGTON

On mature reflection I believe Shermans proposition is the best that can be adopted. With the long line of rail-road in rear of Atlanta Sherman cannot maintain his position. If he cuts loose destroying the road from Chattanooga forward he leaves a wide and destitute country for the rebels to pass over before reaching territory now held by us. Thomas could retain force enough to meet

Hood by giving up the road from Nashville to Decatur and thence to Stevenson and leave Sherman still force enough to meet ~~his~~ Hoods Army if it took the other and most likely course. Such an Army as Sherman has, (and with such a commander) ~~it will~~ is hard to corner or capture.

U. S. GRANT
Lt. Gn.

ALS (telegram sent), IHi; telegram received (at 6:00 P.M.), DNA, RG 107, Telegrams Collected (Bound). *O.R.*, I, xxxix, part 3, 239. On Oct. 12, 1864, 8:00 P.M., Secretary of War Edwin M. Stanton had telegraphed to USG. "The President feels much solicitude in respect to Shermans proposed movement and hopes that it will be maturely considered ~~before receiving your sanction~~. The objections stated in your telegram of last night impressed him with much force and a mis step ~~now~~ by ~~him~~ Sherman might be fatal to his army. This much ~~he~~ the President directed me to say to you when I saw him this evening and although I find on reaching the office that you now think better of ~~it now it is proper~~ the plan you should know how he feels on a point so vital." ALS (telegram sent), DNA, RG 107, Telegrams Collected (Bound); telegram received (on Oct. 13), *ibid.*, RG 108, Letters Received. *O.R.*, I, xxxix, part 3, 222. See telegram to Maj. Gen. William T. Sherman, Oct. 11, 1864.

To Edwin M. Stanton

City Point Va. Oct. 13th *1864.*

HON. E. M. STANTON,
SEC. OF WAR,
SIR:

A proposition has been submitted to me by I. F. Quinby, a Brig. Gen. of Volunteers, for other parties, to build a telegraph line between Cairo, Ill. and New Orleans, La. All that I have seen on the subject has been more to get my views of the practicability of the enterprise, and to learn what Military protection would be given after the wire was up than for any other purpose.

The nature of the country from Cairo to New Orleans is such that by frequently crossing the river with a telegraph line one can be laid so there will be but few roads from the interior striking it. This will much facilitate its protection. The Navy and established Military Garrisons, I think, could as well protect a judiciously located wire from Cairo to New Orleans as we can now protect the wires in rear of most of our Armies. I would recommend therefore, if the proposition comes up, that a contract be entered into to give Military protection to parties whilst building the line, and all the protection to it thereafter that can be given without detriment to the service. Further, that Government will pay for all official dispatches passed over the same at the rates charged individuals. A telegraph line from Cairo to New Orleans would be of such vast importance to the Government in a Military point of view, both in economy of time in transmitting orders, and economy of money in avoiding the use of dispatch boats, that I do not know but further pecuniary assistance than the mere paying for the transmission of dispatches might be afforded.

I think this matter of sufficient importance to give it at least full concideration and, if not deemed entirely impracticable, such support as will insure its accomplishment.

> I have the honor to be
> very respectfully
> your obt. svt.
> U. S. GRANT
> Lt. Gen.

ALS, IHi.

To Maj. Gen. Henry W. Halleck

(Cipher)   City Point Va. Oct. 13th *1864*.
MAJ. GEN. HALLECK, WASHINGTON,

Vessels should be got ready loaded with grain, Ordnance stores, and provisions, say 200.000 rations ~~of each~~ of grain & 500000 rations of provisions, & 100 rounds of Ammunition for 30.000 men with a proper proportion of field Artillery Ammunition for that number of Inf.y. The Ordnance Dept. will have to select the kinds of Ammunition based upon what they know of the Armament of Shermans Army. Soon after it is known that Sherman has struck South these vessels should sail and rendesvous at Ossabaw Sound. I take it his first supplies will have to be received by way of that river. Canby ought to move the force he has in Mobile Bay, with the exception of enough to hold the forts, and any other force he can add to it, to Brunswick and try to strike the Albany & Gulf rail-road, say at Initial Point. Information should be got to Sherman of all preparations made to receive him on the Seaboard. If Foster can send men to Brunswick it will be as well to send him as to send Canby and probably phis preparations can be earlyer made. The forage ration here indicated might be reduced one half if there is any difficulty about securing transportation but the other supplies should rather be increased than diminished. There probably will be no difficulty about securing fifteen to twenty days forage in the country and with a small amount on hand the animals could be kept along until vessels could return for a new supply.

U. S. GRANT

Lt. Gn.

ALS (telegram sent), OClWHi; telegram received (marked sent at 11:00 A.M., received at 3:00 P.M.), DNA, RG 107, Telegrams Collected (Bound). *O.R.*, I, xxxix, part 3, 239–40. On Oct. 14, 1864, 1:00 P.M., Maj. Gen. Henry W. Halleck telegraphed to USG. "Would it not answer your purposes to have the supplies sent direct to Hilton Head, with steamers in readiness there to take them to any point required? This would give to the enemy no intimation of intended operations; and would save most expenses in the demurrage of Ocean transports. The Quartermaster General has storage at Hilton Head and every facility for landing and shipping stores. Moreover, light draft steamers are kept there to run into the sounds & rivers. Should your plans be changed, the stores can be more readily transferred from Hilton Head than from Ossibaw. Genl Meigs has just suggested that the sailing vessels go from here as they are loaded, so as not to attract any attention. Please answer if this arrangement will suit you. I think from Genl Thomas' despatch of last night that Sherman is probably following up Hood towards Dalton. Sheridan appears to have changed his views in regard to the Manassas Gap road on recieving your despatch in regard to operations on Charlottesville & Gordonsville, & has countermanded his orders about the 6th Corps. He will probably be in here to night when I can ascertain his plans more fully." ALS (telegram sent), DNA, RG 107, Telegrams Collected (Bound); telegram received, *ibid.*; *ibid.*, RG 108, Letters Received. *O.R.*, I, xxxix, part 3, 267. At 7:30 P.M., USG telegraphed to Halleck. "It will not be necessary to send supplies to meet Sherman until it is known that he starts South. Then it probably will be much better to send them as you suggest." ALS (telegram sent—misdated Oct. 13), CSmH; telegram received (on Oct. 15, 4:00 P.M.), DNA, RG 107, Telegrams Collected (Bound). *O.R.*, I, xxxix, part 3, 267.

On Oct. 21, 6:30 P.M., USG telegraphed to Halleck. "The stores intended for Sherman might now be started for Hilton Head. There will be no necessity for them going ~~at~~ all at once but let them accumulate there gradually." ALS (telegram sent), CSmH; telegram received (at 7:20 P.M.), DNA, RG 107, Telegrams Collected (Bound). *O.R.*, I, xxxix, part 3, 386.

To Maj. Gen. Henry W. Halleck

(Cipher)   City Point Va. Oct. 13th/64 [*9:00* P.M.]
MAJ. GN. H. W. HALLECK, WASHINGTON

I think it will be advisable for Gn. Thomas now to abandon all the rail-road from Columbia to Decatur thence to Stevenson. This will give him much additional force. Has any change of commander in Mo. been ordered? I do think Price could be driven out in a week with the right man after him.

U. S. GRANT
Lt. Gn.

ALS (telegram sent), OClWHi; telegram received (on Oct. 14, 1864), DNA, RG 107, Telegrams Collected (Bound). *O.R.*, I, xxxix, part 3, 240.

To Maj. Gen. Benjamin F. Butler

City Point Va. Oct. 13th/64
MAJ. GN. BUTLER,

I would not attack the enemy in his intrenchments. The reconnoisance now serves to locate them for any future operation. To attack now we would loose more than the enemy and only gain ground which we are not prepared to hold nor are we prepared to follow up any advantage.

U. S. GRANT
Lt. Gn.

ALS (telegram sent), OClWHi; telegram received (at 1:00 P.M.), DLC-Benjamin F. Butler. *O.R.*, I, xlii, part 3, 213. On Oct. 13, 1864, noon, Maj. Gen.

Benjamin F. Butler had telegraphed to USG. "I forward to you the enclosed Despatch from Genl. Terry as the result so far of his reconnoissance which he began this morning at day light. Shall I order an attack on the works? They extend in a line from the house marked E Cunningham on the map near Darbytown road about two (2) miles ~~on~~ from the intermediate line round to the point near New Market road marked Laurel Hill" ALS (telegram sent), DNA, RG 107, Telegrams Collected (Unbound); telegram received, *ibid.*, RG 108, Letters Received. *O.R.*, I, xlii, part 3, 213. At 1:20 P.M., Butler telegraphed to USG. "Despatch recd.   orders have been sent to Gen Terry to reconniter the ground thoroughly & to return to his position" Telegram received, DNA, RG 108, Letters Received. *O.R.*, I, xlii, part 3, 213. On the same day, Butler telegraphed to USG. "Forwarded ~~by~~ for the information of Gen Grant   I have not heard from Terry since I sent orders not attack the works" ALS (telegram sent), DNA, RG 107, Telegrams Collected (Unbound); telegram received, *ibid.*, RG 108, Letters Received. *O.R.*, I, xlii, part 3, 213, 222. The enclosures are *ibid.*, pp. 218–19, 222; *ibid.*, I, xlii, part 1, 681–82.

To Maj. Gen. Benjamin F. Butler

City Point, Va, Oct. 13th/64

MAJ. GN. BUTLER,

Has the expedition started out this morning returned? What was the result of their observations?

The troops here have been assigned to Gen. Benham to complete work laid to protect this place from raids and to enable a small force to hold it in case it becomes necessary to ~~lea~~ move the greater part of the Army. I would not like to reduce this force unless there is a special necessity for it.

U. S. GRANT
Lt. Gn.

ALS (telegram sent), OClWHi; telegram received (at 7:07 P.M.), DLC-Benjamin F. Butler. *O.R.*, I, xlii, part 3, 214. On Oct. 13, 1864, 7:25 P.M., Maj. Gen. Benjamin F. Butler telegraphed to USG. "The Expedition has returned—Genl Terry is now telegraphing me the results—I will send them as soon as recieved—" LS (telegram sent), DNA, RG 94, War Records Office, Army of the Potomac. *O.R.*, I, xlii, part 3, 214.

On the same day, USG telegraphed to Butler. "I the 158th NY Infy Vols with the Army of the James" Telegram received, DLC-Benjamin F. Butler. At 7:30 P.M., Butler telegraphed to USG. "The 158th. N. Y. *is* with the Army of the James and won its colors handsomely at Battery Harrison—" LS (telegram sent), DNA, RG 107, Telegrams Collected (Unbound).

To Maj. Gen. Benjamin F. Butler

City Point Va. Oct. 13th *1864.*

MAJ. GEN. BUTLER,

Have you Artillery enough on Bermuda to defend it if the enemy should attack? I do not think such a thing likely but would rather judge their examination to be with a view to further reduce their force there to run you North of the James. We want to be watchful however at all points.

U. S. GRANT
Lt. Gn.

ALS (telegram sent), OClWHi; telegram received, DLC-Benjamin F. Butler. *O.R.*, I, xlii, part 3, 214. On Oct. 13, 1864, 8:30 P.M., Maj. Gen. Benjamin F. Butler had telegraphed to USG. "The enemy have reinforced in front of my old line now commanded by Col Potter who thinks they may attack him—I do not— They have been ~~reinforcing~~ reconnoitering this evening will a ballon" Telegram received, DNA, RG 108, Letters Received. *O.R.*, I, xlii, part 3, 214. At 9:15 P.M., Butler telegraphed to USG. "I think we have artillery enough in Bermuda to defend it if they should attack. We have all the artillery necessary on the line and one six (6) gun Napoleon battery for movable artillery—I do not believe in any intention of attack   A deserter I had from in front of our line there said they had orders to look out for an attack from us day befor yesterday" LS (telegram sent), DNA, RG 94, War Records Office, Army of the Potomac; telegram received, *ibid.*, RG 108, Letters Received. Printed as received at 9:20 P.M. in *O.R.*, I, xlii, part 3, 214.

On the same day, USG telegraphed to Butler. "Please give me such information as you have of the result of Gn. Terry's reconnoisance. Such willd rumers were afloat about Varina this evening that I feel much anxiety to know the facts." ALS (telegram sent), OClWHi; telegram received (at 9:15 P.M.), DLC-Benjamin F. Butler. *O.R.*, I, xlii, part 3, 215. At 9:50 P.M., Butler telegraphed to USG. "The operations today as I learn them from Genl Terry are as follows—with two (2) divisions and Kautz Cavalry he went up the Darbytown road, ~~went~~ felt along the enemys lines to the right for something like a mile driving in the enemys pickets with considerable loss to them—He then sent me a telegram which I forwarded to you at 12 o clock M. To that I returned an answer at 12 10 'Despatch recieved contents referred to Genl Grant   will send orders' ~~at 12 10~~—After recieving your orders at 1.30 I despatched to him the following 'I would not attack the enemy in their entrenchments—After carefully reconnoitering the enemy and their position and looking out all the roads retire at leisure.' At 3 o clock I recieved from him that Genl Kautz had found a place in the line where there was apparantly a gap and Ames had gone in with a brigade before my orders were recieved—that he would retire as soon as that fact was settled— Ames was unsuccessful owing to the enemys lines being retired which gave the impression that there was a gap in the line—The enemy then charged Ames and were repulsed handsomely—Terry then retired leisurely followed only by a line of skirmishers for a short distance   The losses in his Corps he says during the day were between three (3) and four hundred (400)   The troops are all back in their camps and every thing quiet—There is not the slightest cause for any anxiety—I had telegraphed for all particulars from Genl Terry but ascertained that being very much tired he was home a bed—" LS (telegram sent), DNA, RG 94, War Records Office, Army of the Potomac; telegram received, *ibid.*, RG 108, Letters Received. Printed as received at 10:20 P.M. in *O.R.*, I, xlii, part 3, 215.

On the same day, Lt. Col. Theodore S. Bowers wrote to Brig. Gen. Henry W. Benham. "Send immediately one of the Regiments now serving with you, and belonging to the Army of Gen. Butler, to report to Col. Potter Commanding forces on Butler's old line, near Bermuda Hundred.—The Regiment will march with promptness to Broadway Landing crossing the ponton bridge at that place. Let the Regiment sent be the strongest you have." ALS, DNA, RG 393, Army of the Potomac, Cav. Corps, Letters Received. *O.R.*, I, xlii, part 3, 203. On the same day, Butler telegraphed to USG. "Now that the enemys line is extended so for to our left is there any objection to my sending to Bermuda one of the two reg'ts Sent to Prince Georges Court House"   Telegram received, DNA, RG 108, Letters Received. *O.R.*, I, xlii, part 3, 215. On the same day, USG telegraphed to Butler. "I have ordered Gn. Benham to send back one of the regiments brought from Bermuda. Please notify Col. Potter that it will reach Bermuda between this and morning and for him to designate where it shall go." ALS (telegram sent), OClWHi; telegram received, DLC-Benjamin F. Butler. *O.R.*, I, xlii, part 3, 215. At 10:20 P.M., Butler telegraphed to USG. "Col. Potter is naturally from his situation a little nervous and I have ordered Gen Weitzel to send over the 12th New Hampshire to him his own Col. Potters own regiment." ALS (telegram sent), DNA, RG 94, War Records Office, Army of the Potomac. *O.R.*, I, xlii, part 3, 216.

On Oct. 14, noon, Maj. Gen. George G. Meade telegraphed to USG. "Conversations with cavalry videttes on the left, yesterday seemed on the part of the enemy to indicate some movement of their cavalry against our rear, as particular enquiry was made as to the location of the colored troops—The day & night have however passed without disturbance.—Deserters continue to repeat reports of the presence of Genl. Whiting with re-inforcements from No. Carolina—I can not ascertain any thing positive upon this point but judge from so many rumours, that it is probable some effert is being made to procure re-inforcements from that state under Whiting—In view of a probable cavalry movement I am unable to report the progress of the works in front of City Point under Genl. Benham, as that officer does not, altho ordered to do so—make any reports to these Hd. Qrs.—" ALS (telegram sent), DNA, RG 393, Army of the Potomac, Cav. Corps, Letters Received; telegram received, *ibid.*, RG 108, Letters Received. Printed as sent at 12:10 P.M. in *O.R.*, I, xlii, part 3, 225. On the same day, USG telegraphed to Meade. "My staff officers have examined the work done by Gen Benham & report it about as defensible as ordinary rifle pits with the work progressing well owing to a threatened attack on Bermuda Hundred I had to order back one of the regts drawn from Gen Butler during the night last night   this diminishes Benhams working force"   Telegram received (at 1:30 P.M.), DNA, RG 393, Army of the Potomac, Cav. Corps, Letters Received; copies (2), Meade Papers, PHi. *O.R.*, I, xlii, part 3, 225.

On Oct. 18, Bowers wrote to Brig. Gen. Seth Williams. "An order is now being issued attaching all the new organizations now serving with Gen Benham to the Army of the Potomac" ALS, DNA, RG 107, Telegrams Collected (Unbound). *O.R.*, I, xlii, part 3, 262.

To Edwin M. Stanton

(Cipher)   City Point Va. Oct. 14th *1864.* [*7:30* P.M.]
HON. E. M. STANTON, SEC. OF WAR, WASHINGTON

I am very glad you have determined to make me a visit here. The best that can be done with dispatches for Sherman is to send them to Thomas to be forwarded as soon as communications are opened.

U. S. GRANT
Lt. Gn.

ALS (telegram sent), CSmH; telegram received (on Oct. 15, 1864, 4:00 P.M.), DNA, RG 107, Telegrams Collected (Bound). *O.R.*, I, xxxix, part 3, 266; (incomplete) *ibid.*, I, xli, part 3, 853. On Oct. 14, 1864, 10:30 A.M., Secretary of War Edwin M. Stanton twice telegraphed to USG. "Sheridan expected to be at Rectortown today. I requested him to come here immediately by rail to confer with him in respect to Missouri and will let you know when he arrives. I expect to make you a visit tomorrow with General Meigs to confer on the matters in hand and am only waiting Sheridans arrival" ALS (telegram sent), DNA, RG 107, Telegrams Collected (Bound); telegram received, *ibid.*, RG 108, Letters Received. *O.R.*, I, xli, part 3, 853; *ibid.*, I, xliii, part 2, 363. "Communication between Sherman and Thomas being broken I have directed copies of your despatches for Sherman to be delivered to General Thomas in order to apprise him of your views—This will I hope meet this will meet your view approbation" ALS (telegram sent), DNA, RG 107, Telegrams Collected (Bound); telegram received, *ibid.*, RG 108, Letters Received. *O.R.*, I, xxxix, part 3, 266.

On Oct. 16, USG telegraphed to Maj. Gen. Benjamin F. Butler. "The Sec. of War and myself will start immediately for Aiken's Landing. We take no horses with us and therefore request you to meet us at the landing." ALS (telegram sent), OClWHi; telegram received (at 12:45 P.M.), DLC-Benjamin F. Butler. *O.R.*, I, xlii, part 3, 251. On the same day, Bvt. Maj. Gen. Godfrey Weitzel telegraphed to USG. "You dispatch received   I start at once for Aikins landing—" Telegram received, DNA, RG 107, Telegrams Collected (Unbound). *O.R.*, I, xlii, part 3, 252. On the same day, Weitzel telegraphed to Lt. Col. Cyrus B. Comstock. "General Butler has gone to Fort Monroe leaving a written order for me to take command of this army during his absence. Bvt Genl. Terry whose brevet as Maj. Genl is of the same date as mine ranks me as Brigadier, but was placed on duty in his brevet rank after I was. Now, ask the General whether I shall assume command under these circumstances, or turn it over to Terry. Please answer at once." ALS (telegram sent), DNA, RG 107, Telegrams Collected (Unbound). On the same day, Comstock telegraphed to Weitzel. "The lieutenant-general commanding directs me to say that, having been first assigned according to your brevet rank as major-general, you will take command of the Army of the James in General Butler's absence." *O.R.*, I, xlii, part 3, 251.

On Oct. 17, USG telegraphed to Maj. Gen. George G. Meade. "The Secy of War & secy of the Treasury with a number of other gentlemen will leave here for your HdQrs at 9 30 a m this morning" Telegram received, DNA, RG 393, Army of the Potomac, Cav. Corps, Letters Received; copies (2), Meade Papers, PHi. *O.R.*, I, xlii, part 3, 255.

To Maj. Gen. Henry W. Halleck

(Cipher) City Point Va. Oct. 14th/64 [*1:00* P.M.]

MAJ. GEN. HALLECK, WASHINGTON,

It looks to me that Hood has now put himself in a position where his army must be to a great extent destroyed. Sherman has Rome and the rich district of country about it and is in a better condition to live, independent of supplies on hand, than Hood. I think we may look now for favorable news from that quarter. What is the condition of affairs in Mo.?[1]

U. S. GRANT
Lt. Gn.

ALS (telegram sent), CSmH; telegram received (at 3:30 P.M.), DNA, RG 107, Telegrams Collected (Bound). *O.R.*, I, xxxix, part 3, 266–67.

1. On Oct. 14, 1864, 4:45 P.M., Maj. Gen. Henry W. Halleck telegraphed to USG. "I have just learned from Col Cummings who left Little Rock September 23d, that Genl J. J. Reynolds left his troops in garrison on White River and started down the Miss. to rejoin Genl Canby on the 21st of September; that Magruder's forces from Texas were at Camden & Montecello, threatening Pine Bluff & Little Rock, that Genl Steele did not expect to send any of his troops north after Price, as to do so he would expose the whole line of the Arkansas to Magruder's army. Col. Cummings does not seem to know whether or not Genl Reynolds expected to return with more troops. How far these statements can be relied on I do not know. I hardly think Genl Steele would state his plans to a line officer so freely. Rosecrans telegram is all I have from Missouri." ALS (telegram sent), DNA, RG 107, Telegrams Collected (Bound); telegram received, *ibid.*; (marked as sent at 5:00 P.M.) *ibid.*, RG 108, Letters Received. *O.R.*, I, xli, part 3, 854.

On Oct. 16, Capt. Robert C. Clowry, St. Louis, telegraphed to Col. Anson

Stager providing information about military operations in Kan., and a copy was transmitted to USG. Telegram received, DLC-Edwin M. Stanton; DNA, RG 107, Telegrams Collected (Unbound); *ibid.*, RG 108, Letters Received. *O.R.*, I, xli, part 4, 6.

To Maj. Gen. Philip H. Sheridan

(Cipher)   City Point Va. Oct. 14th 1864 [*12:30* P.M.]
MAJ. GEN. SHERIDAN, CEDAR CREEK VA.

What I want is for you to threate[n] the Va. Central rail-road & Canal in the manner your judgement ~~thinks~~ tells you is best holding yourself ready to advance if the enemy draw off their forces. If you make the enemy hold a force equal to your own for the protection of those thoroughfares it will accomplish nearly as much as their destruction. If you can not do this then the next best thing to do is to send here all the force you can. I deem a good Cavalry force necessary for your offensive as well as defensive operations. You need not therefore send here more than one Division of Cavalry.

U. S. GRANT
Lt. Gen.

ALS (telegram sent), CSmH; telegram received (marked as sent at 11:30 A.M., received at 4:00 P.M.), DNA, RG 107, Telegrams Collected (Bound). *O.R.*, I, xliii, part 2, 363.

On Oct. 9, 1864, midnight, Maj. Gen. Philip H. Sheridan, Strasburg, Va., telegraphed to USG. "In coming back to this-point I was not followed up until late yesterday when a large force of Cavalry appeared in my rear. I then halted my command to offer battle by attacking the enemy. I became satisfied that it was only all the rebel Cavalry of the valley commanded by Rosser & directed Torbert to attack at daylight this morning & finish this 'Saviour of the valley' The attack was handsomely made   Custer Comdg 3rd Cavalry Divn charged on the back road & merritt Comdg 1st Cavalry Divn on the strasburg pike. Merritt captured 5 pieces of artillery, Custer captured 6 pieces of artillery with caissons, battery forge Ets. The two Divns. captured 47 wagons, ambulances Etc Among the wagons captured are the Hd Qrs wagons of Rosser, Lomax, Wicham and Col Pollard. The number of prisoners will be about 330. The enemy after being charged by our gallant Cavalry were broken & ran. They were followed by our men on the jump 26 miles through Mt Jackson & across North fork of the shenandoah. I deemed it best to make this delay of one day here & settle this new Cavalry Genl. The 11 pieces of artillery captured today make 36 pieces captured in the Shenandoah valley since the (19th) nineteenth of September. Some of the Artly was new & never had been fired. Pieces marked Tredegar works." Telegrams received (2—on Oct. 10, 9:40 P.M.), DNA, RG 107, Telegrams Collected (Bound); *ibid.*, Telegrams Collected (Unbound); copies, *ibid.*, Telegrams Received in Cipher; (2) DLC-Philip H. Sheridan. Printed as received on Oct. 11 in *O.R.*, I, xliii, part 1, 31; *ibid.*, I, xliii, part 2, 327. On Oct. 11, 7:00 P.M., Sheridan, Cedar Creek, Va., telegraphed to USG. "I have seen no sign of the Enemy since the brilliant engagement of the 9th inst. It was a square Cavalry fight in which the enemy was routed beyond my power to describe, He lost everything carried on wheels except one piece of artillery and when last seen it was passing over Rude's Hill near New Market on the keen run twenty six miles from the battle field, to which point the pursuit was kept up, The battery men and horses Etc were captured; the horses were in good condition, but were all exchanged by our own Cavalry men for their broken down animals,) I have given you but a faint idea of the cleaning out of the stock, forage, wheat, provisions Etc, in the valley. The casualties on the 9th will not exceed Sixty men. The one hundred men of the 8th Ohio dispersed while guarding the bridge over the north Shenandoah have come in except the Officers. Lieut. Col. Tolles my chief QrMr. and Asst. Surg. John Ohlenschlager medical Inspector on my staff were both mortally wounded by guerrillas today on their way to join me from Winchester, They were ambuscaded. Three men were killed, five wounded out of an escort of twenty four. The refugees from Early's army, Cavalry and Infantry, are organizing guerrilla parties and are becoming very formidable and are annoying me very much, I know of no way to exterminate them except to burn out the whole country and let the people go north or south If I attempt to capture them by sending out parties they escape to the mountains on fleet horses, Col Powell Comd'g Cavy. Division on the 5th inst. cut down the Railroad bridge over the Rapidan & threw it into the river." Telegram received (on Oct. 12, 1:30 P.M.), DNA, RG 107, Telegrams Collected (Bound); copies, *ibid.*, Telegrams Received in Cipher; (2) DLC-Philip H. Sheridan. *O.R.*, I, xliii, part 1, 32; *ibid.*, I, xliii, part 2, 339–40. On Oct. 12, 9:00 P.M., Sheridan telegraphed to USG. "I have directed the 6th Corps to march to Alexandria via Ashby's Gap to commence the march tomorrow morning, It will take four and a half days, It is now at Front Royal. I will request major Genl Halleck to have transportation ready to embark through to Petersburg, From my best information Early did not follow me down the valley with his Infantry but sent only his Cavalry, I have already informed you of the handsome manner it was smashed up, Information received from Col. Powell at Berryville reports Early, (or Longstreet, I do not yet know which is in command, but think Early is) with the bulk of his force at Craig's Creek between Brown's Gap and Waynesboro. I object to the opening of the R, R, and an advance on the old Rapidan line, on account of The waste of fighting force to protect R. Rds, and the additional waste of force, as some would have to be left in this valley, You see how many troops might then be rendered unavailable, I believe that concentrating at vital points, and the destruction of subsistence resources to be everything, but do not let my views influence your better judgment. I believe that a rebel advance down this valley will not take place, I have not yet started the Cavalry Division. Am waiting the results of Col. Powell's Division which I sent through Chester Gap towards Gordonsville." Telegram received (on Oct. 13, 5:30 P.M.), DNA, RG 107, Telegrams Collected (Bound); (on Oct. 14) *ibid.*, RG 108, Letters Received; copies, *ibid.*, RG 107, Telegrams Received in Cipher; (3) DLC-Philip H. Sheridan. *O.R.*, I, xliii, part 2, 345–46.

To Julia Dent Grant

October 14th *1864.*

DEAR JULIA,

Time is passing and Richmond is still not ours. No efforts have been made in that direction however for some days. I think it cannot be long now before the tug will come which, if it does not secure the prize will put us where the end will be in sight. I keep in good health but I am getting very anxious for a little recreation and home. I have no news for you only that I have just heard that the Commissioner for the exchange of prisoners has again agreed that John Dent shall be delivered at Savannah Georgia with the first lot of prisoners sent from there. We send vessels in a few days for some 4.000 agreed to be delivered at that point. I think his wife may look for him this time but she had better not be too sanguine.— Col. Hillyer writes me that Missy is at his house? I would not let her remain long. She ought to be going to school every day. Tell Jess to send me word what he is learning at school. As soon as he can write he must send me a letter. Love and kisses for you and the children. I sent yesterday pay accounts to Capt. Leet with directions to send you a check for $800 00. I presume you will have received the money by the time you get this. I have been afraid you be without. But it wont hurt if you are without a few days. Be careful as you can, without stinting your self, for I have $2625 00 to pay for some stock I have bought. I told you that I had $1500 00 more Horse rail-road stock? But this is paid for. Do you hear any thing further about the house in Phila?

ULYS.

ALS, DLC-USG.

To Maj. Gen. George G. Meade

City Point Va. Oct. 15th/64

MAJ. GN. MEADE,

Scouts of the enemy are cutting the wire between Powhattan & Jamestown about as rapidly as we can put it up.[1] I am determined to stop this or clear out the country. To effect this object I wish you would send a regiment of Cavalry. Let them go to Powhattan in the morning. I will send from here my escort company to go from there with them and will send instructions by them. The escort knows the roads and country.[2] ~~Rations and~~

U. S. GRANT
Lt. Gn.

ALS (telegram sent), OClWHi; telegram received, DNA, RG 393, Army of the Potomac, Cav. Corps, Letters Received. *O.R.*, I, xlii, part 3, 233. On Oct. 15, 1864, 8:00 P.M., Maj. Gen. George G. Meade endorsed this telegram. "The foregoing despatch is transmitted to Brig. Genl. Gregg who will in accordance therewith send a regiment of cavalry to be at Fort Powhattan tomorrow morning to join the escort of the Lt. Genl. Comd & be governed by the instructions there received.—" AES, DNA, RG 393, Army of the Potomac, Cav. Corps, Letters Received. *O.R.*, I, xlii, part 3, 233. On Oct. 16, noon, Meade telegraphed to USG. "Maj. Genl. Hancock reports the enemy strengthening & adding to his works, on his Genl. Hancocks immediate front—Genl. Hancock last night, directed his batteries to shell at intervals the enemys working parties.—Genl. Hancock likewise reports the enemy as throwing up works on the left bank of the Appomatox between Petersburgh & Fort Clifton.—Genl. Hancock is of the opinion these works are designed for offensive movements, looking to a crossing of the Appomatox on our right flank. I have directed Maj. Michler to examine into this matter & report, but am at present of the opinion these works are more likely to be defensive & to guard against such movement on our part, particularly if there is any thing in the prevailing opinion the enemy are preparing to abandon the South side of the Appomatox.—Quiet prevails on the left of our lines—the defensive works are nearly completed.—I regret to have to report a continuance of desertions to the enemy from this army—Five are reported as having deserted last night from the 2d Div. 9. A. C—and Three on the 14th inst from the 2d Div. 2d A. C.   the latter I regret to say were old soldiers. Generally these desertions which of late have become quite frequent, have been confined to newly arrived recruits, & mostly, substitutes and foreigners.—A Regiment of cavalry was sent this morning to Fort Powhattan in accordance with your instructions received last evening.—A reconnaissance made by Genl. Gregg on the 14th inst in a southerly direction failed to obtain any intelligence of previously reported movements by the enemys cavalry—They ascertained however, that the enemys guerillas had murdered a Mr. Brockwell & his servant residing just without our picket lines, for no other reason, than that he had taken the oath of allegiance to the U. S. and drawn provisions from the Commissary to feed his destitute family.—The authors of this barbarous outrage are unknown, and can not therefore be punished, as their disgraceful crime merits. The victims head- less body was found by our people, brought within our lines & buried.—" ALS (telegram sent), DNA, RG 393, Army of the Potomac, Cav. Corps, Letters Re- ceived; telegrams received (2), *ibid.*, RG 108, Letters Received. *O.R.*, I, xlii, part 3, 245. See *ibid.*, p. 242.

1. On Oct. 12, USG telegraphed to the commanding officer, Fort Powhatan. "I sent Capt. Mason to Ft. Powhattan with about fifty Cavalry to join the Cavalry with you and clear out the country of such persons as are engaged in destroying the wires between you and Jamestown. Send your Cavalry under Capt. M. with such information and guides as you have. The Captain received verbal instruc- tions from me what to do." ALS (telegram sent), OClWHi; copies, DLC-USG, V, 45, 70, 107; DNA, RG 108, Letters Sent. *O.R.*, I, xlii, part 3, 195.

2. See *ibid.*, I, xlii, part 1, 959–60.

To Maj. Gen. Henry W. Halleck

(Cipher)   City Point Va. Oct. 16th *1864.* [*7:30* P.M.]
MAJ. GEN. HALLECK, WASHINGTON

I think no troops have left Richmond on the contrary the Artil- lery that lost their pieces have returned. Kershaws Division and probably some of Breckenridges forces that were not in the previ- ous engagements in the Valley may have gone to meet Sheridan.

U. S. GRANT
Lt. Gn.

ALS (telegram sent), CSmH; telegram received (at 11:35 P.M.), DNA, RG 107, Telegrams Collected (Bound); *ibid.*, Telegrams Collected (Unbound). *O.R.*, I, xliii, part 2, 385.

To Maj. Gen. Henry W. Halleck

City Point, Va. Oct. 16th *1864.*

MAJ. GEN. H. W. HALLECK
CHIEF OF STAFF OF THE ARMY
WASHINGTON, D. C.
GENERAL:

Please cause a general order to be issued from the Adjutant General's Office directing all officers and men in the United States service on recruiting service in the several States, except those detailed by orders from the Adjutant General's Office, to cease recruiting at once and return immediately to their respective commands, conditioned that all Officers to which said order refers, who are absent from their commands on the 10th day of November next, shall be reported by their immediate commanding Officers, through the regular military channels, to the Adjutant General of the Army for muster out of service; and also, positively prohibiting Commanding Officers of Armies, Military Divisions or Departments from detailing officers and men for recruiting service in future.

Very Respect. Your Ob't Servant
U. S. GRANT
Lieut. General

LS, DNA, RG 94, Letters Received, 1081A 1864. See *O.R.*, III, iv, 806.

To Maj. Gen. Ambrose E. Burnside

[*Oct. 17, 1864.*]

... It has been no part of my plan to break up the 9th Corps and it cannot be spared from here. Knowing how unpleasantly you are situated with Gen. Meade, I have not thought it best to order your return to the Army of the Potomac but have waited to see if there was not other service which would seem more agreeable to you which you could be assigned. I should not like to assign you to the command of a single corps unless it embraced a department, other than your old corps. The proceedings of the "Court of Inquiry" were forwarded to Washington without coming through my headquarters. I have not heard the result of the investigation and do not know if it has been published.

Kenneth W. Rendell, Inc., Catalogue No. 100 [*1974*], p. 58.

On Nov. 15, 1864, USG telegraphed to Maj. Gen. Ambrose E. Burnside, Baltimore. "You are authorized to visit Head Quarters" Copies, DLC-USG, V, 45, 70, 107; DNA, RG 108, Letters Sent. *O.R.*, I, xlii, part 3, 624. On Nov. 17, Burnside, Fort Monroe, telegraphed to USG. "I leave at once—We were at the R. R. station in time, but the train was delayed—I Am anxious to see you— Can I do so by stopping at Burlington on Saturday—" ALS (telegram sent),

DNA, RG 107, Telegrams Collected (Unbound); telegram received, *ibid.* Brig. Gen. John A. Rawlins drafted a reply at the foot of the telegram. "Genl Grant will arrive in Baltimore on Steamer Martin in the morning" ADf, *ibid.* On the same day, Maj. Gen. John G. Parke telegraphed to USG. "Gen'l. Burnside started some 15 minutes since on a Locomotive   There was some delay in the arrival of the train—" Copy, *ibid.*, RG 393, 9th Army Corps, Telegrams Sent.

To Maj. Gen. William T. Sherman

From City Point Va. 3.30 P. m. Octo. 17, *1864.*

MAJOR GEN W. T. SHERMAN,

VIA CHATTANOOGA TENN,

The moment I know you have started south stores will be shipped to Hilton Head where there are transports ready to take them to meet you at Savannah.

In case you go south I would not propose holding any thing south of Chattanooga, certainly not south of Dalton. Destroy in such case all of military value in Atlanta.

U S GRANT

Lt Genl

Telegram received (at 5:00 P.M.), DNA, RG 107, Telegrams Collected (Bound); copies, *ibid.*, Telegrams Received in Cipher; *ibid.*, RG 108, Letters Sent; DLC-USG, V, 45, 70, 107. *O.R.*, I, xxxix, part 3, 324. On Oct. 16, 1864, 4:30 P.M., Maj. Gen. William T. Sherman, Ship's Gap, Ga., telegraphed to USG. "I got the despatch in cipher about providing me a place to come out on Salt water but the cipher is imperfect & I cannot make out whether Savannah or Mobile be the point preferred but I also want to know if you are willing that I should destroy Atlanta and the railroad   Hood broke eight miles of road at Big Shanty and about fifteen from Resacca to the Tunnel. The break at Big Shanty is repaired but the other will take some time   I have now taken position where I dont care which way he moves   I think the rebels will now go back south"   Telegram received, DNA, RG 107, Telegrams Collected (Unbound); (on Oct. 17, 1:30 P.M.) *ibid.*, RG 108, Letters Received. *O.R.*, I, xxxix, part 3, 304–5.

On Oct. 22, 8:00 A.M., Sherman, Gaylesville, Ala., telegraphed to USG. "I feel perfectly master of the situation here   I still hold Atlanta and the road, with all bridges and vital points well guarded, and I have [on] hand an army before which Hood has retreated precipitately down the Valley of the Tennessee   It is hard to divine ~~out~~ his future plans *but* by abandoning Georgia, and taking position with his rear to Selma he threatens the road from Chattanooga to Atlanta, and may move to Tennessee by Decatur   He cannot cross the Tennessee except at Muscle Shoals, for all other ports are patrolled by our gunboats. I am now perfecting arrangements to put into Tennessee a force able to hold the line of the Coosa, whilst I break up the RailRoad in front of Dalton, including the city of Atlanta, and push into Georgia and break up all its RailRoads and Depots, capture its horses and negroes, Make desolation every where, destroy the factories at Macon, Milledgeville and Augusta, and bring up with sixty thousand men on the sea shore, above Savannah or Charleston Harbor. I think this far better than merely defending a long line of Railroad. I will leave Genl Thomas to command all my Divisions behind me, and take with me only the best fighting material. Of course I will subsist on the bountiful clover fields, and potato patches, as I am now doing luxuriously. I have now all your dispatches, and there will be time to give me any further instructions   Genl Canby should be most active as against Selma from the direction of Mobile, and I will order similar movements from the Mississippi and Decatur, provided Beauregard follows me, as he will be forced to do by public clamor—" Telegram received (on Oct. 23), DNA, RG 107, Telegrams Collected (Bound); *ibid.*, Telegrams Collected (Unbound); *ibid.*, RG 108, Letters Received; copy, *ibid.*, RG 107, Telegrams Received in Cipher. *O.R.*, I, xxxix, part 3, 394–95.

To Gen. Robert E. Lee

October 18th *1864*

GENERAL R. E. LEE
COMDG. ARMY N. V.
GENERAL.

The accompanying are copies of letters addressed by Judge R. Ould, Commissioner for the exchange of prisoners of war to Hon. E. M. Stanton, Sec. of War, and to Lieut Colonel Jno. E. Mulford, Asst. Comr of Exchange.[1] I have been authorized by the Secretary of War to make such arrangements as can be agreed upon for the mutual relief of prisoners held by the two parties. In the propositions submitted by Judge Ould, I see no one thing to object to. I shall be perfectly willing to receive at any place held by Federal troops all clothing or delicacies sent for the use of prisoners in our hands provided the same privelige is extended for supplying the wants of those held by the Confederate authorities. No objection will be urged to receiving supplies for like distribution at any of our Northern ports direct from Europe, or to allowing purchases in Northern cities for the same purpose. I would suggest, however, as a means of satisfying each party that all goods sent reach their proper destination, that a commissioned officer from each party, to be selected from among the prisoners of war, be paroled to remain within the lines of the party now holding them, whose duty it shall be to receive and receipt for all articles sent for distribution and who shall see that they are distributed according to the wishes of those sending.

Looking entirely to the alleviation of the sufferings of those held in captivity, I will not interpose any obstacle to any plan that may be proposed which gives equal priveliges to both belligerents.

> Very Respectfully
> Your obt. Servt
> U. S. GRANT
> Lieutenant General.

Copies, DLC-USG, V, 45, 70, 107; DNA, RG 108, Letters Sent; USG 3. *O.R.*, II, vii, 1008–9. The enclosures are *ibid.*, pp. 926, 929. On Oct. 15, 1864, Secretary of War Edwin M. Stanton wrote to USG. "A communication signed Ro. Ould Agent of Exchange dated Oct 7th inst mailed at Fortress Monroe and addressed to me is herewith referred to you together with a paper that accompanied it, bearing the same signature dated Oct 6 and addressed to Major Jno E. Mulford Assistant Agent of Exchange. You are authorized and instructed to take such action in reference to said papers & the subject matter to which they relate as you may deem best adapted to the relief of our soldiers held as prisoners by the rebels. You are also authorized to take any steps that you may deem proper to effect the release and exchange of our soldiers and all loyal persons held as prisoners by the rebel authorities   It is the desire of the President that no effort consistent with national safety and honor, be spared to effect the prompt release of all soldiers and loyal persons in captivity to the rebels as prisoners of war or on any other grounds and the subject is committed to you with full authority to act in the premises as you shall deem right & proper"   ALS, DNA, RG 108, Letters Received. *O.R.*, II, vii, 988–89. On the same day, Stanton endorsed the enclosures. "Referred to Lieutenant General Grant with authority to act upon the subject in such manner as he deems proper and with authority to take such measures as he deems consistent with national honor & safety for the release of all soldiers & loyal persons held by the rebels in captivity"   AES, DNA, RG 108, Letters Received. *O.R.*, II, vii, 930. On Oct. 19, Gen. Robert E. Lee wrote to USG. "I have received your letter of the 18th Inst:, accompanying letters from Judge Ould, Commr of Exchange of prisoners, on the part of the Confederate States, and the Hon. E. M. Stanton, Sect. of War, and Lt. Col. Mulford, Ass't. Commr of Exchange of the United States. I understand your letter to be an acceptance of the general proposition submitted by Judge Ould, for the relief of the prisoners held by both parties, and shall transmit it to him, that arrangements may be made for carrying it into effect. The necessary details will be submitted to you, through Col. Mulford for agreement. In order to simplify the matter, and to remove as far as possible, causes of complaint, I suggest that the articles sent by either party should be confined to those necessary for the comfort and health of the prisoners, and that the Officer selected from among them to receive and distribute the articles, should be given only such a parole while so engaged, as to afford him the necessary facilities to attend properly to the matter." Copy, DNA, RG 109, Letterbook of Robert Ould. *O.R.*, II, vii, 1009–10.

1. John E. Mulford rose from capt., 3rd N. Y., as of May 14, 1861, to lt. col. in 1864, but had served as commissioner of exchanges (or asst. agent for exchange) since July, 1863. *O.R.*, II, vi, 141.

To Maj. Gen. Henry W. Halleck

(Cipher) City Point Va. Oct. 18th/64 [*1:30* P.M.]
MAJ. GEN. HALLECK, WASHINGTON,

Gen. Sheridan should follow and break up Longstreets force if he can and either employ all the force the enemy now have in the valley or send his surplus forces here. With the 6th Corps and one Division of Cavalry I think my lines could be closed up to the Appomattoxa above Petersburg and the Danville road cut.

U. S. GRANT
Lt. Gn.

ALS (telegram sent), CSmH; telegram received, DNA, RG 107, Telegrams Collected (Bound). *O.R.*, I, xliii, part 2, 409. On Oct. 17, 1864, 12:30 P.M., Maj. Gen. Henry W. Halleck telegraphed to USG. "Genl Sheridan has just been here. He has not yet fully decided about the Manassas road but will do so in a day or two. He has gone back with cols. Alexander & Thom to make a fuller reconnoissance. Thomas thinks Sherman's movements favorable for cutting off Hood. Nothing whatever from Genl Rosecrans." ALS (telegram sent), DNA, RG 107, Telegrams Collected (Bound); telegram received, *ibid.*; *ibid.*, Telegrams Collected (Unbound); (at 1:30 P.M.) *ibid.*, RG 108, Letters Received. *O.R.*, I, xliii, part 2, 393.

To Maj. Gen. Benjamin F. Butler

City Point Va. Oct. 19th/64
MAJ. GEN. BUTLER,

I have just received information that the enemy are undermining Fort Harrison. It would be well for Gen. Weitzel to ascertain if this is so.

U. S. GRANT
Lt. Gn.

ALS (telegram sent), DNA, RG 107, Telegrams Collected (Unbound); tele-
gram received (at 6:30 P.M.), *ibid.*, RG 393, 10th Army Corps, Miscellaneous
Telegrams Received. Printed as sent at 6:50 P.M. in *O.R.*, I, xlii, part 3, 275.
On Oct. 19, 1864, Maj. Gen. Benjamin F. Butler telegraphed to USG, drafting
his reply on the telegram received. "It is inpossible to undermine fort Harrison
from the Conformation of the Ground"   ADfS, DNA, RG 393, 10th Army
Corps, Miscellaneous Telegrams Received; telegram received, *ibid.*, RG 107,
Telegrams Collected (Unbound); *ibid.*, RG 108, Letters Received. *O.R.*, I, xlii,
part 3, 276. On Oct. 20, Capt. John McEntee wrote to Lt. Col. Theodore S.
Bowers transmitting information from a "Richmond agent" which included mention of C.S.A. plans to retake Fort Harrison. *Ibid.*, p. 282.

On Oct. 19, Butler telegraphed to USG transmitting a telegram announcing
the death of Maj. Gen. David B. Birney. *Ibid.*, p. 276.

To Frederick Dent Grant

———

City Point Va. Oct. 19th *1864.*

DEAR FREDDY,

I have now received two letters from you since you commenced
going to school in Burlington. You must continue to write often as
much for your improvement as that I may hear from you. I would
have written two days ago to your Ma but I supposed she had gone
to St. Louis. I do not know now whether she has gone atall. I received a telegraph from her at Philadelphia saying she had got that
far on the way but did not know whether to go further. I telegraphed her that your Uncle Fred would start at once for St. Louis
and I did not think it was best for her to go but to do as she pleased.
I am glad you are all pleased with your schools and hope you will
learn fast. Does Jess continue to like school and his books? Jess is
a good boy, only sometimes when he forgets, and a smart one too.
He will learn to read by Christmass. Has Nelly returned from New
York? I hope she had a pleasant visit. She & Buck must both write
to me and Jess must tell you all something to write until he learns
so that he can write for himself. Love and kisses for all of you. I
will not write to your Ma until I know where she is.

Your PA.

ALS, DLC-USG.

To Gen. Robert E. Lee

———

October 20 *1864*

GENERAL R. E. LEE, C S. A.
COMDG ARMY N. V.
GENERAL.

Your letter of yesterday, accepting the terms offered for the mutual relief of prisoners of war held by each party, is received. Your understanding of my proposition is perfectly correct. I have no objection to limiting the articles to be sent to simple necessaries, or to extending as much as you will agree to. It is my desire that all prisoners of war should be made as comfortable as it is possible for prisoners under restraint to be, and I will favor any proposition looking to that end.

> I have the honor to be,
> Very Respectfully
> Your Obt Servant
> U. S. GRANT
> Lieutenant General.

Copies, DLC-USG, V, 45, 70, 107; DNA, RG 108, Letters Sent; USG 3. *O.R.*, II, vii, 1018. See letter to Gen. Robert E. Lee, Oct. 18, 1864. On Oct. 23, 1864, USG wrote to Secretary of War Edwin M. Stanton transmitting copies of all his recent correspondence with Gen. Robert E. Lee. LS, DNA, RG 249, Letters Received. *O.R.*, II, vii, 1022–23.

To Gen. Robert E. Lee

———

October 20th *1864.*

GEN. R. E. LEE, C. S. A.
COMD.G ARMY N. VA.
GENERAL,

Understanding from your letter of the 19th that the Colored prisoners who were employed at work in the trenches near Fort Gilmer have been withdrawn I have directed the withdrawal of the Confederate prisoners employed in Dutch Gap canal. I shall always regret the necessity of retaliating for wrongs done our soldiers but regard it my duty to protect all persons received into the Army of the United States, regardless of color or Nationality. When acknowledged Soldiers of the Government are captured they must be treated as prisoners of War or such treatment as they receive inflicted upon an equal number of prisoners held by us. I have nothing to do with the discussion of the slavery question therefore decline answering the arguments adduced to show the right to return to former owners such negroes as are captured from our army. In answer to the question at the conclusion of your letter I have to state that all prisoners of War falling into my hands shall receive the kindest possible treatment, consistent with securing them, unless I have good authority for believing any number of our men are being treated otherwise. tThen, painful as it my be to me, I shall inflict like treatment on an equal number of Confederate prisoners. Hoping that it may never become my duty to order retaliation upon any man, held as a prisoner, of war

> I have the honor to ~~subscribe~~ be
> Very respectfully
> your obt. svt.
> U. S. GRANT
> Lt. Gn. Com

ALS, DNA, RG 109, Documents Printed in *O.R. O.R.*, II, vii, 1018–19. On Oct. 19, 1864, Gen. Robert E. Lee wrote to USG. "In accordance with instructions from the Hon. Secrctary of War of the Confederate States, I have the honor to call your attention to the subject of two communications recently addressed by Major Genl. B. F. Butler, an officer under your command, to the Hon. Robert Ould, Commissioner for the exchange of prisoners. For the better understanding of the matter, I enclose copies of the communications. You will perceive by one of them, that the writer has placed a number of officers and men belonging to the Confederate service, prisoners of war, captured by the United States forces, at labour in the canal at Dutch Gap, in retaliation, as is alleged, for a like number of Federal colored soldiers, prisoners of war in our hands, who are said to have been put to work on our fortifications. The evidence of this fact is found in the affidavits of two deserters from our service. The other letter refers to a copy of a notice issued by a Confederate officer commanding a camp near Richmond, calling upon the owners to come forward and establish their claims to certain negroes in the custody of that officer. The writer of the letter proceeds to state that some of the negroes mentioned in the notice, are believed to be soldiers of the United States Army captured in arms, and that upon that belief, he has ordered to such manual labor as he deems most fitting to meet the exigency, an equal number of prisoners of war held by the United States, and announces that he will continue to order to labor captives in war to a number equal to that of all the United States soldiers who, he has reason to believe, are held to service or labor by the Confederate forces, until he shall be notified that the alleged practice on the part of the Confederate authorities has ceased. Before stating the facts with reference to the particular negroes alluded to, I beg leave to explain the policy pursued by the Confederate Government towards this class of persons when captured by its forces. All negroes in the military or naval service of the United States taken by us, who are not identified as the property of citizens or residents of any of the Confederate States, are regarded as prisoners of war, being held to be proper subjects of exchange, as I recently had the honor to inform you. No labor is exacted from such prisoners by the Confederate authorities. Negroes who owe service or labor to citizens or residents of the Confederate States, and who through compulsion, persuasion, or of their own accord, leave their owners and are placed in the military or naval service of the United States, occupy a different position. The right to the service or labor of negro slaves in the Confederate States, is the same now as when those states were members of the Federal Union. The constitutional relations and obligations of the Confederate government to the owners of this species of property, are the same as those so frequently and so long recognized as appertaining to the government of the United States, with reference to the same class of persons, by virtue of its organic law. From the earliest period of the independence of the American States, it has been held that one of the duties incumbent upon the several common governments under which they have from time to time been associated, was the return to their lawful owners, of slaves recaptured from the public enemy. It has been uniformly held that the capture or abduction of a slave does not impair the right of the owner to such slave, but that the right attaches to him immediately upon recapture. Such was the practice of the American States during their struggle for independence. The government under which they were then associated, restored to the owners slaves abducted by the British forces and subsequently recaptured by the American armies. In the war of 1812 with Great Britain, the course pursued by the United States government was the same, and it recognized the right of the owner to slaves recaptured from the enemy. Both the Continental and United States governments, in fact denied that the abduction of slaves was a belligerent right, and the latter power insisted upon, and ultimately secured by treaty, pecuniary indemnity from the British government, for slaves taken by its forces during the war of 1812   And it is supposed that if a negro belonging to a citizen of a state in which slavery is recognized, and which is regarded as one of the United States, were to escape into the Confederate States, or be captured or abducted by their armies, the legal right of the owner to reclaim him would be as clear now as in 1812, the constitution of the United States being unchanged in this particular, and that instrument having been interpreted in the judicial decisions, legislation and diplomatic acts and correspondence of the United States, as imposing upon that government the duty of protecting, in all cases coming within the scope of its authority, the owners of slaves as well as of any other kind of property, recognized as such by the several states. The Confederate government, bound by the same constitutional obligations, considers, as that of the United States did, that the capture or abduction of a negro slave does not preclude the lawful owner from reclaiming him when recaptured, and I am instructed to say that all such slaves, when properly identified as belonging to citizens of any of the Confederate States, or to persons enjoying the protection of their laws, will be restored, like other recaptured private property, to those entitled to them. Having endeavoured to explain the general policy of the Confederate government with regard to this subject, I beg leave to state the facts concerning the particular transactions referred to in the enclosed communications. The negroes recently captured by our forces, were sent to Richmond with other Federal prisoners. After their arrival it was discovered that a number of them were slaves belonging to citizens or residents of some of the Confederate States, and of this class, fifty nine as I learn were sent with other negroes to work on the fortifications around Richmond, until their owners should appear and claim them. As soon as I was informed of the fact, less than two days afterwards, not wishing to employ them here, I ordered them to be sent into the interior. By a misapprehension of the Engineer officer in charge, they were transferred to our lines South of James River, but when apprised of the error I repeated the order for their removal. If any negroes were included among the number who were not identified as the slaves of citizens or residents of some of the Confederate States, they were so included without the knowledge or authority of the War Department, as already explained, and the mistake when discovered would have been corrected. It only remains for me to say that the negroes employed upon our fortifications, are not allowed to be placed where they will be exposed to fire, and there is no foundation for any statement to the contrary. The author of the communication referred to, has considered himself justified by the report of two deserters, who do not allege that the negroes in question were exposed to any danger, in placing our prisoners at labor in the canal at Dutch Gap under the fire of our batteries. In view of the explanation of the practice of the Confederate government above given, and of the statement of facts I have made, I have now in accordance with my instructions, respectfully to inquire whether the course pursued towards our prisoners as set forth in the accompanying letters has your sanction, and whether it will be maintained?" LS, USMA. *O.R.*, II, vii, 1010–12. On Oct. 20, Brig. Gen. Charles K. Graham telegraphed to USG. "I have sent by an Aide communications received by flag-of-truce,   The bearer of them will be at the point designated at two o'clock p. m. to-morrow the twenty first inst to receive reply." ALS (telegram sent), DNA, RG 107, Telegrams Collected (Unbound); copy, *ibid.*, RG 393, Army of the James, Provisional Div., Letters Sent.

On Oct. 13, Surgeon Francis J. D'Avignon, 96th N. Y., wrote to Maj. Gen. Benjamin F. Butler. "I respectfully state to you that I was a prisoner at Petersburgh, Virginia, and made to sign a parole of honour to not leave the premises of the Hospital—That the Rebel authorities put me in charge of the prisoners sick & wounded—That about the second day of August, after the mine explosion before Petersburgh, about one hundred & thirty wounded of our soldiers were brought to me for treatment. This lot of wounded were looked upon by the Rebels with a great deal of hatred & with an earnest desire to degrade them. For this object General Henry A. Wise, commanding the first military district, issued an order to mix the Negroes with the white soldiers. A non commissioned officer read to me the order, to place one white man, especially an officer, between two negroes. The order was strictly followed & the wounded were crowded. I objected to this crowding & also to place the men promiscuously, against the good judgment of physicians & surgeons to separate those affected with Erysipelas from the others; But to no effect. And I can safely state that this arrangement was a cause of destroying the life of our soldiers. I will remark that I gave my attention to the Black & to the white soldiers, uniformly alike, to the great annoyance & regret of the Southerners. I have also observed that the Rebel Authorities have given up several of the black soldiers to individuals, who claimed them as their former slaves." ALS, *ibid.*, RG 108, Letters Received. On Oct. 21, Butler endorsed this letter. "Respectfully forwarded to Lieut Genl Grant for his information and with the enquiry whether some action ought not to be taken" ES, *ibid.*

To Edwin M. Stanton

(Cipher)   City Point Va. Oct. 20th *1864.* [*7:00* P.M.]
HON. E. M. STANTON, SEC. OF WAR, WASHINGTON.

I had a salute of one hundred guns from each of the Armies here fired in honor of Sheridan's last victory.[1] Turning what bid fare to be a disaster into glorious victory stamps Sheridan what I have always thought him, one of the ablest of Generals. ~~I hope the President will reward his services by making him a Major General in the Regular Army without delay.~~

U. S. GRANT
Lt. Gn.

ALS (telegram sent), CSmH; telegrams received (2—at 8:10 P.M.), DNA, RG 107, Telegrams Collected (Bound). *O.R.*, I, xlii, part 3, 280; *ibid.*, I, xliii, part 2, 423.

On Oct. 19, 1864, 7:30 P.M., Asst. Secretary of War Charles A. Dana telegraphed to USG. "I send the adjoined despatch for your information. Mr Garret derives his intelligence from his agents along line of the rail road, of course much if not most of these statements are matters of rumor rather than of absolute fact" Telegram received, DNA, RG 107, Telegrams Collected (Unbound); *ibid.*, RG 108, Letters Received. The enclosure is in *O.R.*, I, xliii, part 2, 417. On the same day, 10:00 P.M., Maj. Gen. Philip H. Sheridan telegraphed to USG. "I have the honor to report that my army at Cedar Creek was attacked this morning before daylight and my left was turned and driven in confusion. In fact most of the line was driven in confusion with the loss of twenty pieces of artillery—I hastened from Winchester where I was on my return from Washington and formed the armies between Middletown and Newtown having been driven back about four miles—I here took the affair in hand and quickly united the Corps formed a compact line of battle just in time to repulse an attack of the enemy which was handsomely done at about 1 p. m At 3 p m after some changes of the cavalry from the left to the right flank I attacked with great vigor driving and routing the enemy capturing according to last report forty three pieces of artillery and very many prisoners I do not yet know the number of my casualties or the losses of the enemy—Wagons trains, ambulances and caissons in large numbers are in our possession—They also burned some of their trains—Genl Ramseur is a prisoner in our hands severely and perhaps mortally wounded—I have to regret the loss of Genl Bidwell killed and Genls Wright Grover and Ricketts wounded—Wright slightly wounded—Affairs at time looked badly but by the gallantry of our brave officers and men disaster has been converted into a splendid victory—Darkness again intervened to shut off greater results   I now occupy Strasburg   As soon as obtained I will send you further particulars" Telegrams received (2—on Oct. 20), DNA, RG 107, Telegrams Collected (Bound); copies, *ibid.*, Telegrams Received in Cipher; (3) DLC-Philip H. Sheridan. Printed as received at 3:00 P.M. in *O.R.*, I, xliii, part 1, 32–33; *ibid.*, I, xliii, part 2, 410. On Oct. 20, Brig. Gen. John A. Rawlins sent copies of this telegram to all senior commanders. On Oct. 20, 11:30 A.M., Sheridan telegraphed to USG. "We have again been favored by a great victory, a victory won from disaster by the gallantry of our officers and men. The attack on the enemy was made about 3 P. M. by a left half wheel of the whole line with a Divn. of Cavalry turning each flank of the enemy, the whole line advancing. The enemy after a stubborn resistance broke and fled, and were pushed with vigor. The artillery captured will probably be over 50 pieces, this of course includes what were captured from our troops in the early morning. At least 1.600 prisoners have been brought in, also wagons & ambulances in large numbers. This morning the Cavalry made a dash at Fisher's Hill & carried it the enemy having fled during the night leaving only a small rear guard. I have to regret the loss of many valuable Officers killed & wounded, among them Col. Joseph Thoburn Comd'g Divn of Crooks command killed, Col. C. R. Lowell Jr. Com'd'g Reverse Cav'y. Brig. killed Col. J. Howard *Kitchen* Comd'g Brigade wounded, Col. R. G. McKenzie Comd'g Brigade wounded severely, would not leave the field. I cannot yet give exact details. Many of our men captured in the morning have made their escape & are coming in. Ramseur Comd'g Divn in Early's Army died this morning—" Telegrams received (2—on Oct. 21, 7:30 A.M.), DNA, RG 107, Telegrams Collected (Bound); copies, *ibid.*, Telegrams Received in Cipher; (3) DLC-Philip H. Sheridan. Printed as received on Oct. 21, noon, in *O.R.*, I, xliii, part 1, 33; *ibid.*, I, xliii, part 2, 424. On Oct. 21, Rawlins transmitted copies of this telegram to all senior commanders.

1. On Oct. 20, USG telegraphed to Maj. Gen. Benjamin F. Butler and to Maj. Gen. George G. Meade. "I think we can afforad a salute of one hundred guns at sunset this evening over Sheridans victory of yesterday." Telegram received (at 3:30 P.M.), DLC-Benjamin F. Butler; DNA, RG 94, War Records Office, Army of the Potomac; copies (2), Meade Papers, PHi. At 5:30 P.M., Meade telegraphed to USG. "I have just returned to camp, and received the glorious news from Sheridan—To achieve such results after having met the reverse he describes, is one of the most brilliant feats of the war—I heartily congratulate you & him on the result.—" ALS (telegram sent), DNA, RG 94, War Records Office, Army of the Potomac; telegram received, *ibid.*, RG 108, Letters Received. *O.R.*, I, xlii, part 3, 281.

To Maj. Gen. Henry W. Halleck

(Cipher) City Point Va. Oct. 20th *1864.* [*4:00* P.M.]
MAJ. GEN. HALLECK, WASHINGTON

No troops have gone from here to the Valley according to the information we have. Deserters come in to all parts of our line daily from which the position of every Division of Lee's Army can be located. It is probable Sheridan has had to meet Kershaw's Division in addition to the forces he has heretofor defeated. I think that Division does not now exceed 4000 in number.

U. S. GRANT
Lt. Gen.

ALS (telegram sent), CSmH; telegram received (at 5:40 P.M.), DNA, RG 107, Telegrams Collected (Bound). *O.R.*, I, xliii, part 2, 423.

To Maj. Gen. Henry W. Halleck

(Cipher) City Point, Va, Oct. 20th/64 [*7:30* P.M.]
MAJ. GEN. HALLECK WASHINGTON

Has Rosecrans yet come upon Price? If he has not he should be removed at once. Price is in a country where he supports his Army without difficulty and there is no reason why our forces should not move without any delay. Of all the Generals whose names have been mentioned in connection with the successorship, and are available, I prefer Logan. Any body however will be better than Rosecrans.

U. S. GRANT
Lt. Gn.

ALS (telegram sent), CSmH; telegram received (at 8:45 P.M.), DNA, RG 107, Telegrams Collected (Bound). *O.R.*, I, xli, part 4, 126. On Oct. 21, 1864, 4:30 P.M., Maj. Gen. Henry W. Halleck telegraphed to USG. "As it is manifest that no troops can at present be taken from Genl Sheridan's command, and as the vessels collected at Alexandria are wanted elsewhere & involve enormous cost for demurrage, I have directed Genl. Rucker to use them for other purposes. The can be collected again in a week or ten days if required. Nothing satisfactory from Missouri. I can form no clear idea of the condition of affairs from the reports recieved here. Genl Curtis seems to be fighting near Independence, but I hear nothing of Rosecrans, A. J. Smith or Mower's division. No action yet as to change of commanders." ALS (telegram sent), DNA, RG 107, Telegrams Collected (Bound); telegram received, *ibid.*; *ibid.*, Telegrams Collected (Unbound); (at 8:30 P.M.) *ibid.*, RG 108, Letters Received. *O.R.*, I, xli, part 4, 153.

To Maj. Gen. Benjamin F. Butler

By Telegraph from City Pt
Dated Oct 20 *1864.*

To GEN BUTLER

I am in receipt of a Communication from Gen Lee showing that prisoners of war set to work in the intrenchments have been withdrawn. I will send you the communication tomorrow. It becomes incumbent on us of course to with draw the prisoners employed in Dutch Gap canal. Please withdraw them & have them forwarded to join the prisoners of war North.

U. S. GRANT. Lt Gen

Telegram received (at 6:50 P.M.), DNA, RG 107, Telegrams Collected (Unbound). *O.R.*, I, xlii, part 3, 285–86; *ibid.*, II, vii, 1015. On Oct. 20, 1864, 9:50 P.M., Maj. Gen. Benjamin F. Butler telegraphed to USG. "Your telegram concerning the official dispatch of Genl Lee regarding the prisoners at work in the rebel trenches is recieved. Orders have been issued relieving to night the prisoners at Dutch Gap. A copy of the order will be sent you in the morning." LS (telegram sent), DNA, RG 107, Telegrams Collected (Unbound); telegram received, *ibid.*, RG 108, Letters Received. *O.R.*, I, xlii, part 3, 286; *ibid.*, II, vii, 1015–16.

Also on Oct. 20, 6:00 P.M., Butler telegraphed to USG. "Please send me about 500 copies of your Proclamation—Some rebel picket officers have asked for them for distribution among their soldiers—" Telegram received, DNA, RG 107, Telegrams Collected (Unbound).

To Maj. Gen. Benjamin F. Butler

(Confidential)   City Point, Va. Oct. 20th *1864.*
MAJ. GEN. B. F. BUTLER,
COMD.G ARMY OF THE JAMES,
GENERAL,

On Thursday morning, the 27th inst. Gen. Meade will move from our left with the design of seizing and holding the Southside rail-road. To facilitate this movement, or rather to prevent reinforcements going from the North side of James River to Petersburg, I wish you to demonstrate against the enemy in your front substantially as we talked the matter over last evening, and as you proposed. I do not want any attack made by you against intrenched and defended positions. But feel out to the right beyond the front line intrenched by the enemy, and, if you can, turn it.—Have your men go with three days rations in their Haversacks, sixty rounds of ammunition on their persons, and as near without wagons and ambulances as it is possible to go. It probably will be well to move all transportation not absolutely necessary with the Army to the south side of the James. This need not take place before your movement of Thursday but should commence in the morning with your movement.

Let it be distinctly understood by Corps commanders that there is to be no attack made against defended intrenched positions. They should also have their commands fully instructed as to the possibility of the enemy moving out from their right on the James to attack in flank or rear. This demonstration on the part of the enemy is not likely to occur but should be guarded against and should be taken advantage of if attempted.

Your cavalry I believe is not now well commanded: if it was and the opportunity occured, I would favor sending that to the Central road to destroy as much track as possible and return to the James River in rear of your Army. As it is I will leave this to your judgement whether the trip can be made. You being present with your Army can form a judgement after the first few hours of your

movement as to the expediency of attempting this. I shall myself
be with the forces on our extreme left. Such dispatches as you may
want to send to me through the day, or days, we may be out, will
reach me, by courier, from the Hd Qrs. of the 9th Army Corps.

> I am Gen. very respectfully
> your obt. svt.
> U. S. GRANT
> Lt. Gen.

ALS, DLC-Benjamin F. Butler. Dated Oct. 24, 1864, in *O.R.*, I, xlii, part 3, 331–
32. It is possible that this letter is misdated Oct. 20 and that the Oct. 24 date
is correct. USG did not characteristically give Maj. Gen. Benjamin F. Butler
instructions without first discussing plans with Maj. Gen. George G. Meade.
USG conferred with Meade on Oct. 21 and issued instructions to him on Oct. 24
for a movement to take place on Oct. 27.

To Julia Dent Grant

City Point, Va. Oct. 20th *1864.*

DEAR JULIA,

   Your letter from Phila saying that you had determined not to
go to St. Louis is received. Wm Smith also arrived this evening. I
am glad you did not go. It would have been a long, cold, disagreeable trip. Fred. has gone. It was four days between two of my letters
because I supposed you had gone. I received a letter this evening
also from Mr. Morris.[1] Thank him for me for his and his daughter's
kindness in promising to look after our children, and keeping us
advised, during your absence. I should write to Mr. Morris myself, thanking him, but I have so much writing to do. Has dear little
Nelly got home? She ought to be at school. Is Jess learning as fast
as he ought to? Tell Fred he must give me the particulars of his
battles. I do not want him to feel afraid to *pitch in* when boys im-
pose on him but he had better avoid boys who are inclined to quarrel. Has Jess been in a fight yet with any body but his Ma? I know
he fights his Ma some times but it generally ends in a love quarrel.
—I have no special news to write you this evening. I have just had
a salute of one hundred guns fired for Sheridans last victory in

the Valley. I hope we will have one here before a great while to selebrate.

Love and kisses for you and the children. Of course I am satisfied with your sending $50 00 to your father. You may send him as much every month if he needs it. I can about spare $800 00 per month to support you and the children out of which will come our savings. The balanse of my income it will take to support me.

Kisses again.

ULYS.

ALS, DLC-USG.

    1. See letter to E. Morris, Nov. 6, 1864.

To Maj. Gen. George G. Meade

By Telegraph from City Point
Dated Oct 21 *1864.*

To MAJ GEN MEADE

I go out this morning to ride round the works west of the Weldon Road. Will stop the Cars at your Station, and go from there on horse back.

If not otherwise engaged I would be pleased to have you ride with me.

U. S GRANT,
Lt. Genl.

Telegram received, DNA, RG 393, Army of the Potomac, Cav. Corps, Letters Received; copies, *ibid.*, RG 108, Letters Sent; DLC-USG, V, 45, 70, 107; (2) Meade Papers, PHi. *O.R.*, I, xlii, part 3, 290. On Oct. 21, 1864, 9:10 A.M., Maj. Gen. George G. Meade telegraphed to USG. "Have received your despatch & will be ready on your arrival to accompany you." ALS (telegram sent), DNA, RG 393, Army of the Potomac, Cav. Corps, Letters Received; copy, *ibid.*, Army of the Potomac, Letters Sent. *O.R.*, I, xlii, part 3, 290.

    On Oct. 19, noon (sent at 12:10 P.M.), and Oct. 20, noon, Meade had telegraphed to USG. "I have nothing particular to report—The artillery firing last night, was the shelling of the enemys working parties in front of our extreme right—I am going to day to ride over the lines recently constructed in front of City Point, after which if not too late I shall probaly be at City Point.—" "The quiet of the lines during the past 24 hours, has been undisturbed except by the usual artillery firing in front of 2d. corps. (4) Four deserters came in during the night who report nothing new—Some contrabands came in on the left this morning, who state there was to be today at 10. a m an assemblage of masters & slaves at Dinwiddie C. H. for the purpose of collecting slaves to take the places of teamsters & other detailed men in the army.—On inspecting Genl. Benhams lines yesterday I found a battery organised from detachments of recruits & convalescents from various regiments in this army—This organisation I understood was gotten up temporarily when a cavalry raid was anticipated & was formed with your sanction—As this contingency has passed & the men are wanted with their regiments & the pieces required for existing organisations—I directed the men to be returned to their regiments & the pieces turned in to the ordnance officer, who will issue them to batteries requiring guns. As soon as Genl. Benham's lines are completed & the batteries of this army filled, I will send such batteries to arm the lines as may be necessary—This explanation is now made in case this subject is brought to your attention.—" ALS (telegrams sent), DNA, RG 393, Army of the Potomac, Cav. Corps, Letters Received; telegrams received, *ibid.*, RG 108, Letters Received. *O.R.*, I, xlii, part 3, 271, 280–81.

On Oct. 20, Lt. Col. Theodore S. Bowers wrote to Brig. Gen. Seth Williams requesting an explanation of discrepancies in reports of men present for duty, and on Oct. 21, Williams wrote a letter of explanation. *Ibid.*, pp. 281, 290.

To Maj. Gen. Philip H. Sheridan

(Cipher)   City Point Va. Oct. 21st/64

MAJ. GEN. SHERIDAN, CEDAR CREEK, VA.

If it is possible to follow up your great victory until you reach the Central road and Canal do it even if you have to live on half rations. I say nothing about reaching Lynchburg with a portion of your force because I doubt the practiciability of it. If the Army at Richmond ~~cut~~ could be cut off from Southwest Va it would be of great importance to us but I know the difficulty of supplying so far from your base.

U. S. GRANT
Lt. Gn.

ALS (telegram sent), CSmH; telegram received (marked as sent at 3:00 P.M.), DNA, RG 107, Telegrams Collected (Bound). *O.R.*, I, xliii, part 2, 436.

On Oct. 21, 1864, 4:00 P.M., Maj. Gen. Philip H. Sheridan, Cedar Creek, telegraphed to USG. "I pursued the routed forces of the enemy nearly to Mt Jackson which point he reached during the night of the 19th and 20th without an organized regt. of his army. From the accounts of our prisoners who have escaped and citizens the rout was complete. About 2.000 of the enemy broke and made their way down through the mountain on the left. For ten miles on the line of retreat the road and country were covered with small arms thrown away by the flying rebels, and other debris, 48 pieces of captured artillery are now at my Head Quarters. I think that not less than 300 wagons & ambulances were either captured or destroyed. The accident of the morning turned to our advantage as much as though the whole ~~moment~~ movement had been planned. The only regret I have is the capture in the early morning of from 800 to 1.000 of our men. General, I want Getty of the 6th corps, and the brave boys Merritt and Custer promoted by brevets. When I attacked the enemy Merritt & Custer under the direction of Torbert fiercely attacked the enemy's flanks and when he broke closed in after dark and secured the artillery trains Etc, Etc., My loss in killed and wounded will be between three and four thousand. I am now sending to the War Dept. ten battle flags. The loss of artillery in the morning was 7 from Crook 11 from Emory 6 from Wright. From all that I can learn I think that Early's re-enforcements could not be less than 12.000 men." Telegram received (on Oct. 22, 8:00 A.M.), DNA, RG 107, Telegrams Collected (Bound); copies, *ibid.*; *ibid.*, Telegrams Received in Cipher; (3) DLC-Philip H. Sheridan. Printed as received on Oct. 23, 6:00 P.M., in *O.R.*, I, xliii, part 1, 33–34; *ibid.*, I, xliii, part 2, 436–37.

On Oct. 25, 10:00 P.M., Sheridan telegraphed to USG. "I have found it impossible to move on the Central Railroad as you desire, If I do so it must be up the Valley via Swift Run Gap or Brown's Gap, or across via Front Royal and Chester Gap. To move up the valley via the routes designated would be Exceedingly difficult on account of supplies and forage and would demoralize the troops now in magnificent trim. To move by Chester Gap I would have to leave at least 5,000 (the whole of Crook) in the valley. To open the Orange & Alexandria Railroad would require a corps on it to protect it, which would leave me very little to operate with successfully, To advance against Gordonsville & Charlottesville with a line of communication up this valley and through the Blue Ridge is impracticable, I have been meditating Cavalry operations against the Central Railroad as soon as the necessary preparations can be made. The cavalry has lost largely in numbers by expiration of service & is not half as strong as it was six weeks ago. The battle of the 19th still increases in results, we captured 48 pieces of artillery, caissons, horses & all the appointments, 24 of the above number were captured from us in the morning, These I returned & in addition allowed the batteries to refit and exchange & have left 24 pieces of rebel artillery, with caissons complete, which I will send to Washington tomorrow. All the ambulances of the 19th Corps captured by the Enemy were retaken with 56 rebel ambulances in good condition & as many more were destroyed. A number of wagons & ambulances were burned unnecessarily by the Cavalry in the excitement, Not less than 300 wagons and ambulances were captured or burned, The road between Cedar Creek & Fisher's Hill for three miles was blocked by captured artillery and wagons. The rebel army did not stop at Fisher's Hill but continued to Mt Jackson on the night of the battle and on to NewMarket next morning and perhaps further, The Cavalry pursuit was kept up to a point between Edenburg and Mt Jackson, We captured 14 battle flags, 10 of which I sent to the War Dept & have 4 more yet to go, Persons who left the rebel army at Mt Jackson report it broken up and demoralized worse than it ever has been. Rest assured, General, I will strike and strike hard whenever opportunity offers. I am anxious to get the recruits & conscripts for this army. We are now reduced to an effective force of not over 22,000 Infantry. From the accounts of officers Early's Infantry when he attacked me was 25,000, the number of Cavalry not known." Telegram received (on Oct. 26, 6:00 P.M.), DNA, RG 107, Telegrams Collected (Bound); copies, *ibid.*, Telegrams Received in Cipher; (3) DLC-Philip H. Sheridan. *O.R.*, I, xliii, part 1, 34; *ibid.*, I, xliii, part 2, 464–65.

To Edwin M. Stanton

City Point Va. Oct. 22d/64

~~Maj. Gen Halleck~~ Hon E. M Stanton, Washington

Your confidential dispatch of 12.~~15~~30 P. M. this date is received. I do not think it possible that any Brigades or even regiments have gone from here to reinforce Early. The number of deserters coming in daily fixes all the commands of Lee. From deserters of to-day I learn that Early has been reinforced from men who have been returned to the service from hospitals and by relieving detailed men but in no other way. Some troops may also have joined him from Lynchburg & Southwest Va. ~~b~~But after Sheridan's splendid victory it will only count that much more if this proves to be so.

U. S. Grant
Lt. Gn.

ALS (telegram sent), OClWHi; telegram received (sent at 6:30 P.M., received at 10:00 P.M.), DNA, RG 107, Telegrams Collected (Bound). *O.R.*, I, xliii, part 2, 444. A telegram received and a copy in DNA, RG 107, Telegrams Collected (Unbound) indicate that this telegram was addressed to Maj. Gen. Henry W. Halleck; the change of addressee on the original is not in USG's hand. On Oct. 22, 1864, 12:30 P.M., Secretary of War Edwin M. Stanton telegraphed to USG. "There is a strong belief prevailing among the rebel sympathisers here that a large force has been detached against Sheridan and that ~~although~~ while the attack upon him Wednesday was ~~prematur~~ repelled it was because it had been prematurely made before the re inforcements reached Early. I have ~~a~~ an intercepted cipher despatch ~~from Jeff Davis Richmond~~ which favors this view. It is so important to the safety of individuals that I am unwilling to run the risk of its getting ~~into any~~ to the knowledge of any one else but yourself and your cipher operator, and therefore request you to be present when it is translated and immediately destroy it. We have nothing from Sheridan since 11 a m ~~yesterday~~. Thursday" ALS (telegram sent), *ibid.*, Telegrams Collected (Bound); telegram received (at 2:15 P.M.—copied as sent by Halleck), *ibid.*, RG 108, Letters Received. *O.R.*, I, xliii, part 2, 444. At 6:30 P.M., USG telegraphed to Stanton. "The intercepted dispatch alluded to in your dispatch of 2.15 p. m. this date is not yet received. ~~will it be sent me~~" ALS (telegram sent), OClWHi; telegram received (at 10:00 P.M.), DNA, RG 107, Telegrams Collected (Bound). The telegram sent was addressed by USG to Halleck, readdressed in another hand to Stanton. At 9:30 P.M., Stanton telegraphed to USG. "Information received this evening induces me to delay sending the despatches mentioned in my telegram last night ~~in~~ They will be transmitted with other reports by special messenger tomorrow" ALS (telegram sent), *ibid.*; telegram received, *ibid.*, Telegrams Collected (Unbound); *ibid.*, RG 108, Letters Received.

To Maj. Gen. Henry W. Halleck

(Cipher) City Point Va. Oct. 22d/64

MAJ. GEN. HALLECK, WASHINGTON,

I think it would be well to send Canby the orders you have prepared. If he was within telegraphic communication I would not have them sent until it was known Sherman had started.

U. S. GRANT
Lt. Gn.

ALS (telegram sent), CSmH; telegram received (marked as sent at 6:30 P.M., received at 10:00 P.M.), DNA, RG 107, Telegrams Collected (Bound). Misdated Oct. 21, 1864, in USG's letterbooks and *O.R.*, I, xli, part 4, 153. On Oct. 22, 1:30 A.M., and Oct. 23, 2:00 P.M., Maj. Gen. Henry W. Halleck telegraphed to USG. "I had prepared instructions to Genl Canby to move all available forces in Mobile Bay & elsewhere to Brunswick and cut the Savannah & Gulf Rail Road, as directed by you on the 13th, but on learning that Sherman's operations were uncertain I withheld the order. I learn to day that General Canby left New Orleans about the 15th for Arkansas, & will recieve communications at mouth of White River. Shall I now send to him your orders of the 13th, in regard to the Georgia movement? He is of opinion that Price's movement into Missouri was partly intended to draw our forces in that direction so that a part of Magruder's army could cross the Mississippi and reenforce Hood " "Despatches recieved to day from Genl Canby state that he is moving all his available forces *up* the Mississippi River to support Steele and prevent Buckner & Taylor's divisions from crossing the Miss. Intercepted despatches show that Price is expected to return to the Arkansas river and attack Steele, in conjunction with Magruder, while Kirby Smith sends a force across the Miss. to operate in conjunction with Hood. Jeff Davis orders to Kirby Smith are positive that he send a force to assist Forrest in cutting off Sherman's communications in Tennessee. Canby is doing all he can to prevent this. As Sherman must wait sometime near Atlanta for supplies, I think no time will be lost in delaying Canby's instructions a few days. I regard it of vital importance to Sherman that Hood should not be reinforced from west of the Miss." ALS (telegrams sent), DNA, RG 107, Telegrams Collected (Bound); telegrams received, *ibid.*; *ibid.*, Telegrams Collected (Unbound); *ibid.*, RG 108, Letters Received. *O.R.*, I, xli, part 4, 172, 199.

To Julia Dent Grant

City Point, Va, Oct. 22d *1864.*

DEAR JULIA,

I have shipped by Adams' Ex. a box containing some of my old clothing and some very fanciful new clothing. There is also a

pair of fine pistols inside but the box they are in is locked up and
Fred Dent has the key. When he returns I will send it to you. The
pistols are for Jess when he gets to be a General.

I have been in hopes of being able to make you a visit yet this
month but I do not now think it possible. If you have good servants
to leave the children with you might come down to see me for a
few days. I could always send some one as far as Baltimore to meet
you and would go myself to Fort Monroe to bring you from there.
Will you come? Love and kisses for you and the children.

ULYS.

ALS, DLC-USG.

To L. J. Lieberman

———

City Point Va. Oct. 23d 1864.

L. J. LEBERMAN,
CH. COM. ON CLOTHING
DEAR SIR:

Your letter of the 19th inst. asking if I had received a suit of
clothing made to my measure and presented to the Phila Fair by
Rackhill & Wilson is received. The clothing was duly received and
acknowledged by me at the time.[1] I regret you did not receive my
letter. I will again express my thanks to Messrs Rockhill & Wilson
for this liberal donation to a humane and patriotic cause.

Very respectfully
your obt. svt.
U. S. GRANT
Lt. Gn.

ALS, George V. Rountree, Chicago, Ill.

1. On July 17, 1864, USG wrote to Rockhill & Wilson acknowledging re-
ceipt of a suit of clothes from the Philadelphia Sanitary Fair, "for the benefit of
myself, the subscriptions going to the benefit of the sick and wounded soldiers."
Swann Galleries, Inc., 600th Sale, Sept. 27, 1962, p. 25. On Aug. 9, 1865,
USG, Niagara Falls, wrote to Rockhill & Wilson ordering another suit. Stan. V.
Henkels, Sale No. 677, Dec. 15, 1891, no. 2469.

To Abraham Lincoln

City Point Va. Oct. 24th *1864*.

HIS EXCELLENCY A. LINCOLN PRESIDENT,

Mrs. Hulburt of Memphis has asked me for a letter of introduction to you. I do not know the object in view but having met Mrs. Hulburt & her husband frequently during the short period I was in Memphis have no hesitation in complying with her request. Both Mr. H. and his wife expressed the strongest sympathy for our cause immediately upon the occupation of Memphis by the Federal Army. They were sociable and visited, and envited to visit, the officers of our Army, a thing not done at that day by many who are very loud now for the Union.

> Very respectfully
> your obt. svt.
> U. S. GRANT
> Lt. Gn.

ALS, DLC-Robert T. Lincoln. Valeria Hulbert of Memphis, wife of Henry S. Hulbert, a lawyer serving as surveyor of customs at Memphis when the Civil War began, enclosed copies of USG's letter in her patriotic letters of March 4, 1865, to President Abraham Lincoln (Seward Papers, NRU) and Vice President Andrew Johnson (DLC-Andrew Johnson). See Johnson, *Papers*, IV, 412–13; V, 612–14.

To Edwin M. Stanton

City Point, Va. October 24. 1864.

HON. E. M. STANTON, SECRETARY OF WAR.

WASHINGTON, D. C.

The very significant dispatches sent by private hands, and your letter in relation to affairs in New York are received. It is consoling to know that Sheridan defeated the first part of the rebel programme so signally. I am at a loss to know what was expected to be done in the North further than to colonize voters, unless it is to control the polls by violence at stated points where their imported voters are colonized. I had ordered another regiment of regulars to report to Gen. Dix before receiving your letter.[1] I see the absolute necessity of further reinforcing him, and it must be done. I do not like the idea of sending troops from here, but if they can not be spared from elswhere, they must go from here. Cannot two or three of the new regiments now raised in the North be sent there? I would not advise ~~sending~~ taking new NewYork Regiments, but those from Pennsylvania or the New England States would answer. Please telegraph me whether you can send Gen. Dix the necessary reinforcements in the manner here proposed.

Price I presume is now about leaving Mo, having accomplished his mission. If so Rosecranz can send the required troops to New.York.

U. S. GRANT.

Lt. Gen.

Copies, DLC-USG, V, 45, 70, 107; DNA, RG 108, Letters Sent. *O.R.*, I, xliii, part 2, 456–57. On Oct. 23, 1864, Secretary of War Edwin M. Stanton wrote to USG. "The aspect of affairs in New York City and State urgently demands attention, as well for the security of the forts in the harbor of New York, the defence of the lake frontier from invasion, and the preservation of the public peace, ~~as~~ and for the purity of the ballot-box from rebels imported from Canada. I have just had a consultation with General Dix, who has called here for conference upon these subjects. He informs me he has already, in a communication to you as General commanding all the forces of the United States, reported the insecure condition of the forts in New York Harbor. You are aware that there are no troops in Washington or elsewhere, at the disposal of the Department, to meet this necessity. General Dix informs me that during the coming week he will be able to send you five thousand new recruits; but for want of organization, and also for local reasons, they are not a proper force to place in garrison. Allow me to suggest whether, in view of their accession to your army, you cannot spare two or three thousand men temporarily, to be sent to New York and placed under his command. I see no other way of meeting the emergency. By the 15th of November, the necessity will either have passed away, or, by troops from other States, those now to be forwarded can be replaced. Please favor me with your views on this subject at your earliest convenience." LS, DNA, RG 108, Letters Received. *O.R.*, I, xliii, part 2, 452–53.

1. On Oct. 19, Maj. Gen. John A. Dix, New York City, wrote to USG. "I deem it my duty to Call your attention, as General in Chief of the Army, to the want of troops in this City and Harbor. It is but a short time since the 3d U. S. Inftry. was taken from me, and five days ago I received an order to send to you the 7th U. S. Inftry. It is now being relieved by the 17th. The 7th Regt constituted the garrison of Fort Schuyler and Fort Lafayette. The latter has sixty-three rebel prisoners, chiefly blockade-runners, and many of them men of desperate character. The former is one of our most important forts, and is the only protection for the entrance into the Harbor by way of Long Island Sound. My ag-

gregate force here, present for duty to-day, exclusive of musicians, recruits, and daily and extra duty men, is as follows: . . . 359 Fort Columbus is a general recruiting depot and not under my control. It has the 20th N. Y. Battery, aggregate 101, and 21 of the Vet. Res. Corps. The total for duty is 81; and there are 150 deserters, stragglers, wounded and sick, and over 300 rebel prisoners, to take care of. The public property in the City amounts to many millions of dollars; and there is more disaffection and disloyalty, independent of the elements of mischief and disturbance always here, than in any other city in the Union. I have not men enough to man one tenth part of the guns in the harbor, and not enough to do guard duty properly. A few days ago I was ordered to send a Regiment to Hart's Island to take care of prisoners of war about to be sent there But I have not, as you see, a single Regt left. I have deemed it proper to advise you of the condition of things here. I feel that this want of preparation would be very injurious if known, and it is not easy to conceal it long. Fort Richmond, the most important fortification in the Harbor, is shut up, the 5th U. S. Art.y having not men enough to guard properly the exterior batteries. I feel very uneasy under this state of things, without a force adequate to protect the public property in the City or the important forts in the Harbor. I was at Hart's Island the day before yesterday, where there were 2700 recruits. Of these 750 left for the Army of the Potomac the same day. The residue will go as rapidly as they can be prepared for transportation. In fact under existing arrangements there is no other delay in forwarding recruits than that which is necessary to make out their papers." LS, DNA, RG 108, Letters Received. *O.R.*, I, xliii, part 2, 420–21. On Oct. 24, noon, USG telegraphed to Dix. "I will send you one of the reduced regular regiments from here. By recruiting this it may give you force enough. If it does not you can retain some new regiment of volunteers." ALS (telegram sent), CSmH; telegram received (at 1·00 P.M.), DNA, RG 107, Telegrams Collected (Bound); (marked as sent at 12:30 P.M.) *ibid.*, Telegrams Collected (Unbound). *O.R.*, I, xliii, part 2, 464. On the same day, USG telegraphed to Maj. Gen. George G. Meade. "As soon as ~~possible~~ practicable after Thusday next send one of your reduced regular regiments to New York City to report to Gn. Dix for duty." ALS (telegram sent), MiU-C; telegram received, DNA, RG 393, Army of the Potomac, Cav. Corps, Letters Received. Printed as sent at 3:00 P.M. in *O.R.*, I, xlii, part 3, 316. At 3:00 P.M., Meade telegraphed to USG. "I find the 10th Inft. has present Five officers & one hundred & seventy six enlisted men—This number is so small the Regiment can be sent at once to New York if you desire it.—" ALS (telegram sent), DNA, RG 393, Army of the Potomac, Cav. Corps, Letters Received; copies, *ibid.*, Army of the Potomac, Letters Sent; Meade Papers, PHi. *O.R.*, I, xlii, part 3, 316. On the same day, Lt. Col. Theodore S. Bowers telegraphed to Meade. "order the tenth (10th) U. S. Infantry to proceed to New York City without delay, and report to Maj Gen John. A. Dix. for orders." Telegram received, DNA, RG 94, War Records Office, Army of the Potomac. *O.R.*, I, xlii, part 3, 316. At 7:30 P.M., USG telegraphed to Dix. "If the 7th Infantry is not already on its way here detain it." ALS (telegram sent), CSmH; copies, DLC-USG, V, 45, 70, 107; DNA, RG 107, Telegrams Collected (Unbound); *ibid.*, RG 108, Letters Sent.

On Oct. 31, Bowers telegraphed to Brig. Gen. Seth Williams. "A week ago Gen Halleck informed Gen Grant that the 7th Infantry was on its way here— Several days subsequent Gen Grant authorized Gen Dix to retain the regt until further orders if it had not already left New York—We have heard nothing from it since & do not know whether it is on its way or was detained" Telegram received, *ibid.*, RG 393, Army of the Potomac, Cav. Corps, Letters Received. *O.R.*, I, xlii, part 3, 445. On the same day, USG telegraphed to Meade. "order to New York City at once the Brigade of regular Troops in the 5th Corps." Telegram received, DNA, RG 393, Army of the Potomac, Cav. Corps, Letters Received; copies (2), Meade Papers, PHi. *O.R.*, I, xlii, part 3, 444. See *ibid.*, pp. 447–48.

To Maj. Gen. George G. Meade

City Point, Va. Oct. 24th/64

MAJ. GEN. MEADE,

Your note by the hands of Lieut. Dunn is received. I have felt as much pained as you at the constant stabs made at you by a portion of the public press. I know nothing better to give you to use in answer of to these charges than copies of every dispatch sent to Washington by me in which your name is used. These will show at least that I have never expressed dissatisfaction at any portion of your services.

U. S. GRANT
Lt. Gn.

ALS (telegram sent), OClWHi; telegram received, Meade Papers, PHi. *O.R.*, I, xlii, part 3, 317. On Oct. 24, 1864, Maj. Gen. George G. Meade had written to USG. "With extreme reluctance I find myself compelled to call your attention to the following extracts from an article published in the New York Independent of Oct 13th 1864. 'He is the General (myself) x x x x x; who, in the campaign from the Rapidan to the James under Grant, annulled the genius of his Chief, by his own executive incapacity; who lost the prize of Petersburg by martinet delay on the South bank of the James; who lost it again in succeeding contests by tactical incompetence; who lost it again by inconceivable follies of military administration when the mine was exploded; who insulted his Corps commanders & his Army by attributing to them that inability to cooperate with each other, which was traceable solely to the unmilitary slovenliness of their General; who in a word holds his place by virtue of no personal qualifications, but in deference to a presumed, fictitious, perverted political necessity, and who hangs upon the neck of Genl Grant, like an old man of the sea whom he longs to be rid of, and whom he retains solely in deference to the weak complaisance of his constitutional commander in chief. Be other voices muzzled if they must be, ours at least shall speak out on this question of enforced military subservience to political, to partizan, to personal requisitions.—We, at least, if no others, may declare in the name of a wronged, baffled, indignant army, that its nominal commander is unfit, or unwilling, or incapable to lead it to victory, and we ask that Genl Grants hands may be strengthened by the removal of Meade.' It is not necessary to enquire or surmise what source inspired the foregoing grave bill of indictments—nor would

I trouble you in regard to this matter, if this was the first or only instance in which I have cause to complain of misrepresentation But you are aware, that ever since I have had the honor to serve under your immediate direction, I have been held responsible, for all the acts, which a certain portion of the public press have been pleased to designate as failures or blunders. Indeed the extract now quoted is an admirable summary of the various charges which from time to time have been brought against me. Now these Charges are either true or false in either case, the public and those who are near and dear to me, are entitled to know the facts. In the absence of any published official reports or any official record, to which I can refer, I feel justified in appealing to you and asking as a matter of Justice, and a simple concession to truth, that you will furnish me with such evidence, as will place it in my power, to correct the extra-ordinary misapprehension, into which the Editor of the New York Independent appears to have been led, through some malign influence, the origin of which I am utterly unable to account for.—" LS, DNA, RG 108, Letters Received; ADfS, Meade Papers, PHi. *O.R.*, I, xlii, part 3, 316–17.

On Nov. 4, USG telegraphed to Meade. "Have you got the number of the New York Independent of last week containing an article to which you called my attention?" ALS (telegram sent), OClWHi; copies, DLC-USG, V, 45, 70, 107; DNA, RG 108, Letters Sent. On the same day, Meade wrote to USG. "The article referred to was published in the New Yk Independent of Oct 13th—I have the paper." Copies, *ibid.*, RG 393, Army of the Potomac, Letters Sent; Meade Papers, PHi.

To Maj. Gen. George G. Meade

(Confidential)   City Point Va. Oct. 24th *1864.*
MAJ. GEN. G. G. MEADE,
COMD.G ARMY OF THE POTOMAC,
GENERAL,

Make your preparations to march out at an early hour on the 27th to gain possession of the Southside rail-road, and to hold it, and fortify back to your present left. In commencing your advance move in three columns exactly as proposed by yourself in our conversation of last evening, and with the same force you proposed to take. Park, who starts out nearest to the enemy, should be instructed that if he finds the enemy intrenched, and their works well manned, he is not to attack but confront him and be prepared to advance promptly when he finds that by the movement of the other two columns to the right and rear of them they begin to give way. Take three days rations in Haversacks, Sixty rounds of Ammunition on the person of each soldier, and go as near as possible without wagons or ambulances. It might be well to have say twenty rounds of ammunition per man, with a corresponding amount of Artillery ammunition, in wagons ready to be taken to the army if required.

All the depots on the line of the road should ~~should~~ be cleared of stores, and all wagons, ambulances and Artillery horses not moving with the Army sent back to City Point during the night of the 26th.

I will go out to the left at an early hour of the morning your move commences.

> I am General, very respectfully
> your obt. svt.
> U. S. GRANT
> Lt. Gn.

ALS, deCoppet Collection, NjP. *O.R.*, I, xlii, part 3, 317–18.

On Oct. 24, 1864, 1:00 P.M., Maj. Gen. George G. Meade telegraphed to USG. "Deserters who came in last night reported the enemy mining in front of Fort Steadman—An engineer officer & working party were immediately sent to take the requisite measures for ascertaining if such was the case—I think the report has arisen like many of its predecessors in some precautionary measures of the enemy defensive against our mining. With this exception, I have nothing further to report.—" ALS (telegram sent), DNA, RG 393, Army of the Potomac, Cav. Corps, Letters Received; telegram received (at 2:00 P.M.), *ibid.*, RG 108, Letters Received. *O.R.*, I, xlii, part 3, 315.

On Oct. 25, noon, Meade telegraphed to USG. "I have nothing very important to report this morning. Signal officers yesterday evening and this morning report movements of small bodies of the enemy generally to their right. Deserters confirm the previous statements of the extension of the enemys line of works in their right to Hatchers run & the evidence would seem to indicate this line is completed. Last evening two 2 divisions of the second corps were withdrawn from the lines and are now massed in the rear as reserves." Telegram received (at 12:20 P.M.), DNA, RG 108, Letters Received; copies, *ibid.*, RG 393, Army of the Potomac, Letters Sent; (2) Meade Papers, PHi. *O.R.*, I, xlii, part 3, 337–38.

To Julia Dent Grant

City Point Va. Oct. 24th *1864.*

DEAR JULIA,

I received your letter in relation to buying stocks &c. I have bought and paid for $1500 more of horse rail-road stock, and have bought 500 shares of copper stock at $5 25 per share which I still owe for and have to pay 6 pr. ct. interest on the money until it is all paid up. I shall pay $1.000 at the end of this month. This stock I can now sell at $7 00 per share and expect it to be worth $10 00 within the next three months. I do not want to take any of the proceeds of the sale of Wish-ton Wish. That you can dispose of in your own way. What I am anxious to do and what I am trying to do is to save and invest enough to give us an income of $6000 per year and a home. You would then be independent if anything should happen to me. With that income I would not care a cent to increase and would be perfectly willing that you should spend and give to friends every dollar as it would come in. When Richmond is taken I shall move my Hd Qrs. to Washington and stay most of the time with you in Burlington. I shall stay but very little in Washington. Most of the time I shall be visiting the different armies and when not so engaged will be with you. How anxious I am that this time should come. There has not been one hour since this war commenced that I have been relieved from anxiety. It is to much for one person to bear but I do not see but I bear it very well. My health has not given way in the least. Have you concluded to make me a visit? Love and kisses for you and the children.

ULYS.

ALS, DLC-USG.

To Edwin M. Stanton

(Cipher)   City Point Va. Oct. 25th *1864*. [*4:00* P.M.]
HON. E. M. STANTON SEC. OF WAR WASHINGTON

Your dispatch of 2 P. M. in relation to the organization of a new Army Corps from Veterans who have been discharged the service is received. I do not see any suggestion I can make improving the plan proposed by you. I it will prove a success and give us a body of men equal to any now in service.

U. S. GRANT
Lt. Gn.

ALS (telegram sent), CSmH; telegram received (at 6:00 P.M.), DNA, RG 107, Telegrams Collected (Bound). *O.R.*, I, xlii, part 3, 337. On Oct. 25, 1864, 2:00 P.M., Secretary of War Edwin M. Stanton telegraphed to USG. "I propose to issue the following order for the organization of an extra Army Corps. Please examine & favor me with any suggestions you may have immediately   I want to give ~~the~~ public notice ~~now~~, immediately and hope to raise it by first December. . . . Ordered That an army corps to consist of not less than twenty thousand 20 000 infantry and enlisted for not less than One 1 year to be designated the first 1st Corps shall be organized at Washington, commencing the Organization on Wednesday the 9th day of November and continuing until the first day of December   The privates to consist only of able bodied men who have served honorably not less than two 2 years and therefore not subject to draft. The officers to be commissioned by the President from such as have honorably served not less than two 2 years. The accepted recruits will be refunded their transportation to Washington will be credited to the district in which they or their families are domiciled & will be paid a special bounty of five hundred 500 dollars upon being mustered into service. Each recruit who preserves his arms to the end of his term will have the privilege of retaining them   Details of organization will be prescribed by the Adjutant General. The heads of bureau will detail competent officers for the prompt examination & organization Arming, equiping & supplying the corps   (Cipher) IV Major General Hancock is assigned to the command of the corps when organised." ALS (telegram sent), DNA, RG 107, Telegrams Collected (Bound); telegram received, *ibid.*, Telegrams Collected (Unbound); (at 3:00 P.M.) *ibid.*, RG 108, Letters Received. *O.R.*, I, xlii, part 3, 337.

On Nov. 15, 2:00 P.M., USG telegraphed to Stanton. "Has the order been promulgated yet for the organization of a 1st Army Corps about which you telegraphed me some two weeks ago? If it is to be issued I think it would be advisable to issue it at once." ALS (telegram sent), CSmH; telegram received (at 4:00 P.M.), DNA, RG 107, Telegrams Collected (Bound); *ibid.*, Telegrams Collected (Unbound). *O.R.*, I, xlii, part 3, 619. On Nov. 16, 1:00 P.M., Stanton telegraphed to USG. "The order for raising the new Corps was suspended by the President but will be issued in a day or two as soon as I can effect arrangement with the Secretary of the Treasury" ALS (telegram sent), DNA, RG 107, Telegrams Collected (Bound); telegram received (at 3:00 P.M.), *ibid.*, RG 108, Letters Received. *O.R.*, I, xlii, part 3, 626. See *ibid.*, I, xlii, part 3, 628–29, 728.

To Edwin M. Stanton

(Cipher)   City Point Va. Oct. 25th/64 [4:30 P.M.]
HON. E. M. STANTON, SEC. OF WAR, WASHINGTON

I have no objection to permitting every French subject in the South, or in fact every foreigner no matter what his nationality, pass out North or to their native country by way of City Point. Please so inform the Hon. Sec. of State.

U. S. GRANT

Lt. Gn.

ALS (telegram sent), CSmH; telegram received (at 6:00 P.M.), DNA, RG 107, Telegrams Collected (Bound). *O.R.*, I, xlii, part 3, 336; *ibid.*, III, iv, 806. On Oct. 13, 1864, Asst. Secretary of War Charles A. Dana wrote to USG. "I am directed by the Secretary of War to transmit to you the enclosed copies of communications received by the Department of State from Mr L. de Geofroy, the Chargé d'Affaires of France, and to request you to inform this Department of your views as to the advisability of permitting French subjects residing in the insurrectionary districts of the United States to pass through our lines at City Point, or any other place that may be designated for the purpose by you. The Secretary of War believes that unless the proposed arrangement should be found incompatible with important military considerations, it would be expedient to furnish every proper facility for the withdrawal from the South of the class of persons spoken of in these communications." LS, DNA, RG 108, Letters Received. *O.R.*, III, iv, 779. The enclosures are *ibid.*, pp. 779–81.

To Maj. Gen. Henry W. Halleck

———

(Cipher) City Point Va. Oct. 26th/64 ⌊7:00 P.M.⌋

MAJ. GEN. HALLECK, WASHINGTON

An order with an officer to see it enforced should go to Mo. to send from there all the troops not actually after Price, and guards for public stores, to Gen. Thomas, telegraphing Thomas to know at what points he wants them. Memphis now looks to me as if it was in danger.

U. S. GRANT

Lt. Gn.

ALS (telegram sent), CSmH; telegram received (at 8:15 P.M.), DNA, RG 107, Telegrams Collected (Bound). *O.R.*, I, xli, part 4, 246. On Oct. 27, 1864, noon, Maj. Gen. Henry W. Halleck telegraphed to USG. "Your orders have been transmitted to Genl Rosecrans. I have no staff officer of sufficient rank to send with discretionary instructions as to the particular troops to be withdrawn. Moreover, to withdraw any until the pursuit is well underway may cause Genl Rosecrans to stop it. Genl Canby's orders to him are to pursue with *all* his available force to the Arkansas river, or at least till Price encounters Steele & Reynolds. Neither

Thomas nor Washburne consider Memphis in danger. Thomas says Forrest with about ten thousand men is attempting to cross the Tennessee above Decatur. He thinks that with the forces he now has he will soon be able to clean out West Tennessee & North Alabama   Intercepted despatches from Jeff. Davis, dated at Montgomery Sept 30th renew the orders to Kirby Smith to cross the Mississippi & reenforce Forrest & Hood. Despatches of the 9th & 11th report that the rebel force in Ffront of steele is falling back to Camden & Monroe, probably with a view to crossing the Miss. Canby is fully impressed with the importance of preventing this, and is now probably on the Miss. at Vicksburg or the Mouth of White River. I will probably meet you at City Point on saturday morning on official business." ALS (telegram sent), DNA, RG 107, Telegrams Collected (Bound); telegram received, *ibid.*; *ibid.*, Telegrams Collected (Unbound); *ibid.*, RG 108, Letters Received. *O.R.*, I, xli, part 4, 263.

To Maj. Gen. Benjamin F. Butler

City Point Va. Oct. 26th/64

MAJ. GN. BUTLER,

If you desire an Engineer officer to report either to yourself or one of your Corps Commanders for the present occation I can send either Comstock or Babcock. Please answer.

U. S. GRANT
Lt. Gen.

ALS (telegram sent), OClWHi; copies, DLC-USG, V, 45, 70, 107; DNA, RG 108, Letters Sent. On Oct. 26, 1864, 12:25 P.M., Maj. Gen. Benjamin F. Butler telegraphed to USG. *"Confidential* . . . I take leave to send you a copy of the my orders for the movement to morrow—If you will do me the favor to examine them and see if there is anything you object to, therein, and will notify me, there will be time to change—If you can spare him I should be very glad to have Col Comstock with me to morrow—" LS (telegram sent), *ibid.*, RG 393, Dept. of Va. and N. C., Telegrams Sent (Press). *O.R.*, I, xlii, part 3, 366. The enclosure is *ibid.*, pp. 366–68. On the same day, USG telegraphed to Butler. "Your orders are recd,   They meet the case in hand exactly. Col Comstock has been ordered to report to you." Telegram received (at 2:10 P.M.), DLC-Benjamin F. Butler.

To Maj. Gen. George G. Meade

City Point Va. Oct. 26th/64

MAJ. GEN. MEADE,

Gen. Benham's correspondence for the last few days has been such as to make me distrust his capacity for commanding troops if there should be a raid attempted on this place. I have therefore relieved him and ordered him to report to Gen. Delafield[1] for assignment placing Gen. Patrick temporarily in command of all the troops at this place. You can make your own assignment of commander to the Eng. Brigade.

U. S. GRANT
Lt. Gn.

ALS (telegram sent), OClWHi; copies, DLC-USG, V, 45, 70, 107; DNA, RG 108, Letters Sent. On Oct. 26, 1864, Lt. Col. Theodore S. Bowers issued Special Orders No. 112. "Brig. Gen. H. W. Benham, Commanding Engineer Brigade, Army of the Potomac and Defences of City Point, is hereby relieved from such Commands and from duty with the Army of the Potomac, and will report in person to Brig. Gen. Rich'd. Delafield, Chief of Engineers Washington D. C. for orders. Brig Gen. M. R. Patrick, U. S. Vols., is assigned to the command of the troops and defences of City Point and will immediately assume said Command." Copies, DLC-USG, V, 57, 62, 63, 64, 70. *O.R.*, I, xlii, part 3, 357. On the same day, Maj. Gen. George G. Meade telegraphed to USG. "Dispatch in reference to Gen Benham received. Lt. Col. Spaulding now comdg 50th New York will take command of the Engineers brigade by seniority, as his Col Pettes remains in Washington & the colonelcy of the 15th N. Y. remains vacant. Lt Col Spaulding now comdg 5 is an excellent officer but has not rank enough & it will be difficult to give it to him unless he is made Brig Genl of Volunteers but if an appointment of this kind is to be made I would prefer Duane or Comstock" Telegram received, DNA, RG 108, Letters Received.

Copies of letters from Brig. Gen. Henry W. Benham to Bowers, Oct. 15, 23, 25, are *ibid.*, RG 393, Army of the Potomac, Engineer Brigade, Letters Sent. *O.R.*, I, xlii, part 3, 236–37, 309, 342. On Oct. 26, Bowers wrote to Benham suspending the orders for his relief. Copies, DLC-USG, V, 45, 70, 107; DNA, RG 108, Letters Sent. On Oct. 28, Bowers issued Special Orders No. 113 revoking the orders relieving Benham. Copies, DLC-USG, V, 57, 62, 63, 64, 70. *O.R.*, I, xlii, part 3, 409.

1. Richard Delafield, born in 1798 in New York City, USMA 1818, served twice as superintendent, USMA (1838–45, 1856–61), including the period of USG's cadetship. Always serving in the Corps of Engineers, he was appointed brig. gen., chief of engineers, as of April 22, 1864.

To Maj. Gen. George G. Meade

City Point Va. Oct. 26th 1864 [*2:30* P.M.]

MAJ. GN. MEADE,

Your orders for to-morrow have been received and read. The only point on which I would suggest a change is in regard to Park's movements. If he finds the enemy's fortifications in good defensible condition & manned I think he should only confront them until the movement of the other two corps had its effect.

U. S. GRANT
Lt. Gen.

ALS (telegram sent), CSmH; copies, DLC-USG, V, 45, 70, 107; DNA, RG 108, Letters Sent; (2) Meade Papers, PHi. *O.R.*, I, xlii, part 3, *355.* On Oct. 26, 1864, 7:30 P.M., Maj. Gen. George G. Meade telegraphed to USG. "The orders for tomorrow intend that Parke should act in the manner you suggest—that is to say, he will not attack if he finds the enemy in such position & force as renders it injudicious to do so, but as his movement is to be made at day light or just before he will have to make a partal attack to ascertain the exact condition of affairs unless he waits unless he waits until after day light and if he does I am quite sure he will have no chance" Telegram received, DNA, RG 108, Letters Received; copies, *ibid.*, RG 393, Army of the Potomac, Letters Sent; (2) Meade Papers, PHi. *O.R.*, I, xlii, part 3, *355.*

At 9:00 A.M., Meade had telegraphed to USG. "A scouting party sent out by Gen Gregg, down the norfolk RR. captured some scouts of the enemy & brought in a Mr. Heath a Magistrate who has been very active in conscripting for the Rebel army   They also captured at Disputanta a large number of telegraphic dispatches showing the enemy have been taking off the dispatches from the wire running down the river. I send by orderly a few of these despatches containing information of use to the enemy & would suggest some caution being Given to subordinate officers not putting these telegrams in cipher. All these dispatches have been sent to the Pro. Mar. Gen   Six deserters came in last night   have no changes or anything new to report" Telegram received, DNA, RG 108, Letters Received; copies, *ibid.*, RG 393, Army of the Potomac, Letters Sent; (2) Meade Papers, PHi. Printed as sent at 10:00 A.M. in *O.R.*, I, xlii, part 3, *354–55.*

To Julia Dent Grant

City Point Va. Oct. 26th *186[4]*

DEAR JULIA,

To-morrow a great battle will probably be fought. At all events I have made all the arrangements for one and unless I conclude through the day to change my programme it will take place. I do not like to predict results therefore will say nothing about what I expect to accomplish. The cake you sent by Mr. Smith[1] come to hand but the other you speak of having sent by Express has not. In one of your letters you ask if I accepted the house in Chicago? I did not accept or decline. I stated that I had no disposition to give up Ill. as my place of residence but the probability being that my duties hereafter would keep me most of the time in the East I had selected Phila as a place where my children could have the benefit of good schools and I could expect often to visit my family. If they were in Chicago I could not expect to see them often.[2] I have heard nothing further since.

All are well here. Rawlins appears to have entirely recovered. Shall I have Little Rebel sent to you? If you had him you could get a little buggy and sleigh expressly for him and the children could then ride as much as they pleased. I expect when this campaign ends to send all my horses home and stay there most of the time myself when I am not visiting the different Armies. I do wish I could tell when that would be.—Love and kisses for you and the children.

ULYS.

ALS, DLC-USG.

1. See letter to Julia Dent Grant, Oct. 20, 1864.
2. See letter to J. Russell Jones, Oct. 4, 1864.

To Edwin M. Stanton

(Cipher)   City Pt. Va. Oct. 27th *1864*. 9 p. m.
HON. E. M. STANTON SEC. OF WAR, WASHINGTON

I have just returned from the crossing of the Boydtown plank road with Hatcher's Creek. Our line now extends from its former left to Armstrongs Mill thence by the South bank of Hatchers Creek to the point above named. At every point the enemy was found intrenched and his works manned. No attack was made during the day further than to drive pickets and the cavalry inside of the main works. Our casualties have been light probably less than

200 killed wounded & missing. The same probably is true with the enemy. We captured however seven loaded teams on their way from Stoney Creek to the enemy about a dozen beef cattle & a traveling forge and seventy-five to one hundred prisoners. On our right Gen. Butler extended around well towards the Yorktown road without finding a point unguarded. I shall keep our troops out where they are until towards noon to-morrow in hope of inviting an attack.—This reconnoisance, which I had intended it for more, points out to me what is to be done.

U. S. GRANT
Lt. Gn.

ALS (telegram sent), CSmH; telegram received (on Oct. 28, 1864, 5:00 P.M.), DNA, RG 107, Telegrams Collected (Bound); (incomplete) *ibid.*; (2) *ibid.*, Telegrams Collected (Unbound). *O.R.*, I, xlii, part 1, 22–23; (printed as received on Oct. 28, 2:00 A.M.) *ibid.*, I, xlii, part 3, 373.

To Edwin M. Stanton

City Point, Va, Oct. 27th/64 [*9:00* P.M.]

HON. E. M. STANTON SEC. OF WAR WASHINGTON.

I have frequently before found that newspaper authority was not reliable. I am very glad that Custer[1] has been Breveted and Crook made a full Maj. General. I could not believe the papers therefore asked if it was possible that Crook had been overlooked.

U. S. GRANT
Lt. Gn.

ALS (telegram sent), CSmH; telegram received (on Oct. 28, 1864, 5:00 P.M.), DNA, RG 107, Telegrams Collected (Bound). *O.R.*, I, xliii, part 2, 474. On Oct. 26, 8:30 P.M., USG telegraphed to Maj. Gen. Henry W. Halleck. "The papers announce that Custer has been made a Maj. General. Is it possible he has been made a full Major General & Crook who commands a Dept. left only a Major Gn. by Brevet?" ALS (telegram sent—misdated Nov. 26), CSmH; telegram received (at 9:00 P.M.), DNA, RG 107, Telegrams Collected (Bound). *O.R.*, I, xliii, part 2, 467. At 10:30 P.M., Secretary of War Edwin M. Stanton telegraphed to USG. "Crook was appointed a full Major General immediately upon the vacancy created by General Birneys death. Custar was made a *brevet* Major General upon the urgent and repeated solicitation of General Sheridan. The newspapers are not good authority for the action of the Department." ALS (telegram sent), DNA, RG 107, Telegrams Collected (Bound); telegrams received (2), *ibid.*, Telegrams Collected (Unbound); *ibid.*, RG 108, Letters Received. *O.R.*, I, xliii, part 2, 467.

1. George A. Custer, born in 1839 in New Rumley, Ohio, USMA 1861, fought at the first battle of Bull Run as 2nd lt., 2nd Cav., served on the staff of Maj. Gen. George B. McClellan, then as 1st lt., 5th Cav. Appointed brig. gen. as of June 29, 1863, he began to gain fame as a flamboyant commander of cav. Commander of the 3rd Div., Cav. Corps, under Maj. Gen. Philip H. Sheridan, he was appointed bvt. maj. gen. of vols. as of Oct. 19, 1864, for services at the battles of Winchester and Fisher's Hill.

To Edwin M. Stanton

(Cipher) ~~Office of Chief Quartermaster~~,
Armies Operating Against Richmond, Va.,
Oct. 27th 11 p. m. *1864.* 11.30 p. m.

Hon. E. M. Stanton, Sec. of War, Washington,

Your dispatch of 11 a. m. this date is just received. Troops are now very much extended but if possible I will give the furloughs you ask. Will telegraph you again in the course of the day tomorrow.

U. S. Grant
Lt. Gn.

ALS (telegram sent), CSmH; telegram received (on Oct. 28, 1864, 6:00 p.m.), DNA, RG 107, Telegrams Collected (Bound). On Oct. 27, 11:00 a.m., Secretary of War Edwin M. Stanton telegraphed to USG. "The first, third, and fourth regiments of Delaware Volunteers are now near Petersburg—two of them numbering about one hundred each—one numbering about four hundred. They are in the Fifth Corps. The vote of the State will depend on them. If it be possible, please give them leave of absence to go home for the election. One transport can carry them to Baltimore, and they can return the day after the election. Let me know immediately if you can spare them." LS (telegram sent), *ibid.*; telegram received, *ibid.*, RG 108, Letters Received. On Nov. 1, USG telegraphed to Maj. Gen. George G. Meade. "Send the 1st 3d & 4th regiments of Del. Volunteers to Washington at once. These regiments will be returned in ten days." ALS (telegram sent), OClWHi; telegram received, DNA, RG 393, Army of the Potomac, Cav. Corps, Letters Received. *O.R.*, I, xlii, part 3, 471. On the same day, 7:00 p.m., USG telegraphed to Stanton. "I have ordered three Del. regiments to Washington from which place the can be furloughed. I would like to have the furloughs of these regiments made as short as possible." ALS (telegram sent), OClWHi; telegram received (at 10:45 p.m.), DNA, RG 107, Telegrams Collected (Bound). *O.R.*, I, xlii, part 3, 471. See *ibid.*, p. 492.

To Maj. Gen. Henry W. Halleck

(Cipher) City Point, Va. Oct. 27th/64 [*9:00* P.M.]
MAJ. GN. HALLECK, WASHINGTON

Now that Price is on the retreat, without a probability of his bringing up again, Rosecrans should forward all the troops he can to Thomas. This ought to be done without delay. He has 6 or 8 thousand troops around St. Louis and withi[n] a few hours travel of it that can start at once.

U. S. GRANT
Lt. Gn.

ALS (telegram sent), CSmH; telegram received (on Oct. 28, 1864, 6:00 P.M.), DNA, RG 107, Telegrams Collected (Bound); *ibid.*, Telegrams Collected (Unbound). *O.R.*, I, xli, part 4, 263.

On Oct. 31, 3:00 P.M., Maj. Gen. Henry W. Halleck telegraphed to USG. "Telegram just recieved from Genl Curtis states that Genl Rosecrans has recalled his troops from the pursuit of Price. This is contrary to repeated orders. I have just telegraphed that the pursuit *must* be continued." ALS (telegram sent), DNA, RG 107, Telegrams Collected (Bound); telegram received, *ibid.*; (at 3:30 P.M.) *ibid.*, RG 108, Letters Received. *O.R.*, I, xli, part 4, 337.

On Nov. 4, 12:30 P.M., Halleck telegraphed to USG. "I think from present appearances that Price's affair will be over in the course of the next ten days & that Reynolds troops can then be withdrawn from Arkansas. Steeles effective force is now about twenty thousand. Sherman thinks that a movement from the Miss. River toward Selma cutting the Mobile & Ohio R. R. by which Beauregard's army is now supplied will be more advantageous to him than any operations on the coast. If you are of the same opinion Genl Canby's instructions should be to that effect. For the present I think all of Canby's efforts should be directed to prevent Kirby Smith from sending the intended reenforcements across the river to assist Beauregard & Hood against Thomas." ALS (telegram sent), DNA, RG 107, Telegrams Collected (Bound); telegram received, *ibid.*; (marked as sent on Nov. 5, 1:00 P.M., received at 11:30 P.M.) *ibid.*, RG 108, Letters Received. *O.R.*, I, xli, part 4, 424.

To Maj. Gen. Benjamin F. Butler

Clemens House Oct 27th *1864*, 9 o'clock, A. M.
MAJ. GN. BUTLER, AIKINS HOUSE. The movements at this end have not yet resulted in anything more than a little skirmishing and forcing the enemy back towards their lines. The 2d Corps &

the Cavalry have forced the crossing of Hatcher's run and are moving west. The 9th Corps confront the enemy in their works North of Hatchers run. The 5th Corps is moving between the 2d & 9th Corps.

How are you progressing on the right.

U. S. GRANT
Lt. Gn.

ALS (telegram sent), OClWHi; telegram received, DNA, RG 107, Telegrams Collected (Unbound); *ibid.*, RG 393, Army of the Potomac, Cav. Corps, Letters Received. *O.R.*, I, xlii, part 3, 390. On Oct. 27, 1864, 9:30 A.M., Maj. Gen. Benjamin F. Butler, "Near Darbyton Road," telegraphed to USG. "Terry has advanced to Daby Road driving in the Enemys Pickets Weitzel colum was on Darby Road at 8 o clock where it Joins Drill River Road In time and where he ought to be—All going on well" ALS (telegram sent), DNA, RG 107, Telegrams Collected (Unbound); telegram received, *ibid.*, RG 94, War Records Office, Dept. of Va. and N. C., Army of the James, Unentered Papers. *O.R.*, I, xlii, part 3, 390.

To Maj. Gen. Benjamin F. Butler

5.40 p m [*Oct. 27, 1864*]

GEN. BUTLER,

The result on the left has been to find the enemy as far as we have extended to the left. Our troops are now eight miles West of the Weldon rail-road from which point I have just returned. Your dispatch of 3.30 is only just rec'd to late to direct an attack. Hold on where you are for the present.

U. S. GRANT
Lt. Gen

ALS (telegram sent), OClWHi; telegram received, DNA, RG 107, Telegrams Collected (Unbound); (at 5:50 P.M.) *ibid.*, RG 393, Army of the Potomac, Cav. Corps, Letters Received. *O.R.*, I, xlii, part 3, 390–91. On Oct. 27, 1864, 3:10 P.M., Maj. Gen. Benjamin F. Butler, Darbytown, telegraphed to USG. "We have driven in the pickets of the Enemy by Terry as far as Charles City Road. Weitzel has reached at one forty 140 P M the exterior lines on the Williams burgh Road and finds Fields dvision in his front He is going to the right as far as Yorktown Rail road to see where the Enemys right rests. Fields right rested this morning near the Darby town road He has extended therefore four miles Shall I make a trial on this out streched line Casualties few as yet." ALS (telegram sent), DNA, RG 107, Telegrams Collected (Unbound); telegram received, *ibid.*; *ibid.*, RG 108, Letters Received. *O.R.*, I, xlii, part 3, 390.

To Maj. Gen. Benjamin F. Butler

City Point Va. Oct. 27th *1864.*

Maj. Gen. Butler,

I have no special orders further than to direct that your troops keep as near all they now hold as they can favorably to receiving an attack If the enemy can be induced to do such a thing. You need not make any further advance however unless it be in following up a repulse of the enemy. The enemy is now so extended that he must be very weak in the middle. If it was possible to get a force together for the purpose I would try an attack in the morning south of Bakehouse Creek.

U. S. Grant
Lt. Gn.

ALS (telegram sent), OClWHi; telegram received, DNA, RG 393, Army of the Potomac, Cav. Corps, Letters Received. *O.R.,* I, xlii, part 3, 391. On Oct. 27, 1864, Maj. Gen. Benjamin F. Butler, "Near NewMarket Road," telegraphed to USG. "We have not been able to turn the Enemies ~~right~~ left although Weizel has demonstrated to the left of the Williams burg Road   I have therefore ordered him back to the Charles City Road sent one division in the line between darbytown and Charles City and massed two division ~~refused~~ with Cavalry to hold to Whiteoak Swamp. Terry holds from Darby town to our intrenched lines on the NewMarket Roads   Have you any orders"   ALS (telegram sent), DNA, RG 107, Telegrams Collected (Unbound); telegram received, *ibid.,* RG 108, Letters Received. *O.R.,* I, xlii, part 3, 391.

On Oct. 28, 8:40 [A.M.], USG telegraphed to Butler. "You may withdraw your troops to their former position   the some thing is being done on the left." Telegram received, DLC-Benjamin F. Butler; copies, DLC-USG, V, 45, 70, 107; DNA, RG 108, Letters Sent. *O.R.,* I, xlii, part 3, 417. At 9:15 A.M., Butler, "Atlee Farm Near Darby Road," telegraphed to USG. "Dispatch directing with drawal of troops recievd   Orders have been issued"   ALS (telegram sent), DNA, RG 107, Telegrams Collected (Unbound); telegram received, *ibid.,* RG 108, Letters Received. *O.R.,* I, xlii, part 3, 417.

To Maj. Gen. George G. Meade

City Point Va. Oct. 27th/64 12 Midnight

Maj. Gen. Meade,

Your dispatch with those from Hancock just received. Now that the enemy have taken to attacking I regret the necessity of withdrawing but see the cogency of your reasoning. If ammunition could have been taken up on pack animals it might have enabled us after all to have gained the end we started out for. The enemy attacking rather indicates that he has been touched on a weak point. Do not change however the directions you have given.

U. S. GRANT

Lt. Gen.

ALS (telegram sent), OClWHi; copies, DLC-USG, V, 45, 70, 107; DNA, RG 108, Letters Sent; (2) Meade Papers, PHi. *O.R.*, I, xlii, part 3, 374. On Oct. 27, 1864, 9:00 P.M., Maj. Gen. George G. Meade telegraphed to USG. "I forward a despatch just recd from Maj Gen Hancock by which you will see he has concluded to withdraw in which opinion I fully concur as I doubt the practicalbilty of supplying him with ammunition & re inforcing him in time tomorrow. Besides were this practicable it would be a simple matter for the enemy re cross a part of their force over ha Hatchers Run and attack my weakened right wing, my wings being seperated by more than six miles whereas they have less than two to move from one point to the other   after Hancock has re-crossed I will tomorrow leisurely withdraw to our entrenchments and if the enemy is disposed to Come out of his lines and attack on this side I will give him battle. Gen Hancock claims a decided success having repulsed all the enemys attacks and made many prisoners. He regrets the necessity of withdrawing but places it on the difficulty of being in time re-inforced and supplied in the ammunition." Telegram received, DNA, RG 108, Letters Received; copies, *ibid.*, RG 393, Army of the Potomac, Letters Sent; (2) Meade Papers, PHi. Printed as sent at 11:15 P.M. in *O.R.*, I, xlii, part 3, 374. The enclosure is *ibid.*, p. 382.

At 8:00 P.M., Meade had telegraphed to USG. "Soon after we left Maj Genl Hancock he made his preperations and was about ~~assaulting~~ assaulting the bridge over the Boydtown plank road in his front when he received a heavy attack on his right and rear. The enemy having crossed Hatchers run & ~~de~~ advanced through the roads between his position and Crawfords, Brig Genl Egan comdg the Division immediately desisted from his assault in his front and turning met the advancing enemy. At the same time Mott on the left was assaulted and Gregg in the rear. From that time till dark the fighting was sharp and severe with varying results. at dark, Gen Hancock maintained his position in the open ground though he was obliged to yield the advanced line he held near the bridge to meet the direction of the attack on his right. Mott also was driven in to the plank road but Gregg maintained his position staidly covering the left ~~near~~ rear. Hancock lost a number of prisoners on the skirmish line in the Early part of the action but took several hundred during the fight probably more than he lost. At one time two piece of his artillery were given up but soon re-taken as soon as troops could be collected for the purpose. on the whole I should judge from the reports of Staff officers in the adsence of any despatches that Gen Hancock made a glorious fight and although having to yield some ground punished the enemy severely. In accordance with your instructions he was directed to withdraw tomorrow morning but since receiving the above intelligence I have notified him I could send ayers division to reinforce him and if the condition of his command and other circumstances justified it I wished him to hold on tomorrow but if in his judgement it was more Judicious to withdraw he could do so tonight. One difficulty in his remining is the want of ammunition his train not having accompanied him and the continuous fighting having nearly exhausted the sixty (60) rounds carried on the mens persons. The defile communicating with him will be so filled with troops going to him and ambulances returning that it would be difficult if not impossible to Supply him tonight. Crawford moved up the run after driving in their skirmishers & confronted the enemy on its bank but owing to the very dense thicket through which he had to move and the slashed timber in the run did not succeed in finding a practicable place to attack. He consulted however with Griffin on this fault. Griffin after minutely examining the enemy position on this side found him so Strongly entrenched he deemed it useless to attempt to carry any part of the line. so soon as I hear from Genl Hancock I will advise you ~~if~~ of what it is prosposed to do tomorrow. I have no return of causaulties but have reason to believe Hancocks losses have been severe. On this side the medical ~~dir~~ Director estimates the wounded of the 5th and 9th corps at about two hundred (200)." Telegram received, DNA, RG 108, Letters Received; copies, *ibid.*, RG 393, Army of the Potomac, Letters Sent; (2) Meade Papers, PHi. Printed as sent at 10:50 P.M. in *O.R.*, I, xlii, part 3, 373–74.

Also on Oct. 27, USG telegraphed to Brig. Gen. Nelson A. Miles. "Can you tell me what the heavy firing now heard is?" ALS (telegram sent), OClWHi; copies, DLC-USG, V, 45, 70, 107; DNA, RG 108, Letters Sent. On Oct. 28, 4:30 A.M., Meade telegraphed to USG. "The following despatch ~~was~~ received during the night is forwarded for your information—Genl. Miles has been directed to send the prisoners mentioned to City Point.—" ALS (telegram sent), *ibid.*, RG 107, Telegrams Collected (Unbound); telegram received (at 4:30 A.M.), *ibid.*, RG 108, Letters Received. *O.R.*, I, xlii, part 3, 402.

To Edwin M. Stanton

City Point
9 a m Oct 28 1864

Hon E M Stanton
Sec'y of War

The enemy attacked our left (Hancock) last evening with great vigor—

I cannot give the results yet though the fight was sanguinary on both sides and resulted in a considerable number of captures—

Genl H thinks he captured more prisoners than he lost—I will try to give you full particulars during the day

U S Grant
Lt Genl

Telegram received (at 6:00 P.M.), DNA, RG 107, Telegrams Collected (Bound); *ibid.*, Telegrams Collected (Unbound); copy, *ibid.*, Telegrams Received in Cipher. *O.R.*, I, xlii, part 1, 23; *ibid.*, I, xlii, part 3, 401.

To Edwin M. Stanton

City Point
Oct 28th 1864

HON E M STANTON
SEC'Y OF WAR

The attack on Genl Hancock now that a report is received proves to be a decided success—He repulsed the enemy and remained in his position holding possession of the field until midnight when he commenced with-drawing—Orders had been given for the with-drawal of the 2nd Corps before the attack was made— We lost no prisoners except the usual stragglers who are always picked up—Our captures for the day on the south side foots up 910—The rebel Genl Dearing[1] is reported killed—Genl Meade in his report says "I am induced to believe the success of the operation which was most decided was mainly due to the personal exertions of Maj Gen Hancock and the conspicuous gallantry of Brig Genl Eagan[2]

U S GRANT
Lt Genl

Telegrams received (2—at 6:20 P.M.), DNA, RG 107, Telegrams Collected (Bound); *ibid.*, Telegrams Collected (Unbound); copies, *ibid.*, RG 108, Letters Sent; DLC-USG, V, 45, 70, 107. *O.R.*, I, xlii, part 1, 23; *ibid.*, I, xlii, part 3, 402.

1. James Dearing, born in 1840 in Campbell County, Va., resigned from USMA in 1861 to fight for the South. In Oct., 1864, he commanded a brigade of cav., Maj. Gen. William H. F. Lee's Div., under Maj. Gen. Wade Hampton. *Ibid.*, p. 1192. The report of his death was incorrect.

2. Thomas W. Egan, born in 1834 in N. Y., was appointed lt. col., 40th N. Y., as of July 1, 1861, and rose to brig. gen. as of Sept. 3, 1864. He was later appointed bvt. maj. gen. as of Oct. 27, 1864, for his services at the battle of Boydton Plank Road.

To Maj. Gen. George G. Meade

By Telegraph from City Point
Dated Oct 28 *1864.*

To MAJ GEN MEADE

From your dispatch of Last night It seems the enemy crossed Hatchers run below Hancock Position. where was crawford during this time—If he had followed your repeated instructions to warren this could not have happened—Even after Hancock was attacked, crawford must have been in a position where by boldly pushing up he could have annihilated all of the enemys south of the run—there may be an explanation for all this or I may misunderstand what did occur—Before telegraphing to washington the particulars of yesterdays operations I would like a partial report—

U. S. GRANT
Lt. Gen

Telegram received, DNA, RG 393, Army of the Potomac, Cav. Corps, Letters Received; copies (2), Meade Papers, PHi. *O.R.*, I, xlii, part 3, 402–3. On Oct. 28, 1864, 11:00 A.M., Maj. Gen. George G. Meade twice telegraphed to USG. "Hancocks command & Crawfords Division had recrossed Hatchers run by 7. a m—I have directed Maj. Genls. Warren & Parke to remain in position sufficiently long, to send all impedimenta to the rear & collect stragglers & then to with draw leisurely to their former positions in our entrenched lines—I find my despatch of yesterday evening requires some modification—Maj. Genl. Hancock did not substantially yield any ground—he held the Boydtown plank road bridge till midnight—He is also unaware of the loss of any prisoners—except the usual stragglers scattered in the woods whom it was impossible to collect—He was compelled for want of transportation to leave a number of his most severely wounded—These were carefully collected & placed in the houses on the field, & surgeons with supplies left with them—The whole number of prisoners reported to the P. M. Genl up to this time is 689—these are exclusive of 200 turned over by the 2d corps to the cavalry not yet brought in, & 21 sent to City Point by Brig Genl. Miles—Prisoners report the death of Maj. Genl. Dearing—I am induced to believe, the success of the operation, which was most decided, was mainly due to the personal exertions of Maj Genl Hancock, and the conspicuous gallantry of Maj Genl Egan.—" "Your despatch in relation to Genl—Crawfords movements is received—The enquiry you make is quite natural, but I judge from all I can learn, the difficulty of Crawfords reaching the scene of action in time was two fold—first the character of the country, represented as worse than the Wilderness and secondly the fact that Crawford was at that time engaged with the enemy, and trying to get across the run to take the line confronting Griffin in reserve—The distance between Hancock & Crawford was also owing to a bend in the stream greater than was at first supposed—no connection between the two having been made as was erroneously reported.—You may perhaps remember hearing just before we left Hancock severe sharp & continued musketry firing—this was Crawford—again when I spoke of the enemys crossing the run on Hancock's right, I referred to their coming through that piece of woods, which if you remember we stopped on the edge of, for a little while before we left—Indeed I am now satisfied, if we had continued on the road we started on, much longer, we should have struck the enemy—When I first heard of the attack on Hancock, Genl Warren had just returned from Crawford & so well satisfied were we both that Crawford could not get to him in time, that I immediately started Ayres to move up the road from Armstrongs mill, but it was then so late that it was dark by the time Ayres had crossed the run at Armstrongs & I accordingly halted him to hear from Hancock—I am of the popinion that Crawfords position & movements, were of essential value to Hancock by keeping in check a considerable force of the enemy, who would otherwise have not only joined in the attack but cut off the road communicating with him—This explanation will I trust relieve your mind of any impression unfavorable to Genl. Crawford, who I really believe, was disposed to do all in his power—There is no doubt now it would have been better, if Crawford had been sent at once to Hancock by the road we took—but in ignorance of the distance either that Hancock would have to go, or had gone in sending Crawford to Hancocks support, I directed he should move up the bank of the stream, with the hope that in co-operation with Griffin we might dislodge the enemy from the line of works he occupied resting on the runs —The character of the country caused delay in Crawfords progress, and his subsequently striking the enemy, for he found him on the right bank of the stream, and had to drive ~~him~~ his skirmishers across—When he had done so he found the passage of the stream obstructed by felled timber & the enemy posted on the other side He then made efforts to find a practicable place for assaulting & was engaged in this & connecting with Griffin on the other side below the enemys line when Hancock was attacked.—The special report required will be made at once— ~~d~~Do you wish it in writing or by telegraph?—" ALS (telegrams sent), DNA, RG 393, Army of the Potomac, Cav. Corps, Letters Received; telegrams received, *ibid.*, RG 108, Letters Received. *O.R.*, I, xlii, part 3, 403, 404. On the same day, USG telegraphed to Meade. "All I want is about the general result of the operations of yesterday, by telegraph, so that I can send a dispatch to Washington." ALS (telegram sent), OClWHi; telegram received, DNA, RG 393, Army of the Potomac, Cav. Corps, Letters Received. *O.R.*, I, xlii, part 3, 404. On the same day, Meade telegraphed to Lt. Col. Theodore S. Bowers a lengthy report of the events of the previous day. ALS (telegram sent), DNA, RG 393, Army of the Potomac, Cav. Corps, Letters Received; copy, Meade Papers, PHi. *O.R.*, I, xlii, part 1, 35–37; *ibid.*, I, xlii, part 3, 404–6.

On Oct. 29, 1:00 P.M. (sent at 1:20 P.M.), Meade telegraphed to USG. "The different corps of the army engaged in the recent reconnaissance returned yesterday afternoon to their several positions—since which all is quiet—Late in the morning small bodies of the enemys cavalry appeared & followed the withdrawal evidently simply as observers.—Signal officers reported at intervals during the afternoon the return of ~~of~~ bodies of the enemy to their lines & towards Petersburgh.—I forward a despatch received at 12 M today from Maj. Genl—Hancock" ALS (telegram sent), DNA, RG 393, Army of the Potomac, Cav. Corps, Letters Received; telegram received, *ibid.*, RG 108, Letters Received. *O.R.*, I, xlii, part 3, 423. The enclosure is *ibid.*

On Oct. 30, 11:00 A.M., Meade telegraphed to USG. "I have nothing par-

ticular to report to day.—If you are going to be at home I will come down to City
Point.—" ALS (telegram sent), DNA, RG 393, Army of the Potomac, Cav.
Corps, Letters Received; copies, *ibid.*, Army of the Potomac, Letters Sent; Meade
Papers, PHi. *O.R.*, I, xlii, part 3, 435.

On Oct. 31, 2:00 P.M. (sent at 2:40 P.M.), Meade telegraphed to USG.
"About 8. P. M last evening the enemy made a dash on the picket line of the 2d
corps west of the Plank road—They were quickly repulsed & the line re-
established—Maj. Genl. Hancock reports about 60 men lost as his causualties.—
I forward you a despatch just received from Maj. Genl. Hancock in relation to
the affair of the 27th inst—Genl—Hancock does not mention in it that the bridge
was held till after midnight & that two regiments of his command remained in
possession of the field till after 8. oclok the next morning, when they withdrew
followed by a force of the enemys cavalry." ALS (telegram sent), DNA, RG
393, Army of the Potomac, Cav. Corps, Letters Received; telegram received, *ibid.*,
RG 108, Letters Received. *O.R.*, I, xlii, part 3, 444. The enclosure is *ibid.*, p.
448. On Nov. 1, 4:00 P.M., USG telegraphed to Maj. Gen. Henry W. Halleck
transmitting Meade's telegram. Telegram received (at 11:00 P.M.), DNA, RG
107, Telegrams Collected (Bound).

To Julia Dent Grant

City Point, Va. Oct. 28th *1864.*

DEAR JULIA,

I have just rec'd letters from Mr. Morris & Mrs. Hillyer telling
me that you had gone to St. Louis. I hope you will find your father
improved and feel no doubt but you will from the last news I heard
from there. Whils[t] you are aut see if Sappington has commenced
suit to get that rascal White off the farm. I do want to see him
ousted. You may tell Ford to ship Little Rebel to you in Burlington. I wrote to you about that but presume the letter had not reached
Burlington before you left. I will write to Buck as present head of
the family to-morrow. Next time I will write to Missy & Jess in
answer to the letter Jess did not write.—Give my love to all at your
fathers and also remember me to Dr. & Mrs. Barrett. I have no
special news to write. The battle which we had yesterday resulted
much in our favor back of Petersburg but North of the James
Gen. Butler lost I fear much more than the enemy did. I will work
this thing all out right yet. It is about the last of the Confederacy
however when Richmond is gone and knowing this they will hold
on desperately. You will find that Fred. knows just as much about

traveling as most of grown people. You do not want any better escort than he is. Love and kisses.

ULYS.

ALS, DLC-USG.

To Brig. Gen. John A. Rawlins

City Point, Va. Oct. 29th *1864.*

BRIG. GEN. J. A. RAWLINS,
CHIEF OF STAFF,
GENERAL,

The ~~importance~~ necessity of reinforcing the Armies actually confronting the principle Armies of the enemy, Lee's & Beaurigard's, is of such vital importance that you are selected to go West as bearer of orders intended to accomplish this end. Your position as "Chief of Staff" makes it proper to entrust you with authority to issue orders in the name of the "~~Gen. in Chief~~" "Lieut General" to further the object of your mission. Now that Price is retreating from Missouri it is believed that the whole force sent to that state from other Departments can be spared at once. The fact however that a conciderable force is pursuing ~~p~~Price, and may go so far that some time may elapse before they can be returned to Missouri and be distributed for the proper protection of the state, has induced me to make two separate orders, one for the withdrawel only of the command of Maj. Gn. A. J. Smith, the other embracing also the command of Maj. Gen. Mower. You will deliver which ever of these orders you deem best, or in case of doubt telegraph to these Hd Qrs. for instructions. The destination of troops withdrawn will depend on circumstances. If it is found that the enemy under Hood or Beaurigard have actually attempted an invasion of Tennessee, or those under Forrest are approaching the Ohio River, you will send them directly to Maj. Gn. Thomas to confront and frustrate such movement. Under other circumstances they will be sent to join this Army. The aim will be to get all the troops possible, especially veterans, with the Armies operating against Richmond. Gen.

Sherman will be instructed that no force except that already South of the Tennessee, and such as Gn. Canby can send, will be used between the Tenn. River and the Atlantic & the Gulf of Mexico. If he goes South and draws Hood after him he must take care of himself without the support of a pursuing column. I am satisfied on full and mature reflection that Sherman's idea of striking across for the sea coast is the best way to rid Ten. & Ky. of threatened danger and to make the war felt. I do not believe that Gen. Sherman can maintain his communications with Atlanta with his whole force. He can break up such an extent of roads that the enemy will be effectually cut in two for several months by which time Augusta & Savannah can be occupied. Augusta cuts the same line of road that Atlanta does with the advantage of water communication with the Atlantic. This also has the advantage of cutting the Southern line of railroads as well as the Central.

You will remain in Missouri until all the troops ordered from there are actually in motion. If in your judgement any other troops than those mentioned in orders can be spared from there you will telegraph the fact here and orders will be given for their removal.

Being all the time in telegraphic communication with Hd Qrs. you will communicate regularly and ask for such instructions as suggest themselves to you from time to time.

I am General, very respectfully your obt. svt.

U. S. GRANT

Lt. Gn.

ALS, USG 3. *O.R.*, I, xli, part 4, 305–6. On Oct. 29, 1864, Lt. Col. Theodore S. Bowers issued Special Orders No. 114. ". . . III   Maj. Gen. W. S. Rosecrans, commd'g. Department of the Missouri, will at once order Maj. Gen. A. J. Smith, with his entire Command, to proceed immediately by rail road or by marching, which ever is most practicable, to the nearest point for river transportation, and there embark and forward them with all possible dispatch, to report to Maj. Gen. G. H. Thomas, Commd'g. Army and Department of the Cumberland. An immediate & prompt compliance with this order is required: IV. Maj. Gen. W. S. Rosecrans, commd'g. Department of the Missouri, will at once order Maj. Gen J. A. Mower, with his entire Command, to proceed immediately by rail road or by marching, which ever is most practicable, to the nearest point for river transportation, and there embark and forward them with all possible dispatch to report to Maj. Gen. G. H. Thomas, commanding Army and Department of the Cumberland. An immediate and prompt compliance with this order, is required.

V. Brig. Gen. John A. Rawlins, Chief of Staff, will, under written instructions from the Lieutenant General Commanding, proceed to the Head Quarters of Maj. Gen. W. S. Rosecrans, Commanding Department of the Missouri, and to such other points, as he may deem necessary to the execution of his instructions. He will remain in the Department of the Missouri until the order or orders entrusted to him for Maj. Gen. Rosecrans are complied with and his instructions executed; and should he deem it necessary is authorized as Chief of Staff, to issue, by Command of the Lieutenant General such orders, as will secure the carrying out of the instructions he has received or may receive. The orders he is hereby, or by his instructions authorized to issue may be directed to Maj. Gen. Rosecrans, or to the officer or officers in immediate Command of the troops afficted by them. Upon the execution of said instructions, Gen. Rawlins, will rejoin these Head-Quarters." Copies, DLC-USG, V, 57, 62, 63, 64. *O.R.*, I, xli, part 4, 306–7.

On Oct. 29, Asst. Secretary of War Charles A. Dana wrote to Brig. Gen. John A. Rawlins. "I have lately been in the Shenandoah Valley, and send, for the General's consideration and yours, the result of my observations, and of my conversations with Sheridan and other officers. The active campaign in the Valley seems to be over for this year. The enemy is so decidedly beaten and scattered, and driven so far to the South, that he can scarcely be expected to collect his forces for another attempt during the present season. Besides, the devastation of the Valley, extending as it does for a distance of about one hundred miles, renders it almost impossible that either the Confederates or our own forces should make a new campaign in that territory; and when Sheridan has completed the same process down the Valley to the vicinity of the Potomac, and when the stores of forage which are yet to be found in Loudoun County and in some parts of Fauquier, and the animals that are still there, are all destroyed or removed, the difficulty of any new offensive operations on either side will have been greatly increased. The key to the Valley is, in Sheridan's judgment, the Opequan Creek, which is rather a deep cañon than an ordinary water-course. Sheridan's idea I understand to be to fall back to the proper defensive point upon that creek, and there to construct fortifications which will effectually cover the approach to the Potomac.—The opening of the Winchester Railroad to this point—an affair of not more than eight or ten days—will render it possible to supply the garrison with safety and economy; and this line of railroad communication can be defended with a less force than is now required to escort the wagon trains which supply Sheridan from Martinsburg and Harper's Ferry. As soon as this is accomplished—say by the 10th of November—it will, in my judgment, be perfectly practicable to hold the Valley, and to defend the approach to the Potomac and to the railroad in that direction, with from five thousand to ten thousand men; that is to say, with the infantry and cavalry forces of the Department of West Virginia—thus leaving the Sixth and Nineteenth Corps disposable for operations elsewhere. A movement against Gordonsville and the Orange and Alexandria Railroad cannot well be made from the Valley, but, if it is decided upon, must, I think, be undertaken by way of Manassas and Culpeper. It is plain that, as soon as Sheridan has taken up the purely defensive position on the Opequan Creek of which I have spoken above, and has got himself properly fortified, it will be a great deal easier for him to march the movable part of his army to Manassas, and to advance from there, where he can constantly keep himself supplied by means of a good railroad, than to move with his wagon train up the Valley, in order to debouch through any of the gaps leading eastward toward Gordonsville. This is especially true when we consider that any effective movement upon that place presupposes a permanent occupation of the railroad, and not a mere temporary raid, whose interruption of the enemy's communications is felt for a few days only. I dare say these facts and considerations have already been brought to the General's notice, either by his own examination of the matter, or by the reports of other correspondents; but they nevertheless seem to me to be of importance enough to bear repeating." LS, DNA, RG 108, Letters Received. *O.R.*, I, xliii, part 2, 487–88. On Oct. 31, Dana telegraphed to Bowers. "I sent a letter to Gen. Rawlins by a messenger from Capt Leet's office on Saturday. Please open it." ALS (telegram sent), DNA, RG 107, Telegrams Collected (Unbound). On the same day, Rawlins, Washington, telegraphed to Bowers. "The letter from asst. Sec. Dana sent me by special Mail Messenger you will please hand the Lieut Genl to read" ALS (telegram sent), *ibid*.

On Nov. 3, 4:00 P.M., and Nov. 4, 12:30 P.M., Maj. Gen. Henry W. Halleck telegraphed to Rawlins. "I am satisfied that all the troops you can lay hand on in Missouri should be sent forward with the least possible delay to reenforce Genl Thomas. He is probably opposed by Hood's entire army, & the cavalry of Wheeler & Forest." "Genl curtis has orders to assume command of the troops under Genl Sanborn and to pursue Price to the Arkansas River or till he meets Steele or Reynolds forces, then to send all troops to their proper commands. It is important that the troops in pursuit of Price should not be with drawn till he is either broken up or driven out of the country." ALS (telegrams sent), *ibid.*, Telegrams Collected (Bound); telegrams received, USG 3. *O.R.*, I, xli, part 4, 418, 429.

On Nov. 4, 4:00 P.M. and 10:30 P.M., Rawlins, St. Louis, telegraphed to USG. "I reached here yesterday morning Genl. Rosecrans was absent with his army but returned here last night. I have seen him and delivered your orders— The commands embraced in them were already marching to the Mississippi river Gen. Smith to st. Charles & Gen ~~Mower~~ Mower now Gen McArthur to this city under orders previously communicated to him by Genl. Halleck. These two divisions numbering about nine thousand men will reach their respective destinations on the river within six days where transportation will be ready for their immediate embarkation By order of Gen Sherman McArthur relieved Mower in command of his division and the two divisions of Gen. Shermans army in this dept are placed under command of Gen Smith who has had all the necessary orders Gen. Rosecrans informs me to expedite their movement to the point designated by Thomas—Winslow's Cavalry is with Gen Sanborn to whom orders have been sent by Rosecrans for its return to the Mississippi River the moment [it] can safely be withdrawn from the pursuit of Price which seems to be the case now as Price from all accounts has been pretty completely broken up and dispersed—This Cavalry will reach the river for Embarkation in about ten days from this date—In addition to the troops of Gen. Sherman Rosecrans will send to Gen Thomas one regt. of colored Infantry which is all he thinks can be spared from here with safety to this state and government stores owing to the great activity of guerillas in different parts of the state especially in the Northern counties—Mower reports in person to Gen Sherman Rosecrans seems to appreciate fully the condition of affairs on the Mississippi and Tennessee [&] will use every exertion I have no doubt to forward troops there I have received this morning a despatch from Gen: Halleck. It requires no answer other than is contained in this Gen. Smith is here" "Since my despatch of this forenoon I have seen Gen Smith who says he has all the necessary orders from Rosecrans for the return of the whole of Shermans troops to Gen Thomas, and that he will be able to get away from here by the tenth (10th) inst with all except the cavalry, which numbers about two thousand effective men, now with Genl Sanborn. This he will not be able to get away before the fifteenth inst. His whole force exclusive of this cavalry is nine 9 thousand effective men   I shall procure from Rosecrans a complete statement of the force he will have in his Department, after Sherman's troops leave. Sherman's cavalry constituted a part of Pleasantons force in the battles with Price.—Smith being so anxious to get off and so alive to the importance of doing so, at the earliest possible moment together with Rosecrans disposition to facilitate his purpose to the fullest extent, I deem it unnecessary for me to remain longer, and unless you think otherwise I shall be prepared to leave here for City Point on sunday evening next. With your permission I would like to return by the way of New York City and remain over there for three or four days to see my physician, providing nothing of importance is likely to transpire in that time. I shall await here your answer to this, and further orders—" Telegrams received, DNA, RG 107, Telegrams Collected (Bound); *ibid.*, Telegrams Collected (Unbound); (on Nov. 5) *ibid.*, RG 108, Letters Received; copies, *ibid.*, RG 107, Telegrams Received in Cipher; *ibid.*, RG 393, Dept. of Mo., Telegrams Sent; USG 3. *O.R.*, I, xli, part 4, 429–30. On Nov. 5, 4:00 P.M., USG telegraphed to Rawlins. "You can now return via NewYork, as you request. Report your arrival in Washington City by telegraph and await reply." Copies, DLC-USG, V, 45, 70, 107; DNA, RG 107, Telegrams Received in Cipher; *ibid.*, RG 108, Letters Sent; *ibid.*, RG 393, Dept. of Mo., Telegrams Received. *O.R.*, I, xli, part 4, 438. On Nov. 4, Maj. Gen. Williams S. Rosecrans telegraphed to Bowers. "I have the honor to acknowledge the receipt of spc. ord. 114 p. III & IV., Armies of the United States Oct. 29. 1864. by the hand of Brig Genl Rawlins and to state for the information of the Genl-in-chief that in pursuance of telegraphic orders of the same tenor from Genl. Halleck chf of staff Maj Genl A. J. Smith was ordered to move from Harrisenburg to Pleasant Hill Mo on the 29th Ult and from thence on Sunday the 30th to the Missouri River at Glasgow Arrow Rock and Booneville. But finding the chances of reaching the Mississippi by marching better than by the Missouri which is so low that navigation is very difficult, one division was ordered to move directly to the Mississippi near St Louis by the South of the river and the other to cross the Missouri at Glasgow & move on the North side of that river to a point of embarkation near St Charles. Boats will be in readiness with ample supplies to meet them on their arrival and transport them to Genl Thomas who desires them come in fighting order to Johnsonville on the Tennessee. Both Divisions are now under the command of Maj Genl A. J. Smith. Mower was relieved by McArthur and ordered to report to Genl Sherman some three weeks ago. The Genl in chief may be assured that neither Genl Smith nor myself will leave any thing undone which in our opinion will expedite the movement of the troops or their arrival at their destination in fighting trim." Telegram received, DNA, RG 108, Letters Received. *O.R.*, I, xli, part 4, 428–29.

Rawlins correspondence regarding troop movements on Nov. 5 is *ibid.*, pp. 438–40. On Nov. 6, 1:00 P.M. and 10:00 P.M., Rawlins telegraphed to USG. "The 72nd Regt Ills Vols Infantry at Cairo enroute for Sherman I have ordered to Paducah   It numbers about Six hundred effective men   The 61st Ills Vols Infantry is on Steamer with orders for Paducah." ALS (telegram sent), DNA, RG 107, Telegrams Collected (Unbound); telegram received (at 3:00 P.M.), *ibid.*, Telegrams Collected (Bound). "I have just received from Genl Rosecrans the following communication . . . General Rosecrans has ordered here the six Regts and two batteries he says he can send for immediate embarkation, under orders to proceed to Paducah Ky, and report to the commanding officer there until the arrival of Genl A. J. Smith, then to report to him, unless they receive other orders from Genl. G. H. Thomas. Four of these Regts and the two Batteries will get away from here within two days from this, and the other two within four or five days. They will number over four thousand effective men. ~~Winslows~~ Winslows Cavalry will be returned to Genl Sherman by Gen'l Rosecrans as soon as they get back from the pursuit of Price if they come this way. I will here state that General Rosecrans has shown since I met him here every disposition to hurry forward troops to Genl Thomas and for that purpose to strip his command to the least possible number. He will be enabled to send more when the pursuit of Price ends. I shall leave here on my return tomorrow," ALS (telegram sent), *ibid.*, Telegrams Collected (Unbound); telegram received (on Nov. [7], 3:00 P.M.), *ibid.*, Telegrams Collected (Bound); (on Nov. 7, 9:30 P.M.) *ibid.*, RG 108, Letters Received. *O.R.*, I, xli, part 4, 453–54. See *O.R.*, I, xxxix, part 3, 684.

On Nov. 14, Rawlins, Washington, telegraphed to USG. "I have arrived here. The weather being fine will ~~start~~ leave on todays mail boat for City-Point." Telegram received, DNA, RG 107, Telegrams Collected (Unbound).

To Julia Dent Grant

                                        City Point, Va, Oct. 230th *1864.*

DEAR JULIA,

Gen. Rawlins starts for St. Louis this morning bearer of orders to Gen. Rosecrans. He will be in St. Louis several days. If you are prepared to return about the same time he is returning you might take advantage of that occation to come back with him. I shall be compelled to spend two or three days in Washington about the 10th of November and will endeavor, will go, to Burlington before returning. I received letters from Mr. Morris and Mrs. Hillyer notifying me that you had started for St Louis. Poor Fred, I am afraid he will never get an uninterrupted quarters schooling.

My love to all at your father's. I hope you found him much improved. If he recovers sufficiently to travel why not take him to Burlington with you? Love and kisses.

                                        ULYS.

ALS, DLC-USG.

To Julia Dent Grant

———

[*Oct.–Nov., 1864*]

DEAR JULIA,

I have just rec'd a letter from Mr. Barnard[1] saying that he and Amanda would leave soon to pay you a visit and requested a pass for him to visit City Point to be sent to your care. Having just written to you but last night I need only add that it is now night and at Sunrise I start to superintend operations which will take place West of Petersburg in the morning. Love and kisses again for you and the children. I thought likely you would come down after my invitatio[n] and pay me a visit of a few days. But this visit will probably prevent your doing so. I will be glad to see you if you can come. If you can not I will go to Burlington as soon as I can.

ULYS.

ALS, DLC-USG.

1. See letter to William P. Fessenden, Dec. 6, 1864.

To Edwin M. Stanton

———

(Cipher)   City Point, Va, Nov. 1st 1864 [*3:30* P.M.]
HON. E. M. STANTON, SEC. OF WAR, WASHINGTON,
I ordered the brigade of regular troops to New York City two days ago. The force sent there from this place will number ofbout 1200 in all. In addition to this Gen. Dix was directed to retain the 7th Infantry which had been previously ordered here. Do you not think this sufficient force.

U. S. GRANT
Lt. Gn.

ALS (telegram sent), OClWHi; telegram received (at 6:30 P.M.), DNA, RG 107, Telegrams Collected (Bound); *ibid.*, Telegrams Collected (Unbound). *O.R.*, I, xlii, part 3, 470; *ibid.*, I, xliii, part 2, 520. See telegram to Secretary of War Edwin M. Stanton, Oct. 24, 1864. On Nov. 1, 1864, 10:30 A.M., Secretary of War Edwin M. Stanton telegraphed to USG. "It is absolutely necessary there should be at New York an adequate military force to protect the public property

and man the forts. Governor Seymour has under a specious pretext ordered out
his National Guard under command of a man named Green. No time should be
lost in placing at General Dixs command under ~~a~~ loyal suitable officers not ~~leess~~
less than five or six thousand troops   Western men should be sent if possible.
If General Butler could be spared it would be well to send him." ALS (telegram
sent), DNA, RG 107, Telegrams Collected (Bound); telegram received (at 11:00
A.M.), *ibid.*, RG 108, Letters Received. *O.R.*, I, xlii, part 3, 470; *ibid.*, I, xliii,
part 2, 519.

On the same day, USG telegraphed to Maj. Gen. George G. Meade. "Have
the troops ordered to New York a few days since gone"   Telegram received (at
3:00 P.M.), DNA, RG 393, Army of the Potomac, Cav. Corps, Letters Received.
O.R., I, xlii, part 3, 471. At 3:00 P.M., Meade telegraphed to USG. "The regulars are to leave tomorrow for City-Point.—. . . They were ordered yesterday to
leave without delay—the transportation arrangements have kept them today"
ALS (telegram sent), DNA, RG 393, Army of the Potomac, Cav. Corps, Letters
Received; telegram received, *ibid.*, RG 108, Letters Received. *O.R.*, I, xlii, part
3, 471.

At 3:30 P.M., USG telegraphed to Maj. Gen. Benjamin F. Butler. "I am just
in receipt of dispatch from the Sec. of War asking me to send more troops to the
City of New York, and if possible to let you go there until after the election   I
wish you would start for Washington immediately and be guided by orders from
thire in the matter." ALS (telegram sent), OClWHi; telegram received, DNA,
RG 107, Telegrams Collected (Unbound). *O.R.*, I, xlii, part 3, 481. At 5:35
P.M., Butler telegraphed to USG. "Despatch recieved   Will Start in an hour—"
ALS (telegram sent), DNA, RG 107, Telegrams Collected (Unbound). *O.R.*,
I, xlii, part 3, 481.

To Maj. Gen. William T. Sherman

City Point Va
6 p m Nov 1st 1864

MAJ GENL SHERMAN
ROME GA

Do you not think it advisable now that Hood has gone so far
north, to entirely settle him before starting on your proposed campaign? With Hoods Army destroyed you can go where you please
with impunity—I believed, and still believe that if you had started
south whilst Hood was in the neighborhood, of you he would have
been forced to go after you   Now that he is so far away, he might
look upon the chase as useless and go in one direction, whilst you
are pushing in the other—If you can see the chance for destroy-

ing Hoods Army, attend to that first & make your other move secondary

U S GRANT
Lt Gen

Telegram received (at 10:45 P.M.), DNA, RG 107, Telegrams Collected (Bound); copies, *ibid.*, Telegrams Received in Cipher; *ibid.*, RG 108, Letters Sent; *ibid.*, RG 393, Military Div. of the Miss., Telegrams Received in the Field; DLC-USG, V, 45, 70, 107; (2) DLC-William T. Sherman. *O.R.*, I, xxxix, part 3, 576. On Nov. 1, 1864, 9:00 A.M., Maj. Gen. William T. Sherman, Rome, Ga., telegraphed to USG. "As you foresaw and as Jeff Davis threatened the enemy is now in the full tide of execution of his grand plan to destroy my communication and defeat this army   His infantry about 30.000 with Wheelers and Roddys cavalry from seven to 10.000. are now in the neighborhood of Tuscumbia and Florence and the water being low is able to cross at will. Forrest seems to be scattered from Eastport to Jackson Paris and the lower Tenn. & Thomas reports the capture by him of a gunboat and five transports. Thomas has, near Athens & Pulaski, Stanleys Corps about 15.000 strong and Schofields Corps en route by rail and has at least twenty to 25000 men with new regiments & conscripts arriving all the time, also, Rosecrans promises the two divisions of Smith and Mower belonging to me but I doubt if they can reach Tenn. in less than ten (10) days. If I were to let go Atlanta and Northern Georgia and make for Hood, he would, as he did here, retreat to the Southwest leaving his militia now assembling at Macon and Griffin to occupy our conquests and the work of last summer would be lost. I have retained about 50.000 good troops and have sent back full 25000 and having instructed Thomas to hold defensively Nashville Chattanooga and Decatur, all strongly fortified and provisioned for a long siege and I will destroy all the R. R. of Ga. and do as much substantial damage as is possible, reaching the Sea-coast near one of the points hitherto indicated—trusting that Thomas with his present troops and the influx of new troops promised, will be able in a very few days to assume the offensive   Hoods cavalry may do a good deal of damage and I have sent Wilson back with all dismounted cavalry; retaining only about 4500. This is the best I can do and shall therefore when I can get to Atlanta the necessary stores move as soon as possible" Telegram received (at 7:45 P.M.), DNA, RG 107, Telegrams Collected (Bound); (on Nov. 2, 8:00 A.M.) *ibid.*, RG 108, Letters Received; copies, *ibid.*, RG 107, Telegrams Received in Cipher; *ibid.*, RG 393, Military Div. of the Miss., Telegrams Received. *O.R.*, I, xxxix, part 3, 576–77. See telegram to Maj. Gen. William T. Sherman, Nov. 2, 1864.

On Nov. 2, Sherman, Rome, 12:30 P.M., and Kingston, 6:00 P.M., telegraphed to USG. "Your despatch recd. If I could hope to overhaul Hood I would turn against him with my whole force,   Then he retreats to the South-West drawing me as a decoy from Georgia which is his chief object. If he ventures North of the Tenn. I may turn in that direction and endeavor to get between him and his line of retreat, but thus far he has not gone above the Tenn   Thomas will have a force strong enough to prevent his reaching any country in which we have an interest and he has orders if Hood turns to follow me, to push for Selma   No single army can catch him and I am convinced the best results will

follow from thwarting Jeff Davis cherished plan of making me leave Georgia
Thus far I have confined my efforts to thwart his plans and reduced my baggage
so that I can pick up and start in any direction, but would regard a pursuit of
Hood as useless: Still if he attempts to invade Middle Tenn. I will hold Decatur
and be prepared to move in that direction, but unless I let go Atlanta my force
will not be equal to his" "If I turn back the whole effect of my campaign will
be lost ~~and~~—By my movements I have thrown Beauregard to the West and
Thomas will have ample time and sufficient troops to hold him until reinforcements reach him from Mo. and recruits   We have now ample supplies at Chattanooga & Atlanta to stand a months interruption to our communications, and I
dont believe the confederate army can reach our line save by cavalry raids and
Wilson will have cavalry enough to check-mate that. I am clearly of opinion that
the best results will follow me in my contemplated movement through Georgia"
Telegrams received (the first on Nov. 2, the second on Nov. 3, 10:30 A.M.),
DNA, RG 107, Telegrams Collected (Bound); *ibid.*, Telegrams Collected (Unbound); *ibid.*, RG 108, Letters Received; copies, *ibid.*, RG 107, Telegrams Received in Cipher; *ibid.*, RG 393, Military Div. of the Miss., Telegrams Received;
DLC-William T. Sherman. *O.R.*, I, xxxix, part 3, 594–95.

To Julia Dent Grant

———

City Point, Va, ~~O~~Nov 1st *1864*.

DEAR JULIA,

I have just received a second letter from Mr. Morris saying
that our children were all well and happy. I am under many obligations to him for the interest he seems to take and will try to write
to him to-morrow acknowledging the obligation   I hope you found
your father much improved in health. I have had no letter from you
since you left Burlington but suppose you have written. Give my
love to all at your father's house. I belive I wrote to you that I
should be compelled to go to Washington about the 10th of this
month and will take a run up home.—Love and kisses dear Julia.

ULYS.

ALS, DLC-USG.

To Maj. Gen. William T. Sherman

(Cipher) City Point Va Nov. 2d/64

Maj. Gen. Sherman, Rome Ga,

Your despatch of 9 a. m. yesterday is just received.[1] I dispatched you the same date advising that Hoods Army, now that it had worked so far North, be looked upon more as the objective. With the force however you have left with Thomas he must be able to take care of Hood and destroy him. I do not really see that you can withdraw from where you are to follow Hood without giving up all we have gained in territory. I say then go on as you propose.

U. S. Grant
Lt. Gn.

ALS (telegram sent), Elkins Collection, Free Library of Philadelphia, Philadelphia, Pa.; telegram received (sent at 11:30 A.M., received at 3:00 P.M.), DNA, RG 107, Telegrams Collected (Bound). *O.R.*, I, xxxix, part 3, 594. On Nov. 2, 1864, 9:30 P.M., Maj. Gen. William T. Sherman, Kingston, Ga., telegraphed to USG. "Despatch of 11.30 a. m received. I will go on and complete my arrangements and in a few days notify you of the day of my departure—Gen Thomas reports today that his cavalry reconnoitred within three miles of Florence yesterday and found Beauregard entrenching—I have ordered him to hold Nashville Chattanooga & Decatur all well supplied for a siege. All the rest of his army to assemble around Pulaski and to pursue Beauregard cautiously and carefully—At the same time for A J Smith and all reenforcements to get up to enable him to assume a bold offensive and to enable Wilson to get a good mount of Cavalry. I think Jeff Davis will change his tune when he finds me advancing into the heart of Georgia instead of retreating and I think it will have an immediate effect on your operations at Richmond" Telegram received (on Nov. 3, 12:30 P.M.), DNA, RG 107, Telegrams Collected (Bound); *ibid.*, Telegrams Collected (Unbound); *ibid.*, RG 108, Letters Received; copies, *ibid.*, RG 107, Telegrams Received in Cipher; *ibid.*, RG 393, Military Div. of the Miss., Telegrams Received. *O.R.*, I, xxxix, part 3, 595.

On Nov. 6, Sherman wrote to USG. "I have heretofore telegraphed and written you pretty fully, but I still have some thoughts in my busy brain that should be confided to you as a key to future developments. The taking of Atlanta broke upon Jeff Davis so suddenly as to disturb the equilibrium of his usually well-balanced temper; so that at Augusta, Macon Montgomery and Columbia (S. C.) he let out some of his thoughts which otherwise he would have kept to himself. As he is not only the President of the Southern Confederacy, but also its commander in chief—we are bound to attach more importance to his words than we would to those of a mere civil magistrate. The whole burden of his song consisted in the statement that Shermans communications must be broken and his Army destroyed. Now it is a well settled principle that if we can prevent his succeeding in his threat, we defeat him, and derive all the moral advantages of a victory. Thus far, Hood and Beauregard conjointly, have utterly failed to interrupt my supplies or communications with my base. My railroad and telegraph are now in good order, from Atlanta back to the Ohio river. His losses at Allatoona, Resacca, Ships Gap and Decatur exceed in number, (his losses in men) ours at the Block-houses at Big Shanty, Allatoona Creek and Dalton, and the rapidity of his flight from Dalton to Gadsden, takes from him all the merit or advantage claimed for his skillful and rapid lodgement made on my Railroad. The only question in my mind is whether I ought not to have dogged him far over into Mississippi,—trusting to some happy accident to bring him to bay and to battle. But I then thought that by so doing I would play into his hands by being drawn or decoyed too far away from our original line of advance. Besides I had left at Atlanta a Corps and railroad guards back to Chattanooga, which might have fallen an easy prey to his superior Cavalry. I felt compelled to what is usually a mistake in war—divide my forces—send a part back into Tennessee, retaining the ballance here,   As I have heretofore informed you I sent Stanley back directly from Gaylesville and Schofield from Rome; both of whom have reached their destination, and thus far Hood who had brought up at Florence, is farther from my communications than when he started. And I have in Tennessee a force numerically greater than his; well commanded and well organized, so I feel no uneasiness on the score of Hood reaching my main communications. My last accounts from General Thomas, are to 9.30 last night; when Hoods Army was about Florence in great distress about provisions, as he well must be. But that devil Forrest was down about Johnsonville, and was making havoc among the Gun boats and Transports, but Schofields troops were arriving at Johnsonville, and a fleet of Gun boats reported coming up from below able to repair that trouble. But you know that that line of supplies was only opened for Summers use, when the Cumberland could not be depended upon. We now have abundant supplies at Atlanta, Chattanooga and Nashville with the Louisville and Nashville R. Road, and the Cumberland river unmolested, so that I regard Davis threat to get his Army on my rear or on my communications as a miserable failure. Now as to the second branch of my proposition. I admit that the first object should be the destruction of that Army, and if Beauregard moves his Infantry and Artillery up into that pocket about Jackson and Paris, I will feel strongly tempted to move Thomas directly against him and myself move rapidly by Decatur on Purdy to cut off his retreat. But this would involve the abandonment of Atlanta and a retrograde movement which would be very doubtful of expediency or success, for as a matter of course Beauregard who watches me with his Cavalry and his friendly Citizens would have timely notice and would slip out and escape to regain what we have earned at so much cost. I am more than satisfied that Beauregard has not the men to attack fortifications or meet me in battle: and it would be a great achievement for him to make me abandon Atlanta by mere threats and manoeuvres. These are the reasons which have determined my former movements. I have employed the last ten days in running to the rear the sick and wounded and worthless, and all the vast amount of Stores accumulated by our Army in the advance—aiming to organize this branch of my Army into four well commanded Corps, encumbered by only one Gun to a thousand men, and provisions and ammunition which can be loaded up in our mule teams so that we can pick up and start on the shortest notice. I reckon that by the 10th inst this end will be reached, and by that date I also will have the troops all paid, the Presidential election over and out of our way, and I hope the early storms of

November now prevailing, will also give us the chance of a long period of fine healthy weather for campaigning. Then the question presents itself—'What shall be done?'—On the supposition always that Thomas can hold the line of the Tennessee, and very shortly to be able to assume the offensive as against Beauregard, I propose to act in such a manner against the material resources of the South as utterly to Negative Davis' boasted threat and promises of protection. If we can march a well appointed Army right through his territory, it is a demonstration to the World, foreign and domestic, that we have a power which Davis cannot resist. This may not be War, but rather Statesmanship, nevertheless, it is overwhelming to my mind that there are thousands of people abroad and in the South who will reason thus—'If the North can march an Army right through the South, it is proof positive that the North can prevail in this contest,' leaving only open the question of its willingness to use that power. Now Mr Lincolns election which is assured, coupled with the conclusion thus reached makes a complete logical whole. Even without a battle, the result operating upon the minds of sensible men, would produce fruits more than compensating for the expense, trouble and risk. Admitting this reasoning to be good, that such a movement 'per se' be right, still there may be reasons why one route would be better than another. There are three from Atlanta South East, Sout and South West all open, with no serious enemy to oppose at present. The first would carry me across the only East and West Railroad remaining in the Confederacy, which would be destroyed and thereby sever the communications between the Armies of Lee and Beauregard. Incidentally I might destroy the enemys Depots at Macon and Augusta, and reach the Sea shore at Charleston or Savannah, from either of which points I could reinforce our Armies in Virginia. The second, and easiest route would be due South, following substantially the Valley of Flint river, which is very fertile and well supplied, and fetching up on the navigable waters of the Apalachicola, destroying *en-route* the same Railroad taking up the Prisoners of War still at Andersonville, and destroying about four hundred Thousand (400.000) Bales of Cotton near Albany and Fort Gaines. This however would leave the Army in a bad position for future movements. The third down the Chattahoochee to Opelika and Montgomery, thence to Pensacola or Tensas Bayou in communication with Fort Morgan. This latter route would enable me at once to cooperate with Genl Canby in the reduction of Mobile and occupation of the line of the Alabama. In my judgement the first would have a material effect upon your Campaign in Virginia—the second would be the safest of execution, but the third would more properly fall within the sphere of my own command, and have a direct bearing upon my own enemy Beauregard. If therefore I should start before I hear further from you or before further developments turn my course, you may take it for granted that I have moved *via* Griffin to Barnsville. that I break up the road between Columbus and Macon *good* and then if I feint on Columbus, will move *via* Macon and Millan to Savannah, or if I feint on Macon you may take it for granted I have shot of towards Opelika, Montgomery, and Mobile bay or Pensacola. I will not attempt to send Couriers back, but will trust to the Richmond papers to keep you well advised. I will give you notice by telegraph of the exact time of my departure. General Steedman is here to clear the Rail road back to Chattanooga, and I will see that the road is broken completely between the Etowah and Chattahoochee including their bridges; and that Atlanta itself is utterly destroyed." Copies, DNA, RG 393, Military Div. of the Miss., Letters Sent in the Field; *ibid.*, Telegrams Received. *O.R.*, I, xxxix, part 3, 658–61.

1. See telegram to Maj. Gen. William T. Sherman, Nov. 1, 1864.

To Edwin M. Stanton

(Cipher)   City Point Va. Nov. 3d 1864
HON. E. M. STANTON, SEC. OF WAR, WASHINGTON,

The troops sent to New York have been selected by Gens. Terry & Weitzel and they say they have taken the most reliable men of their Corps.[1] There are several New York regiments among those going, a thing I wished to avoid, but I suppose they had to be selected to fulfill the other conditions of their orders. Lack of transportation here will delay their reaching New York as soon as I would have liked, but to prevent any further delay than can be avoided I have ordered the troops as far as Fortress Monroe on the river transportation to meet the Ocean Steamers there and avoid the necessity of the latter running to this place.

U. S. GRANT
Lt. Gn.

ALS (telegram sent), CSmH; telegram received (at 2:00 P.M.), DNA, RG 107, Telegrams Collected (Bound). *O.R.*, I, xlii, part 3, 491; *ibid.*, I, xliii, part 2, 533.

1. On Nov. 2, 1864, 5:00 P.M., USG telegraphed to Bvt. Maj. Gen. Alfred H. Terry. "Send a good large brigade of Infantry with two batteries of Napolien guns to report to Gen Butler at New York at once. If you have Western troops they will be preferabl[e.] Answer what troops you send." ALS (telegram sent), OClWHi; copies, DLC-USG, V, 45, 70, 107; DNA, RG 108, Letters Sent. *O.R.*, I, xlii, part 3, 489. At 7:00 P.M., Terry telegraphed to USG. "Your dispatch is just received   I have but four Western regiments   in two of these there ~~are~~ is much dissatisfaction because as the men think their time has expired, & I ~~should~~ do not think they are as much to be trusted just now as some others. To make a ~~large~~ brigade large I shall have to add regiments to it   Please indicate the number you wish sent." ALS (telegram sent), DNA, RG 107, Telegrams Collected (Unbound); telegram received (at 8:00 P.M.), *ibid.*, RG 108, Letters Received. A telegram sent by USG at 8:00 P.M., although deciphered as sent to Maj. Gen. Henry W. Halleck, was probably intended for Terry. "select a reliable force of about 3000 infanty and 2 Batteries"   Telegram received, *ibid.*, RG 107, Telegrams Collected (Unbound). At 9:50 P.M., Terry telegraphed to USG. "Col Dodge the Quartermaster of this army reports that he can obtain no transportation for the troops which I am to send away. I take it for granted that they are to go direct to the point named by water"   ALS (telegram sent), *ibid.*; telegram received (on Nov. 3, 2:00 A.M.), *ibid.*, RG 108, Letters Received. On Nov. 3, Terry telegraphed to USG listing the regts. and batteries sent. LS (telegram sent), *ibid.*, RG 107, Telegrams Collected (Unbound). *O.R.*, I, xlii, part 3, 504. An undated telegram from Terry to USG was probably sent on Nov. 3 or 4. "In

the list of troops to go under General Hawley which I sent to you were the 96 & 118 N. Y. Regiments, but the transportation furnished was not sufficient to take them. The other regiments, however, when they came to embark were stronger than they were estimated so that the full number required have gone. The first steamer for the infantry reported at 2 oclk yesterday afternoon the last one at 12½ oclk this morning They were sent to Hampton Roads as fast as loaded, the last one leaving at 2 oclk this A. M." ALS (telegram sent), DNA, RG 107, Telegrams Collected (Unbound). On Nov. 4, USG telegraphed to Terry. "The force sent is sufficient. The two Regiments mentioned in your dispatch, will not go." Copies, DLC-USG, V, 45, 70, 107; DNA, RG 108, Letters Sent.

To Maj. Gen. Benjamin F. Butler

(Cipher) City Point, Va, Nov. 3d *1864.* [*9:00* P.M.]
MAJ. GEN. BUTLER, NEW YORK CITY.

Troops were ordered from here promptly. 3100 Infantry went from the 10th & 18th Corps selected by the Corps Commanders for their reliability and two batteries as you requested. The Brigade of regulars had been previously ordered from the Army of the Potomac. Want of ocean transports has delayed the shipment of these troops but the advance of them must reach you to-morrow.[1]

U. S. GRANT
Lt. Gn.

ALS (telegram sent), CSmH; telegram received (at 11:00 P.M.), DLC-Benjamin F. Butler. *O.R.,* I, xlii, part 3, 503–4; *ibid.,* I, xliii, part 2, 537. On Nov. 2, 1864, 1:00 P.M., Maj. Gen. Benjamin F. Butler, Washington, telegraphed to USG. "I am here in obedience to your order. Am ordered to report in New York to General Dix. From the state of things as I can learn them, we should have at least five thousand (5000) good troops and at least two batteries of Napoleons. There is necessity for haste in getting them off. They can easily be spared from the 10th and 18th Corps. A show of force may prevent trouble. I have directed the Qr Master at Fort Monroe to have ready all transportation there, making use of that provided for Col Mulford except the 'Atlantic' and 'Baltic.' I would desire that the particular brigades or regiments to be sent should be left to the selection of Generals Terry & Weitzel. They will have ample enough to hold their lines after reliable troops are sent to me. Shall leave to-night for New York, Fifth Avenue Hotel—" LS (telegram sent), DNA, RG 107, Telegrams Collected (Unbound); telegram received, *ibid.*; (at 4:00 P.M.) *ibid.,* RG 108, Letters Received. *O.R.,* I, xlii, part 3, 489. On Nov. 3, Butler, New York City, telegraphed to USG. "*Confidential* . . . Have arrived no troops have here yet come Will you inform me when I can expect them and what troops—I believe all will be quiet here— Certainly if there is a force here. Did you receive telegram from me yesterday"

ALS (telegram sent), DLC-Benjamin F. Butler; telegram received (at 4:10 P.M.), DNA, RG 107, Telegram Collected (Bound); *ibid.*, Telegrams Collected (Unbound); *ibid.*, RG 108, Letters Received. *O.R.*, I, xliii, part 2, 537.

On Nov. 7, 4:30 P.M., USG telegraphed to Butler. "Have all troops sent from here reached you." Copies, DLC-USG, V, 45, 70, 107; DNA, RG 108, Letters Sent. *O.R.*, I, xliii, part 2, 568. On the same day, Butler telegraphed to USG. "All have arrived & been disposed of as best We may" Telegram received (at 9:35 P.M.), DNA, RG 107, Telegrams Collected (Unbound). *O.R.*, I, xliii, part 2, 568.

1. On Nov. 3, Lt. Col. Theodore S. Bowers telegraphed to Col. George S. Dodge. "All available boats in the Harbor, will report to you in an hour. On these you will at once embark the Infantry ordered East, and send it to Fortress Monroe, where it will be transferred to sea going vessels, that are expected to be waiting there. No vessels have yet been provided for the Artillery, but every effort, is being made to procure them. Get the Infantry off with all possible dispatch." Copies, DLC-USG, V, 45, 70, 107; DNA, RG 108, Letters Sent. *O.R.*, I, xlii, part 3, 504. At 2:00 P.M., Bowers telegraphed to Lt. Col. Orville E. Babcock, Fort Monroe. "Three thousand infantry are now embarking here for Fortress Monroe. Vessels are to arrive there to take them to New York. Dispatch is important. The Gen. desires that you remain at Fort Monroe ~~until you are satisfied that~~ long enough to see that the troops are transferred and got off without delay. Then go." ALS (telegram sent), Rawlins Papers, ICHi; copies, DLC-USG, V, 45, 70, 107; DNA, RG 108, Letters Sent. *O.R.*, I, xlii, part 3, 492. At 7:00 P.M., Babcock telegraphed to Bowers. "Your despatch received. Col Webster has ordered a sufficient number of the sea going steamers now here to be unloaded at once to be ~~in~~ readi~~ness~~y for the troops as they arrive   Shall we take these transports or will others be sent here? I have directed that the transports here be got in readiness. Please let me know when the troops leave for this point. I will let you know when they are all off" Telegram received, DNA, RG 108, Letters Received. *O.R.*, I, xlii, part 3, 492. At 9:00 P.M., Bowers telegraphed to Babcock. "Provide transportation at Fort Monroe for the Infantry. The boats from here are not sea going, and the troops must be transfered. Most of the Infantry left here this evening and the remainder will go early in the morning. The Artillery will get off in the morning on boats that will go through. No provision need be made for it." Telegram received, DNA, RG 107, Telegrams Collected (Unbound); copies, *ibid.*, RG 108, Letters Sent; DLC-USG, V, 45, 70, 107. *O.R.*, I, xlii, part 3, 492–93. On Nov. 4, Bowers telegraphed to Babcock. "Your last dispatch received. The last boat will be off in a few minutes. All O. K." Copies, DLC-USG, V, 45, 70, 107; DNA, RG 108, Letters Sent. *O.R.*, I, xlii, part 3, 506. At 6:30 P.M., Babcock telegraphed to Bowers. "All but the Iolas have arrived and will be off by 2 a. m. of the 5th. So rough here we had to send boats off Craney Island to transfer   All the boats with artillery horses have to go to Portsmouth to have stalls put in, this will cause delay. The qr.mr. will fit them as soon as possible   I shall go to Baltimore tomorrow evening, Gen Hawley goes tonight with infantry Letter by morning mail" Telegram received (on Nov. 5), DNA, RG 108, Letters Received. *O.R.*, I, xlii, part 3, 506. On Nov. 5, 1:15 P.M., Bowers telegraphed to Babcock. "Dispatch received. The Artillery must go at once, and cannot wait to have stalls put in the vessells. If it is unsafe to carry the horses without, debark them, and send the men and guns, leaving the horses at Fort Monroe or Ports-

mouth" Copies, DLC-USG, V, 45, 70, 107; DNA, RG 108, Letters Sent. *O.R.*, I, xlii, part 3, 517. At 3:15 P.M., Babcock telegraphed to Bowers. "Your despatch received The horses would all be killed if sent without stalls. So Only four peices of artillery remain here and the horses of one battery They will all leave tonight without fail. One steamer with 360 Infantry broke down off the Capes last night and came back her men have been transferred and will leave on boat with Genl Butlers horses in one hour. I go to Baltimore on steamer." ALS (telegram sent), DNA, RG 107, Telegrams Collected (Unbound). See telegram to Maj. Gen. Henry W. Halleck, Nov. 5, 1864.

To William Dennison

City Point, Va. Nov. 4th 1864

Hon. W. Dennison
Post Master General
Washington, D. C.
Dear Sir.

I have the honor to acknowledge the receipt of your letter of date 31st Oct. and am glad to be able to inform you, that so far as my knowledge extends the Army is well and satisfactorily supplied with mails. Our soldiers receive their mail matter with as much regularity & promptness, as is possible for Armies in the field, and with perhaps as much certainty and security, as the most favored portions of the Country.

When the expedition started from Cairo in February 1862 against Fort Henry Col. A. H. Markland voluntairily joined me and was assigned to the duty of keeping up the mails to and from the Army in the field. After the fall of Fort Donelson, Markland was commissioned as Special Agent of the Post Office Department, and has been on duty with me, or with Officers under my Command most of the time since. A system of receiving and forwarding mails was adopted and enlisted men detailed for the purpose of carrying into effect, which they did under Col. Marklands supervision, with signal fidelity and acciptanse, and without any expense to the Post Office Department, that I am aware of.

The policy I then adopted of prohibiting civilians from having anything to do with the mails within the lines of the Army, and of

detailing intelligent, reliable enlisted men for the purpose, my subsequent experience has confirmed.

Should there be any necessity for adopting a diffrent policy
within the lines of any of the Armies, under my Command I will
comply with your request to inform you of what is desired.

I am Very truly,

Your Ob't. serv't.

U. S. GRANT Lt. Gen.

Copies, DLC-USG, V, 45, 70, 107; DNA, RG 108, Letters Sent. *O.R.*, I, xlii,
part 3, 506. William Dennison, born in Cincinnati in 1815, a businessman,
lawyer, and politician, served as governor of Ohio 1860–62, and succeeded
Montgomery Blair as postmaster gen. in 1864. On Oct. 31, Dennison had written to USG. "I have requested Col Markland to express to you my earnest purpose of promptly furnishing you, and the army at all times, all the assistance in
my power connected with the postal service in the army and my desire, that you
will inform me from time to time, of your wishes in relation to that subject. The
Col will explain more fully. Any changes in the 'personel' of the agents will be
made at your request—and none will be made without my communicating with
you, and upon your concurrence. Your experience in the Military postal service
having been greater than that of any other Army Officer, you will greatly oblige
me by communicating to me any views you may have on that subject that I may
refer to them in the annual Report of this Department to Congress"   Copy, DNA,
RG 28, Postmaster Gen., Letters Sent.

On Dec. 20, USG telegraphed to Absalom H. Markland. "I would be
pleased to have you obtain the authority from the P. M. Gen. to go to Savannah
and arrange for the regular transmission and distribution of the mails for Gen'l.
Sherman's Army. I understand Mr's Markland desires to accompany you. If so
she has permission." Copies, DLC-USG, V, 45, 71, 107; DNA, RG 108, Letters
Sent. *O.R.*, I, xliv, 765.

On June 20, Lt. Col. Theodore S. Bowers had issued Special Orders No. 39
concerning mail to and from the Armies before Richmond. Copies, DLC-USG,
V, 57, 62, 67. *O.R.*, I, xl, part 2, 236–37.

To Edwin M. Stanton

———

From City Point Nov 5 1864.

HON E M STANTON

The Richmond Whig of today contains the following paragraph 'From Mobile—The Mobile Tribune of Saturday received
yesterday states that on Wednesday a regiment of Yankee Infantry
landed at Escambria Bay below Hilton. They were attacked by a
company of the 8th Mississippi Regiment which were stationed at

in the neighborhood on picket duty & while the engagement was going on part of the Yankee Cavalry got in the rear capturing about fifty (50) of the men.—The enemy destroyed all of our camp equipage wagons &c and also everything in and about Hilton.' Another Richmond paper speaking of the same affair says the Salt works at Hilton were destroyed—The only other information of importance from these sources is a statement that the Rebels evacuated Plymouth after the loss of the Albemarle

U S Grant
Lieut Genl U S A

Telegram received (at 8:35 p.m.), DNA, RG 107, Telegrams Collected (Bound); copies, *ibid.*, RG 108, Letters Sent; DLC-USG, V, 45, 70, 107. Printed as sent at 8:35 p.m. in *O.R.*, I, xxxix, part 3, 640.

To Maj. Gen. Henry W. Halleck

(Cipher) City Point, Va, Nov. 5th 1864 [*4:30* p.m.]
Maj. Gen. H. W. Halleck, Washington,

At the time Gen. Butler called for three thousand ~~additional~~ Infantry and two batteries additional to what had been already sent there was great scarcity of sea going transportation. The troops however were all sent as fast as possible to Fortress Monroe to be transfered to sea vessels as fast as they arrived. The very rough weather ~~has prod~~ of the past few days has produced some delay but I understand the last of the Inf.y left Fortress Monroe at 2 ʙA. m. to day. Oughing to the rough sea the vessels having on board the artillery were being detained to build stalls for the horses. As soon as I learned this I ordered them to sea at once and leave their horses behind. This may make it necessary for Gen. Butler to press into service for a few days such horses as he may require.

U. S. Grant
Lt. Gn.

ALS (telegram sent), OClWHi; telegram received (at 6:00 p.m.), DNA, RG 107, Telegrams Collected (Bound). *O.R.*, I, xlii, part 3, 517; *ibid.*, I, xliii, part 2, 544. See telegram to Maj. Gen. Benjamin F. Butler, Nov. 3, 1864.

On Nov. 10, 1864, 1:45 p.m., Secretary of War Edwin M. Stanton telegraphed to USG. "Orders have been made requiring the immediate return of all troops to the field and the utmost diligence of the Department will be directed to that object. General Dix reports that all of Butlers troops except five hundred regulars can return. A copy of his despatch is given. Before ordering Butler back I will wait a day until the New York election is more definitely ascertained." ALS (telegram sent), DNA, RG 107, Telegrams Collected (Bound); telegram received (marked as sent at 2:00 P.M., received at 2:45 P.M.), *ibid.*, RG 108, Letters Received. *O.R.*, I, xlii, part 3, 581. The enclosure is *ibid.*, pp. 569–70. On Nov. 12, noon, USG telegraphed to Maj. Gen. Benjamin F. Butler. "I want Gen. Dix to keep from the regulars the force he deems necessary and send the balance here. If any of the regular regiments are sent I want those that are the fullest." ALS (telegram sent), CSmH; telegram received, DLC-Benjamin F. Butler. *O.R.*, I, xliii, part 2, 617.

On Nov. 15, 11:30 A.M., USG telegraphed to Maj. Gen. John A. Dix. "Have the troops sent to New York ~~yet~~ started back yet? I wish you would urge Provost Marshals in your Dept. to forward~~ing~~ all troops and recruits to the field without delay." ALS (telegram sent), CSmH; copies, DLC-USG, V, 45, 70, 107; DNA, RG 107, Telegrams Received in Cipher; *ibid.*, RG 108, Letters Sent. Printed as received at 11:45 A.M. in *O.R.*, I, xliii, part 2, 633. On the same day, Dix telegraphed to USG. "Your despatches rec'd   Genl Butlers troops have gone & all despatch will be used in forwarding the others"   Telegram received, DNA, RG 108, Letters Received; copy, *ibid.*, RG 393, Dept. of the East, Telegrams Sent. *O.R.*, I, xliii, part 2, 633.

To Maj. Gen. George G. Meade

By Telegraph from City Point
Dated November 5 1864.

To GEN MEADE

In view of the fact that elections are to be held in the armies on tuesday[1] next the enemy may make an attack expecting to find us unprepared and to prevent as far as possible the holding of elections—

Every precautions should be taken to have all troops so in hand that they can be used if required—

U S GRANT
Lt Gen

Telegram received, DNA, RG 393, Army of the Potomac, Cav. Corps, Letters Received; copies (2), Meade Papers, PHi. *O.R.*, I, xlii, part 3, 517. On Nov. 5, 1864, USG sent an identical telegram to Bvt. Maj. Gen. Alfred H. Terry. Telegram received, DNA, RG 393, 24th Army Corps, Letters Received; copy, Louis Bell Papers, New Hampshire Historical Society, Concord, N. H.

1. Nov. 8.

To Robert Ould

November 6th 1864

JUDGE RO. OULD
AGENT OF EXCHANGE
SIR:

Your communication of the 30th of October inquiring whether the United States Authorities will consent to a shipment of cotton from a southern port to a northern city with the view of purchasing blankets etc. for the immediate relief of prisoners etc, is just this moment received. I hasten to reply, to send back by the same messenger who brought your's.

I would propose, that the United States authorities send a vessel to receive the cotton at any place you may designate between the lines of the two parties, and ship it to such Northern City as you may designate.

A Confederate prisoner of war will be allowed to accompany the vessel going after the cotton, and to stay with it until it is sold. He will also be allowed to make the purchases with the proceeds and distribute them. A commissioned United States Officer will accompany the Officer selected by you, during the whole of this transaction.

This much I can answer you without referring to higher authority. If it is insisted on, that a southern vessel to run from a Southern to a Northern port direct I will have to refer the matter to the Treasury Department for the views of the President.

Respectfully Your Ob't. serv't.
U. S. GRANT. Lt. Gen.

Copies, DLC-USG, V, 45, 70, 107; DNA, RG 94, Letters Received, 51A 1865; *ibid.*, RG 108, Letters Sent. *O.R.*, II, vii, 1101. On Oct. 30, 1864, C.S.A. Agent of Exchange Robert Ould had written to USG. "I beg leave respectfully to inquire whether the U. S. Authorities will consent to a shipment of cotton from one of our ports to one of the Northern Cities, with the view of purchasing there, with the proceeds of sale, blankets &c, for the immediate relief of our prisoners confined in Northern prisons. Of course we would give you due notice of the name of the vessel carrying the cargo, as well as the time of her sailing, together with such other particulars as you might request." Copies, DNA, RG 94, Letters Received, 51A 1865; *ibid.*, RG 109, Ould Letterbook; Ould Letterbook, Virginia State Library, Richmond, Va. *O.R.*, II, vii, 1063.

To Edwin M. Stanton

———

City Point V[a.]
Nov. 6th [2] P. M. 1864

Hon Edwin M. Stanton
Secy of War.

In the death of Brig Genl Gordon [*Ransom*] the country has sustained a great loss. He was always regarded as one of the most brave and capable commanders in the West and had he lived no doubt would have been promoted to the rank of Major General— May I now ask that Brevet appointment be given him dating from the time he received his last wound? the 9th of April/64 and that the appointment be sent to his mother.

U S Grant
Lt Genl

Telegram received (at 3:55 P.M.), DNA, RG 107, Telegrams Collected (Bound); copies, *ibid.*, Telegrams Received in Cipher; *ibid.*, RG 108, Letters Sent; DLC-USG, V, 45, 70, 107. *O.R.*, I, xxxix, part 3, 657. On Dec. 12, 1864, President Abraham Lincoln nominated Thomas E. G. Ransom as bvt. maj. gen. to date from Sept. 1.

To Maj. Gen. Henry W. Halleck

———

(Cipher)   City Point Va. Nov. 6th *1864.* [*10:15* A.M.]
Maj. Gen. Halleck, Washington,

Your dispatch of 1.~~30~~ p. m. yesterday is answered by my dispatch of yesterday[1] not probably received until yours was sent off. I think Memphis is just as likely to be endangered by Beaurigards movement as Nashville. ~~The~~ The best way to drive him back in my opinion is that being pursued and that recommended by Sherman. I have been regreting for several days that I did not see where a column of 10.000 men could be got from to move from Vicksburg to Meridian & Selma. I am inclined to think the whole affair on the lower Tennessee has been disgraceful to those on our side engaged.

U. S. Grant
Lt. Gn.

ALS (telegram sent), OClWHi; telegram received (marked as sent at 10:30 A.M., received at 11:30 A.M.), DNA, RG 107, Telegrams Collected (Bound). *O.R.*, I, xxxix, part 3, 657.

1. On Nov. 5, 1864, 4:30 P.M., USG telegraphed to Maj. Gen. Henry W. Halleck. "I do not see how Canby can raise the men to make the move proposed for him by Sherman in his dispatch of 7.30 p. m. the 3d. It may be advisable to send Canby a copy of Sherman's dispatch with instructions that if he can render the co-operation asked for to do so." ALS (telegram sent), OClWHi; telegram received (at 6:30 P.M.), DNA, RG 107, Telegrams Collected (Bound). *O.R.*, I, xxxix, part 3, 640. See *ibid.*, pp. 613–14.

To Maj. Gen. Henry W. Halleck

City Point, Va, Nov. 6th *1864*. [*2:00* P.M.]
MAJ. GEN. HALLECK, WASHINGTON,

Last night a little after 11 oclock the enemy attacked the Picket line in front of Gibbon's & Motts Divisions of sSecond corps and carried about forty of the pitts occupied by Pickets. Stubborn fighting was kept up from that time until near daylight resulting in the enemy being driven to their own lines with conciderable slaughter. ABesides the dead & wounded carried back by the enemy quite a number are still lcft in the picket trenches & vicinity. Forty two prisoners were also captured and some entrenching tools. Gen. Gibbons loss is estimated at fifteen or twenty captured. Gen. Mott says his loss will be small but does not yet give numbers.

U. S. GRANT
Lt. Gn.

ALS (telegram sent), OClWHi; telegram received (at 3:30 P.M.), DNA, RG 107, Telegrams Collected (Bound). *O.R.*, I, xlii, part 3, 528.

To Maj. Gen. Henry W. Halleck

(Cipher) City Point, Va, Nov. 6th 1864 [*6:00* P.M.]
MAJ. GEN. HALLECK, WASHINGTON,

What I understood to be Gen. Sherman's desire was that Canby should act on Beaurigards communications from the Miss. river.

By all means under existing state of affairs he should not move a
soldier from the Mississippi to the southern coast. As large a force
as he can send ought to go as far as Meredian or Selma if they can
get there. But the road from Jackson East should be well broken
and as much damage as possible done to the Mobile & Ohio.

U. S. GRANT

Lt. Gn.

ALS (telegram sent), PPRF; telegram received (at 7:30 P.M.), DNA, RG 107,
Telegrams Collected (Bound). *O.R.*, I, xxxix, part 3, 658. On Nov. 6, 1864,
1:00 P.M., Maj. Gen. Henry W. Halleck telegraphed to USG. "What I meant
about Canby was whether considering the uncertaintity of Sherman's movements
and the large force with which Beauregard was operating against Thomas and
the Miss. River, it would not be best for Canby to give up sending troops to the
coast of Georgia, & operate against Beauregard the best he could from the Miss.
River. I understand that the Mobile & Ohio R R has been repaired as far north
as Corinth which is made Beauregard's depot, and that the Miss. & Tenn. R R.
is repaired to Holly Springs. I also learn from Genls Dana & M. L. Smith that the
enemy are preparing to occupy the left bank of the Miss so as to secure the crossing of Kirby Smith's forces to the east side. Genl Curtis reached Fayetteville Ark
on the 2d and raised the rebel siege of that place. He then pushed on for Fort
Smith, where Genl Thayer is besieged, & will probably reach there to-night or
to-morrow. Whether Steele is doing anything I cannot learn. At any rate Price
will be disposed of within the next two or three days, and it seemed to me that
if canby were relieved from the proposed expedition to the Georgia coast, he
could with Reynold's forces, what Steele could spare & what he could collect on
the Miss. River so operate on Beauregard's communications as to greatly relieve
Sherman and Thomas. From all the despatches & telegrams recieved here, it
seems that Beauregard is collecting into west Tennessee & northern Miss. every
man he can raise in Miss. Ala. & Geo." ALS (telegram sent), DNA, RG 107,
Telegrams Collected (Bound); telegram received, *ibid.*; (at 4:00 P.M.) *ibid.*,
RG 108, Letters Received. *O.R.*, I, xxxix, part 3, 658; *ibid.*, I, xli, part 4, 448.

To Maj. Gen. George G. Meade

———

By Telegraph from City Point
Dated Nov 6 *1864.*

To MAJ GEN MEADE
By Gen Hancocks report of last nights attack am I to understand
that the enemy carried 100 yards of the main line held by Motts
Divn and all the pickets of 20 posts or only one hundred yards of
the picket line itself and about 20 pickets   I would also enquire

whether the Officer & 40 men left in our hands were the killed & wounded or if they are prisoners of war exclusive of the enemys loss in killed & wounded

U S GRANT

Lt Gen

Telegram received, DNA, RG 393, Army of the Potomac, Cav. Corps, Letters Received; copies (2), Meade Papers, PHi. *O.R.*, I, xlii, part 3, 529. On Nov. 6, 1864, 12:15 A.M. and 2:00 A.M., Maj. Gen. George G. Meade telegraphed to USG. "Gen Hancock reports that a few minutes before 12 a sharp musketry fire broke out near Fort Morton & that the firing is apparently picket firing accompanied by the opening of the mortor batteries. The firing has very much slackned. The firing has now nearly ceased" Telegram received, DNA, RG 108, Letters Received; copies, *ibid.*, RG 94, War Records Office, Army of the Potomac; *ibid.*, RG 393, Army of the Potomac, Letters Sent; (2) Meade Papers, PHi. *O.R.*, I, xlii, part 3, 528. "Following just recd from Gen Hancock" Telegram received, DNA, RG 108, Letters Received. *O.R.*, I, xlii, part 3, 528. The enclosure is *ibid.* At 10:30 A.M., Meade telegraphed to USG. "Maj. Genl—Hancock reports his picket line was attacked last night at 11.40 P—M both in Gibbons & Motts fronts On the former some 8 men were captured & on Motts line the enemy succeeded in capturing some 20 posts & about 100 yards of the line which he held till just before daylight when he was repulsed with heavy loss in killed & wounded leaving one officer & 40 men of the Holcombe Legion in our hands— The rest of the lines were quiet during the day & night.—" ALS (telegram sent), DNA, RG 393, Army of the Potomac, Cav. Corps, Letters Received; telegram received, *ibid.*, RG 108, Letters Received. *O.R.*, I, xlii, part 3, 528.

At 11:00 A.M. and 12:30 P.M., Meade telegraphed to USG. "In reply to your despatch I forward Hancocks report I understand the enemy took one hundred yards of Motts picket line caputing 20 men—that Mott recaptured the picket line killing & wounding a number of the enemy & capturing one officer & 40 men exclusive of the killed & wounded.—Hancock as soon as fully advised will make a more detailed report.—" ALS (telegram sent), DNA, RG 393, Army of the Potomac, Cav. Corps, Letters Received; telegram received, *ibid.*, RG 108, Letters Received. *O.R.*, I, xlii, part 3, 529. The enclosure is *ibid.* "I forward a despatch just received giving details of the affair of last night—" ALS (telegram sent), DNA, RG 94, War Records Office, Army of the Potomac; telegram received, *ibid.*, RG 108, Letters Received. The enclosure is in *O.R.*, I, xlii, part 3, 532.

To Maj. Gen. George G. Meade

―――――

City Point, Va, Nov. 6th/64

MAJ. GEN. MEADE,

I think it will be advisable to have Gen. Gregg make a pretty strong reconnoisance to-morrow well down ~~towards Reams Station~~

the rail-road to ascertain if any movent towards our rear is in contemplation. I feel pretty confident an effort will be made at some
point Monday night or Teusday.

U. S. GRANT
Lt. Gn.

ALS (telegram sent), OClWHi; telegram received, DNA, RG 393, Army of the
Potomac, Cav. Corps, Letters Received. *O.R.*, I, xlii, part 3, 529. On Nov. 6,
1864, 6:15 P.M. (sent at 6:30 P.M.), Maj. Gen. George G. Meade telegraphed
to USG. "Your despatch received, & orders in accordance therewith sent to Genl
—Gregg.—" ALS (telegram sent), DNA, RG 393, Army of the Potomac, Cav.
Corps, Letters Received; copies, *ibid.*, Army of the Potomac, Letters Sent;
Meade Papers, PHi. *O.R.*, I, xlii, part 3, 530.

To Bvt. Maj. Gen. Alfred H. Terry

City Point, Va, Nov. 6th/64

MAJ. GEN. TERRY.

It will be well for you to push Cavalry out to-morrow as far
towards the Chickahominy as they can go, and as near to the enemy.
It is possible there will be an effort made to-morrow night or Teusday by the enemy. They will not venture on a direct attack but may
attempt to get in your rear with a small force.

U. S. GRANT Lt. Gn.

ALS (telegram sent), OClWHi; copies, DLC-USG, V, 45, 70, 107; DNA, RG
108, Letters Sent. *O.R.*, I, xlii, part 3, 537. On Nov. 6, 1864, 8:45 P.M., Bvt.
Maj. Gen. Alfred H. Terry telegraphed to USG. "Your despatch is received. I yesterday having in view the possibility of attack at this time I directed the cavalry
pickets to be pushed further out than they recently have been. Since the reception of your order I have directed Col West who commands the division to push
out Spears Brigade toward the Chickahominy ~~paying~~ at an hour before daylight
to-morrow moring paying particular attention to the Charles City & Long Bridge
roads & looking out for the White Oak Bridge. This brigade will be relieved at
~~midday~~ mid-day by Evans Brigade. these two brigades will releive each alter-
nately other in the performance of this duty as long as may be thought necessary.
the third brigade of the division will remain to do the ordinary picket duty." ALS
(telegram sent), DNA, RG 107, Telegrams Collected (Unbound); telegram received, *ibid.*, RG 108, Letters Received. *O.R.*, I, xlii, part 3, 538. At 9:40 P.M.,
Terry telegraphed to USG. "Major Stevens ~~has~~ returned with his party yesterday
afternoon. His report has just come to me. I will forward it immediately   He
brought in fourteen prisoners & a number of sheep horses & cattle. He lost no

men." ALS (telegram sent), DNA, RG 107, Telegrams Collected (Unbound). On the same day, Terry endorsed to USG the lengthy report of Maj. Atherton H. Stevens, Jr., 4th Mass. Cav. AES, *ibid.*, RG 108, Letters Received. The report is printed in *O.R.*, I, xlii, part 1, 683–85.

On Nov. 7, 12:55 A.M., Terry telegraphed to Lt. Col. Theodore S. Bowers. "A small demonstration has just been made upon our cavalry near Flussers Mills. A party of the enemy's infantry estimated at 200 men drove in the pickets, & attacked the supports. They were driven back, & our line reestablished. Col West comdg the cavalry divison has sent out in that quarter Spears brigade which was to go out just before daylight." ALS (telegram sent), DNA, RG 107, Telegrams Collected (Unbound); telegram received (misdated Nov. 6), *ibid.*, RG 108, Letters Received. Printed as sent at 12:25 A.M. in *O.R.*, I, xlii, part 3, 550.

To E. Morris

City Point, Va, Nov. 6th *1864.*

MR. E. MORRIS,
DEAR SIR:

Your two letters informing me of the condition of my children and the attention they are receiving, in the absence of their mother, were duly received. I feel very greatfull to you for the trouble you took in accompanying Mrs. Grant as far as Phila on her way West and for your subsequent kindness in looking after my family and informing me. I have received but one letter from Mrs. G. since she reached Mo. She found her father much improved and in a fair way of recovery. She probably left St. Louis this evening on her return home. All the letters I have ~~received from~~ written her since the receipt of your first have been directed to St. Louis. As I am not now writing to her, and may not until I hear again from her, may I tax your kindness further by asking you to inform her, on arrival in Burlington, that I am well and think it probable I may be able to spend next Sunday[1] at home. I do not want this fact known to any one but yourself and Mrs. Grant. Our papers are received by the enemy as early as by ourselves and learning that I was to be absent in advance they might prepare for some annoyance. I am not vain enough to suppose that another might not command these Armies as well as myself but bringing in a commander suddenly upon an immergency he might not do as well as he would after commanding for some time.

With again thanking you for your kindness I subscribe myself

Sincerely Yours

U. S. GRANT

ALS, Ritzman Collection, Aurora College, Aurora, Ill. Probably addressed to Edmund Morris, born in Burlington, N. J., in 1804, who edited newspapers in Pa. and N. J. before 1856, afterwards a frequent contributor to the *New York Tribune* and other newspapers. Known as an antislavery advocate, he also wrote frequently on farming.

1. Nov. 13, 1864.

To Elihu B. Washburne

City Point Va. Nov. 6th *1864.*

HON. E. B. WASHBURN,
DEAR SIR:

Your letter of the 24th asking for a Pass for Corwith to visit this place come duly to hand and was thrust in my pocket to answer immediately. Some how I forgot it until to-day   in trying to get up even with all the letters which I thought ought to be answered I examenid my coat pockets to find if there was any thing there and found among others yours. This is rather a poor excuse but it is the fact and I have none other. I shall be very glad to see Mr. Corwith and enclose to you the pass.

I received a letter last evening from your little sons asking me for some trophy of the battle field, to be sent by his father, which he might keep. I have a revolver taken at Fort Donelson and carried by me from Shiloh to the present time, generally in my trunk, which I will send to you by first opportunity to give him.

We have no special news here. The enemy made a slight night attack last night and were badly punished in a small way.

Yours Truly

U. S. GRANT

Lt. Gn.

ALS, DLC-USG, I, B.

To Edwin M. Stanton

(Cipher) City Point, Va, Nov. 7th *1864. [3:00* P.M.]
HON. E. M. STANTON, SEC. OF WAR WASHINGTON.

Unless you insist on it I will make no report to go before Congress. This campaign not being ended whilst Richmond is in the possession of the enemy I could not properly make a report further than is embraced in subordinate reports now in the Department at Washington without giving information that would be valuable to the enemy. I also doubt the propriety of my absenting myself from here for five or six days as I should have to do to make a report.

U. S. GRANT
Lt. Gen.

P. S. Private: I think I will spend Christmas in Richmond and there get my report ready for Congress before they get through with the holidays and meet at the beginning of the new year

U. S. GRANT[1]

ALS (telegram sent), OClWHi; telegram received (at 4:00 P.M.), DNA, RG 107, Telegrams Collected (Bound). *O.R.*, I, xlii, part 3, 541. The postscript is copied in DNA, RG 107, Telegrams Received in Cipher. On Nov. 8, 1864, 10:30 P.M., Secretary of War Edwin M. Stanton telegraphed to USG. "Your report can lay over until the Campaign is ended. I am perfectly contented to wait for the conditions mentioned in your Post script." ALS (telegram sent), *ibid.*, Telegrams Collected (Bound); telegram received (marked as sent at 11:30 A.M., received at noon), *ibid.*, RG 108, Letters Received.

1. The absence of the postscript on USG's original and letterbook copies, and also on the telegram received, combined with the uncharacteristic phrasing and sentiment, suggest that it may not have been written by USG but inserted in the process of telegraphic transmission.

To Maj. Gen. Henry W. Halleck

City Point, Va, Nov. 7th 12 p. m. *1864*.
MAJ. GEN. HALLECK, WASHINGTON.

Under the circumstances pointed out in Gen. Rosecrans dispatch of this date[1] I think as he does, that the pursuit after Price might as well be discontinued. Please so direct him.

U. S. GRANT
Lt. Gn.

ALS (telegram sent), OClWHi; telegram received (on Nov. 8, 1864, 2:05 A.M.), DNA, RG 107, Telegrams Collected (Bound). *O.R.*, I, xli, part 4, 463.

1. On Nov. 7, Maj. Gen. William S. Rosecrans telegraphed to Maj. Gen. Henry W. Halleck recommending that the pursuit of C.S.A. Maj. Gen. Sterling Price be discontinued because of C.S.A. activity in the rear of the pursuing U.S. cav. *Ibid.*, p. 470.

To Maj. Gen. Henry W. Halleck

Cipher   City Point Va. Nov. 7th/64 [7:00 P.M.]
MAJ. GN. HALLECK, WASHINGTON,

I suppose there is no doubt but Thomas will be sustained in giving Schofield the command over Stanley ~~on account of the latter being senior in rank. If any question is likely to be raised~~ The latter is senior in rank but a corps is a very big command for him. ~~and to~~ To insure it being ~~well~~ advantageously used he should always have a superior with him to direct. If Schofield is likely to be embarassed by Stanley feeling soured at serving under a junior, and therefore not giving a hearty support, authority had better be given Schofield to remove the latter when, in his judgement, the good of the service requires it.

U. S. GRANT
Lt. Gn.

ALS (telegram sent), CSmH; telegram received (at 7:40 P.M.), DNA, RG 107, Telegrams Collected (Bound); DLC-John M. Schofield. *O.R.*, I, xxxix, part 3, 684.

To Maj. Gen. Henry W. Halleck

City Point Va
Nov 7th 1864.

Maj Gen Halleck
Chf of Staff

Our loss in killed wounded and missing in the attack on our picket line, the night of the 5th proves to be only twenty 20.

Deserters from that portion of the enemys line making the attack, say theirs was about two hundred. Our captures were forty two prisoners, and some entrenching tools. The enemy have asked permission to bury their dead under flag

U. S. Grant
Lt Gen

Telegram received (at 11:00 P.M.), DNA, RG 107, Telegrams Collected (Bound); copies, *ibid.*, RG 108, Letters Sent; DLC-USG, V, 45, 70, 107. *O.R.*, I, xlii, part 1, 23; *ibid.*, I, xlii, part 3, 542.

On Nov. 7, 1864, noon (sent at 3:30 P.M.) and 4:30 P.M., Maj. Gen. George G. Meade telegraphed to USG. "I have nothing of consequence to report, all having been quiet during the past 24 hours—A deserter who came in to the 2d corps lines estimates the enemy's loss in the affair of night before last at about Two hundred—Maj Genl. Hancock reports his loss in killed wounded & missing as under 20.—" "Lt. Genl. Anderson has applied to Maj. Genl. Hancock for a flag of truce for an hour or two to bury the dead lying between the lines—It will hardly be practicable to have one this evening, but with your permission authority can be given to Hancock to arrange one tomorrow morning.—" ALS (telegrams sent), DNA, RG 393, Army of the Potomac, Cav. Corps, Letters Received; telegrams received, *ibid.*, RG 108, Letters Received. *O.R.*, I, xlii, part 3, 542. On the same day, Lt. Col. Cyrus B. Comstock wrote to Meade. "Lieutenant-General Grant approves your proposal in reference to a flag of truce for burying the dead." *Ibid.*

On Nov. 8, 10:30 A.M. (sent at 10:40 A.M.), Meade telegraphed to USG. "There was picket firing last evening for about an hour in front of Fort Meickle—no result. The rest of the lines quiet.—Lt. Genl. Anderson confed army applied thro' Maj. Genl. Hancock for permission to remove the wounded & bury the dead lying between the lines since the affair of the 8th inst—Maj. Genl. Hancock was authorised to grant a truce from 9 to 10. a m today. Genl. Gregg reported last night the return of the cavalry reconnaissance. One brigade went over the Rail Road 8 miles beyond Reams station, and another brigade went down the Jerusalem plank road beyond the crossing of the Nottoway—No signs of the enemy in force were discovered or could be heard—About 9 prisoners principally scouts were picked up.—" ALS (telegram sent), DNA, RG 393, Army of the Potomac, Cav. Corps, Letters Received; telegram received, *ibid.*, RG 108, Letters Received. *O.R.*, I, xlii, part 3, 557–58.

To Maj. Gen. William T. Sherman

———

(Cipher)   City Point, Va, Nov. 7th *1864*. 10.30 p. m.
Maj. Gen. W. T. Sherman, Atlanta Ga,

Your dispatch of this evening received. I see no present reason
for changing your plan. Should any arise you will see it or if I do
will inform you. I think everything here favorable now. Great
good fortune attend you. I believe you will be eminently succesful
and at worst can only make a march less fruitful of results than is
hoped for.

U. S. Grant
Lt. Gen.

ALS (telegram sent), Forbes Magazine Collection, New York City, N. Y.; telegram received (at 11:35 p.m.), DNA, RG 107, Telegrams Collected (Bound).
O.R., I, xxxix, part 3, 679. On Nov. 7, 1864, 6:00 p.m., Maj. Gen. William T.
Sherman, Kingston, Ga., telegraphed to USG, sending a copy to Maj. Gen. Henry
W. Halleck. "By the 10th the election will be over, the troops all paid and all our
surplus property will be back to Chattanooga. On that day or the following if affairs remain as now in Tenn. I propose to begin the movement which I have
hitherto fully described   I can hear of no large force to our front and according
to Thomas, Hood remains about Tuscumbia and he feels perfectly confident of
his ability to take care of him. You can safely communicate with me for the next
Three days"   Telegram received (at 9:30 p.m.—addressed to Halleck), DNA,
RG 108, Letters Received. Printed as received at 8:15 p.m. in *O.R.*, I, xxxix, part
3, 679.

To Bvt. Maj. Gen. Alfred H. Terry

———

City Point, Va. Nov. 7th *1864.*
Maj. Gen. Terry, Comd.g Army of the James,

I see our papers announce that large numbers of the A[rmy]
have gone home to vote. These papers get through to the enemy
within an hour of after reaching our lines. Information gained by
this means the enemy may try to take advantage of. If we are prepared I hope he may. I see by a Richmond paper that they think this
depletion is mostly from the Army of the James; at least they say
they now know that most of the forces from the North side have
gone. That nothing is left but a skelleton line to hold our works. I

think from this there is sufficient probability of you being attacked to justify requiring the greatest vigilence on the part of every Division and Brigade commander and the most perfect readiness to form and move their commands. If the enemy should attack and be repulsed he should be followed up at once and no officer should hold back for orders to do so.

U. S. GRANT
Lt. Gn.

ALS (telegram sent), OClWHi; copies, DLC-USG, V, 45, 70, 107; DNA, RG 108, Letters Sent; *ibid.*, RG 393, Army of the Potomac, Cav. Corps, Letters Received; *ibid.*, 24th Army Corps, Letters Received. *O.R.*, I, xlii, part 3, 550–51. On Nov. 7, 1864, 12:40 P.M., Bvt. Maj. Gen. Alfred H. Terry telegraphed to USG. "Your despatch is just received. I will see that the most extreme vigilance is exercised. The only point about which I have aniety is our right & rear. I think however that sufficnt precautions have been taken for this point. The cavalry are well out coving it, the redoubt at Camp Holly has six guns four of them twenty pdrs. that at Signal Hill ten guns: that at Four Mile Church Six guns   at the small work between the two last named there are two guns. All these works have good infantry garrisons. I have increased the force in the new line in front of Deep Bottom so that there are now there two thousand men   they occupy the right of the line running nearly as far to the left as the Grover House. In case of attack ~~We~~ in that direction Weitzel will move troops at once down the Kingsland Road Ames 10th Corps will move a column down the Newmarket Road Weitzel will change direction to the left & Ames to the right & form line of battle on a crest between, & running at right at angles with the Two roads: the left resting on one of the redoubts the ~~right~~ connecting with the left of the men in the new Deep Bottom line. I think the position will then be very strong. I have been over the ground with Weitzel this moring." ALS (telegram sent), DNA, RG 107, Telegrams Collected (Unbound); telegram received, *ibid.*, RG 108, Letters Received. Printed as received at 1:35 P.M. in *O.R.*, I, xlii, part 3, 551.

To Edwin M. Stanton

From City Point Nov 9 *1864.*

HON E M STANTON

The following official statement of the vote polled in the army of the Potomac yesterday has just been received from Gen Meade— Maine total vote 1677 Lincolns's majority 1143. New Hampshire 515 Lincoln's maj. 279—Vermont 102 Lincoln maj 42. Rhode Island 190 Lincolns maj 134. Pennsylvania 7 counties to hear from 11.122 Lincoln maj 3494—West Virginia 82 Lincoln maj. 70—

Ohio—684. Lincoln maj. 306—Wisconsin 1065 Lincoln maj 633 —Michigan 1917 Lincoln maj 745   Maryland 1428 Lincoln maj. 1160

U. S. S. S.[1] 124 Lincoln maj 89—New York 305 Lincoln maj. 113. Majority for Lincoln—8208.

U. S. GRANT
Lt Gen—

Telegram received (at 10:45 P.M.), DNA, RG 107, Telegrams Collected (Bound). *O.R.*, I, xlii, part 3, 570. Also on Nov. 9, 1864, USG endorsed to Secretary of War Edwin M. Stanton the statement of regt. voting prepared for Maj. Gen. George G. Meade from which the figures were taken. ES, DNA, RG 107, Letters Received from Bureaus. At 11:00 A.M., Meade telegraphed to USG. "Unusual quiet prevailed yesterday along the lines—The returns of the election were sent to you as received during the night—I am now preparing a consolidated return showing the votes in each regiment by states, which when completed will be telegraphed—Early yesterday morning my attention was called to the existence & circulation of spurious poll books in Pa regiments   I immediately notified all comd. officers of the fact & directed the soldiers should be put on their guard— During the day two men were arrested in the 2d corps charged with circulating these false papers & there being reason to believe one of the state Agents was connected with the transaction I have directed he should be detained, till an investigation now being made by the Judge Advocate of this army, shows whether or not there is ground for further action.—" ALS (telegram sent), *ibid.*, RG 393, Army of the Potomac, Cav. Corps, Letters Received; telegram received, *ibid.*, RG 108, Letters Received. *O.R.*, I, xlii, part 3, 572. See *ibid.*, pp. 558, 570–72, 582, 595–96.

On Nov. 8, USG telegraphed to Meade. "Have the returns of the Army vote been received yet. I would like to send them to the War Department to night if possible"   Copies (2), Meade Papers, PHi. At 10:30 P.M., Meade telegraphed to USG. "I forward returns from the 9th Corps and from the regiments serving at these Head Quarters: all that have been received up to this hour." Copies, *ibid.*; DNA, RG 393, Army of the Potomac, Letters Sent. On the same day, USG telegraphed to Stanton. "The 9th Corps gives a Republican Majority of 2125. No other returns are yet received." ALS (telegram sent), IHi; telegram received (marked as sent Nov. 9, received 9:50 A.M.), DNA, RG 107, Telegrams Collected (Bound). Printed as sent on Nov. 9 in *O.R.*, I, xlii, part 3, 570.

1. U.S. Sharpshooters.

To Maj. Gen. Philip H. Sheridan

(Cipher)   City Point, Va. Nov. 9th 1864
MAJ. GEN. SHERIDAN, CEDAR CREEK, VA,

Do you not think it advisable to notify all citizens living East of the Blue Ridge to move out North of the Potomac all their stock, grain and provisions of every discription? There is no doubt about the necessity of clearing out that country so that it will not support Mosby's gang and the question is whether it is not better that the people should save what they can. So long as the war lasts they must be prevented from raising another crop both there and as high up the valley as we can controll.

U. S. GRANT
Lt. Gn

ALS (telegram sent), CSmH; telegram received (marked as sent on Nov. 10, received at 10:30 A.M.), DNA, RG 107, Telegrams Collected (Bound). *O.R.*, I, xliii, part 2, 581. On Nov. 11, 1864, 10:00 A.M., Maj. Gen. Philip H. Sheridan, Kernstown, telegraphed to USG. "A small division of my cavalry has just returned from the east side of the Blue Ridge. It went through Manassas Gap to Rectortown and then down the country, coming back by way of Ashbys Gap. They brought back three hundred head of cattle, a lot of sheep and horses; burned all the graineries; destroyed all the provision they could on the road. They report that the country is full of grain & forage   This will be a warning which will probably be taken advantage of by any Union citizens living in that country   I think it best General; to settle the question of which way the people go *practically*. Orders on the subject [are no]t very effective and cause great annoyance. I have no news from the enemy since I took up my new position. He has not made his appearance in even small scouting parties"   Telegram received (at 8:00 P.M.), DNA, RG 107, Telegrams Collected (Bound); (on Nov. 12) *ibid.*, RG 108, Letters Received; copies, *ibid.*, RG 107, Telegrams Received in Cipher; (2) DLC-Philip H. Sheridan. *O.R.*, I, xliii, part 2, 602–3.

To Julia Dent Grant

City Point, Va, Nov. 9th *1864*.

DEAR JULIA,

I wrote to Mr. Morris telling him that I expected to be in Burlington next Sunday to spend the day. At that time I expected to go to Washington, where all my records are kept, to remain a few days to write my report for Congress. The campaign not being ended I asked the Sec. of War to let me off and he has consented. I will not therefore be home at the time designated.

I have received but one letter from you since you left N. J. Did you meet Gen. Rawlins in St. Louis? He was to have gone out to see you and as he returned about the time your letter announced you would I supposed you would come in company with him.

The election has passed off quietly, I understand, and I hope the choise of the people will be quietly submitted to. If there was less clamer and dessenting in the North the rebellion would be much sooner put down. The hopes of the South are constantly fed by the sayings of our Northern people.

Love and kisses for you & the children. Gen. Rawlins expects to stay about four days in New York City and then return here. If you wish to come and spend a week at that time do so. Bring Jess with you if you come. I would rather you would spend Christmass Holidays with me however and bring all the children. Love and kisses again.

Ulys.

ALS, DLC-USG.

To Edwin M. Stanton

(Cipher)   City Point, Va, Nov. 10th *1864*. [*10:30* P.M.]
HON. E. M. STANTON, SEC. OF WAR, WASHINGTON.

Enough now seems to be known to say who is to hold the reins of Government for the next four years. Congratulate the President for me for the double victory. The election having passed off quietly, no bloodshed or rioit throughout the land, is a victory worth more to the country than a battle won. Rebeldom and Europe ~~both will feel it~~ will so construe it.

U. S. GRANT
Lt. Gn.

ALS (telegram sent), CSmH; telegrams received (2—at 10:30 P.M. and 11:15 P.M.), DNA, RG 107, Telegrams Collected (Bound). *O.R.*, I, xlii, part 3, 581.

To Edwin M. Stanton

City Point, Va, Nov. 10th *1864*.

HON. E. M. STANTON,
SEC. OF WAR,
SIR:

I would respectfully recommend the promotion of Brig. Gen. R. Ingalls, now Brigadier General of Volunteers, to the same grade, by brevet, in the regular army, to take rank as such from the 16th day of June 1864, the date of his assuming the duties of Chief Quartermaster of the combined armies operating against Richmond. This is also the date of the crossing of the James River after the campaign from the Rapidann, by the Army of the Potomac. For his promotion, by Brevet, in the intermediate grades between that of Major, (Gen. Ingalls present army rank,) and that of Brigadier General, I would respectfully recommend that dates given in a previous recommendation for his promotion be followed.

For the skillful manner in which Gen. Ingalls has conducted the affairs of his Department he deserves this recognition of his services. He was the first officer of his Dept. I believe, who proved capable of organizing and running all the machnery in it for the Army of the Potomac. There has been no other Army in the United States where the duties of Quartermaster have been nearly as well performed. The services of General Ingalls are too well understood at Washington to make it necessary for me to add more than my testamony that since I have been directly with the Armies where he has acted as Chief Quartermaster his services have been all that could be asked, and such as but few could perform.

Very Respectfully
your obt. svt
U. S. GRANT
Lt. Gn.

ALS, DNA, RG 94, ACP, 2163 ACP 1878. *O.R.*, I, xlii, part 3, 582. On Dec. 2, 1864, 5:30 P.M., USG telegraphed to Secretary of War Edwin M. Stanton. "I asked to have Gn. Ingalls brevet dated 15th of June because that was the day the Army crossed the James river and established the Depot at City Point." ALS (telegram sent), CSmH; telegram received (at 6:00 P.M.), DNA, RG 107, Telegrams Collected (Bound). On Dec. 12, President Abraham Lincoln nominated Rufus Ingalls as bvt. lt. col., bvt. col., and bvt. brig. gen., all to rank from July 6.

To Edwin M. Stanton

City Point, Va, Nov. 10, 64

HON E. M. STANTON
SECRETARY OF WAR WASHINGTON D. C.

SIR, I have the honor to acknowledge the receipt this date, of communication from the State Department to you, and referred by you for my consideration relative to "the embarkation of French subjects who wish to leave the insurgent states" and to respectfully say in reply, that I will afford al necessary assistance and protection to the French vessel proposed to be sent to Aikins landing. I desire to be apprized of the time the vessel will be ready to proceed, that I may place an Officer of the United States Army on board and give the necessary directions for her safe conduct.

Whilst I am ready any day to carry out this plan, if you so direct, I would prefer to send a vessel, or vessels, from here to Aikins landing (the highest point on the river to which a flag of truce boat can go) and receive and convey to Fortress Monroe, Norfolk or Baltimore, all French subjects who may come there for the purpose named in the communications.

I have the honor to be Sir
Very Respectfully
your obt. serv't.
U. S. GRANT.
Lieut, Gen.

Copies, DLC-USG, V, 45, 70, 107; DNA, RG 108, Letters Sent. See telegram to Edwin M. Stanton, Oct. 25, 1864.

On Nov. 11, 1864, USG wrote to Asst. Secretary of War Charles A. Dana. "The communication of John Hitz Consul General of Switzerland, enclosing request of G. Honegger, 'for a permit for his wife and children to come north by flag of truce boat' refered to by you for my action has been received. Our Agent of Exchange at Aikins Landing has been directed to receive the parties named and convoy them to Fort Monroe" Copies, DLC-USG, V, 45, 70, 107; DNA, RG 108, Letters Sent.

To Maj. Gen. Henry W. Halleck

(Cipher)   City Point, Va. Nov. 10th *1864*. [*11:00* A.M.]
Maj. Gen. Halleck, Washington,

I suppose without my saying anything about it all the troops now in the North will be hurried to the field, but I wish to urge this as of the utmost importance. Shermans movement may compell ~~the~~ Lee to send troops from Richmond and if he does I want to be prepared to annoy him.

U. S. Grant
Lt. Gn.

ALS (telegram sent), CSmH; telegram received (at noon), DNA, RG 107, Telegrams Collected (Bound). *O.R.*, I, xlii, part 3, 582. On Nov. 11, 1864, 3:00 P.M., Maj. Gen. Henry W. Halleck telegraphed to USG. "Troops sent north have been ordered back to their commands. When will you be up to make annual Report." ALS (telegram sent), DNA, RG 107, Telegrams Collected (Bound); telegram received, *ibid. O.R.*, I, xlii, part 3, 595. On Nov. 11, 5:00 P.M., USG telegraphed to Halleck. "The sec. of War has excused me from making a report until the end of the campaign. I could not go now as the enemy have been very busy last night & to-day moving troops apparently with the intention of attacking both South of the Appomattox & North of the James, probably the latter to be the main attack if any is made." ALS (telegram sent), CSmH; telegram received (at 5:30 P.M.), DNA, RG 107, Telegrams Collected (Bound). Printed as received at 5:40 P.M. in *O.R.*, I, xlii, part 3, 595.

To Maj. Gen. George G. Meade

By Telegraph from City Point
Dated Nov 10 *1864*.

To Gen Meade

Owing to the reported movement of a portion of Hills Corps to the north side of the Appomattex I have ordered Gen Benham to send back to Bermuda the 205th Pa[1] which belongs to Genl Butlers command—

Benham has left 2500 men which is a sufficient force—

U S Grant
L Gen

Telegram received, DNA, RG 393, Army of the Potomac, Cav. Corps, Letters

Received; copies, *ibid.*, RG 108, Letters Sent; DLC-USG, V, 45, 70, 107; (2) Meade Papers, PHi. *O.R.*, I, xlii, part 3, 583.

On Nov. 10, 1864, USG telegraphed to Bvt. Maj. Gen. Alfred H. Terry. "I have ordered back to Bermuda Hundred the 205 Pa. This Reg't numbers 1000 men and will give you the means of drawing from Col Potter if you should require reinforcements North of the James." Copies, DLC-USG, V, 45, 70, 107; DNA, RG 108, Letters Sent. *O.R.*, I, xlii, part 3, 590.

1. At 7:30 P.M., Lt. Col. Theodore S. Bowers wrote to Brig. Gen. Henry W. Benham. "Order the 205th Regiment Pennsylvania Infantry Volunteers to proceed immediately (via Broadway Landing.) to Bermuda, and there report to Colonel Potter, Commanding Defences, for orders." ALS, DNA, RG 94, War Records Office, Army of the Potomac, Engineer Branch. *O.R.*, I, xlii, part 3, 584.

To Bvt. Maj. Gen. Alfred H. Terry

City Point, Va. Nov. 10, 1864

MAJ. GEN. TERRY,
ARMY OF THE JAMES

The enemy have a Cavalry force near Hopeville Church, probably sent there, to prevent such raids, as that of last week. If your Cavalry is in good condition I think it will be well to drive them out. As large a force, as you can send, should go for the purpose.

U. S. GRANT. Lt. Gen.

Telegram, copies, DLC-USG, V, 45, 70, 107; DNA, RG 108, Letters Sent. *O.R.*, I, xlii, part 3, 589. On Nov. 10, 1864, Bvt. Maj. Gen. Alfred H. Terry telegraphed to USG. "The cavalry are in good condition & about 1500 men could be taken out. Is the Hopesville Church referred to, the one north of the York River rail road about two miles from Tunstalls Station and six miles from White House?" ALS (telegram sent), DNA, RG 107, Telegrams Collected (Unbound); telegram received, *ibid.*, RG 108, Letters Received. *O.R.*, I, xlii, part 3, 589. Both USG and Terry referred to Hopewell Church. On the same day, USG telegraphed to Terry. "The Hopeville Church referred to is about two miles from Jones Bridge. I do not want the Cavalry to cross the Chickahominy but to get out near to it and above Jones' bridge, sweeping down from there to below the bridge." Copies, DLC-USG, V, 45, 70, 107; DNA, RG 108, Letters Sent. Printed as received at 5:40 P.M. in *O.R.*, I, xlii, part 3, 589.

At 12:10 A.M., Terry had telegraphed to Lt. Col. Theodore S. Bowers. "A small party of the enemys cavalry made a dash on on pickets near Flussers Mills & the junction of the Charles City & Long Bridge Roads. They were soon repulsed without loss" ALS (telegram sent), DNA, RG 107, Telegrams Collected (Unbound). *O.R.*, I, xlii, part 3, 589.

To Bvt. Maj. Gen. Alfred H. Terry

———

City Point, Va. Nov. 10. 1864

MAJ. GEN. TERRY

Your forces on Bermuda must be watchful. The movement of a portion of Hills Corps North of the Appomattox may indicate an attack there, or they may have gone on North of the James to attack you. If we are not surprised there is no danger of the result.

U. S. GRANT. Lt. Gen.

Telegram, copies, DLC-USG, V, 45, 70, 107; DNA, RG 107, Telegrams Collected (Unbound); *ibid.*, RG 108, Letters Sent; (2) *ibid.*, RG 393, Army of the Potomac, Cav. Corps, Letters Received. *O.R.*, I, xlii, part 3, 590. On Nov. 10, 1864, 8:27 P.M., Bvt. Maj. Gen. Alfred H. Terry telegraphed to USG. "I have received your despatches relative to the movement of a portion of Hills Corps I was about to order the cavalry to move on Hopewell Church at so as to strike it at daylight to-morrow morning. Will this movement of Hill make any change in your order relative to Hopewell Church." ALS (telegram sent), DNA, RG 107, Telegrams Collected (Unbound); telegram received, *ibid.*, RG 108, Letters Received. *O.R.*, I, xlii, part 3, 590. On the same day, USG twice telegraphed to Terry. "It will now be better to keep your Cavalry to watch the movements of the enemy. They had better push out in the morning to discover if any movement is on foot, but not to go on the Expedition ordered to-day," Copies, DLC-USG, V, 45, 70, 107; DNA, RG 108, Letters Sent. *O.R.*, I, xlii, part 3, 590. "I think there is no possible probability of the enemy attacking your front anywhere from the New Market road to the Fort at sSignal Hill. It would be advisabl therefore to have all the reserves from that line, leaving only a thin support for it, in readiness to move to any point." ALS (telegram sent), CSmH; copies, DLC-USG, V, 45, 70, 107; DNA, RG 108, Letters Sent. *O.R.*, I, xlii, part 3, 590. On the same day, Terry telegraphed to USG. "Your despatch is recived I will take all possible precautions" ALS (telegram sent), DNA, RG 107, Telegrams Collected (Unbound).

To Edwin M. Stanton

———

Cipher City Point, Va, Nov. 11th/64 [*4:30* P.M.]

HON. E. M. STANTON

All the Northern papers of the 10th and especially the New York Times contain the most contraband news I have seen published during the war. The Times lays out Sherman's programme exactly and gives his strength. It is impossible to keep these papers from reaching the enemy and no doubt by to-morrow they will be making the best arrangements they can to meet this move.

U. S. GRANT

Lt. Gn.

ALS (telegram sent), CSmH; telegram received (at 5:30 P.M.), DNA, RG 107, Telegrams Collected (Bound). *O.R.*, I, xxxix, part 3, 740. On Nov. 11, 1864, 9:30 P.M., Secretary of War Edwin M. Stanton telegraphed to USG. "I have seen with indignation the newspaper articles referred to and others of like kind, but they come from Shermans army and generally from his own officers and there is reason to believe he has not been very guarded in his own talk. I saw today in a Paymasters letter to another officer his plans as stated by himself—Yesterday I was ~~show~~ told full details given by a member of his staff to a friend in Washington. Matters not spoken of aloud in the Department are bruited by ~~Sherman~~ officers coming from Shermans army in every western printing office and street. If he cannot keep from telling his plans ~~from~~ to paymasters, and his staff are permitted to send them broad cast over the land the Department cannot ~~protect him~~ prevent their publication." ALS (telegram sent), DNA, RG 107, Telegrams Collected (Bound); telegram received (on Nov. 12), *ibid.*, RG 108, Letters Received. *O.R.*, I, xxxix, part 3, 740.

On Nov. 11, USG telegraphed to Maj. Gen. George G. Meade and to Bvt. Maj. Gen. Alfred H. Terry. "If possible to prevent todays papers getting into the hands of the Enemys prevent it. They all contain news from the west most decidedly contraband"   Telegram received, DNA, RG 393, Army of the Potomac, Cav. Corps, Letters Received; *ibid.*, 9th Army Corps, Letters Received; copies, *ibid.*, 2nd Div., Letters Received; *ibid.*, 2nd Army Corps, Letters Received; *ibid.*, 24th Army Corps, Letters Received; *ibid.*, RG 108, Letters Sent; DLC-USG, V, 45, 70, 107; (2) Meade Papers, PHi. *O.R.*, I, xlii, part 3, 597. On the same day, Terry twice telegraphed to USG. "No papers have yet arrived here. I think that the ~~shortest~~ best way to prevent them from getting into the hands of the enemy will be to seize them all at Aiken's Landing & Deep Bottom. I will give orders to that effect." "~~I believe that~~ aAll the newspapers coming to this side of the river have been seized & are in the custody of the Provost Marshals." ALS (telegrams sent), DNA, RG 107, Telegrams Collected (Unbound).

To Bvt. Maj. Gen. Montgomery C. Meigs

City Point, Va, Nov. 11th *1864.*

BVT. MAJ. GEN. M. C. MEIGS
Q. M. GEN. U. S. A.
DEAR GENERAL,

I have just seen your letter to General Ingalls in reply to Capt. Eddy's setting forth his grievances. I had no idea of interfering or putting in a word in the matter knowing that you had acted from a sense of duty and that if, through mistakes, you had done Capt. E. an injustice you would correct it by simply pointing out to you wherein you had been mistaken or misinformed. Capt. Eddy could write to you as well as to me, or to Gen. Ingalls intending his letter for me, on this subject. Personally I like Capt. Eddy but I cannot let this influanc[e] me ~~in~~ to ~~protecting~~ him from the just consequences of his own neglect.

Yours Truly
U. S. GRANT
Lt. Gn.

ALS, DLC-Montgomery C. Meigs.

To Maj. Gen. George G. Meade

City Point Va. Nov. 11th/64

MAJ. GEN. MEADE,

The enemy have been movin[g] on Gen. Terry's front all day apparently massing troops to our right. At same time there appears to be troops masse[d] North of the James below our left on the river. These are probably the troop[s] reported yesterday to have left Hill's Corps. If the enemy should attack Terry it will be out of the Question to reinforce him from you but be prepared to attack at Petersburg either by moving to the left or on some weak point in front as may seem best. The movements of the enemy may mean nothing but they will bear watching.

U. S. GRANT
Lt. Gn.

ALS (telegram sent), PHi; telegram received, DNA, RG 393, Army of the Potomac, Cav. Corps, Letters Received. *O.R.*, I, xlii, part 3, 597.

On Nov. 11, 1864, 1:00 P.M., Maj. Gen. George G. Meade telegraphed to USG. "I have nothing particular to report beyond the usual picket firing on 2d corps front.—Signal officers report a movement of the enemy towards their left within their lines—I send you the despatches. I am not able to judge from them that this movement is any thing but a change of position in some of the troops—corps comdrs have been notified to be on the qui-vive & if any thing further occurs it will be duly reported.—I have this morning turned over to Lt. Col: Taylor from Washington, the political prisoners arrested in this army, to be taken by him under the orders of the War Dept to Washn—" ALS (telegram sent), DNA, RG 393, Army of the Potomac, Cav. Corps, Letters Received; telegram received, *ibid.*, RG 108, Letters Received. *O.R.*, I, xlii, part 3, 596.

To Bvt. Maj. Gen. Alfred H. Terry

City Point, Va Nov. 11, 1864

MAJ. GEN. TERRY

Let me know the preparation you are making in consequence of the movements of the enemy. Movements South of the Appomattox and your front indicate some attempt on the part of the enemy. I am really anxious to see them take the iniatiative but don't want to give them the advantage of a surprise

U. S. GRANT Lt. Gen.

Telegram, copies, DLC-USG, V, 45, 70, 107; DNA, RG 108, Letters Sent. *O.R.*, I, xlii, part 3, 604. On Nov. 11, 1864, Bvt. Maj. Gen. Alfred H. Terry telegraphed to USG. "Your despatchs received   As to the Bermuda lines, Graham has four thousand infantry besides his artillerists. In case of attack there Weitzel will at once on hearing firing move two thousand men over the river. more can be sent if necessary. In case of attack on our right & rear Weitzel can move four thousand men still leaving his lines in front sufficiently manned,   Ames has a movable column organized of between four & five thousand men ready to move in any direction. One brigade of cavalry is held in reserve ready to be thrown anywhere to fight dismounted. One brigade is doing the ordinary picket duty, & one brigade is covering our right & rear near the junction of the Charles City & Long Bridge Roads. I have had a strong rifle pit dug ~~between~~ running from the redoubt on the New Market road next east of the Four Mile Church Redoubt to the Deep Bottom Line, so that if the cavalry give us a resonable warning of an attack in that direction our troops can be put in an almost impregnable position. General Weitzel thinks that the enemy are reliving some of the local defense battalions by regular troops. Deserters for some days past have told him that such was ~~Lee's intention~~ the intention. He thinks that not more than three regiments have come across the river & it has been reported to me since I commenced writing this that small bodies of troops have been seen moving back to Richmond ~~I belie think that~~ All commanders are on the alert & I do not think that we are ~~not~~ in danger of a surprise." ALS (telegram sent), DNA, RG 107, Telegrams Collected (Unbound); telegram received, *ibid.*, RG 108, Letters Received. *O.R.*, I, xlii, part 3, 604–5.

Earlier on the same day, Terry twice telegraphed to USG, first at 11:30 A.M. "All has been quiet here this morning but I have just received the following dispatch from General Weitzel." "Since sending my last despatch I have received the following from Genl Weitzel"   ALS (telegrams sent), DNA, RG 107, Telegrams Collected (Unbound); telegrams received, *ibid.*, RG 108, Letters Received. *O.R.*, I, xlii, part 3, 604. The enclosures are *ibid.*, p. 606.

To Julia Dent Grant

City Point, Va. Nov. 11th *1864.*

DEAR JULIA,

This is the second letter I have written to you directed to Burlington besides one sent to Mr. Morris more for you than him. But as yet I have not even heard whether you have left St. Louis. In fact I have received but one letter from you since you left New Jersey. Why have you not written? Notwithstanding I shall not go to Washington to write my report I may find time to run home and spend a day or two within the next ten days.—Miss Steele[1] has written to me asking if I will not let her and you come down here to see the Army after the meeting of Congress. I have not answered but I presume it would be agreeable to have company.—I suppose the children were delighted to see you back? Jess particularly. Did you tell Mr. Ford to send Little Rebel on? If you did not I will write for him. He can be kept any place and it will be a great comfort to the children to have him.—Have you heard any thing from the house in Phila? I [would not] have thought of it but Mr. Steward,[2] Chairman of the Christian Commission, wrote to me that in a few days you would have a call from some gentlemen, admirers of your husband, on business. I supposed the business related to the house you were to be presented with.—Love and kisses for you and the children.

ULYS.

ALS, DLC-USG.

1. Probably a member of the family which included Maj. Gen. Frederick Steele and his half-brother, U.S. Representative John B. Steele of N. Y. *Frederick Steele: Forgotten General* (Stanford, Calif., 1971), p. 14. See John Y. Simon, ed., *Personal Memoirs of Julia Dent Grant* (New York, 1975), p. 134.

2. George H. Stuart, born in Ireland in 1816, a successful Philadelphia merchant, played a major role in religious and philanthropic organizations and served as president of the U.S. Christian Commission during the Civil War.

To Robert Ould

Head Quarters Armies of the United States
November 12th. 1864

JUDGE RO. OULD
AGENT FOR EXCHANGE
SIR,

Your communication of yesterday is received. All that you ask will be complied with. I will send instructions immediately to the Federal Commander in Mobile Bay to notify Gen. Maury[1] of his readiness to receive and ship to NewYorkCity one thousand bales of cotton to be consigned to one of the parties you name, who shall have every facility asked by you. My instructions in this matter, will have to go by way of Washington and NewYork cities, and may be ten days in reaching their destination. All shipments of clothing, provisions, &c for distribution among prisoners of war will be sent from the place of purchase to the point of delivery free of charge, as you suggest.

Very Respectfully
Your Ob't. Serv't.
U. S. GRANT. Lt. Gen.

Copies, DLC-USG, V, 45, 70, 107; DNA, RG 94, Letters Received, 51A 1865; *ibid.*, RG 108, Letters Sent. *O.R.*, II, vii, 1122. On Nov. 11, 1864, Robert Ould wrote to USG. "Your communication of the 6th Inst. in reply to mine of the 30th Ult. has been received. The Confederate Government will deliver on board one of your vessels near Mobile, one thousand bales of cotton, to be forwarded to the City of New York and there sold, the proceeds to be applied to the benefit of our prisoners in accordance with the recent agreement. The cotton will be ready to be delivered within a week. Whenever the Federal vessel is ready to receive it, notification can be given to Major General Maury commanding at Mobile. I venture to suggest some details, all of which I believe are in accordance with the tenor of your letter of the 30th Ulto. 1. Major General Trimble now at Fort Warren has been selected as the Confederate officer to whom the consignment shall be made at New York, who will there make the necessary and proper arrangements for the sale of the cotton and the purchase of the articles needed by our prisoners. In the event of the disability of Major General Trimble, Brig. Gen. Wm. W. R. Beale, is designated as his alternate. The selected officer shall be put on such a parole as will enable him to discharge the duties assigned to him with facility and effectiveness. 2. Such officer shall be allowed to make his purchases at those points where they can be made with the greatest advantage. 3. As the Confederate Government proposes to forward without charge such supplies as you may send for the relief of your prisoners, we take it for granted that the cost of transportation from the place of purchase will be borne by the U. S. Government. The officer selected by us will make all necessary arrangements for such transportation. 4. The reception of the supplies and their subsequent distribution amongst the prisoners on both sides, shall be certified by a Committee of officers confined in the prisons so supplied. Such a parole will be given to such officers as will enable them to carry out this agreement with due facility. They will report through the proper agents, their proceedings to their respective governments. 5. Receipts will be given when the cotton is delivered on board your vessel, and a bill of lading forwarded to Major Gen. Trimble or his alternate. 6. I will thank your authorities to furnish to Gen. Trimble or his alternate as near as may be the number of prisoners confined in your respective prisons, in order that he may duly apportion the supplies. Similar information as to our prisons will be furnished whenever it is asked. I trust that these details will be agreeable to you. If they are found to be inconvenient or defective, they can be amended by the consent of both parties. I will thank you for a reply to this communication at your earliest convenience." LS, DNA, RG 108, Letters Received. *O.R.*, II, vii, 1117–18.

On Nov. 16, 2:30 P.M., Secretary of War Edwin M. Stanton telegraphed to USG. "It is objectionable on several grounds to let General Trimble have any parole or trust or indulgence in relation to supplies for prisoners or any other purpose. He cannot be trusted and is the most dangerous rebel in our hands. General Beale is believed to be unexceptionable and may be designated as the officer or a agent under your arrangement with Mr Ould." ALS (telegram sent), DNA, RG 107, Telegrams Collected (Bound); telegram received, *ibid.*, RG 108, Letters Received. *O.R.*, II, vii, 1131. On Nov. 27, C.S.A. Maj. Gen. Isaac R. Trimble, Fort Warren, wrote to USG. "Pardon me for intruding a moment on your time. It would be a source of regret to you, I am sure, if the arrangement between yourself and General Lee (conceived and agreed to in a humane and liberal spirit, and which I to-day see noticed in the public prints with commendation) should fail to produce the good results intended by you and him from failure or oversight on the part of either Government to grant the necessary facilities for its prompt execution. The rigors of winter in the North are approaching and there is but little time left to do all that is to be done, viz, to ascertain the relative wants of each prison, to purchase or contract for clothing and blankets, to inspect and ship them, and distribute fairly among so many prisons. Most of this labor can be done or prepared for before the cotton reaches New York, so as to ship all articles as soon as sales are made. You can well understand what time can be saved by going to work at once with proper activity and with the proper number of agents. Therefore (though in ignorance of what facilities may have been the subject of stipulation, and from a desire to avoid all causes of delay) I venture to address [you] on the subject as one who having originated the work may feel a desire to see it carried out to a humane result, and ask of you the favor of doing what you can with propriety to procure for me, if not already allowed, permission to associate with me six or more Confederate officers (among them General W. N. R. Beall) 'on parole,' to aid in effecting the satisfactory execution of the business. Similar facilities will, of course, be granted by Confederate authorities." *Ibid.*, p. 1164. On Nov. 30, Lt. Col. Theodore S. Bowers wrote to Trimble. "I am directed by Lieut. Gen Grant to acknowledge the receipt by him of your communication of date Nov. 27th and to say in reply that Judge Ould named you as Agent, on the part of the Confedrate authorities for carrying out the agreement for the relief of prisoners etc. and Gen. Beall as you alternate. Of the two named the government of the United States has selected Gen. Beall, as the Agent, and in that selection the Lieut. General acquiesces He directs me to say further that he has no objection to allowing the Agent six Assistants if the Confederate authorities allow thesame number to the Agent of the United States" Copies, DLC-USG, V, 45, 70, 107; DNA, RG 108, Letters Sent. See *O.R.*, II, vii, 1191–92.

On Nov. 29, Lt. Col. John E. Mulford, U.S. asst. agent for exchange, wrote to Maj. Gen. Benjamin F. Butler discussing problems involved in delivering supplies to prisoners in C.S.A. hands. LS, DNA, RG 108, Letters Received. *O.R.*, II, vii, 1170. On Dec. 7, Butler endorsed this letter. "Respectfully forwarded to Lt Genl Grant for his information and respectfully calling his attention to the suggestion of Lt Col Mulford" AES, DNA, RG 108, Letters Received.

On Dec. 1, Lt. Col. Frederick T. Dent wrote to C.S.A. Brig. Gen. William N. R. Beall. "Yours of the 26th of Nov 1864 was not half an hour since handed me and has been submitted to Lt Gen Grant. He desires me to say that he is in receipt of a letter from the Sec of War stating that you (not Gen Trimble) have been selected. I am also aware of the fact that the Lieut General suggested the change. I am glad of it for many reasons and possibly Billy may have had some hand in bringn about the things—So you will perceive that you are not forgotten even though we stand on opposite sides of the fence—a thing I regret Still I know you to be a foeman worthy of my steel—when in the opposing hands—I hope this war will soon end and that we may meet again as of yore My little family are at Wilmington Del Mrs D has not forgotten cousin Billy Beale we often talk of you and your sisters and Shinka. Should you in the course of your travels be in Wilmington the Madam would be much pleased to see you No 506 Market street, you will ~~have~~ before this reaches you have received information from the War Dept in relation to the subject of your note so that I send you no news but am delighted to send my congratulations for your escape from longer durance to a possition where you can be usefull to your comrades in misfortune—" ALS, Museum of the Confederacy, Richmond, Va.

On Dec. 24, Beall, New York City, telegraphed to USG. "I have heard nothing from the [c]otton no orders in reference to it had been recd by Admiral Farragut [u]p to his departure from the fleet about the third inst—Please have Capt Beall Hampstead a prisoner at Johnsons Island paroled to assist me in my duties here. Two u s officers are paroled in the South and I am the only Confederate officer paroled North Please ans" Telegram received (at 7:00 P.M.), DNA, RG 107, Telegrams Collected (Bound).

1. Maj. Gen. Dabney H. Maury, District of the Gulf. See letter to Maj. Gen. William T. Sherman, Nov. 10, 1862, note 4; *O.R.*, II, vii, 1200–1.

To Edwin M. Stanton

(Cipher)   City Point, Va, Nov. 12th *1864*. [*2:00* P.M.]
HON. E. M. STANTON, SEC. OF WAR, WASHINGTON

The publications refered to in my dispatch seemed to originate in an Indianapolis paper on the authority of Army officers direct from Chattanooga. I ~~have order~~ will send a Staff officer West in the morning to ascertain who these officers are and order them here.[1] I think I will send them to the Dry Tortugas for duty, without commands, for a while as a warning to all others that they are not to report Military movements in advance of their being made.

U. S. Grant
Lt. Gen.

ALS (telegram sent), CSmH; telegram received (at 4:20 P.M.), DNA, RG 107, Telegrams Collected (Bound). *O.R.*, I, xxxix, part 3, 749. See telegram to Edwin M. Stanton, Nov. 11, 1864.

Also on Nov. 12, 1864, 9:00 P.M., USG telegraphed to Secretary of War Edwin M. Stanton. "Would it not be well to send a dispatch to Gen. Dix stating that dispatches are just received from Sherman from Kingston stating that he still held Atlanta and the road to his rear having sent back sufficient force to take care of Hood?" ALS (telegram sent), CSmH; telegram received (on Nov. 13, 2:50 P.M.), DNA, RG 107, Telegrams Collected (Bound). *O.R.*, I, xxxix, part 3, 750. On Nov. 13, 5:00 P.M., Stanton telegraphed to USG. "Your despatches of the 12th and 13th have just reached me. I will send a telegram to Dix. Every exertion is being made to get the troops forward rapidly. McClellan has resigned his resignation accepted and Sheridan appointed in his place on account of his great achievement of the 19th October" ALS (telegram sent—misdated Nov. 14), DNA, RG 107, Telegrams Collected (Bound); telegram received (on Nov. 13, 8:00 P.M.), *ibid.*, RG 108, Letters Received. *O.R.*, I, xlii, part 3, 612.

1. On Nov. 12, Lt. Col. Theodore S. Bowers issued Special Orders No. 126 sending Lt. Col. Horace Porter to Indianapolis. Copies, DLC-USG, V, 57, 62, 63, 64. On Nov. 14, Bvt. Maj. Gen. Alvin P. Hovey, Indianapolis, telegraphed to Asst. Secretary of War Charles A. Dana. "I have used every exertion to ascertain who furnished information in reference to Gen Shermans allieged movement. The information was given to the editors of the Indianapolis Journal by a soldier whose name and destination were both unknown and no trace of him can be found" Telegram received (at 8:50 P.M.), DNA, RG 108, Letters Received.

To Maj. Gen. Henry W. Halleck

———

(Cipher)   City Point, Va. Nov. 12th/64 [*9:00* P.M.]
Maj. Gn. Halleck, Washington,

I presume you have sent instructions to Foster in accordance with Sherman's request? I think it will have a good effect to make the attempt to get into Pocataligo even if it should not succeed entirely. If the troops can not get through they can keep the enemy off of Sherman a little as Derby held the Editor of the Santiago Herald,[1] or as Sturges kept Forrest off of our communications in Middle Tenn.[2]

U. S. GRANT
Lt. Gn.

ALS (telegram sent), CSmH; telegram received (on Nov. 13, 1864), DNA, RG 107, Telegrams Collected (Bound). *O.R.*, I, xxxix, part 3, 750.

1. George H. Derby of Mass., USMA 1846, who served in the U.S. Army until his death in 1861, was best known as a humorist and author of *Phoenixiana* (1856) and *Squibob Papers* (1860). In the former, he described his encounter with the enraged editor of the *San Diego Herald*. "We held 'the Judge' down over the press by our nose (which we had inserted between his teeth for that purpose), and, while our hair was employed in holding one of his hands, we held the other in our left, and, with the sheep's foot brandished above our head, shouted to him, 'Say Waldo!' " (Chicago, 1897), II, 45.

2. On June 10, 1864, Maj. Gen. Nathan B. Forrest, with about 3,500 men, attacked and defeated Brig. Gen. Samuel D. Sturgis, with about 8,000 men, at the battle of Brice's Crossroads or Guntown, Miss. Sturgis spent the remainder of the war awaiting orders. On Oct. 14, 1865, USG wrote to Secretary of War Edwin M. Stanton. "I would respectfully recommend the promotion of Bvt. Col. S. D. Sturges to the rank of Brig. Gn. by Brevet. Notwithstanding his failure at Guntown Miss. I know him to be a good and efficient officer, far above the average of our Cavalry Colonels. From the begining of the War he has suffered from having served in Kansas and coming in contact with and in opposition, ~~with~~ to, civilians, Senator Lane probably in the lead." ALS, DNA, RG 94, ACP, 1398 1881.

To Maj. Gen. Henry W. Halleck

City Point, Va, Nov. 12th *1864.*

MAJ. GEN. HALLECK,
CHIEF OF STAFF OF THE ARMY,
GENERAL,

Inclosed I send you copies of correspondence between Judge Ro. Ould, Agt. of Exchange, and myself. The correspondence explains itself. Please forward instructions to the commanding officer in Mobile Bay to notify Gen. Maury when he will be ready to receive the cotton specified; also to require an officer to receipt for it, giving "bills of lading" consigning it to one or either of the rebel officers named by Judge Ould, the officer receipting for the cotton accompanying it until it is turned over to the party to whom it is consigned. You will see by the correspondence with Gen. Lee on this subject that the officer paroled to attend to this business, is to be accompanied by a Federal Officer whilst he is at large. Please make a detail of an officer for this duty. You can arrange the wording of the parole given as you wish to carry out the agreement.

I have tried to be very liberal with the rebel authorities in this matter, because, as we get the same privileges, I thought it would better secure the main object: supplying the wants of our suffering soldiers in the South.

Very respectfully
Your ob't. serv't.
U. S. Grant. Lt. Gen.

ALS (incomplete facsimile), Paul C. Richards Autographs, *The Presidents of the United States*, [1982], p. 83; copies, DLC-USG, V, 45, 70, 107; DNA, RG 94, Letters Received, 51A 1865; *ibid.*, RG 108, Letters Sent. *O.R.*, II, vii, 1121–22.

To Edwin M. Stanton

(Cipher) City Point, Va, Nov. 13th 1864 [*8:30* A.M.]
HON. E. M. STANTON, SEC. OF WAR WASHINGTON.

As soon as troops begin to arrive here rapidly so as to insure against offensive operations on the part of the enemy I want to run up home for a day or two. I can go and return before troops enough will have arrived for me to take the offensive. I would not if I could just now do any thing to force the enemy out of Richmond or Petersburg. It would liberate to much of a force to ~~go~~ oppose Sherman with.

U. S. Grant
Lt. Gn.

ALS (telegram sent), CSmH; telegram received (at 3:10 P.M.), DNA, RG 107, Telegrams Collected (Bound). *O.R.*, I, xlii, part 3, 612.

To Maj. Gen. George G. Meade

By Telegraph from City Point
Dated Nov 13 *1864.*

To MAJ GEN MEADE
Admiral Porter & the Asst Secy of the Navy are here[1] & will start
back in a few minutes   I go with them to Fortress Monroe & will
be absent until tomorrow night leaving you in command in the in-
terval[2]   please inform Capt Emery that his brother is in Hampton Roads a prisoner aboard the Florida[3]   if he wishes to do so
permit him to visit his brother

U S GRANT
Lt. Gen

Telegram received, DNA, RG 393, Army of the Potomac, Cav. Corps, Letters
Received; copies (2), Meade Papers, PHi. *O.R.*, I, xlii, part 3, 612.
    On Nov. 12, 1864, 11:45 A.M., and Nov. 13, 12:30 P.M. (sent at 1:00
P.M.), Maj. Gen. George G. Meade telegraphed to USG. "The quiet of the lines
was undisturbed yesterday & last night. No further movements of the enemy reported since the despatches sent yesterday—After comparing all the signal officers reports, they amount to seeing the movement of about 5 or 6000 men with
some artillery,—wagons, & ambulances on the Boydtown Plank road going west
ward.—Deserters yesterday morning, who came in the night previous, say it was
rumoured their lines were to be extended to the right—A Deserter who came in
this morning belonging to Weisegar's brigade Mahon's Divn had been on picket
two days & knew nothing of any movement of his brigade or Div. Taking all the
information I possess which is simply that some of Mahone's Div. about the
Jerusalem plank road have been withdrawn from the lines Johnston extending
to supply their places & that yesterday about a div. moved to their right, I am
led to beleive that the enemy have extended their lines toward the south side
R.R. probably on some rumor of an intended movement on our part. This would
account for the movements reported by Terry as they would naturally expect
operations on both flanks & move accordingly   I have had no information of any
part of Hills corps going north of the Appomattox except when deserters reported
the withdrawal of some of Mahone's brigades, as previously stated, they said a
rumour was prevalent that the Division was going North of the James—Subsequent deserters however have not confirmed this & troops instead of being seen
going into Petersburgh have been reported coming out.—Genl. Gregg reports
one of his scouting parties yesterday encountered a scouting party of the enemy,
guerillas & he had two men wounded.—He reports numerous guerillas outside his
picket line—He has been directed to take measures to capture or drive them
away.—" "The lines were yesterday & last night all quiet except some artillery
firing on the right.—Deserters yesterday reported no movement of the enemy,
but said it was understood Mahon's Division had been withdrawn from the
trenches & was going into winter quarters. Brig Genl. Gregg reports a scouting
party of the cavalry, overtook & killed Five guerillas in the neighborhood of

Disputantia Station on the Norfolk R. Rd—yesterday." ALS (telegrams sent—the first incomplete), DNA, RG 393, Army of the Potomac, Cav. Corps, Letters Received; telegrams received, *ibid.*, RG 108, Letters Received. *O.R.*, I, xlii, part 3, 607–8, 612.

1. On Nov. 11, Asst. Secretary of the Navy Gustavus V. Fox telegraphed to USG. "I wish to go down to see you sunday noon. If you are not to be there, please notify me." Copy, DNA, RG 45, Miscellaneous Letters Sent. At 11:30 P.M., USG telegraphed to Fox. "Will you leave Washington Sunday at noon or will you be here at that time? I ask because I want to see Adm.l Porter if I can get away and will arrange to meet you at Fortress Monroe & come up with you." ALS (telegram sent), CSmH; telegram received (on Nov. 12, 1:45 A.M.), DNA, RG 45, Miscellaneous Letters Received; *ibid.*, RG 107, Telegrams Collected (Bound). *O.R.* (Navy), I, xi, 60. On Nov. 12, 9:00 A.M., Fox telegraphed to USG. "We shall be at Hampton Roads at 7 A. M. tomorrow morning unless it is stormy weather which will cause some delay   Admiral Porter joins us there" Telegram received, *ibid.*, RG 108, Letters Received.

2. On Nov. 13, USG wrote to Bvt. Maj. Gen. Alfred H. Terry. "I am going to Fort Monroe. Will be absent until to morrow evening. Should anything occur you will receive orders from Gen. Meade," Copies, DLC-USG, V, 45, 70, 107; DNA, RG 108, Letters Sent. *O.R.*, I, xlii, part 3, 615.

On Nov. 12, Terry had twice telegraphed to USG. "I have no Richmond papers of yesterday or to-day but I will try to obtain some"   "I have been obtained & forwarded to you to-day's Richmond papers. I have not yet been able to get yesterday's papers." ALS (telegrams sent), DNA, RG 107, Telegrams Collected (Unbound).

3. Capt. Campbell D. Emory, USMA 1861, was then serving as act. aide to Meade; C.S.A. Asst. Surgeon Thomas Emory was taken prisoner when the C.S.S. *Florida* was captured on Oct. 7 off Bahia, Brazil, by the U.S.S. *Wachusett*. The two ships arrived at Hampton Roads on Nov. 11. See *O.R.* (Navy), I, iii, 256, 270.

To J. Russell Jones

City Point, Va, Nov. 13th *1864.*

DEAR JONES,

Bass [*Sappington*] writes to me that he has shipped "old Jack" to you. I hope he reached you all safe. If you will ride him with a curb bit and spur you will find him the best saddle horse you ever rode. He drives perfectly gentle too, but he is thick skined and cares nothing for a whip. To drive him with any pleasure you want a stick with a spike in the end of it to use as a spur. You will find him tolerably fast and very durable. He is also perfectly safe for your wife or children to either ride or drive. Use him freely as you would your own horse.

Every thing is very quiet here and seems likely to remain so until I make it otherwise. The rebels are reinforcing to a conciderable extent by bringing in men who have heretofore been detailed in workshops &c. and by collecting the old men and little boys. It is better that it should be so. When the job is done then it will be well done. The overwhelmming majority received by M. Lincoln, and the quiet with which the election went off, will prove a terrible damper to the rebels. It will be worth more than a victory in the field both in its effect on the rebels and in its influance abroad. Admiral Porter is now tightening the blockade so closely that I think with the two, the election and the capture of blockade runners, England will soon withdraw her support from the rebel cause.

I suppose you and Washburn are as happy over the result of the election as "Clams in high tide'? My respects to W. and all other friends.

Yours Truly
U. S. GRANT

ALS, ICHi. On the same day, USG wrote another private letter in which he discussed the need for the C.S.A. to recruit the Negro. "Him they are afraid of, and they will never use him unless as a last desperate alternative. . . . The immense majority which Mr. Lincoln has received is worth more to us than a victory in the field, both in its effects on the rebels, and in its foreign influence." *Richardson*, p. 454.

To Edwin M. Stanton

City Point, Va. Nov. 14. 1864.

HON. E. M. STANTON
SECRETARY OF WAR
WASHINGTON, D. C.
SIR!

Herewith I respectfully return the papers submitted by Thomas H. Yeatman in behalf of Samuel and W. W. Worthington for proceeds of 1036 bales of cotton seized on the Mississippi river by my order, and by you referred to me for remarks.

The order within set forth as the one on which said cotton was seized is correct. This cotton with a large amount of other cotton, was by my order (and prior to the receipt of the Treasury Regulations on the subject) sent to Memphis and there turned over to the Quarter Masters Department and sold for the benefit of the Government, and the funds realized borne and accounted for on proper Quarter Masters papers. This addition to the Quarter Masters fund of the Department I then commanded, as well as justice to the men who volunteered to run the Vicksburg batteries, and served as pilots, engineers and laborers on the steamers during that, dangerous service, induced me to order payment to them for such services (above their pay as soldiers) by the Quarter Masters Department as well as free transportation to their homes and return on furloughs granted them. I never supposed that the Quarter Masters Department would be liable to refund the amount, received for this cotton to the persons holding the receipts for it, any more than they could be required to pay for horses and mules taken in an enemy's country, under existing orders from the Adjutant Generals Office. The receipts were given so, as to enable the parties, if they could prove themselves loyal before courts authorized by Government to decide such cases, to show by whom and by what authority their cotton was seized. This adjudication has not been had in this case, and entertaining the same opinion now, that I entertained, when I made the orders referred to, I cannot recommend the refunding of the amount realized on the sale of this cotton.

There is another thing in this case that I depricate and regard as highly censurable. It is, that persons who have filled the responsible position of Treasury Agent (as has the attorney in this case) should take advantage of the information acquired in their position of trust and confidence, to get up claims against the Government. All claims gotten up or advocated by them should be regarded with suspicion, and fully investigated before being allowed.

> Very Respectfully
> Your Obt. Servt.
> U. S. GRANT, Lt. Gen.

Copies, DLC-USG, V, 45, 70, 107; DNA, RG 108, Letters Sent. See John Jolliffe, *Argument Before the Secretary of War in the Cases of Samuel Worthington and Dr. William W. Worthington* (Washington, [1866]).

To Julia Dent Grant

———

City Point, Va. Nov. 14th *1864.*

DEAR JULIA,

As soon as troops begin to arrive here so that there will be no likelyhood of an attack on us I will run up home for a day or two. I expect the troops to begin to arrive to-morrow so I think you need not look for an other letter from me until you see me in person. Gen. Rawlins left Washington to-day for City Point. As he says nothing of you being with him I presume you are not coming. I do not know even that you have left Mo. as I have had but one letter from you since you left Burlington. If I should be so neglectful I would get a regular c[ussn']. I shall go to Burlington however and see the childre[n] if you are not there.

Love and kisses for you and the children.

ULYS.

ALS, DLC-USG.

To Edwin M. Stanton

———

Cipher   City Point, Va, Nov. 15th 1864 [*2:30* P.M.]
HON. E. M. STANTON, SEC. OF WAR.

I would recommend the appointment of Brevt. Maj. Gen. Weitzel to full Maj. Gn. of Volunteers. I want to have him assigned to the command of the 10th Corps. This assignment however I do not wish made at present. It is my intention to transfer all the White troops from the 10th and all Colored troops of other Corps to it and then assign Weitzel to the command.

U. S. GRANT
Lt. Gn

ALS (telegram sent), CSmH; telegram received (at 3:50 P.M.), DNA, RG 107, Telegrams Collected (Bound); *ibid.*, Telegrams Collected (Unbound). *O.R.*, I, xlii, part 3, 619.

On Nov. 18, 1864, 3:00 P.M., Maj. Gen. Benjamin F. Butler telegraphed to Brig. Gen. John A. Rawlins. "General Grant told me yesterday that an order should be issued transferring the Colored troops of the Ninth (9th) Corps to me Please therefore order over two (2) regiments to report to General Graham at Point of Rocks and I will order two (2) regiments of the Provisional Brigade to report to Genl Parke as soon as the Colored regiments arrive—I ask this movement in this form in view of the threatened attack on Bermuda line Please order them to night" LS (telegram sent), DNA, RG 107, Telegrams Collected (Unbound); telegram received, *ibid.*, RG 108, Letters Received. Printed as transmitted to Maj. Gen. George G. Meade (received at 3:30 P.M.) in *O.R.*, I, xlii, part 3, 638. On the same day, Rawlins telegraphed to Meade. "Gen Grant has decided to issue an order transferring the Colored troops of the 9th Corps to Gen Butlers Command. You will therefore please order two (2) Regiments of Colored troops to report to Gen Graham at Point of Rocks at once Gen Butler has been ordered to send 2 Regiments of white troops to report to Gen Parke when these colored Regiments report to Gen Graham." Telegram received, DNA, RG 107, Telegrams Collected (Unbound); (at 3:55 P.M.) *ibid.*, RG 393, Army of the Potomac, Cav. Corps, Letters Received; copies, *ibid.*, RG 108, Letters Sent; DLC-USG, V, 45, 70, 107; (2) Meade Papers, PHi. *O.R.*, I, xlii, part 3, 638. Also on Nov. 18, Butler telegraphed to Rawlins transmitting a telegram from Brig. Gen. Charles K. Graham reporting rumors of the evacuation of Petersburg, which Rawlins in turn transmitted to Meade. Telegram received (at 3:30 P.M.), DNA, RG 94, War Records Office, Army of the Potomac; *ibid.*, RG 108, Letters Received; copies (2), Meade Papers, PHi. *O.R.*, I, xlii, part 2, 656. At 3:30 P.M., Rawlins telegraphed to Butler. "Your dispatches received and information of rumors of enemy's contemplated movements transmitted to Gen. Meade. Gen. Meade has been ordered to send at once two Regiments of colored troops to report to Gen. Graham at Point of Rocks. Upon these so reporting you will please send the two Regiments you propose to report to Gen. Parke." Copies, DLC-USG, V, 45, 70, 107; DNA, RG 108, Letters Sent. *O.R.*, I, xlii, part 3, 652.

On Nov. 25, Butler telegraphed to Rawlins. "Will you please ~~telegraph~~ send me the order transferring the colored troops of the 9 Corps to my command in ex change for ~~white~~ an equal number of white troops, that I may commence the transfer immediately" ALS (telegram sent), DNA, RG 94, War Records Office, Dept. of Va. and N. C., Army of the James, Unentered Papers. On the same day, Lt. Col. Ely S. Parker issued Special Orders No. 136. "The following permanant transfer of troops is hereby ordered: The U. S. colored troops of the 9th Army Corps, Army of the Potomac to the Army of the James, and Col Potter's brigade of the Army of the James to the Army of the Potomac. The necessary orders for immediate carrying out of this order will be made by the respective Commanders of said Armies." Copies, DLC-USG, V, 57, 62, 63, 64; Meade Papers, PHi. *O.R.*, I, xlii, part 3, 702. On Dec. 2, USG telegraphed to Butler. "Has Col. Potter been sent to the Army of the Potomac? I do not care to have him go but Gen. Meade is desirous of knowing, if he is to go or not in order that he may know whether to assign a commander to the troops you sent to him." ALS (telegram sent), CSmH; telegram received, DLC-Benjamin F. Butler. *O.R.*, I, xlii, part 3, 781. On the same day, Butler telegraphed to USG. "Col Potter has been assigned to the Command of a Brigade in the 18th Corps and I would not like to Spare him if you do not object to the Assignment" ALS (telegram sent), DNA, RG 107, Telegrams Collected (Unbound). *O.R.*, I, xlii, part 3, 782.

To Edwin M. Stanton

City Point, Va, Nov. 15th *1864.*

HON. E. M. STANTON,
SEC. OF WAR,
SIR:

Copy of Brig. Gn. L. Thomas' Spl. Ord. 144, present series, dismissing Capt. J. R. Locke, 64th U. S. Colored Inf,y. together with copy of letter from the Sec. of the Western Sanitary Commission exhonerating him from the charges made in the order, are before me. As the order specifies Capt. Locke has been dismissed for improper appropriation of Sanitary goods entrusted to him, justice would demand his reinstatement. If, as charged by Gen. Thomas, a general unfitness exists ~~the~~ Capt. Locke should be allowed to resign as there is evidence he attempted to do prior to his dismissal. I would respectfully suggest however before demanding the resignation of Capt. Locke the opinion of Col. J. Eaton, 63d U. S. Colored Inf.y, as to his fitness be had.

It would appear that Gen. Thomas has received his impressions in this matter principally from Brig. Gen. N. B. Buford whos judgement I would not take, knowing him well from the begining of this war, in any Military matter. I think the charge of general unfitness had better be left to the judgement of one less subject to the same charge.

Very respectfully
your obt. svt.
U. S. GRANT
Lt. Gn.

ALS, DNA, RG 94, Colored Troops Div., Letters Received, L118/64. James R. Locke of Springfield, Ill., chaplain, 2nd Ill. Cav., from Aug. 6, 1861, had long been active in relief for the freedmen and in recruiting Negro troops. At the time of his dismissal he was serving as superintendent of freedmen at Helena, Ark., as well as capt., 64th U.S. Colored. On Nov. 22, 1864, Judge Advocate Gen. Joseph Holt wrote a lengthy report, which President Abraham Lincoln endorsed on Nov. 26. "Report approved. Let Captain Locke be reinstated according to the recommendation of the Leiutenant General and the Judge Advocate General." ES, *ibid.* See Lincoln, *Works*, VIII, 122.

To Maj. Gen. Benjamin F. Butler

City Point, Va, Nov. 15th *1864*.

MAJ. GEN. B. F. BUTLER
COMD.G ARMY OF THE JAMES,
GENERAL,

As I am about leaving City Point to be absent for five or six days I have just sent instructions to Gen. Meade of which the enclosed is a copy. These instructions contain all that is necessary for you if the contingency upon which they are based should arise. All that I would add is that in case it should be necessary for you to withdraw from North of the James you abandon all of your present lines except at Deep Bottom and Dutch Gap. Just occupy what you did prior to the movement which secured our present position.

Preparitory to this remove at once, within the line to be held, all heavy guns that cannot be drawn of readily. Open the rear of all enclosed works so that when we want to retake them they will not be directed against us. Gen. Barnard, Chief Eng. in the Field, by my direction, informed the Chief Eng. Army of the James, of the work to be done in this respect.

> Very respectfully
> your obt. svt.
> U. S. GRANT
> Lt. Gn.

ALS, DNA, RG 94, War Records Office, Dept. of Va. and N. C., Army of the James, Unentered Papers. *O.R.*, I, xlii, part 3, 625.

To Maj. Gen. John A. Dix

City Point, Va, Nov. 15th *1864*.

MAJ. GEN. J. A. DIX,
COMD.G DEPT. OF THE EAST,
GENERAL,

I understand General Butler whilst in New York, had one Mr. Bergholz, a citizen of Columbia S. C. arrested and sent to Fort

Hamilton. I have never seen Mr. B. but have heard from him and of him and believe he is and always has been a friend of the Government. He is a German, Prussian I think, who left the North for the South prior to the War and on account of having accumulated some property there felt himself compelled to remain until fearing the conscription probably, he has left. Before hearing that Mr. B. was in arrest I had sent a pass to him to visit me at my Head Quarters for the purpose of getting from him more particular an minute information upon matters in the South than that already received from him in writing.

If there are not special charges against him of which I know nothing I wish you would have Mr. Bergholz released and permitted to visit me at Hd Qrs. without exacting from him an oath of allegiance.

> Very respectfully
> your obt. svt.
> U. S. Grant
> Lt. Gn.

P. S. I have no doubt but Mr. Bergholz may have had a permit to leave the South, obtained solely on account of intimacy between himself and Mr. Trenholms the rebel Sec. of the Treasury.

> U. S[.] G.

ALS, DNA, RG 109, Union Provost Marshals' File of Papers Relating to Individual Civilians. See letter to Mrs. Mary M. Bergholz, Nov. 15, 1864. On Nov. 19, 1864, Maj. Gen. John A. Dix, New York City, wrote to USG. "I have the honor to acknowledge the receipt of your letter of the 15th inst. in regard to the arrest of Mr. Bergholz by Maj. Genl. Butler, of which I had previously received no intimation whatever. Had I been apprized of it, I should have directed him (Mr. B.) to be sent to my Head Qrs. for examination. I have always regarded the arrest of citizens as a high prerogative; and, even when in the field, have required persons taken into custody by my subordinate commanders to be reported to me immediately with a written statement of the grounds of arrest. Mr. Bergholz was sent to Fort Hamilton without any notice to me and without any charges against him. Genl. Butler had no geographical command, and the arrest and confinement of Mr. Bergholz was altogether without authority. I enclose herewith authenticated copies of the report of Major Woodruff, commanding at Fort Hamilton, and of the order under which Mr. Bergholz was sent there by Genl. Butler." ALS, *ibid.*, RG 108, Letters Received. The enclosures are *ibid.*

To Maj. Gen. George G. Meade

City Point, Va, Nov. 15 *1864.*

Maj. Gen. G. G. Meade,
Comd.g A. P.
General,

The movements now being made by the Army under Gen. Sherman may cause General Lee to detach largely from the force defending Richmond to meet him. Should this occur it will become our duty to follow. In such case the Army of the James will be promptly withdrawn from North of James River and put in the trenches about Petersburg, thus liberating all of your Infantry and Cavalry, and a sufficient amount of Artillery. To prepare for such imergency therefore I would direct that you hold yourself in readiness to start in the shortest time with twelve days rations, six being carried on the person, and forty rounds of ammunition in waggons. Select from your command the best batteries to accompany you not exceeding one gun to one thousand men. It is not intended that these preparations shall be made to start at a moments notice but that the articles shall be where they can be reached and loaded, and all preparations made for starting, by the time your troops can be relieved ~~after~~ by the troops of General Butler after such movement on the part of the enemy is discovered.

A Copy of this will be furnished Gen. Butler with instructions to carry out his part promptly, moving night as well as day, if the contingency should arise.

Very respectfully
your obt. svt.
U. S. Grant
Lt. Gen.

ALS, deCoppet Collection, NjP. *O.R.,* I, xlii, part 3, 620.
On Nov. 15, 1864, USG telegraphed to Maj. Gen. George G. Meade. "Will you please send one of your Cipher operators here to remain at my Hd Qrs. during my absence. I shall have to take my Cipher operator with me." ALS (telegram sent), Kohns Collection, NN; copies, DLC-USG, V, 45, 70, 107; DNA, RG 108, Letters Sent; (2—dated Nov. 16) Meade Papers, PHi. On Nov. 16, 9:00 p.m., Meade telegraphed to USG. "I have now but one cipher operator with me

Mr. Caldwell who is the chief in charge of all. I will send him tomorrow as he can readily be spared during your absence, but I should like him to come back on your return"   ALS (telegram sent), DNA, RG 94, War Records Office, Army of the Potomac; copies, *ibid.*, RG 393, Army of the Potomac, Letters Sent; Meade Papers, PHi.

On Nov. 15, Lt. Col. Theodore S. Bowers telegraphed to Meade. "Please have the ambulances & wagons left behind by the 6th Corps except those with the artillery returned into Depot & the men now with them sent to the 6th Corps the artillery will continue a portion of your Command as heretofore & subject to such use as you wish to put it to:"   Telegram received, DNA, RG 393, Army of the Potomac, Cav. Corps, Letters Received; copies, *ibid.*, RG 108, Letters Sent; DLC-USG, V, 45, 70, 107; (2) Meade Papers, PHi. *O.R.*, I, xlii, part 3, 620.

On Nov. 16, 10:00 A.M., Meade telegraphed to USG. "There is nothing to report from this army—If you have no objection & will be at home this morning I wish ~~you~~ to visit you at City Point"   ALS (telegram sent), DNA, RG 393, Army of the Potomac, Cav. Corps, Letters Received; telegram received, *ibid.*, RG 107, Telegrams Collected (Unbound). The response from Brig. Gen. John A. Rawlins was noted at the foot of the telegram received. "The General desires you to come down this morning if you can." Copy, *ibid.*

To Bvt. Maj. Gen. Alfred H. Terry

City Point, Va, Nov. 15th *1864*.

MAJ. GEN. TERRY,
COMD.G ARMY OF THE JAMES
GENERAL,

Please pass Mrs. Carrington by flag of truce through our lines and deliver her to the pickets of the enemy, with her baggag[e] &c. without inspection. Mrs. C. is the mother of Gen. Carrington who has been in our service and is now U. S. Atty. for the Dist. of Columbia. Gn. Carrington is permitted to accompany Mrs. Carrington to our lines.

Please furnish transportation for person and baggage

Very respectfully
your obt. svt.
U. S. GRANT
Lt. Gn.

ALS, ViHi. On Nov. 15, 1864, USG prepared a pass. "Pass Gen. Carrington and Mother, with baggage to Aiken's Landing, or terminous of line, on Steamer bearing U. S. Mail for Army of the James." ADS, *ibid.* An undated telegram from Bvt. Maj. Gen. Alfred H. Terry to USG was probably sent the same day.

"Your dispatch is received   I will send an officer with my spring wagon to meet Mrs Carrington at Bermuda Landing to-morrow morning." ALS (telegram sent), DNA, RG 107, Telegrams Collected (Unbound). Edward C. Carrington, born in 1825, the son of Edward C. Carrington and Eliza H. Preston Carrington, served as capt., 1st Va., in the Mexican War, practiced law in D. C., where he served as brig. gen. of militia, then was appointed U.S. district attorney for D. C. by President Abraham Lincoln. See Lincoln, *Works*, VII, 419; *ibid.* (*Supplement*), 252, 262; *Washington Post*, June 4, 1892; Lee A. Wallace, Jr., "The First Regiment of Virginia Volunteers 1846–1848," *Virginia Magazine of History and Biography*, 77, 1 (Jan., 1969), 46.

To Maj. Gen. George H. Thomas

(Cipher)   City Point, Va, Nov. 15th 1864 [*11:00* A.M.]
MAJ. GEN. G. H. THOMAS, NASHVILLE TEN.

If Hood commences falling back it will not do to wait for the full equipment of your Cavalry to follow. He should in that event, be pressed with such force as you can bring to bear.

U. S. GRANT
Lt. Gn.

ALS (telegram sent), CSmH; copies, DLC-USG, V, 45, 70, 107; DNA, RG 107, Telegrams Received in Cipher; *ibid.*, RG 108, Letters Sent; *ibid.*, RG 393, Dept. of the Cumberland, Telegrams Received. *O.R.*, 1, xlv, part 1, 895. On Nov. 15, 1864, 4:00 P.M., Maj. Gen. George H. Thomas telegraphed to USG. "Your telegram this A. M. just recd. Am watching Hood closely, and should he move after Sherman I will follow him with what force I can raise at hand   The reports this morning are that he is moving in the direction of Waynesboro. A cavalry force has been sent to ascertain the true state of affairs" Telegram received (at 9:10 P.M.), DNA, RG 107, Telegrams Collected (Bound); (on Nov. 16, 10:30 A.M.) *ibid.*, RG 108, Letters Received; copies, *ibid.*, RG 107, Telegrams Received in Cipher; *ibid.*, RG 393, Dept. of the Cumberland, Telegrams Sent. *O.R.*, I, xlv, part 1, 895.

On Nov. 13, 1864, 8:00 P.M., Thomas had telegraphed to USG, sending a copy to Maj. Gen. Henry W. Halleck. "I have nothing new to report tonight in the situation of affairs at the front   The enemy up to this morning has made no effort to advance beyond Shoal Creek   Gen Wilson reports tonight that the cavalry arms and equipments enquired for some weeks since have not yet reached Louisville. Their non arrival will delay us in preparing for the field" Telegram received (at 10:40 P.M.), DNA, RG 107, Telegrams Collected (Bound); (at 12:00 P.M.) *ibid.*, RG 108, Letters Received; copy, *ibid.*, RG 107, Telegrams Received in Cipher. Printed as sent at 10:00 P.M. in *O.R.*, I, xxxix, part 3, 764.

On Oct. 4, 11:00 P.M., Thomas, Nashville, had telegraphed to USG, sending a copy to Secretary of War Edwin M. Stanton. "I reached this place yesterday P. M. having been ordered here by Gen Sherman to organize the troops in the district to drive Forrest from our lines of communication whilst he with the main army watched the movements of the main rebel army in the vicinity of Atlanta. While at Chattanooga I succeeded in getting Gen Morgans d[ivis]ion of the 14th Corps as far as Athens on the 2d inst with orders to move to Bainbridge & seize Forrests ponton bridge at that place which he used when he came into Tennessee. I then came to this place and despatched Maj Gen Rosseau with a mounted force of cavalry & infantry of about 7000 men along Ala. R. R. to meet Forrest who was reported at Spring Hill on the 2d inst. Gen Rousseaus troops are beyond Columbia tonight and he reports this P M that Forrest retreated via Mt Pleasant towards Florence, He will push after him rapidly as roads will permit & Washburne with 3000 cavalry will start from Tenn tomorrow morning to strike Gen Rousseaus line of march near Pulaski & join in the pursuit. Two gunboats have also been ordered up The Tenn to go as far as possible; They will probably reach Florence as the river has risen very much within the past few days & if Forrest does not succeed in crossing tonight I believe we shall be able to destroy him. He has done very little damage to the Ala. R. R. between Pulaski & Columbia—He destroyed five miles of the road and two bridges between Columbia and Franklin. We have the telegraph repaired to Pulaski & will soon have it through to Athens; R R to Athens can be repaired in one week; Bridge over the Elk River and Sulphur trestle cannot be repaired within month but as all the troops in that region of the country can be supplied from Pulaski & Athens we shall not suffer much inconvenience. Nashville & Chattanooga R R has not been injured at all by Forrest Following information just recd by telegraph from Chattanooga 'Teleg. lines now working to Alatoona—Rebels have captured Big Shanty & are northward bound, Sherman is after them R. R. torn up & burned for ten miles—Chattahoochee bridge destroyed by high water and hundreed feet bridge at Ressacca also carried away by high water Gen Corses Div. is at Rome and great portion of Jno E Smiths division is at Alatoona This force can hold the line of the Etowah and resist the further progress of the enemy north whilst Sherman can move upon his rear Sherman has ample facilities for crossing the Chattahoochee by several bridges constructed by the army in its advance on Atlanta; he fortunately also has an ample supply of ammunition & provisions in Atlanta so that he will not be materially affected by the present state of the R. R. Reinforcements are beginning to arrive at this place & I hope soon to have some of them so posted as to prevent a repetition of Forrests recent raid; should he escape across the river" Telegram received (on Oct. 5, 3:00 P.M.), DNA, RG 107, Telegrams Collected (Bound); *ibid.*, RG 108, Letters Received; copy, *ibid.*, RG 107, Telegrams Received in Cipher. Printed as sent at 8:30 P.M. in *O.R.*, I, xxxix, part 3, 78–79. Through Oct. 20, Thomas telegraphed almost daily to Stanton or Halleck, sending copies to USG. Because USG did not respond directly to these telegrams, already available in *O.R.*, they will not be printed.

To Mrs. Mary M. Bergholz

Nov. 15th *1864*.

Mrs. M. M. Bergholz,
My Dear Madam,

I have just this evening rec'd your letter of the 13th and at once wrote to Gen. Dix to release your husband. I presume it will be done the very day you receive this. But you had better call on Gen. Dix at once and find out what the probabilities are in the matter.

You speak of troubles never coming singly? What was your other troubles? I hope nothing from having received a letter from me? I have sent a pass for Mr. Bergholz to come to City Point and in my letter to Gen. Dix have asked him to release him to come here.

Hoping you will have no serious trouble I remain

AL (signature clipped), DLC-USG, I, B. On Sept. 19, 1864, USG had issued a pass. "Mrs. M. M. Bergholz & son have permission to pass through the Federal lines south per 'Flag of Truce' steamer 'New York.'" ADS, DLC-Benjamin F. Butler. See letters to Mary M. Bergholz, Nov. 20, Dec. 22, 1864; letter to Maj. Gen. William T. Sherman, Dec. 19, 1864.

Calendar

1864, AUG. 16. USG endorsement. "Respectfully forwarded to the Sec. of War with the request that Gen. Barnard be assigned to duty with his Brevet rank, and for the reasons stated."—AES, DNA, RG 94, Letters Received, 1068B 1864. Written on a letter of the same day from Bvt. Maj. Gen. John G. Barnard to USG. "The fact that though 'Chief Engineer' of the combined armies I am not the ranking Officer of my Corps on *Engineer duty* with those armies (Gen. Benham ranking me as a Brigadier General), renders it proper I think, independently of other considerations, that I should be assigned to duty with my brevet rank, as Major General. Should you concur in this I request that you will forward this application, with your recommendation, to the Hon. Secretary of War."—ALS, *ibid.*

1864, AUG. 16. USG endorsement. "Owing to the great amount of inland navigation in the Dep't. of N. C. & Va. a fleet of light draft gun boats, such as this flotilla furnishes, I deem very essential. Whether they do better service attached to the land or water service is a question. I am inclined to believe they are of more service attached to the Army. Prize money is a great temptation to do many things on the inland waters, that ought not to be done, and the Army receives no prize money. Gen Butler however should not be allowed to fit out Gunboats, at the expense of Government, without special Authority from the Secretary of War."—ES, DNA, RG 107, Letters Received, W2336 1865. Written on a letter of Aug. 3 from Maj. Gen. Benjamin F. Butler to Asst. Secretary of War Charles A. Dana reporting the use of soldiers on armed vessels belonging to the Q. M. Dept.—LS, *ibid.* On Aug. 19, Dana endorsed this letter. "Respectfully returned to Lieut: Genl Grant, with the information that the proceeds of prizes, captured by gun-boats, attached to the army are distributed among their crews precisely as in the naval service, with the exception, that, whereas in the naval service, the prize money is shared among all vessels within a certain distance of the property captured, the army gun-boats divide the same among those vessels alone which are actually engaged in the capture."—ES, *ibid.* On Feb. 7, 1865, USG again endorsed this letter. "I would *now* respectfully recommend that what is known as the Naval Brigade be turned over to the Navy, and the officers and men connected with it be returned to their Regiments as soon as their places can be supplied by the Navy. I would further recommend the discharge of the two chartered vessels now with this Brigade."—ES, *ibid.* On Feb. 14, Col. Edward D. Townsend wrote to USG stating that Secretary of War Edwin M. Stanton approved the recommendation made in USG's endorsement.—LS, DNA, RG 108, Letters Received.

1864, AUG. 17. Secretary of War Edwin M. Stanton to USG. "I enclose herewith a letter of the Honorable Wm. H. Seward, Secretary of State, introducing Col. Estvan, correspondent of the Augsburg Gazette, who desires permission to visit the armies of the United States. This Department grants no passes, except at the instance or with the approval of the Commanding Generals. You will please therefore report whether, in your opinion, the pass requested by Col. Estvan shall be granted. He comes highly recommended, as you will see, and accredited by the State Department. An early answer is requested."—Copy, DLC-Edwin M. Stanton. The correspondent may be Bela Estvàn, author of *War Pictures from the South* (New York, 1863).

1864, AUG. 18, 10:30 A.M. To Maj. Gen. Edward O. C. Ord. "Please send an ambulance or horse to Pitken's station to take Mr Chagham Esq to front. Mr C leaves in half hour."—Telegram received, Ord Papers, CU-B.

1864, AUG. 20. USG endorsement. "Respectfully returned to the Secretary of War, and attention invited to the opinions within expressed. McCandless was mustered out by reason of the expiration of the term of service of his Regiment about the 1st of June."—ES, DNA, RG 94, Letters Received, 894A 1864. Written on a letter of Aug. 4 from Col. Edward D. Townsend to USG. "The Secretary of War directs me to send you the enclosed copy of a letter from Colonel Wm. McCandless, declining the appointment of Brigadier General."—ALS, *ibid.* On July 30, William McCandless, Philadelphia, wrote to Brig. Gen. Lorenzo Thomas. "I have the honor to acknowledge the receipt of a communication from the Secretary of War dated the 21st inst informing me of my promotion to the position of Brigadier General of Volunteers. This appointment I decline to accept. In order that my motives for so doing may be clearly understood, I will state that, when those who administer the Government, re adopt the original intention, of prosecuting this War for the restoration of the Union, I, together with hundreds of Officers and thousands of men (at present out of service) will be found ready and willing to reenter. Until such time I consider the the post of honor to be the private station."—Copy, *ibid.* See letter to Edwin M. Stanton, May 13, 1864.

1864, AUG. 21. To Maj. Gen. George G. Meade. "Gen Sheridan asks that Surg Ghiselin on duty with your Med Dir may be assigned as his Med Dir   Are you willing to spare him for this purpose"—Telegram received, DNA, RG 94, War Records Office, Army of the Potomac; copies, *ibid.*, RG 108, Letters Sent; DLC-USG, V, 45, 68, 107; (2) Meade Papers, PHi. On the same day, 9:20 P.M., Meade telegraphed to USG. "I have no objection to the assignment of Surgeon Ghiselin to duty as Medical Director of Major General Sheridans' command."—Copy (telegram sent), DNA, RG 94, War Records Office, Army of the Potomac; telegram received, *ibid.*, RG 108, Letters Received.

1864, AUG. 23. USG endorsement. "Approved and respectfully forwarded to the Qr. Mr. Gn. of the Army, Washington D. C."—AES, DNA, RG 92, Letters Received from Hd. Qrs. Written on a letter of Aug. 21 from Brig. Gen. Rufus Ingalls to Maj. Robert S. Davis, adjt. for Maj. Gen. Benjamin F. Butler, requesting assignments for q. m. officers.—LS, *ibid.*

1864, AUG. 23.   Special Orders No. 78, Armies of the U.S. *"Commissaries of Subsistence* will sell subsistence stores, to all citizens properly authorized to be within the lines of the Armies operating against Richmond, who are not entitled to draw rations, such sales to be made in compliance with paragraph '1230' Revised Army Regulations. Citizens will not be allowed to purchase a greater amount of stores, than is required for their own use, nor more, than a supply for ten days at any one time. *The Quarter Masters Department* will also sell to such citizens forage, in such quantities, and at such rates, as may be determined on, by the Chief Qr. Mstr."—Copies, DLC-USG, V, 57, 62, 68; ICarbS. *O.R.,* I, xlii, part 2, 424–25.

1864, AUG. 24.   USG endorsement. "Respectfully forwarded to the Secretary of War, with the request that this resignation be accepted. Col Rowley has been a member of my Staff for over two years, and has on all occasions discharged the duties entrusted to him with zeal, fidelity and ability, and to my fullest satisfaction. His health however, has become so impaired that his withdrawal from service is necessary to save his life."—ES, DNA, RG 94, ACP, 482R CB 1864. Written on a letter of Aug. 3 from Maj. William R. Rowley, Galena, to USG tendering his resignation.—ALS, *ibid.* On Aug. 26, USG wrote to Secretary of War Edwin M. Stanton. "I respectfully request that Captain Ely S. Parker, Assistant Adjutant General of Volunteers be assigned to duty on my Staff as Military Secretary with the rank of Lieutenant Colonel, vice W. R Rowley resigned."—LS, *ibid.,* 731 1887. On Aug. 30, Col. Edward D. Townsend issued General Orders No. 249 announcing the appointment as USG had requested.—Copy (printed), *ibid.*

1864, AUG. 25.   Capt. George K. Leet, Washington, to Lt. Col. Theodore S. Bowers. "Scouts report that no troops had moved to or from the Valley up to Tuesday night, 23d. Rebels are hauling considerable grain by Wagon to Beaver Dam Station."—ALS (telegram sent), DNA, RG 107, Telegrams Collected (Bound); telegram received, *ibid.,* Telegrams Collected (Unbound). *O.R.,* I, xlii, part 2, 471.

1864, AUG. 26.   To Secretary of War Edwin M. Stanton. "If the vacancy created by the appointment of Med. Inspector Barns as Surgeon General has not been filled I would respectfully recommend Surgeon M. Mills or Surgeon J. M. KCuyler for the place my preference being in the order in which they are here named knowing as I do Dr Mills the best."—ALS (telegram sent), CSmH; telegram received (sent at 8:30 P.M., received Aug. 28, 1864, 6:40 A.M.), DNA, RG 107, Telegrams Collected (Bound). Surgeon Madison Mills received the promotion as of Dec. 1.

1864, AUG. 27, 12:15 P.M.   Maj. Gen. Henry W. Halleck to USG. "The Governor of Ohio wishes for important reasons that private Ernst Greino, of the one hundred & thirtieth Ohio militia, now at Fort-Powhattan, be furloughed to the seventh of September, the date his term expires. I send this to you as Genl Butler is absent."—ALS (telegram sent), DNA, RG 107, Telegrams Collected (Bound); telegram received, *ibid.*; *ibid.*, Telegrams Collected (Unbound). On Aug. 28, USG telegraphed to Maj. Gen. Edward O. C. Ord. "Grant a furlough to private Earnest Greino 130th Reg't Ohio militai stationed atF̶t̶ Fort Powhattan for twenty 20 days—It is desirable that he should return to Ohio as early as possible"—Telegram received, Ord Papers, CU-B.

1864, AUG. 28. USG endorsement. "Respy returned to the Secretary of War with the recommendation that Gustavus Wieland be discharged"— Copy, DLC-USG, V, 58. Written on documents concerning Gustavus Wieland, a prisoner at St. Louis captured at Vicksburg while serving with the 28th La., whose discharge was recommended by a board of examination and by Maj. Gen. Ethan Allen Hitchcock.—*Ibid.* On Aug. 19, 1863, Wieland had signed a parole stating that he was an alien who lived in Philadelphia.— ADS, DNA, RG 109, Union Provost Marshals' File of Papers Relating to Individual Civilians.

1864, AUG. 28, 3:30 P.M. To Col. Edward D. Townsend. "It would be very inconvenient to spare Capt Harwood at this time."—ALS (telegram sent), CSmH; telegram received (at 11:45 P.M.), DNA, RG 94, Letters Received, 907A 1864; *ibid.*, RG 107, Telegrams Collected (Bound). On Aug. 27, Townsend had telegraphed to USG. "Please inform this office if the services of Captain Franklin Harwood U.-S. Engineers, can be spared for duty at West-Point"—LS, *ibid.*, Telegrams Collected (Unbound); telegram received, *ibid.*; *ibid.*, RG 108, Letters Received.

1864, AUG. 28. Maj. Gen. Henry W. Halleck to USG. "I transmit herewith a very long communication from Gov. Andrews in regard to the 4th Mass. Cavalry, with accompanying papers. When Genl Gillmore was ordered to Fort Monroe, he was directed to leave in the Dept of the South such troops as his medical officers reported as least requiring a change of climate. As he left there only a single battalion of cavalry it became necessary to divide some regiment, and in selecting the battalion of the 4th Mass. Cavalry which had served less time than any others in a southern climate, it is presumed that Genl Gillmore followed the advice of his medical officers. On this head Governor Andrews has no cause of complaint, for the division of a regiment was necessary & the selection made was, so far as appears, entirely proper. In regard to alleged conduct of the Major, and the improper treatment of the Colonel in Genl Butler's Department by not giving him his proper command, there is no information here other than the Gov's letter. I, therefore, forward the papers for such action as you may deem proper. In regard to the companies left in Genl Foster's Dept., one is at Hilton Head, one at Folly Island & one in Florida; men and officers present 198; present and absent 384. I presume this force is very necessary for pickets & scouts. If the battalion were brought away it would be necessary to send another in

its place, which would cause a similar division of some other regiment."—
LS, DNA, RG 108, Letters Received.

1864, AUG. 29. USG endorsement. "Respectfully returned to the Secretary of War. There is no objection to the arrangement proposed by the Chief Engineer."—ES, DNA, RG 94, Letters Received, 375E 1864. Written on a letter of Aug. 10 from Brig. Gen. Richard Delafield, chief engineer, to Secretary of War Edwin M. Stanton concerning the assignment of an officer to the "Board of Engineers for San Francisco defences . . ."—ALS, *ibid.*

1864, AUG. 30. USG endorsement. "Respectfully returned to the Secretary of War. The services of Gen. Cortez are not required or desired."—ES, DNA, RG 107, Letters Received from Bureaus. Written on a letter of July 14 from José D. Cortés, New York City, to Secretary of State William H. Seward offering his services in directing U.S. art. at Petersburg.—Copy (translation), *ibid.* Cortés, who claimed to be a Mexican gen., had been expelled from Mexico as an impostor and "pernicious stranger."—*O.R.*, I, xxxiv, part 2, 216–17.

1864, AUG. 30. To Asst. Secretary of War Charles A. Dana. "I have had a large number of the enclosed order printed for circulation among the troops of the enemy in my front. I desire that you have printed at Washington a sufficient number for the use of Generals Sherman and Sheridan, and such other commanders in the field as can use them to advantage, and forward the same to them"—LS, DNA, RG 94, Letters Received, 913A 1864. See *O.R.*, III, iv, 703. USG enclosed a copy of Special Orders No. 82, Aug. 28, issued by Lt. Col. Theodore S. Bowers. "Hereafter deserters from the Confederate Army, who deliver themselves up to the United States Forces, will, on taking an oath that they will not again take up arms during the present rebellion, be furnished subsistence and free transportation to their homes, if the same are within the lines of Federal occupation. If their homes are not within such lines, they will be furnished subsistence and free transportation to any point in the Northern States. All deserters who take the oath of allegiance, will, if they desire it, be given employment in the Quartermaster's and other Departments of the Army, and the same remuneration paid them as is given to civilian employes for similar services. Forced military duty, or service endangering them to capture by the Confederate Forces, will not be exacted from such as give themselves up to the United States military authorities."—Copies (printed), DNA, RG 94, Letters Received, 913A 1864; DLC-USG, V, 57, 62, 68. *O.R.*, I, xlii, part 2, 555–56. A draft of these orders in USG's hand was offered at Anderson Auction Co., Sale No. 285, March 22, 1904.

1864, SEPT. 1. To Maj. Gen. Edward O. C. Ord. "In the case of the two (2) officers found drunk on duty—act as you propose"—Telegram received,

Ord Papers, CU-B; copies, DLC-USG, V, 45, 68, 107; DNA, RG 108, Letters Sent. On the same day, Ord had telegraphed to USG. "Two of my Officers were brought in Very drunk one a Vol Capt from Picket the other a Reg Lt Comdg a Batty—if you agree I will dismiss both & send them off subject to approval of the President"—ALS (telegram sent), *ibid.*, RG 107, Telegrams Collected (Unbound); telegram received, *ibid.*; *ibid.*, RG 108, Letters Received.

1864, SEPT. 1.   To Maj. Gen. Edward O. C. Ord. "Does Capt Sharpe go North tomorrow?"—Telegram received, Ord Papers, CU-B. On the same day, Ord telegraphed to USG. "Capt Sharpe starts North tomorrow morning"—ALS (telegram sent), DNA, RG 107, Telegrams Collected (Unbound); telegram received, *ibid.*

1864, SEPT. 2.   To Col. James A. Hardie. "Gen Hancock with whom Colonel Egan is serving desires him to be the first (1st) one (1) promoted from the second (2d) Corps. ~~viz~~. His gallantry has been conspicuous; & he would be pleased to see him made a Brigadier General."—Telegram received (at 9:20 P.M.), DNA, RG 94, ACP, E205 CB 1866; (press) *ibid.*, RG 107, Telegrams Collected (Bound). On the same day, 9:20 A.M., Hardie had telegraphed to USG. "There is an application before the department for the appointment of Colonel T. W. Egan, 40th New-York Vols to be Brigadier General. The testimonials are numerous. ~~and~~ The President's thinks it a strong case. Shall the appointment be made?"—ALS (telegram sent), *ibid.*; telegram received (at 12:30 P.M.), *ibid.*, Telegrams Collected (Unbound); *ibid.*, RG 108, Letters Received. Also on Sept. 2, Lt. Col. Theodore S. Bowers telegraphed to Maj. Gen. Winfield S. Hancock. "The claims of Col. T. W. Egan 40th New York are being pressed on the President for a Brigadier Generalcy. Gen Grant desires to know what his merits are, and whether you desire his promotion in advance of others in your Corps."—ALS (telegram sent), *ibid.*, RG 107, Telegrams Collected (Bound). On the same day, Hancock telegraphed to Bowers. "Col Egan is entitled to promotion. He was the first on my list made sometime since of those officers who commanded troops. He should date if possible from the day he took the enemy's redoubt by assault at the 'North Anna'—May 23rd 1864. I recommended my 'chief of staff first.' I desire him promoted"—ALS (telegram sent), *ibid.*, RG 94, War Records Office, Army of the Potomac. Misdated Sept. 21 in *O.R.*, I, xlii, part 2, 956. Thomas W. Egan was appointed brig. gen. as of Sept. 3.

1864, SEPT. 2.   Special Orders No. 86, Armies of the U.S. "Brig. Gen. O. S. Ferry U. S. V. is hereby relieved from duty in the Dept. of Va & N. C. and will report in person to Maj. Gen. D. N. Couch Commanding Department of the Susquehanna. Cap't. H. L. Johnson, Ass't. Adj't. Gen. Vol's., has permission to accompany him."—DS, DNA, RG 94, War Records Office, Army of the Potomac. *O.R.*, I, xlii, part 2, 660. See *ibid.*, pp. 562, 647; *ibid.*, I, xliii, part 1, 782.

1864, SEPT. 3.   USG endorsement. "Respectfully forwarded to the Secretary of War"—ES, DNA, RG 94, ACP, D731 CB 1864. Written on a letter of Aug. 27 from Maj. Gen. Gouverneur K. Warren to Brig. Gen. Seth Williams recommending an appointment as brig. gen. for Col. Andrew W. Denison, 8th Md.—ALS, *ibid.* Denison received an appointment as bvt. brig. gen. as of Aug. 19.

1864, SEPT. 3[?].   James Forsyth, provost marshal, Troy, N. Y., to USG. "There is a A number of Reenlisted Volunteers of the state of New York who have not been credited to any locality of the state, & who have not received any local bounty   they are in the following Regements Fifty first (51) N. Y. S. V; forty first (41) do; seventeenth (17th) do; first N Y Cavalry S. V; fifth N Y. battery; first N. Y light artillery; If one hundred of these men sign a consent to be accredited to the City of Rennselaer N. Y. they can obtain a local bounty each of five hundred (500) dollars as soon as the Consents are received, & the Credits made here, & it does not effect the number drafted from the State at large, but merely adjusts the credit to the locality named & the business requires despatch as the consents should be here before the draft in this district which will take place about the twelfth (12) inst. It will be best to detail some person to obtain the consent & forward them as obtained, now too late for the men to obtain the bounty except through your kindness. Please answer at once if this is acceptable."— Telegram received (dated Sept. 2), DNA, RG 107, Telegrams Collected (Unbound); (dated Sept. 3) *ibid.*, RG 108, Letters Received.

1864, SEPT. 4.   USG endorsement. "Forwarded for information of the Sec. of War."—AES, DLC-Edwin M. Stanton. Written on a letter of Sept. 3 from Col. George H. Sharpe to Lt. Col. Theodore S. Bowers. "I submit a memorandum of the information within the last twenty four hours. The enemy is lying from their right to their left on our front as follows:—Wilcox, Mahone, Heth, Johnson, Hoke. Pickett's Division is still between the Appomattox and the James, and I think that but one brigade of Field's Division remains on the north side of the James. Wights Brigade of Mahone's Division rests on the railroad, and then come in order from their right to their left, Mahone's old Brigade, Saunder's Brigade, Harris' Brigade, & Finnegan's Brigade   It is quite certain that two brigades of Field's Div. (Law's & Anderson's) are lying in the ravine between the plank road and the lead works. Supposing I am correct that there is but one brigade of Field's Division on the north side of the James, this would leave two brigades of Field's Division to be accounted for; but it is to be remarked that the Texas' Brigade of this Div. is exceedingly small, and probably is not reckoned as more than a regiment, event at the present low estimates.

Young's Cavalry Brigade is lying five miles west of the Weldon R. R., on the Dinwiddie C. H. road, for the purpose of giving protection to the wagon trains which take that route from Stony Creek Depot to Petersburg. This brigade has been lately strengthened by the Seventh Georgia cavalry, from the South. The regiment is about twelve hundred strong—the strongest reg't that we know of in their army, but has only from 25 to 50 horses, the regiment doing duty on foot until horses can be provided, of which they do not seem to think the prospect is good. As a specimen of the enemy's late losses I submit some well attested facts. The Seventh S. C. Cavalry which came here in June, and was added to Geary's Brigade, then numbered one thousand men for duty, and has now about four hundred men, of whom less than fifty are mounted. The brigade numbers about fifteen hundred men, and is about as strong as any in the service. An intelligent deserter, from the 21st South Carolina, in Hagood's Brigade, which came here with Beauregard and had not seen severe fighting before coming here, says that when it came north his brigade numbered thirty seven hundred men; that several days ago, being at Weldon in the hospital, he met Col. Gillard of the 27th regt, in the same brigade, to whom he remarked that the brigade must be considerably reduced in numbers. The Colonel said, 'Yes, if the sick and slightly wounded were all present the brigade would now number about eight hundred men.' They have not only lost heavily in fighting, but many of them have deserted, and gone singly to their homes. A late deserter from the Second Maryland says that his regiment has seventy men for duty, and that they lost eighty eight men in the assault on the Weldon R. R. Quite an intelligent man, born in Pennsylvania, from Colquitt's Georgia Brigade, says that the lieutenant commanding his company knew of his intention to desert, and that he will come into our lines himself at the first opportunity. In regard to the railroads north of Richmond I have the following information:—The trains on the Central R. R. run regularly from Richmond through to Staunton. There is but one train daily each way —going up in the morning and down in the evening. Freight trains on the same road run three times a week each way from Staunton to Richmond. A passenger train is also sent once a day from Gordonsville to Orange C. H., beyond which point the Orange and Alexandria R. R. is not used. The Fredericksburg R. R. is used at this moment only as far as Hanover Junction. The North Anna bridge, however, is being rapidly repaired, and it is announced that the line will be ready by the 15th inst to run through to Hamilton's Crossing, which is four miles from Fredericksburg. I notice an announcement in a late Richmond paper showing that a Col. Gordon had been appointed a brigadier General and assigned to the command of Vaughn's Brigade of in Hood's Army. Vaughn's Brigade is one of the Bbrigades formerly doing duty in Western Virginia, and which under Breckenridge was united to General Early's Command prior to his advance towards Maryland. I do not know, however, how long it has been absent from Early, as I am not aware of any prisoners being taken from it since the battle of Piedmont, when the brigade lost eight hundred men."—LS, *ibid.*

1864, SEPT. 5. USG endorsement. "Respectfully forwarded to the Secretary of War, with the recommendation that Capt. Patten be promptly tried by Court Martial or dismissed the service by special orders."—ES, DNA, RG 94, ACP, P464 CB 1863. Written on a letter of Aug. 31 from Brig. Gen. Rufus Ingalls to Lt. Col. Theodore S. Bowers stating that Capt. Henry D. Patton, q. m., had refused to report for duty and recommending that Patton be tried by court-martial or dismissed.—LS, *ibid.* Patton was dismissed as of Sept. 12.

1864, SEPT. 5. U.S. Representative Elihu B. Washburne to USG. "Russ Jones and myself start for the front this afternoon."—ALS (telegram sent), DNA, RG 107, Telegrams Collected (Unbound).

1864, SEPT. 6. USG endorsement. "Respectfully forwarded to the Secretary of War with the recommendation that this resignation be accepted"— ES, DNA, RG 94, ACP, B117 CB 1868. Written on a letter of Sept. 6 from 1st Lt. James T. Baden, 5th Cav., City Point, to Secretary of War Edwin M. Stanton resigning because of illness and injuries resulting from a fall from a horse.—ALS, *ibid.* The resignation was accepted as of Sept. 12.

1864, SEPT. 7. USG endorsement. "Approved, and respectfully forwarded to the Adjutant General of the Army, Washington D. C."—ES, DNA, RG 94, Letters Received, 1227B 1864. Written on a letter of Sept. 5 from Capt. Abner R. Benedict, 4th Inf., City Point, to Lt. Col. Theodore S. Bowers requesting that hd. qrs. of the regt. be established in New York City, which would facilitate recruiting and training troops for the field.— LS, *ibid.*

1864, SEPT. 8. USG endorsement. "Approved and respectfully forwarded to the Adjutant General of the Army Washington, D. C."—ES, DNA, RG 94, ACP, B1266 CB 1864. Written on a letter of Aug. 7 from Capt. William T. W. Ball, commissary, tendering his resignation if he could not be transferred to a post in the North for health reasons.—ALS, *ibid.* Ball's resignation was accepted as of Sept. 30.

1864, SEPT. 8. Lt. Col. Theodore S. Bowers to Brig. Gen. Marsena R. Patrick, provost marshal. "The attention of Lieut. Gen. Grant, having been called to the large quantities of liquor being brought within the lines of the Armies operating against Richmond, he directs, that from and after this date you prohibit all kinds of spiritous winous or Malt liquors from being brought, above Fort Monroe Va except such as belong to the Commissary or Medical Departments."—Copies, DLC-USG, V, 45, 69, 107; DNA, RG 108, Letters Sent. *O.R.,* I, xlii, part 2, 837. On Sept. 10, Capt. George K. Leet wrote to William R. Rowley, referring to Bowers. ". . . Joe has prevailed upon the General to issue an order prohibiting liquor from being taken within the lines of the Armies down there. He says it is the most intemperate, drunken Army in the World. . . ."—ALS, Rowley Papers, IHi.

1864, SEPT. 8.   Special Orders No. 89. "Hereafter rations will not be sold to citizens residing within the lines of the Armies operating against Richmond, unless such persons take the oath of allegiance. Gratuitous issues of provisions will not be made to citizens except on certificates, that they are destitute and have no means of purchasing, and in such cases issues will be made in accordance with General Orders No. 30, A. G. O. War Department. Citizens who are inimical to the Government or refuse to take the oath of allegiance will be sent into the enemys lines. Those citizens, who take the oath of allegiance will be sent to the Northern states, if they desire to go there."—Copies, DLC-USG, V, 57, 62, 69. *O.R.*, I, xlii, part 2, 745. On Oct. 5, Lt. Col. Ely S. Parker wrote to Brig. Gen. Marsena R. Patrick, provost marshal, Army of the Potomac. "Special Orders No 89 dated Sept 8th 1864 from these Headquarters, relating to the expulsion of such citizens from within our lines, as are inimical to our Government—or refuse to take the oath of allegiance, you will now carry into execution—without any further delay   Those who desire to go to Richmond you can send by boat to Aikens Landing, and thence to Coxs Ferry, at which point they can pass into the Rebel lines. all others you can turn loose outside of our picket lines, at any convenient point. You will permit parties removing, to take with them whatever personal property they may have"—Copies, DLC-USG, V, 45, 69, 107; DNA, RG 108, Letters Sent; *ibid.*, RG 393, Army of the Potomac, Staff Officers, Letters Received. *O.R.*, I, xlii, part 3, 80.

1864, SEPT. 9.   William F. Hathaway, Philadelphia, to USG. "As an entire stranger you may think very strange of my addressing you this note; In so many words—I simply wish to know if it is possible for me to obtain the privelege of Photographing in the limits of the Army—You may say why not come and fight: in reply—I have to acknowledge that I have partially lost the use of my right arm—My will is good—My Only *Son* was with you through the whole of the Vicksburge Campaign in the 42d. Ohio Regt. Col Shelden (—Wm. F. Hathaway Son' name—)   If I had another Son—I would say go—and help put down this awful Rebellion—I went to Culpeper, on the same day that Your Honor went to take command of the Army of the Potomac—as a Photogrepher in the 5th. Army Corps   But your valuable Order of the 16th of last April sent me Home—Therefore I had only about 4 weeks—in Camp—I made a goodly number of pictures for the 4the Maryland—7th. do—the 4the Col. Bowman—the 7th Col Phillips—All expressed a strong wish for me to remain with them—but the Order said go.—I have had 23 years experiance in the Photographic arts,—and could I obtain a chance to be with the Army this fall and Winter, I could aside from doing the business for such of the Officers & Soldiers as might wish pictures—Make you many valuable Views—And should be very happy to do so—Should you deem this worthy of an Answer—and can if in your judgement grant me the favor—some weeks hence you will confer a favor . . . P. S—Pardon me for troubling you at this time, when you are so Gloriously defending the County and crushing the Rebellion"—ALS, OClWHi. On Oct. 11, Lt. Col. Theodore S. Bowers endorsed this letter. "You are hereby permitted to visit the Army on the James, for the purpose of taking photographs, subject to the restrictions after your arrival, deemed necessary for the good of the service by the Provost Marshal at City Point . . . The 'Army on the James' means the Armies operating against Richmond."—AES, *ibid.*

1864, SEPT. 10.   To Col. Edward D. Townsend. "I respectfully request to be furnished with the organization of the different Corps, Departments & Commands comprising the Armies of the United States. For want of this information, I frequently find it difficult to ascertain to what Command Regiments and Independent Companies belong. I would also request, that an abstract of the effective force of the several Armies, as shown by the monthly returns be furnished me monthly."—Copies, DLC-USG, V, 45, 69, 107; DNA, RG 108, Letters Sent. On Sept. 25, Townsend sent a consolidated return of the armies.—DS, *ibid.*, Letters Received.

1864, SEPT. 10.   Col. Edward D. Townsend to USG. "A sufficient number of Surgeons for Hospital inspection have reported at this Office—"—LS (telegram sent), DNA, RG 107, Telegrams Collected (Unbound); telegram received, *ibid.*, RG 108, Letters Received.

1864, SEPT. 11.   Maj. Gen. Benjamin F. Butler to USG. "I have read McClellans letter—It wont do"—Telegram, copy, DNA, RG 107, Telegrams Collected (Unbound). The letter of George B. McClellan, Sept. 8, accepting the Democratic nomination for president, somewhat at odds with the party platform, is in Edward McPherson, *The Political History of the United States During the Great Rebellion* (Washington, 1865), p. 421.

1864, SEPT. [11].   Maj. Gen. John Gibbon to USG. "Col Washburne is not with this corps nor is the 14th Mass cavalry. One squadron of the 4th Mass cavy is here & some of it with the 10th corps."—Telegram received, DNA, RG 107, Telegrams Collected (Unbound).

1864, SEPT. 12.   To Maj. Gen. Benjamin F. Butler. "Geo. Key, living on Miles Crenshaws place about 1½ miles North of James River (Crenshaw's place is marked on the map.) is engaged in conducting deserters through to Richmond. Mr Taylor living on the Upper Harrison place, next to Shirley, is similarly engaged, If it can be arranged to have these two men arrested I would like it."—Telegram, copies, DLC-USG, V, 45, 69, 107; DNA, RG 108, Letters Sent. Butler drafted an undated telegram to USG on what appears to be the second page of this telegram. "The matters of the arrest of Crenshaw and Taylor shall be attended to."—ADfS, *ibid.*, RG 107, Telegrams Collected (Unbound).

1864, SEPT. 13.   Brig. Gen. Henry W. Benham, Engineer Brigade, to USG. "I have the honor to lay before you in writing the substance of my verbal report to you this morning—in relation to the regiments of this Brigade. This Brigade has for the greater part of the past three years—consisted of the 15th and 50th Regiments of N. Y. Engineers—to which at different times the Battalion of Regular Engineers has been attached. In June of last year the 15th Regiment, consisting partly of two years and partly of three years men—was reduced, by the going out of the two years men to about 360 men which I formed into three companies of Engineers, to which two other companies have since been added making as they do now nearly 5 full companies of 150 men each—and leaving still seven companies vacant to complete it to an Engineer Regiment of 12 companies. During the past year also the 50th N. Y. Engineers has been filled up to a full regiment of 12 companies of 150 men each, and though the three years men, 170 only go out on the expiration of their enlistment—on the 17th inst. yet additional recruits have already arrived here—about or quite sufficient to fill up the 50th Regiment to its full organization, while the officer of that regiment, to whom these recruits are consigned, reports to me that about one thousand men or more enlisted for this 50th Engineer Regiment, are now at Elmira N. Y. awaiting transportation here. Under these circumstances, as these men cannot of course be placed in that Regiment I would respectfully submit for your consideration, and for your orders if approved—that these extra men should be assigned to fill up the vacant companies of the 15th N. Y. Engineers, a regiment from the same state—As I would also ask for your recommendation to Governor Seymour, should you deem proper to give it—to secure the efficiency of the new 15th Regt. that Lieut Col J. Spaulding now of the 50th Regt. should be appointed Colonel of the 15th Regt, and that Capt Stephen Chester, now senior captain, and Capt. T. Lubey, of the 15th and Capt Wm. W. Folwell of the 50th should be appointed to two of the three other field Officer of the 15th Regt., according to their present relative rank. Also that Major W. Brainerd, senior Major of the 50th shall be appointed Lieut Colonel vice Spaulding, and that Capt J. H McDonald shall be Major of the 50th vice Brainerd. These appointments would in my opinion secure the highest efficiency in their peculiar duties—for both the regiments of the Brigade."—LS, OClWHi.

1864, SEPT. 16.   Maj. Gen. George G. Meade endorsement. "Respectfully forwarded for the information of the Lt. Genl—Comdg, he having verbally communicated to me the report that Mr. Lamb had improperly suppressed a number of the Wash. Chronicle on political grounds, & this investigation having been directed by m̶y̶e̶ on the communication above referred to."—AES, DNA, RG 108, Letters Received, P377½ 1864. Written on documents indicating that John M. Lamb had ordered and distributed 3,000 copies of the *Washington Chronicle* of Sept. 4.—*Ibid.*

1864, SEPT. 16. S. S. Putnam & Co., Neponset, Mass., to USG. "We have by this mail taken the liberty of fowarding to your address a package of Circulars like the enclosed feeling that if by any means they could find their way into the Rebel Lines, they might be the means of bringing to their notice some of the plain, and forceble truths of one of their most able and prominent leaders. It is extremely doubtful if they have, or a majority of them have even seen this article before, and as it is a Shot from one of their own Guns, it would have all the more affect. Should this meet with your approbation, and you deem it advisable, we would take great pleasure in fowarding some thousands more of the same"—LS, USG 3.

1864, SEPT. 17. Bvt. Maj. Gen. William H. Emory, "Near Berryville, Va.," to Brig. Gen. John A. Rawlins. "A letter received by Col. Sharp, Commanding 3d Brigade 2d Division of the 19th Army Corps, from a Staff Officer of Major Genl. Canby, conveys the information to this corps that there are being organized two Divisions, which with the 3d Division now in Louisiana are to comprize the 19th Army Corps, and that he supposes the Two Divisions now here are to be assigned to some other Corps. The effect of this announcement on this Corps is such that I think it right to address the General in Chief directly on the subject in place of sending it through the Commander of the Corps and the Commander of the Division of the West Mississippi whose distance is so great that the mischief may be done before they can remedy it, which I know from the high character of these Officers, they would do promptly, as soon as the facts are brought to their notice. Those facts are as follows; The whole of the original 19th Army Corps composed of the 1st and 2d Divisions now here and at Harpers Ferry, numbering some Thirteen Thousand fighting men, embrace all the Regiments, with the exception of Two or Three, scattered about the Dep't of the Gulf, that belongs to the 19th Army Corps proper. The 3d Division left behind was a Division transferred bodily from ~~from~~ the 13th Army Corps, just before our departure from New-Orleans, and formed no part of the original 19th Army Corps. The 13th Army Corps was abolished as an organization; and the effect of the present movement will be, what could never have been designed; to in fact abolish the 19th Army Corps as an organization and substitute in its place, the 13th Army Corps: for it is of the fragments of this Corps, that the Two Divisions in question must be composed. The good feeling between the 13th and 19t[h] Army Corps, would no doubt make the 19th Army Corps glad to have the 13th Corps as their successors, but it must be evident that the transfer of 19th Army Corps proper, with all its insignia, its records of Battles—for although involvved in some ill-designed campaigns, it has never yet been really whipped—must act as a damper, if it does not demoralize Thirteen Thousand of as well disciplined and as good fighting men as the Army has, in its ranks. These men now here have campaigned together for nearly Three Years; They understand each other and support each other with great cordiality in Battle, and to break up this organization at this time, and transfer their History and their Records to an organization which the Government has seen fit, once to discontinue, would in my opinion much lessen the efficiency of these men and be injurious to the Public Service   I therefore respectfully suggest that they may be permitted to retain their present designation and organization. Or if the act has gone past recall, that they be retained as an organization and numbered as the 1st 3d or some other Corps which has ceased to exist and has no identity   There are now in this Corps Seven Brigades and quite enough Regiments, if filled up to complete Two more Brigades and the Officers are quite sure, they could fill their Regiments promptly if they could be permitted to go home for that purpose"—LS, ICarbS. *O.R.*, I, xliii, part 2, 97–98.

1864, SEPT. 17.   Lt. Col. John T. Sprague, N. Y. AG, Albany, to USG. "There are now organizing in this state some thirty (30) companies of infantry   to what new York regiments can they be attached so as to secure all the officers their commissions"—Telegram received (at 8:15 P.M.), DNA, RG 107, Telegrams Collected (Bound).

1864, SEPT. 19.   Capt. George K. Leet to Brig. Gen. Marsena R. Patrick. "You will please report to these Headquarters, the names and probable, or positive, method of desertion, if the same has been, or can be, ascertained, of all deserters who may hereafter arrive at this point from the North. It is particularily desired to have reported, such as have deserted to the enemy and by him sent through to the North."—Copies, DLC-USG, V, 45, 69, 107; DNA, RG 108, Letters Sent. *O.R.*, I, xlii, part 2, 912.

1864, SEPT. 20, 11:00 P.M.   To Maj. Gen. Henry W. Halleck. "The Richmond Sentinel of today has the following. 'A slight ripple of excitement was produced here yesterday by the report that a Yankee raiding party was advancing on Gordonsville, and were within a few miles of that place—The result of all our inquiries on this head is, that this [re]port originated in the fact that ~~Early~~ early yesterday a party of [Yan]kee raiders whose number is not [known visite]d Rapidan Bridge & after [destroying it] proceeded to Liberty Mills five or six miles above, which they also destroyed. From this latter place they are believed to have gone back to Culpepper'—"—Telegram received (Sept. 21, 12:15 A.M.), DNA, RG 107, Telegrams Collected (Bound); copies, *ibid.*, Telegrams Received in Cipher; *ibid.*, RG 108, Letters Sent; DLC-USG, V, 45, 69, 107. *O.R.*, I, xlii, part 2, 934–35; *ibid.*, I, xliii, part 2, 118.

1864, SEPT. 20, 2:30 P.M.   To Maj. Gen. Henry W. Halleck. "Please give Genl Washburn a twenty (20) days leave of absence"—Telegram received (at 6:00 P.M.), DNA, RG 94, Letters Received, 989A 1864; *ibid.*, RG 107, Telegrams Collected (Bound); copies, *ibid.*, Telegrams Received in Cipher; *ibid.*, RG 108, Letters Sent; DLC-USG, V, 45, 69, 107. At 11:35 A.M., U.S. Representative Elihu B. Washburne had telegraphed to USG. "Genl. Washburne wants leave for thirty days—~~Secretary refers, me to you.~~ He says he can leave now without prejudice to the service   Secretary refers me to you. Please telegraph me here. Bully for Sheridan."—ALS (telegram sent), DNA, RG 107, Telegrams Collected (Unbound); telegram received, *ibid.*

1864, SEPT. 22.   USG endorsement. "Respy. returned to the Com. Gen of Prisoners, Washington D C. Many of the prisoners captured at Vicksburg declined being paroled for the reason they wished to avoid further service in the rebel Army, but I gave them no promises or pledges of any kind—I would recommend however, that all the prisoners sent north from Vicksburg, after the capture of that place, who desire to take the oath of allegiance, be permitted to do so, and be set at liberty"—Copy, DLC-USG, V, 58. *O.R.*, II, vii, 610. Written on a letter of Aug. 18 from Ind. AG Lazarus Noble to Maj. Gen. John A. Logan stating that about 300 prisoners at Indianapolis, captured at Vicksburg, claimed to be La. Unionists forced into C.S.A. service, who wanted to take an oath of allegiance rather than be exchanged on parole.—*Ibid.*, pp. 608–9. On Sept. 17, Col. William Hoffman, commissary gen. of prisoners, endorsed this letter to USG.—*Ibid.*, p. 609. On Sept. 25, USG telegraphed to Hoffman. "The petition of prisoners captured at Vicksburg with decision endorsed thereon has been returned by mail & will reach you tomorrow"—Telegram received (at 2:40 P.M.), DNA, RG 107, Telegrams Collected (Bound); *ibid.*, RG 249, Letters Received; copies, *ibid.*, RG 108, Letters Sent; DLC-USG, V, 45, 69, 107.

1864, SEPT. 23.   To Maj. Gen. David Hunter. "Certainly you Can Come and see me here—"—Telegram received, DNA, RG 107, Telegrams Collected (Unbound). *O.R.*, I, xliii, part 2, 153. On the same day, Hunter, Washington, had telegraphed to USG. "May I come and see you at City Point"—ALS (telegram sent), DNA, RG 107, Telegrams Collected (Unbound); telegram received, *ibid.*, RG 108, Letters Received. *O.R.*, I, xliii, part 2, 153.

1864, SEPT. 23.   To Maj. Gen. Gouverneur K. Warren. "Please send word to Mr. Fox, Sutlers Clerk 1st Mich. 3d Brig. 1st Div. your Corps, that Mrs. Fox arrived this evening and requests, that he come in to night or early in the morning, as she desires to go back again in the morning. She will be found at the public house next to the Sanitary Commission rooms."—Telegram, copy, DLC-USG, V, 69.

1864, SEPT. 25.   USG endorsement. "Approved and respectfully forwarded."—AES, DNA, RG 94, ACP, M1352 CB 1864. Written on a letter

of Sept. 19 from Maj. Gen. George G. Meade to Secretary of War Edwin
M. Stanton transmitting a list of forty-seven recommendations for bvt. commissions.—LS, *ibid.*

1864, SEPT. 27.   Maj. Gen. Henry W. Halleck to USG. "Respectfully
forwarded to Lt Genl Grant"—AES, DNA, RG 108, Letters Received. Written on a statement of Sept. 23 of George C. Wilde. "I left Richmond, Va.,
on the 9th Aug., being at that time one of the Reporters of the 'Enquirer,'
and having good opportunity to know what was progressing there. At that
time Genl. Lee's army consisted of A. P. Hill's Corps, a fragment of Longstreet's, and a portion of the troops formerly guarding Charleston, the latter
under the command of General Beauregard. I am sure that this whole force
did not number but little over 40.000 men. Hill's corps was never 20.000
strong, and battle had considerably thinned its numbers. Ewell's corps, under Early, was in the valley. 6.000 and upwards of infantry belonging to
Longstreet passed up the Central road about the 16th Aug. to join Early.
I do not know what force the latter had, but if he had 22.000 infantry, he
had more than he got credit for in Richmond. Lee's army does not expect to
hold either Richmond or Petersburg by numbers, but rely on the strong
earthworks erected around each city. They hope to be able to repel any
direct assault. On the north of Richmond, the earthworks were garrisoned
by a few battalions of artillery, commencing at the battery near Mechanics-
ville, and running southeast. Directly east, this side of Seven Pines, there
were sundry strong earthworks, and farther off east, towards Deep Bottom,
was a brigade of cavalry made up of sundry detached battalions, and one
regiment from S. C., under Genl. Gary. These, when that part of the defences were threatened, were reënforced by General Hampton's cavalry,
and such infantry as could be spared from Chaffins Bluff. At the latter a
small brigade under Genl. Eppe Hunton was stationed, but no land or water
attack was ever made on the place, which, on the water side, is quite strong.
The City Battalion that used to guard the Prisons in Richmond were
stationed at Chaffin Bluff as part of Hunton's force. At Drewry's Bluff there
were occasionally, in addition to the garrison of 900 men, sometimes two
brigades in the rifle-pits and extending across, towards Petersburg. This
force was lessened or increased as Grant's movements north or south of the
James river seemed to demand. Though it may seem strange, yet owing to
the conformation of the country, and the positions occupied by Genl. Grant's
troops, he can get troops quicker in the vicinity of Richmond, and on the
north side of James river, than Genl Lee can. When the canal across the
river is finised by Butler, Genl. Grant's facilities for moving troops quicker
than Lee will be much increased. If the Weldon R. R. is held, and the south
side destroyed, or the Danville injured as it was once by Kautz's troops,
Petersburg will be isolated as well as Richmond. The C. S. Army this winter will have bacon and bread in Richmond, but a large number of the citizens will have to leave to get bread and a shelter, as a majority of the Peters-

burg have already done. The policy of the C. S. Government is to hold the claims of the soldiers superior to that of the citizen. The latter will be left to shift for themselves as they best can. If once Genl. Grant gets into Richmond, he will find no difficulty about the loyalty of the people. The majority are heartily sick of the war. Genl Davis (Jeff.) is personally unpopular, but is held in estimation because the leader of the Confederacy. He rides out in the evening alone, or accompanied by his daughter or private Secretary—Harrison. No attempt was ever made to assassinate him that I ever heard of. Such a thing could be done, because there is nothing to prevent it in the way of guards &c. around him. He professes to be desirous of peace, and may be so for aught I know. If Genl Lee's army numbers all told (with Early's and Longstreet's Corps added) more than 65.000 men of all arms, then myself and others who ought to know have been much mistaken in our estimate of its strength. The soldiers of the C. S. Army believe, (or are made to believe) that by fighting they will conquer an honorable peace, and secure Southern Independence. Many, very many of them are sick and tired of the war, not being originally in favor of it, but compelled by law and the pressure of public opinion to go in the army. Very few 'Original Secessionists' figure *now* in the war either as officers or privates. They have retired to soft places."—Copy, *ibid.*

1864, SEPT. 28. Joseph H. Campbell, Green Island, Albany County, N. Y., to USG. "Pardon me, a stranger, for thus addressing you but I wish to be informed if I can get back to the army? Last June my mother was lying at the point of death—and yielding to the appeals of brothers and sisters I blush to confess it—absented myself without leave. I would gladly return—yea, more I will serve my remaining time—(2½ years) without compensation and in any capacity, but to be taken as a deserter I would rather suffer ten thousand deaths Dare I hope for a reply and advise."—ALS, DNA, RG 108, Letters Received.

1864, SEPT. 28. Charles F. Raymond, Norwalk, Conn., to USG discussing his invention of a breech-loading double cannon for chain shot.—ALS, USG 3.

1864, SEPT. 30. USG endorsement. "Respectfully returned to the Secretary of War. Let it be ascertained whether Capt. W. Boyd of Pemberton Scouts, is still at Johnson's Island, get from him a statement of this matter, and if it corroborates the within, then have Wyatt arrested and tried, using the Scout as States Evidence."—ES, DNA, RG 94, Letters Received, 951M 1865. Written on a letter of Aug. 23 from 1st Lt. William A. Lilly, 43rd Ohio, accusing Lt. Col. William J. Wyatt of betraying the garrison of Holly Springs, Miss., to C.S.A. forces on Dec. 20, 1862.—ALS, *ibid.* Lilly based his charge on information received from C.S.A. Capt. James W. Boyd, 6th Tenn., once in charge of secret service, Army of Tenn., then a prisoner at

Johnson's Island, Ohio. In subsequent letters, however, Boyd identified the betrayer of Holly Springs as Lt. Col. Elijah Willard, 109th Ill.—*Ibid.* See *ibid.*, Baker-Turner Records, 718 B; General Orders No. 12, Feb. 1, 1863. For Boyd, see *Civil War Times Illustrated*, XVI, 7 (Nov., 1977), 47–49.

1864, SEPT. 30.   USG endorsement. "Respy returned to the Sec of War. I have no objections to passing Mr Broadwell on the mission herein named —on the contrary would highly favor any measure calculated to relieve the condition of prisoners in the hands of the rebels."—Copy, DLC-USG, V, 58. *O.R.*, II, vii, 815, 920. Written on a letter of Sept. 12 from M. M. Broadwell, 103 Pearl St., New York City, to Col. William Hoffman, commissary gen. of prisoners, proposing to furnish prisoners of war of both sides with blankets and clothing.—*Ibid.*, pp. 814–15. On Sept. 24, Asst. Secretary of War Charles A. Dana referred this letter to USG.—*Ibid.*, p. 815. On Oct. 5, Broadwell wrote to Dana stating that he planned to leave for Richmond in a few days and requesting that clothing for the prisoners be prepared for shipment.—ALS, DNA, RG 108, Letters Received. On Oct. 9, Dana endorsed this letter. "Respectfully referred to Lieutenant-General Grant, commanding Armies of the United States, with the remark that as official propositions touching this subject have recently been received from Mr Ould Rebel Agent of Exchange, there seems at present no necessity for the intervention of Mr Broadwell."—AES, *ibid.* On Nov. 12, Broadwell wrote to USG's hd. qrs. "Applies either to be permitted an interview with Maj R Ould C S A, or to send a by flag of truce enclosed (open) communication to the Major, asking his consent to his (Mr B's) being made a Commissioner for the supplying of prisoners"—DLC-USG, V, 48. Some time between Nov. 17 and Nov. 21, Lt. Col. Theodore S. Bowers endorsed this letter. "Respy. returned. The interview asked for with Mr Ould cannot be permitted, neither can the enclosed communication for Mr Ould be forwarded to him   Your persistence in the matter, after the disclosures contained in the memorandum which unintentionally on your part, came to the attention of the Lt Gen Commanding the first time you were at City Point, and what he said to you on your on your 2d visit, shows your desire for gain to be so great, that he believes you would go to the very verge of honesty, if not beyond, to secure it; and he desires therefore that you understand that no proposition coming from you will be looked upon with favor by him, but on the contrary will be discountenanced in every way consistant with the cause of honor and official position."—Copy, *ibid.*, V, 58.

1864, SEPT. 30.   Maj. Gen. Henry W. Halleck to USG. "Respectfully referred to Lt Genl Grant for his information. Genl Foster was directed some time ago to make no exchanges, except *on the field* of prisoners just captured."—AES, DNA, RG 108, Letters Received. Written on copies of letters of Sept. 25 and 26, 1864, from Maj. Gen. John G. Foster, Hilton Head, S. C., discussing the deplorable condition of prisoners in C.S.A. custody.—Copies, *ibid.* *O.R.*, II, vii, 874–75, 879.

1864, SEPT. 30.   Lt. Col. Ely S. Parker endorsement. "Respectfully returned. General Order No. 37. Headquarters Army of the Potomac, being general in its operation, applying to all Regiments or Batteries is approved. The right of any Officer Comd'g troops, to reverse any order or action of his subordinate is undoubted. In this [c]ase Gen. Hancock might properly have reversed Gen. Gibbon's action, but such action, having been approved by a superior Commander, the order must be respected by Gen. Hancock, until he can get the same revoked by authority higher than the Comand'g. General. The right of any Officer to appeal from decisions of his superior, and carry it through to the highest Mility authority, cannot be denied, but until a final reversion is obtained all orders must be respected and obeyed."—ES, DNA, RG 94, Letters Received, 1243P 1864. *O.R.*, I, xlii, part 3, 14. Written on a letter of Sept. 28 from Maj. Gen. Winfield S. Hancock to Lt. Col. Theodore S. Bowers. "I have the honor to solicit your attention to the enclosed copy of an order published by Major General Gibbon on the 30th ult. with an endorsement thereon, and to the printed order of the Major General Commdg the Army of the Potomac confirming and approving Genl. Gibbons order. It will be seen that Genl. Gibbon deprived three (3) Regiments of his Division of the privilege of bearing colors; (they having lost their colors at the battle of Reams Station Aug. 25th) that I approved of the principle but requested that if it was adopted the rule might be made general and affect other Corps as well as my own; and finally that General Meade over-ruled my suggestion and singled out these Regiments, the 8th N. Y. H. Arty, 164th New York Vols and 36th Wisconsin Vols to be published to the Army as having rendered themselves unworthy to carry colors. This without regard to the fact that in the same action other Regiments of my command lost colors, and that but a few days before several Regiments of another Corps had met with the same misfortune—Under the circumstances I respectfully submit that the three Regiments have been proceeded against with unnecessary severity, and a slur cast upon the Corps which I have the honor to command which in view of the past might well have been omitted. It is perhaps known to you that this Corps had never lost a color nor a gun previous to this campaign, though oftener and more desperately engaged than any other Corps in this Army, or perhaps in any other in the Country. I have not the means of knowing exactly the number of guns and colors captured but I saw myself nine in the hands of one Division at Antietam, and the official reports show that thirty four fell into the hands of the Corps at Gettysburg. Before the opening of this Campaign it had at least captured over half a hundred colors from the enemy and never yeilded one, though at the cost of over twenty five thousand (25.000) casualties—During this campaign you can judge how well the corps has performed its part. It has captured more guns and colors than all the rest of the Army combined—Its reverses have not been many and they began only when the Corps had diminished to a remnant of its former strength—after it had lost twenty five (25) Brigade Commanders and over one hundred and twenty five (125) Regimental Commanders, and over twenty thousand (20,000) men—I submit that with the record of this Corps it is in the highest degree unjust, by a retrospective order to publish a part of it as unworthy to bear colors—It is not necessary perhaps to speak more particularly as to the injustice done the regiments, the principle discussed covering their case. I may say however that these Regiments first saw service in the field after the battle of Spotsylvania. At Coal Harbor the Colonel of the 36th Wiss. Vols, as gallant a soldier as ever lived, fell dead on the field, as did the Colonel of the 8th N. Y. H. Arty. The Colonel of the 164th fell mortally wounded beside his flag on the breastworks of the enemy. These Regiments have since that action suffered severely—one of them at least having lost two Commdg Officers. I respectfully request that their colors may be restored to them. They are entitled to the same privilege as other Regiments, that is, the right to strive to avoid the penalties of Gen'l Order No. 37 C. S. Head Quarters Army of the Potomac."—ALS, DNA, RG 94, Letters Received, 1243P 1864. *O.R.*, I, xlii, part 2, 1071–72. Additional documents pertaining to the matter are in DNA, RG 94, Letters Received, 1243P 1864.

1864, SEPT. 30.   Hanson A. Risley, special agent, U.S. Treasury Dept., to USG. "Mr. B. H. Morse assistant special agent goes by my advice to the vicinity of the army of the Potomac to receive for this Department any property captured from the enemy or seized by military authority, which officers or others connected with the army, have to turn over under General Order of the War Dept. 88. and also to collect and receive abandoned property, in pursuance of the act of March 12. 1863. He has been duly appointed by the Secretary of the Treasury, for that purpose. Wm Silvey. Esq. also asst. special agent, has recently visited the army to perfect arrangements for collecting the debris of the army, and transporting it to a place of sale. Mr. Morse is under instructions, not to interfere with any arrangement made by Mr. Silvey. but to aid and facilitate them. I commend Mr. Morse to your protection and favorable regard"—LS (press), DNA, RG 366, 7th Special Agency, Letters Sent.

1864, OCT. 1, 2:00 P.M.   Col. James A. Hardie to USG transmitting a telegram of Sept. 27 from Bvt. Maj. Gen. Montgomery C. Meigs to Secretary of War Edwin M. Stanton inquiring if all the boats gathered in Chesapeake Bay were still needed.—LS (telegram sent), DNA, RG 107, Telegrams Collected (Bound); telegram received, *ibid.*, RG 108, Letters Received. *O.R.*, I, xlii, part 3, 3. On Oct. 2, 10:30 A.M., Lt. Col. Ely S. Parker telegraphed to Hardie. "In reply to yours of 2 P. M. yesterday, the Lieut Gen. directs that the water transportation ~~need~~ will not be ~~accumulated~~ required until ~~he so directs~~—ordered by him—"—LS (telegram sent), Rawlins Papers, ICHi; telegram received, DNA, RG 107, Telegrams Collected (Bound).

1864, OCT. 1.   Rear Admiral David D. Porter, Mound City, to USG. "By a late order, I believe, of General Butler's, all persons in Norfolk over 16 years of age, who have not taken the oath of allegiance, are ordered to proceed beyond our lines on or before the 16th of October. This rule affects an old gentleman of 75 years of age, by the name of George Loyall, the father-in-law of my fleet captain, Captain Pennock. Mr. Loyall, it is true, has not taken the oath of allegiance to the U. S. Government, but he is perfectly inoffensive in act or deed. I know him well, he is a most respectable and honorable gentleman, and is highly appreciated by all who know him. He is in very feeble health and with no means of subsistence out of Norfolk. A banishment would, without doubt, cause his death and give great pain to Mrs. Captain Pennock, a most estimable lady. You will confer a great favor on me by revoking the order in the case of Mr. Loyal, and lay me under many obligations."—Typescript, DNA, RG 45, Area 5.

1864, OCT. 2.   Lt. Col. Ely S. Parker to USG. "Col Marsh 186th N. Y Vols a new reg't, is at Ft Monroe. Adjt Gen Sprague directed him to report to Adjt. Genl. at Washington—Gen Van Vleit ordered ~~them~~ the Col. to await further orders at Ft Monroe. Shall I send orders for him to come forward—"—ALS (telegram sent), DNA, RG 107, Telegrams Collected (Unbound). On the same day, Parker telegraphed to Lt. Col. E. Jay Marsh, 186th N. Y. "You will report at these Hdqrs without delay with your reg't."—ALS (telegram sent), *ibid.*

1864, OCT. 7.   W. H. Womble, Johnsonville, Tenn., to USG offering to raise mounted troops for local defense.—ALS, DLC-Andrew Johnson. On Oct. 17, Lt. Col. Theodore S. Bowers endorsed this letter to Governor Andrew Johnson of Tenn.—AES, *ibid.* See letter to Salmon P. Chase, Sept. 26, 1863.

1864, OCT. 8.   Maj. Gen. Benjamin F. Butler to Brig. Gen. John A. Rawlins. "Please order all men of the 142nd, 112th, and 169th New York to come up to me at once from the landing at City Point—There has been very unfair means used by Officers from the Army of the Potomac in relation to these men—They have tampered with them endeavoring to get them into Regiments in the Army of the Potomac—Please order all men for ~~New York~~ Regiments not actually in the Army of the Potomac to report to me at Varina & send them with transportation to that Point—While we are here fighting I had a little rather the Army of the Potomac would not steal our men—"—LS, DNA, RG 108, Letters Received. *O.R.,* I, xlii, part 3, 142–43. On Oct. 12, 7:00 P.M., Butler telegraphed to USG. "There are at City Point about three hundred unoganised Recruits of the the 142 New York   They have been some days at City Point, have been coaxed by those who desire to get them. The Captains that have been commissioned have deserted them and cannot be found   they were orderd to the 142d Regt by the War department   They have elected officers and are a mob. If they Can be ~~assigned to m~~ sent to the Regiment to which they belong they will be assigned to good companies with good officers and will be serviceable in a fortnight otherwise they are worse than useless for months   We have suffered so much from these new Organsations rendering men useless that I trust where there is no organisation we shall not wait for a mob to make one   Please order them to me and I will send for them tomorrow moring"—ALS (telegram sent), DNA, RG 107, Telegrams Collected (Unbound). *O.R.*, I, xlii, part 3, 184. On Oct. 13, Rawlins telegraphed to Butler. "The men will be sent to the Regiment, to which they were assigned by the War Department. There is no evidence, that these men have been tampered with here. They certainly have not been by the Provost Officers, in charge of them here. Please send an Officer to take charge of them, and conduct them to their Reg't,"—Copies, DLC-USG, V, 45, 69, 107; DNA, RG 108, Letters Sent. *O.R.*, I, xlii, part 3, 213. On Oct. 18, Lt. Col. Theodore S. Bowers wrote to Brig. Gen. Marsena R. Patrick. "The men in your charge with paprs assigning them to the 142d Regt NewYork Vols. will be sent forward to that Reg't. The other men desiring to join the 56th NewYork Vols. or the 20th NewYork State Militia, will be assigned to the latter Reg't., as the 56th is not in either of the Armies here. The question, as to the authority of the assignment of these men to the 142d NewYork Vols. has been referred to the War Dep't. for decision."—Copies, DLC-USG, V, 45, 69, 107; DNA, RG 108, Letters Sent.

1864, OCT. 8.   Capt. George K. Leet, Washington, to USG. "Two Scouts who returned from Spottsylvania Co. this morning report following. Cars have not been running on the Central R. R. since last Saturday. Reports say that the transportation is all being used to convey Government property from Richmond to Danville, preparatory to the evacuation of Richmond. The impression prevails that Richmond cannot be held a month longer. Every available man is being sent to Richmond to aid in its defence. All old men & boys who are able to carry muskets are ~~pla~~ put in the trenches."—ALS (telegram sent), DNA, RG 107, Telegrams Collected (Bound); telegram received, *ibid.*, RG 393, Army of the Potomac, Cav. Corps, Letters and Telegrams Received.

1864, OCT. 9.   USG endorsement. "Respectfully forwarded to the Secretary of War."—ES, DNA, RG 94, ACP, G560 CB 1864. Written on a letter of Sept. 22 from Lt. Col. Michael R. Morgan to USG recommending twenty commissary officers for bvt. promotions.—LS, *ibid.*

1864, OCT. [9–14].   USG endorsement. "Respy returned to the sec of war. At the time this building was ordered to be taken possessin of for the use of the Pay Department, the demand for buildings for hospitals was so great that no other suitable building could be obtained. It was supposed by me that the building belonged to disloyal owners, and I know nothing to the contrary now, other than what is stated in these papers"—Copy, DLC-USG, V, 58. Written on a letter of Aug. 10 from F. S. Ayres, Memphis, to Maj. Gen. Cadwallader C. Washburn stating his loyalty and asking rent for U.S. Army use of his building in Memphis.—*Ibid.*; *ibid.*, V, 48. On June 29, Paymaster Thomas K. Osgood wrote to Washburn in support of the Ayres claim.—ALS, DNA, RG 109, Union Provost Marshals' File of Papers Relating to Individual Civilians.

1864, OCT. 9.   USG endorsement. "This Communication together with the battle-flags named in it, are respectfully forwarded to Headquarters of the Army Washington, D. C."—ES, DNA, RG 94, Letters Received, 181V 1864. Written on a letter of Oct. 1 from Col. George S. Dodge, chief q. m., Army of the James, to Lt. Col. Theodore S. Bowers. "I have the honor to forward herewith to the Lieu't. Genl. Comd'g the U. S. Armies, with the Compliments of Maj. Genl. Butler, three captured battle flags, one of the 8th N. C. one of the 61st N. C. and one unknown.—"—LS, *ibid.* On Oct. 11, Col. Edward D. Townsend, AGO, wrote to USG acknowledging receipt of the letter and flags.—LS, *ibid.*, RG 108, Letters Received.

1864, OCT. 10.   To Maj. Stewart Van Vliet, q. m. "Please examine such steamers as Mr H Kidder reports to you with the view of chartering them should they be required. Mr. Kidder has had experience in navigating the waters for which these vessels are likely to be wanted and can select them better perhaps than any one els."—ALS, Maine Historical Society, Portland, Me.

1864, OCT. 10.   Secretary of State William H. Seward to USG. "I enclose an extract from a letter of a patriotic and intelligent citizen of Georgia, of high standing, recommending a military movement in the Southern part of that State. From the same source, I also learn that, in his judgment, a force of ten thousand men would be ample for the purpose. It is suggested that your views upon the subject be communicated to the President."—LS, DNA, RG 108, Letters Received; ADf, *ibid.*, RG 59, Correspondence Regarding Prisoners of War. The lengthy unsigned enclosure is *ibid.*, RG 108, Letters Received. Another lengthy anonymous letter of Oct. 10 to President Abraham Lincoln, possibly written by the same person, is *ibid.*

1864, OCT. 11.   Bvt. Maj. Gen. Montgomery C. Meigs to USG. "Referring to the papers transmitted to this Office by Brig Gen Ingalls, Chief Q. M. &c relative to the construction of wooden pavilion Hospitals at City Point to replace the tents now used for that purpose, I have the honor to state that orders have been given to send forward a supply of material sufficient for commencing the work. It has been found from actual experience, here, in the construction of hospitals of similar character to those contemplated that the cost of a hospital for one corps, or 960. Beds, will be in round numbers $70.000.—or not less than $280.000. for four corps, with 3840. beds. This estimate includes all & only the constructions contemplated by instructions from the War Dept. July 20th 1864,—relative to construction of Gen— Hospitals, including labor, steam apparatus pipes &c—. Under these circumstances, I respectfully present for your consideration the question whether it will not be better to erect only a portion of the structures proposed, and send a greater part of the sick and wounded to hospitals already built at vast expense."—LS, DNA, RG 108, Letters Received.

1864, OCT. [11?].   Maj. Gen. Benjamin F. Butler to USG. "The 184th New York is at Wilsons Wharf (Fort Pocahontas)"—Copy, DNA, RG 107, Telegrams Collected (Unbound).

1864, OCT. 11, 4:30 P.M.   Capt. George K. Leet, Washington, to USG. "Scouts from Falmouth this morning report following. 'Part of the troops lately sent to Early have returned to Richmond. The rebels are moving supplies from Gordonsville to Hanover Junction. R. R. bridge over North Anna is not yet repaired and freight & passengers have to be transferred at that place.' They bring no other information"—ALS (telegram sent), DNA, RG 107, Telegrams Collected (Bound); telegram received, *ibid. O.R.,* I, xliii, part 2, 340.

1864, OCT. 12.   To Secretary of War Edwin M. Stanton. "Will you please send me The election news so far as heard from"—Telegram received (at 4:55 P.M.), DNA, RG 107, Telegrams Collected (Bound). On the same day, President Abraham Lincoln telegraphed to USG. "Sec. of War not being in, I answer yours about election—Pennsylvania very close, and still in doubt on home vote—Ohio largely for us, with all the members of Congress but two or three—Indiana largely for us—Governor, it is said by 1.5-000; and 8. of the eleven Members of congress—Send us what you may know of your army vote."—ALS (telegram sent), *ibid.;* telegrams received (2), *ibid.,* Telegrams Collected (Unbound). Lincoln, *Works,* VIII, 45.

1864, OCT. 12.   USG endorsement. "Respectfully forwarded to the Sec. of War with recommendation that Col. Curtin be promoted by Brevet."— AES, DNA, RG 94, ACP, C1162 CB 1864. *O.R.,* I, xlii, part 3, 181. Written on a telegram of Oct. 12 from Maj. Gen. John G. Parke to USG. "Col John G Curtin 45th regt Penn Vols has heretofore been recommended both for ~~adjutant~~ a Brevet & promotion—No more deserving appointment could be made—He is an invaluable Brigade commander—Unless promoted or Breveted he will loose the command of his Brigade by the return of a Senior colonel who has been absent from duty for twelve out of the last fifteen months and is not as well fitted for the position"—Telegrams received (2), DNA, RG 94, ACP, C1162 CB 1864; *ibid.,* RG 107, Telegrams Collected (Bound); *ibid.,* Telegrams Collected (Unbound). *O.R.,* I, xlii, part 3, 181.

1864, OCT. 12.   USG endorsement. "Col. Myers having organized the Signal Corps I would give the seniority to him in preference to anyone else. If, however, there is any reason, unknown to me, why Col. M. should not receive the promotion I would then recommend the appointment of Maj. Fisher to the Chief place in his Corps."—Typescript, Atwood Collection, InU. Written on a letter of Oct. 10 from Maj. Gen. George G. Meade to Secretary of War Edwin M. Stanton. "I am advised the office of Chief Signal Officer is vacant. Should this appointment be open to selection, without desiring to prejudice the claims or merits of others, I beg leave to bring to your notice the pre-eminent fitness for this place of Maj. B. F. Fisher new chief Signal Officer of this Army. My knowledge of Maj. Fisher's Capacity and service extends for some time back, and during the recent campaign since crossing the Rapidam, Maj. Fisher as Chief Signal Officer, has rendered most valuable and efficient service, and by his zeal and energy finds himself in my judgment most worthy of promotion."—Typescript, *ibid.* Also attached was a letter of Oct. 8 from Maj. Gen. Andrew A. Humphreys to Maj. Benjamin F. Fisher. "I have no hesitation in expressing my entire satisfaction with the manner in which you have performed the duty of Chief Signal Officer with this Army. You have been zealous, prompt, active, careful and intelligent, and the Signal Department has been well conducted under your direction."—Typescript, *ibid.*

1864, OCT. 12. To Maj. Gen. Andrew A. Humphreys. "You have authority to visit Washington"—Telegram received (at 10:00 A.M.), DNA, RG 94, War Records Office, Army of the Potomac. On Oct. 9, Humphreys wrote to Lt. Col. Theodore S. Bowers. "I telegraphed General Halleck last evening for authority to visit Washington on private matters, but as I have received no answer presume I shall have no reply until Monday. Under the circumstances I would request the authority from the Lieutenant General." —Copy, *ibid.*, RG 393, Army of the Potomac, Letters Sent.

1864, OCT. 13. USG endorsement. "Respectfully forwarded for the information of the Secretary of War."—ES, DNA, RG 94, Letters Received, 1372C 1864. Written on a letter of Oct. 11 reporting that sixteen men of the 5th N. H. had deserted to the enemy the previous night.—LS, *ibid.* On Oct. 12, Maj. Gen. George G. Meade endorsed this letter. "Respectfully forwarded for the information of the Lieutenant General Commanding. It is understood that the men within reported as having deserted to the enemy have recently been sent to this Army as recruits or substitutes."—ES, *ibid.*

1864, OCT. [13–17]. USG endorsement. "Respy. forwarded to the Sec of War. Several cases of dissatisfaction and apparently just complaint on the part of Volunteers and recruits, have occurred, from (as they allege) their not having been allowed the privilege of selecting the regiments to which they should be assigned. In the present case the men seem to have enlisted in the belief that they should form one company instead of being scattered over a regiment, and if this was not attainable, with the strong wish to join the Regt from their immediate District, the 118th N. Y. This privilege has not been conceded them—for what reason does not appear—Since volunteers enlist with the understanding that they can select the regiment that they prefer, instructions to state authorities that will insure or protect them in the exercise of this privilege, will add to the efficiency of the service"— Copy, DLC-USG, V, 58. Written on a statement of Brig. Gen. Marsena R. Patrick, provost marshal, concerning the case of H. D. W. C. Hill and others stating that a co. raised for the 118th N. Y. had been wrongfully assigned to the 142nd N. Y.—*Ibid.; ibid.,* V, 48.

1864, OCT. 13. USG endorsement. "Respectfully returned to Maj Gen. Meade. The advantages to be gained will not compensate for the amount of work. Hence the change should not be made."—ES, DNA, RG 393, Army of the Potomac, Letters Received. Written on a letter of Oct. 12 from Maj. Nathaniel Michler to Brig. Gen. Seth Williams. "The Major General Commanding directed me to make an examination of that part of our line extending from Fort Alex Hays west towards the new works near the Pegram House, to ascertain whether said line can be shortened, and, if so, whether any particular advantage would be gained by the change; for his information I have the honor to submit the following report: The present line from Fort Alex Hays to the Redoubt at the Chapel House is three and three quarter miles; the most direct line between the same works is three miles, and the greatest distance of the latter in front of the former, measured on a line nearly north from Fort Wadsworth, is six tenths of a mile; this line would cross the Weldon Railroad near Will's. A third line from Fort Alex Hays to the W. W. Davis' House, and thence to the work near Pegram's, would be four and a quarter miles without allowing for any irregularities of the ground; the present line between the two extreme points (Pegram and Alex Hays) is nearly five miles:—the two would probably therefore be about the same length. The first line is already completed, seven redoubts having been constructed; heavy slashing has been done along it, and abattis and fraises have been arranged; the whole forming very substantial obstacles. It is generally concealed from the enemy's view, and no movements of our troops can be seen by them; nor are the troops behind the works constantly annoyed by the opposite fire. Although the second line would be three quarters of a mile shorter, and the ground over which it runs is admirably adapted for the purpose, being almost a perfectly level plain, still it does not possess in other respects the advantages of the first; it will be more exposed, and in my opinion will require a larger force to hold. The distance gained to the front is a little over a half of a mile, which, as no regular siege operations are in progress, will not be commensurate to the amount of labor required to entrench a new line. Three additional Redoubts would have to be constructed, each taking from five to six days to complete with the ordinary details of about eight hundred men per day for each. The connecting lines would of course be thrown up at the same time. The main line of the enemy's works is nearly two miles in advance of our line of pickets between Fort Alex Hays and the Railroad, and his picket line about half a mile, the latter running immediately in front of Fisher's House. The third line by the W. W.

Davis would require the enemy's Pickets to be driven back upon their main works.—The ground in front of the work at the Chapel House is open to a short distance beyond the W. W. Davis House and is commanded by our guns; if the latter place is occupied, a line of timber will immediately cover our front, and conceal any movement of the enemy."—LS, *ibid.* On the same day, Maj. Gen. George G. Meade endorsed this letter. "Respectfully forwarded for the information of the Lt. Genl. Comd—in consequence of a verbal intimation received thro' Lt. Col. Babcock. A. D. C—Immediately after the recent movement & before the present lines to the left were commenced my attentions was turned to shortening the line as herein indicated, but I came to the same general conclusion as is claimed by Maj. Michler that it would require as many men to hold the shorter line as the present one, owing to the defensible character & the facility for using artillery of the present line—In view of this consideration & the amount of work done the project was abandoned."—AES, *ibid.*

1864, OCT. 13.   USG endorsement. "I know Private Ruggles well and the services he rendered in Miss. as a Scout. With an independent company of such men as himself he would be worth more in the Shenandoah Vally and over the district of country over which Mosby roams than a regiment of Cavalry. I would recommend that he be authorized to raise a battalion of men and be put in the Dept. of West Va."—AES, DNA, RG 94, Enlisted Branch, Letters Received, RSZ 517–65. Written on a letter of Aug. 15 from Maj. Gen. John A. Logan to Capt. Lewis M. Dayton, aide to Maj. Gen. William T. Sherman, recommending that Private C. Lorain Ruggles, 20th Ohio, be allowed to raise a co. of scouts since he had been so effective in secret service.—LS, *ibid.* On Dec. 21, 1865, Ruggles, Columbus, Ohio, wrote to USG. "I have the honor to submit my case, papers herewith inclosed, for final disposition. After having been detailed by you, I was serving with Genl Howard in South Carolina and was cut off from the main command by the enemy, in March 1865 and joined the 97th Ill. Inft. and went with it to Mobile, and there with it embarked for Texas alrriving at Galveston in June, and from there went to Columbus Texas, and remained at this pt. or with said 97th Ill. Vols. Col Staton, until December 2d 1865, when I recd. transportaton of Genl. Grierson to Columbus Ohio for Muster out. The Mustering Officer here refers me you for further orders before they will muster me out. I therefore request that such orders be given for my dischg"—ALS, *ibid.* On Feb. 12, 1866, Ohio AG Benjamin R. Cowen wrote to USG. "I have the honor to represent to you that Corp. Lorain Ruggles, late of Co. H., 20th Regt. who represents himself to have been on secret service under your order, during your operations against Vicksburg, and subsequently with other general officers. His regiment has been mustered out, & he is here unable to procure his discharge, or descriptive list. The latter is in the hands of the A. A. Pro. Mar. Gen. for Ohio, who declines to give it to Ruggles because the latter is unable to produce the orders under which he operated while on detached service. I respectfully request you to take such measures as will procure Ruggles an honorable discharge, and his back pay. At his suggestion & request I write you, as he claims to have written before, but received no answer. He remains here to await your action."—ALS, *ibid.* Endorsements indicate that Ruggles was properly discharged. See E. C. Downs, *Four Years a Scout and Spy* (Zanesville, Ohio, 1866), pp. 359–66, 388. On July 9, 1866, USG wrote to Edward C. Downs. "In the work of which you speak, you are at liberty to refer to me concerning the value of the services rendered by Mr. Ruggles as a scout and spy. His reports were always reliable, and were held in high estimation by me."—*Ibid.*, p. 9.

1864, OCT. 14, 1:00 P.M.   To Maj. Gen. Henry W. Halleck. "I wish you would order Allen's Batter H R. I. here. I will send back in return to be recruited up Batteries A. & B. R. I. These two number but One officer & seventy-nine men."—ALS (telegram sent), CSmH; telegram received (at 3:30 P.M.), DNA, RG 107, Telegrams Collected (Bound). *O.R.*, I, xlii, part 3, 225. See *ibid.*, pp. 153–54, 410.

1864, OCT. 15.   Asst. Secretary of War Charles A. Dana to USG. "Gen. Dix in NewYork requests that no more released rebel prisoners & deserters be allowed to go North till after Nov 8, as they are all in favor of a cessation of hostilities"—ALS (telegram sent), DNA, RG 107, Telegrams Collected (Bound); telegram received, *ibid.*, Telegrams Collected (Unbound); *ibid.*, RG 108, Letters Received. *O.R.*, II, vii, 989. On Oct. 16, Lt. Col. Theodore S. Bowers wrote to Brig. Gen. Marsena R. Patrick, provost marshal. "Hereafter all Deserters from the enemy will be sent to Fort Monroe, Va., and delivered to the Commanding Officer there, who will retain them until orders are received by him from these Headquarters to send them to the North."—ALS, DNA, RG 393, Army of the Potomac, Staff Officers, Letters Received.

1864, OCT. 15.   Maj. Gen. Henry W. Halleck to USG. "Resp. forwarded to Lieutt. General Grant for his decision."—Copy, DNA, RG 108, Register of Letters Received. *O.R.*, II, vii, 896. Written on a letter of Sept. 30 from Maj. Gen. Cadwallader C. Washburn to Col. William Hoffman proposing to accept an offer to exchange prisoners in order to gain the release of 350 men of the 16th Army Corps held at Cahaba, Ala.—*Ibid.*, pp. 895–96.

1864, OCT. 17.   USG endorsement. "This man might get information of value if successful in reaching Wilmington and returning. His attention should be called to collecting the forces at Wilmington; at & in the forts about the mouth of Cape Fear river, the works about the city the condition of the roads towards Fort Fisher and particularly if an attack is expected and if so from what direction."—AES, DNA, RG 94, Letters Received, 564D 1864. Written on a letter of Oct. 8 from Private Henry W. Dodge, Signal Corps, Georgetown, D. C., to 1st Lt. Edmund H. Russell, Signal Corps, offering his services as a spy to report conditions at Wilmington,

N. C.—ALS, *ibid.* On Oct. 24, Maj. Gen. Henry W. Halleck endorsed this letter. "Respectfully referred to Lt Genl Grant. If you think any important information not already procured through the navy & deserters, is likely to be obtained by this man, I see no objections to his undertaking this expedition. He *voluentarily* offers himself as a Spy."—AES, *ibid.*

1864, OCT. 17.   W. E. Boardman, secretary, U.S. Christian Commission, to USG. "An admirable system of Extra Diet Kitchens has grown up within the year past under direction of the Medical authorities, and under the auspices of the Christian Commission in Gen Shermans Department. Mrs. Anne Wittenmyer in connection with our Field agents has had general management, and by precise administration and the efficient services of those under her, very many soldiers have been lifted to the ranks, from the graves every month. She is desirous of consulting with you about the extension of this system to the whole army field, and we know that argument is unnessary to induce your attention to the matter. Taking the occasion of Mrs. W visit to you Mr Stuart requests me to mention a conversation had with you in reference to the extension of your 'Special Order No 32' dated 'In the Field, Chatanooga Dec. 12, 1863,' and to say that if it suits your pleasure and convenience, you will confer a great favor by the proposed extension so as to make it cover the whole army."—ALS, DNA, RG 94, U.S. Christian Commission, Letters Sent (Press).

1864, OCT. 18.   To Maj. Gen. Ethan Allen Hitchcock. "Captain Carswell McClellan, A. A. G., with Brig. Gen. Cutler, 4th Div. 5th Corps, was captured some time since and paroled for special exchange.—He is now at Camp Parole, Annapolis. I desire to have him exchanged for an officer of equal rank."—LS, DNA, RG 249, Letters Received. See *O.R.*, I, xlii, part 1, 472.

1864, OCT. 18.   Maj. Gen. Benjamin F. Butler to USG. "If you please to have one of your Staff inspect our base Hospital of the 18th Corps at Point of Rocks perhaps it will be seen that with small expense we can make a hospital that will serve all purposes of the Field in connection with our hospital boats—It has provided for three thousand"—ALS (telegram sent), DNA, RG 393, Dept. of Va. and N. C., Telegrams Sent (Press); telegram received (at 11:10 A.M.), *ibid.*, RG 107, Telegrams Collected (Unbound). Printed as sent at 11:10 A.M. in *O.R.*, I, xlii, part 3, 268.

1864, OCT. 18.   Lt. Col. Theodore S. Bowers to Maj. Gen. Benjamin F. Butler. "The first of a number of regiments of colored troops from Ky. have just arrived—At what point will you have them landed—"—Telegram received, DNA, RG 107, Telegrams Collected (Unbound). On the same day, 10:30 A.M., Butler telegraphed to Bowers. "I propose to disembark at Deep Bottom the colored troops coming to me. They will be there at a place easy of access now healthy and with good water and a fine place for drill—"—

ALS (faded telegram sent), *ibid.* Printed as sent at 10:10 A.M., received at 10:30 A.M., in *O.R.*, I, xlii, part 3, 268.

1864, OCT. 19. USG endorsement. "Respectfully forwarded for the information of the Assistant Secretary of War."—ES, DNA, RG 107, Letters Received from Bureaus. Written on a letter of Oct. 16 from Capt. Alfred F. Puffer, aide to Maj. Gen. Benjamin F. Butler, to Lt. Col. Theodore S. Bowers. "The Commanding General directs me to inform you that Passes to come North by Flag of Truce have been forwarded to Mr. Tabouelle, Chancellor of the French Consulate, and Mr. Dumas, also to Mr. Fred. Wm. Hairewinkel and Family, in accordance with requests from the War Department transmitted through Head Quarters Armies of the United States—"— ALS, *ibid.*

1864, OCT. 19. Special Orders No. 108, Armies of the U.S. "The following named regiments and detachments are hereby assigned to the Army of the Potomac, and will immediately report to Maj. Gen. Geo. G. Meade, Comd'g. for orders. 186th New York Vols. Col. Bradley Winslow. 39th New Jersey Vols. Col. Wildrick 188th New York Vol.s Maj. Davison (6 comps) 18th New Hampshire Vols. Capt A K Potter (5 comps) 8th Delaware Vols., Capt R. I. Holt (3 comps) 61st Massachusetts Vols., Lieut C. S. Wolcott (5 comps) Captain A Webster, Asst Quarter master Vols., is hereby assigned to special duty at these Headquarters."—Copies (altered from tabular form), DLC-USG, V, 57, 62, 63, 64, 70.

1864, OCT. 20. To Maj. Gen. George G. Meade. "Mrs Spencers a hospital nurse and at the same time a Sanitary Agt wishes a pass to go to the front for the purpose of leaving tobacco & other articles with Commissaries for distribution among the men in the trenches—I declined giving the pass but should think there was no objection"—Telegram received, DNA, RG 94, War Records Office, Army of the Potomac; copies (2), Meade Papers, PHi. On the same day, 7:10 P.M., Meade telegraphed to USG. "I have directed General Patrick to give Mrs. Spencer's concerning whom you telegraphed me this evening, a pass to visit the front."—Telegram sent, DNA, RG 94, War Records Office, Army of the Potomac; copy, *ibid.*, RG 393, Army of the Potomac, Letters Sent.

1864, OCT. 21. Asst. Secretary of the Navy Gustavus V. Fox to USG. "Requisition for ordnance and ordnance stores received today all of which will leave by special boat tomorrow except the rifle guns which shall be ~~got~~ obtained from the North at the earliest moment"—Telegram received, DNA, RG 107, Telegrams Collected (Unbound); *ibid.*, RG 108, Letters Received; copy, *ibid.*, RG 45, Miscellaneous Letters Sent.

1864, OCT. 23. USG endorsement. "Approved and respectfully forwarded to the Adjutant General of the Army, Washington, D. C."—ES, DNA, RG

94, ACP, 756P CB 1864. Written on a letter of the same day from Col. Perley P. Pitkin to Brig. Gen. Rufus Ingalls tendering his resignation in order to accept a position as Vt. q. m.—ALS, *ibid.*

1864, OCT. 25. USG endorsement. "I have known Mr. C. W. Ford for many years most favorably. He has been from the start an ardent supporter of the Government and is universally known as an honest upright business-man. I would have no hesitation in recommending him for the place he asks." —AES, DNA, RG 94, ACP, F431 CB 1864. Written on a letter of Oct. 13 from Charles W. Ford, St. Louis, to Secretary of War Edwin M. Stanton applying for appointment as post sutler, Jefferson Barracks.—ALS, *ibid.*

1864, OCT. 25. To Maj. Gen. Benjamin F. Butler. "Mr G. Odine of Boston, & Dr Groves of Chelsa are here, & will go up on the 'Greyhound' in the morning to see you, Will you please have an ambulance at the landing to take them to your HdQrs."—Telegram received, DLC-Benjamin F. Butler.

1864, OCT. 25. Lt. Col. Adam Badeau to Maj. Gen. George G. Meade. "Mr. Romero the Mexican minister, and Gen. Doblado with a staff officer will visit your hdqrs today with letters for you. They leave here on the 10.55 train"—ALS (telegram sent), DNA, RG 107, Telegrams Collected (Unbound); telegram received, *ibid.*, RG 94, War Records Office, Army of the Potomac. *O.R.*, I, xlii, part 3, 337. On Oct. 26, Badeau telegraphed to Maj. Gen. Benjamin F. Butler. "Gen Grant directs me to say Mr. Romero, minister from Mexico and Gen Doblado will visit your headquarters this morning. The"—ALS (telegram sent), DNA, RG 107, Telegrams Collected (Unbound); telegram received (at 9:10 A.M.), DLC-Benjamin F. Butler.

1864, OCT. 26. Lt. Col. Theodore S. Bowers endorsement. "Respectfully referred to Brig. Gen. Rufus Ingalls, Chief Quarter Master Armies operating against Richmond, who will please cause an investigation of this case, and apply the proper punishment, and who will also take measures to correct any abuses that may exist on the Mail boats."—ALS, DNA, RG 108, Letters Received. Written on a letter of Oct. 13 from Chaplain Henry M. Turner, 1st U.S. Colored, to Maj. Robert S. Davis, adjt. for Maj. Gen. Benjamin F. Butler. "I feel it my duty to report and out rage, which surpasses any that I ever experienced under the same circumstances, This out rage was perpetrated by one Mr Joseph Wear, on the 12th inst, which while coming from Fort Monroe to Bermuda Hundred on the steam boat Manhattan, Having procured a pass from the Provost Marshall at Bermuda, *as per order*, to visit the sick and wounded of my regiment, at Hampton and Portsmouth Hospitals, and especially to see after our Adjutant who was severely wounded, I proceeded to do the Same, by taking passage on the boat Manhattan, on the morning of the 9th inst, Being informed on my arrival at Fort Monroe that our Adjutant was dead, I defered my visit

to Hampton Hospital, untill Tuesday the 11th inst, and immediately left for
Norfolk,   There, I spent monday (though quite sick) in seeing after my
soldeirs,   Tuesday morning I left Norfolk for Fort Monroe, and visited the
officers and soldeirs of my regiment, and preached at night to a very large
audience,   So early on wednesday morning 12 inst, I had my pass re-
stamped by the Provost Marshall and took passage on the Manhattan again
for Bermuda Hundred,   Remaining on the boat but a short time, my attention was called to the wives of two of our Soldeirs, Anna Thomas the
wife of George Thomas of my regiment, and Clara Bell, the wife of Some
soldeir in the 6th U S C Troops, who is supposed to be mortally wounded
in the hospital at point of Rocks,   They having no place to sit, but on the
wet bow of the boat, among some two or three Hundred soldeirs to be black
gaurded and insulted, were told by one of the deck hands to go into a room
next to the Kitchen room, Where they would be releived from the soldeirs
insults, but which room ~~as~~ was as dirty and as Greesy as the Kitchen,
However, I offered them my protection and sit there with them, and wrote
a correspondence to one of the papers for which I write,   The hour for dinner having arrived the bell was rang, and several tables were served to the
white passengers,   And being informed that I could get nothing to eat untill all the white people were done, I waited very willingly, for I knew, this
was the general custom on boats,   And after a long time, I was informed by
a colored man that dinner was ready,   I ~~finding~~ invited the two ladies to
accompany me to dinner,   But finding the regular door for entrance locked,
I was told to go the front of the boat, and go down throug[h] the gaurd
door, (I think they called it) as colored people were not allowed to go
through the door marked *Gents Cabin*,   with this order I complied without
a murmuring thought,   But going down the steps, I soon found it so dark,
that I could neither ~~tell~~ see where I was, nor tell where to go, but a man
came down, and Said follow me,   I took the ladies by the hand and done
So, and he finally led us into the eating Saloon, where it was light,   I
looked upon the table, and saw it nearly covered with bread crumbs, and
dirty dishes,   A~~a~~nd around it sit, all sorts of colored people, some with
coats off, sleeves rolled up, &c &c   And on the table sit a plate of cold beef,
Some bread, some cold potatoes, a little Butter, and a few tumblers with
water,   I said to the ladies, this is a poor dinner for 50 cts, for I was told
by the colored man who announced dinner being ready, that the price was
50 cts,   By the time I commenced eating the said Mr Joseph Wear cheif
Steward came to two men at the end of the table, and requested pay for
dinner,   they asked him how mutch, he said a dollar,   To this they
drumbled out something, I did not understand what, But I heard him very
loudly Say, God damn you, you know it ~~know~~,   after geting his money he
came to me, Saying, I will have none of your damn Jaw about it neither,
He then said to me, 'fare for your dinner,'   do you pay for these two women,
meaning the two with me,   I Said, yes Sir, what is it,   Three dollars he
replied,   Said I, what a dollar ~~a dollar~~ a peice for Such a dinner as this,
Yes, he said,   Well Sir, I did not know that, I Said,   Well you know it

know dont you, was his reply,   Then runing my hand into my pocket to get
out his money, I remarked, I think it an out rage to charge a dollar for such
a dinner as this,   He remarked, God damn you, if you dont like it, get out
of here damn quick,   So on the ladies accout, I gave him three dollars,
which he took, and ~~wh~~ walked off, saying, you will never get on this boat
again, and if you give me any impudence, I will Knock you damned head
off,   I then replied very sharply I reckon I will get on this boat again, you
dont command it,   Shortly after I got up, and coming out lit a segar, and
passing him, Said, Will you tell me who sits the price on the boat,   Said
he, I do,   Said I, Sir what is your name,   Said he, What do you want to
know that for,   Said I, I wish to call the captain's attention to it, for I think
such prices an out rage,   At this point, he drew his knife and followed me,
Saying, go out of here, God damn you, go out of here, and with a drawn
Knife he followed me to the outer door,   I Said nothing but walked out,   I
have been traviling on boats for many years, but never was so maltreated
in my life,   But it is due to the Captain and clerk &c, to say they treated
me very gentlemanly,   ~~And~~ But all the army officers on the boat, who was
made acquainted with the circumstance, told me to report his conduct to
your honor   Besides, there was a captain of the second Corps, whose body
servant eat at the Same table, and who only paid 50 cts for his servants
dinner,   After he thus acted, I found that he was universally detested by
~~all~~ many who knew him, for I talked with several,   His name was given to
me by one of the engeneers of the same boat, which he said was Joseph Wear
(or Ware)   to all of the above, I do most positively affirm."—ALS, *ibid.* For
Turner, first Negro chaplain appointed in the U.S. Army, see M. M. Ponton,
Life and Times of Henry M. Turner (Atlanta, 1917; reprinted, Westport,
Conn., 1970), pp. 51–53. On Oct. 21, Butler endorsed Turner's letter.
"Respectfully forwarded to Brig. General Rawlings Chief of Staff that he
may see that the proper correction is made—I learn that Ware is under arrest—Chaplain Turner is a gentlemanly correct proper and as well behaved an officer as there is in the United States service—This is not the first
or second time that colored soldiers have been insulted on this line of boats—
There must be something radically wrong in the manner the line is man-
aged—I have recieved repeated complaints not only of the treatment of
colored soldiers but of white officers—I respectfully request that investigation be made that proper food properly served for a proper price be given
to passengers on the boats, or what would be preferable that I may be allowed to put on a line of boats between Fortress Monroe and my Head Qrs
I can then control them so that there will be no complaints of this sort—
One of the most respectable gentleman in New York told me that upon this
line of boats the clerk refused to deliver any tickets for supper until after all
the officers of the boat had their meals—that ~~then~~ the clerk invited such
persons as he chose, generally of his own class down to supper with him
and then after they had eaten the supper room was thrown open to the general passengers—The boats seem to be from what I hear of them a mass of
filth outrage extortion and insult and I respectfully ask the Lieut General

Com'd'g leave to put on a line of boats between here and Fortress Monroe that shall do business in such a manner that all persons whether white or black can recieve proper and civil treatment. A gentleman of my own staff has paid a dollar for a dinner which consisted of a single potatoe and a peice of beef and bread that being all he could get—The time is not far distant when the rebels will employ colored men for soldiers and if we allow the wives and officers of our colored soldiers to be treated in the way this communication shows, if I were the husband I would go to the enemy—To expect the Negro to come to us is useless, unless we show that we are willing to give him a higher and better position as a man than he recieves from a Southern master—If this complaint set forth in Chaplain Turners communication were a sporadic incident I would not have troubled you by so long a letter, but it is a part of a policy inaugurated in the Army of the Potomac by McClellan and kept up ever since and serious enough in my judgment to be very carefully investigated and summarily corrected."—ES, DNA, RG 108, Letters Received. On Oct. 27, Capt. Charles E. Scoville, "Office of Pro. Mar. Genl.," endorsed this correspondence. "Respectfully returned to Brig. Genl. Ingalls, Chief Quarter Master, Armies operating ags Richmond, with the information that on or about the 20th Inst, at the request of Col Pitkin, the Steward of the Str Manhattan was arrested by my Guard. The Col requested that he might be retained in custody until He could hear from Genl Butler. After abt three days confinement Col Pitkin again saw me Stated that He had heard nothing from Genl Butler, but had in the meantime learne[d] that the charges against the Steward were sustaind by the Capt of the Manhattan, (by others) that the Capt declared that the Steward should not again come onto his Boat. Whereupon the Col requested that the Steward should be released from further confinement, Sent beyond the lines of the Army. Which request was carried into effect abt. the 23d Inst. Capt Blood is mistaken when stating that I informed him, that the Steward was arrested for incivility to a Colored Chaplain. I know nothing of the particulars concerning the arrest of Mr. Weir. In this case as in others, my Guard was simply lent to Col Pitkin, to make such arrests, as he deemed necessary for the interests of the Service"—AES, *ibid.* On Oct. 28, Brig. Gen. Rufus Ingalls endorsed this correspondence. "Respectfully referred to General Patrick, Provost Marshal General, who will please make such investigation and report as he may deem proper, and who is desired to return these papers to Gen'l Rawlins for the information and action of the Lieut. General commanding the Armies. The harsh and uncalled for endorsement of Maj. Gen'l Butler, obliges me to submit the following remarks in vindication of myself, my Department, and the Army of the Potomac. By a glance at paper herewith, marked 'A,' it will be observed that the matter complained of had already been summarily disposed of and closed *before* Genl. Butler's communication reached these Head Quarters. Why then this endorsement full of unjust, not to say utterly unfounded imputations? These Mail boats were detailed from those already in the public service best qualified for such duty. They receive no extra compensation from the government for *mail* service, but are allowed to charge for meals and lodgings actually provided by them. There are officers and guards of the Provost Marshal's Dep't. on these boats for thes enforcement of established rules and orders, and *fewer* complaints have been made by passengers on this line, than on any other probably in the world of anything like equal magnitude. Quite all the complaints have emenated from or come through Gen'l Butler, and I have used all my power to make the line satisfactory to *him*; but it doubtless never will please him until it is put exclusively under his orders, although there ought to be ability enough here to run it on proper principles. The line is a very important one, and, I claim is conducted as economically, as strictly and as properly as possible—. There is no sort of necessity for having the line asked for by General Butler, as, I trust, the Lieut. General will readily perceive. When Gen'l Butler requires boats for any particalar service they are promptly detailed. I state this very emphatically, because I want the matter well understood and *settled*. There are many complaints on all lines over which so many people pass. Doubtless most of them have good foundation, but very many of them are frivolous, made by over-exacting parties— sometimes officers exceed their rights and aim by brow-beating Stewards and officers of vessels, to secure extra attention. Some even think that they must be furnished food and bed *gratis*, instead of either paying like men for what they call for and eat, or carrying their own rations as do soldiers—Had this Colored Chaplin called upon the officer of the guard, or the master of the vessel, or even reported the matter to the Provost Marshal General, or any other person having *direct* authority in the case, Gen'l. Butler would not have been troubled. Such matters come properly within the province of the Provost Marshal Generals Department. Without ignoring the rights of my own race, I still have invariably sought to protect those of the Colored soldiers and employés, since the organization of the Army of the Potomac—. I have been fully supported in my efforts by every commander of that Army. I wish we had many more of these colored . . ."—E (incomplete), *ibid.* On Feb. 9, 1865, Turner wrote to Butler. ". . . Sir, permit me to inform you that there never was a man more beloved than you were by the colored troops. . . ."—*Private and Official Correspondence of Gen. Benjamin F. Butler . . .* (n.p., 1917), V, 546.

1864, OCT. 26. Secretary of State William H. Seward to USG. "This note will be handed to you by Mr. Ransom Van Valkenburgh, a reliable and trustworthy man, who comes to the Army to aid in collecting the soldiers' vote of the State of New York. Pray give him suitable facilities—"—LS (press), Seward Papers, NRU.

1864, OCT. 27. Brig. Gen. Rufus Ingalls to USG. "The cars have been ordered to leave at once for Warren Station"—ALS (telegram sent), OClWHi.

1864, OCT. 28. To Maj. Gen. Benjamin F. Butler. "Gen Williams of California a particular friend of Gen Halleck goes up this morning to visit you He has with him his son & three ladies Will you please send conveyance to take them from aikens landing I am sorry that I cannot accompany them"—Telegram received, DLC-Benjamin F. Butler.

1864, OCT. 30. To Maj. Gen. Benjamin F. Butler. "When your despatch was rec'd I was absent, I would like to see you this evening, Your coming down will save me going up,"—Telegram received, DLC-Benjamin F. Butler.

1864, Nov. 1. USG endorsement. "Respectfully forwarded to the Secretary of War, with the recommendation that the suggestions of Gen. Patrick Provost Marshal General of the Armies operating against Richmond be carried into effect."—ES, DNA, RG 107, Letters Received from Bureaus. On Oct. 28, Brig. Gen. Marsena R. Patrick, provost marshal, wrote to Lt. Col. Theodore S. Bowers. "I have the honor to request that you present the following suggestions to the Lieutenant General Commanding, for his consideration, with a view of effecting a much needed reform in the Trade Regulations. Under the rules and regulations of the Treasury Department, concerning commercial intercourse with and in states and parts of states declared in insurrection, sutlers belonging to the army are, by Article XXIV, limited in the amount of goods which they are permitted to transport to their commands, to twenty five hundred dollars ($2500.) worth per. month, or double the amount for two months. In view of the increase in price of all articles sold by sutlers, from that at which they were sold when these rules were established, and with a view of introducing into the Army a generous supply of goods, by authorized dealer's, thereby breaking down a monopoly which exists in consequence of Department Officers granting special permits to parties who may bring within the Department large stocks of goods, to be resold to sutlers, I would recommend such a change to be made in the rules and regulations aforesaid, as will permit sutlers to transport to their commands such an amount of goods as will be required, and that for all goods, so taken, in excess of twenty five hundred dollars ($2500) per. month, they should be required to pay three (3) per. cent tax, or such other tax as the law requires in such cases."—LS, *ibid.*

1864, Nov. 1. Bvt. Maj. Gen. Godfrey Weitzel to Lt. Col. Theodore S. Bowers. "I have the honor most urgently to request that Major G. E. Cowen, 1st La. Cavalry, now on leave at Fairhaven Massachusetts be at once ordered to report to me for duty He can be spared from the Dept. of the Gulf. He is one of my original staff, has served with me a year, and desires this I need him much. I hope this order will be sent him by telegraph."—ALS (telegram sent), DNA, RG 107, Telegrams Collected (Unbound); telegram received, *ibid.*, Telegrams Collected (Bound). On the same day, USG telegraphed to Secretary of War Edwin M. Stanton transmitting the text of Weitzel's telegram and adding his endorsement. "Approved & submitted for the action of the Secy of War"—Telegram received (at 10:20 P.M.), *ibid.*

1864, Nov. 1.   U.S. Representative Samuel Knox of Mo. and six others, St. Louis, to USG. "The assignment to this dept. of Lieut. Col. J. H Hammond vice A. D. Greene removed will be very acceptable to the loyal people of this state"—Telegram received (at 2:30 P.M.), DNA, RG 107, Telegrams Collected (Bound). On Sept. 21, AGO Special Orders 313 relieved Maj. Oliver D. Greene, then serving as adjt. and chief of staff for Maj. Gen. William S. Rosecrans. Col. John V. D. Du Bois replaced Greene, who spent two years awaiting orders.—*O.R.*, I, xli, part 3, 286, 358. On Feb. 6, 1865, Greene, Louisville, wrote to USG a lengthy letter asking an assignment to duty.—ALS, DNA, RG 94, ACP, 3819 ACP 1884. On March 7, USG endorsed this letter. "Respectfully forwarded to the Secretary of War. I know nothing of this case but what appears from the within papers, but I would recommend that Major Green be assigned to duty. unless there is good reason for not doing so"—ES, *ibid.*

1864, Nov. 2.   To President Abraham Lincoln. "The following despatch from Gen Meade in reply to your telegram of three forty (340) is forwarded for your information . . . 'Hd Qrs A of P. Nov 2nd   LIEUT GENL U S GRANT   The dispatch of the President directing that the execution of the sentence of Death in the case of Private Nathan Wilson twenty second (22) Mass Volunteers has been received—There is no Soldier of that name given under sentence of death in this Army & the Presidents order was no doubt intended to apply to the case of Private Nathaniel M. Wilcox company C. twenty second (22d) Mass Volunteers who was to have been executed on friday next. The suspension of his execution will at once be ordered   GEO. G. MEADE MAJ GEN.''—Telegram received, DLC-Robert T. Lincoln; (2) DNA, RG 107, Telegrams Collected (Bound). On the same day, 3:40 P.M., Lincoln had telegraphed to USG. "Suspend until further order the execution of Nathan Wilcox, of 22nd Mass. Regt Fifth Corps, said to be at Repair Depot."—ALS (telegram sent), *ibid.*; telegram received, *ibid.*, Telegrams Collected (Unbound); *ibid.*, RG 108, Letters Received. Lincoln, *Works*, VIII, 87. See *ibid.*, p. 86. The name appears as Wilson in the telegrams received. At 4:30 P.M., USG had telegraphed to Maj. Gen. George G. Meade transmitting Lincoln's telegram.—Copies, DLC-USG, V, 45, 70, 107; DNA, RG 108, Letters Sent; Meade Papers, PHi. Before responding to USG at 5:30 P.M., Meade telegraphed directly to Lincoln at 5:00 P.M.—Telegram received, DLC-Robert T. Lincoln; DNA, RG 107, Telegrams Collected (Bound); (2) *ibid.*, Telegrams Collected (Unbound); copy, Meade Papers, PHi.

1864, Nov. 2.   USG endorsement. "Respectfully returned to the Secretary of War. I concur in the views of Generals Delafield and Halleck, and

recommend that a Board be convened to take the subject under consideration."—ES, DNA, RG 94, Letters Received, 471E 1864. Written on a letter
of Oct. 7 from Brig. Gen. Richard Delafield to Secretary of War Edwin M.
Stanton proposing that officers wear less conspicuous uniforms so as not to
attract enemy sharpshooters.—LS, *ibid.* On Oct. 13, Maj. Gen. Henry W.
Halleck endorsed this letter. "Much of that here recommended is already
practically carried out in the field, our officers wearing the soldier's blouse
in the summer & the soldier's overcoat in the winter. Many also dispense
with the shoulder strap when in the field. While it is necessary that officers
wear some distinctive marks of their ranks, these could be made less conspicuous than at present. In regard to uniform color and shape of over coats,
&c I fully concur with Genl Delafield. I therefore respectfully recommend
that a Board of officers be organized to prepare modifications, in this respect,
of the Army Regulations."—AES, *ibid.*

1864, Nov. 3.   To Capt. John McEntee. "Call on Gen. Weitzel for flag of
truce, and such instructions as you may require. Show him the letter to Mulford"—Telegram, copies, DLC-USG, V, 45, 70, 107; DNA, RG 108, Letters Sent. On Nov. 2, Lt. Col. Theodore S. Bowers wrote to Col. John E.
Mulford, asst. agent of exchange. "Gen. Patrick Provost Marshal General
will hand over to you the body of Gen. Ramseiur of the C. S. A. which is
accompanied by and in charge of Maj. R. R. Hutchinson, and private A. E.
Johnson, both prisoners of War. You will please take charge of the matter,
and deliver the body under flag of truce to the Confederate authorities. Maj.
Hutchison and private Johnson will be permitted to accompany the flag of
truce and see that the body is properly and truly delivered to the Confederate authorities, after which they will be returned to Gen. Patrick for shipment north as prisoners of War   Under no circumstances can their desire
to go beyond our flag be gratified."—ALS, *ibid.*, RG 393, Army of the
Potomac, Miscellaneous Letters Received. On Nov. 2, Brig. Gen. Marsena
R. Patrick ordered McEntee to convey the body of Maj. Gen. Stephen D.
Ramseur to C.S.A. forces.—LS, *ibid.*

1864, Nov. 4.   USG endorsement. "Respectfully returned to the Adjutant
General of the Army, Washington, D. C. I have no objection to making an
exception from the General rule in this case. I therefore recommend, that
Gen. Foster be authorized, to raise the Regiment, within requested."—ES,
DNA, RG 94, Vol. Service Div., 1027 (VS) 1864. Written on a letter of
Oct. 20 from Col. Milton S. Littlefield, 21st U.S. Colored Troops, Hilton
Head, S. C., to Secretary of War Edwin M. Stanton asking permission to
organize a regt. of white Fla. vols.—LS, *ibid.*

1864, Nov. 4.   Special Orders No. 119, Armies of the U.S., concerning
reports of engineer officers.—Copies, DLC-USG, V, 57, 62, 63, 64. *O.R.*,
I, xlii, part 3, 507. These orders superseded Special Orders No. 91, Sept.

12.—DS, DNA, RG 94, War Records Office, Army of the Potomac. *O.R.*, I, xlii, part 2, 795.

1864, Nov. 4. "An European Officer" to USG. "It is *nearly a year,* since you put yourself *at the head* of the *army of the Potomac* & *marched onto Richmond*! Instead of 'The Hundred Days' *two hundred* have dawned & faded but you are *not nearer the fullfilment of the capture of the 'promised Land'*! How long yet shall the soil of Virginia be watered with the blood of tens of thousands? How long yet shall the nation spend its hundreds of millions' to feed & clothe your army & to reinforce it—only to be beaten & check-mated at every move? I will give *two reasons, why you should resign* & make place for a man who shall show himself the equal of General Lee in *the theory* & *practise* of the *science of war*! *1st.* your brain is *not a mathematical brain*; it lacks *comprehensioness, profundity*, the faculty *of grasping highly original* & *intricate problems* & *analecting them correctly in all their details*! *2d.* you do *not* understand to make use of hundreds of thousands of men; nor the art of disciplining them into a compact machine—nor, *how* & *when to circumvent the enemy's position* & *plans*! Want of space & time forbid me to say more.—I hope for this poor, bleeding nations sake! that you may disapoint my horoscope of your head & that *you may annihilate Lee's army* & *conquer Virginia*! God Love The Republic!"—AL, DLC-Edwin M. Stanton.

1864, Nov. [6–8]. USG endorsement. "Respy referred to the Com Gen of Prisoners with the request that J. R Petway be extended the benefits allowed deserters from the enemy, under order No. 82 from these Head Quarters on compliance with the requirements of said order."—Copy, DLC-USG, V, 58. Written on a letter of Oct. 12 from Mrs. C. M. J. Williamson, Vicksburg, requesting the release of her son, J. R. Pettway, from Fort Delaware because he surrendered voluntarily at Vicksburg.—*Ibid.*, V, 48.

1864, Nov. 7. USG endorsement. "Respectfully forwarded to the Secretary of War approved and recommended"—ES, DNA, RG 94, ACP, W1256 CB 1864. Written on a letter of Sept. 21 of Col. Charles L. Peirson, 39th Mass., recommending 1st Lt. E. E. White for appointment as q. m.—LS, *ibid.*

1864, Nov. 8. To Maj. Gen. George G. Meade and all corps commanders. "The following despatch just recd from the Secy of Navy   It might be of interest to the enemy to receive a copy"—Telegram received, DNA, RG 393, 9th Army Corps, Telegrams Received; copy, Meade Papers, PHi. On the same day, Secretary of the Navy Gideon Welles telegraphed to USG. "Sends copy of dispatch from Commd'r Collins Comd'g U S Ship 'Wachusett' who reports his arrival at St Thomas with the 'Florida' "—DLC-USG, V, 48. See *O.R.* (Navy), I, iii, 254–55.

1864, Nov. 8.   Maj. Gen. Oliver O. Howard, Atlanta, to USG. "I write you this letter confidentially, constrained only by a sense of duty and with no view to personal advantage. The Orders (No. 277. General) just received by telegram, virtually dissolves the ~~Army~~ Department of the Tennessee & retains in the Army two Army Corps viz: the 15th & 17th Corps. The 16th Corps is dissolved and two thirds of the Army transferred to Maj. Gen. Canby. Being already on the Missippi he is better located than Gen. Sherman now is for immediate influence in the river Valley, but, General I fear he is not the man for that important trust. Good hearted, well meaning, gentlemanly as he is, still I fear from my observation that rumors affect him too much, that he ties up steamers to wharves regardless of expense to the government, that he scatters his troops without feeling properly impressed with the vitality of certain points & the comparative unimportance of others. Gen. Sherman's directions are usually full & explicit, so that his control of the Miss. river even when absent is better than that of most men present. Maj. Gen. Dodge, I learn visited you when away with his wound. I have heard that he felt disappointed in not having the 16th Corps, but I assure you he is a worthy officer & one I am pleased to command a Division or Corps under me, but Gens. A. J. Smith Dodge & Dana were on my hands & I recommended the Senior and believed him better for the post to which he was assigned. But there is no want of confidence in Gen. Dodge   It is intimated that Gen. Logan may not return to the 15th. Gen. Osterhaus is now commanding it and does quite well. He ɫ is brave & energetic and I am reluctant to disgust him by putting him back & more reluctant to send the efficient & excellent commander Gen. Woods (Chas. R) back to a brigade— he has commanded a division so long—But I am always free to say that, other things being equal I prefer an American Corps commander to a German. I had already made arrangements to establish a Dept. Hd. Qrs. at Memphis & now I have not time to change—Lt. Col. Clark will take this letter to you and receive from you an~~d~~y instructions—or suggestions for the Dept. which will be thankfully received. Gen. Sherman is at Kingston & I cannot consult with him before Col Clark will be obliged to leave. I find the Army of the Tenn. just suited to my spirit, brave, confident and in earnest." —ALS, DNA, RG 108, Letters Received. *O.R.*, I, xxxix, part 3, 702.

1864, Nov. 9.   USG endorsement. "Recommended and respectfully forwarded to the Secretary of War. Lieut. Cate deserves promotion."—ES, DNA, RG 94, ACP, C1156 CB 1863. Written on a letter of the same day from Lt. Col. Michael R. Morgan, chief commissary, to USG. "I have the honor to ask that you request for Lt. T. J. Cate, 36th U. S. C. T., the appointment of Captain & C. S. Vols. He merits that reward for having built the extensive bakery for soft bread at this point.—I do not think it is excelled by any similar bakery in the U. S.—It will turn out bread for one hundred thousand men, per day.—He deserves all the credit for the bakery. I promised him at the start that if in the erection of this bakery he gave me satisfaction, I would make the above request of you. Lt. Cate is now and has been for a long time acting as a Commissary of Subsistence."—LS, *ibid*. No appointment followed.

1864, Nov. 9. To Bvt. Maj. Gen. Godfrey Weitzel. "The communication of Gen. Graham, with your endorsement thereon, was daily received. I deem it inexpedient to make the request you suggest, on the navy at present, but will confer with you further on the subject at such time, as in my judgement will seem to warrant the carrying out of the plan proposed."—Copies, DLC-USG, V, 45, 70, 107; DNA, RG 108, Letters Sent.

1864, Nov. 9. Maj. Gen. Winfield S. Hancock to USG. "The chf of arty 2d corps reports that it would be very disadvantageous to the service to spare Lt Grordon who is ord officer of the arty of this corps at this time. He has not only to supply all the ord. required for the arty except the heavy guns but for all the forts and redoubts on the line of the enemys works in front of Petersburg. This with u̶s̶ us is a daily matter on account of the continaul firing. To educate another officer to the experience of Lt Gordon would take some time and in the interim the service might seriously suffer. If we were not in the lines before Petersburg I would present no objections whatever to his advancement in any way. The enemy fired this evening upon our reliefs marching out on picket supposing probably an attack was intended by us"—Telegram received, DNA, RG 108, Letters Received; copy, *ibid*., RG 393, 2nd Army Corps, Letters Sent.

1864, Nov. 9. William S. Hillyer, New York City, to USG. "The most exciting political contest in the history of the Republic is ended. The result was generally anticipated and few intelligent men are disappointed. But the intense feeling engendered by the bitter chargs and recriminations made by the leaders of each party against the other, has placed the defeated party in a condition where they should be tenderly conciliated. Mr Lincoln will get the electoral vote of almost the entire loyal states but his popular majority will probably not exceed ten per cent of the votes cast. Now the vote cast for McClellan is nineteen twentieths at least an earnest loyal vote in favor of the suppression of this rebellion by whatever means are necessary. If it were not so, if the McClellan vote was a disloyal vote as overzealous Republicans would teach—then the contest for the Union would be hopeless for with a United South and nine twentieths of the North against the war it would be a hopeless and useless struggle. But this is not so; the issue so far as my observation has gone and my knowledge of the private views of the democratic leaders has taught me (and I know many of them intimately) has been under whose administration will this rebellion most certainly be suppressed and the Union restored? You stated in one of your published letters that what was most required to suppress the rebellion was a *United North* This is evident to every reflecting patriot   We must have some of the enthusiasm and unity which characterized the nation when whigs republicans and democrats joined hands in forgetfulness of past differences and stood shoulder to shoulder in the determination to avenge the insult to the old flag at Fort Sumter—How can this [be] effe[cte]d? it will require a judicious administration of the executive department but it striks me that me that one thing can be done by you, or through your influence which will do more to allay popular prejudice and reunite the popular heart, than any other single act. *Recall Gen McClellan* to command. If you have not a suitable fighting command let him take charge of this department   I do not think that any man doubts his loyalty. Put McClellan in command and there will be little if any opposition to a draft. It will conciliate and appease the democrats and his approval of any military order will silence all objection   I make this earnest appeal to you General of my own motive and without the knowledge of any other person. I feel that the fate of the country may be in your hands. You can survey men and measures without the prejudice which blinds politicans   you have no private ends or personal ambition to subserve   I know you so well, that I know you can judge men fairly even when they have wronged you. A paper is just handed me stating that McClellan has resigned. Don't if you can prevent it let his resignation be accepted   Do tender him some command and write him a kind letter, personally urging its acceptance. If he accepts it you will have added great moral strength to the nations arm. If he declines you will have shorn him of all power to do evil were he so disposed. You know that I can have no object in this urgent appeal but the country's good   I have no acquaintance with Gen McClellan & am influenced by no motive of personal friendship   I have just returned from a business trip to Kentucky   while in Louisville I received a letter from Rawlins explaining the conduct of Mr Broadhead to whom I gave a letter of introduction   I was very much mortified, at the information and have terminated by connection with him. I wrote him in Washington on his return and before I had recd. Rawlins note but he did not give me the true reason of his returning your pass   I shall endeavour in future to be more careful in selecting my assoc[iates.] I am giving my attention now especially to developing man[n's] patent accoutrements and securing their adoption in the army. It is very strange that there should be so much trouble in securing the adoption of what every officer I have met in the army approves   My wife has been quite sick of late but is recovering. She had a repetition of the accident of last summer,   Tell Rawlins I will write to him as soon as I know where to address him. I see by the papers that he had arrived in St Louis. I thought that Rosecrans had a tough customer to deal with in John. What are the prospects for Richmond? Your last move was a *little expensive* to me"—ADfS, Robert C. W. Hillyer, San José, Costa Rica.

1864, Nov. [10–12].   USG endorsement. "Respy. returned to the AG. of the Army, Washington D. C. and attention invited to accompanying report of General Patrick, Provost Marshal General   There was no necessity of bothering the Department at Washington with this matter, as all possible redress would have been furnished at these Headquarters had the communication been properly forwarded   The assertion that there is no system at City Point on recieving and forwarding recruits could only have been made from ignorance of the facts. Perhaps no depot, or rendezvous in the United States is conducted with more care or system than that under the direction of General Patrick at this place. Mistakes do occur—complaints are made— but neither are often attributable to Gen Patrick or his assistants   The difficulty arises from the fact that hundreds of men are recieved here without any rolls or evidence to show for what organization they are intended. These men are held, and every effort made to ascertain what regiments they were assigned for   Again, hundreds of men arrive here, when enlisted for a particular arm of the service, or organization, and find that the rolls assign them differently. In the latter case the rolls are followed to the great dissatisfaction of the recruits. There are now at City Point over 600 men that there is no means of knowing where they belong, or to what regiment assigned. I am making arrangement to assign them (independant of assignments made at rendezvous, and of which I know nothing) to regiments of states from which they claim to come   Unless greater care and system is observed by those forwarding recruits here, it will be impossible to prevent complaint."— Copy, DLC-USG, V, 58. Written on a letter of the commanding officer, 48th N. Y., concerning problems with the receipt of substitutes and recruits, accompanied by a report of Brig. Gen. Marsena R. Patrick.—*Ibid.*

1864, Nov. [10–12].   USG endorsement. "Respy. forwarded to the Provost Marshal General of the Army, Washington D. C. for his information and with the hope that vigilent measures will be adopted to prevent this class of men being recieved into our service. In many cases the men are deceived, and in all cases the Government is defrauded of a good soldier"— Copy, DLC-USG, V, 58. Written on a letter of Nov. 8 of Brig. Gen. Marsena R. Patrick concerning C.S.A. deserters enlisted in U.S. service.—*Ibid.*; *ibid.*, V, 48.

1864, Nov. 12.   Maj. Gen. John Gibbon to Lt. Col. Cyrus B. Comstock. "I beg leave to submit certain propositions in regard to the organization of our armies, which I deem worthy the attention of our highest authorities and of Congress. *Appointment of officers. No efficient* military force can be kept up unless a regular *military* principle is employed in the appointment of officers. The only proper rule is to promote for gallantry and efficiency in the field, on the recommendation of the military superiors. For the want of such a rule our troops are *now* suffering, and the evil will increase the longer it lasts. Now, politics and personal influence have more to do with promotion than military merit. We require a stricter discipline, and we can never have it until we have officers who know and appreciate its importance. Plenty of these can be obtained amongst our volunteers if the right course is adopted. Now, each Gov. of a State. appoints his own officers, and very few require *military* recommendations, in consequence of which we do not get *military officers*. The Gov.s. of States should have nothing to do with the appointment of officers after the Regt. is once mustered into the U. S. Service. In many instances where the political or personal interest is strong it is impossible to prevent poor appointments or to get good ones made by rewarding military merit. Such a system will not make soldiers, but will ruin any army in the world; It is now fast impairing the efficiency of this. *General officers.* Although the General Government has in its hands the appointment of General officers it also was, at the commencement of the war, influenced more by political than military considerations in making these appointment, and it was only when it became evident that we must have military appointments that the system was *partially* changed. This necessity in regard to Genl. officers is apparent to the world at large. The necessity among the lower grades is just as great, though not as easily seen except by those who serve with the troops. The necessity for a reorganization amongst our Genl. officers will be apparent by examining the list of those now in service. It will be found that nearly all the earlier appointments have proved failures, and most of them are now laid aside, whilst their appropriate commands in the field are held by juniors. They should at once be mustered out of the service to give place to more recent appointments and more capable men. The Government owes them nothing. They were appointed for doing nothing and have done nothing ever since. There are exceptions of course to this, but one could not go far amiss in deciding who to muster out, especially if assisted in the decision by a Board of competent officers. In consequence of the plethora of General officers so many of whom are practically retired from active service many of our Div.s. are commanded by Brig. Genls. and most of our Brigs. by Cols. Lt. Cols. and Majors.,   The Government is forced to resort to the Brevet system to reward officers who have distinguished themselves in the field. *The system of Brevets.* The present system of Brevets is a very unjust one and not at all calculated to fulfil what should be the object of such a system—the *reward* of merit. A high title is a very good thing in its way, but when accompanyed with no right of command or pay is no adequate reward for field service. 'The servant is worthy of his hire' and it certainly is very unjust to deprive the officer who does the service, of his pay and give it to him who does it not. By the present system a brevet officer cannot exercise the command of his brevet unless specially assigned by the President, nor even then can he draw the pay. *Recruiting.* Some system ought to be at once adopted by which our old Regimental organizations ~~could~~ can be filled up, so as to take the best advantage of the discipline instilled into the officers and men who have had over three years experience in the field, instead of filling the army with new Regiments, led by new and incompetent officers. Men under such circumstances are apt to be uselessly slaughtered or captured, simply for a want of that knowledge in the officer which can be acquired only by long service in the field, and in the end three times the number of men would not produce the same effect as if the third were placed in the old organizations. This is a fact which our people cannot be too soon made aware of, and they will be convinced of it only by the presistent representations of our military men.

The object of this communication is simply to impress upon our authorities the *absolute necessity* of some well recognised system of organization for our armies and I shall be satisfied if it tends in the most remote degree to the accomplishment of that most desireable end. I beg you will lay this communication before the Genl.-in-chief for his consideration."—ALS, DNA, RG 108, Letters Received. On Nov. 15, Maj. Gen. George G. Meade endorsed this letter. "Respectfully forwarded. There is no doubt that some of the objections to the present system of appointments of officers raised by Maj Genl Gibbon are valid, but it is questionable whether the same objections cannot be brought against the plan proposed to be substituted by him, where personal influences can be brought to bear against the superior officer having the power to recommend, which is virtually the appointment. I should my self prefer, in case the present law is modified, to give to Boards of Officers the examination into the qualifications & military record of the Officers entitled to promotion, and the right to overslaugh such as are found wanting —As to restricting the power and prerogative of the Executive in the appointment of General Officers, I consider not only out of the question, but by no means desirable or proper."—ES, *ibid.*

1864, Nov. 12.   Brig. Gen. Truman Seymour, near Winchester, Va., to Lt. Col. Cyrus B. Comstock. "As the season for active operations at the north will soon virtually close, I beg to submit to you a few points—enforced upon my attention while serving in the Department of the South, as Chief of Staff to Maj. Genl Hunter—and that may be worthy, perhaps, of laying before the Lieut General. 1. Our armies are operating, of necessity, upon exterior lines. The Rebels occupy a line from Georgia to Virginia— an army at each extremity—with but two lines of communication between them. When beaten at these extremities, they will naturally fall back upon some intermediate point, and (,if resistant to the last moment of despair) still maintain their present and prospective advantages of interior lines   2. These lines of communication approach the Coast at Branchville. S. C. within striking, and readily accessible, range. By placing a mass upon these lines at that point Lee's & Hoods armies are separated forever—and the advantages of interior lines forever remain with us. 3. Neither Charleston or Savannah are necessary as bases for such a movement. The Sea-Coast islands between those points will suffice. The Edisto, Ashepoo and Combahee (Port Royal) are all navigable for good-sized vessels nearly, or quite, to the Charleston & Savannah R. R. and our force can be thrown thus upon that Railroad—then concentrate at Walterboro' (say 15 miles) and move upon Branchville (15 or 20 m)   With the Ashepoo, navigable within 5 miles of Walterboro, as a line of supply—with the Edisto on one flank (passable only by two or three bridges nearly up to Branchville) and the difficult and marshy line of the Combahee on the other—a force could operate with the greatest possible advantages. Branchville occupied, and a small force landed in Bull's Bay (15 m N. of Charleston) Charleston itself would almost necessarily fall—or could be opened to our possession (then desireable) by the navy. 4. The necessity of unloosening our clasp upon these vital lines of communication would compel both Lee & Hood to detach largely. Eventually the seat of War would be transferred to S. Carolina. The movement could be made with great rapidity—would be comparitively unresisted—and can be effected when nothing decisive can be elsewhere accomplished. And I am strongly impressed with the belief that it must be made before the War ends, on sound military principles—and eventually, of necessity. 5. As a new draft will probably soon be made, could there be a better disposition made of 50,000 of these men than to send them to Genl Foster, with the above-indicated plan in view, and where they can be rapidly disciplined during inactivity elsewhere? In other words, cannot the *best work* be done here, when other work must be put aside? I trust you will pardon my seeming impertinence in writing this to you—The suggestions have met the thorough approval of so many capable officers, and have seemed so sound in principle, that you will not accuse me of any other design, I trust, than to hit our Enemy whereever we can do him essential damage."—LS, DNA, RG 108, Letters Received. On Nov. 18, Lt. Col. Theodore S. Bowers issued Special Orders No. 131 assigning Seymour to duty in the 6th Army Corps under Maj. Gen. Philip H. Sheridan.—Copies, DLC-USG, V, 57, 62, 63, 64. *O.R.*, I, xliii, part 2, 642.

1864, Nov. 13.   USG endorsement. "Respectfully forwarded to the Secretary of War, for his information."—ES, DNA, RG 107, Letters Received from Bureaus. Written on a letter of Nov. 12 from Capt. John McEntee, office of the provost marshal, to Lt. Col. Theodore S. Bowers reporting that I. M. Hatch, sent into C.S.A. lines posing as a deserter to discover what happened to such persons, had been sent to Ky. with other deserters and that they had entered U.S. lines posing as C.S.A. deserters.—ALS, *ibid.* Printed as addressed to Bvt. Maj. Gen. Alfred H. Terry in *O.R.*, I, xlii, part 3, 608–9.

1864, Nov. [13–16].   USG endorsement. "I recommend that the arrangement within proposed be carried into effect. The reciept of these articles will give great satisfaction to the troops. Care should be taken to prevent liquor from being sent"—Copy, DLC-USG, V, 58. Written on a letter of Bvt. Brig. Gen. Stewart Van Vliet, New York City, concerning the sending of Christmas gifts to soldiers.—*Ibid.*; *ibid.*, V, 48.

1864, Nov. 14.   USG endorsement. "Respectfully forwarded to the Sec. of War. I have no recommendation to make on this application."—AES, DNA, RG 107, Letters Received from Bureaus. Written on an undated petition addressed to USG. "We the undersigned most respectfully represent that we have long known August V. Boudroux and Todul Junaux who were conscripted on the miss River near Donaldsonville a short time before the fall of Vicksburg and sent there by the Rebel authorities, That they were driven into the rebel army by force of arms and against their will,

That these men are and always have been known to us as true and Loyal citizens of the United States, and are still so. and that since their capture at Vicksburg under your most able Generalship they have been confined as prisoners of war at Camp Morgan near Indianopolis Indiana where they have since remained protesting against being exchanged and praying to be released. They are both poor men with large families that are now destitute and refugees within the Federal lines. They never owned Negro property and were never disunionists. we know all this and more to be true and correct and most earnestly beseech and pray you to approve this their application and petition for their release, and we further are willing severally to bind ourselves as their security in any reasonable amount for their future good conduct as loyal and peacable citizens of the United States. We therefore most humbly pray that you will approve their application for rlease, allowing them to return to New Orleans to their families"—DS, *ibid.* On Sept. 14, J. E. Wallace, New Orleans, wrote to USG. "Enclosed please find also some papers to Sec Stanton which are submitted to your investigation. Should you approve the application which I trust you will please forward all of the papers to Hon. E. M. Stanton if necessary—"—ALS, *ibid.*

1864, Nov. 15, 3:30 P.M. To Maj. Gen. Henry W. Halleck. "Please order Brig. Gen. E. Upton, as soon as sufficiently recovered from his wounds, to report to Maj. Gen. Thomas for duty. Gen. Upton is in Batavia N. Y."— ALS (telegram sent), CSmH; telegram received (at 11:05 P.M.), DNA, RG 107, Telegrams Collected (Bound). *O.R.,* I, xliii, part 2, 630; *ibid.,* I, xlv, part 1, 894. See *ibid.,* I, xliii, part 2, 637; *ibid.,* I, xlv, part 1, 921.

1864, Nov. 15. USG endorsement. "Respectfully referred to Maj Genl G. H Thomas who is Authorised to act in this matter according to his discretion."—Copy, DNA, RG 109, Union Provost Marshals' File of Papers Relating to Individual Civilians. Written on a letter of Nov. 7 from Meredith P. Gentry, Shelbyville, Tenn., to USG. "Please find enclosed a Copy of a Letter from the President of the U. S. addressed to me in reply to my Letter which you were so kind as to deliver for me. His letter did not come to hand until after you had left Tennessee to take Command in person of the Army of the Potomac, and when Genl Shermans preparations for his Southern Campaign so completely ocupied the Rail Road and all other Routes of travel as to preclude the possibility of my going South at that time   In fact Genl Sherman had Caused notification to be published in the Newspapers that no application for such purpose would be granted by him to any person whatever. I have waited thus long reluctant to trouble you with such an application when I knew that every moment of your time must be fully ocupied by the important duties inciden[t] to your high and responsible position, and with the hope that some lull in the Military Storm would come when I might with less impropriety venture to ask your attention to my Case. But I am Surraunded by Circumstances now which compell me to ask you to read the Copy of the Presidents Letter and if you think it right to do so, to send me such a paper as will relieve me from my parole, and pass me safely to Augusta Georgia   I have been living since I saw you in perfect retirement on my Plantation Ten Miles from this Village and nothing has since occurred which could operate as a reason for complying or not complying with my request which did not exist at the time of my interview with you. But as you can have no personal knowledge on this subject except my assurance to you, this difficulty can be overcome by confering Authority upon the commandant of this Post to give in the needful pass, leaving it to his direction to withhold it if he should think it imprdent to grant it. A State of things may make it impossible to travel by the usual Rail Road Rout, therefor it would be best to leave it to his direction to give the pass by either of several Routs—overland by Huntsville, by Chattanooga, or by the River to Memphis, and from there overland. I want a pass for my Daughter Mary A Gantry, a grown young Woman, for my Son Charles a Lad of thirteen and myself. If you have not forgotten the Contents of my Letter to the President, I requested to be relieved of my Parole obligation—permitted to go to Georgia and when my business should be compleated there, return to Tennessee. As I can not foresee how long my business may detain me, I suggest that you use some phrases in a reply to this, that would secure me a pass from whatever Officer may then command the Federal Forces in that region. Begging you to believe that it is with very great reluctance that I trouble you with a matter, which in comparison with the great affairs that Constantly claim your attention is of such small importance"—Copy, *ibid.* Gentry had served as a Whig U.S. Representative from Tenn. (1839–43, 1845–53) and as a member of the C.S.A. Congress (1862–63). USG carried his letter requesting to go south to President Abraham Lincoln, who wrote to Gentry on March 13, 1864, authorizing USG to grant Gentry's request.—Lincoln, *Works,* VII, 242.

1864, Nov. 15.   USG endorsement. "Respectfully returned. I see no objection to granting the within request, and therefore recommend that the insane person be sent to Hilton Head, S. C. from where Maj. Gen. Foster will send him into the Confederate lines by flag of Truce."—ES, DNA, RG 94, Letters Received, 615D 1864. The letter endorsed is missing. On Nov. 23, Col. Edward D. Townsend, AGO, wrote to Dorothea L. Dix. "Your application of the 9th instant for a pass to send the son of R Middleton of Charleston, S. C, an insane person, through the lines to Porcher Miles of South Carolina, having been referred to Lieut. General Grant., has been returned with the following remark . . . This is approved by the Secretary of War and accordingly the necessary passes will be furnished upon application to the War Department and the necessary instructions given to General Foster"—Copy, *ibid.,* Letters Sent.

Index

All letters written by USG of which the text was available for use in this volume are indexed under the names of the recipients. The dates of these letters are included in the index as an indication of the existence of text. Abbreviations used in the index are explained on pp. xvi–xx. Individual regts. are indexed under the names of the states in which they originated.

DATE DUE
